Biology 2 FOR OCR

Mary Jones

CAMBRIDGE UNIVERSITY PRESS
Cambridge, New York, Melbourne, Madrid, Cape Town, Singapore, São Paulo, Delhi

Cambridge University Press
The Edinburgh Building, Cambridge CB2 8RU, UK

www.cambridge.org
Information on this title: www.cambridge.org/9780521732994

First published 2009

Printed in the United Kingdom at the University Press, Cambridge

A catalogue record for this publication is available from the British Library

ISBN 978-0-521-73299-4 paperback with CD-ROM

ACKNOWLEDGEMENTS
Project management: Sue Kearsey
Front cover photograph: The Borneo Anglehead Agamid lizard (*Gonocephalus borneensis*) / Tom Fayle / www.tomfayle.com
Page layout, illustration and preparation of interactive pdfs: Geoff Jones

Contents

Advice

Introduction

Cambridge OCR Advanced Sciences

The new *Cambridge OCR Advanced Sciences* course provides complete coverage of the revised OCR AS and A2 Level science specifications (Biology, Chemistry A and Physics A) for teaching from September 2008. There are two books for each subject – one covering AS and one covering A2. Some material has been drawn from the existing *Cambridge Advanced Sciences* books; however the majority is new.

The course has been developed in an innovative format, featuring Cambridge's new interactive PDFs on CD-ROM in the back of the books, and free access to a dedicated website. The CD-ROM provides additional material, including detailed objectives, hints on answering questions, and extension material. It also provides access to web-based e-learning activities (A Level and background revision from GCSE) to help students visualise abstract concepts, understand calculations and simulate scientific processes.

The books contain all the material required for teaching the specifications, and can be used either on their own or in conjunction with the interactive PDFs and the website.

In addition, *Teacher Resource CD-ROMs*, with book PDFs plus extra material such as worksheets, practical activities and tests, are available for each book. These CD-ROMs also provide access to new *Cambridge OCR Advanced Sciences* Planner website with a week-by-week adaptable teaching schedule.

Biology 2 for OCR – the A2 biology text

This book covers the entire OCR A2 Biology specification for first examination in 2010. Chapters 1 to 6 correspond to Unit F214, *Communication, Homeostasis and Energy*. Chapters 7 to 16 correspond to Unit F215, *Control, Genomes and Environment*. Each chapter covers one of the numbered sections within the four Modules in Unit F214, and within the four Modules in Unit F215. The content of the chapters is arranged in the same sequence as in the specification.

The book builds on the material covered in *Biology 1 for OCR*. The language is kept simple, to improve accessibility for all students, while still maintaining scientific rigour throughout. Care is taken to introduce and use all of the specialist terms that students need to acquire during their A2 biology studies. Key terms are highlighted in bold.

The depth and breadth of treatment of each topic is pitched at the appropriate level for OCR A2 students. The accompanying CD-ROM also contains some material that goes a little beyond the requirements of the specification, which should interest and stretch more able students.

Some of the text and illustrations are based on material in the endorsed text *Biology 2*, which covered the earlier OCR specification, while some is completely new. All of it has been reviewed and revised, ensuring that relevant new findings relating to particular topics are included. In addition to the main content in each chapter, there are How Science Works boxes, describing issues or events related to the biological material, which begin to explore the relevance of these aspects of biology to individuals and to society.

Self assessment questions (SAQs) in each chapter provide opportunities to check understanding. Many of them require the student to think back to work done during their AS course, or in other parts of the A2 specification. They therefore help students to make links between different areas of biology and to address the synoptic aspects of the A2 biology course. Stretch and challenge questions are included which require students to pull together their ideas about a topic, and to organise and discuss these in a well-structured and broad-ranging answer. Past examination questions at the end of each chapter allow students to practise answering exam-style questions. The answers to these, along with exam-style mark schemes and hints on answering questions, are found on the accompanying CD-ROM.

Acknowledgements

We would like to thank the following for permission to reproduce images:

Cover Tom Fayle; p. 1*t* NHPA/Yves Lanceau; pp. 1*b*, 103*r* Eye of Science/Science Photo Library; p. 6 NHPA/Andy Rouse; p. 7*t* © SHOUT/Alamy; p. 7*b* Ria Novosti/Science Photo Library; p. 8 NHPA/Mark Bowler; pp. 11, 238*t* Manfred Kage/Science Photo Library; p. 14*l* Biophoto Associates/Science Photo Library; p. 14*r* Steve Gschmeissner/Science Photo Library; p.18 Sovereign, ISM/Science Photo Library; p. 23 © Amazon-Images/Alamy; pp. 30, 43, 196, 258*l* © Peter Arnold, Inc./Alamy; p. 35 © Medical-on-Line/Alamy; p. 36 Saturn Stills/Science Photo Library; p. 38 © colinspics/Alamy; p. 42 M.I. Walker/Science Photo Library; p. 45 Simon Fraser/Freeman Hospital, Newcastle upon Tyne/Science Photo Library; pp. 48*l*, 80, 97, 234 CNRI/Science Photo Library; p. 48*r* Astrid & Hans-Frieder Michler/Science Photo Library; pp. 49, 142b © PHOTOTAKE Inc/Alamy; pp. 54, 131*t*, 131*b*, 249 © blickwinkel/Alamy; p. 59 © Duomo/CORBIS; pp. 66*l*, 194*r* Dr Jeremy Burgess/Science Photo Library; p. 66*r* Dr Kenneth R. Miller/Science Photo Library; pp. 67, 134*r* © Sinibomb Images/Alamy; p. 86 © Hulton-Deutsch Collection/CORBIS; pp. 100, 146*l* Dr Gopal Murti/Science Photo Library; p. 103*l* Pascal Goetgheluck/Science Photo Library; pp. 104*l*, 244*r*, 254 Science Photo Library; p. 104*tr* Mauro Fermariello/Science Photo Library; pp. 104*br*, 130 Dr Keith Wheeler/Science Photo Library; p. 105 St Bartholomew Hospital/Science Photo Library; p. 168 Sinclair Stammers/Science Photo Library; p. 109 John Adds; pp. 124*t*, 215*l* © vario images GmbH & Co.KG/Alamy; p. 124*c* © Redmond Durrell/Alamy; p. 124*b* © Arco Images GmbH/Alamy; p. 132*tl* © fotoFlora/Alamy; p. 132*bl* © Suzanne Long/Alamy; p. 132*tr* © Paul Collis/Alamy; p. 132*br* Mike Powles; p. 134*l* © David R. Frazier Photolibrary, Inc./Alamy; pp. 139*l*, 191, 206 Geoff Jones; pp. 139*r*, 143, 194*l*, 216, 220 © Nigel Cattlin/Alamy; p. 140*tl* © David Hosking/Alamy; p. 140*tr* © John Robertson/Alamy; p. 140*br* NHPA/Stephen Dalton; p. 141*l* NHPA/Mike Lane; p. 141*r* Brian Bowes/Science Photo Library; p. 142*t* Dr Meriel G. Jones, University of Liverpool; p. 145 © Art Kowalsky/Alamy; p. 146*r* © doug steley/Alamy; p. 156 Health Protection Agency/Science Photo Library; p. 158 AJ Photo/Science Photo Library; p. 162 Colin Cuthbert/Science Photo Library; p. 174 Golden Rice Humanitarian Board; pp. 181*tl*, 181*bl*, 259 © Steve Bloom Images/Alamy, p. 181*tr* © Mira/Alamy; p. 181*br* © Images of Africa Photobank/Alamy; p. 182*tl* © David Poole/Alamy; p. 182*bl* © Greg Vaughn/Alamy; p. 182*tr* © Worldwide Picture Library/Alamy; p. 182*br* © imagebroker/Alamy; p. 187 © David Burton/Alamy; p. 188*tl* © Fabrice Bettex/Alamy; p. 188*bl* © Ron Niebrugge/Alamy; p. 188*tr* © Yellow Dog Photography/Alamy; p. 188*br* © Phil Degginger/Alamy; p. 199 © Allan Williams/Alamy; p. 208*bl*, 208br © Bracknell Forest Borough Council; p. 208*t* © Frank Blackburn/Alamy; p. 210*l* NHPA/Martin Harvey; p. 210*r* © Greg Lyons, LyonsPhotoImage.com; p. 211*t* © Pep Roig/Alamy; p. 211*c*, 212*tl*, 212*bl* © Charles Darwin Foundation/Isabela Project; p. 211*b* © Wolfgang Kaehler/Alamy; p. 212r David M. Dennis; p. 215*r* © Michael Grant/Alamy; p. 223 © Bettmann/CORBIS; p. 238*b* Biology Media/Science Photo Library; p. 242 BSIP, Sercomi/Science Photo Library; p. 244*l* M.I. Walker, Wellcome Images; p. 250 © Linda Alstead/Alamy; p. 252 © FLPA/Alamy; p. 255 Photo Researchers/Science Photo Library; p. 258*r* © Penny Boyd/Alamy; extension ch. 7 Sinclair Stammers/Science Photo Library.

We would like to thank OCR and CIE for permission to reproduce exam questions, and UK Sport, American Chemical Society and Jane Goodall Institute (JGI) for permission to reproduce URLs.

Chapter 1

Communication

e-Learning

Objectives

Safety in numbers

This photograph shows a slime mould, growing on a decaying tree. It is sometimes known as the dog vomit fungus.

In fact, slime moulds are not fungi at all, although they were for a long time classified in that kingdom. They have an amazing life history, which makes it difficult to classify them into any of the five kingdoms. They are now placed in the Protoctista.

Slime moulds spend most of their lives as single cells, each like an amoeba. They crawl slowly around in damp leaf litter or rotting wood, capturing and digesting other microorganisms, such as bacteria, by phagocytosis.

But when food begins to run short, their behaviour drastically changes. A hungry slime mould cell secretes a chemical called cyclic AMP (cAMP), which acts as a signal to other slime mould cells in the vicinity. These other cells also begin to secrete cAMP, and to move towards areas where the cAMP concentration is greatest. Gradually, more and more of them collect up together in a heap.

Once the pile of slime mould cells has around 100 000 members, they begin to behave like a multicellular organism. This organism crawls slowly along, secreting slimy mucus as it goes – hence the name. After a few days, the cells begin to specialise to form a 'fruiting body'. Some of the cells form a disc that holds the slime mould organism firmly to a surface, such as a piece of rotting wood. Some of them form a hollow tube leading upwards from the disc, and yet others move up through the tube and form a bulge at the top (see photograph below).

The cells at the top of the tube now round themselves up individually, and each produces a cellulose cell wall. They are now spores, and can remain in this state for a long time, even in difficult conditions such as extreme temperatures or drought. Eventually, the fruiting body bursts, propelling the spores up into the air, where they are carried away by the wind. Any spore that lands in a suitable place 'hatches' into a single-celled slime mould, and the life cycle begins again.

Coordinating cell activities

Most animals and plants are complex organisms, made up of many millions of cells. They are said to be **multicellular**. Different parts of the organism perform different functions. It is important that information can pass between these different parts, so that their activities are coordinated.

Sometimes, the purpose of this information transfer is to regulate the levels of some substance within the organism, such as the control of blood glucose levels in mammals. Or it may be to change the activity of some part of the organism in response to a stimulus, such as salivating when you smell good food cooking, or moving away from someone you do not want to talk to.

In both plants and animals, chemicals called **hormones** (in plants they are sometimes known as plant growth regulators) help to transfer information from one part to another. In many animals, including mammals, **nerves** transfer information in the form of electrical impulses. Both of these methods, hormonal and nervous, involve information from one cell being passed on to another, a process called **cell signalling**. We will look in detail at how cell signalling occurs in the nervous system in Chapter 2, and the hormonal (endocrine) system in Chapter 3.

Homeostasis

One of the most crucial functions of the nervous and hormonal systems in mammals is to control internal conditions, maintaining a stable internal environment. This is called **homeostasis**.

'Internal environment' means the conditions inside the body, in which cells function. For a cell, its immediate environment is the tissue fluid that surrounds it. Many features of this environment affect the activities of the cell. They include:

- **temperature** – low temperatures slow down metabolic reactions; high temperatures can cause proteins to denature, causing damage to enzymes and to cell membranes
- **amount of water** – lack of water in the tissue fluid causes water to move out of cells by osmosis, which can cause metabolic reactions in the cells to slow down or even stop; too much water in the tissue fluid causes water to move into cells by osmosis, which can cause the cell to swell and burst
- **concentration of glucose** – glucose is the fuel for respiration in many cells, so a lack of it causes respiration to slow down or halt, as the cells now have no energy source; too much glucose in the tissue fluid can cause water to move out of cells by osmosis, having the same effect as described above.

SAQ

1 Explain why low temperatures slow down metabolic reactions.

Hint

Answer

The principles of homeostasis

It is easiest to understand how homeostasis works by looking at one particular example. Humans are mammals, and we share one of the most distinctive mammalian characteristics – the ability to control core body temperature. (Birds are the only other group of organisms able to do this to the same extent.) Whatever the temperature of the environment outside the body, the cells within it are kept at a temperature close to 37 °C. This ensures that metabolic reactions taking place inside the cells do not speed up or slow down just because the external temperature changes.

SAQ

2 Suggest the advantages to an organism of having a relatively constant core temperature.

Hint

Answer

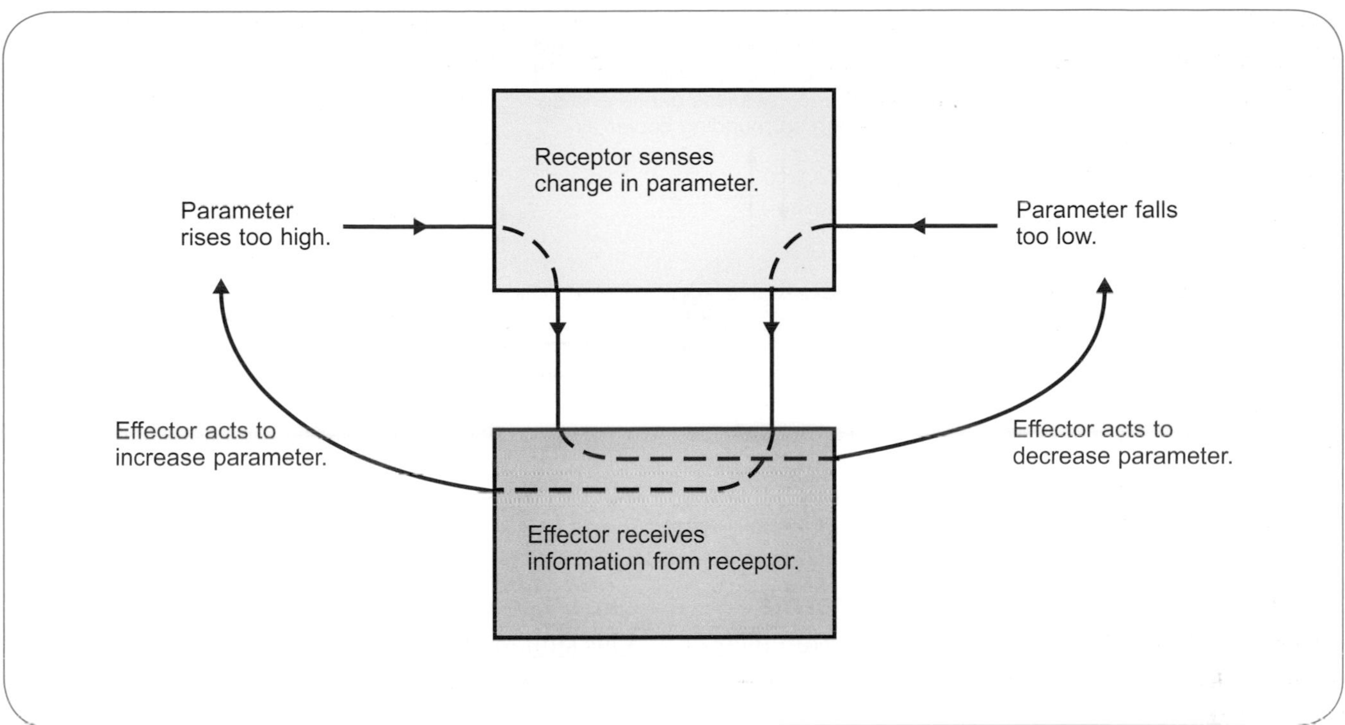

Figure 1.1 Negative feedback.

The control of core temperature, like water content and glucose concentration, involves a mechanism called **negative feedback**. The general principles of negative feedback are shown in Figure 1.1. A negative feedback system requires a **receptor** and an **effector** and an efficient means of communication between them. The receptor monitors the factor that is being controlled – in this case, the temperature of the blood. If the value of this factor is not within a suitable range, the receptor communicates with the effector. The effector then causes an action that brings the factor back towards normal.

In the control of temperature, the communication between receptor and effector involves both the nervous system and hormonal system. In general, the nervous system brings about rapid, short-term changes, whereas hormones act more slowly but have longer-term effects.

Because there is inevitably a short time delay between a change in the factor, its detection by the receptor, communication with the effector and the action of the effector, the control does not happen instantly. This results in an oscillation around a set value, rather than an absolutely unchanging one.

There are a few examples of **positive feedback** in living organisms. For example, if a person breathes air that has a very high carbon dioxide content, this produces a high concentration of carbon dioxide in the blood. This is sensed by carbon dioxide receptors, which cause the breathing rate to increase. So the person breathes faster, taking in even more carbon dioxide, which stimulates the receptors even more, so the person breathes faster and faster. You can see that positive feedback does not have a role to play in homeostasis. It pushes a parameter further and further away from the norm, rather than keeping it constant.

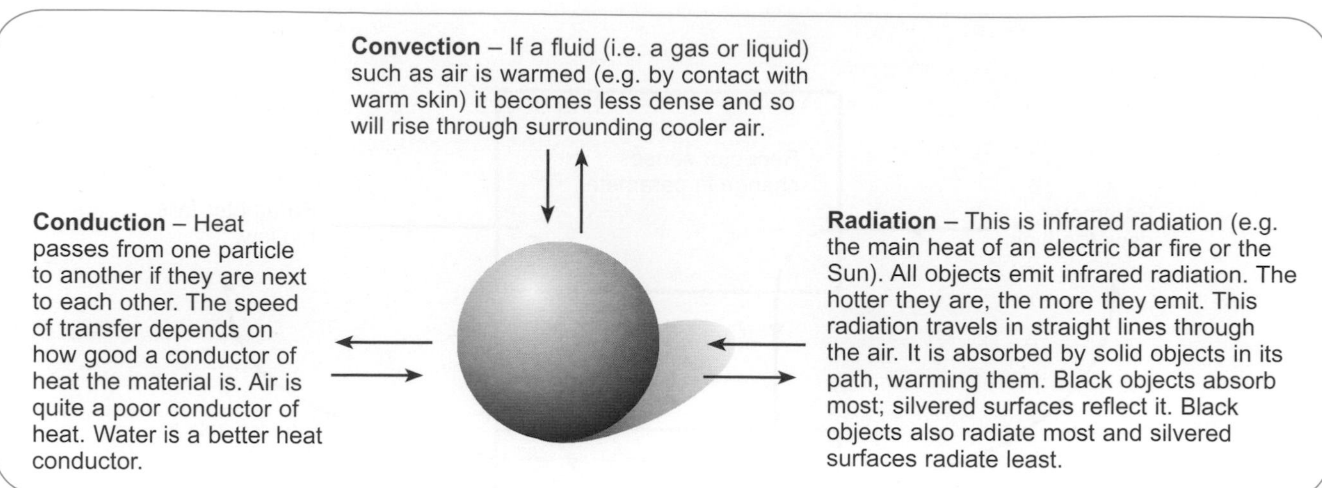

Convection – If a fluid (i.e. a gas or liquid) such as air is warmed (e.g. by contact with warm skin) it becomes less dense and so will rise through surrounding cooler air.
Conduction – Heat passes from one particle to another if they are next to each other. The speed of transfer depends on how good a conductor of heat the material is. Air is quite a poor conductor of heat. Water is a better heat conductor.
Radiation – This is infrared radiation (e.g. the main heat of an electric bar fire or the Sun). All objects emit infrared radiation. The hotter they are, the more they emit. This radiation travels in straight lines through the air. It is absorbed by solid objects in its path, warming them. Black objects absorb most; silvered surfaces reflect it. Black objects also radiate most and silvered surfaces radiate least.

Figure 1.2 Heat is transferred by conduction, convection and radiation.

Temperature regulation in endotherms

All mammals are able to generate heat within their bodies, and so are said to be **endothermic**. ('Endo' means 'inside'.) Body temperature is controlled by ensuring a balance between heat input and heat output (Figure 1.2 and Figure 1.3).

We are perhaps better at keeping our bodies warm in a cold environment than we are at keeping them cool in a hot one. We have several different ways of keeping warm, but if the external temperature rises above our internal one, the only physiological way to keep cool is by sweating.

Temperature receptors

The **hypothalamus** (right in the middle of the head, at the base of the brain) never stops monitoring the temperature of the blood flowing through it. The temperature it monitors is our **core temperature** – the temperature inside the body. This should remain at around 37 °C, although this value varies between different people. It also depends on the level of activity and the time of day and – for women – the stage of the menstrual cycle.

The hypothalamus receives information about temperature from other sources as well. The skin contains receptors that monitor the changes in skin temperature, which is the first to change if there is a change in environmental temperature. These **peripheral** ('around the outside') **receptors** are able to give 'early warning' about a possible change in core temperature. When you walk from a warm room into a cold one and 'feel cold', it is nerve impulses from these peripheral temperature receptors in the skin that you are responding to. Your core temperature will not have changed at all.

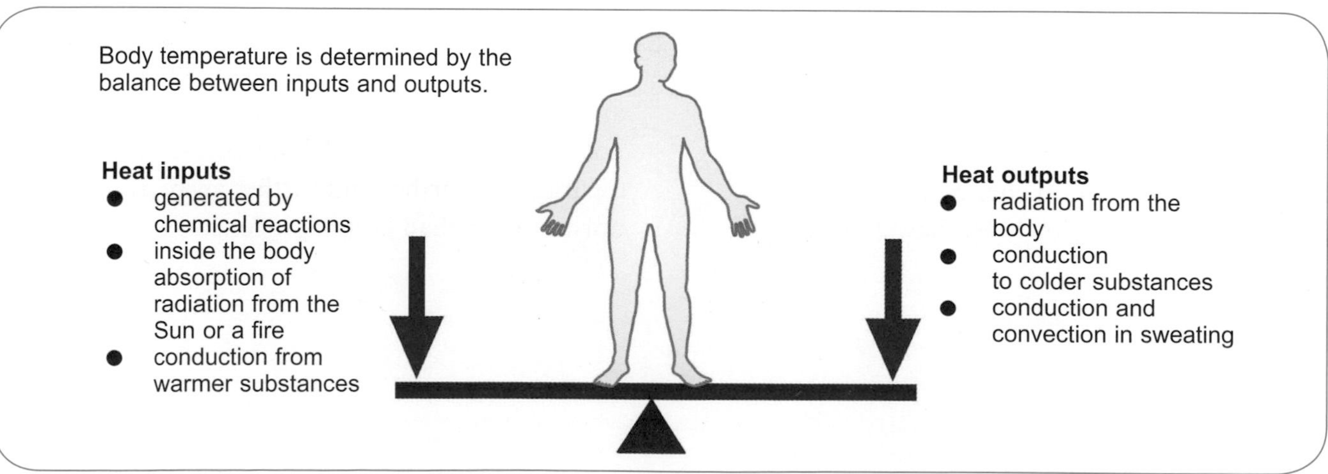

Figure 1.3 Heat inputs and heat outputs.

When core temperature might fall

If core temperature falls, or if skin temperature receptors signal that environmental temperature has fallen, this information is picked up by the hypothalamus. The hypothalamus sends electrical impulses along motor neurones (nerve cells) to some of your muscles and to the skin.

The nerve impulses from the hypothalamus cause some of the muscles repeatedly to contract and relax very rapidly, which we call **shivering**. This involves respiration inside the cells, as glucose is oxidised to release energy that is used to make ATP. Some of the energy, however, is lost as heat. Shivering therefore generates heat inside the muscles. The heat is transferred into the blood as it passes through the muscles, and is then carried around the rest of the body in the bloodstream.

The nerve impulses also affect the smooth muscle in the walls of **arterioles** that supply blood to capillaries near the skin surface (Figure 1.4). This muscle contracts, narrowing the lumen of the arterioles and shutting off blood supply to the surface capillaries. This is known as **vasoconstriction**. It ensures that less heat is lost to the surroundings by radiation from the warm blood at the surface of the skin.

Sweat glands in the skin reduce their output of sweat. **Erector muscles**, each attached to the base of a hair follicle, contract and pull the hairs up on end. We are not very hairy, so this does nothing to keep us warm. In other mammals, it increases the thickness of the layer of air trapped next to the skin. Air is a poor conductor of heat, so this insulates the body from changing temperatures around it. We just get goose bumps.

We can also change our behaviour to prevent body temperature falling too low. The obvious thing is to put on more clothes, increasing insulation of the body surface. We can move into a warmer place, drink hot drinks or eat hot food. Jumping up and down increases the rate of respiration, and therefore heat generation, in the muscles. Wrapping your arms around yourself and huddling up reduces your surface area, so that less heat leaves your body by radiation.

Extension

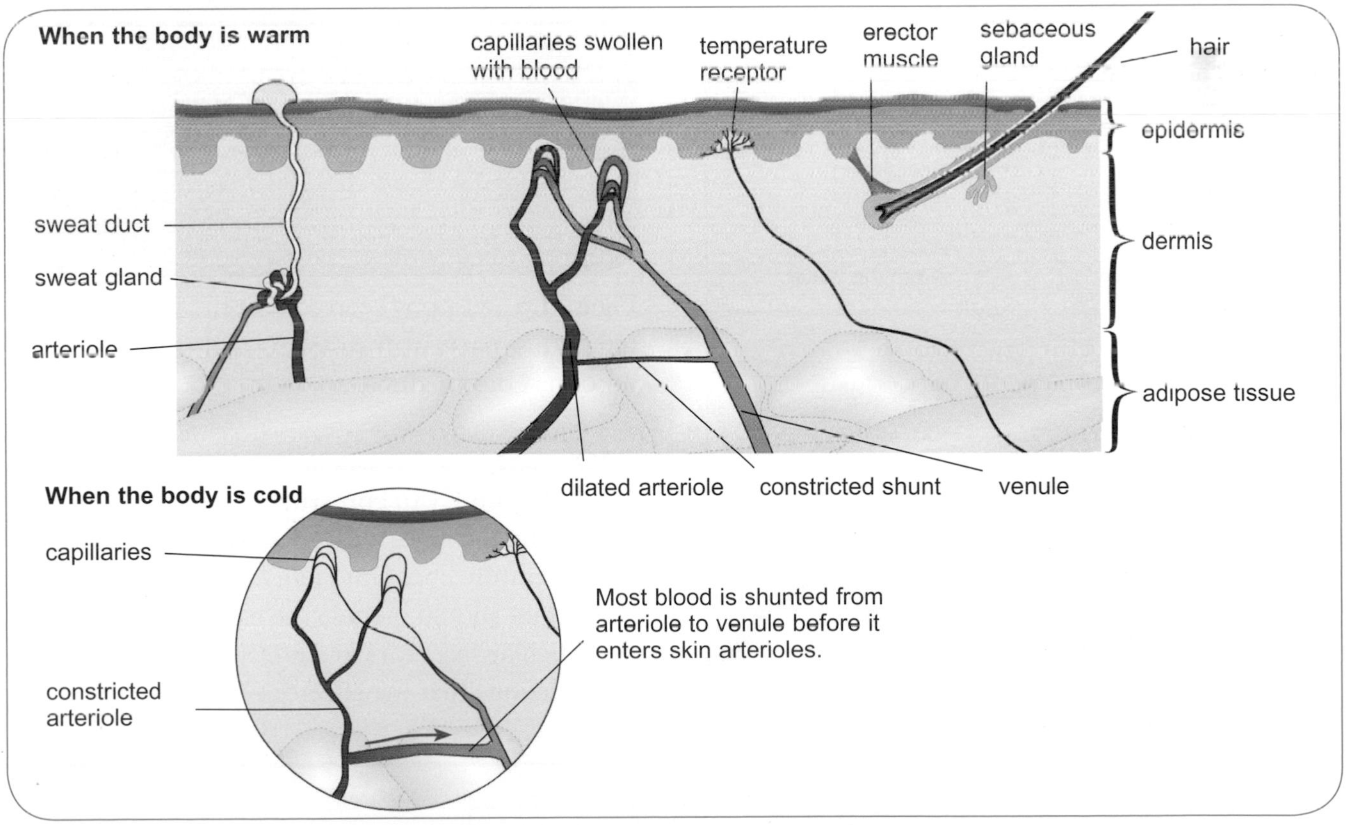

Figure 1.4 Section through skin to show vasodilation and vasoconstriction.

When core temperature might rise

When a rise in environmental temperature is detected by skin receptors, or a rise in blood temperature is detected by receptors in the hypothalamus, the hypothalamus sends impulses along a different set of neurones. These impulses make all of the actions just described go into reverse.

The arterioles supplying blood to the skin now dilate as the smooth muscle in their walls relaxes. This is called **vasodilation**. It allows more blood to flow close to the skin surface, so that heat can radiate from it or be conducted to the air. This is why a pale skin tends to go pink in hot conditions.

Sweat glands secrete more sweat (Figure 1.5). Plasma from the blood passing through the blood vessels that supply them is extracted in the sweat glands and passes up through the sweat ducts to the skin surface. This liquid is mostly water, but also contains many of the solutes present in blood plasma, in particular sodium ions, chloride ions and urea. As it lies on the surface of the skin, the water in it evaporates. Water has a high latent heat of vaporisation and so, as it changes from liquid to gas, it absorbs heat from the skin.

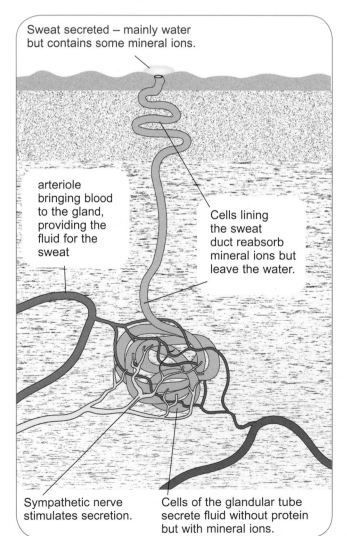

Sweat secreted – mainly water but contains some mineral ions.

arteriole bringing blood to the gland, providing the fluid for the sweat

Cells lining the sweat duct reabsorb mineral ions but leave the water.

Sympathetic nerve stimulates secretion.

Cells of the glandular tube secrete fluid without protein but with mineral ions.

Figure 1.5 A sweat gland.

Behaviour can also help (Figure 1.6). On a very hot day, we often tend to be less inclined to do vigorous exercise, which reduces heat generation by muscles. We wear fewer clothes, allowing heat to be lost more easily from the skin surface. We move into the shade, or into a cool room. We drink iced drinks and eat cool salads instead of hot food.

Figure 1.6 Hippos keep cool in the water during the hottest parts of the day. At night, they move up onto the land to graze.

SAQ

3 Use Figure 1.1 to construct a flow diagram showing the negative feedback loop that keeps temperature constant in an endotherm. Your diagram should include the names of the particular receptors and effectors, and the actions that the effectors take.

Answer

Extension

Hypothermia

Hypothermia is a condition in which the body temperature drops significantly below normal – usually considered to be below 35 °C – and where the normal temperature regulation mechanisms are unable to bring it back up.

Hypothermia can be caused by exposure to extreme cold – for example, being outdoors when air temperature is low and where there is a strong wind, causing wind chill. Walkers trapped by injury on a mountainside can quickly suffer a dangerous fall in body temperature, as they are unable to move to generate heat and keep warm. Crawling inside a plastic survival bag can make a huge difference to the likelihood of survival.

Getting thoroughly wet can also increase the risk of hypothermia, because heat is taken from the body by the water as it evaporates.

Elderly people may suffer hypothermia if they are unable or unwilling to spend money on heating. Their metabolic rate is generally lower than that of younger people, and they may not be very mobile. They may not eat enough to provide their cells with sufficient fuel for respiration. Every winter in the UK, elderly people die from hypothermia.

A person suffering from hypothermia may not recognise it. They will have been feeling very cold, but now feel sleepy and relaxed. This is a danger sign to others, who should recognise that their companion is at risk and act quickly.

The first thing to do is to stop any further heat loss, by wrapping the victim in warm, dry blankets and providing a hot water bottle if possible. Search and rescue dogs are sometimes trained to snuggle up to casualties in exposed conditions, to help to keep them warm. In most cases, a person suffering from hypothermia who is taken into a warm environment will recover if they simply lie there for a few hours. Sugary drinks should not be given until body temperature is close to normal, because cells cannot metabolise sugar if they are too cold.

In one particular instance, however, hypothermia can be useful. Heart surgery can only be done when the heart is not beating, and stopping the heart means that body cells run short of oxygen. By packing the anaesthetised patient in ice, as in the photo below, cells are cooled to such a low temperature that their metabolic rate slows right down, and they have much less need of oxygen. This avoids the use of a heart-lung machine to keep oxygenated blood moving to the body cells during the operation. This technique can only be used for short operations, not ones that would last for much more than 10 minutes.

Search and rescue dogs are sometimes trained to snuggle up to casualties to help to keep them warm.

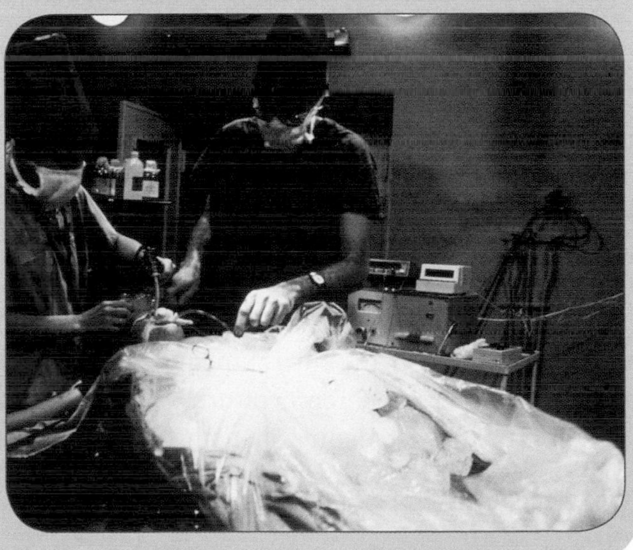

Temperature regulation in ectotherms

'Ecto' means 'on the outside', and **ectotherms** are animals that obtain most of their heat from outside their bodies. They do not generate large amounts of heat inside the body. All animals except mammals and birds are ectotherms. They need much less food than endotherms of the same size, because they don't use it to generate heat (Figure 1.7). Ectotherms tend to be inactive when they are in a cold environment, because their cells are also at this cold temperature and metabolic reactions take place slowly.

Figure 1.7 Snakes are ectotherms, so do not use food to produce heat. This rice rat will be the only food the snake needs for several months.

Even though ectotherms cannot control their body temperature physiologically, they can – just like us – use behaviour to do so. You may have seen butterflies resting with wings outstretched, facing the sun. This helps them to absorb heat and increase their body temperature (Figure 1.8), allowing them to become active.

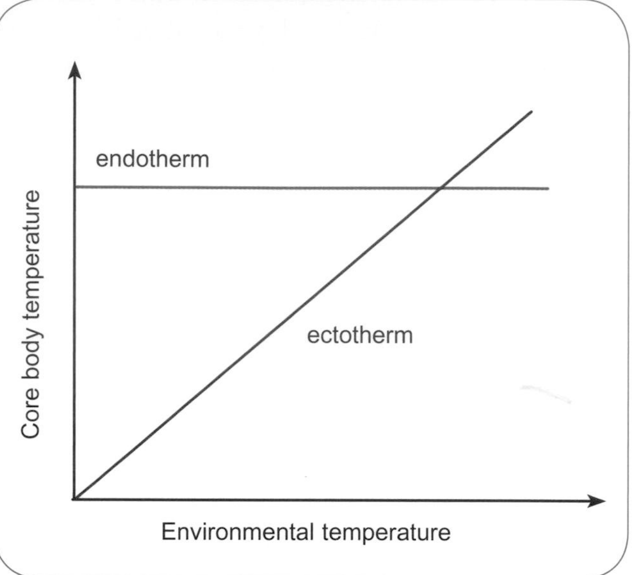

Figure 1.8 Relationship between environmental temperature and core body temperature in an ectotherm and an endotherm.

Summary

Glossary

- Multicellular organisms need communication systems to ensure that all parts of the body work together. Cells communicate by cell signalling. This may involve the neuronal and hormonal systems.
- Homeostasis is the maintenance of a constant internal environment.
- Negative feedback is a mechanism that keeps a particular parameter oscillating around a set point or norm. It involves receptors that detect a change in the parameter, and effectors that take action to push the parameter back towards the norm when deviation occurs.
- Positive feedback amplifies the movement of a parameter away from the norm, and it is not involved in homeostasis.
- Mammals and birds are endotherms, and maintain a constant core body temperature that is independent of the environmental temperature. Temperature receptors in the hypothalamus monitor core temperature. Temperature receptors in the skin monitor surface temperature and communicate with the hypothalamus via neurones. The hypothalamus causes effectors in the muscles and the skin to act in ways that bring temperature back towards the norm.

continued

- When core temperature falls below the norm, vasoconstriction reduces the blood flow near the skin surface and therefore reduces heat loss by radiation. Sweat production decreases. Erector muscles contract and raise hairs on end, which increases insulation in many mammals. Shivering generates heat within the body. Behavioural changes increase heat production within the body and decrease heat loss from it.
- When core temperature rises above the norm, vasodilation increases heat loss by radiation from the body surface. Sweating increases, producing a cooling effect as the water in sweat evaporates from the skin surface. Behavioural changes decrease heat production and increase heat loss.
- All other animals are ectotherms, which do not generate heat within the body in response to falling temperature. Their body temperature is dependent on the environmental temperature, but they do use behaviour to help to keep their temperature within a desirable range.

Stretch and challenge question

1 Discuss the advantages and disadvantages of being endothermic.

Questions

1 a The ability to remove excess heat is an important limiting factor in extending the duration of exercise.

Figure 1 shows the change in core body temperature during exercise.

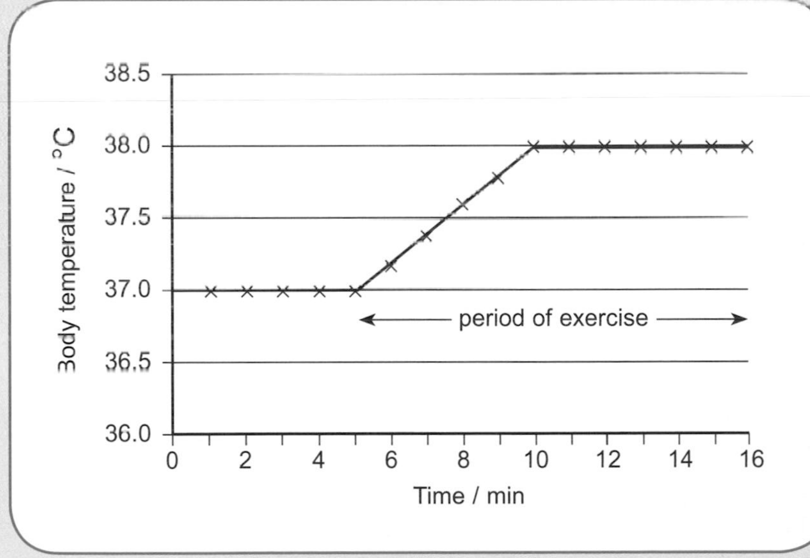

Figure 1

i Describe how the body normally removes excess heat when the core temperature rises above 37 °C. [2]

ii Explain why heat is produced during exercise. [2]

continued

b Core body temperature is normally maintained at a set point (norm) of 37 °C.

i Why is it important to maintain the core temperature at a set point (norm) of 37 °C? [3]

ii Suggest a reason for the slightly higher set point (norm) during exercise. [1]

Hint

c
- As environmental temperature varies, core body temperature must be controlled if the set point is to be maintained.
- Human populations originating in different temperature zones of the world have adapted to the temperature ranges found in these zones.
- Differences in mean body mass have evolved to make it easier to maintain the set point.

Hint

In an investigation, the mean body mass of a sample of the population in different temperature zones of the world was measured.

The results are shown in Figure 2.

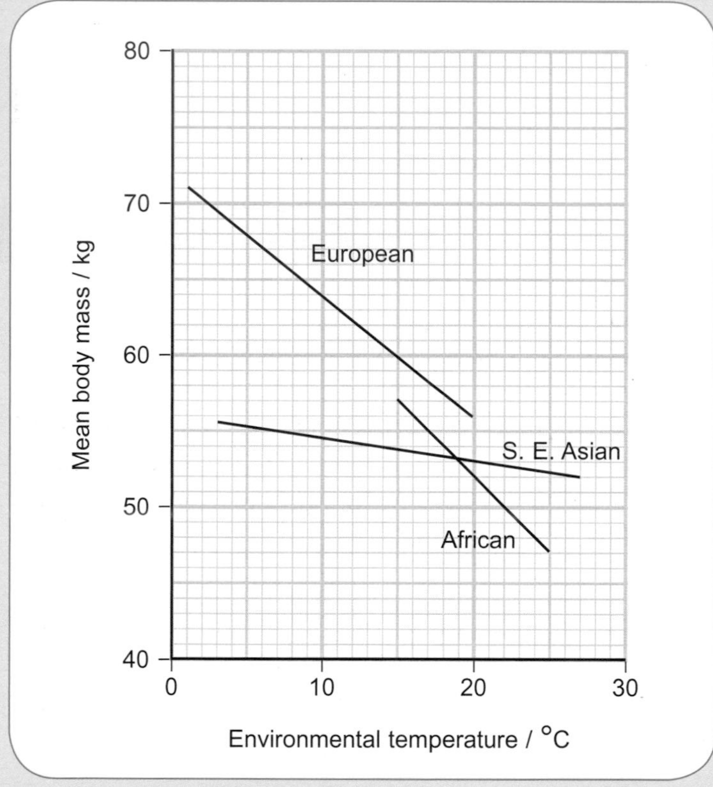

Figure 2

i Calculate the percentage difference in the mean body mass of the European population at an environmental temperature of 5 °C compared with 15 °C. Show your working. Give your answer to the nearest whole number. [2]

ii Describe and explain the relationship between body mass and environmental temperature shown in the European population in Figure 2. [3]

iii Explain how the relationship between body mass and environmental temperature evolved in populations originating from different temperature zones. [2]

iv Suggest two other environmental influences on body mass. [2]

OCR Human Biology A (2867) June 2005 [Total 17]

Answer

Chapter 2

Nerves

e-Learning

Objectives

The human nervous system is made up of the brain and spinal cord, which form the **central nervous system**, and nerves, which form the **peripheral nervous system**. Nerves themselves, and also much of the central nervous system, are made up of highly specialised cells called **neurones**.

Information is transferred along neurones in the form of **action potentials**, sometimes known as nerve impulses. These are fleeting changes in the electrical charge on either side of the plasma membranes.

Neurones

Figure 2.1 shows the structure of a **motor neurone**. This type of neurone transmits action potentials from the central nervous system to an effector such as a muscle or a gland.

The cell body of a motor neurone lies within the spinal cord or the brain. The nucleus of a neurone is in the cell body (Figure 2.2). Often, dark specks can be seen in the cytoplasm. These are groups of ribosomes involved in protein synthesis.

Many thin cytoplasmic processes extend from the cell body. In a motor neurone, all but one of these are quite short. These short processes conduct impulses *towards* the cell body, and they are called **dendrites**. One process is much longer, and this conducts impulses *away from* the cell body. This is called the **axon**. A motor neurone with its cell body in your spinal cord might have its axon running all the way to a toe, so axons can be very long.

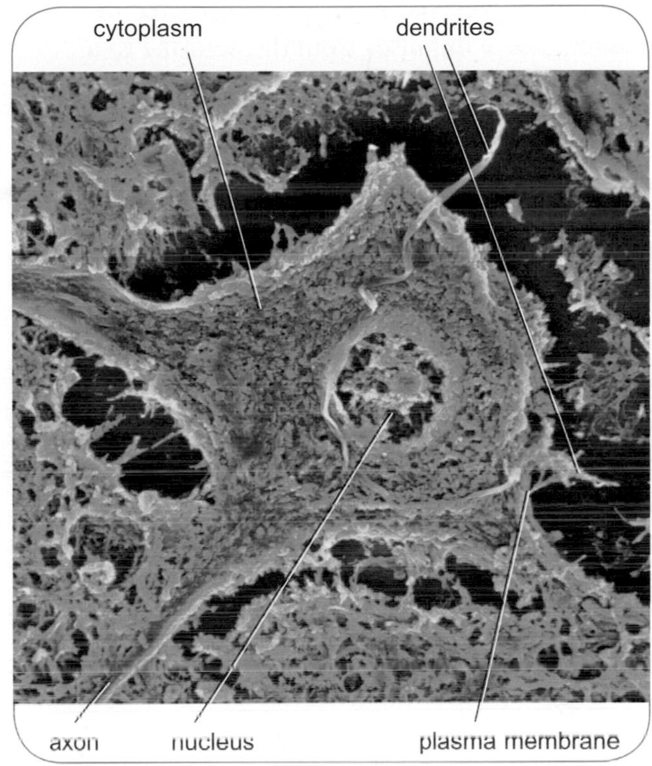

Figure 2.2 An electron micrograph of the cell body of a motor neurone within the spinal cord (× 1390).

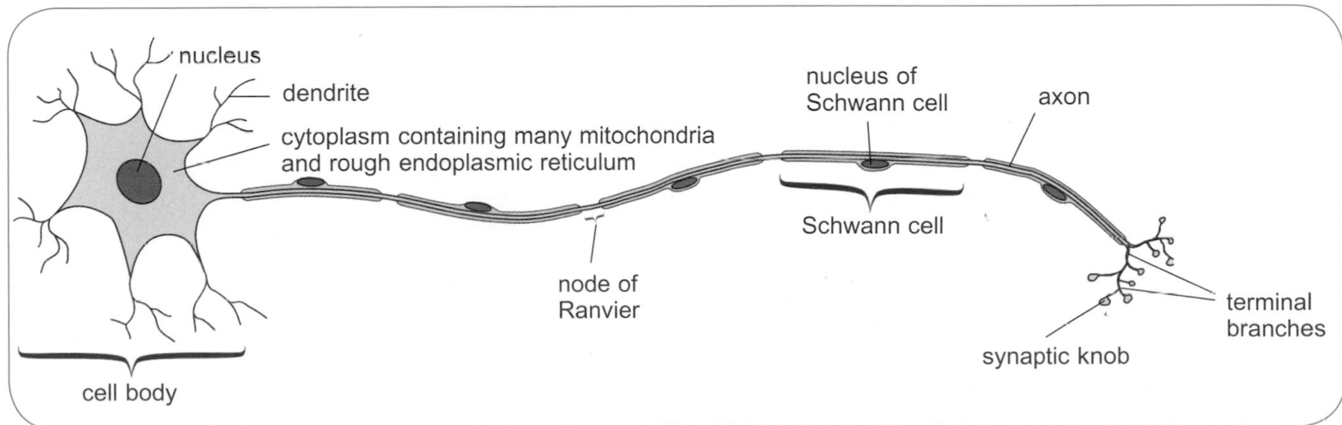

Figure 2.1 A motor neurone.

Within the cytoplasm, all the usual organelles, such as endoplasmic reticulum, Golgi apparatus and mitochondria, are present. Particularly large numbers of mitochondria are found at the tips of the terminal branches of the axon, together with many vesicles containing chemicals called **transmitter substances**. These are involved in passing nerve impulses from the neurone to a muscle.

Sensory neurones (Figure 2.3) carry impulses via a **dendron** from sense organs to the brain or spinal cord. Their cell bodies are inside structures called dorsal root ganglia, just outside the spinal cord.

Intermediate neurones, sometimes called **relay neurones** (Figure 2.3), have their cell bodies and their cytoplasmic processes inside the brain or spinal cord. They are adapted to carry impulses from and to numerous other neurones.

SAQ

1 Describe two differences between the structures of a motor neurone and a sensory neurone.

Answer

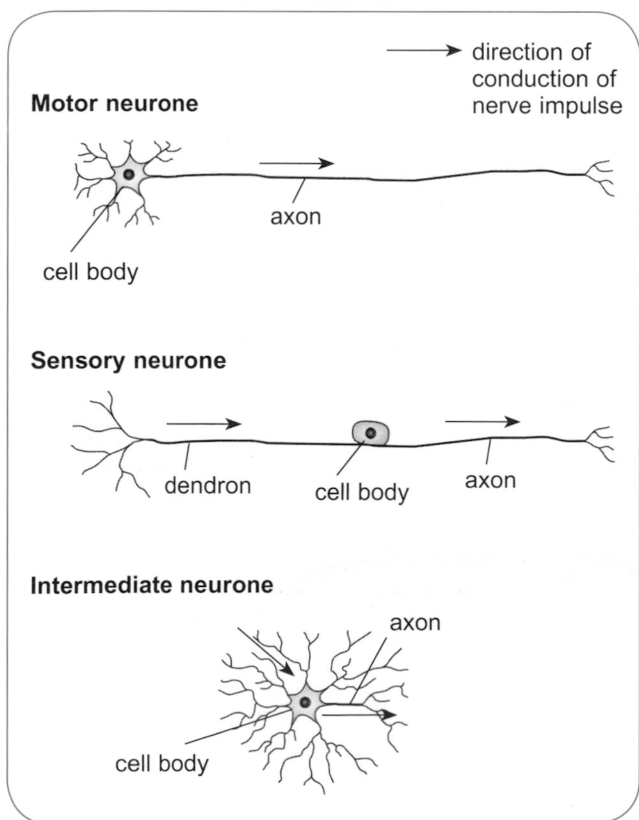

Figure 2.3 Types of neurones.

Myelin

In some neurones, cells called **Schwann cells** wrap themselves around the axon all along its length. Figure 2.4 shows one such cell, viewed as the axon is cut transversely. The Schwann cell spirals around, enclosing the axon in many layers of its plasma membrane. This enclosing sheath, called the **myelin sheath**, is made largely of lipid, together with some proteins.

There are small uncovered gaps along the axons, where there are spaces between the Schwann cells. These are known as **nodes of Ranvier**. They occur about every 1–3 mm.

About one third of our motor and sensory neurones are myelinated. The sheath increases the speed of conduction of the nerve impulses, and this is described on page 19.

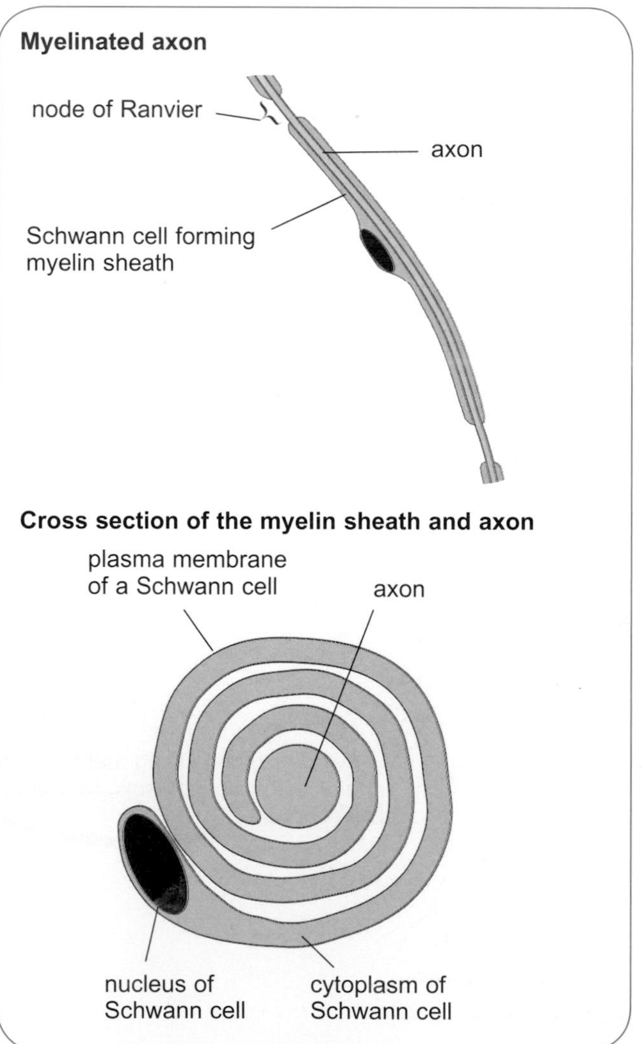

Figure 2.4 A myelinated axon.

A reflex arc

Figure 2.5 shows how sensory, intermediate and motor neurones are arranged in the body to form a **reflex arc**. In the example in Figure 2.5, a **spinal reflex arc** is shown, in which the nerve impulses are carried into and out of the spinal cord. Other reflex arcs may involve the brain.

A reflex arc is the pathway along which impulses are carried from a receptor to an effector, without involving any conscious thought. An **effector** is a part of the body that responds to a stimulus. Muscles and glands are effectors.

The impulse arrives along the sensory neurone and passes through the dorsal root ganglion into a the spinal cord. Here it may be passed directly to the motor neurone, or to an intermediate neurone and then the motor neurone. The impulse sweeps along the axon of the motor neurone, arriving at the effector within less than one second of the receptor having picked up the stimulus.

The response by the effector can be extremely rapid. It is called a **reflex action**. A reflex action is a fast, stereotyped response to a particular stimulus. Reflex actions help us to avoid danger, by allowing us to respond immediately to a potentially harmful situation without having to spend time thinking about it. For example, a sharp pinprick on the bottom of your foot will probably result in contraction of muscles in your leg, pulling the leg away from the stimulus.

SAQ

2 Some reflex actions appear to be innate (inborn). They appear to be 'hard-wired' into our brains from birth. Other reflex actions are learned during our lifetimes.

a Think of a reflex action that almost everyone shows, and that is therefore likely to be innate. Name:
- the stimulus
- the receptor
- the effector
- the response.

b Do the same for a reflex action that you have learned.

c What, if any, are the survival values of the reflex actions you have described?

Answer

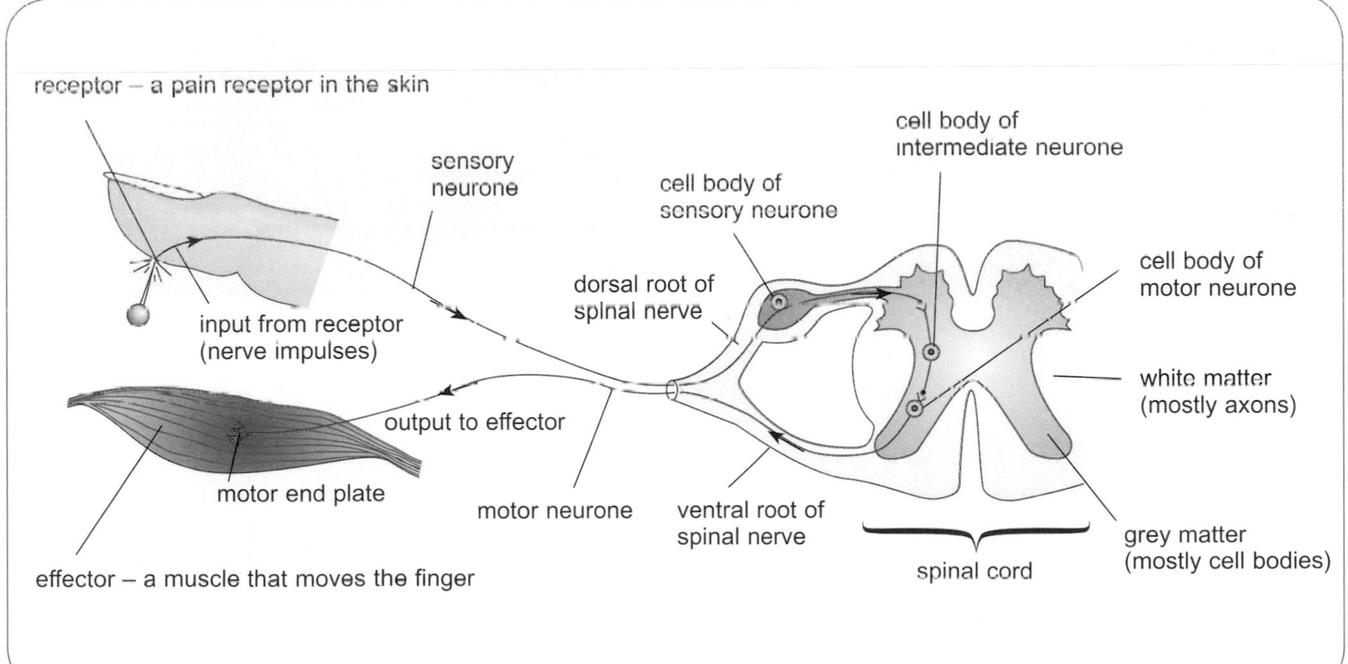

Figure 2.5 A spinal reflex arc.

Structure of a nerve

Axons of neurones are almost always found in bundles. There may be several thousand of them, lying side by side and surrounded by a protective covering called the **perineurium** (Figure 2.6). It is rather like a cable with lots of electrical wires inside it.

Some nerves contain only sensory neurones, some only motor neurones, and some contain a mixture of both. These are respectively known as sensory nerves, motor nerves and mixed nerves. In each type of nerve, some of the axons are myelinated and some not.

Transmission of nerve impulses

Neurones transmit impulses as electrical signals. These signals travel very rapidly from one end of the neurone to the other. They are not a flow of electrons, like an electric current. Rather, the signals are very brief changes in the distribution of electrical charge across the plasma membranes. These changes are caused by the very rapid movement of sodium ions and potassium ions into and out of the axon.

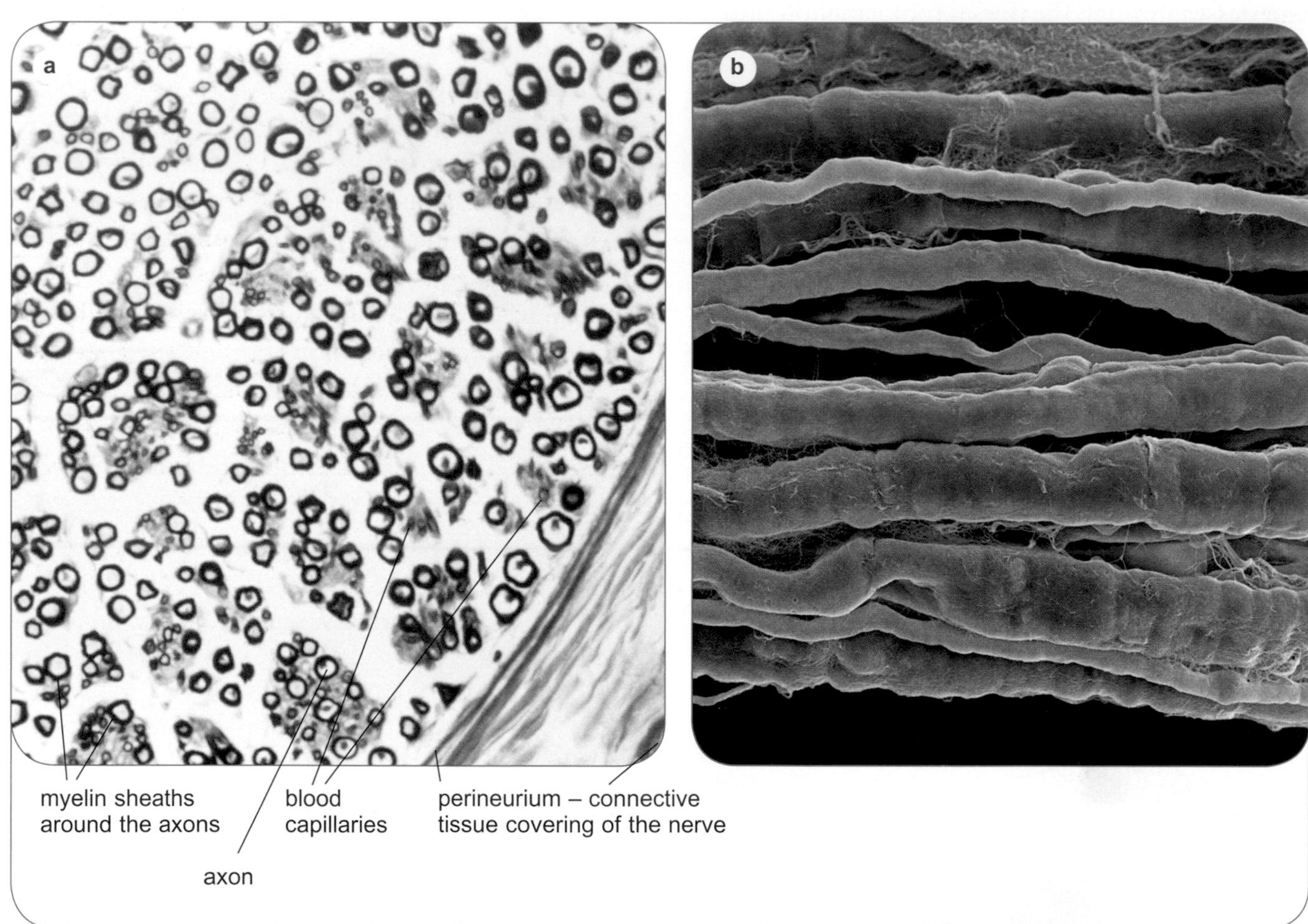

Figure 2.6 **a** A light micrograph of a transverse section across a small part of a nerve (× 960). **b** This is a scanning electron micrograph of a few of the axons in a nerve. Each axon belongs to a different neurone. You can see that the axons are not all the same size (× 4000).

Resting potential

Even a resting neurone is very active. The sodium–potassium pumps in its plasma membrane (Figure 2.7) constantly move sodium ions out of the cell and potassium ions into it. These movements are against the concentration gradient, so they involve active transport. Large amounts of ATP are used.

The sodium–potassium pump removes three sodium ions, Na^+, from the cell for every two potassium ions, K^+, it brings into the cell. Some of these sodium and potassium ions leak back to where they came from, diffusing through other parts of the plasma membrane. The membrane is leakier for potassium ions than sodium ions. As a result of all of this, there are more positive ions outside the membrane than inside. There is a positive charge on the outside of the membrane compared to the inside.

This difference in charge on the two sides of the membrane is called the **resting potential**. In most neurones, it is about −70 mV (millivolts) on the inside compared with the outside.

Action potentials

As well as the sodium–potassium pump, the plasma membranes of neurones have other protein channels that will let sodium ions and potassium ions pass through. Some of these are **voltage-gated channels**. This means that whether they are open or closed depends on the potential difference (voltage) across the membrane. When the membrane is at its resting potential, with a potential difference of −70 mV inside, these voltage-gated channels are closed.

Other channels are caused to open or close depending on stimuli such as touch. Imagine a touch receptor in your hand. The receptor is actually the end of a sensory neurone. When the receptor receives a stimulus (touch) some sodium channels in the plasma membrane open. The sodium ions that had been pumped out now flood back into the cell. They do this because there is an **electrical gradient** for them – the membrane has more positive charge on the outside than on the inside, so the ions tend to move to equal out the charges on the two sides. There is also a **chemical gradient** – there are more sodium ions outside than inside, so they tend to diffuse inwards down their concentration gradient. This 'double gradient' is known as an **electrochemical gradient**.

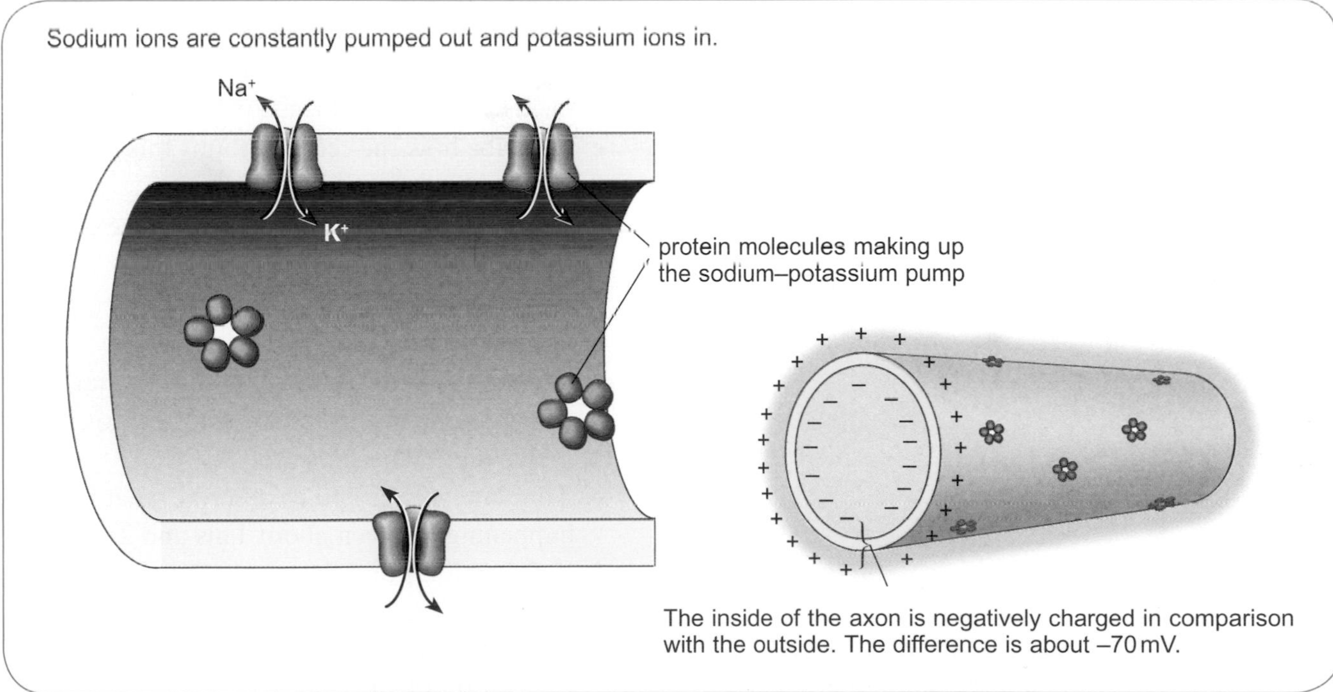

Figure 2.7 Activity in a 'resting' neurone.

Within a very short space of time, the resting potential has gone. There is no longer a negative charge inside the axon compared with the outside. The axon membrane is now **depolarised**.

So many sodium ions flood in so quickly that they 'overshoot'. For a brief moment, the axon actually becomes positively charged inside, rather than negatively. Then the sodium channels close, so sodium ions stop moving into the axon.

At this point, in response to the voltage changes that have been taking place, the potassium channels open. Potassium ions therefore diffuse out of the axon, down their electrochemical gradient. This movement of the potassium ions removes positive charge from inside the axon to the outside, so the charge across the membrane begins to return to normal. This is called **repolarisation**.

So many potassium ions leave the axon that the potential difference across the membrane briefly becomes even more negative than the normal resting potential. The Na^+/K^+ channels then close, and the sodium–potassium pumps restore the normal distribution of sodium and potassium ions across the membrane, which restores the resting potential.

This sequence of events is called an **action potential**. These changes in electrical charge can be measured and displayed using an oscilloscope. Figure 2.8 shows what an action potential looks like, and Figure 2.9 shows what's happening at the Na^+ and K^+ channels during the action potential.

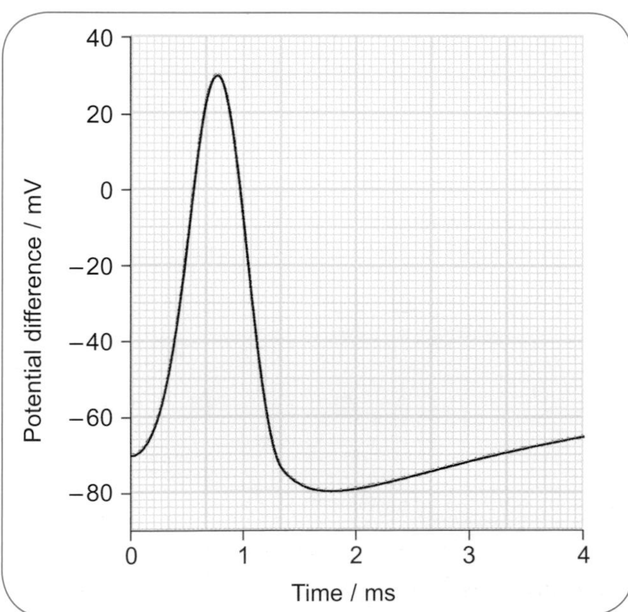

Figure 2.8 Changes in potential difference across a membrane during an action potential.

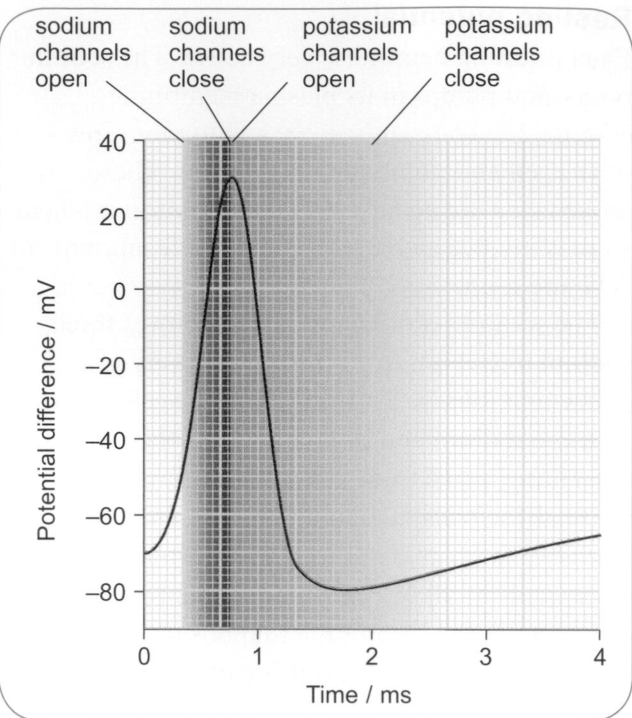

Figure 2.9 The behaviour of ion channels during an action potential.

SAQ

3 Make a copy of Figure 2.8.

a On your graph, draw a horizontal line right across it to represent the resting potential.

b The resting potential is said to be −70 mV inside. What does this mean?

c Describe how the cell maintains this resting potential.

d As an action potential begins, the line on the graph shoots upwards from −70 mV to +30 mV.

i Why is this called depolarisation?

ii Annotate your graph to describe what is happening in the axon membrane to cause this rapid depolarisation.

e Annotate your graph to describe what is happening between about 1 ms and 2 ms.

f If the action potential starts at time 0, how long does it take between the start of depolarisation and the restoration of the resting potential?

Answer

Transmission of an action potential

The graphs in Figure 2.8 and Figure 2.9 show the events that take place at one point in the axon membrane. However, the function of a neurone is to transmit information, in the form of action potentials, along itself. How do action potentials move along a neurone?

An action potential at any point in an axon's membrane triggers the production of an action potential in the part of the membrane just next to it. Figure 2.10 shows how it does this. The temporary depolarisation of the membrane where the action potential is, causes a 'local circuit' to be set up between the depolarised region and the resting regions on either side of it. This depolarises these adjoining regions and so causes voltage-gated sodium and potassium channels to open. Sodium ions flood in, and a few milliseconds later potassium ions flood out, causing an action potential. In this way, the action potential sweeps all along the membrane of the neurone.

In normal circumstances, nerve cell axons only transmit an action potential in one direction. A 'new' action potential is only generated ahead of the action potential, not behind it. This is because the region behind it is still recovering from the action potential it has just had. The distribution of Na^+ and K^+ in this region is still not back to normal. It is therefore temporarily incapable of generating an action potential. The time it takes to recover is called the **refractory period**.

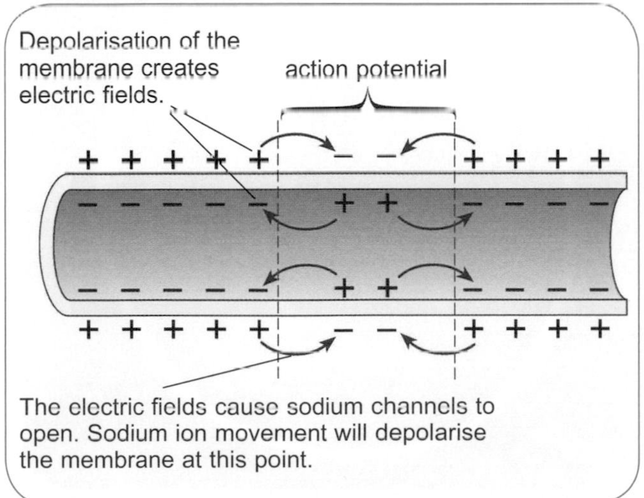
Depolarisation of the membrane creates electric fields.
action potential
The electric fields cause sodium channels to open. Sodium ion movement will depolarise the membrane at this point.

Figure 2.10 How local circuits cause an action potential to move along an axon.

How action potentials carry information

Action potentials are always the same size. A light touch on your hand will generate exactly the same size of action potentials as a strong touch. Either an action potential is generated, or it is not. This is sometimes known as the 'all-or-nothing' law.

So how *does* your brain distinguish between a light touch and a strong touch? This is done using a different frequency of action potentials. A heavy touch generates more frequent action potentials than a light touch. The brain interprets a stream of closely spaced action potentials as meaning 'strong stimulus' (Figure 2.11).

Moreover, a strong stimulus is likely to stimulate more neurones than a weak stimulus. While a weak stimulus might result in action potentials being generated in just one or two neurones, a strong stimulus could produce action potentials in many more.

The brain can therefore interpret the *frequency* of action potentials passing along the axon of a sensory neurone, and the *number* of neurones carrying action potentials, to get information about the *strength* of the stimulus detected by the

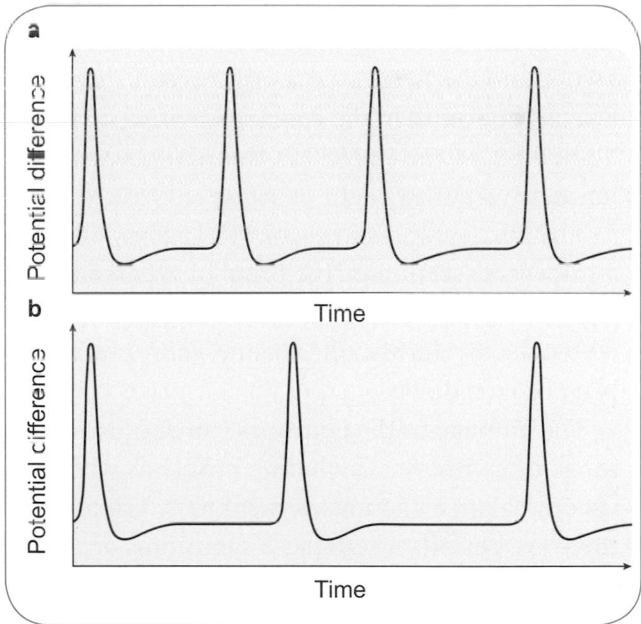
a
Potential difference
Time
b
Potential difference
Time

Figure 2.11 **a** A high frequency of impulses is produced when a receptor is given a strong stimulus. **b** A lower frequency of impulses is produced when a receptor is given a weak stimulus. Notice that the size of each action potential remains the same. Only their frequency changes.

receptor. The *nature* of the stimulus – whether it is light, heat or touch, for example – is deduced from the *position* of the sensory neurone bringing the information. If the neurone is from the retina of the eye, then the brain will interpret the information as meaning 'light'. If for some reason a different stimulus, such as pressure, stimulates a receptor cell in the retina, the brain will still interpret the action potentials from this receptor as meaning 'light'. This is why rubbing your eyes when they are shut can cause you to 'see' patterns of light.

Speed of conduction

The speed at which an action potential sweeps along an axon is not the same for every neurone. It depends partly on the diameter of the axon, and partly on whether or not it is myelinated (Figure 2.12).

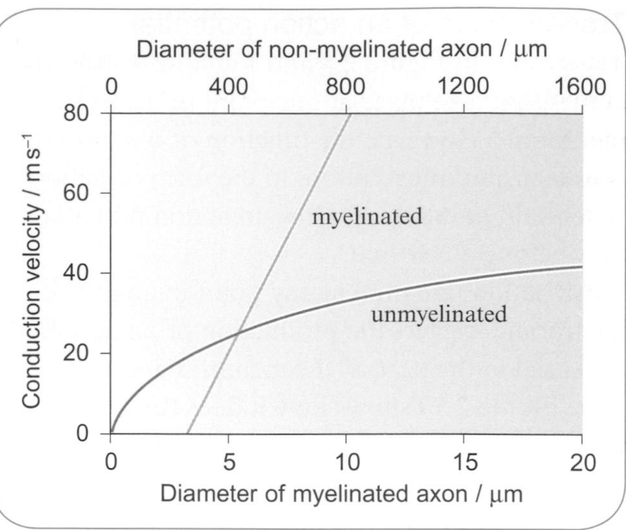

Figure 2.12 Speed of transmission in myelinated and non-myelinated axons of different diameters.

Multiple sclerosis

Multiple sclerosis, MS, is a chronic (long-lasting) disease that generally occurs in people between the ages of 20 and 40. No-one knows what causes it, but for some reason the body's own immune system attacks the myelin sheaths around neurones in the brain and spinal cord. Some researchers think that this inappropriate immune response might be triggered by a virus.

The photograph shows an MRI scan showing a transverse section of the brain of a person with multiple sclerosis. The white areas are places where the myelin sheaths around neurones have been broken down.

The damage to the neurones can cause a wide range of symptoms, including problems with vision, balance and muscle weakness. Usually, there are periods where these symptoms occur, interspersed with periods when the person is almost entirely free of them. In some, the symptoms get progressively worse, but in others the disease remains relatively mild over a long period of time.

At the moment, there is no treatment that completely cures MS, although several different drugs can be used to help to relieve the symptoms. Research is focused on finding ways of quietening the T lymphocytes that are responsible for the attacks of the immune system on the myelin sheaths.

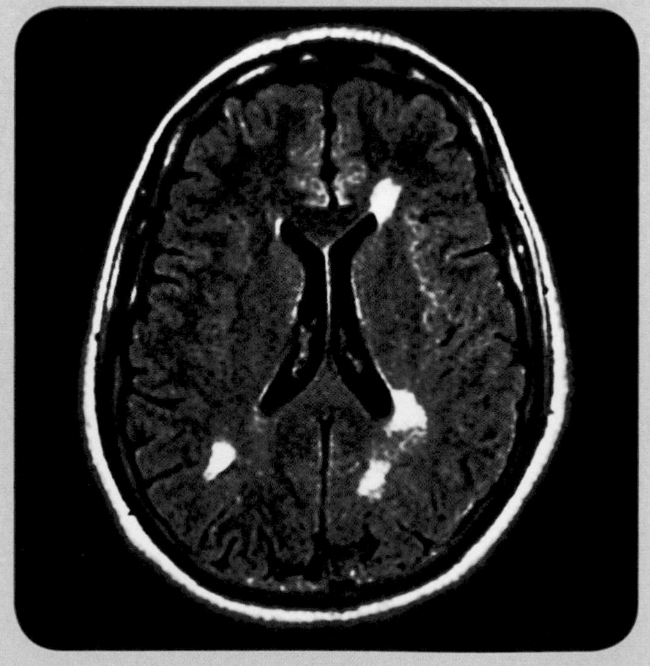

The wider the axon, the faster the speed of transmission. For example, in a relatively small human axon it may be no more than $15\,m\,s^{-1}$. Earthworms have 'giant axons' which can transmit action potentials at around $25\,m\,s^{-1}$. This enables an action potential to sweep along the whole length of the body very quickly, so the earthworm can respond very rapidly to a peck from a bird and escape into its burrow (Chapter 16).

Giant axons work well for an earthworm, but humans use a different system for speeding up the transmission of nerve impulses. Myelin insulates axons, and this speeds up the rate of transmission of an action potential along them. Sodium and potassium ions cannot flow through the myelin sheath, so it is not possible for depolarisation or action potentials to occur in parts of the axon that are surrounded by it. These can only happen in the gaps between the sheath, at the nodes of Ranvier.

Figure 2.13 shows how an action potential is transmitted along a myelinated axon. The local circuits that are set up stretch from one node to the next. Thus action potentials 'jump' from one node to the next, a distance of between 1 and 3 mm. This is called **saltatory conduction**. It can increase the speed of transmission by up to 50 times.

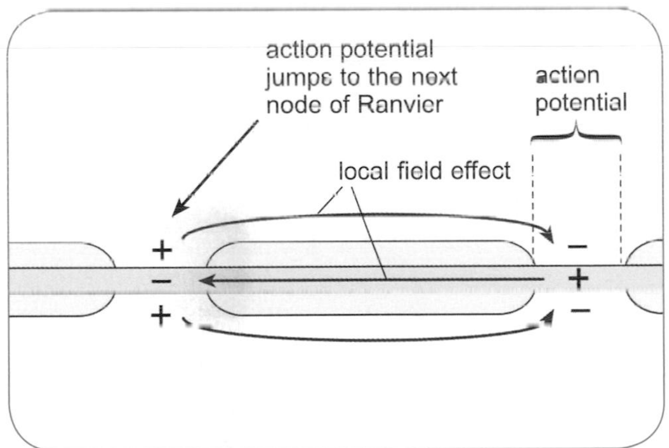

Figure 2.13 Saltatory conduction of an action potential along a myelinated neurone.

Types of receptors

On page 13, we saw how pressure acting on a skin receptor can produce an action potential in a sensory neurone. The receptor transforms mechanical energy in whatever is causing the pressure to electrical energy in the neurone. It is acting as a transducer. Receptors all work by converting a particular form of energy into nerve impulses. Table 2.1 summarises the type of energy that is transformed by different receptors.

Extension

Receptor	Sense	Form in which energy is received
rod or cone cells in retina	sight	light
taste buds on tongue	taste	chemical potential
olfactory cells in nose	smell	chemical potential
Pacinian corpuscles in skin	pressure	movement and pressure
Meissner's corpuscles in skin	touch	movement and pressure
Ruffini's endings in skin	temperature	heat
proprioceptors (stretch receptors) in muscles	placement of limbs ('body awareness')	mechanical displacement – stretching
hair cells in semicircular canals in ear	balance	movement
hair cells in cochlea	hearing	sound

Table 2.1 Some examples of energy conversions by receptors. Each type of receptor converts a particular form of energy into electrical energy in a nerve impulse.

Synapses

Where two neurones meet, they do not quite touch each other. There is a very small gap, usually about 20 nm wide, between them. This gap is called a **synaptic cleft**. The parts of the neurones near to the cleft, plus the cleft itself, make up a **synapse** (Figure 2.14).

How impulses cross a synapse

Action potentials cannot jump across synapses. Instead, the signal is passed across by a chemical, known as a **transmitter substance**. In outline, an action potential arriving along the plasma membrane of the presynaptic neurone causes it to release transmitter substance into the cleft. The transmitter substance molecules diffuse across the cleft, which takes less than a millisecond as the distance is so small. This may set up an action potential in the plasma membrane of the postsynaptic neurone.

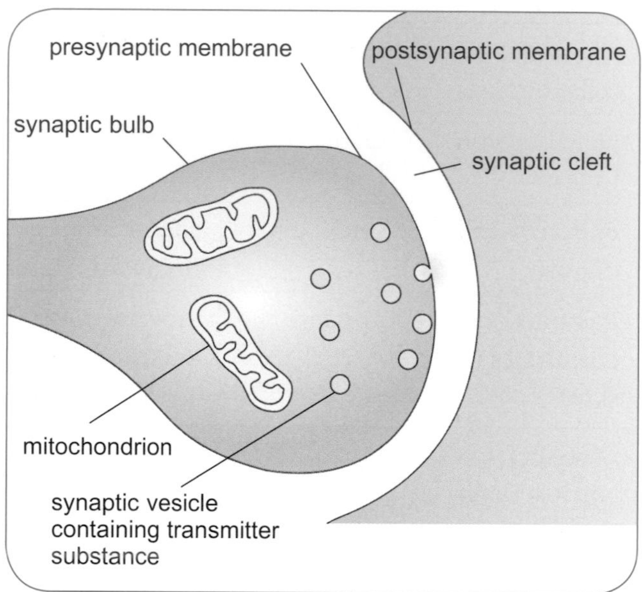

Figure 2.14 A synapse.

This is shown in Figure 2.15. The cytoplasm of the presynaptic neurone contains vesicles of transmitter substance. More than 40 different transmitter substances are known. **Noradrenaline** and **acetylcholine** (sometimes abbreviated to **ACh**) are found throughout the nervous system, while others such as **dopamine** and **glutamate** occur only in the brain. We will look at synapses which use acetylcholine as the transmitter substance; they are known as **cholinergic synapses**.

You will remember that, as an action potential sweeps along the plasma membrane of a neurone, local circuits depolarise the next piece of membrane. This opens voltage-gated Na^+ channels and propagates the action potential. In the part of the membrane of the presynaptic neurone that is next to the synaptic cleft, the action potential also causes **calcium ion channels** to open. So the action potential causes not only sodium ions but also calcium ions to flood into the cytoplasm.

This influx of calcium ions causes vesicles of acetylcholine to move to the presynaptic membrane and fuse with it, emptying their contents

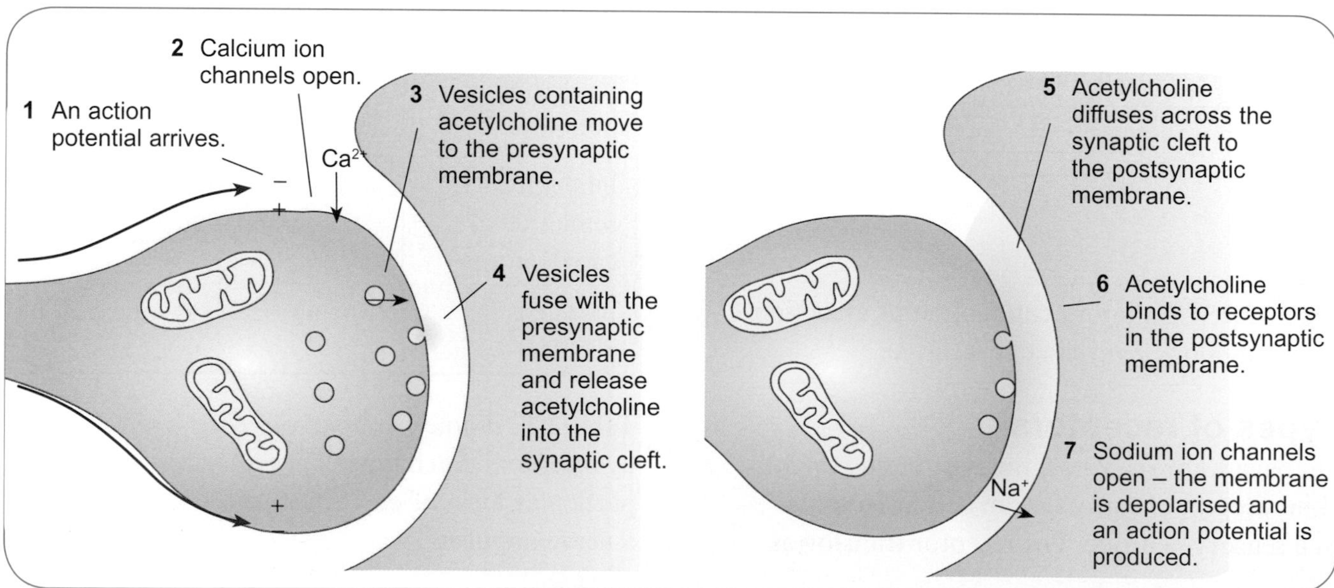

Figure 2.15 How an impulse crosses a synapse.

into the synaptic cleft. (This is an example of exocytosis.) Each action potential causes just a few vesicles to do this, and each vesicle contains up to 10 000 molecules of acetylcholine. This rapidly diffuses across the cleft, usually in less than 0.5 ms.

The plasma membrane of the postsynaptic neurone contains receptor proteins. Part of the receptor protein molecule has a complementary shape to part of the acetylcholine molecule, so that the acetylcholine molecules can bind with the receptors. This changes the shape of the protein, opening channels through which sodium ions can pass (Figure 2.16). Sodium ions rush into the cytoplasm of the postsynaptic neurone, depolarising the membrane and starting off an action potential.

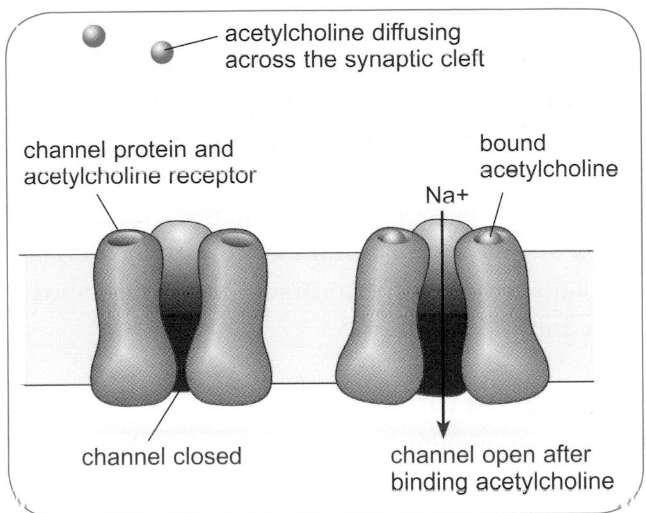

Figure 2.16 How an acetylcholine receptor works.

Action potentials in plants

Plants have action potentials, too. They do not have specific 'nerve cells', but many of their cells transmit waves of electrical activity that are very similar to those transmitted along the neurones of animals. The action potentials generally last much longer and travel more slowly than in animal neurones (see graph below).

Almost all animal and plant cells have sodium–potassium pumps, which maintain an electrochemical gradient across the plasma membrane, and it is this that produces the resting potential. As in animals, plant action potentials are triggered when the membrane is depolarised. Just as in animals, there is a refractory period following each action potential.

Many different types of stimuli have been shown to trigger action potentials in plants. In Venus fly traps, for example, the touch of a fly on one of the hairs on the leaf starts an action potential that travels across the leaf and causes it to fold over and trap the fly. This is quite fast as plant responses go, taking only about 0.5 s between the stimulus and the action.

Chemicals coming into contact with the plant's surface also trigger action potentials. For example, dripping a solution of acid of a similar pH to acid rain onto soya bean leaves causes action potentials to sweep across them. In potato plants, Colorado beetle larvae feeding on the leaves has been shown to induce action potentials, of the shape shown in the graph here. These travel only slowly, from the leaves down the stem and all the way to the tubers beneath the soil. At the moment, we don't know what effect, if any, these action potentials have, but it is thought that they might bring about changes in the metabolic reactions taking place in some parts of the plant.

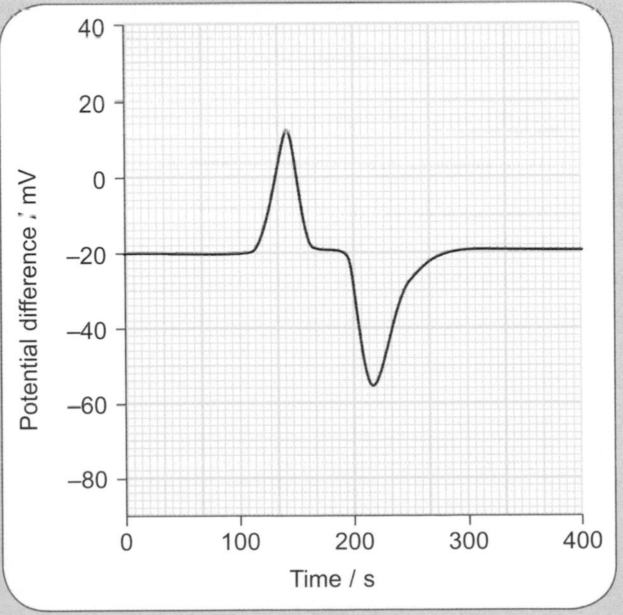

A **neuromuscular junction** is a synapse between the end of a motor neurone and a muscle. Here, the plasma membrane of the muscle fibre is the postsynaptic membrane, and acetylcholine sets up an action potential in it in just the same way as in a postsynaptic neurone. The action potential sweeps along the plasma membrane of the muscle fibre and causes the fibre to contract. This is described more fully in Chapter 15.

Recharging the synapse

If the acetylcholine remained bound to the postsynaptic receptors, the sodium ion channels would remain open. Action potentials might fire continuously, or it might be impossible to reinstate the resting potential across the membrane, so that there could be no new action potentials generated. To prevent either of these events from happening, and also to avoid wasting the acetylcholine, it is recycled. The synaptic cleft contains an enzyme, **acetylcholinesterase**, which splits each acetylcholine molecule into acetate and choline.

The choline is taken back into the presynaptic neurone, where it is combined with acetyl CoA to form acetylcholine once more. This resynthesis requires energy from ATP, supplied by mitochondria. The acetylcholine is then transported into the presynaptic vesicles, ready for the next action potential. The entire sequence of events from initial arrival of the action potential to the re-formation of acetylcholine, takes about 5–10 ms.

The functions of synapses

It isn't at first obvious why we have synapses. Action potentials could move much more swiftly through the nervous system if they did not have to cross synapses. In fact, synapses have numerous functions.

Ensuring one-way transmission

Signals can only pass in one direction at synapses. This ensures that signals can be directed along specific pathways, rather than spreading at random through the nervous system.

Interconnecting nerve pathways

Synapses allow a wider range of behaviour than could be generated in a nervous system in which neurones were directly 'wired up' to each other. At most synapses, many different neurones converge, so that many different possible pathways for the impulses are brought together. It may be necessary for action potentials to arrive along several neurones simultaneously before an action potential can be set up in another. The arrival of impulses at certain synapses actually *reduces* the likelihood of an action potential starting up in that neurone. These are called 'inhibitory' synapses.

Think for a moment of your possible behaviour when you see someone you know across the street. You can call out to them and walk to meet them, or you can pretend not see them and hurry away. It is events at your synapses that help to determine which of these two responses, or any number of others, you decide to make.

Your nervous system is receiving information from various sources about the situation. Receptors in your eyes send action potentials to your brain that provide information about what the person looks like and whether or not they have seen you. Inside your brain, information is stored about previous events involving this person, and also about what you were about to do before you saw them. All of these pieces of information are stored in the myriad of synaptic connections between your brain cells. They are integrated with each other, and as a result action potentials will or will not be sent to your leg muscles to take you towards your acquaintance.

Electric eels

The electric eel, *Electrophorus electricus*, is a fresh-water fish that lives in rivers in South America. It is a carnivore, and it captures its prey by giving it a high-voltage electric shock.

The eels have highly specialised effector cells, called electrocytes, that produce the electrical discharge. The electrocytes maintain a resting potential across themselves, negative inside, using the sodium–potassium pump.

Each electrocyte has a motor neurone that forms a synapse with it. The electrocytes are disc-shaped, and the motor neurone synapses with one of its surfaces. When an action potential arrives at the presynaptic membrane (on the motor neurone), acetylcholine is released and diffuses across the cleft, just as in an ordinary synapse. The acetylcholine slots into receptors on the postsynaptic membrane (on the electrocyte) and depolarises it.

But this only happens on one side of the electrocyte. The other side of the cell, where there is no synapse with a motor neurone, remains polarised. Momentarily, there is a difference in electrical potential on the two sides of the cell.

This difference is only 0.15 V, but electric eels greatly amplify it by having lots of electrocytes – as many as 200 000 – stacked up together, each facing in the same direction. It is like connecting a lot of electrical cells in series. The potential difference (voltage) produced by each cell adds up, producing a voltage that is enough to stun and often kill quite large prey.

This only works if all of the electrocytes discharge exactly in unison. This happens as the result of an 'electrocytes fire!' signal from the brain. When the eel detects prey, action potentials are sent off from the brain along the motor neurones that lead to the electrocytes. As each electrocyte has its own motor neurone, it is important that an action potential arrives at the end of each motor neurone simultaneously. But the electrocytes are not all the same distance from the brain. So, to achieve perfect synchronisation, motor neurones leading to electrocytes that are closer to the brain take a longer route than they might need to, or are narrower than others, slowing down the nerve impulses in them.

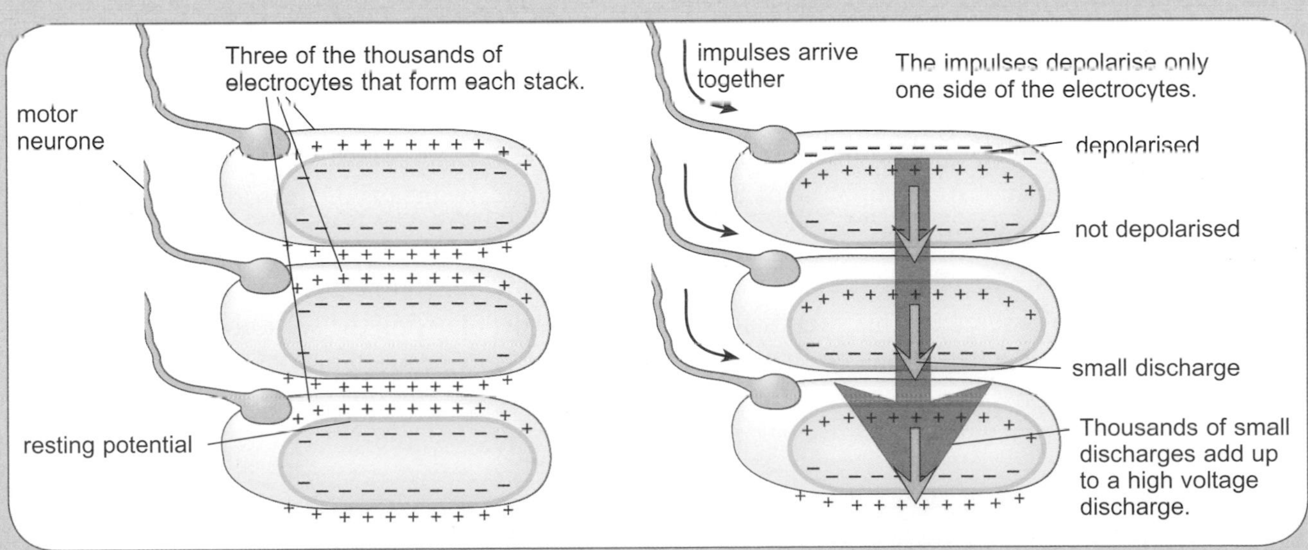

Three of the thousands of electrocytes that form each stack.
motor neurone
resting potential
impulses arrive together
The impulses depolarise only one side of the electrocytes.
depolarised
not depolarised
small discharge
Thousands of small discharges add up to a high voltage discharge.

Memory and learning

Despite much research, we still do not fully understand how memory operates. But we do know that it involves synapses. For example, if your brain frequently receives information about two things at the same time – say, the sound of a particular voice and the sight of a particular face – then new synapses form in your brain that link the neurones involved in the passing of information along the particular pathways from your ears and eyes. In future, when you hear the voice, information flowing from your ears along this pathway automatically flows into the other pathway too, so that your brain 'pictures' the face that goes with the voice.

Effects of other chemicals at synapses

Many drugs and other chemicals act by affecting the events at synapses.

Nicotine, found in tobacco, has a molecule with a similar shape to acetylcholine, which will fit into the acetylcholine receptors on postsynaptic membranes (Figure 2.16). This produces similar effects to acetylcholine, initiating action potentials in the postsynaptic neurone or muscle fibre. Unlike acetylcholine, however, nicotine is not rapidly broken down by enzymes, and so remains in the receptors for longer than acetylcholine. A large dose of nicotine can be fatal.

The **botulinum toxin** (Botox) is produced by an anaerobic bacterium which occasionally breeds in contaminated canned food. It acts at the presynaptic membrane, where it prevents the release of acetylcholine. Eating food that contains this bacterium is often fatal. However, the toxin does have important medical uses. In some people, for example, the muscles of the eyelids contract permanently, so that they cannot open their eyes. Injections of tiny amounts of the botulinum toxin into these muscles can cause them to relax, allowing the lids to be raised. Botox injections are widely used to smooth wrinkles in skin, especially around the eyes.

Organophosphorous insecticides inhibit the action of acetylcholinesterase, thus allowing acetylcholine to cause continuous production of action potentials in the postsynaptic membrane. Many flea sprays and collars for cats and dogs contain these insecticides, so great care should be taken when using them, for the health of both the pet and the owner. Contamination from organophosphorus sheep dip (used to combat infestation by ticks) has been linked to illness in farm workers. Several nerve gases also work in this way.

Summary

Glossary

- Neurones are highly specialised cells that transfer electrical impulses, in the form of action potentials, from one part of the body to another. Sensory neurones transfer impulses from receptors to the central nervous system, and motor neurones transfer them from the central nervous system to effectors.
- The axons of some neurones are sheathed with myelin, which insulates them and speeds up conduction of action potentials along them.
- Neurones maintain a resting potential of about −70 mV inside, by means of the sodium–potassium pump in the plasma membrane.
- If the plasma membrane is depolarised, voltage-gated sodium ion channels open and an action potential may be generated. This sweeps along the axon by depolarising the section of membrane just ahead of it. In myelinated axons, the action potential jumps between nodes of Ranvier.

continued

- During an action potential, the membrane briefly reaches a potential difference of +30 mV as sodium ions rush in through the voltage-gated sodium channels. Then voltage-gated potassium channels open, and the membrane returns to a potential difference that is negative inside, as potassium ions move out. The membrane cannot transmit another action potential until all the ion channels have returned to their normal state, and this period of time is called the refractory period.
- All action potentials are the same size. The stronger the stimulus, the greater the frequency of action potentials, and the more neurones carry action potentials.
- Receptors are cells that detect changes in the environment and change a particular form of energy – for example, light or sound – into electrical energy in an action potential.
- Synapses are found where two neurones meet. The arrival of an action potential along the plasma membrane of the presynaptic neurone causes calcium ion channels to open and calcium ions then rush into the cytoplasm. This causes vesicles of transmitter substance – for example, acetylcholine (ACh) – to move to the presynaptic membrane and fuse with it. The transmitter diffuses across the cleft and slots into receptors in the postsynaptic membrane. This opens sodium channels and sodium ions flood in, depolarising the postsynaptic membrane. If the depolarisation is great enough, an action potential is triggered in the postsynaptic neurone.
- Acetylcholinesterase in the synaptic cleft quickly breaks down acetylcholine into acetate and choline, which are reabsorbed into the presynaptic neurone and used to resynthesise acetylcholine.
- Synapses ensure that action potentials pass in only one direction, and that they can travel along a range of different pathways, but not at random. They are also involved in memory.

Stretch and challenge questions

1 Describe the roles of: Hint

a sodium ion channels

b potassium ion channels

c calcium ion channels

in the transmission of information along and between neurones.

2 Compare the structure of a motor neurone to that of a 'typical' animal cell, such as a liver cell. How does the specialised structure of a neurone relate to its function? Hint

Questions

1 The table shows how the speed of nerve impulse conduction varies with the diameter of myelinated and non-myelinated axons in different organisms.

Organism	Type of axon	Axon diameter / μm	Speed of impulse / m s^{-1}
crab	non-myelinated	30	5
squid	non-myelinated	500	25
cat	myelinated	20	100
frog	myelinated	16	32

a Describe the trends shown in the table. [2] Hint

b Explain how nerve impulses are transmitted along axons accounting for the differences shown in the table. [7]

c Explain the term *refractory period* and outline its importance in nerve impulse conduction. [4]

OCR Biology A (2804) June 2005 [Total 13]

Answer

2 Parkinson's disease is a disorder of the nervous system. People with this condition are unable to produce enough of the neurotransmitter substance dopamine. This chemical is required in neurone circuits in the brain that control movement.

a Outline two roles of synapses in the nervous system. [2]

The diagram illustrates the events at a synapse where the neurotransmitter is dopamine.

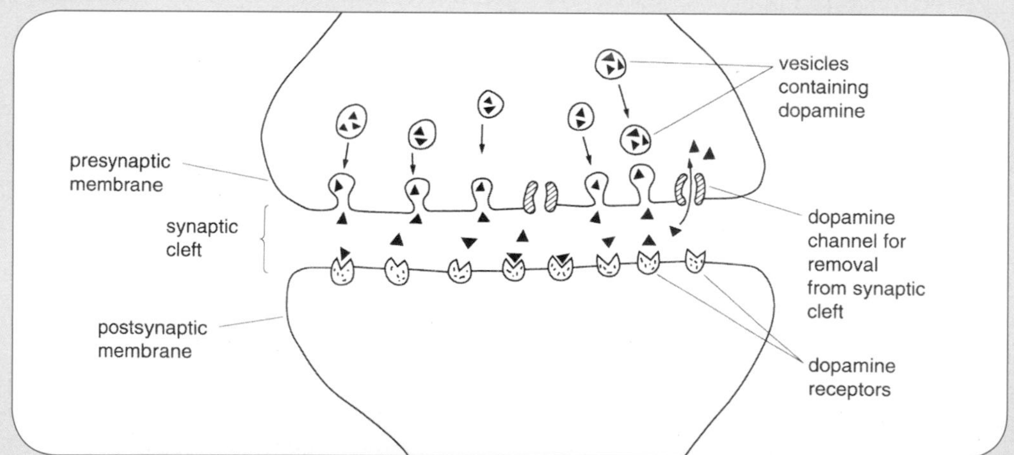

b Using only the information in the diagram, list three ways in which the events occurring at this synapse are the same as at a cholinergic synapse. [3]

c For the proper functioning of neurone circuits, neurotransmitters have to be removed from the receptors in the postsynaptic membrane and from the synaptic cleft. Explain why this is so. [2]

OCR Biology A (2804) June 2006 [Total 7]

Answer

Chapter 3

Hormones

e-Learning

Objectives

The nervous system is not the only one responsible for communication between different parts of the body. Many animals, including mammals, also have another system, the **endocrine system**, which transmits information from one cell or organ to another. This system is made up of **endocrine glands**, which secrete chemicals called **hormones**. The hormones travel in blood plasma from the gland where they are made, all over the body. The tissues that they affect are called their **target tissues**.

A gland is a group of cells that produces and releases one or more useful substances, a process known as **secretion**. Endocrine glands contain secretory cells that pass their secretions directly into the blood. 'Endocrine' means 'secreting to the inside', a reference to the fact that endocrine glands secrete hormones into blood capillaries inside the gland.

We also have glands of another type, called **exocrine glands** (Figure 3.1). These secrete substances into a **duct,** which carries them to a

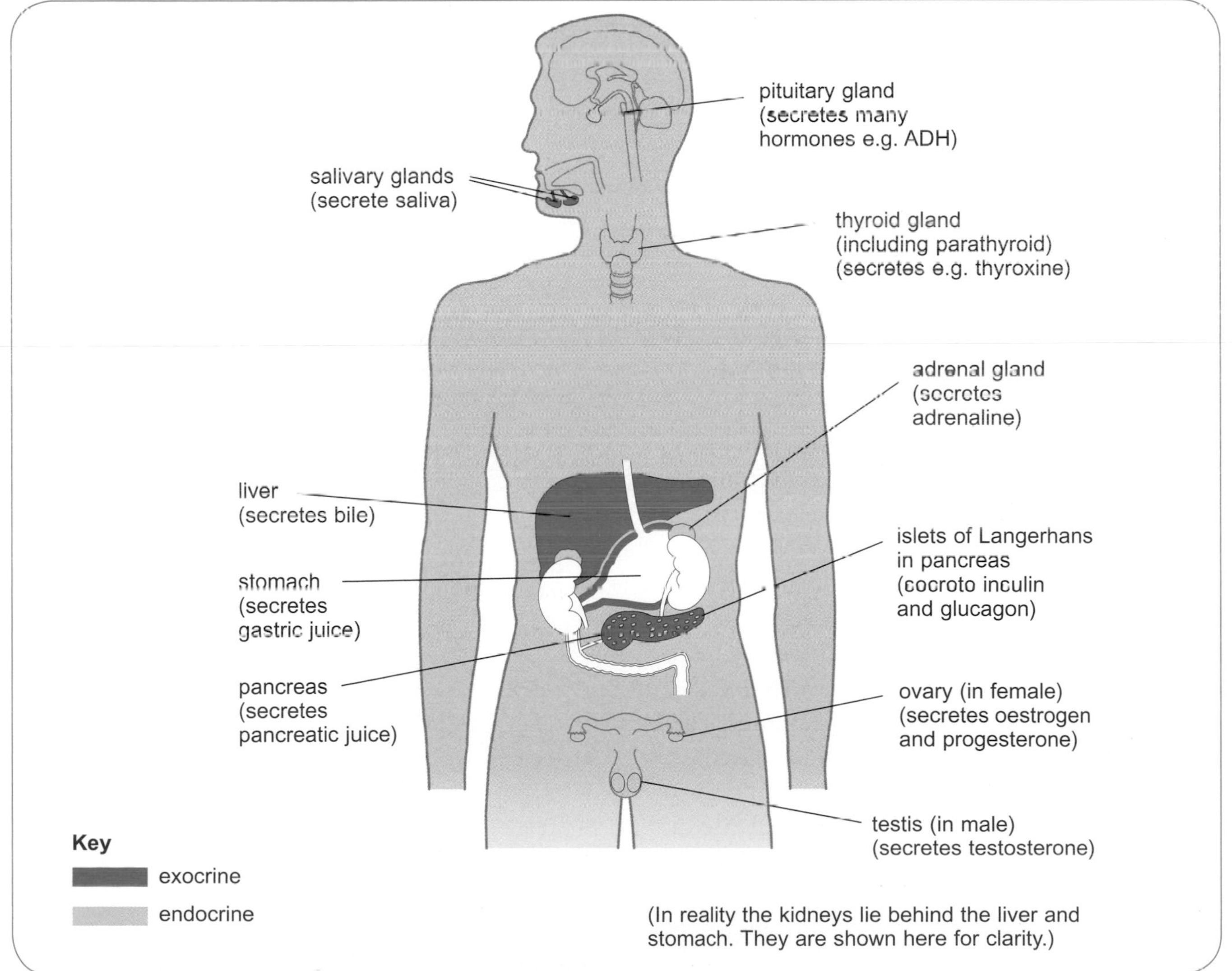

Figure 3.1 The positions of some exocrine and endocrine glands in the human body.

particular part of the body. 'Exocrine' means 'secreting to the outside'. There are many different exocrine glands in the body. One example is the salivary glands, which secrete saliva into salivary ducts that carry the saliva into the mouth.

Mammalian hormones

Mammalian hormones are usually relatively small molecules. Many, such as insulin, are polypeptides or proteins. Others, such as testosterone, are steroids. Adrenaline is a catecholamine, produced from amino acids.

After they have been secreted from an endocrine gland, hormones are transported around the body in the blood plasma. The concentrations of hormones in human blood are very small. For any one hormone, the concentration is rarely more than a few micrograms per cm^3 of blood. Their rate of secretion from endocrine glands is also low, usually of the order of a few micrograms or milligrams a day. These small quantities of hormone can, however, have very large effects on the body.

Most endocrine glands can secrete hormones very quickly when an appropriate stimulus arrives. In particular, adrenaline is secreted from the adrenal glands within less than one second of the arrival of a stimulus that elicits fear or excitement.

Many hormones have a very short life in the body. They are broken down by enzymes in the blood or in cells – often in the liver – or are lost in the urine. Insulin, for example, lasts for only around 10 to 15 minutes. Adrenaline lasts for between 1 to 3 minutes.

Although the blood carries hormones to all parts of the body, they only affect their particular target cells. These cells contain receptors for the hormone. The receptors for protein hormones, such as insulin, are in the plasma membrane. The hormones bind with the receptor on the outer surface of the membrane, and bring about a response without actually entering the cell. Steroid hormones, however, are lipid-soluble and they diffuse through the plasma membrane into the cytoplasm. The receptors for steroid hormones are in the cell cytoplasm.

SAQ

1 Explain why steroid hormones can pass easily through the plasma membrane while protein hormones cannot.

Hint

Answer

First and second messengers

Hormones affect their target cells by attaching to a specific receptor molecule, which sets into action a series of events within the cell. This is an example of cell signalling. We will look in particular at how **adrenaline** (sometimes known as **epinephrine**) affects the activity of liver cells (Figure 3.2 and Figure 3.3).

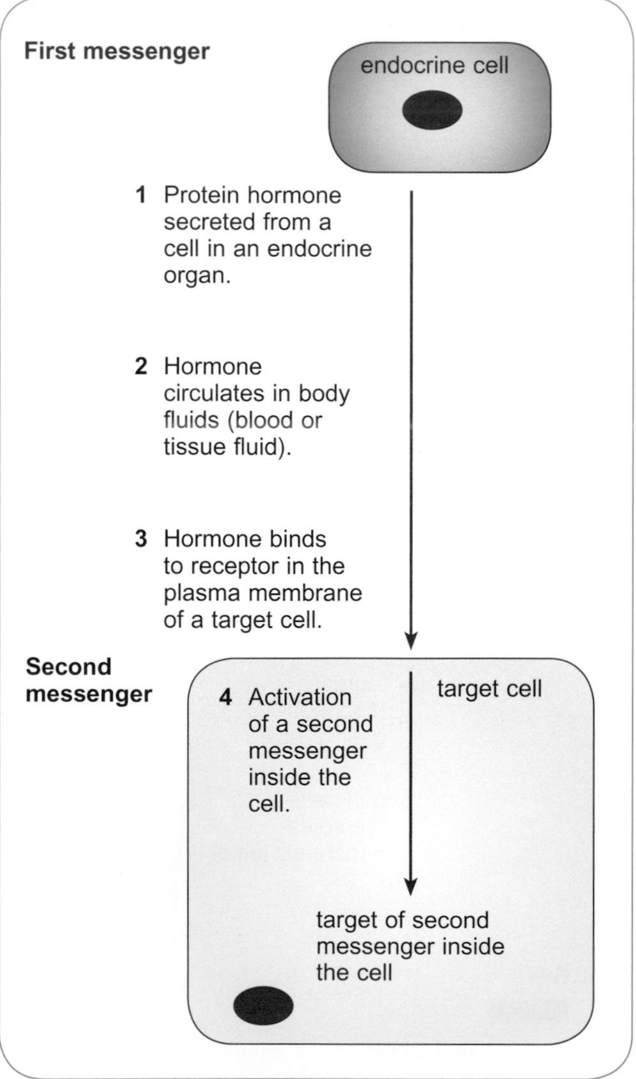

Figure 3.2 First and second messengers.

Adrenaline is secreted by the **adrenal glands** – which lie just above the kidneys – in response to excitement, danger or stress. It has a number of target organs and tissues, including the sino-atrial node in the heart, smooth muscle in the wall of the alimentary canal and the muscles in the iris of the eye. Adrenaline brings about changes that prepare the body for vigorous activity, such as might be needed if escaping from danger or fighting against it.

Adrenaline is a catecholamine, synthesised from amino acids and not soluble in lipids. Its target cells – for example, liver cells – therefore have receptors in their plasma membranes, into which adrenaline slots. The binding of adrenaline with its receptor alters the shape of the receptor, causing it to interact with another protein in the membrane called a **G-protein**. This causes the G-protein to split, and one part of it combines with an inactive enzyme called **adenylyl cyclase**. This activates the enzyme, which converts ATP to **cyclic AMP** (cAMP for short) (Figure 3.3).

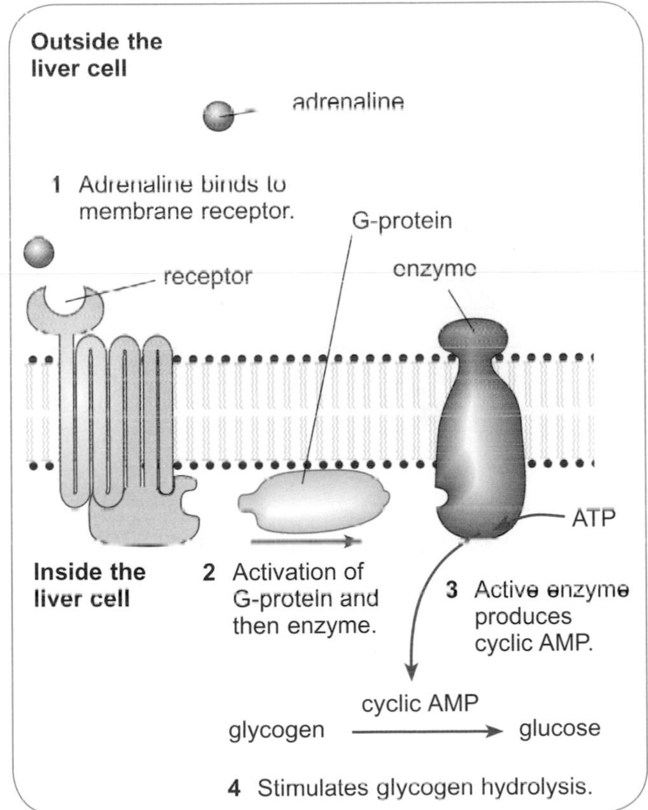
Outside the liver cell
adrenaline
1 Adrenaline binds to membrane receptor.
G-protein
receptor
enzyme
ATP
Inside the liver cell
2 Activation of G-protein and then enzyme.
3 Active enzyme produces cyclic AMP.
cyclic AMP
glycogen
glucose
4 Stimulates glycogen hydrolysis.

Figure 3.3 How adrenaline affects liver cells.

Extension

Now the cAMP binds to another inactive protein, this time an enzyme called **protein kinase**. Once again, the binding changes the shape of the enzyme, which activates it. The activated protein kinase in turn activates yet another enzyme, this time **glycogen phosphorylase kinase**, and this then binds to an enzyme called **glycogen phosphorylase**. Finally, glycogen phosphorylase catalyses the breakdown of glycogen in the liver cell, converting it to glucose.

The secretion of adrenaline has therefore brought about the production of glucose in liver cells, which can be transported in the blood to muscles so that they can respire quickly and generate ATP needed for contraction – to flee or fight the perceived danger. In this response, the adrenaline is known as a **first messenger** and the cAMP is a **second messenger**.

Adrenaline has different effects on other target cells, because the enzymes that are activated by cAMP are not the same in different kinds of cells. For example, it increases the rate of firing of the cells in the sino-atrial node, increasing heart rate. It causes contraction of smooth muscles in arterioles supplying blood to the alimentary canal, reducing the volume of blood flowing through them so that more blood can be diverted to the muscles.

SAQ

2 If you are in a frightening situation, adrenaline will be secreted and cause your heart rate to increase. This can go on for several hours. If adrenaline has a lifespan of only 1–3 minutes in the body, how can its effect continue for so long?

Answer

Extension

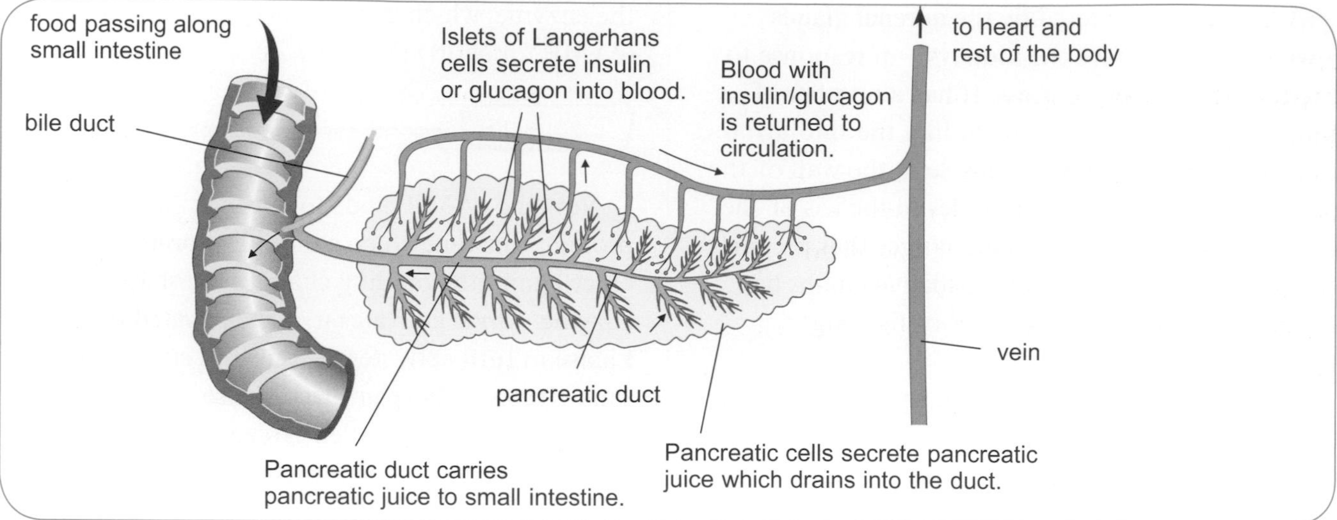

Figure 3.4 The position of the pancreas and its associated organs.

The pancreas

Figure 3.4, Figure 3.5 and Figure 3.6 show the structure of the pancreas.

The pancreas is a very unusual gland, because parts of it function as an exocrine gland, while other parts function as an endocrine gland.

The exocrine function is the secretion of **pancreatic juice**, which flows along the pancreatic duct into the duodenum. Pancreatic juice contains several enzymes, including:

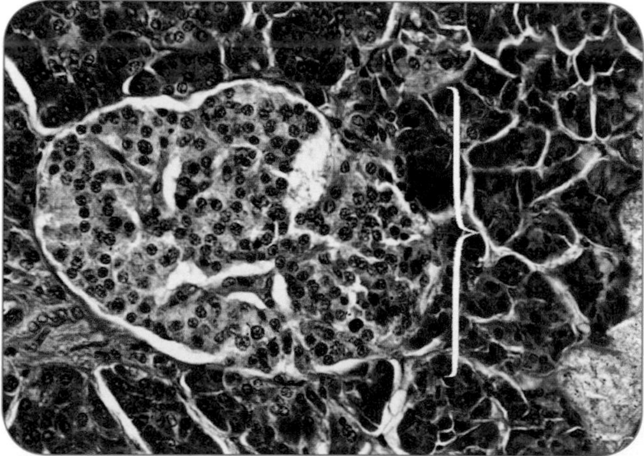

Figure 3.5 The group of cells in the centre of this light micrograph form an islet of Langerhans (bracketed). These cells secrete insulin and glucagon directly into the blood capillaries in the islet. The islet is surrounded by cells that secrete pancreatic juice, which does not enter the blood but is collected into branches of the pancreatic duct (×410).

- lipase, which catalyses the hydrolysis of lipids to fatty acids and glycerol
- amylase, which catalyses the hydrolysis of starch to maltose
- trypsin, which catalyses the hydrolysis of proteins to polypeptides.

Extension

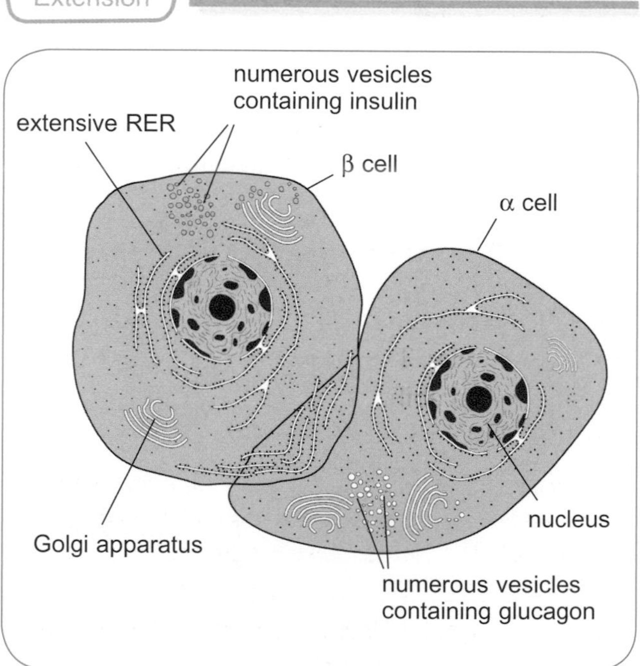

Figure 3.6 These diagrams are based on electron micrographs of alpha cells and beta cells. They look very similar, and it is difficult to tell them apart, but the insulin in beta cells tends to form dark, crystalline deposits that are easier to make out than the glucagon in the alpha cells.

The control of blood glucose by insulin and glucagon

Carbohydrate is transported through the human bloodstream in the form of glucose, in solution in the blood plasma. For storage, glucose can be converted to the polysaccharide **glycogen**, a large, insoluble molecule made up of many glucose units linked together by α1–4 glycosidic bonds with α1–6 branches. Glycogen can be stored inside liver cells and muscle cells.

In a healthy person, each 100 cm^3 of blood normally contains between 80 and 120 mg of glucose. If blood glucose concentration drops much below this, then cells may run short of glucose for respiration, and be unable to carry out their normal activities. This is especially important for any cells that can use *only* glucose for respiration, including brain cells. Very high blood glucose concentrations can also cause severe problems, as the water potential of the blood becomes lower than that inside body cells, which therefore lose water to the blood by osmosis.

After a meal containing carbohydrate, glucose from the digested food is absorbed from the small intestine and passes into the blood. As this blood flows through the pancreas, the **alpha** and **beta cells** in the **islets of Langerhans** detect the raised glucose levels. Alpha cells respond by stopping secretion of **glucagon**, while beta cells respond by secreting more **insulin** into the blood plasma. The insulin is carried to all parts of the body, in the blood.

Insulin affects many cells, especially those in the liver and muscles. The effects on these cells include:

- an increased ability of muscle cells and adipose tissue to absorb glucose from the blood. Glucose can only enter cells through transporter proteins. Muscle cells have glucose transporters called GLUT4, and these are normally kept in the cytoplasm. When insulin is detected by a muscle cell, the transporters are moved into the plasma membrane of the cell, where they form channels allowing glucose to enter (Figure 3.7). (Liver cells and brain cells have a different kind of glucose transporter, which is always present in the plasma membrane and is not affected by insulin, so they are always able to take up glucose.)

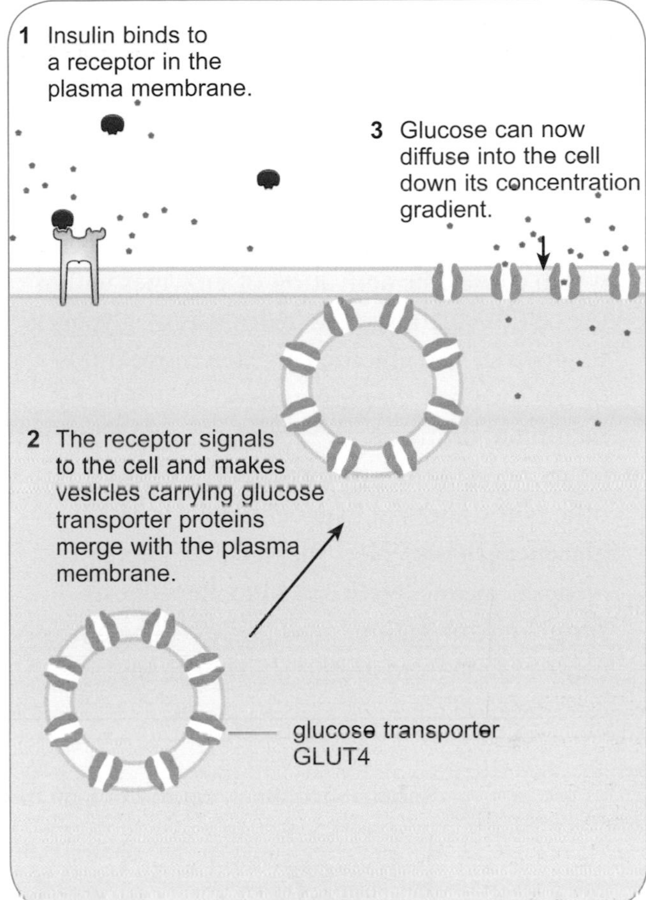

1 Insulin binds to a receptor in the plasma membrane.
3 Glucose can now diffuse into the cell down its concentration gradient.
2 The receptor signals to the cell and makes vesicles carrying glucose transporter proteins merge with the plasma membrane.
glucose transporter GLUT4

Figure 3.7 How insulin increases membrane permeability to glucose.

- an increase in the rate of production of glycogen from glucose inside liver cells. The arrival of insulin molecules at the receptors on the plasma membranes of liver cells causes the activation of the enzyme **glucokinase**, which phosphorylates glucose. This traps the glucose within the cell, because phosphorylated glucose cannot pass through the transporters in the plasma membrane. The arrival of insulin also brings about the activation of two other enzymes (phosphofructokinase and glycogen synthase), which together cause the glucose molecules to form α1–4 glycosidic bonds between each other, producing glycogen molecules.

Both of these effects cause the concentration of glucose in the blood to fall. This is sensed by the beta cells in the pancreas, and they reduce their secretion of insulin. You will recognise that this is a negative feedback mechanism.

The fall in blood glucose is also detected by the alpha cells in the pancreas, and these respond by secreting more glucagon. Glucagon has several effects, including:

- an increase in the rate of breakdown of glycogen in liver cells. Glucagon binds with receptors in the liver cell plasma membranes, which causes the activation of enzymes within the cell that catalyse the hydrolysis of glycogen to glucose. The glucose can then move out of the liver cell through glucose channels, by facilitated diffusion.
- an increase in the production of glucose from other substances in liver cells. This is called **gluconeogenesis**. 'Neo' means 'new', and 'genesis' means 'birth', so gluconeogenesis simply means making new glucose. The glucose can be made from amino acids or lipids.

Both of these actions cause the concentration of glucose in the blood to rise. This is detected by the alpha cells in the pancreas, and they respond by reducing their secretion of glucagon.

Together, the secretion of insulin and glucagon work as part of a negative feedback system, in which any deviation of blood glucose concentration from the norm brings about actions that move it back towards the norm. This is summarised in Figure 3.8.

Blood glucose levels never remain absolutely constant, even in the healthiest person. One reason for this is the inevitable time delay between a change in the blood glucose and the onset of actions to correct it. Time delays in control systems result in oscillations, where things do not stay absolutely constant but sometimes rise slightly above and sometimes drop slightly below the set point.

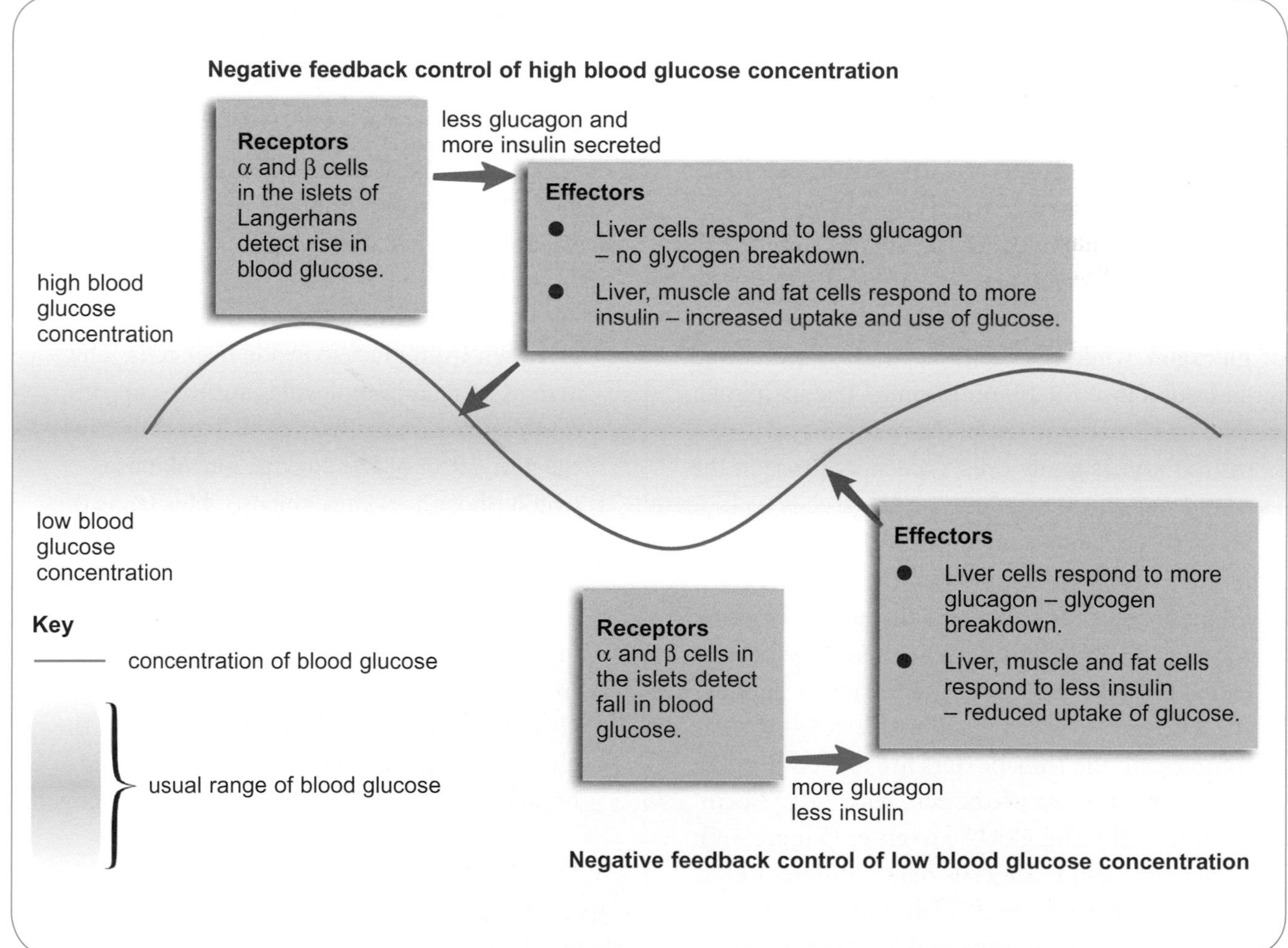

Figure 3.8 The negative feedback control mechanism for blood glucose concentration.

The control of insulin secretion

We have seen that the beta cells in the islets of Langerhans release insulin in response to raised blood glucose levels. How do they sense this, and how is the amount of insulin that is released controlled?

We still do not fully understand how insulin secretion is controlled. It is a complex process, and research continues to discover new factors that influence it. The description that follows is only a part of a more complex complete picture.

The beta cells contain several types of channels in their plasma membranes, each of which allows a particular type of ion to pass through. These include potassium ion, K^+, channels and calcium ion, Ca^{2+}, channels (Figure 3.9).

Normally, the K^+ channels are open, allowing K^+ ions to pass through the membranes freely. They diffuse from inside the cell to the outside. This helps to maintain a slight positive charge on the outside of the membrane with respect to the inside.

When glucose levels around the beta cell are raised, more glucose than usual passes into the cell through glucose transporter proteins. As the glucose enters the cell, it is phosphorylated by the enzyme glucokinase. The phosphorylated glucose is then metabolised to form ATP.

The K^+ channels are sensitive to the amount of ATP in the cell, and they respond to this increase by closing. So now the K^+ ions cannot diffuse out. As a result, the difference in electrical potential between the outside and inside of the membrane becomes less.

Now the Ca^{2+} channels come into the picture. They normally remain closed, but the change in potential difference causes them to open. Calcium ions flood into the cell from the tissue fluid outside it.

The Ca^{2+} ions affect the behaviour of the vesicles containing insulin inside the cell. These vesicles are moved towards the plasma membrane, where they fuse with the membrane and empty their contents outside the cell.

SAQ

3 List four examples of cell signalling that are involved in the control of blood glucose concentration.

Hint

Answer

4 Compare the mechanisms involved in the release of insulin from a beta cell and the transmission of nerve impulses in neurones.

Hint

Answer

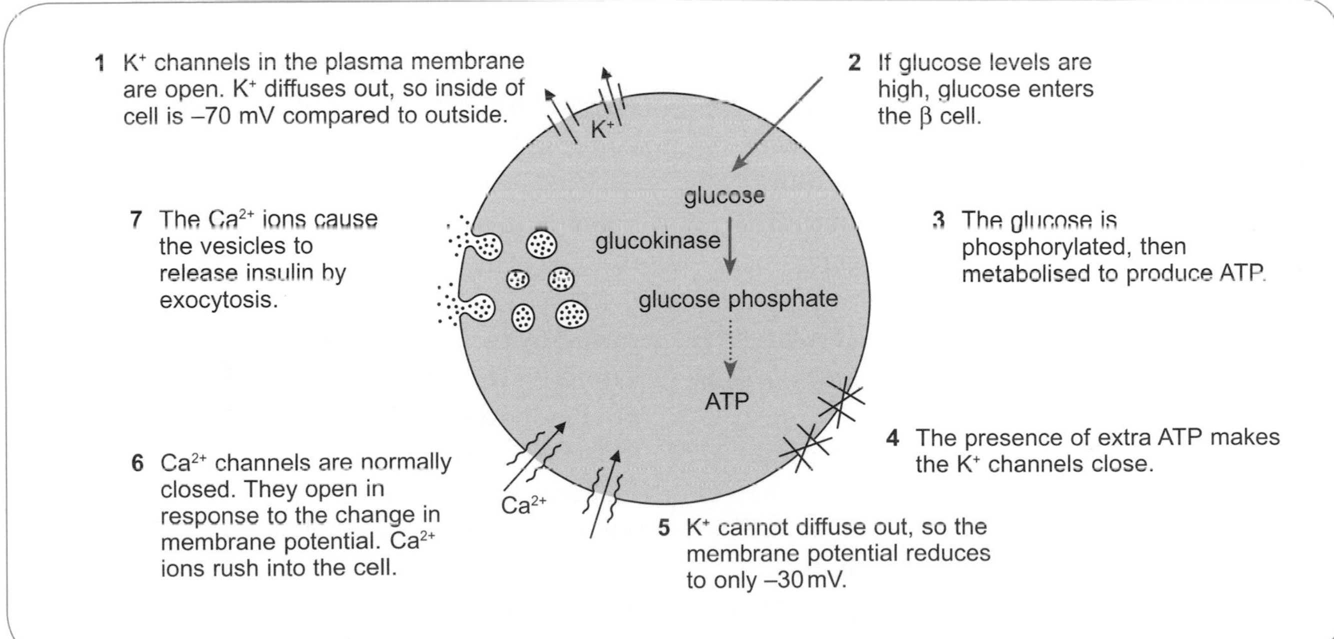

1 K⁺ channels in the plasma membrane are open. K⁺ diffuses out, so inside of cell is –70 mV compared to outside.
K⁺
2 If glucose levels are high, glucose enters the β cell.
glucose
glucokinase
glucose phosphate
ATP
3 The glucose is phosphorylated, then metabolised to produce ATP.
4 The presence of extra ATP makes the K⁺ channels close.
5 K⁺ cannot diffuse out, so the membrane potential reduces to only –30 mV.
6 Ca²⁺ channels are normally closed. They open in response to the change in membrane potential. Ca²⁺ ions rush into the cell.
Ca²⁺
7 The Ca²⁺ ions cause the vesicles to release insulin by exocytosis.

Figure 3.9 How insulin secretion is controlled.

Diabetes mellitus

Diabetes mellitus, usually just called diabetes, is an illness in which the blood glucose control mechanism has partly or completely broken down. It is very important to diagnose and control this disease as early as possible, because wildly swinging blood glucose levels are highly dangerous to many body organs. Good treatment can keep things well under control and allow people with diabetes to live almost entirely normal lives.

There are two types of diabetes. **Type 1 diabetes**, sometimes known as insulin-dependent diabetes, begins at a very early age. The pancreas appears to be incapable of secreting enough insulin, so that blood glucose levels may soar after a carbohydrate-containing meal. **Type 2 diabetes**, also known as non-insulin-dependent diabetes, typically begins later in life. The pancreas does secrete insulin, but the liver and other target organs do not respond to it adequately.

Risk factors for diabetes

The risk factors for Type 1 diabetes are not known. It is thought that the development of this illness may be affected by a person's genes, but there also seem to be some environmental risk factors. In particular, it has been suggested that the person's own immune system may attack their beta cells, although why this should happen is not yet understood.

Type 2 diabetes is most likely to develop in people with an excessively high body weight, especially those with a BMI (body mass index) above 27. (To calculate your BMI, divide your weight, in kilograms, by your height, in metres, squared.) People with 'apple-shaped' figures (most fat carried around the middle) are at greater risk than those with 'pear-shaped' figures (most fat carried around the hips and thighs). A sedentary lifestyle also increases the risk.

There is even more evidence for a genetic link for Type 2 diabetes than there is for Type 1. The first contributory gene was tracked down in the year 2000. It lies on chromosome 2. Since then, others have been discovered and it is expected that more will be found as research progresses.

Symptoms of diabetes

Many people have Type 2 diabetes for years without knowing it. First symptoms can go unrecognised. The person may feel tired or thirsty all the time, but as the development of these symptoms is slow they may just creep up stealthily and be unnoticed.

An understanding of what is going wrong can explain these symptoms. Imagine that a diabetic person eats a meal containing a lot of sugar. As this is absorbed, blood glucose levels go well above normal, but the liver and muscle cells are not alerted and do not take corrective action.

The very high blood glucose levels mean that the kidneys (Chapter 4) are not able to stop glucose being excreted in the urine. Instead of being stored in the liver as glycogen, much of the glucose is lost from the body. Later, when the glucose in the blood has been used in respiration, and if the person does not eat again, blood glucose levels may drop well below normal. The liver cells have not stored any as glycogen, so they cannot release glucose to bring up the level in the blood. The person feels very tired and may even become unconscious.

Having a high blood glucose level is known as **hyperglycaemia**. It is usually defined as a level above about 250 mg per 100 cm^3 (15 $mmol\,dm^{-3}$). In the short term, hyperglycaemia makes the person feel unwell. They may have a dry mouth and blurred vision. They may also feel very thirsty, because the high concentration of glucose in the body fluids reduces their water potential; this is detected by the hypothalamus, which sends nerve impulses to parts of the brain that control feelings of thirst. The person may be confused. Sometimes hyperglycaemia is associated with **ketoacidosis**, caused by the presence of substances called ketone bodies in the blood. The ketone bodies are produced from fatty acids in the liver, and can be used as respiratory substrates. However, in diabetes they may be produced faster than they are used and high concentrations of them can be dangerous. Up to 10% of diabetic people admitted to hospital with ketoacidosis die.

Having a low blood glucose level is known as **hypoglycaemia**. The person feels exceptionally tired and may become confused and show irrational behaviour. Hypoglycaemia is not restricted to people with diabetes. Many normal people can become mildly hypoglycaemic if they have not eaten for a while, and be quite unaware that their mood and behaviour have changed as a result. However, a person with diabetes is more likely to suffer severe attacks of hypoglycaemia. If caught early, hypoglycaemia is easily treated by eating something sugary.

SAQ

5 A glucose tolerance test can be used to diagnose diabetes. A person fasts overnight, and then is given a drink containing a known mass of glucose. Their blood glucose levels are measured over the next few hours. The graphs show the results of glucose tolerance tests carried out on a normal person and a person with Type 2 diabetes.

a These questions are about the graphs for the normal person. Hint

i Explain why the blood glucose concentration rises during the first 20 minutes.

ii Explain why the insulin level also rises during this time.

iii Suggest two reasons why the blood glucose level begins to fall after 45 minutes.

iv Suggest why the insulin level does not begin to fall as soon as the blood glucose level begins to decrease.

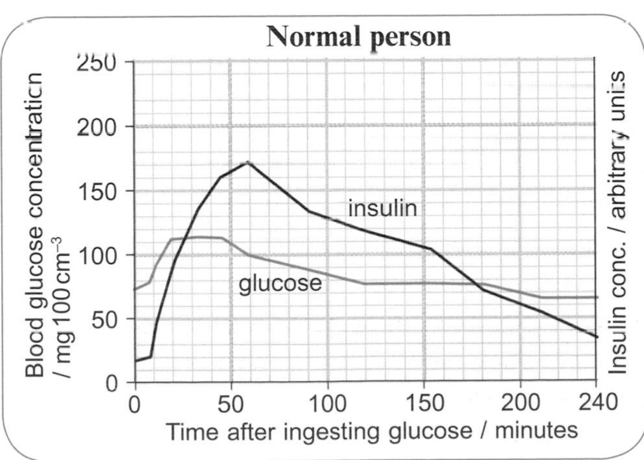

b Now look at both graphs.

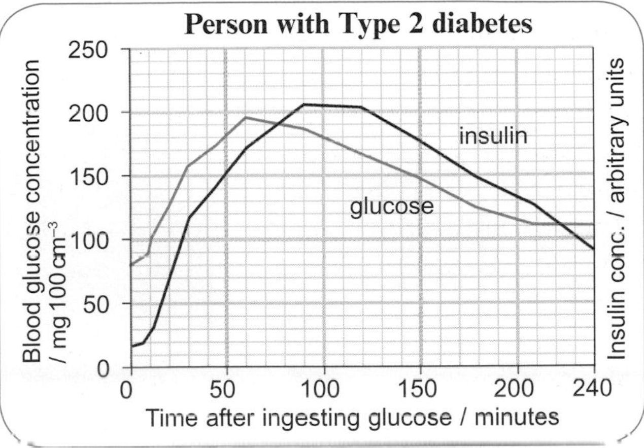

i Describe how the pattern of blood glucose concentration for the person with diabetes differs from that for the normal person.

ii Describe how the pattern of blood insulin concentration for the person with diabetes differs from that for the normal person.

iii Suggest explanations for these differences. Answer

Treating diabetes

As yet, there is no cure for diabetes. However, research into the use of gene therapy and also the use of stem cells gives hope for the future.

The management of diabetes mellitus revolves around keeping blood glucose concentrations reasonably constant. The patient may need to check their blood glucose regularly, which is generally done with a simple sensor providing a digital readout (Figure 3.10).

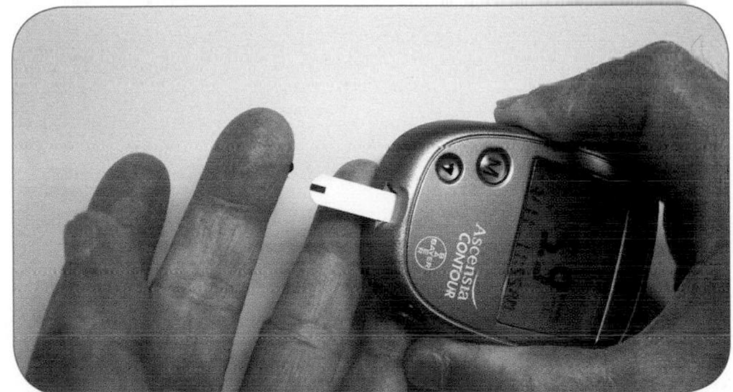

Figure 3.10 This biosensor gives an automatic readout of blood glucose concentration from just a tiny drop of blood.

Urine can also be checked for glucose, using a dipstick, for example (Figure 3.11). If the illness is under control, then there should be no more than very small amounts of glucose present in urine.

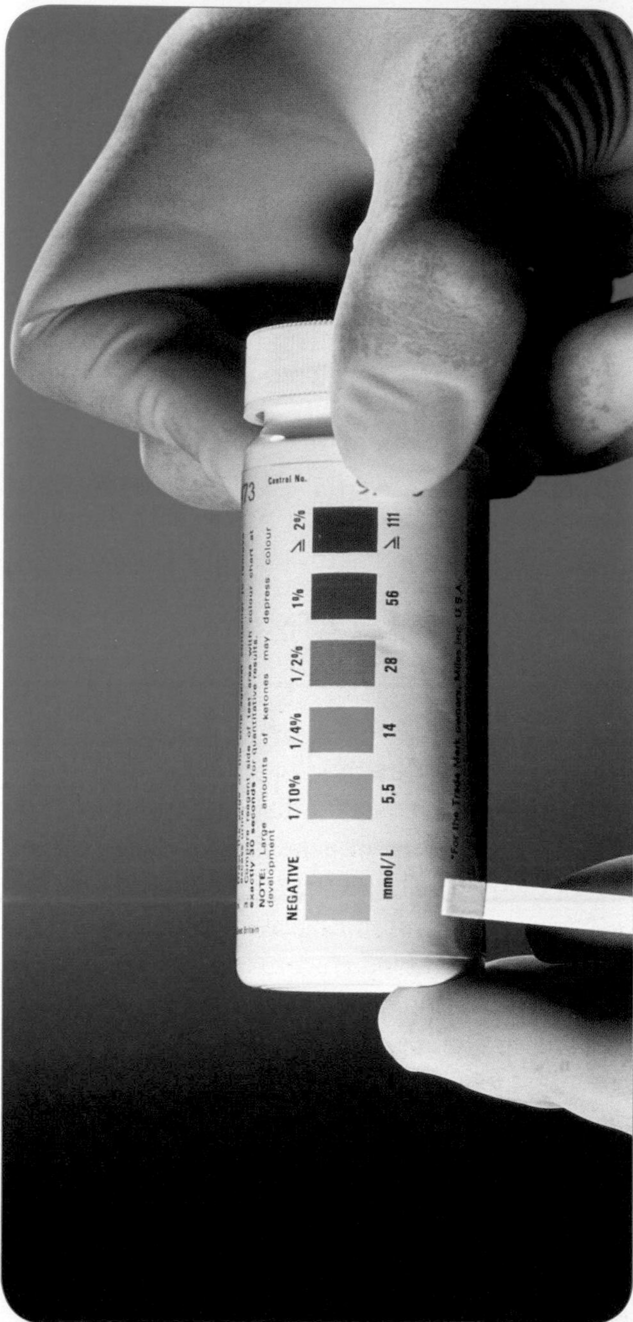

Figure 3.11 The colour produced on the dipstick can be matched up to a colour on the scale given on the chart, to read off the approximate glucose concentration of whatever the stick was dipped into.

In Type 2 diabetes, a well-controlled diet may be able to keep symptoms at bay. If the patient is obese, then weight loss through diet and exercise will be the first target. It is often possible to manage Type 2 diabetes, at least in the early stages, through diet alone. The person needs to eat small meals at reasonably regular intervals, never flooding their blood with excess glucose and never allowing blood glucose levels to drop too low. Polysaccharides are a better carbohydrate source than sugars, because it takes time for them to be digested and then absorbed, spreading out the time over which sugars are absorbed into the blood and avoiding a sharp 'spike' in blood glucose concentration.

SAQ

6 Suggest why testing the level of glucose in blood is more useful than testing the level of glucose in urine.

Answer

Almost all people with Type 1 diabetes, and many with Type 2 diabetes, use insulin injections to help them to control their blood glucose level. Different people may need one, two, three or more injections each day. Most insulin now available is produced by transgenic (genetically modified) bacteria or yeast. Some people still prefer to use insulin obtained from the pancreases of pigs, but this is now in very short supply.

GM insulin is made by genetically modified *Escherichia coli* bacteria. The human gene for insulin has been inserted into them, and they use the genetic code on this gene to make human insulin. Previously, all insulin had to be taken from slaughtered animals, usually pigs. It was thought that the GM insulin would be better for most people, because it is identical to human insulin; pig insulin is slightly different. However, some people have found that that the GM insulin does not seem to suit them as well as pig insulin. For example, a few people find that they seem to be less aware when their blood glucose levels

SAQ

7 The graph shows the changes in blood glucose concentration in a person who ate 50 g of carbohydrate as wholemeal bread and others who ate 50 g of carbohydrate as lentils and as soya beans.

a Explain the shape of the curve when bread was eaten. Hint

b Describe the differences between this curve and the ones showing the results after lentils and soya were eaten. Hint

c Suggest reasons for these differences. Answer

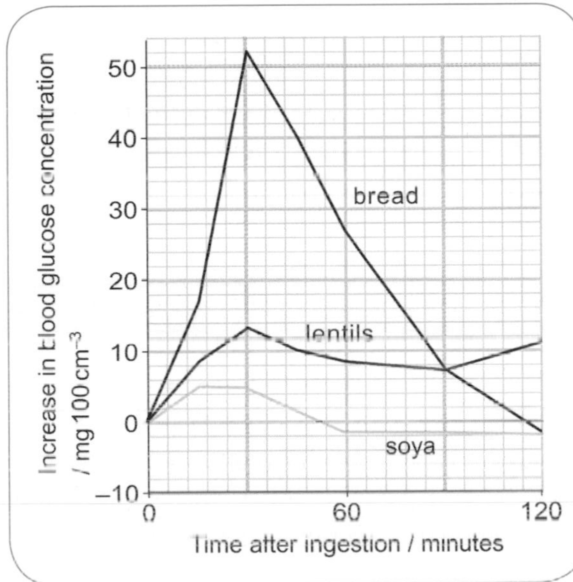

are going too high or too low, and therefore run a higher risk of running into problems with hypo or hyperglycaemia than when they used pig insulin. The reasons for this difficulty are not at all clear. In general, GM insulin is considered to be a better choice. It is cheaper, does not use pigs – which is unacceptable to some people – and is easier to produce to a repeatable standard and concentration.

For most people with diabetes, however, the real hope is that stem cell technology will soon advance to a stage where their illness can actually be cured, rather than simply managed. Stem cells are cells that have not fully differentiated, and are able to divide and then form specialised cells. It may one day be possible to transplant stem cells into a pancreas that has no functioning beta cells, and persuade these stem cells to form new beta cells that can secrete insulin.

However, there are still several hurdles to be overcome before this becomes a commonplace treatment. As we saw in *Biology 1*, the stem cells that have so far been found in adults can each differentiate into only a narrow range of types of cells, and at the moment this does not include beta cells. Cells obtained from blastocysts, however, are totipotent, meaning that they have the ability to differentiate into any type of specialised cell. In theory, transplanting embryonic stem cells into someone's pancreas could provide them with new beta cells. In practice, this is proving very difficult to achieve.

In 2007, however, there was a major breakthrough. This did not use stem cells to make new beta cells, but took an entirely different approach. The trial involved fifteen young people with Type 1 diabetes. The plan was to remove from their bodies the white blood cells that were thought to be attacking their own beta cells.

First, some of their own stem cells that constantly divide to replace white blood cells were harvested. Then the young people were given chemotherapy to destroy their white blood cells that were attacking their pancreases. Finally, the harvested stem cells were replaced. The hope was that these stem cells would make new white cells that did not attack the beta cells in the pancreas.

The results were encouraging, with evidence that new white cells were made, but much more will need to be done before any treatment such as this becomes commonplace.

This is an area of research where things are changing fast, and by the time you read this there may be other good news about the potential of **stem cell therapy** for the treatment of diabetes.

Controlling heart rate

As we saw in *Biology 1*, the beating of the heart is myogenic – that is, heart muscle naturally contracts and relaxes rhythmically without any requirement for nerve impulses. Each contraction is initiated at the sino-atrial node (SAN), and electrical activity sweeps through the wall of the heart from here, ensuring that each part of the heart contracts at an appropriate moment.

But what determines the pace that is set by the SAN? You know that your heart beats faster when you are exercising or when you are frightened. These effects are brought about by information transferred through the body to the SAN through nerves and hormones.

The SAN receives nerve impulses along two different nerves. One is called the **vagus nerve** (a **parasympathetic nerve**), and action potentials arriving along the vagus slow down the rate at which the SAN fires. The other is a **sympathetic nerve**, and this speeds up heart rate. (Chapter 15 has more information about these nerves.) The neurones in both of these nerves arise from the cardiac centre in the brain, and their activity is affected by numerous factors. For example, if the concentration of carbon dioxide in the blood increases, or the concentration of oxygen decreases, then action potentials will pass along the sympathetic nerve, speeding up heart rate.

The hormone **adrenaline** has a similar effect to stimulation by the sympathetic nerve. Adrenaline, as we have seen, is secreted by the adrenal glands in times of stress, and it speeds up the rate of the SAN and hence heart rate.

SAQ

8 Suggest why it is useful for heart rate to increase when carbon dioxide levels in the blood are high or when oxygen levels are low.

Answer

Beta blockers

Beta blockers are drugs that are often prescribed for people with high blood pressure, or who suffer from angina. They reduce the risk of a heart attack.

Beta blockers work by binding with the receptors for noradrenaline and adrenaline, blocking them so that noradrenaline and adrenaline cannot bind. So, if you are feeling nervous and your sympathetic nervous system is sending nerve impulses that would normally speed up your heart rate, the noradrenaline cannot bind with the receptors in the membranes of the cells in the SAN and therefore does not affect the SAN's activity.

Beta blockers are very valuable in the treatment of heart disease, because they prevent the heart rate from rising too high and therefore reduce strain on it. They also help to reduce high blood pressure, by preventing nerve impulses reaching the smooth muscle in the walls of arterioles, which would otherwise make these muscles contract. They have also proved useful in the prevention of some migraines.

These drugs can also improve performance in sports that require steadiness and concentration, such as shooting and archery, because they help a person to stay calm and reduce tremors in muscles. Snooker players may benefit from using beta blockers, as they make it easier to keep absolutely steady while making a shot. They are banned in snooker competitions and in many others, as they could give an unfair advantage.

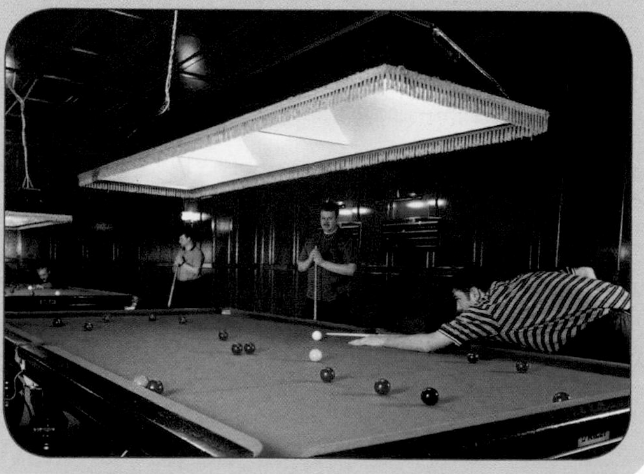

Summary

Glossary

- Hormones are chemicals that are secreted by endocrine glands, and are carried in the blood all over the body. They affect target organs, whose cells contain receptors specific for each hormone.
- Exocrine glands – for example, salivary glands – secrete substances into a duct, rather than directly into the blood.
- Protein-based hormones, which are insoluble in lipids, bind with a receptor in the plasma membrane. Lipid-soluble hormones pass through the membrane and bind with a receptor in the cytoplasm.
- Adrenaline is secreted by the adrenal glands in response to fear or excitement, and binds with a G-protein-coupled receptor in the plasma membranes of a liver cell. This brings about the production of cAMP inside the cell, which in turn results in the conversion of glycogen to glucose. Adrenaline is an example of a first messenger, and cAMP is a second messenger.
- The islets of Langerhans in the pancreas have an endocrine function, secreting insulin and glucagon. The rest of the pancreas is exocrine, secreting pancreatic juice into the pancreatic duct.
- Insulin is secreted in response to high blood glucose levels, and brings about actions in liver cells and muscle cells that reduce blood glucose level. Glucagon is secreted in response to low blood glucose levels, and causes liver cells to increase glucose production.
- High blood glucose levels cause potassium ion channels to close in the membranes of beta cells in the pancreas. This causes calcium ion channels to open, so calcium ions flood into the beta cell. This results in the secretion of insulin from the cell.
- Type 1 diabetes occurs when the beta cells do not make insulin. Type 2 diabetes results when insulin is produced, but the target cells do not respond to it adequately.
- Type 1 diabetes requires treatment with insulin, which is now mostly obtained from genetically modified bacteria. It may eventually be possible to treat diabetes with stem cells that divide to produce cells that differentiate into insulin-producing beta cells.
- Heart rate is controlled by altering the rate of firing of the SAN. Adrenaline speeds it up. Nerve impulses arriving along the sympathetic nerve also increase heart rate. Nerve impulses arriving along the vagus (parasympathetic) nerve decrease the rate.

Stretch and challenge question

1 Discuss the role of cell signalling in the functioning of the endocrine system.

Hint

Questions

1 **a** Explain the term *endocrine gland*. [2]

b The diagram is a flow diagram of the role of the pancreas in controlling blood glucose concentration. Study the diagram and answer the questions below.

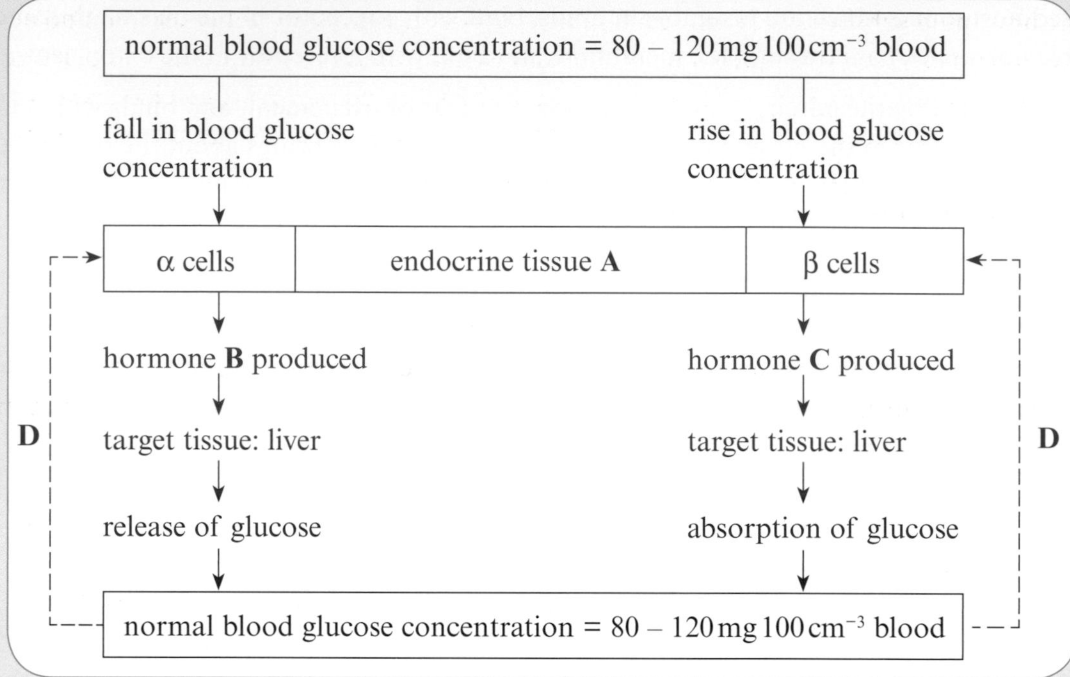

i Name the endocrine tissue labelled **A**. [1]

ii Name the hormone, **B**, produced by the α cells. [1]

iii Name the hormone, **C**, produced by the β cells. [1]

iv Name the process represented by the dotted lines labelled **D**. [1]

v Describe how hormone **B** brings about a rise in blood glucose concentration when it reaches the liver. [5]

c Untreated diabetes is a condition that can lead to blood glucose concentrations often rising above 120 mg 100 cm^{-3} of blood. Genetic engineering has been used to improve the treatment of diabetes.
Explain the advantages of using genetic engineering in the treatment of diabetics. [3]

OCR Biology A (2804) June 2005 [Total 14]

Answer

Chapter 4

Excretion

e-Learning

Objectives

Many of the metabolic reactions occurring in the body produce unwanted substances. Some of these are toxic (poisonous). The removal from the body of these unwanted products of metabolism is known as **excretion**.

There are several excretory products formed in our bodies, but two are made in much greater quantities than the others. These are **carbon dioxide** and **urea**.

Carbon dioxide is produced continuously by almost every cell in the body, by the reactions of aerobic respiration. The waste carbon dioxide is transported from the respiring cells to the lungs, in the bloodstream. It diffuses from the blood into the alveoli of the lungs, and is excreted in the air that we breathe out (*Biology 1*, page 52).

Urea, however, is produced in only one organ – the **liver**. It is formed from excess amino acids, and is transported from the liver to the kidneys, in solution in blood plasma. The kidneys remove urea from the blood and excrete it, dissolved in water, as **urine**.

The liver

The liver is one of the largest organs in the body. Almost 30% of the blood that is pumped with each heartbeat flows through the liver. A total of 1450 cm^3 of blood passes through it every minute. It has an enormous variety of functions involving many different metabolic reactions.

The liver lies just beneath the diaphragm, towards the right-hand side of the body (Figure 4.1). It is made up of several lobes.

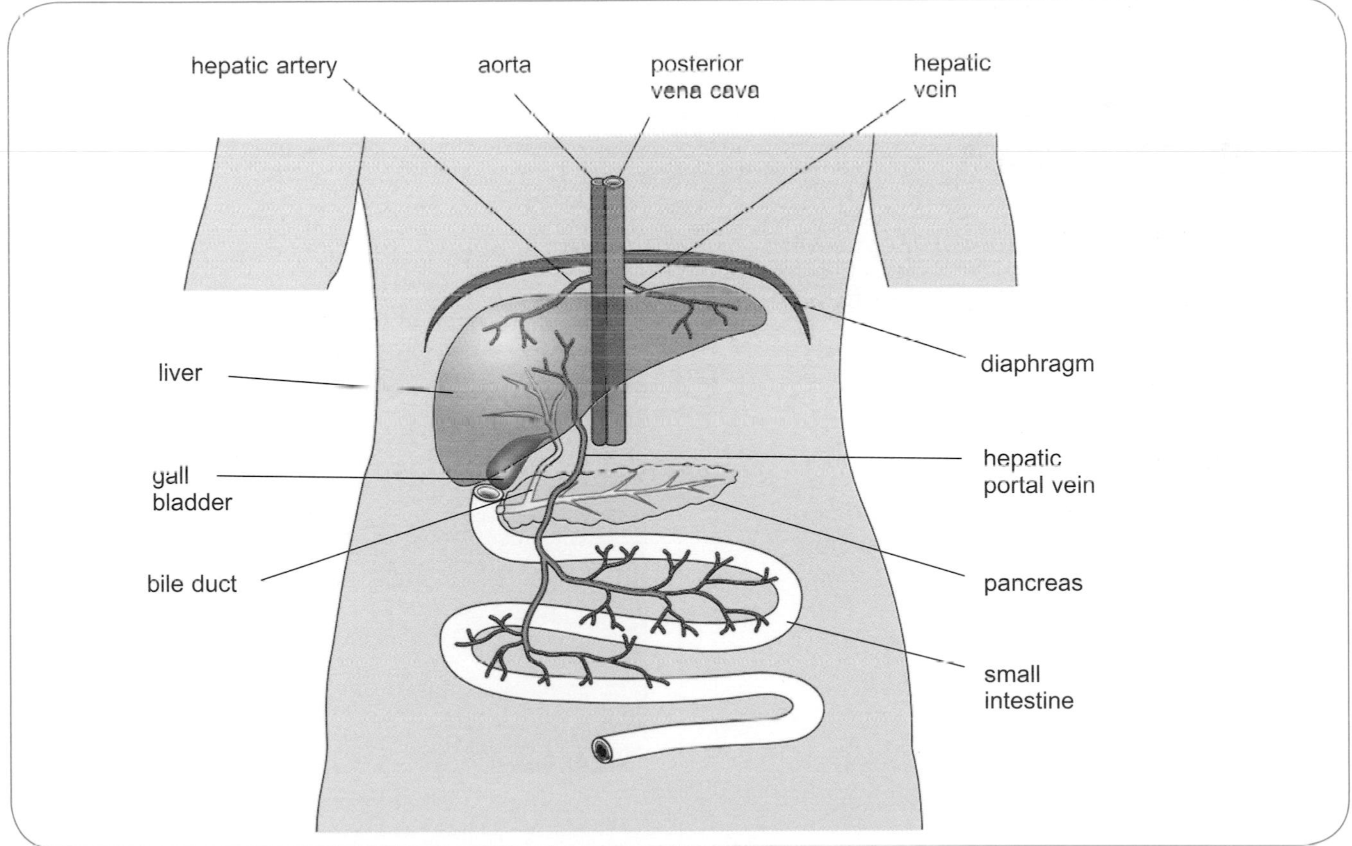

Figure 4.1 The structure of the liver and its associated organs.

Blood supply

The blood supply to the liver is unlike that of any other organ in the body, because it arrives in two different blood vessels (Figure 4.2). One of these is the **hepatic artery**, which leads directly from the aorta and delivers oxygenated blood to the liver. The other is the **hepatic portal vein**. This leads from the small intestine (duodenum and ileum) and delivers blood that is rich in absorbed nutrients. The hepatic portal vein carries about three times as much blood per minute as the hepatic artery.

The blood in the hepatic portal vein has already passed through a set of capillaries, in the wall of the small intestine, and so it is at a much lower pressure than the blood in the hepatic artery. It is deoxygenated.

A single vessel, the **hepatic vein**, carries blood away from the liver to the vena cava, which then transports it back to the heart.

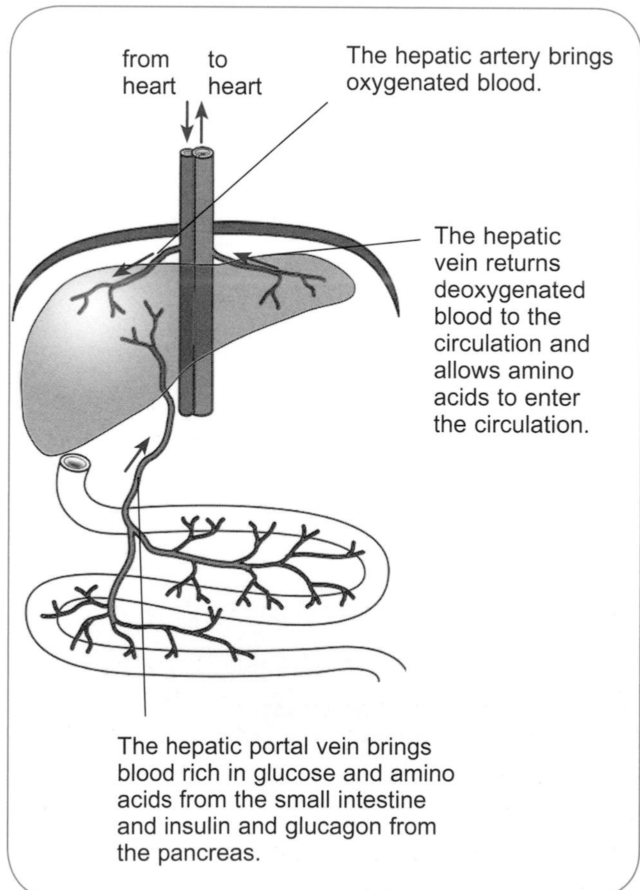

from heart
to heart
The hepatic artery brings oxygenated blood.
The hepatic vein returns deoxygenated blood to the circulation and allows amino acids to enter the circulation.
The hepatic portal vein brings blood rich in glucose and amino acids from the small intestine and insulin and glucagon from the pancreas.

Figure 4.2 The blood supply of the liver.

SAQ

1 Suggest one difference, other than pressure and oxygen concentration, between the blood carried to the liver in the hepatic artery and that carried in the hepatic portal vein.

Hint

Answer

Histology of the liver

Histology is the study of tissues. Figure 4.3 and Figure 4.4 show the structure of the tissues that make up the liver.

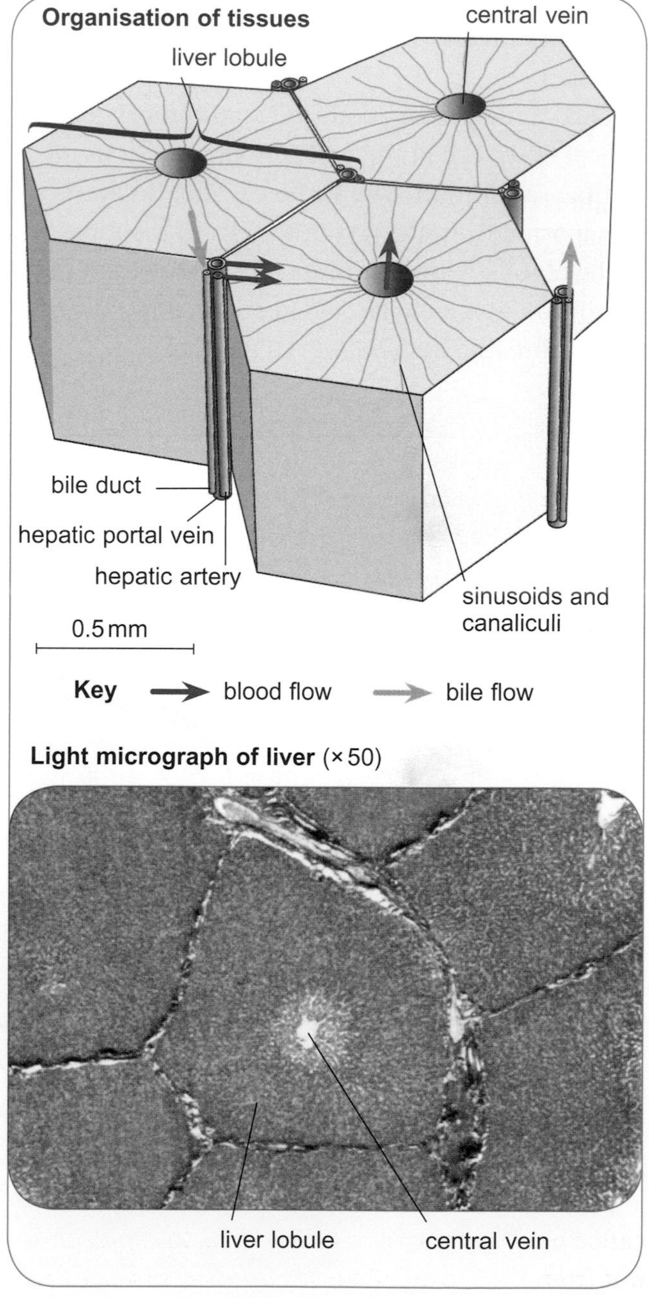

Figure 4.3 Histology of the liver.

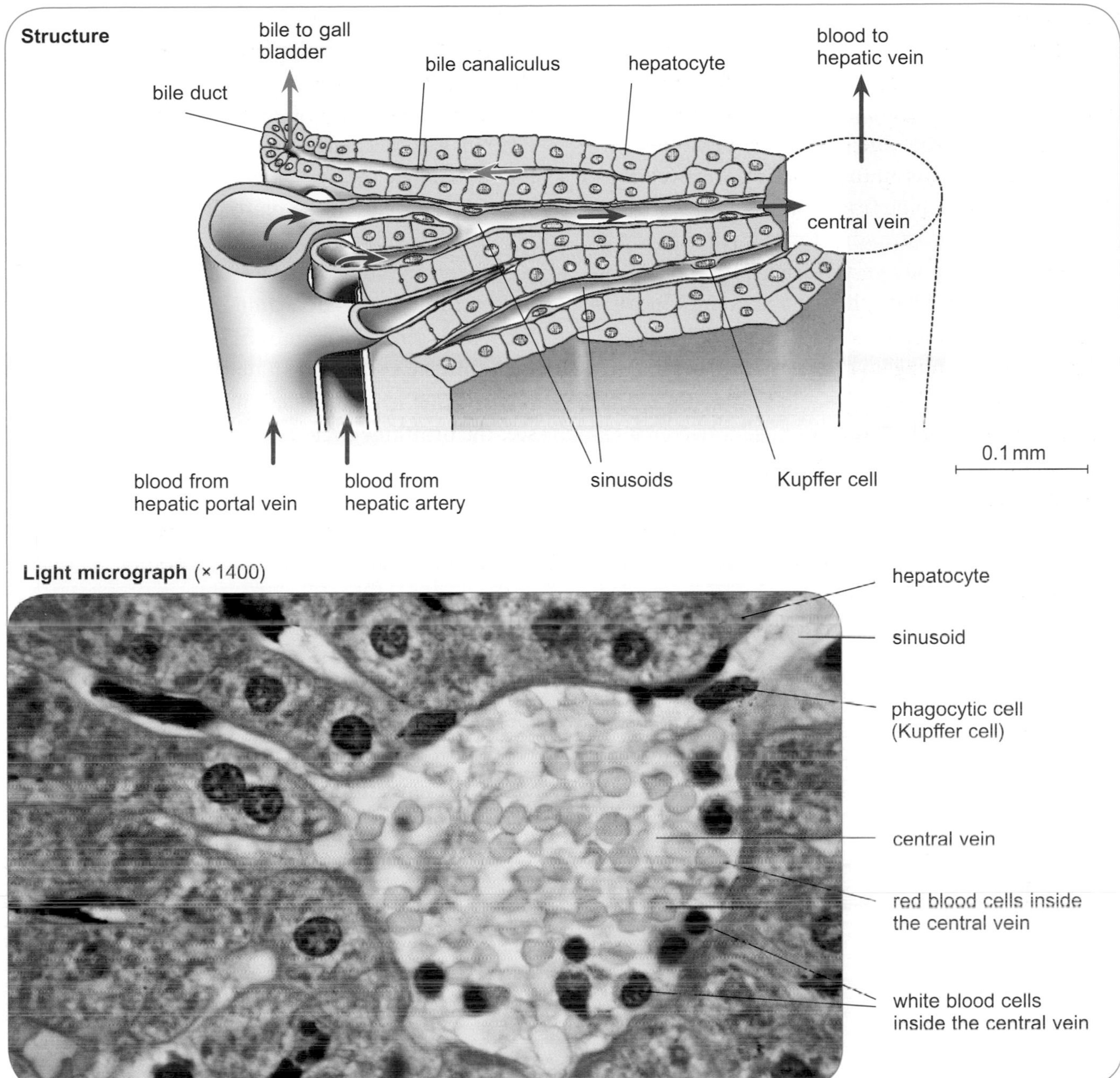

Figure 4.4 The structure of a liver lobule.

The liver is made up of many **lobules**, up to 100 000 in a human. In the centre of each lobule is a branch of the hepatic vein. Between the lobules are branches of the hepatic artery and branches of the hepatic portal vein. Blood flows from here, through the lobules, and into the branch of the hepatic vein.

Each lobule is made up of many liver cells, called **hepatocytes**, arranged in rows that radiate out from the centre of the lobule like spokes from a wheel. The channels that carry blood between these rows of cells are called **sinusoids**. Other channels carry **bile**, which is produced by some of the hepatocytes, and these channels are called **bile canaliculi**. The bile flows from the centre of the lobule towards the outside (that is, in the opposite direction to the blood flow), where it enters a branch of the **bile duct**. The rows of hepatocytes are never more than two cells thick, so that each individual cell is in close contact with the blood in the sinusoids.

The sinusoids are lined with large, phagocytic macrophages (*Biology 1*, page 175). These macrophages capture and destroy bacteria that have entered the liver in the hepatic portal vein, in blood that has come from the small intestine. These macrophages are sometimes known as **Kupffer cells**. They are very efficient. If a bacterium comes into contact with the plasma membrane of a Kupffer cell, the chances are that it will be taken inside the cell by phagocytosis within 0.01 second.

The formation of urea

The human body is unable to store any excess protein that we eat. As many of us eat much more protein than we need, something needs to be done with the excess. This happens in the liver, and it is called **deamination** (Figure 4.5).

In deamination, excess amino acids (from excess protein) are broken down. The amino group is removed, and forms **ammonia**, NH_3. The rest of the amino acid forms a keto acid, which can be respired to release energy or converted to fat to be stored.

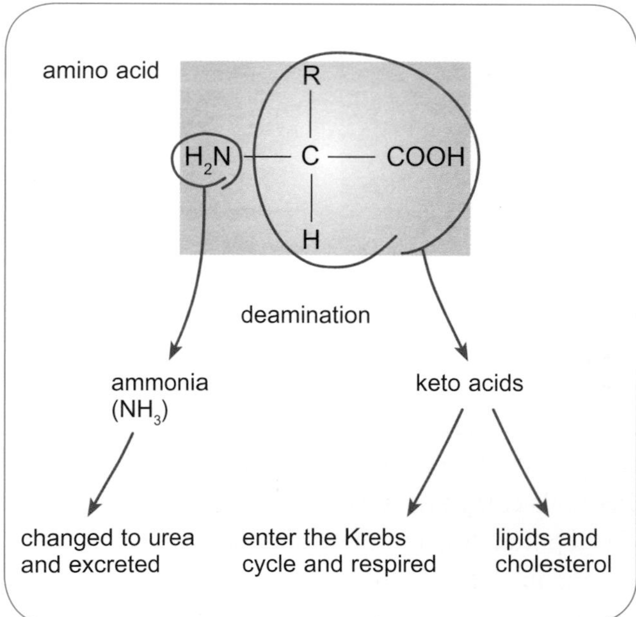

Figure 4.5 Deamination of excess amino acids.

Ammonia is very soluble and very toxic, so it cannot be allowed to remain in the body. Still in the liver, it is combined with carbon dioxide to form **urea**, $CO(NH_2)_2$. Urea, although still toxic, is much less soluble and much less dangerous than ammonia. The liver releases urea into the blood, where it dissolves in the plasma and is transported all over the body. It is removed from the blood as it passes through the kidneys.

Figure 4.6 shows how ammonia is converted to urea. This series of metabolic reactions is called the **ornithine cycle**. Ornithine is an amino acid, but not one that is used in making proteins. As you can see, the ornithine cycle requires input of energy in the form of ATP.

SAQ

2 Aquatic organisms such as fish do not convert the ammonia produced by deamination into urea, but simply excrete it as ammonia into their environment.

a Explain why it is possible for them to do this, whereas terrestrial animals cannot.

b Suggest the advantages to aquatic animals of excreting ammonia rather than urea.

Answer

Extension

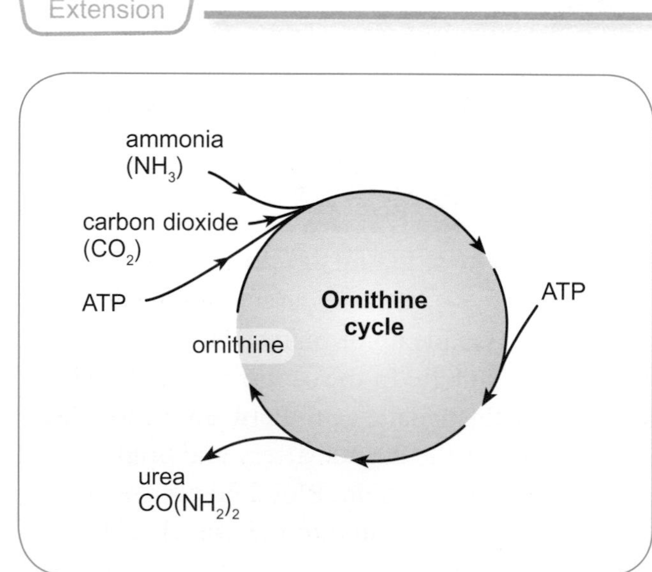

Figure 4.6 The ornithine cycle.

Detoxification of alcohol

Many potentially dangerous substances that find their way into the body are broken down by the liver. This generally happens in the smooth endoplasmic reticulum inside the hepatocytes.

Alcoholic drinks contain **ethanol**, C_2H_5OH. Ethanol molecules are small and lipid-soluble, so they very easily diffuse across plasma membranes and enter cells. Ethanol gets into the blood very rapidly after drinking, because it can simply diffuse across the walls of the stomach. Ethanol is a toxic substance, and can cause considerable damage to cells. The liver helps to avoid this by breaking down ethanol into harmless substances.

The enzyme that catalyses the breakdown of ethanol is **ethanol dehydrogenase** (Figure 4.7), also known as **alcohol dehydrogenase**. Ethanol is first converted to ethanal by this enzyme, and then to ethanoate by **aldehyde dehydrogenase**. This can enter the Krebs cycle (Chapter 6) in mitochondria and be metabolised to produce ATP.

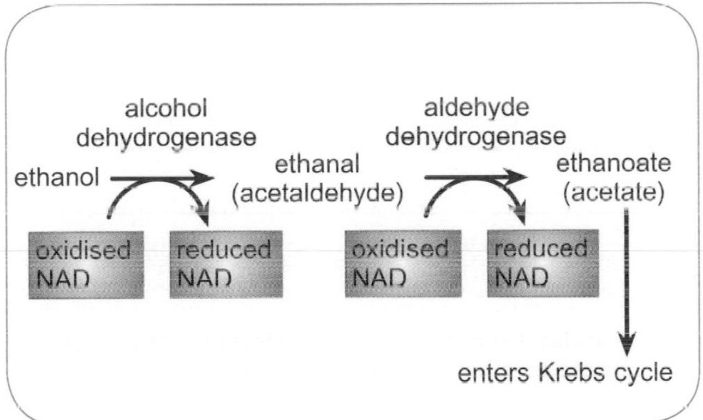

Figure 4.7 Detoxification of alcohol in the liver.

If large quantities of alcohol are consumed on a regular basis, then the tissues within the liver can be damaged. You can see, in Figure 4.7, that the breakdown of ethanol produces reduced NAD. In its oxidised state, NAD is involved in oxidising fatty acids in the liver cells. If the NAD has been reduced, then it cannot do this. The fatty acids accumulate and are converted to fats, which are deposited in the liver. There is a strong correlation between the amount of alcohol consumed and the amount of fat deposited in a person's liver. The fat is stored in the hepatocytes, and can severely reduce their efficiency at carrying out their other functions. This condition is known as **fatty liver** (Figure 4.8). (Alcohol consumption is not the only cause of fatty liver – other risk factors include diabetes and obesity.)

A combination of this effect, plus the direct damage done to hepatocytes by ethanol, can lead to a condition known as **cirrhosis**. The damaged hepatocytes are replaced by fibrous tissue. The structure of the blood supply is lost, so that some blood that arrives in the hepatic portal vein simply goes straight past and into the hepatic vein, without ever passing through the sinusoids on the way.

A liver affected by cirrhosis cannot carry out its normal functions. The liver has a very wide range of roles, involving many different metabolic reactions, so damage to it has far-reaching effects on the body. For example, the hepatocytes can no longer convert ammonia into urea, so ammonia concentration in the blood increases and can cause major damage to the central nervous system. In severe cases, coma and even death may result.

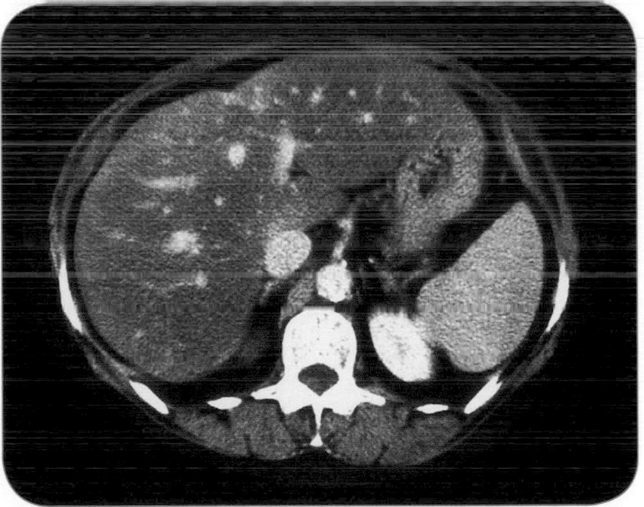

Figure 4.8 This is an MRI scan of a person suffering from fatty liver. The fat deposits can be seen as yellow patches in the liver.

Detoxification of other substances

The liver breaks down many hormones that are produced within the body. Although these are not toxic, it is important that they do not remain in the blood for too long, or else the effects that they cause would go on and on forever. Examples of hormones broken down in the liver include thyroxine, oestrogen and testosterone. Liver damage can therefore lead to the accumulation of one or more hormones in the body, which in turn may cause disruption to processes that are affected by these hormones. Drugs taken for medicinal reasons, such as antibiotics, barbiturates and paracetamol, are also broken down in the liver.

The elimination of the breakdown products of hormones or drugs (and also some unchanged hormones) from the body is done via the kidneys.

Liver disease – a new epidemic

For many people, alcohol is an easily available, enjoyable, legal drug. Alcohol is a depressant, and it affects the activity of parts of the brain that normally inhibit some of our behaviour. Drinking alcohol can help you to feel more relaxed and sociable. There is no evidence that moderate drinking of alcohol has any harmful effects on health.

But unfortunately this benign image of alcohol is leading to an increasing amount of unsafe drinking, especially among young people. And the results are already showing up in the statistics for alcohol-related deaths. In particular, we are seeing a significant rise in the number of deaths of people between the ages of 35 and 54 years, as a direct result of drinking alcohol.

What is happening? Although some of these deaths are the result of changes in a person's behaviour after drinking alcohol – for example, road traffic deaths or deaths due to aggression – the great majority are from liver disease. There has been a big increase in binge drinking; many young people regularly drink large quantities of alcohol over a short time period. This puts enormous stress on the liver, whose cells have to attempt to break down large quantities of ethanol very quickly. There is a very high risk that the liver will be irreversibly damaged. Cases of liver cirrhosis have soared. It is an incurable disease. There is great concern that thousands of young people in the UK are unwittingly shortening their life span by their drinking habits.

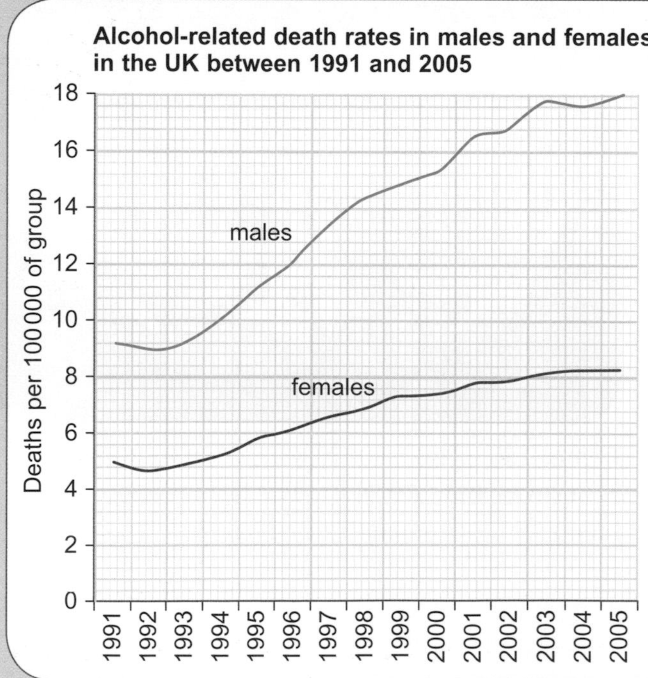

The kidneys

The two kidneys lie at the back of the abdominal cavity (that is, close to the backbone). A long white tube runs from each of them to the **bladder** (Figure 4.9). These are the **ureters**, and they carry urine away from the kidneys to the bladder, where it is stored before being expelled via the **urethra**.

Each kidney is supplied with blood though a **renal artery**, which branches off from the aorta. A **renal vein** returns blood to the vena cava.

Figure 4.10 shows the gross structure of a human kidney. Kidney tissue is a deep, dark red. Seen with the naked eye, the surface of a kidney section shows it to be made up of an outer **cortex** and an inner paler **medulla**. A whitish area, the **pelvis**, lies in the centre of one edge.

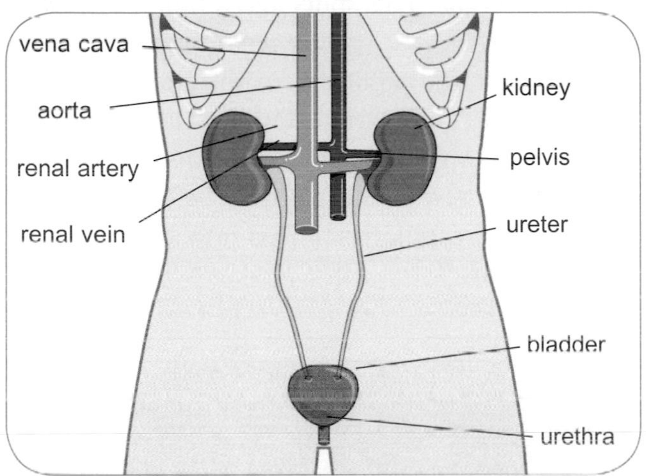

Figure 4.9 Position of the kidneys and associated structures in the human body.

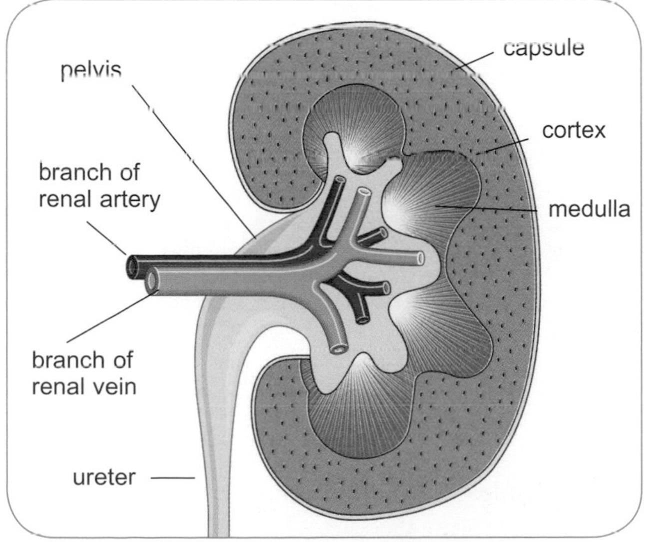

Figure 4.10 A kidney cut in half vertically.

The structure of a nephron

Each kidney is made up of thousands of tiny tubules called **nephrons** (Figure 4.11 and Figure 4.12). These are much too small to be seen with the naked eye, and even with a microscope you will not find it easy to see them clearly. This is because the nephrons take a very winding route from the outer parts of the cortex to the pelvis, so that when a kidney is cut through, the cut passes through tiny bits of many different nephrons (Figure 4.13).

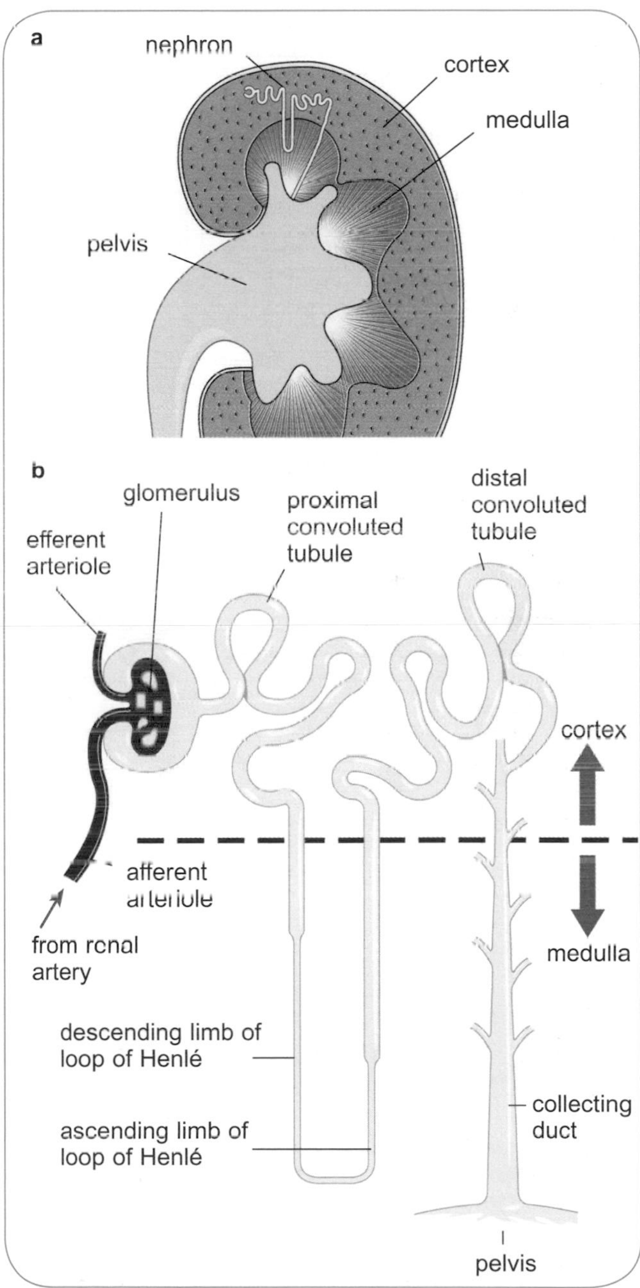

Figure 4.11 **a** Section through a kidney to show the position of one nephron. **b** A nephron.

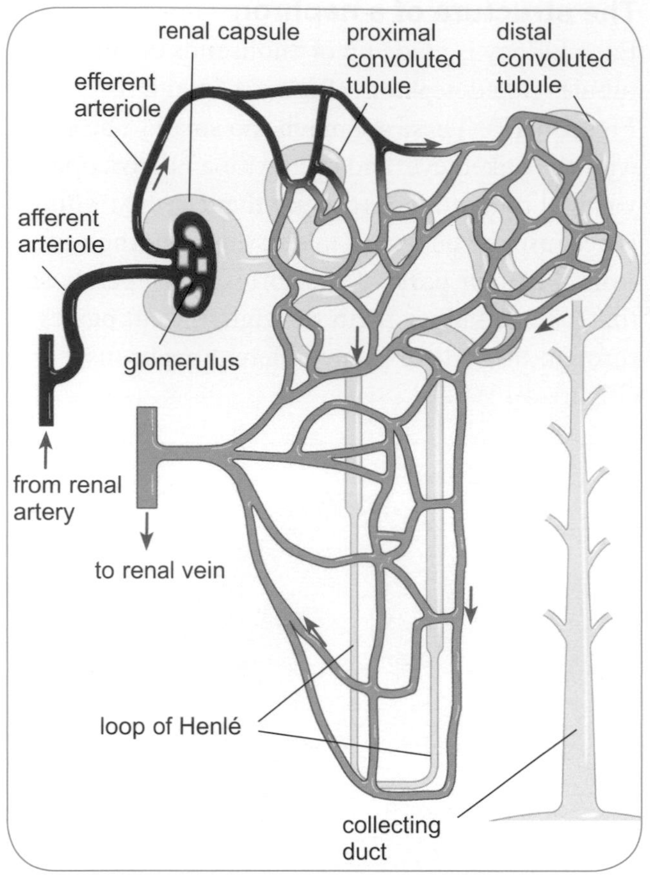

Figure 4.12 The blood supply associated with a nephron.

Each nephron begins as a cup-shaped structure called a **renal (Bowman's) capsule**. The renal capsules of all the nephrons are in the cortex of the kidney. From the renal capsule, the tube runs towards the centre of the kidney, first forming a twisted region called the **proximal convoluted tubule** and then a long hairpin loop in the medulla, the **loop of Henlé**. The tubule then turns back up through the cortex and forms another twisted region called the **distal convoluted tubule**. Finally, it joins a **collecting duct**, which leads down through the medulla and into the pelvis of the kidney. Here the collecting ducts join the ureter.

Blood vessels are closely associated with the nephrons. Each renal capsule is supplied with blood by a branch of the renal artery called an **afferent arteriole**. This splits into a tangle of capillaries in the 'cup' of the renal capsule, called a **glomerulus**. The capillaries of the glomerulus rejoin to form an **efferent arteriole**. This leads off to form a network of capillaries running closely alongside the rest of the nephron, before linking up with other capillaries to feed into a branch of the renal vein.

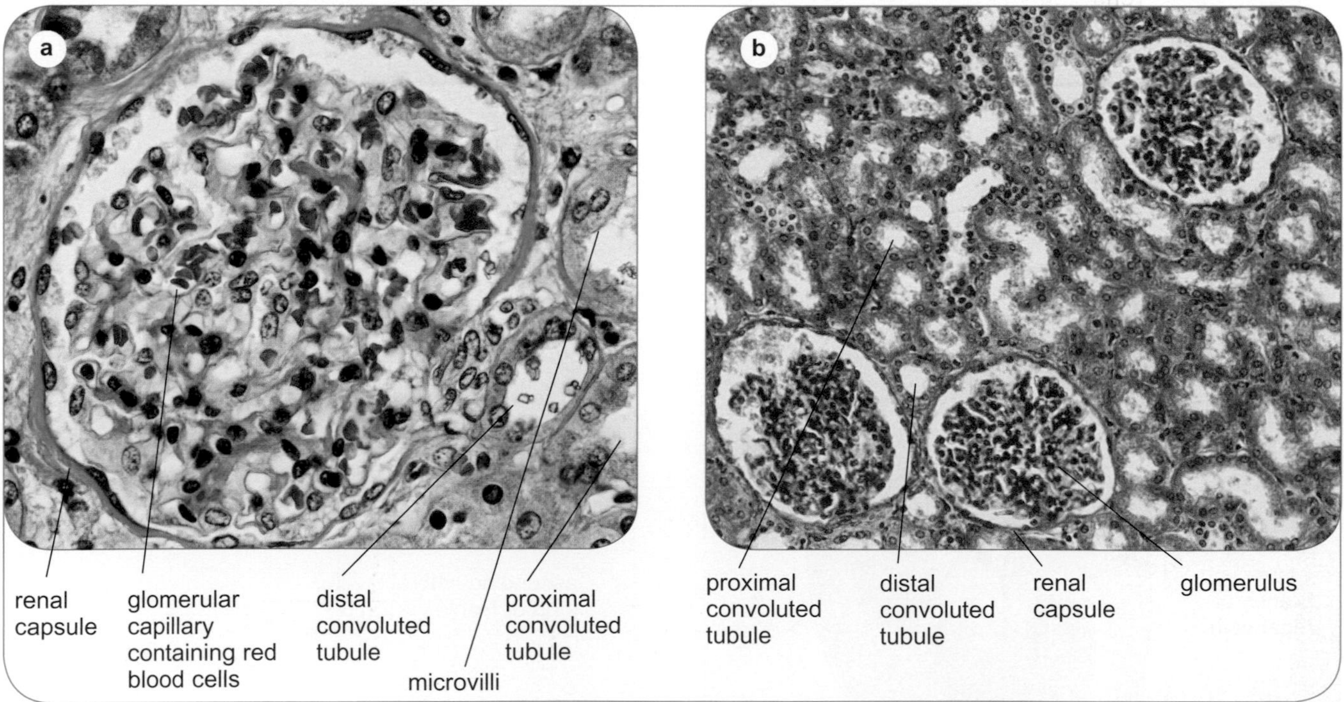

Figure 4.13 **a** Light micrograph of a section through a renal capsule (× 570). **b** Light micrograph of a section through the cortex of a kidney (× 300).

Ultrafiltration

Ultrafiltration, as the name suggests, involves filtration on a micro-scale. This process filters out small molecules from the blood and these pass into the lumens of the nephrons.

Ultrafiltration happens in the renal capsules. The blood in the glomerular capillaries is separated from the lumen of the renal capsule by two cell layers and a basement membrane (Figure 4.14).

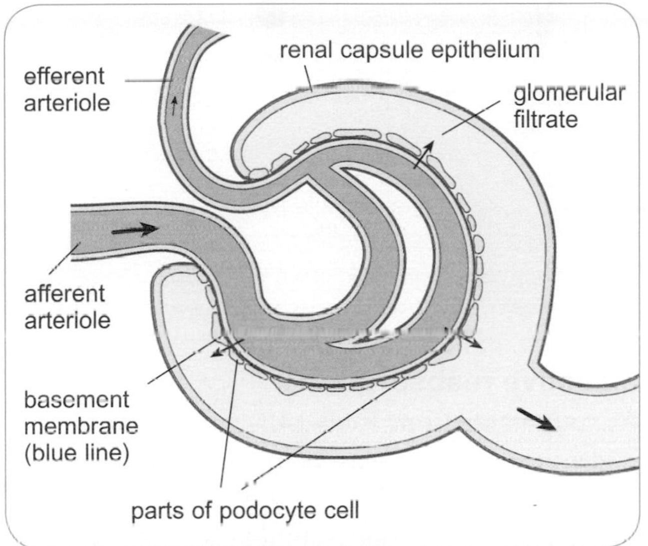

Figure 4.14 A renal capsule.

The first cell layer is the lining, called the endothelium, of the blood capillary. This, like that of most capillaries, has many small pores in it through which plasma can seep out. Lying closely against the endothelium is a basement membrane, and against that is the layer of cells making up the lining of the renal capsule. These cells are called **podocytes**. 'Pod' means 'foot', and these cells have a very unusual structure. They have many projecting fingers (or feet) that wrap themselves closely around the capillary loops of the glomerulus (Figure 4.15). Tiny slits are left between the interlocking podocyte fingers.

The diameter of the afferent arteriole that brings blood to the glomerulus is greater than the diameter of the efferent arteriole that carries it away. This results in a build-up of hydrostatic pressure inside the glomerular capillaries. As a result, blood plasma is forced out through the pores in the capillaries, through the basement membrane and then through the slits between the podocytes. The fluid that seeps through, into the cavity of the renal capsule, is known as **glomerular filtrate** (Figure 4.16).

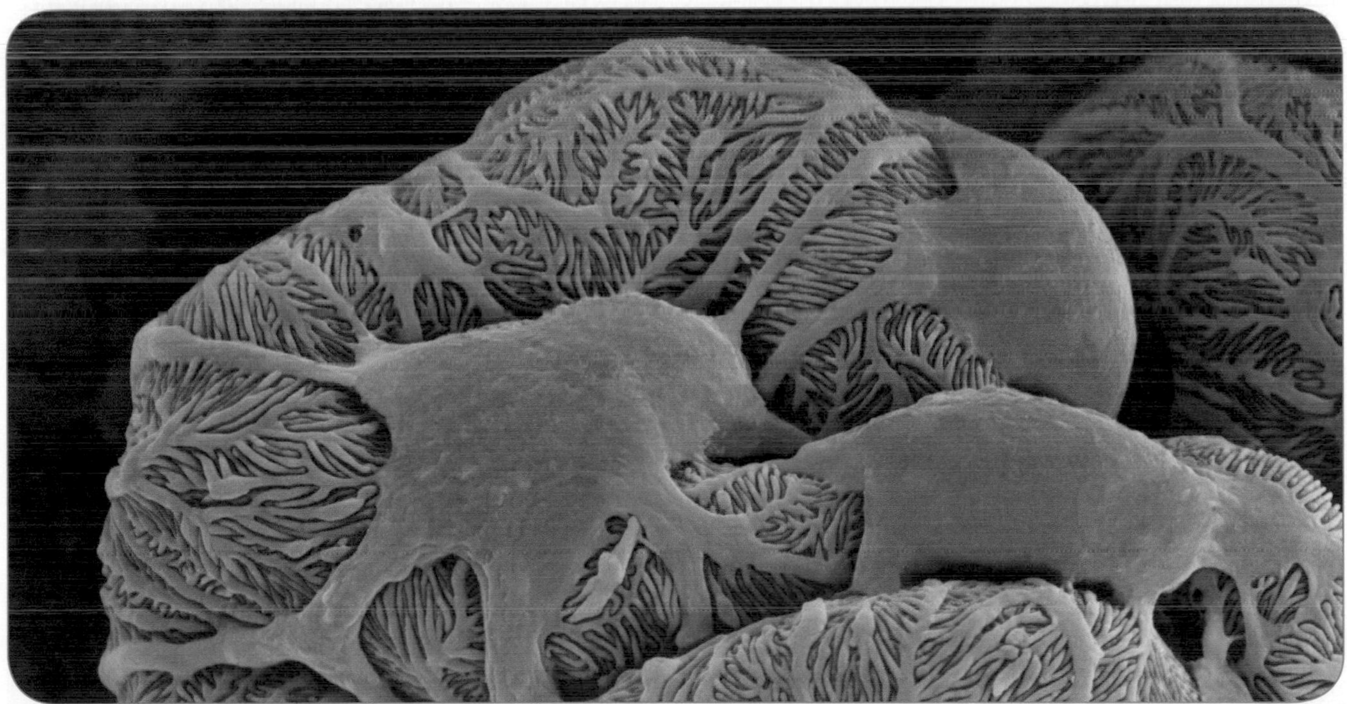

Figure 4.15 A false colour scanning electron micrograph of podocyte cells (× 3900). The podocytes are the blue cells, with their 'fingers' wrapped around the purple blood capillary.

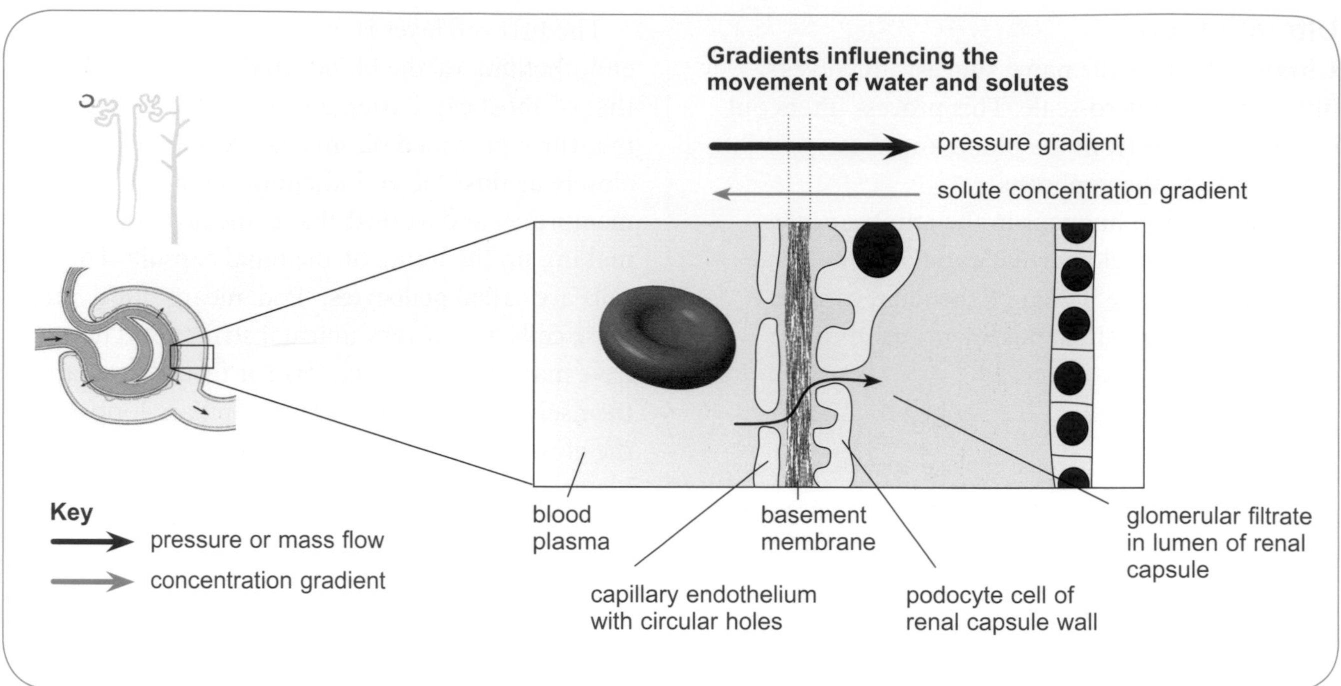

Figure 4.16 Ultrafiltration.

No cells can get through this filter. And not quite all the components of blood plasma can pass through, either. Large proteins with a relative molecular mass of more than about 65 000 to 69 000 remain dissolved in the blood. Table 14.1 shows the composition of blood plasma and glomerular filtrate.

Selective reabsorption

As you can see from Table 14.1, glomerular filtrate is identical to blood plasma minus most proteins. It is therefore inevitable that it will contain many substances that the body should keep, as well as others that need to be got rid of. **Selective reabsorption**, which happens as the filtrate flows along the nephron, takes these wanted substances back into the blood.

Most of this reabsorption takes place in the **proximal convoluted tubule**. The walls of this part of the nephron are made up of a layer of cuboidal cells with microvilli on their inner surfaces (Figure 4.17).

Substance	Concentration in blood plasma / $g\,dm^{-3}$	Concentration in glomerular filtrate / $g\,dm^{-3}$
water	900	900
inorganic ions	7.2	7.2
urea	0.3	0.3
uric acid	0.04	0.04
glucose	1.0	1.0
amino acids	0.5	0.5
proteins	80.0	0.05

Table 14.1 Comparison of the composition of blood plasma and glomerular filtrate.

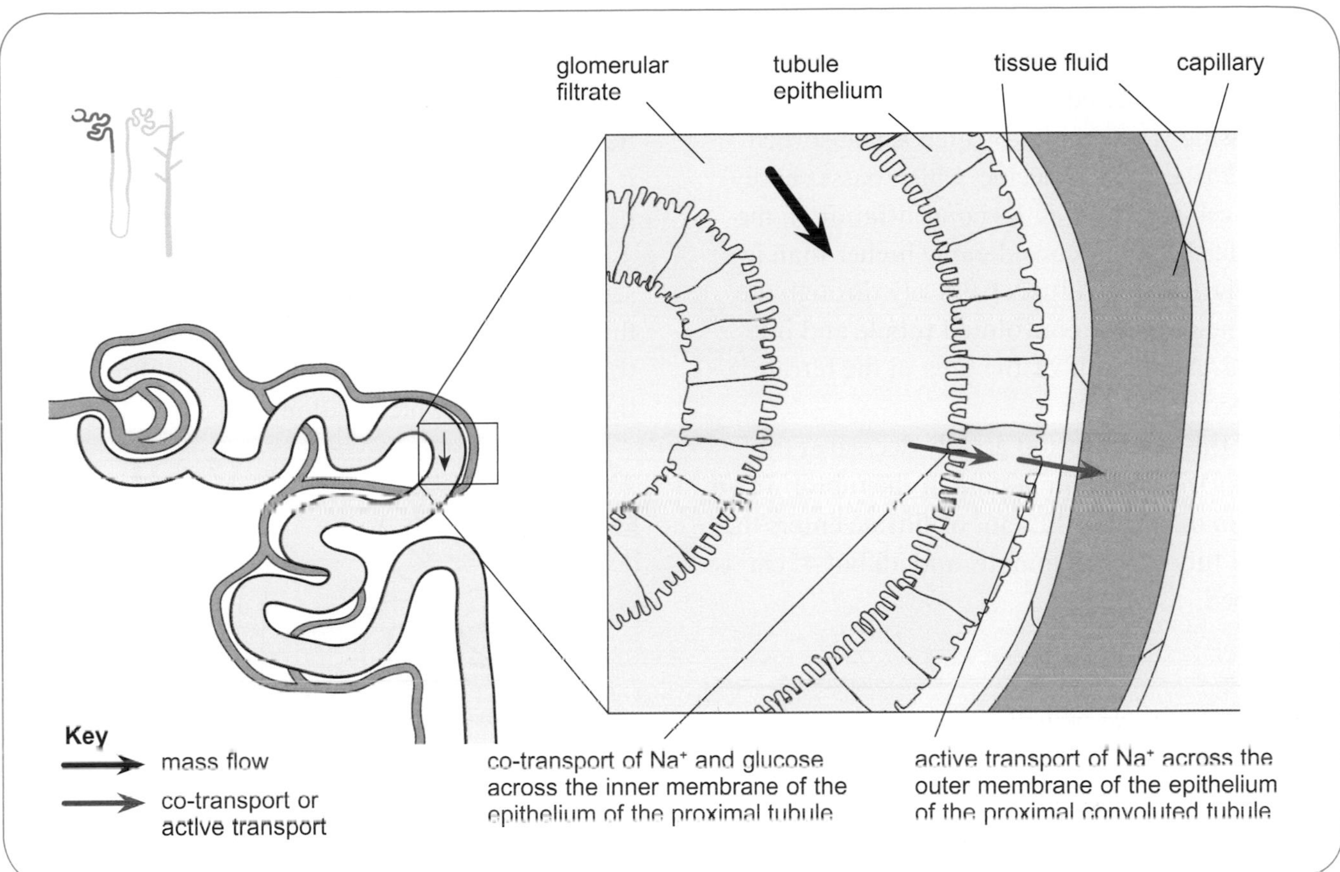

Figure 4.17 Selective reabsorption from the proximal convoluted tubule.

Blood capillaries lie very closely against the outer surface of the tubule. The blood in these capillaries has come directly from the glomerulus, so it has much less plasma in it than usual and has lost much of its water and many of the ions, small proteins and other substances that it was carrying as it entered the glomerulus. It still contains all its cells, and its large soluble proteins.

The outer membranes of the cells of the proximal convoluted tubule walls actively transport sodium ions out of the cytoplasm. This lowers the concentration of sodium ions inside the cells. As a result, there is a concentration gradient for sodium ions from the contents of the tubule (relatively high concentration) into the cytoplasm. The sodium ions diffuse down this gradient from the fluid inside the tubule into the cells, passing through transporter proteins in their plasma membranes.

There are several different varieties of these transporters, and each one transports something else at the same time as sodium ions. They can even do this against a concentration gradient. For example, a sodium ion diffusing through one kind of transporter might carry a glucose molecule with it, *up* the concentration gradient for glucose. This is called **co-transport**. The passive movement of the sodium ion down its gradient provides the energy to move the glucose molecule up *its* gradient. So, indirectly, the active transport of sodium ions out of one side of the cell provides the energy needed to transport glucose molecules into the other side.

In this way, all of the glucose in the proximal convoluted tubule is reabsorbed into the blood. Amino acids, vitamins, sodium ions and chloride ions are also reabsorbed here.

The removal of all these solutes from the glomerular filtrate greatly increases its water potential. But the water potential inside the cells in the nephron walls, and inside the blood capillaries, is *decreasing* as these solutes move into them. So a water potential gradient builds up. Water molecules move down this gradient, out of the nephron and into the blood. About 65% of the water in the filtrate is reabsorbed here. As the blood flows away, the water and other reabsorbed substances are carried away with it.

Surprisingly, quite a lot of urea is reabsorbed too. Urea is a small molecule, which passes easily through cell membranes. Its concentration in the glomerular filtrate is considerably higher than in the capillaries so it diffuses passively through the wall of the proximal convoluted tubule and into the blood. About half of the urea in the filtrate is reabsorbed in this way.

All of this reabsorption greatly decreases the volume of the liquid remaining in the tubule. In an adult human, around 125 cm^3 of filtrate enters the proximal tubules each minute, and all but 45 cm^3 is reabsorbed.

SAQ

3 Although almost half of the urea in the glomerular filtrate is reabsorbed from the proximal convoluted tubule, the concentration of urea in the fluid that remains inside the nephron actually increases.
Explain why.

Answer

The loop of Henlé

About one third of our nephrons have long **loops of Henlé**, dipping down in the medulla of the kidneys. The function of these loops is to create a very high concentration of sodium ions and chloride ions in the tissue fluid in the medulla. As you will see, this allows a lot of water to be reabsorbed from the contents of the nephron as they pass through the collecting duct. This means that very concentrated urine can be produced, conserving water in the body and preventing dehydration.

The first part of the loop of Henlé is called the **descending limb** and the second part is the **ascending limb**. These differ in their permeabilities to water. The descending limb is water-permeable, while the ascending limb is impermeable to it (Figure 4.18).

It is a bit easier to understand how it works if you begin at the 'wrong' end – in the ascending limb. The cells in the upper part of this limb actively transport sodium and chloride ions out of the nephron and into the surrounding tissues. This increases the water potential of the fluid inside the nephron and decreases the water potential outside it. Water cannot pass out of the nephron at this point, because the walls are impermeable to it.

Now think about the descending limb. We have seen that its walls are permeable to water. As the fluid from the proximal convoluted tubule flows through the descending limb, it passes through the tissues into which sodium and chloride ions

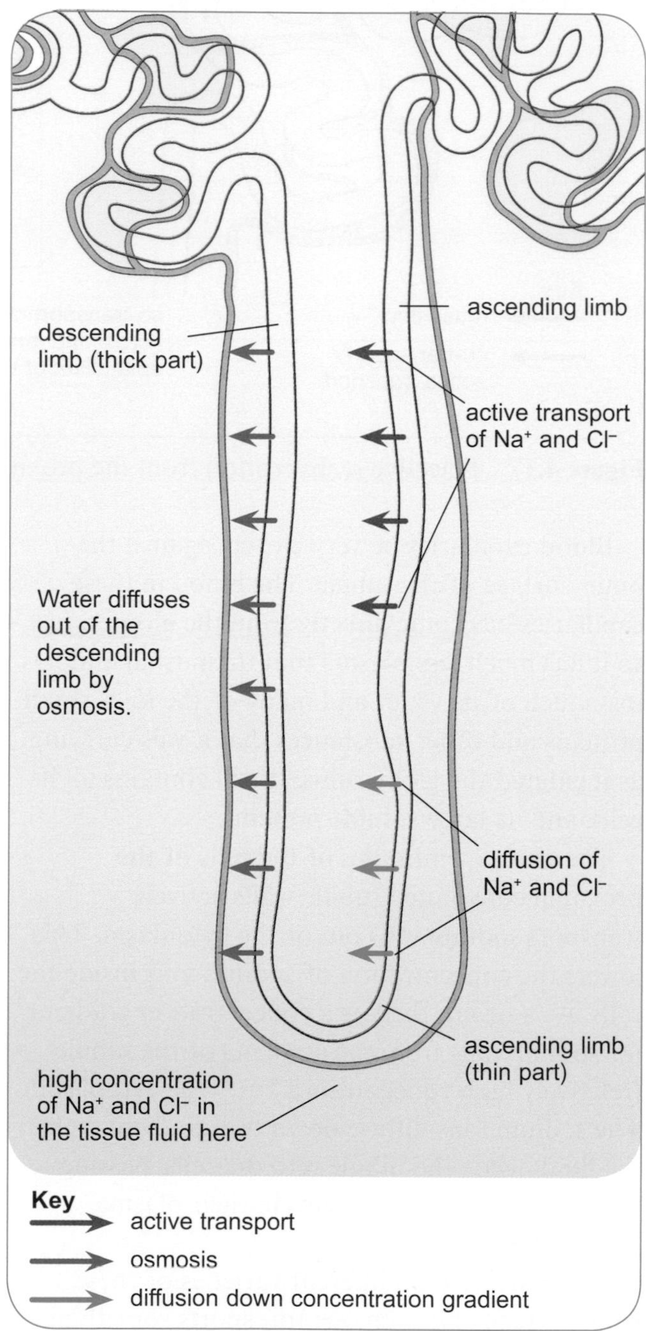

Figure 4.18 The loop of Henlé.

have been pumped. So there is a water potential gradient, and water moves down this gradient from inside the descending limb into the tissues outside it.

The fluid that now begins to go up the ascending limb is very concentrated – it has lost a lot of its water, so the concentration of the ions that remain is large. This makes it relatively easy to pump these ions out of the tubule as the fluid moves up.

Having the two limbs of the loop running next to each other like this, with the fluid flowing down one side and up the other, enables the maximum concentration of solutes to be built up both inside and outside the tube at the bottom of the loop. It is called a **counter-current** system.

The longer the loop of Henlé, the greater the concentration of solutes that can be built up at the bottom of the loop. We have seen that about one third of our nephrons have long loops. In desert-living mammals, such as gerbils, almost all of the loops are very long. This is useful because, as we shall see, the very low water potential that they build up in the medulla helps water to be conserved and not lost in the urine.

Reabsorption in the distal convoluted tubule and collecting duct

The fluid now continues along the nephron, entering the distal convoluted tubule and finally the collecting duct. The cells in the walls of the distal convoluted tubule actively transport sodium ions out of the fluid, while potassium ions are actively transported into it.

As the fluid flows through the collecting duct, deep in the medulla, it passes through the same regions as the deep part of the loops of Henlé. The very low water potential in this region once more provides a water potential gradient, so that water moves out of the collecting duct and into the tissues around it. It moves into the blood capillaries (the vasa recta) and is transported away (Figure 4.19).

The loop of Henlé helps to conserve water. The lower the water potential it can build up, the greater will be the water potential gradient between the fluid inside the collecting ducts and the tissues outside the duct. This enables more water to be drawn out of the collecting duct, resulting in a smaller volume of more concentrated urine. Desert mammals have many long loops (Figure 4.20).

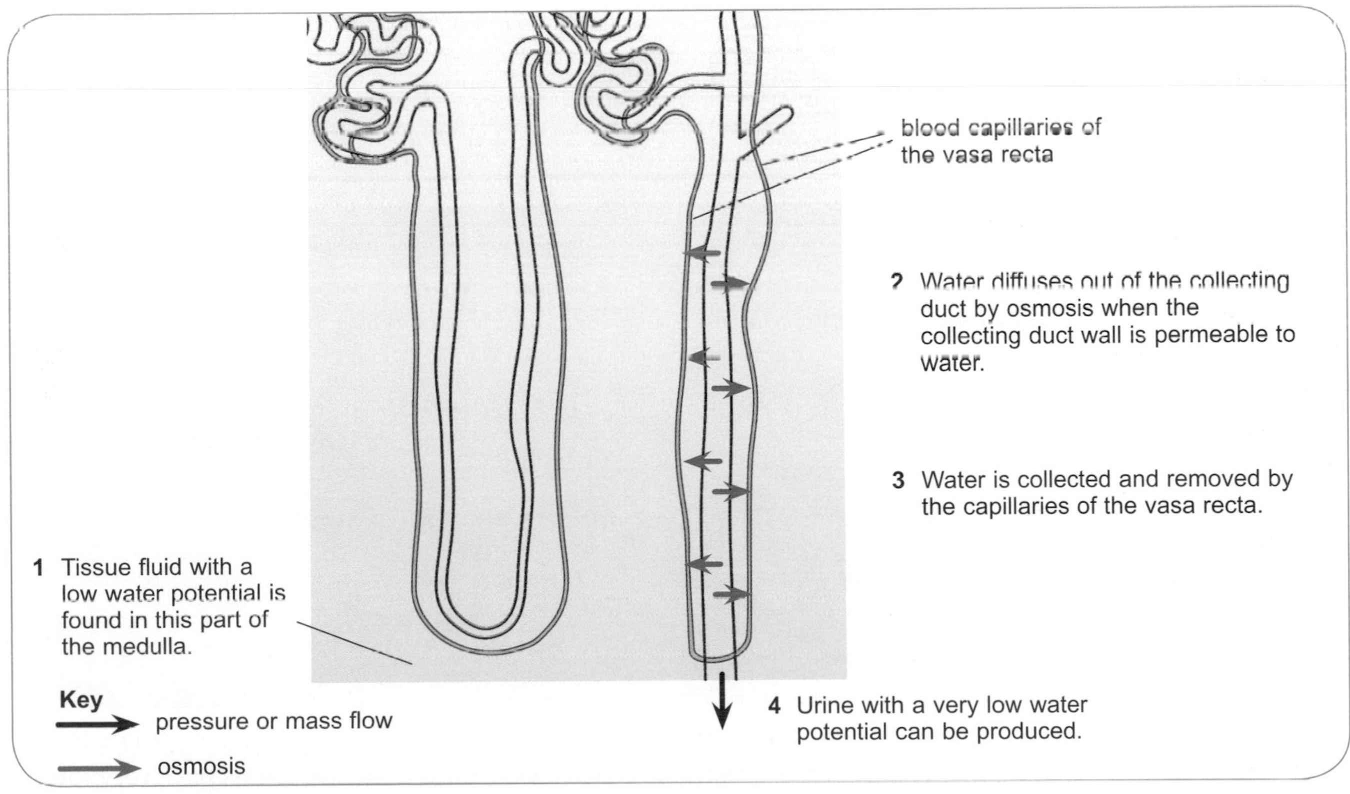

blood capillaries of the vasa recta
2 Water diffuses out of the collecting duct by osmosis when the collecting duct wall is permeable to water.
3 Water is collected and removed by the capillaries of the vasa recta.
1 Tissue fluid with a low water potential is found in this part of the medulla.
Key
pressure or mass flow
osmosis
4 Urine with a very low water potential can be produced.

Figure 4.19 Reabsorption of water from the collecting duct.

SAQ

4 The graph shows the relative concentrations of four substances as they pass along a nephron.

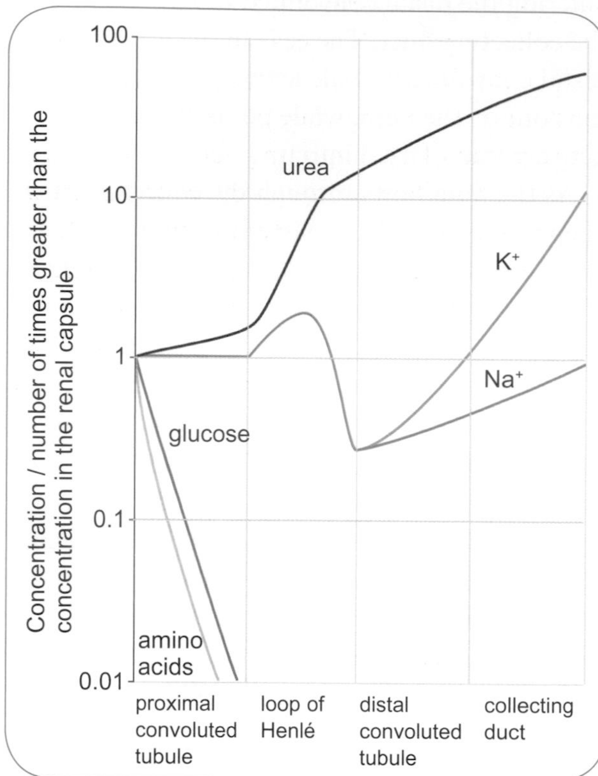

a What is unusual about the y-axis of the graph? Why is it shown this way?

b Take each curve in turn, and explain why it is this shape.

Hint

Answer

5 The graph shows the rates at which fluid flows through different parts of a nephron.

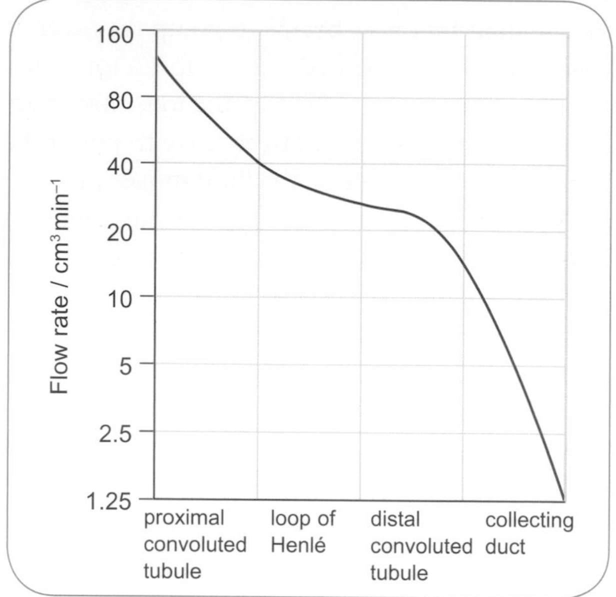

If water flows into an impermeable tube like a hosepipe, it flows out of the far end at the same rate as it flows in. However, this clearly does not happen in a nephron. Suggest an explanation for the shape of the graph.

Answer

Figure 4.20 The Egyption jerboa, *Jaculus jaculus*, lives in dry desert. It is active at night, and spends the day underground, which helps to reduce water loss from its body. One third of its nephrons have very long loops of Henlé.

Osmoregulation

Osmoregulation is the control of the water content of the body. This is a vital part of homeostasis, and it involves the kidneys, the pituitary gland and the hypothalamus. It works by means of negative feedback.

The hypothalamus contains sensory neurones called **osmoreceptors**. They are sensitive to the water potential of the blood that passes through the hypothalamus. Their cell bodies produce a hormone called **anti-diuretic hormone, ADH**. ADH is a small peptide, made up of just nine amino acids.

However, the osmoreceptor cells don't secrete this hormone directly into the blood. Instead, the ADH passes along their axons, which terminate in the posterior pituitary gland (Figure 4.21).

If the water potential in the blood is too low (that is, does not contain enough water), some of this ADH will be released from the ends of these axons, just like a transmitter substance at a synapse. However, ADH is released into the blood, not into a synaptic cleft. The ADH is therefore secreted from the posterior pituitary gland, even though it was synthesised in the hypothalamus.

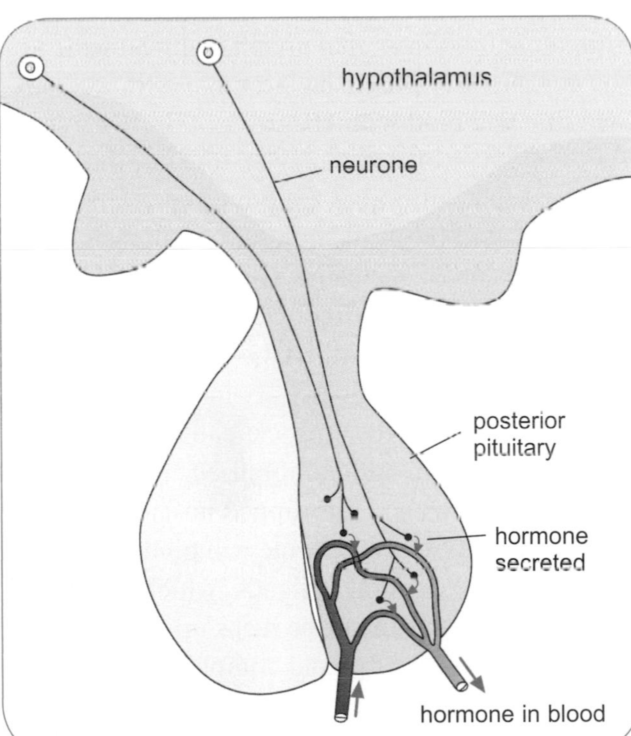

Figure 4.21 ADH is produced in the hypothalamus and moves along axons to be released into the blood from the posterior pituitary gland.

We have seen that water is reabsorbed from the fluid in the nephron and back into the blood as the fluid passes through the collecting ducts. Water is drawn out of the collecting ducts by osmosis, moving down its concentration gradient. The water balance of the body can be controlled by adjusting the water permeability of the plasma membranes of the collecting duct cells. Make them more permeable, and more water is reabsorbed and less is lost in the urine. Make them impermeable and no water is reabsorbed, so more is lost in the urine.

These cells are the target cells for ADH. ADH molecules slot into receptors on their plasma membranes. This causes little groups of protein molecules in their cytoplasm, called **aquaporins**, to move to the plasma membrane and insert themselves into it (Figure 4.22). They form channels that allow water molecules to pass through.

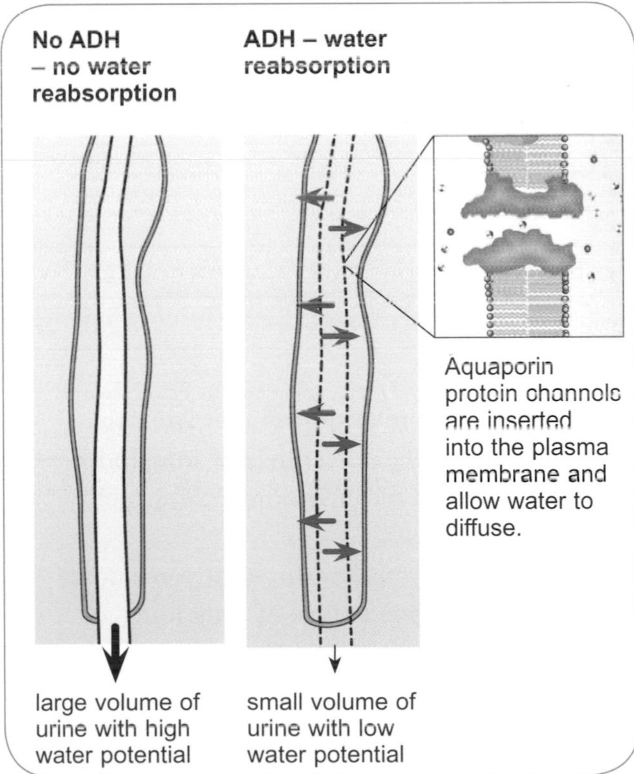

Figure 4.22 ADH and water reabsorption.

So, with ADH in position, water can move freely out of the collecting ducts and back into the blood. A smaller volume of urine is therefore formed, and the body conserves water.

Everything goes into reverse if the blood contains too much water. The osmoreceptors in the hypothalamus are not stimulated, and so only a little ADH is released into the blood. Much less ADH binds to receptors in the plasma membranes of the collecting duct cells, and the aquaporins move back into the cytoplasm. Now the walls of the collecting ducts are quite impermeable to water, so most of the water in the fluid inside the collecting ducts flows along and into the bladder. Large volumes of dilute urine are produced.

SAQ

6 The table shows the percentage of nephrons that have long loops of Henlé in five mammals, and also the maximum concentration of the urine that they can produce.

Mammal	Percentage of long loops	Maximum concentration of urine (arbitrary units)
beaver	0	0.96
desert mouse	100	9.2
human	14	2.6
jerboa	33	12.0
pig	3	2.0

a Describe any relationship that you can see between the percentage of long loops of Henlé and the environment in which a mammal lives.

b Describe any relationship that you can see between the percentage of long loops of Henlé and the maximum concentration of urine produced.

c Suggest reasons for the relationships you have described.

Answer

Using urine for diagnosis

A sample of a patient's urine can be very helpful in the diagnosis of illness. Urine contains many of the waste products of metabolism, and if a doctor knows what these are then he or she is often given useful clues about the nature of a patient's illness. It is much easier and less invasive to collect a urine sample than to take a blood sample.

But urine can also be used for diagnosis of a person who is not ill. It is an excellent way of making an early diagnosis of pregnancy, and it can also contain evidence of the misuse of drugs.

Pregnancy testing

Any couple who are trying for a baby will want to know as soon as possible if the woman has become pregnant. There are now many different pregnancy testing kits on the market which can be used at home. Most of them use **monoclonal antibodies** to test for the presence of a hormone called **human chorionic gonadotrophin (HCG)** in her urine.

Monoclonal antibodies are antibodies – immunoglobulins – that are all identical with one another. For pregnancy testing, antibodies are used that will bind with HCG.

For one type of pregnancy-testing kit, these HCG-specific antibodies are bound to atoms of gold. The antibody–gold complexes are then used to coat the end of a dipstick (Figure 4.23).Another type of monoclonal antibody is also made, which will specifically bind with HCG–antibody–gold complexes. These antibodies are impregnated into a region further up the dipstick, called the Patient Test Result region, and immobilised.

To use the dipstick, it is dipped into a urine sample. Any HCG in the urine will bind to the antibodies at the end of the stick, which will be carried upwards as the urine seeps up the stick. As the HCG–antibody–gold complexes reach the test result region of the stick, they bind with the immobilised antibodies there and are held firmly in position. As more and more gold atoms arrive there, a pink colour (or another colour, dependent on the brand) builds up.

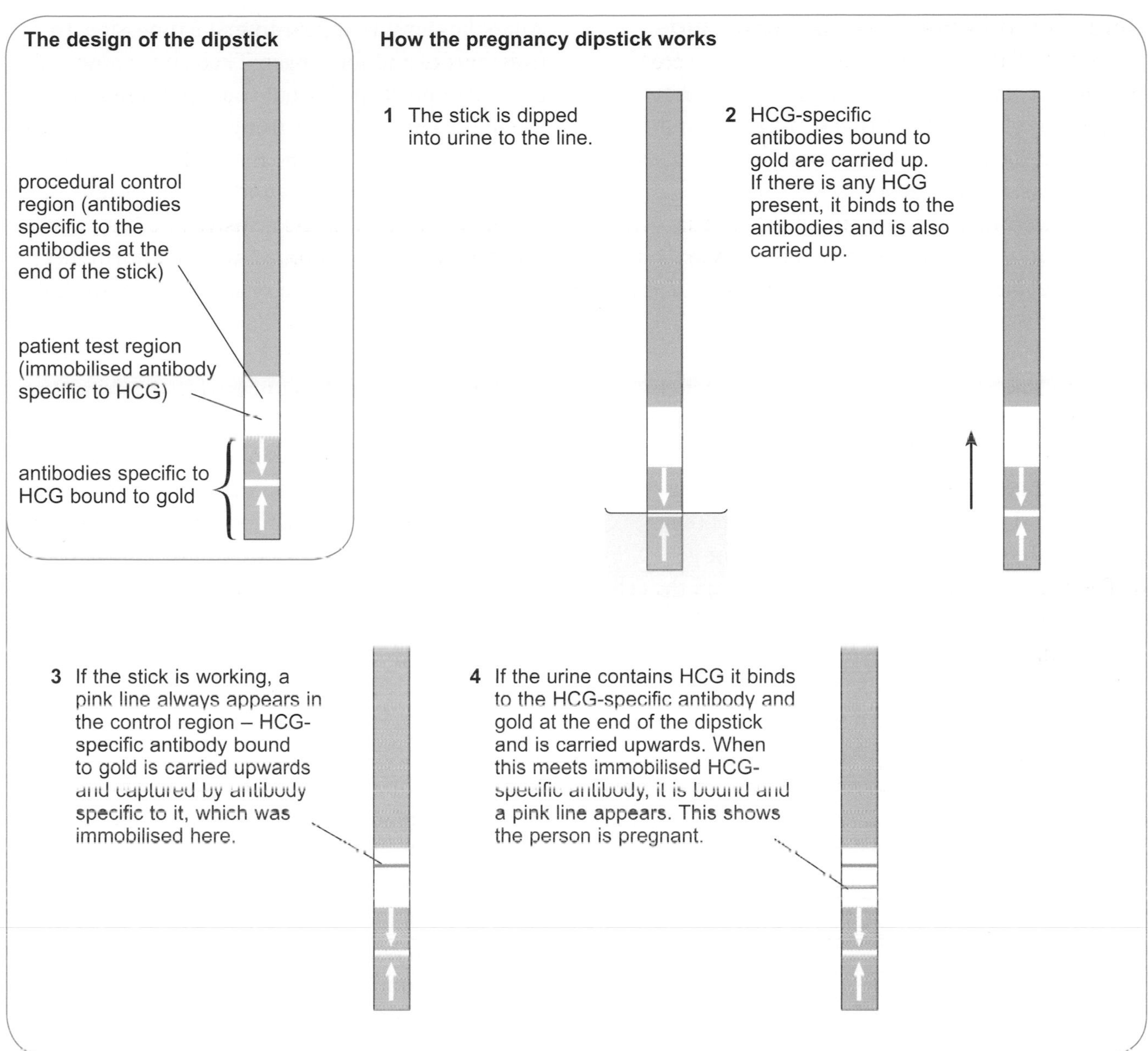

The design of the dipstick
procedural control region (antibodies specific to the antibodies at the end of the stick)
patient test region (immobilised antibody specific to HCG)
antibodies specific to HCG bound to gold
How the pregnancy dipstick works
1 The stick is dipped into urine to the line.
2 HCG-specific antibodies bound to gold are carried up. If there is any HCG present, it binds to the antibodies and is also carried up.
3 If the stick is working, a pink line always appears in the control region – HCG-specific antibody bound to gold is carried upwards and captured by antibody specific to it, which was immobilised here.
4 If the urine contains HCG it binds to the HCG-specific antibody and gold at the end of the dipstick and is carried upwards. When this meets immobilised HCG-specific antibody, it is bound and a pink line appears. This shows the person is pregnant.

Figure 4.23 How one type of pregnancy-testing kit works.

The stick also contains an area called the Procedural Control Region, which contains yet another type of immobilised monoclonal antibody. These are from goats, and they are anti-mouse antibodies. They bind with the antibody–gold complexes even if these have not encountered any HCG in the urine sample. This strip therefore goes pink even if the test result is negative.

SAQ

7 Suggest the purpose of the Procedural Control Region.

Answer

Extension

Detecting misuse of anabolic steroids

Steroids are substances that are synthesised from cholesterol, and their molecules are very similar to cholesterol molecules (Figure 4.24). Several hormones, including progesterone, oestrogen and testosterone, are steroids.

Many steroid hormones stimulate **anabolic** reactions in body cells – that is, reactions in which large molecules are built from smaller ones. They are known as **anabolic steroids**.

Steroids are soluble in lipids, and they are therefore able to move relatively easily through plasma membranes, despite the large size of their molecules. As we have seen (Chapter 3), they then combine with a receptor molecule in the cytoplasm. This sets off a chain of events that results in the transcription of a particular gene, which in turn increases protein synthesis in the cell.

Testosterone, the hormone responsible for many male secondary sexual characteristics, and other similar substances such as stanazolol, have very great effects on protein synthesis within cells. They also increase aggression, which could be of advantage to a sportsperson in making them more competitive.

Athletes and others have illegally used anabolic steroids to increase their muscle size and strength.

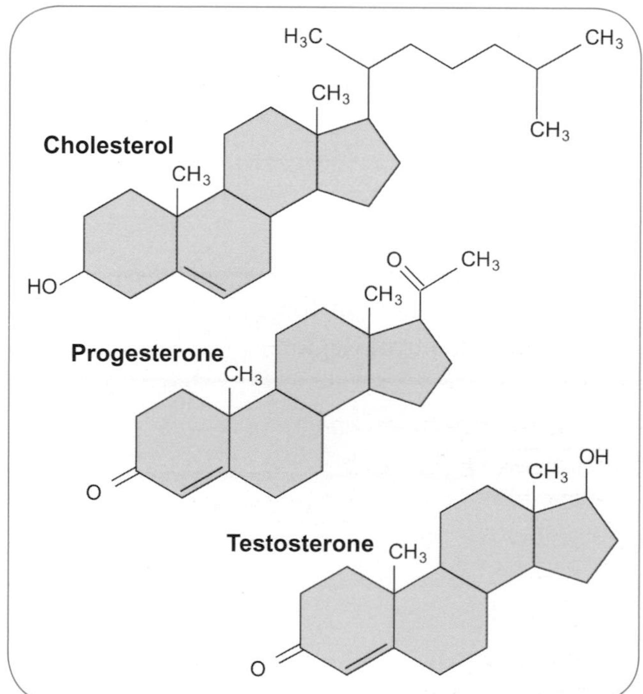

Figure 4.24 Steroids.

Anabolic steroids appear to make it possible to train harder and for longer. Their use is now banned in most sports, but some people have found the temptation of using them so great that they are willing to run the risk of being found out.

The use of anabolic steroids is dangerous. In the long term, they decrease the body's own production of testosterone and other hormones and decrease the immune system's ability to deal with pathogens. They can damage the liver, whose cells take up the hormone and break it down to substances that are then excreted in the urine. In some cases, they can affect physiology so much that athletes put their lives in danger. Although never proved, many people suspect that the death of the American sprinter Florence Griffith-Joiner at the age of 38, from a heart attack, may have been linked to drug use.

Athletes from many different sports are now randomly tested, both in and out of competition, to check whether they have been taking anabolic steroids. The tests are thorough and the athletes must turn up for them, but the interpretation can be unclear. For example, in 2003 a number of sprinters and tennis players were found to have a substance called nandrolone in their urine that was above the officially permitted level. Nandrolone is synthesised in the body from anabolic steroids, so its presence in abnormally large quantities suggests that these banned substances have been taken. However, it has proved difficult to be certain of just how much nandrolone is abnormal, or exactly where the nandrolone in a person's body might have come from. This makes it very difficult to be certain that the person really has been using anabolic steroids illegally.

It is obviously desirable that every country and every sport should have similar rules and regulations about which drugs are not allowed. A World Anti-doping Code is published every few years, listing the drugs and their derivatives whose presence in urine should be regarded as an infringement of the code. You can find details of the latest version of this code and the current list of banned drugs at:
www.uksport.gov.uk/pages/world_anti_doping_code/

The results of the tests done on UK athletes and the names of anyone who has been found guilty of illegal drug use are posted on the UK Sport website – go to the following address and click on 'drug results' to find the latest ones: www.uksport.gov.uk/pages/drug_free_sport/

Two samples of urine are taken. One is sent to an approved laboratory for testing, and the other is stored in carefully controlled conditions. If the first sample is found to be positive, then the second sample is also tested. In many sports, a positive result – or the failure to turn up for a test on three successive occasions – is enough to ban the person from competing in their sport, either for a set period of time or for life.

Extension

The BALCO scandal

BALCO was a company based in California in the USA. It started out by offering urine testing to athletes, with the purpose of detecting mineral deficiencies. They would then be offered a personalised supplement regime, aimed at helping them to perform better in their sport.

However, when Victor Comte took charge of BALCO in the late 1980s, he took the company in a different direction. Instead of legal supplements, he began to supply athletes with illegal performance-enhancing drugs.

The athletes were given advice about how to avoid detection, and BALCO's activities went undetected for many years. However, eventually a number of positive drug tests on athletes began to throw suspicion on BALCO. A 'shopping list' of drugs that could be supplied by BALCO was revealed – individual athletes were recommended to take a particular combination of drugs at particular time intervals, and charged high prices. Drugs to be taken over a five-month period might include erythropoetin (16 bottles at $65 a bottle), human growth hormone (15 bottles at $65 a bottle) and the so-called designer steroid THG (45 doses at $25 each). The drugs regime varied between athletes and between sports. An athlete who obtained a world record was expected to pay a bonus of $20 000 to BALCO.

Victor Comte and other members of the company were taken to court in 2004, found guilty and sentenced to several months in prison. The outcomes for many of the athletes involved have been, if anything, rather more serious.

The world-class sprinter Dwain Chambers was one of the UK athletes who obtained illegal drugs through BALCO. He tested positive for THG in late 2003, and was banned from competition for two years. But the highest-profile athlete was Marion Jones. She represented the USA, and she was almost unbeatable over 100 m and 200 m for many years. Although she was suspected of taking illegal drugs, she denied all involvement until she finally failed a test in 2006, showing that she had been taking erythropoetin. This steroid boosts the formation of red blood cells, helping the blood to carry more oxygen to muscles and therefore enhancing endurance. She continued to deny any wrongdoing, but eventually admitted to using steroids in October 2007. She was given a two-year ban and stripped of the three gold and two bronze medals that she had won at the Sydney Olympics in 2000. (The photograph shows Marion Jones winning the gold medal for the 100 m at the Sydney Olympic Games.) Her team-mates on the relay also lost their medals. In January 2008, she was sentenced to six months in prison.

Kidney failure

Kidney failure is a condition in which the kidneys stop working properly. It may be acute, suddenly happening in the space of a few days or even a few hours. Or it can be chronic, developing slowly over many years.

Acute kidney failure may happen when the patient already has some other illness or following surgery. Sometimes it is caused by inflammation in the glomeruli or as a result of sepsis (infection of the blood and body tissues by bacteria). Chronic kidney failure is usually caused by inflammation in the glomeruli. There is often no clear reason to explain why this happens. It is most common in older people, and people with diabetes stand a greater risk of chronic kidney failure than others.

A person with kidney failure feels very ill, because toxic waste products build up in the blood rather than being removed from the body. Blood tests will probably show an imbalance in inorganic ions and water, which also contributes to a general feeling of being unwell.

Someone with acute kidney failure will often recover completely, and need no further treatment. But in cases of chronic failure, the patient may need to be treated using renal **dialysis**.

In **haemodialysis**, blood from the patient's vein is passed through very small tubes made from a partially permeable membrane. On the other side of the membrane, dialysis fluid flows along in the opposite direction (Figure 4.25). This fluid has the water potential and concentration of ions and

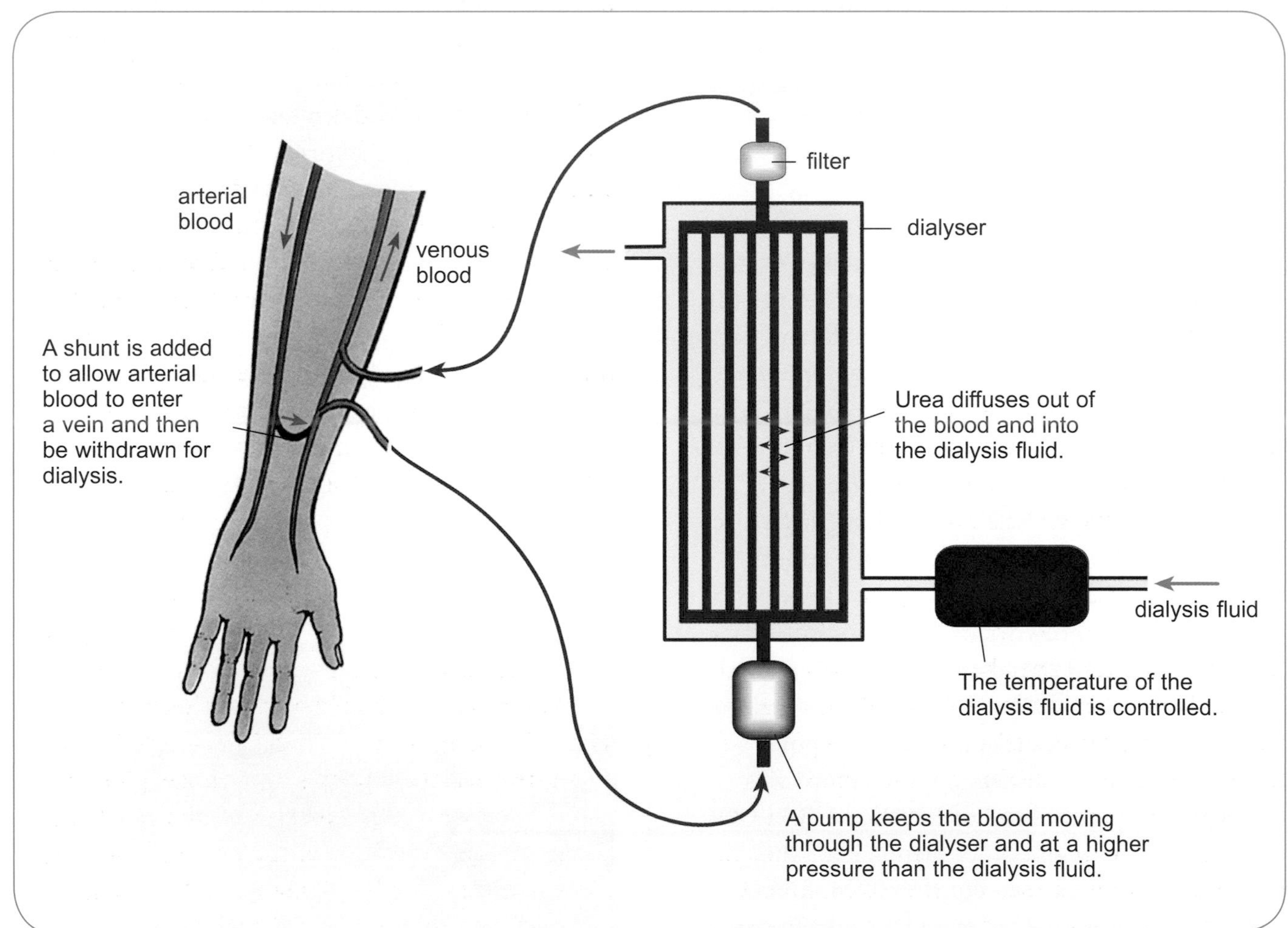

Figure 4.25 Haemodialysis.

glucose that the patient's blood should have if their kidneys were working properly (Table 4.2). As their blood flows through the tubes, water, ions and glucose are able to diffuse freely through the membrane so that concentrations of each of them become the same as in the dialysis fluid. Blood cells and protein molecules are too large to pass through the membrane, so they remain in the blood.

Component	Concentration in dialysis fluid /mmol dm^{-3}	Concentration in blood plasma /mmol dm^{-3}
Na^+	130	139
K^+	2.0	4.5
Ca^{2+}	1.7	1.2
Mg^{2+}	0.5	1.0
Cl^-	98	98
HCO_3^-	38	25
glucose	5	4.2
urea	0	7.5

Table 4.2 Composition of dialysis fluid and blood plasma.

Peritoneal dialysis is now used more commonly than haemodialysis. The peritoneum is the layer of tissue that lines the abdominal cavity. This cavity contains fluid, which bathes the internal organs. In peritoneal dialysis, a catheter is inserted into the peritoneal cavity and dialysis fluid is passed through it, filling the cavity. It is left there for some time, allowing exchange between the blood and the fluid, and then drained off. It takes around half to three quarters of an hour for the fluid to be introduced to the abdomen, take up wastes from the blood and then be drained off again. In most cases, patients can walk around with the fluid inside them, though they do need to have fluid introduced and removed several times each day.

Haemodialysis is more efficient than peritoneal dialysis at removing unwanted substances from the blood, but it does take several hours and a patient has to be connected to a dialysis machine for all of this time, several times a week. Kidney dialysis machines are very expensive and in short supply. Another disadvantage of haemodialysis is that it can normally only be done intermittently, so between treatments the patient has to take great care over what they eat, to avoid large build-ups of urea or other toxic substances.

Peritoneal dialysis frees the patient from being connected to an immoveable machine, but it does have to be done more often than haemodialysis. Its big advantage is that it is a continuous process, so there should be no large swings in blood volume or content. However, it does carry a relatively high risk of infection, because pathogens sometimes get into the abdomen through the catheter.

There is no doubt that most people with chronic kidney failure would like to have a **kidney transplant**. The major difficulty here is that there are simply nowhere near enough kidneys available. To be suitable for transplant, a kidney must come from a healthy person and have a tissue type that is a close match to the recipient (patient), so that the immune system does not reject it. As a person can survive perfectly well with one kidney, it is sometimes possible to take a kidney from a living relative, if they have a close tissue match with the patient.

The shortage of kidneys for transplant has fuelled a global trade in kidneys. International rings have been uncovered where people living in poverty are persuaded to sell a kidney for cash. The kidneys are then sold on to the recipient. This raises a number of ethical questions. It can be argued that these people are being exploited, and that they run a greater risk of illness if their remaining kidney fails or if the operation is done badly. On the other hand, many of the people involved are very poor, and the money they get for the sale may be as much as year's salary for them.

Another avenue leading to a possible solution to the problem of a shortage of kidneys is to produce them in other animals. Pigs – whose physiology is surprisingly similar to that of humans – could perhaps be used to supply kidneys for transplant. This would be a **xenotransplant** – a transplant from a different species. But there are many potential problems with this idea, not least the ethical and religious issues associated with the use of pig organs, as well as the possibility of the transfer of viruses from pigs that could cause a new disease in humans.

SAQ

8 Table 4.2 shows the concentration of eight solutes in the dialysis fluid used in a kidney machine and their concentration in the patient's blood plasma, before these fluids enter the machine. All of these substances have particles that are small enough to pass through the pores in dialysis tubing.

a List the substances that will diffuse from the patient's blood into the dialysis fluid.

b List the substances that will diffuse from the dialysis fluid into the patient's blood.

c What other substance, present in large quantities in both fluids but not listed in the table, will diffuse through the dialysis tubing?

d Explain why the dialysis fluid must contain glucose.

e Suggest one source of HCO_3^- ions in the patient's blood. Hint

f State two solutes that will be present in the patient's blood but that will not pass through the dialysis tubing. Hint

Answer

Extension

Summary

Glossary

- Excretion is the removal of metabolic wastes from the body, including carbon dioxide from respiration and nitrogen waste such as urea from the deamination of excess amino acids.
- The liver is made up of cells called hepatocytes, arranged in rows to form lobules. Blood brought to the liver in the hepatic portal vein and the hepatic artery flows through sinusoids between hepatocytes, while bile made in the liver flows along canaliculi. Blood is taken away from the liver in the hepatic vein.
- Urea is formed in hepatocytes and released into the blood, which carries it to the kidneys for excretion. Urea is made by the ornithine cycle, in which ammonia from deamination is combined with carbon dioxide.
- The liver breaks down toxins such as alcohol, and also hormones.
- The kidneys are made up of thousands of nephrons, each of which begins as a renal capsule in which a glomerulus is found. Ultrafiltration separates soluble blood components with small molecules from the rest of the blood. The filtrate flows along the nephron.
- Selective reabsorption takes back wanted substances into the blood from the nephron. Most reabsorption occurs in the proximal convoluted tubule, where all of the glucose, most of the water and many other substances such as inorganic ions and vitamins are reabsorbed.

continued

- The loop of Henlé uses a counter-current system to produce a very low water potential in the deep medulla of the kidney. This allows water to move out of the collecting duct and into the tissues of the medulla by osmosis, concentrating the urine.
- The secretion of ADH by the posterior pituitary gland increases the permeability of the collecting duct walls to water and so allows more water to be reabsorbed. This happens when osmoreceptors in the hypothalamus detect a low water potential in the blood.
- Urine can be tested for the presence of human chorionic gonadotrophin, a hormone produced during pregnancy. Urine samples can also be used in the detection of illegal usage of steroid hormones in sport.
- Chronic kidney disease can be treated with haemodialysis or peritoneal dialysis. A better and more long-term solution is a kidney transplant, but supplies of kidneys for transplant are too small and it is difficult to find a good tissue match between the potential donor and the recipient.

Stretch and challenge questions

1 a Describe the role of the liver in the control of blood glucose concentration and in the removal of metabolic wastes and toxins. Hint

b How does the structure of the liver adapt it for these functions?

2 What is meant by negative feedback? Explain the role of negative feedback in the control of the glucose content and water content of body fluids. Hint

Questions

1 Human kidneys process 1200 cm^3 of blood every minute. Approximately 125 cm^3 of fluid is filtered from this blood into the renal capsules, resulting in 1500 cm^3 of urine being produced each day.

a i Calculate the volume of filtrate, in cm^3, produced by the kidneys in a day. Show your working. [2]

ii Calculate the <u>percentage</u> of the filtrate that is reabsorbed into the bloodstream. Show your working. [2]

b i State why there are no proteins in the filtrate in the renal capsule. [1]

ii Explain why there is glucose present in the filtrate in the renal capsule but not in the urine. [2]

iii Explain why the concentration of urea is greater in the urine than it is in the filtrate in the renal capsule. [2]

iv Name <u>two</u> other nitrogenous waste products found in urine. [2]

c When little water is ingested, when heavy sweating occurs or when a large amount of salt is absorbed in the diet, the water potential of the blood plasma becomes more negative.

Describe the sequence of events that results in the water potential of the blood plasma returning to normal. [7]

OCR Biology A (2804) January 2005 (modified) [Total 18] Answer

continued

2 a Analysis of the substances contained in a urine sample is useful in monitoring kidney function. The diagram shows a diagrammatic section of the glomerulus and Bowman's capsule in a nephron.
The effective filtration pressure (EFP) in the glomerulus depends on:
- the blood pressure in the glomerular capillaries (BP)
- the water potential of the plasma in the glomerular capillaries (WP)
- the pressure of the fluid in the Bowman's capsule (CP).

These pressures are shown by arrows in the diagram.

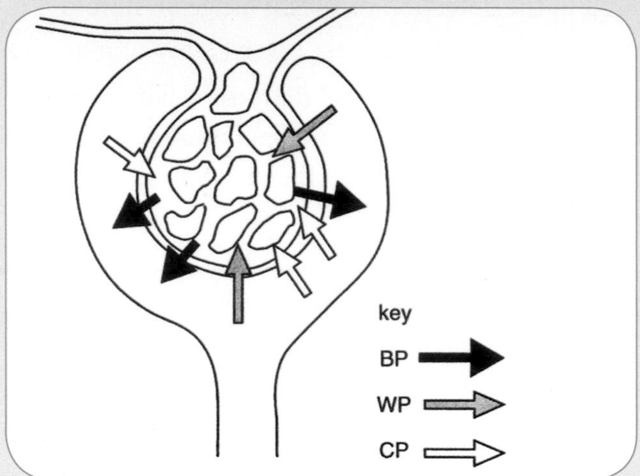

i Explain how each of the pressures shown in the diagram is produced. [3]

ii Suggest a simple equation, using the symbols given in **a i**, to show how these pressures interact to produce the EFP. [1]

Hint

b The table shows the mean concentration of some of the substances in blood plasma, the glomerular filtrate and urine of an individual over 24 hours.

	Mean concentration / $g\,dm^{-3}$		
Substance	**Plasma**	**Glomerular filtrate**	**Urine**
protein	80.00	10.00	10.00
glucose	3.00	3.00	2.00
amino acids	0.50	0.50	0.00
urea	0.30	0.30	0.15

i Name the process which forms urine from the glomerular filtrate in the Bowman's capsule. [1]

ii The table shows an abnormally high concentration of protein and glucose in the urine.
Suggest an explanation for the abnormal concentrations of protein and glucose. [6]

Hint

c Explain how the volume of water excreted in urine is controlled. [9]

OCR Human Biology A (2867) June 2005 [Total 20]

Answer

Chapter 5

Photosynthesis

e-Learning

Objectives

In *Biology 1*, we looked at the human diet – what we need to eat and why. Humans, like all animals and fungi, are **heterotrophs**. This means that we need to eat food containing organic molecules, especially carbohydrates, fats and proteins. These organic molecules are our only source of energy.

Plants, however, do not need to take in any organic molecules at all. They obtain their energy from sunlight. They can use this energy to build their own organic molecules for themselves, using simple inorganic substances. They first produce carbohydrates from carbon dioxide and water, by **photosynthesis**. They can then use these carbohydrates, plus inorganic ions such as nitrate, phosphate and magnesium, to manufacture all the organic molecules that they need. Organisms that feed in this way – self-sufficient, not needing any organic molecules that another organism has made are **autotrophs**.

So heterotrophs depend on autotrophs for the supply of organic molecules on which they feed. Some heterotrophs feed directly on plants, while others feed further along a food chain. But eventually all of an animal's or fungus's food can be traced back to plants, and the energy of sunlight.

In this chapter, we will look in detail at how plants transfer energy from sunlight to chemical energy in organic molecules. In Chapter 6, we will see how all living organisms can then release the trapped energy from these molecules and convert it into a form that their cells can use. This process is called **respiration**, and it involves oxidation of the energy-containing organic substances, forming another energy-containing substance called **ATP**. Every cell has to make its own ATP. You can find out more about ATP in Chapter 6.

An overview of photosynthesis

Photosynthesis happens in several different kinds of organisms, not only plants. There are many kinds of bacteria that can photosynthesise. Photosynthesis also takes place in **phytoplankton**, tiny organisms that float in the upper layers of the sea and lakes. Here, though, we will concentrate on photosynthesis in green plants, because this is the ultimate source of almost all of our food.

You should already be familiar with the overall equation for photosynthesis:

$$6CO_2 + 6H_2O \longrightarrow C_6H_{12}O_6 + 6O_2$$

However, in reality photosynthesis is a complex **metabolic pathway** – a series of reactions linked to each other in numerous steps, many of which are catalysed by enzymes. These reactions take place in two stages. The first is the **light-dependent stage**, and this is followed by the **light-independent stage**. Both of these stages take place inside chloroplasts (Figure 5.1).

Extension

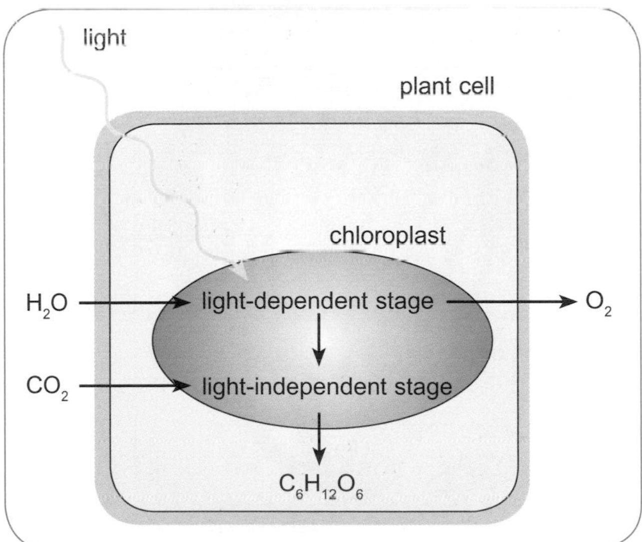

Figure 5.1 The stages of photosynthesis.

The structure of a chloroplast

Figure 5.2 shows the structure of a typical chloroplast. Chloroplasts are found in only some types of plant cells, especially in palisade mesophyll tissue and spongy mesophyll tissue in leaves. Each cell may have ten or more chloroplasts inside it.

A chloroplast is surrounded by two membranes, forming an **envelope**. There are more membranes inside the chloroplast, which are arranged so that they enclose fluid-filled sacs between them. The membranes are called **lamellae** and the fluid-filled sacs are **thylakoids**. In some parts of the chloroplasts, the thylakoids are stacked up like a pile of pancakes, and these stacks are called **grana**. The 'background material' inside the chloroplast is called the **stroma**.

Embedded tightly in the membranes inside the chloroplast are several different kinds of **photosynthetic pigments**. These are coloured substances that absorb energy from certain wavelengths (colours) of light. The most abundant pigment is **chlorophyll**, which comes in two forms, **chlorophyll *a*** and **chlorophyll *b*** (Figure 5.3).

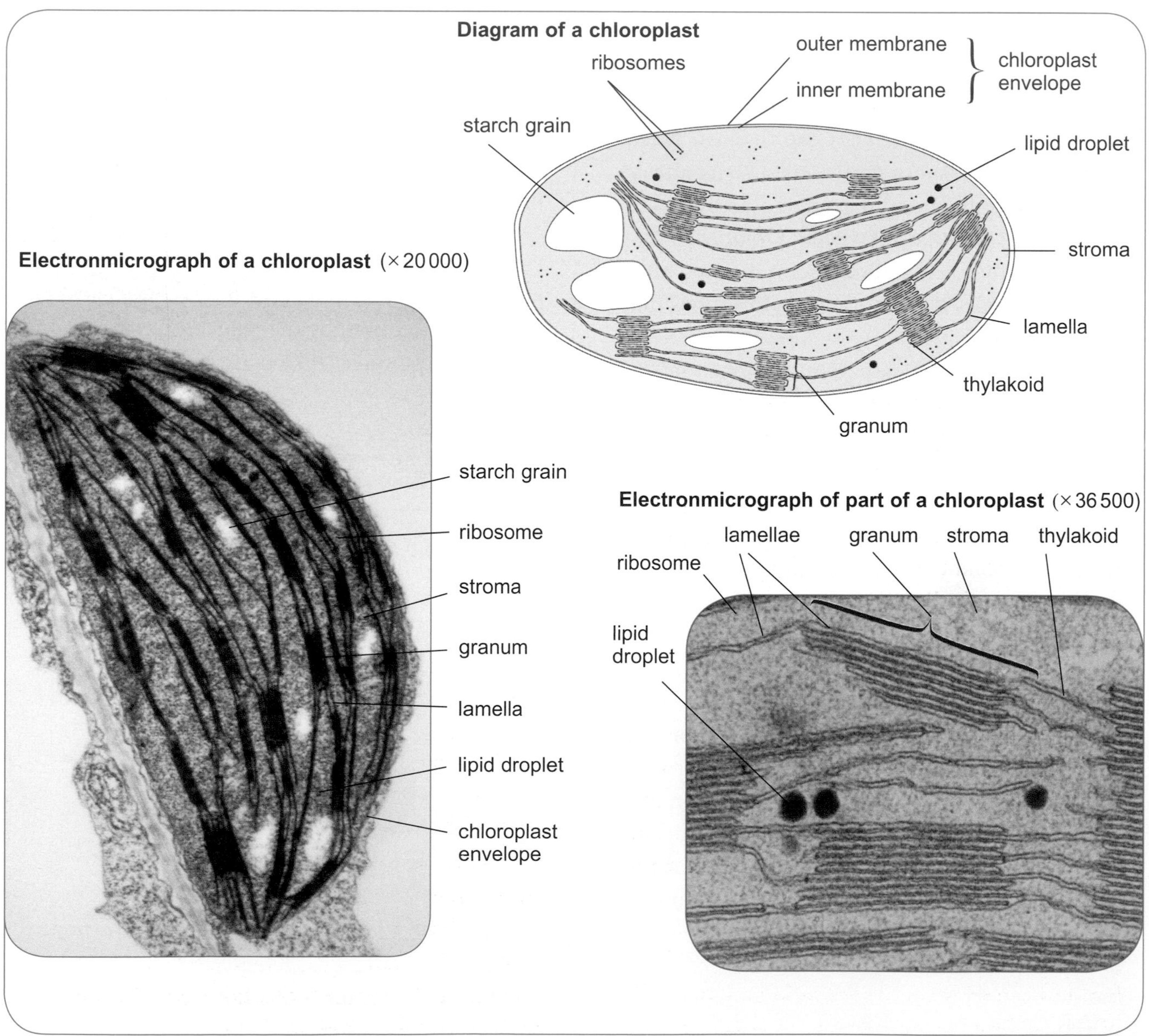

Figure 5.2 The structure of a chloroplast.

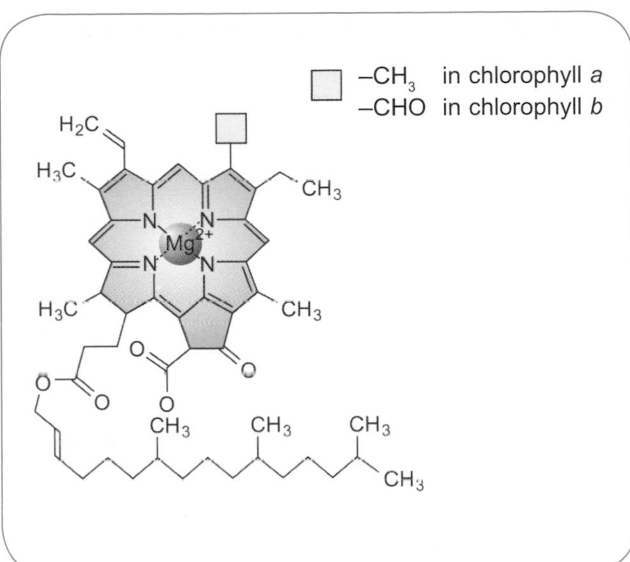

Figure 5.3 A chlorophyll molecule.

Chloroplasts often contain **starch grains**, because starch is the form in which plants store the carbohydrate that they make by photosynthesis. They also contain **ribosomes** and their own small circular strand of **DNA**. (You may remember that chloroplasts have evolved from bacteria that first invaded eukaryotic cells over a thousand million years ago.)

Biofuels

The ability of plants to transfer light energy into chemical energy means that they can be used to provide fuels for us to use – for example, for generating electricity or in vehicle engines. As stocks of fossil fuels run down, and as carbon dioxide levels in the atmosphere continue to increase, there has been a sharp increase in the use of crop plants to produce fuels rather than food. For example, rape seed is being increasingly used to produce biodiesel, rather than food for animals or humans.

At first sight, this would appear to very good for the environment. Using plants to provide fuels is theoretically 'carbon-neutral'. The carbon dioxide that is given out when the fuels are burnt is matched by the carbon dioxide that the plants take in as they photosynthesise and grow. However, if we take into account the energy that is used in harvesting the plants, converting the biomass to a useful form of fuel and transporting that fuel to points of sale, then there is still a net emission of carbon dioxide to the atmosphere.

But the greatest problem is the effect that the increasing quantity of crops grown to produce biofuels is having on the availability and price of food. For example, as huge areas of land in

the USA are taken over to grow corn (maize) to produce fuel, there is less maize on sale for cattle feed or to make foods for humans. Prices have increased, in some cases so much so that poorer people, especially in neighbouring countries like Mexico, are finding it much more difficult to buy enough food for their needs.

We also need to consider effects on ecosystems. Producing large quantities of biofuels will take up large areas of land. There is a danger that some countries will cut down forests to provide extra land for this purpose, damaging habitats and endangering species that live there.

Photosynthetic pigments

A pigment is a substance whose molecules absorb some wavelengths (colours) of light, but not others. The wavelengths it does not absorb are either reflected or transmitted through the substance. These unabsorbed wavelengths reach our eyes, so we see the pigment in these colours.

The majority of the pigments in a chloroplast are chlorophyll *a* and chlorophyll *b*. Both types of chlorophyll absorb similar wavelengths of light, but chlorophyll *a* absorbs slightly longer wavelengths than chlorophyll *b*. This can be shown in a graph called an **absorption spectrum** (Figure 5.4).

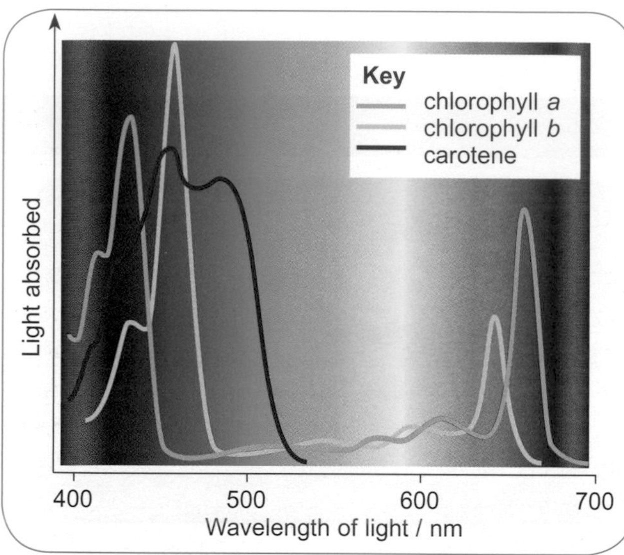

Figure 5.4 Absorption spectra for chlorophyll and carotene.

Other pigments found in chloroplasts include **carotenoids**, such as carotene. These absorb a wide range of short wavelength light, including more blue-green light than the chlorophylls. They are **accessory pigments**. They help by absorbing wavelengths of light that would otherwise not be used by the plant. They pass on some of this energy to chlorophyll. They probably also help to protect chlorophyll from damage by very intense light.

SAQ

1 a Use Figure 5.4 to explain why chlorophyll looks green.

b What colour are carotenoids?

Answer

The two stages of photosynthesis

The light-dependent stage of photosynthesis happens on the thylakoid membranes. Light energy is absorbed by chlorophyll. Some of this energy is then used to make ATP (Figure 5.5). Water molecules are split to produce hydrogen ions, electrons and oxygen. The hydrogen ions and electrons are picked up by a coenzyme called **NADP**, forming **reduced NADP**. The oxygen is a waste product and is excreted from the chloroplast.

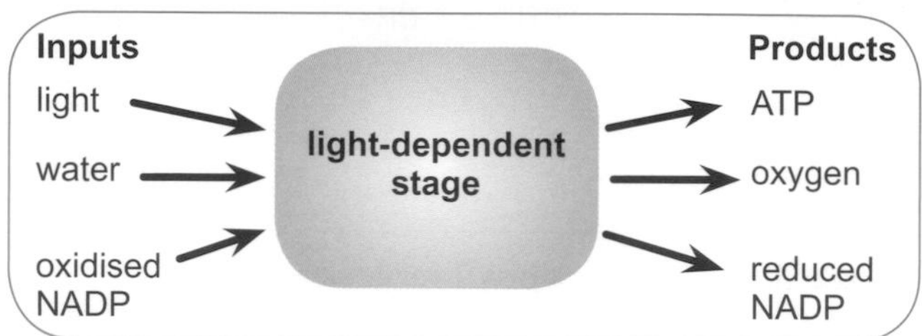

Figure 5.5 Simplified overview of the light-dependent stage of photosynthesis.

The ATP and reduced NADP produced in the light-dependent stage are now used in the light-independent stage, which takes place in the stroma of the chloroplast. This contains a compound called **RuBP**, which combines with carbon dioxide to form a compound that reacts to form a three-carbon sugar called **triose phosphate**. The reactions follow a cycle, at the end of which RuBP is regenerated. These reactions are known as the **Calvin cycle** (Figure 5.6).

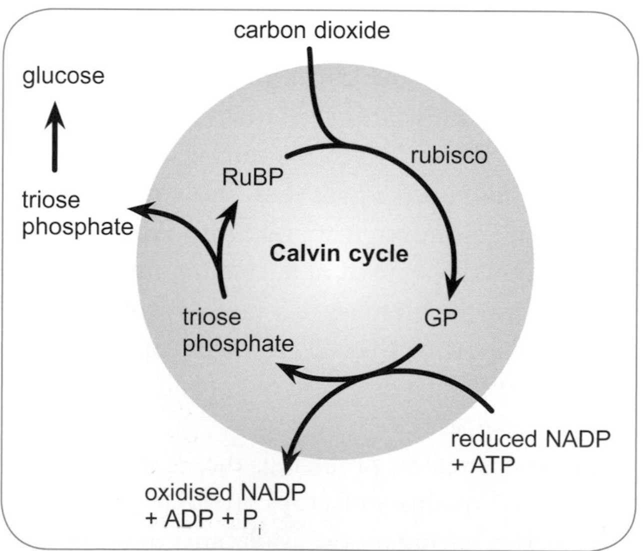

Figure 5.6 Simplified overview of the light-independent stage of photosynthesis.

Now that you have an overall picture of what happens in photosynthesis, we need to look at each stage in more detail.

The light-dependent stage

As we have seen, this stage of photosynthesis takes place on the thylakoids inside the chloroplast. It involves the absorption of light energy by chlorophyll, and the use of that energy and the products from splitting water to make ATP and reduced NADP.

Photosystems

The chlorophyll molecules are arranged in clusters called **photosystems** in the thylakoid membranes (Figure 5.7). Each photosystem spans the membrane, and contains protein molecules and pigment molecules. Energy is captured from photons of light that hit the photosystem, and is funnelled down to a pair of molecules at the **reaction centre** of the photosystem complex.

There are two different sorts of photosystem, **PSI** and **PSII**, both with a pair of molecules of chlorophyll *a* at the reaction centre.

Extension

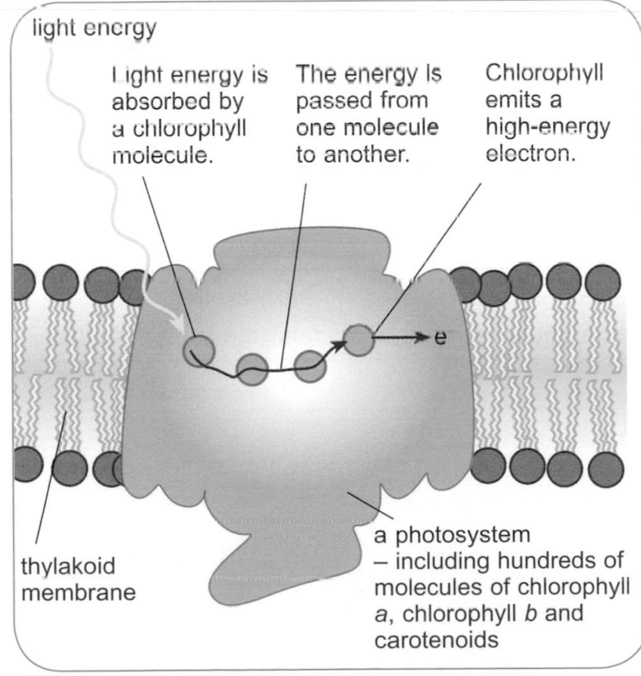

Figure 5.7 A photosystem in a thylakoid membrane.

Photophosphorylation

Photophosphorylation means 'phosphorylation using light'. It refers to the production of ATP, by combining a phosphate group with ADP, using energy that originally came from light:

ADP + phosphate $\longrightarrow$ ATP

Photophosphorylation happens when an electron is passed along a series of **electron carriers**, forming an **electron transport chain** in the thylakoid membranes. The electron starts off with a lot of energy, and it gradually loses some of it as it moves from one carrier to the next. The energy is used to cause a phosphate group to react with ADP.

Extension

Cyclic photophosphorylation

This process involves only PSI, not PSII. It results in the formation of ATP, but not reduced NADP (Figure 5.8).

Light is absorbed by PSI and the energy passed on to electrons in the chlorophyll *a* molecules at the reaction centre. In each chlorophyll *a* molecule, one of the electrons becomes so energetic that it leaves the chlorophyll molecules completely. The electron is then passed along the chain of electron carriers. The energy from the electron is used to make ATP. The electron, now having lost its extra energy, eventually returns to chlorophyll *a* in PSI.

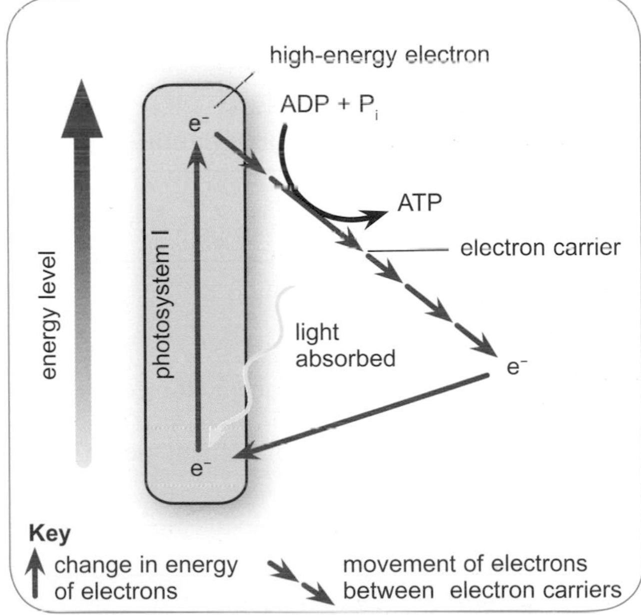

Figure 5.8 Cyclic photophosphorylation.

Non-cyclic photophosphorylation

This process involves both kinds of photosystem. It results not only in the production of ATP, but also of reduced NADP.

Light hitting either PSI or PSII causes electrons to be emitted. The electrons from PSII pass down the electron carrier chain, generating ATP by photophosphorylation. However, instead of going back to PSII, the electrons instead replace the electrons lost from PSI.

The electrons emitted from PSI are not used to make ATP. Instead, they help to reduce NADP.

For this to happen, hydrogen ions are required. These come from another event that happens when light hits PSII. PSII contains an enzyme that splits water when it is activated by light. The reaction is called **photolysis**:

$$2H_2O \longrightarrow 4H^+ + 4e^- + O_2$$

The hydrogen ions are taken up by NADP, forming reduced NADP. The electrons replace the ones that were emitted from PSII when light hit it. The oxygen diffuses out of the chloroplast and eventually out of the leaf, as an excretory product.

The Z-scheme

The **Z-scheme** is simply a way of summarising what happens to electrons during the light-dependent reactions. It is a kind of graph, with the *y*-axis indicating the 'energy level' of the electron (Figure 5.9).

Start at the bottom left, where light hits photosystem II. The red vertical line going up shows the increase in the energy level of electrons as they are emitted from this photosystem. You can also see where these electrons came from – the splitting of water molecules. (In fact, it probably isn't the same electrons – but the electrons from the water replace the ones that are emitted from the photosystem.)

If you keep following the vertical line showing the increasing energy in the electrons, you arrive at a point where it starts a steep dive downwards. This shows the electrons losing their energy as they pass along the electron carrier chain. Eventually they arrive at photosystem I.

You can then track the movement of the electrons to a higher energy level when PSI is hit by light, before they fall back downwards as they lose energy and become part of a reduced NADP molecule.

The light-independent stage

Now the ATP and reduced NADP that have been formed in the light-independent stage are used to help to produce carbohydrates from carbon dioxide. These events take place in the stroma of the chloroplast. As we have seen, the cyclic series of reactions is known as the Calvin cycle (Figure 5.10).

SAQ

2 Copy and complete the table to compare cyclic and non-cyclic photophosphorylation. (If a box in a particular row is not applicable, write n/a.)

	Cyclic photophosphorylation	**Non-cyclic photophosphorylation**
Is PSI involved?		
Is PSII involved?		
Where does PSI obtain replacement electrons from?		
Where does PSII obtain replacement electrons from?		
Is ATP made?		
Is reduced NADP made?		

Answer

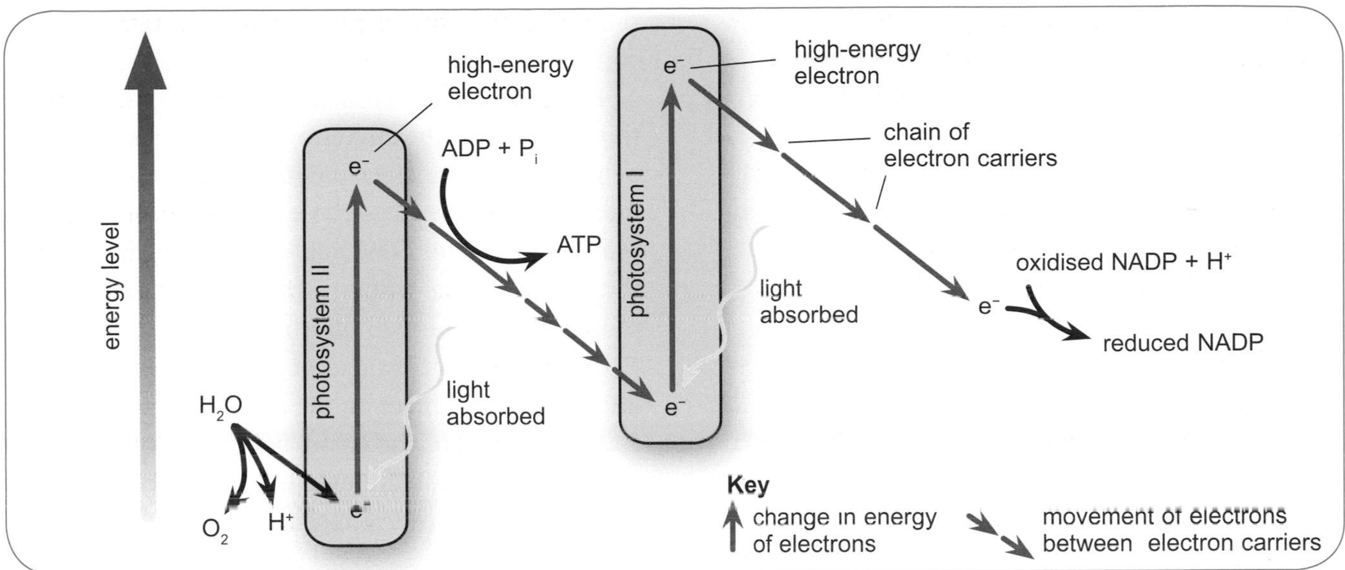

Figure 5.9 The Z-scheme, summarising non-cyclic photophosphorylation.

The chloroplast stroma contains an enzyme called **rubisco** (its full name is ribulose bisphosphate carboxylase). This is thought to be the most abundant enzyme in the world. Its function is to catalyse the reaction in which carbon dioxide combines with a substance called **RuBP** (ribulose bisphosphate).

RuBP molecules each contain five atoms of carbon. The reaction with carbon dioxide therefore produces a six-carbon molecule, but this immediately splits to form two three-carbon molecules. This three-carbon substance is **glycerate 3-phosphate**, usually known as **GP**.

Now the two products of the light-dependent stages come into play. The reduced NADP and the ATP are used to provide energy and phosphate groups, which change the GP into a three-carbon sugar called **triose phosphate** (**TP**). This is the first carbohydrate that is made in photosynthesis.

There are many possible fates of the triose phosphate. Five-sixths of it are used to regenerate RuBP. The remainder can be converted into other

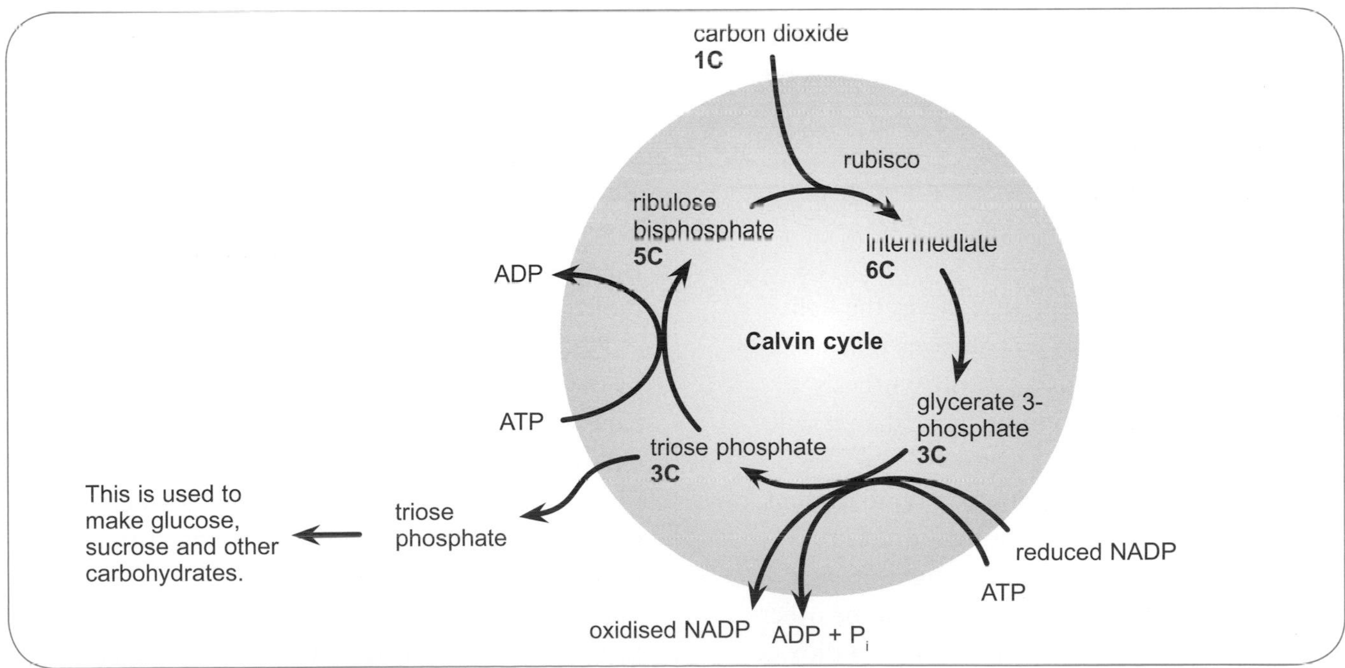

Figure 5.10 The Calvin cycle.

carbohydrates. For example, two triose phosphates can combine to produce a hexose phosphate molecule. From these, glucose, fructose, sucrose, starch and cellulose can be formed.

The triose phosphate can also be used to make lipids and amino acids. For amino acid production, nitrogen needs to be added, which plants obtain from the soil in the form of nitrate ions or ammonium ions.

SAQ

3 Suggest what happens to the ADP, inorganic phosphate and NADP that is formed during the Calvin cycle.

Answer

Factors affecting the rate of photosynthesis

Photosynthesis requires several inputs. It needs raw materials in the form of carbon dioxide and water, and energy in the form of sunlight. The light-independent stage also requires a reasonably high temperature, because the rates of reactions are affected by the kinetic energy of the molecules involved.

If any of these requirements is in short supply, it can limit the rate at which the reactions of photosynthesis are able to take place.

SAQ

4 The rate of the light-dependent reactions is not directly affected by temperature. Can you suggest why this is?

Answer

Light intensity

Light provides the energy that drives the light-dependent reactions, so it is obvious that when there is no light, there is no photosynthesis. If we provide a plant with more light, then it will photosynthesise faster.

However, this can only happen up to a point. We would eventually reach a light intensity where, if we give the plant more light, its rate of photosynthesis does not change. Some other factor, such as the availability of carbon dioxide or the quantity of chlorophyll in its leaves, is preventing the rate of photosynthesis from continuing to increase.

This relationship is shown in Figure 5.11. Over the first part of the curve, we can see that rate of photosynthesis does indeed increase as light intensity increases. For these light intensities, light is a **limiting factor**. The light intensity is limiting the rate of photosynthesis. If we give the plant more light, then it will photosynthesise faster.

But, from point X onwards, increasing the light intensity has no effect on the rate of photosynthesis. Along this part of the curve, light is no longer a limiting factor. Something else is. It is most likely to be the carbon dioxide concentration.

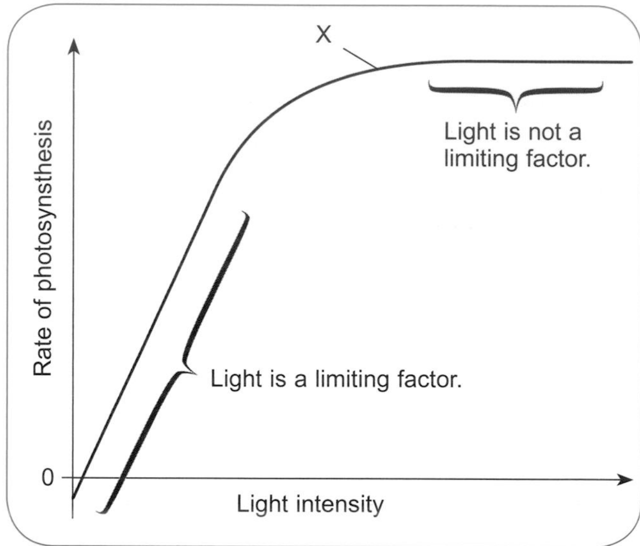

Figure 5.11 The effect of light intensity on the rate of photosynthesis.

Carbon dioxide concentration

The concentration of carbon dioxide in the air is very low, only about 0.04%. Yet this substance is needed for the formation of every organic molecule inside every living thing on Earth.

Plants absorb carbon dioxide into their leaves by diffusion through the stomata. During daylight, carbon dioxide is used in the Calvin cycle in the chloroplasts, so the concentration of carbon dioxide inside the leaf is even lower than in the air outside, providing the diffusion gradient that keeps it moving into the leaf.

Carbon dioxide concentration is often a limiting factor for photosynthesis. If we give plants extra carbon dioxide, they can photosynthesise faster.

Figure 5.12 shows the relationship between carbon dioxide concentration and rate of photosynthesis. Figure 5.13 shows the effect of carbon dioxide at different light intensities.

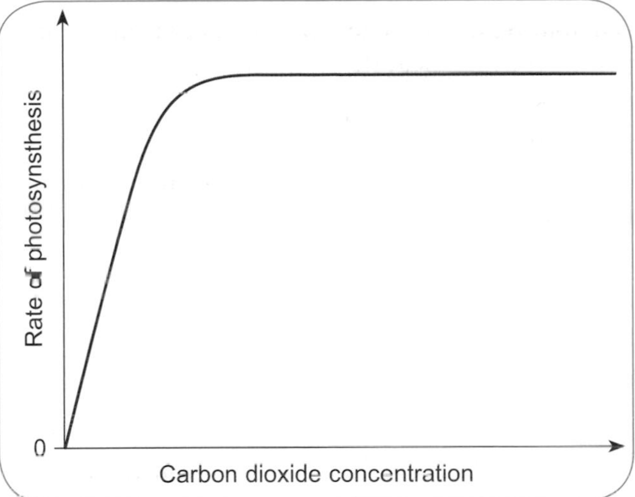

Figure 5.12 The effect of carbon dioxide on rate of photosynthesis.

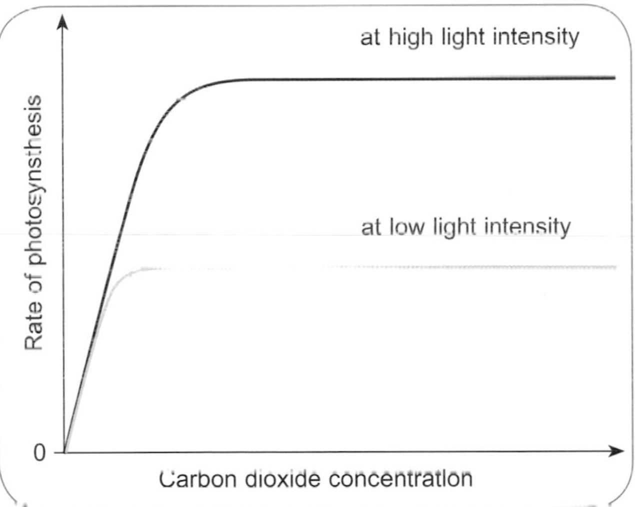

Figure 5.13 The effect of carbon dioxide concentration on the rate of photosynthesis at different light intensities.

SAQ

5 a Over which part of the curve in Figure 5.12 is carbon dioxide a limiting factor for photosynthesis?

b Suggest why the curve flattens out at high levels of CO_2.

Answer

Temperature

Temperature affects the kinetic energy of molecules. The higher the temperature, the faster molecules move, and the more frequently they collide with one another. They also collide with more energy. The greater frequency and energy of collisions means that the reaction rate increases.

In photosynthesis, though, this effect is only seen in the light-independent reactions. The rate of the light-dependent reactions is not directly affected by temperature, because the energy that drives them comes from light, not the kinetic energy of molecules.

In living organisms, most reactions are catalysed by enzymes, so we also need to consider the effect of temperature on them. Just like any molecules, their kinetic energy increases as temperature increases. However, as you will remember, beyond a certain temperature (different for different enzymes) they begin to lose their shape, and therefore their catalytic properties. Plant enzymes often have lower optimum temperatures than enzymes found in mammals, because they have evolved to work in the environmental temperatures in which the plant normally lives.

Things are complicated, however, by a peculiar property of the enzyme rubisco. Rubisco has an unfortunate tendency to stop doing what is supposed to do – catalyse the combination of carbon dioxide with RuBP – and start doing something else when temperature rises. It switches to catalysing a reaction in which *oxygen* is combined with RuBP. This is very wasteful, as it wastes RuBP. It is called **photorespiration**, and it can seriously reduce the rate of photosynthesis in many plant species, when temperature and light intensity are high. (Photorespiration is a misleading name, as it is not really respiration at all.)

The effect of light on the Calvin cycle

The Calvin cycle is the light-independent stage of photosynthesis. It is given that name because it does not require energy input from light. It *does* however, need energy input from the light-dependent stage, in the form of ATP and reduced NADP.

Imagine that light is shining on a chloroplast. The light-dependent stage is generating ATP and reduced NADP, and the reactions of the Calvin cycle are working continuously.

Now the light is switched off. The light-dependent stage stops, so the supply of ATP and NADP to the Calvin cycle also stops. These substances are needed to fuel the conversion of GP to TP. So now GP can no longer be converted into TP, and the GP just builds up. The rest of the cycle keeps running, until most of the TP is used up. Then it grinds to a halt.

Figure 5.14 shows what happens to the relative amounts of GP and TP when the light is switched off. As we would expect, the levels of TP plummet, while the levels of GP rise. If the light is switched on again, they go back to their 'normal' relative levels.

The effect of carbon dioxide concentration on the Calvin cycle

Carbon dioxide is a vital input to the Calvin cycle. If carbon dioxide is in short supply, then less GP is made, and therefore less TP.

The lack of carbon dioxide means that there is less for RuBP to react with, so RuBP might be expected to build up, and this does happen.

But remember that RuBP has to be replaced from TP. The lower rate of synthesis of TP means that there is less available to convert to RuBP or to other carbohydrates, amino acids or lipids. Normally, the plant will prioritise the replacement of RuBP, ensuring that its levels remain reasonably high. If the low carbon dioxide concentration continues over a long period of time, however, then there is little point in the plant maintaining high concentrations of RuBP, as it does not have much carbon dioxide to combine with. Some species of plants appear to adapt to this situation by allowing the level of RuBP to fall.

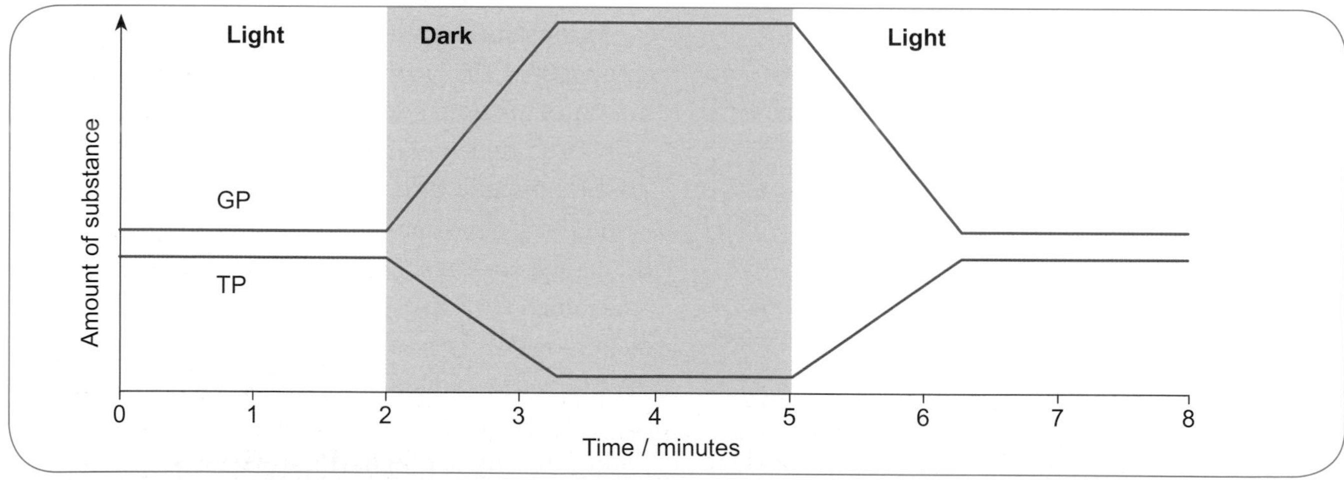

Figure 5.14 The effect of light and dark on the relative levels of TP and GP in a chloroplast.

SAQ

6 a Explain why the Calvin cycle stops running when there is no light and the TP is used up.

b Make a copy of Figure 5.14. Add another line to show what you would expect to happen to the levels of RuBP during this eight-minute period.

Answer

7 What effect would you expect a rise or a fall in temperature to have on the relative levels of GP, TP and RuBP? (Assume that the temperature does not go high enough to denature enzymes.) Explain your reasoning.

Answer

Summary

Glossary

- Autotrophs make their own organic nutrients using inorganic materials. Heterotrophs require organic nutrients that have been made by other organisms. Plants are autotrophs. Animals and fungi are heterotrophs.
- In photosynthesis, energy from light is transformed into chemical energy in organic molecules. This energy can then be released from the organic molecules by respiration.
- Photosynthesis is a two-stage process. In the light-dependent reaction, light is absorbed by chlorophyll and used to split water and produce ATP and reduced NADP. In the light-independent stage, this ATP and reduced NADP are used to produce carbohydrates from carbon dioxide.
- Photosynthesis takes place in chloroplasts. A chloroplast has an envelope surrounding it. Membranes in the stroma form thylakoids, which are stacked to form grana. The light-dependent reaction takes place on the thylakoids, and the light-independent reaction in the stroma.
- Photosynthetic pigments such as chlorophyll absorb energy from light. The energy causes electrons to be emitted from the pigments. Chlorophyll molecules are found in photosystems, of which there are two kinds – PSI and PSII.
- In cyclic photophosphorylation, electrons emitted from PSI are passed along a chain of electron carriers, releasing their energy which is used to make ATP. The electrons return to PSI.
- In non-cyclic photophosphorylation, electrons are emitted from both PSI and PSII. The electrons from PSII pass down the electron transport chain and ATP is formed. These electrons are then taken up by PSI. The electrons from PSI, together with hydrogen ions from the splitting of water, are used to reduce NADP. The electrons lost from PSII are replaced by electrons produced from the splitting of water.
- In the Calvin cycle, the enzyme rubisco catalyses the reaction of RuBP with carbon dioxide. This results in the formation of two molecules of GP. Energy from ATP and NADP is used to convert GP to TP. Most of the TP is used to regenerate RuBP, while the rest is converted to other carbohydrates, lipids or amino acids.
- Low levels of light, low levels of carbon dioxide and low temperatures can all reduce the rate of photosynthesis. A factor that is holding back the rate is called a limiting factor. Increasing the level of the limiting factor increases the rate of photosynthesis.
- Although the light-independent reaction does not require light, it does require ATP and NADP that have been made in the light-dependent reaction. When there is no light, the lack of ATP and NADP causes GP to accumulate and levels of TP and RuBP to fall. Low carbon dioxide levels lead to a fall in GP and TP levels, and an initial accumulation of RuBP. Changes in temperature do not affect the relative levels of these compounds.

Stretch and challenge question

1 Describe how the structures of:

Hint

a a leaf

b a palisade cell

c a chloroplast

are adapted for photosynthesis.

Questions

1 In an experiment to investigate the effect of light intensity on the rate of photosynthesis, the following procedure was carried out by some students.

- Discs were cut from the photosynthetic tissue of the brown alga *Fucus serratus*, a common rocky shore seaweed, using a cork borer.
- Ten discs were placed in each of four beakers filled with 50 cm^3 of sea water. The discs are denser than sea water and therefore sink to the bottom of the beaker.
- Each beaker was illuminated with a bench lamp placed at different distances (d) from the beaker.
- The time in minutes, at which the third disc from each batch reached the surface (t) was recorded.
- The rate of photosynthesis was determined by calculating $\frac{1000}{t}$.

A student's set of results is shown in the table.

Distance of beaker from lamp (d) / cm	**Light intensity $\frac{1}{d^2}$**	**Time for third disc to reach the surface (t) / min**	**Rate of photosynthesis $\frac{1000}{t}$**
5	0.04	23	43.5
10	0.01	36	27.8
15	0.004	52	19.2
20		88	

a Calculate the values for light intensity and rate of photosynthesis when the distance between beaker and lamp was 20 cm. [2]

b Explain why the discs float after being illuminated for a length of time. [3]

c Using the data in the table, describe the relationship between light intensity and the rate of phototsynthesis. [2]

d State the environmental factor limiting the rate of photosynthesis in this experiment. [1]

e State the evidence from the table you used to support your answer to **d**. [1]

f Suggest why the student is <u>not</u> likely to find an increase in the rate of photosynthesis when two lamps are placed 5 cm from the beaker. [2]

OCR Biology A (2804) June 2004 (part) [Total 11]

Answer

Chapter 6

Respiration

e-Learning

Objectives

All living cells, and therefore all living organisms, need energy in order to survive. Energy is required for many different purposes. Every living cell, for example, must be able to move substances across its membranes against their concentration gradients, by **active transport**. Cells need to use energy to drive many of their **metabolic reactions**, such as building protein molecules from amino acids, or making copies of DNA molecules. Energy is used to move chromosomes around during mitosis and meiosis. Most animals also have specialised **muscle cells**, which use energy to make themselves contract and so produce movement. This is described in detail in Chapter 16.

Cells obtain energy by metabolic pathways known as **respiration**. Respiration releases chemical potential energy from glucose and other energy-containing organic molecules.

ATP

ATP stands for **adenosine triphosphate**. Every living cell uses ATP as its immediate source of energy. When energy is released from glucose or other molecules during respiration, it is used to make ATP.

Figure 6.1 shows the structure of an ATP molecule. ATP is a phosphorylated nucleotide. It is similar in structure to the nucleotides that make up RNA and DNA.

SAQ

1 Outline why energy is needed for each of these processes.

Hint

a the transport of sucrose in a plant

b the transmission of an action potential along a nerve axon

c the selective reabsorption of glucose from a kidney nephron.

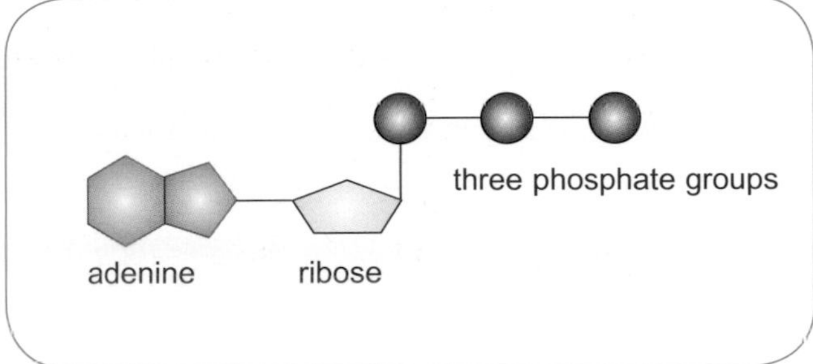

Figure 6.1 The structure of ATP.

ATP molecules contain energy. When one phosphate group is removed from each molecule in one mole of ATP, 30.5 kJ of energy is released (Figure 6.2). This is a hydrolysis reaction, and it is catalysed by enzymes called **ATPases**. Most cells contain many different types of ATPases.

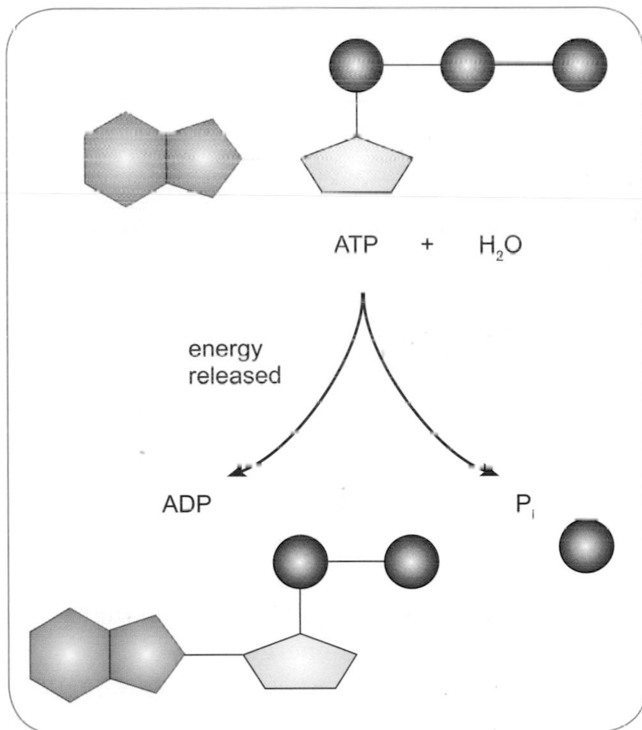

Figure 6.2 Energy is released when ATP is hydrolysed.

The products of the reaction are ADP (adenosine diphosphate) and a phosphate group (P_i).

$$ATP + H_2O \rightleftharpoons ADP + P_i \quad 30.5\,kJ \text{ released}$$

More energy can be obtained if a second phosphate group is removed. AMP stands for adenosine monophosphate.

$$ADP + H_2O \rightleftharpoons AMP + P_i \quad 30.5\,kJ \text{ released}$$

The each-way arrows in these equations mean that the reaction can go either way. ATPases may catalyse the synthesis of ATP, or its breakdown. ATP is used for almost every energy-demanding activity in the body. The amount of energy contained in one ATP molecule is often a suitable quantity to use for a particular purpose. One glucose molecule would contain too much, so a lot would be wasted if all the energy in a glucose molecule was released to make a particular event happen. ATP can provide energy in small packages. Also, the energy in ATP can be released very quickly and easily, at exactly the right time and in exactly the right place in a cell, just when and where it is needed. ATP is often known as the 'energy currency' of a cell. Each cell has to make its own ATP – it cannot be transported from one cell to another.

Glycolysis

Glycolysis is the first group of reactions that takes place in respiration. It means 'breaking glucose apart'. Glycolysis is a metabolic pathway that takes place in the cytoplasm of the cell. Glucose is broken down in a series of steps, each catalysed by an enzyme. In the process, a small proportion of the energy in each glucose molecule is released, and used to make a small amount of ATP. Figure 6.3 shows the main steps in glycolysis.

The first steps in glycolysis involve adding phosphate groups to a glucose molecule. This produces a hexose sugar with two phosphate groups attached to it, **hexose bisphosphate**. The process is called **phosphorylation**. It raises the energy level of the hexose, making it able to participate in the steps that follow.

The hexose bisphosphate is then split into two molecules of a three-carbon sugar, **triose phosphate**.

The triose phosphates are then oxidised to **pyruvate**, by having hydrogen removed from them. The enzyme that catalyses this reaction is called a **dehydrogenase**. It can only work if there is another molecule present that can take up the hydrogens that it removes. This molecule is called **NAD**, which stands for nicotinamide adenine dinucleotide. NAD is a **coenzyme** – a substance

SAQ

2 **a** What are the similarities between an ATP molecule and a nucleotide in DNA?

Hint

b What are the differences between them?

Answer

3 The bar chart shows the relative rate of use of ATP by a cell for its various energy-requiring activities.

a Explain why the sodium–potassium pump requires an input of energy.

b Explain why the synthesis of proteins, DNA and RNA requires energy.

c Suggest what the 'other uses of ATP' could be.

Answer

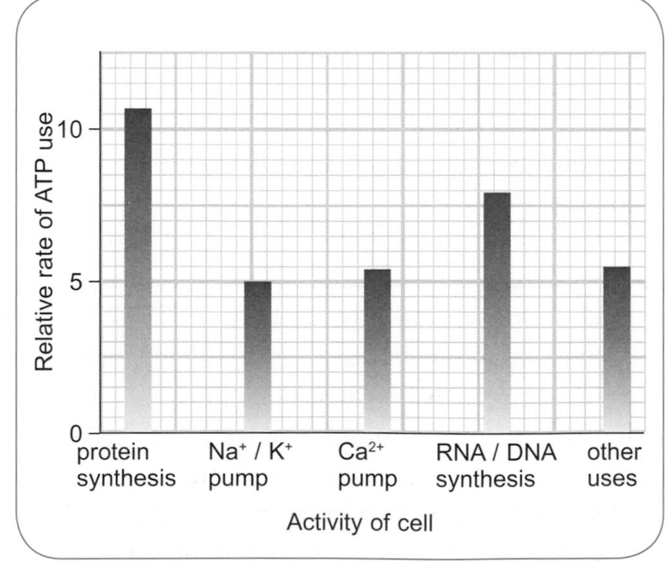

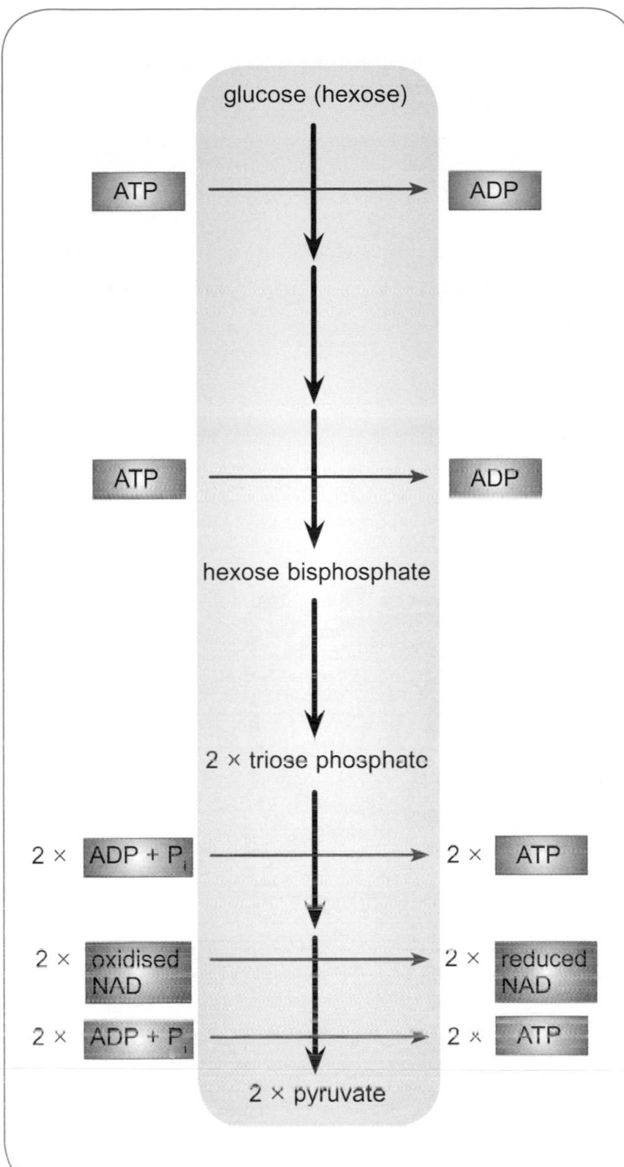

Figure 6.3 The main steps in glycolysis.

that is needed to help an enzyme to catalyse its reactions. The addition of hydrogen to a substance is called **reduction**, so NAD becomes **reduced NAD** (Figure 6.4).

If you look at Figure 6.3, you will see that something else happens when triose phosphate is oxidised to pyruvate. Two ADP molecules are converted to ATP for each triose phosphate. This uses some of the energy that was in the original glucose molecule. Glycolysis transfers some of the energy from within the glucose molecule to energy in ATP molecules.

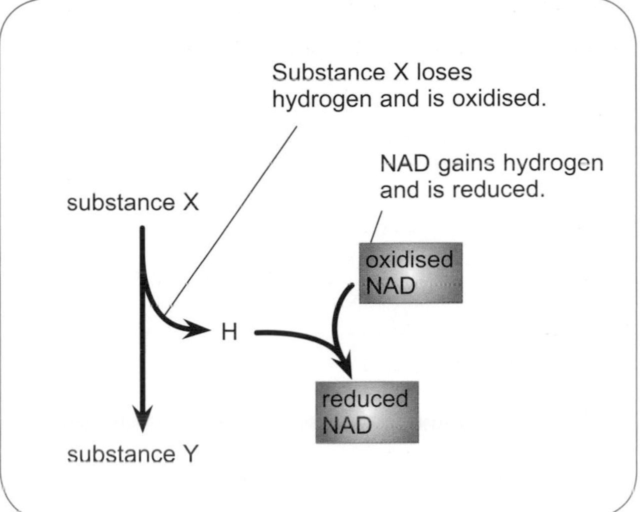

Figure 6.4 Oxidation and reduction.

SAQ

4 Look at Figure 6.3 to answer these questions.

a Explain why ATP is actually used up during the first step in glycolysis.

b How many ATP molecules are used?

c How many ATP molecules are produced during glycolysis, from one glucose molecule? Hint

d What is the net gain in ATP molecules when one glucose molecule undergoes glycolysis? Answer

Extension

Into a mitochondrion

What happens to the pyruvate depends on the availability of oxygen in the cell. If there is plenty, then **aerobic respiration** can take place. The pyruvate is moved into a mitochondrion. This is done by active transport (so again, we are using up ATP before we can make it).

Figure 6.5 shows the structure of a mitochondrion. Like a chloroplast, it is surrounded by an **envelope** of two membranes. The inner membrane is folded, forming **cristae**. The 'background material' inside a mitochondrion is called the **matrix**.

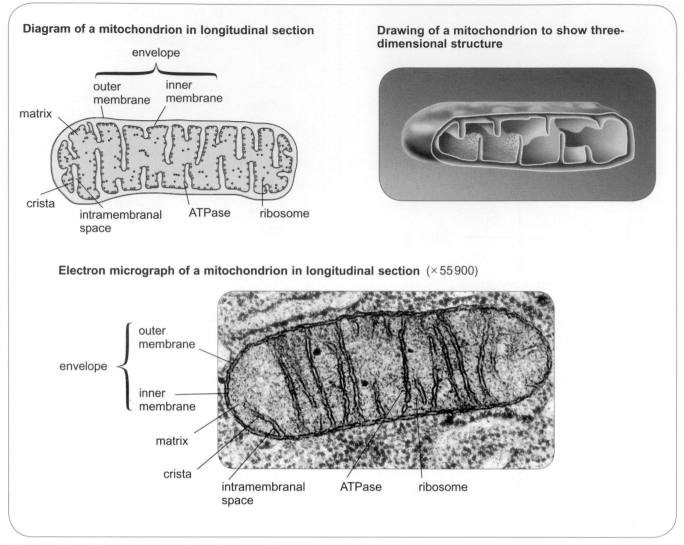

Diagram of a mitochondrion in longitudinal section

envelope
outer membrane
inner membrane
matrix
crista
intramembranal space
ATPase
ribosome

Drawing of a mitochondrion to show three-dimensional structure

Electron micrograph of a mitochondrion in longitudinal section (×55 900)

envelope
outer membrane
inner membrane
matrix
crista
intramembranal space
ATPase
ribosome

Figure 6.5 The structure of a mitochondrion.

The link reaction

Once inside the mitochondrion, the pyruvate undergoes a reaction known as the **link reaction**. This takes place in the matrix.

During the link reaction, carbon dioxide is removed from the pyruvate. This is called **decarboxylation**, and it is catalysed by decarboxylase enzymes. The carbon dioxide is an excretory product, and it diffuses out of the mitochondrion and out of the cell. Pyruvate is a three-carbon substance, so the removal of carbon dioxide leaves a compound with two carbon atoms.

At the same time as the carbon dioxide is removed, hydrogen is also removed from pyruvate. This is again picked up by NAD, producing reduced NAD.

The remainder of the pyruvate combines with **coenzyme A** (often known as CoA) to produce **acetyl CoA** (Figure 6.6).

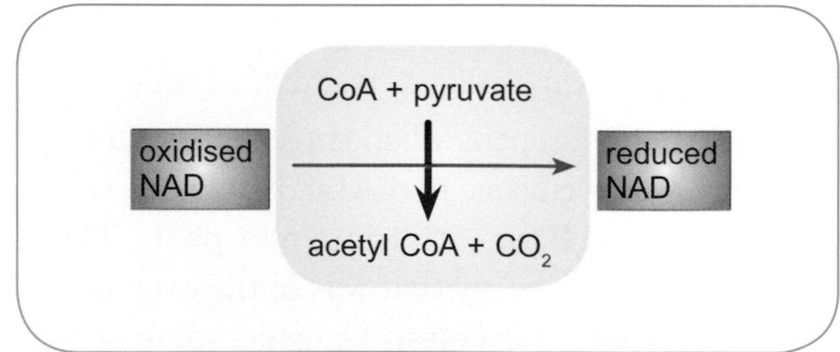

Figure 6.6 The link reaction.

The Krebs cycle

The link reaction is given that name because it provides the link between the two main series of reactions in aerobic respiration – glycolysis and the **Krebs cycle**.

The Krebs cycle takes place in the matrix of the mitochondrion. It is a series of reactions in which a six-carbon compound is gradually changed to a four-carbon compound.

First, the acetyl coA made in the link reaction combines with a four-carbon compound called **oxaloacetate**. You can see in Figure 6.7 that coenzyme A is released at this point, ready to combine with more pyruvate. It is has served its function of passing the two-carbon acetyl group from pyruvate to oxaloacetate.

This converts oxaloacetate into a six-carbon compound called **citrate**. In a series of small steps, the citrate is converted back to oxaloacetate. As this happens, more carbon dioxide is released and more NAD is reduced as it accepts hydrogen. In one stage, a different coenzyme, called **FAD**, accepts hydrogen. And at one point in the cycle a molecule of ATP is made.

Each of the steps in the Krebs cycle is catalysed by a specific enzyme. These enzymes are all present in the matrix of the mitochondrion. Those that cause oxidation are called oxidoreductases or dehydrogenases. Those that remove carbon dioxide are decarboxylases.

Remember that the whole purpose of respiration is to produce ATP for the cell to use as an energy source. At first sight, it looks as though the contribution of the Krebs cycle to this is not very large, because only one ATP molecule is produced during one 'turn' of the cycle. This direct production of ATP is called **substrate-level phosphorylation**. However, as you will see, all those reduced NADs and reduced FADs are used to generate a very significant amount of ATP – much more than can be done from glycolysis.

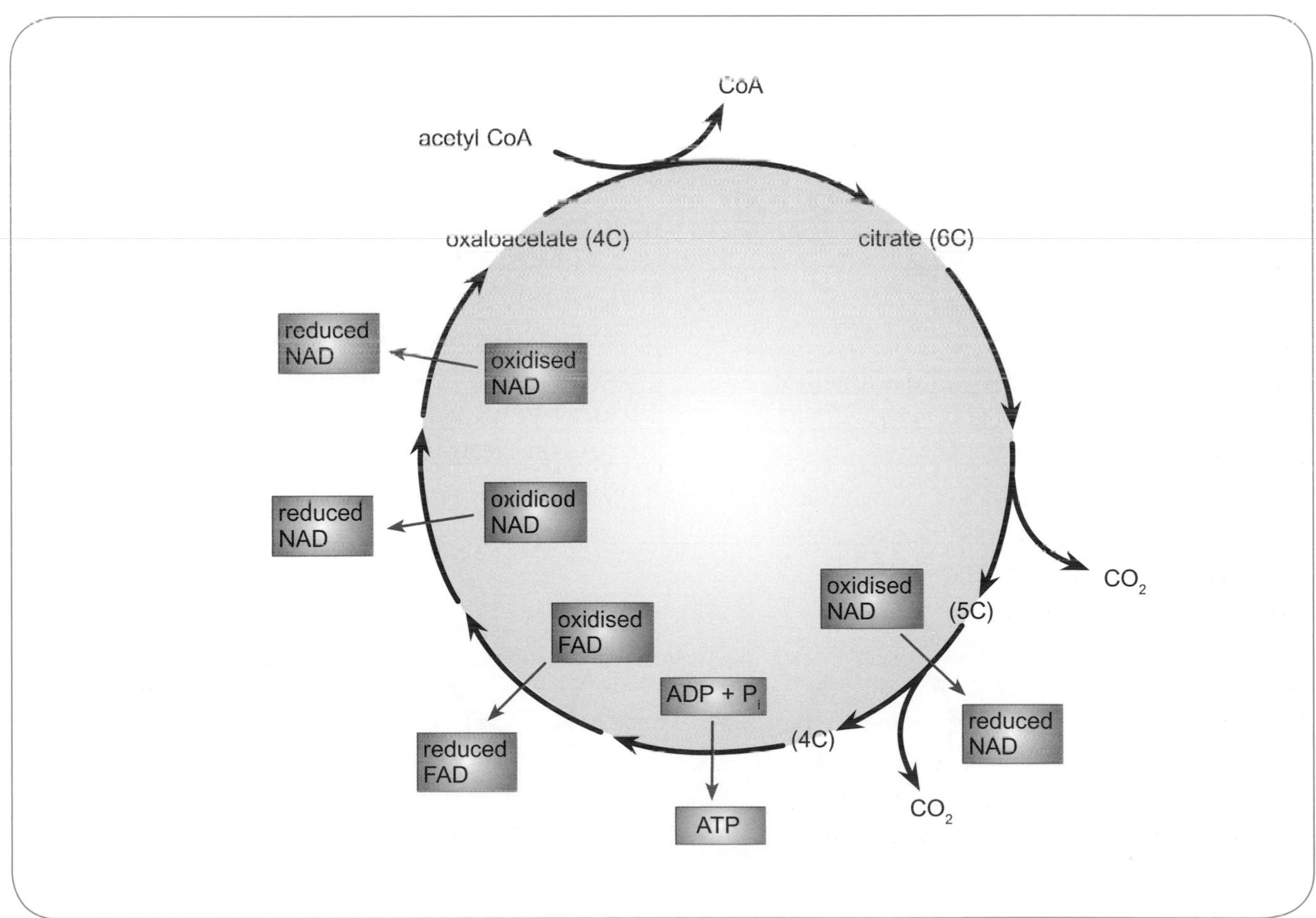

Figure 6.7 The Krebs cycle.

Figure 6.8 shows how glycolysis, the link reaction and the Krebs cycle link together.

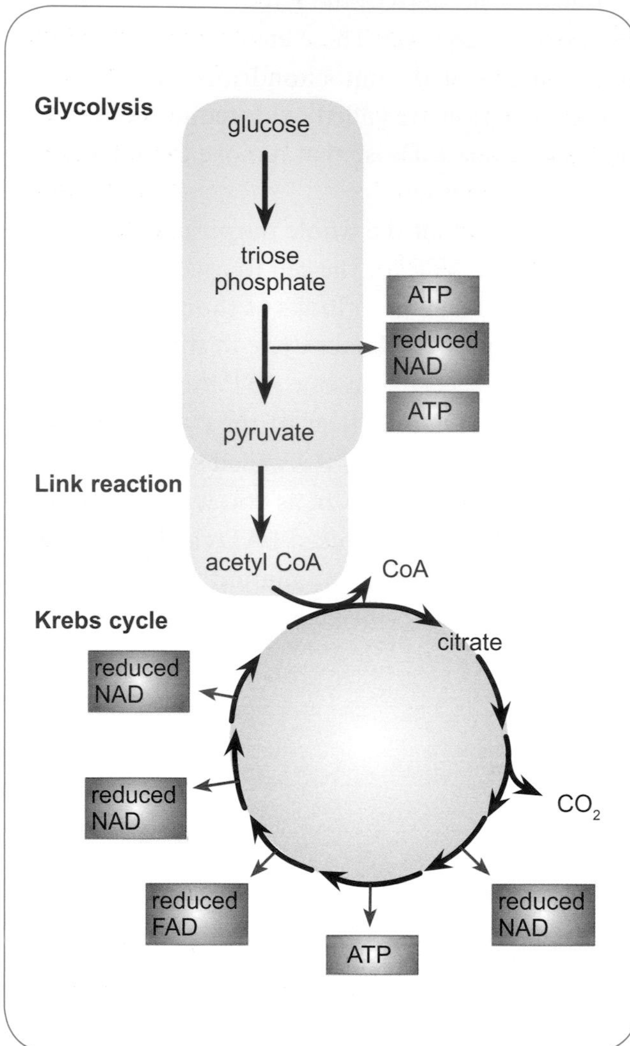

Figure 6.8 Summary of glycolysis, the link reaction and the Krebs cycle.

Oxidative phosphorylation

The last stages of aerobic respiration involve oxidative phosphorylation: the use of oxygen to produce ATP from ADP and P_i. (You'll remember that photophosphorylation was the production of ATP using light.)

The electron transport chain

Held in the inner membrane of the mitochondrion are molecules called **electron carriers**. They make up the **electron transport chain**.

You have already come across a chain like this in photosynthesis. It is indeed very similar, and you will see that it works in a similar way.

Each reduced NAD molecule – which was produced in the matrix during the Krebs cycle – releases its hydrogens. Each hydrogen atom splits into a hydrogen ion, H^+ (a proton) and an electron, e^-.

$$H \longrightarrow H^+ + e^-$$

The electrons are picked up by the first of the electron carriers (Figure 6.9). The carrier is now reduced, because it has gained an electron. The reduced NAD has been oxidised, because it has lost hydrogen. The NAD can now go back to the Krebs cycle and be re-used as a coenzyme to pick up hydrogen again.

The first electron carrier passes its electron to the next in the chain. The first carrier is therefore oxidised (because it has lost an electron) and the second is reduced. The electron is passed from one carrier to the next all the way along the chain.

As the electron is moved along, it releases energy which is used to make ATP.

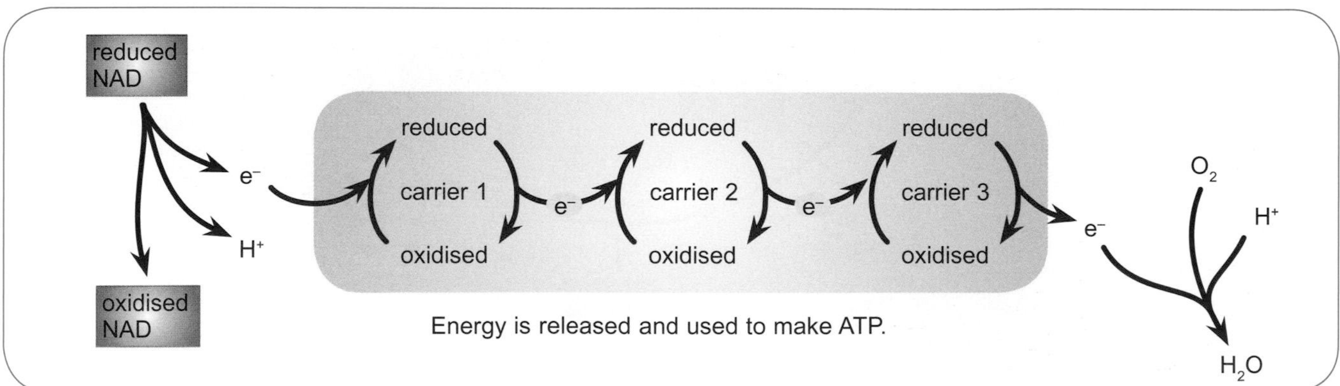

Figure 6.9 The electron transport chain.

At the end of the electron transport chain, the electron combines with a hydrogen ion and with oxygen, to form water. This is why we need oxygen. The oxygen acts as the final electron acceptor for the electron transport chain.

ATP synthesis

We have seen that when hydrogens were donated to the electron transport chain by reduced NAD, they split into hydrogen ions and electrons. These both have an important role to play.

The electrons release energy as they pass along the chain. Some of this energy is used to pump hydrogen ions across the inner membrane of the mitochondrion and into the space between the inner and outer membranes (Figure 6.10). (You may have already read about this happening in photosynthesis, in Chapter 5.) This builds up a concentration gradient for the hydrogen ions, because there are more of them on one side of the inner membrane than the other. It is also an electrical gradient, because the hydrogen ions, H^+, have a positive charge. So there is now a greater positive charge on one side of the membrane than the other. There is an **electrochemical gradient**.

The hydrogen ions are now allowed to diffuse down this gradient. They have to pass through a group of protein molecules in the membrane that form a special channel for them. Apart from these channels, the membrane is largely impermeable to hydrogen ions. The channel proteins act as ATPases. As the hydrogens pass through, the energy that they gained by being actively transported against their concentration gradient is used to make ATP from ADP and P_i.

This process is sometimes called **chemiosmosis**, which is rather confusing as it has nothing to do with water or water potentials.

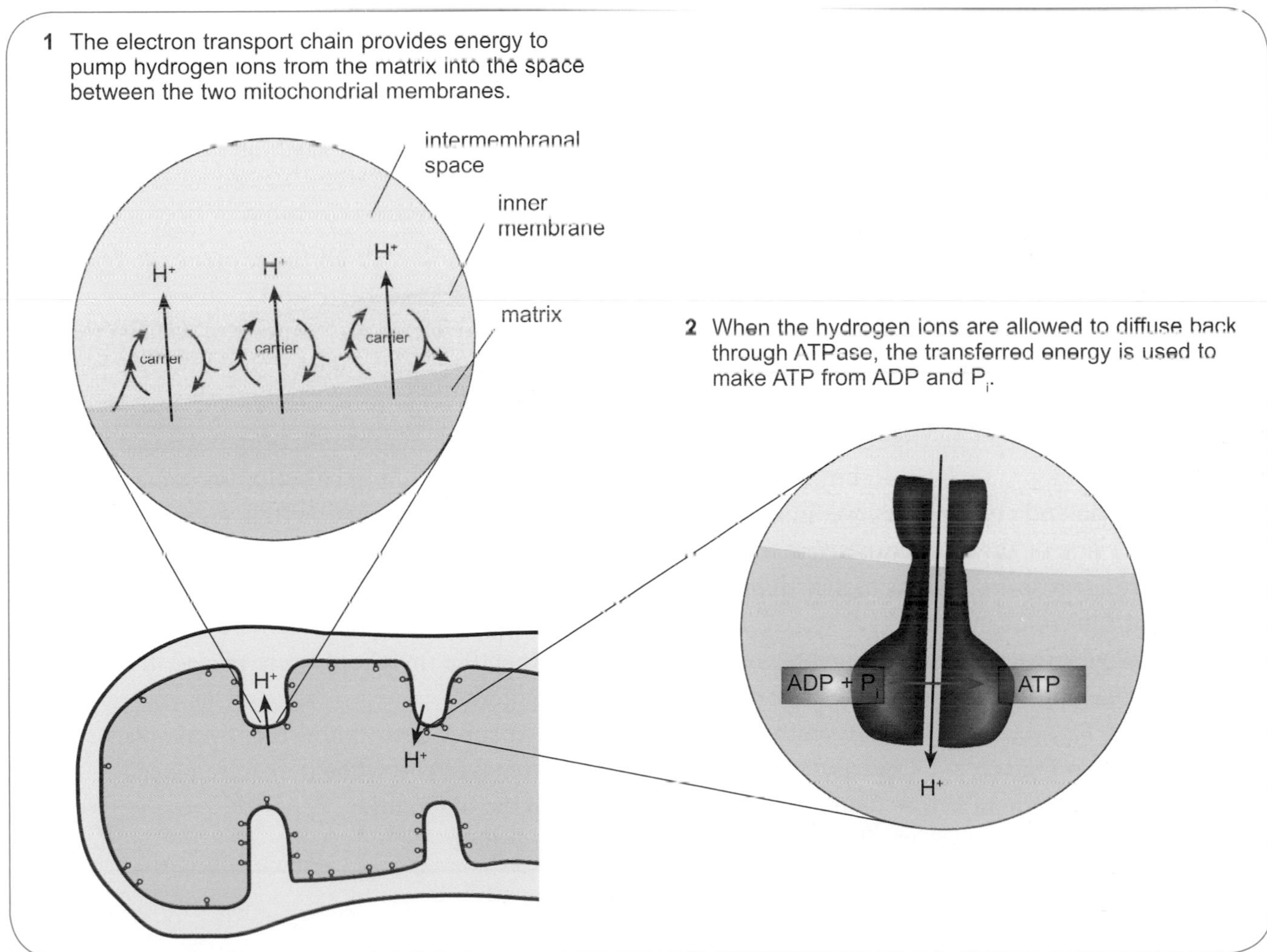

Figure 6.10 Oxidative phosphorylation.

The evidence for chemiosmosis

The processes by which ATP is made in photophosphorylation (in photosynthesis) and oxidative phosphorylation (in respiration) are very similar. In both cases, energy is used to pump hydrogen ions across a membrane, building up a gradient for them. They are then allowed to diffuse back down this gradient through ATPases, which make ATP.

The theory of chemiosmosis was first put forward by a British scientist, Peter Mitchell, in a paper he published in 1961. At the time, it was a great breakthrough, as no-one had any idea how an electron transport chain could produce ATP. Initially, researchers thought there must be some unknown, high-energy phosphorylated compound that could add a phosphate group to ADP. But now, so much evidence has been collected that supports the chemiosmotic theory that it is generally accepted, and all other theories have been discounted.

To understand the evidence for chemiosmosis, you'll need to remember that the pH of a solution is a measure of the concentration of hydrogen ions, H^+, that it contains. A solution with a high concentration of H^+ is acidic, and has a low pH. A solution with a low concentration of H^+ is alkaline, and has a high pH.

There are many different pieces of evidence that we could look at. Here are three particularly convincing ones.

1 There is a pH gradient across the membranes involved in ATP production. In both mitochondria and chloroplasts, we find that the pH on one side of the membranes that contain the electron transport chain is higher than on the other. This indicates that hydrogen ions are being moved actively across the membrane.

2 Membranes in mitochondria and chloroplasts can make ATP even if there is no electron transport taking place – so long as we can produce a pH gradient across them. The experiment described here involves chloroplasts, but similar ones have been done using mitochondria.

First, thylakoids were isolated from chloroplasts. They were kept in the dark throughout the rest of the experiment. The thylakoids were removed and placed in a pH4 buffer solution. They were left there for long enough for the concentration of H^+ inside and outside the thylakoids to become equal (Figure 6.11).

Some of these thylakoids were then placed in a fresh pH4 buffer, which also contained ADP and P_i. They did not make ATP.

Next, some more of the pH4 thylakoids were placed in a pH8 buffer. Again, the solution also contained ADP and P_i. The thylakoids made ATP.

SAQ

5 **a** Across which membranes in a mitochondrion would you expect there to be a pH gradient?

b Which side would have the lower pH?

Hint

c Across which membranes in a chloroplast would you expect there to be a pH gradient?

d Which side would have the lower pH?

Answer

6 This question is about the experiment described on this page and Figure 6.11.

a Explain why it was important to keep the thylakoids in the dark.

b Explain why the pH inside and outside the thylakoid membranes becomes equal when they are left in pH4 buffer for some time.

c Does a pH4 buffer contain a greater or smaller concentration of H^+ than a pH8 buffer?

d In which direction was there a H^+ gradient when the thylakoids were placed in the pH8 buffer?

e Explain why and how the thylakoids were able to make ATP when they were placed in the pH8 buffer solution.

Answer

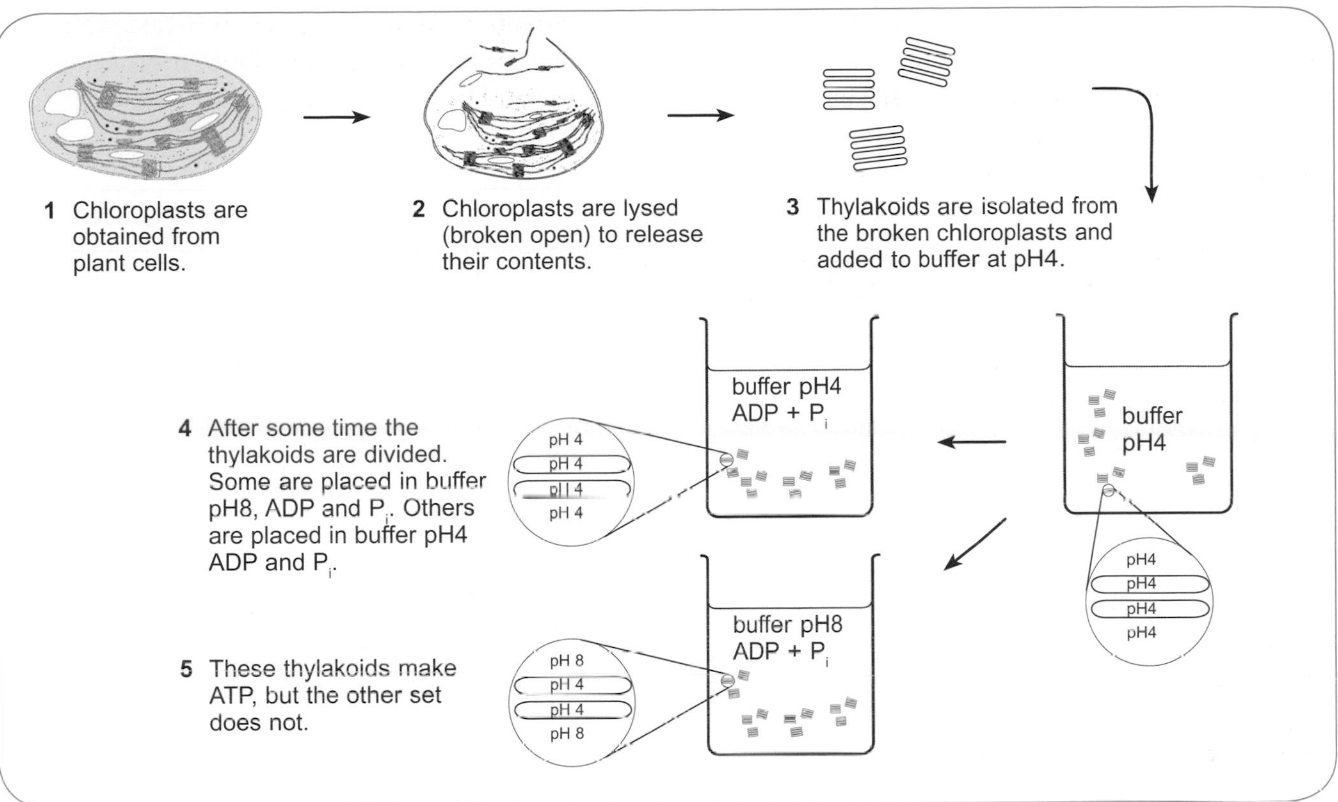

1 Chloroplasts are obtained from plant cells.
2 Chloroplasts are lysed (broken open) to release their contents.
3 Thylakoids are isolated from the broken chloroplasts and added to buffer at pH4.
buffer pH4
pH4
pH4
pH4
pH4
buffer pH4
ADP + P
pH 4
pH 4
pH 4
pH 4
4 After some time the thylakoids are divided. Some are placed in buffer pH8, ADP and P. Others are placed in buffer pH4 ADP and P.
buffer pH8
ADP + P
pH 8
pH 4
pH 4
pH 8
5 These thylakoids make ATP, but the other set does not.

Figure 6.11 An experiment that provides evidence for the chemiosmotic theory.

3 Chemicals that prevent hydrogen ions being transported across the membrane also stop ATP being produced.

Dinitrophenol is a chemical that acts as a carrier for hydrogen ions across membranes. If dinitrophenol is added to thylakoids, no hydrogen ion gradient is built up. This is because as fast as the membranes pump hydrogen ions across them during electron transport, the dinitrophenol allows the ions to diffuse back again straight away. In these circumstances, even though electron transport is still happening as normal, no ATP is made. This shows that it is the hydrogen ion gradient (pH gradient), not the electron transport itself, that is responsible for making ATP.

How much ATP?

We have seen that, in aerobic respiration, glucose is first oxidised to pyruvate in glycolysis. Then the pyruvate is oxidised in the Krebs cycle, which produces some ATP directly. Hydrogens removed at various steps in the Krebs cycle, and also those removed in glycolysis, are passed along the electron transport chain where more ATP is produced.

For every two hydrogens donated to the electron transport chain by each reduced NAD, three ATP molecules are made. The hydrogens donated by FAD start at a later point in the chain, so only two ATP molecules are formed.

However, we also need to remember that some energy has been put into these processes. In particular, energy is needed to transport ADP from the cytoplasm and into the mitochondrion. (You can't make ATP unless you have ADP and P_i to make it from.) Energy is also needed to transport ATP from the mitochondrion, where it is made, into the cytoplasm, where it will be used. Taking this into account, we can say that overall the hydrogens from each reduced NAD produce about two and a half ATPs (not three) while those from reduced FAD produce about one a half ATPs (not two).

Now we can count up how much ATP is made from the oxidation of one glucose molecule. Table 6.1 shows the balance sheet. If you want to work this out for yourself, remember that one glucose molecule produces two pyruvate molecules, so there are two turns of the Krebs cycle for each glucose molecule.

Process		ATP used	ATP produced
Glycolysis	phosphorylation of glucose	2	
	direct phosphorylation of ADP		4
	from reduced NAD		5
Link reaction	from reduced NAD		5
Krebs cycle	direct phosphorylation of ADP		2
	from reduced NAD		15
	from reduced FAD		3
Totals		2	34
Net yield			32

Table 6.1 ATP molecules that can theoretically be produced from one glucose molecule. Note: these are maximum values, and the actual yield will vary from tissue to tissue.

Using energy to keep warm

Going through the ATPases is not the only way that hydrogen ions (protons) can move down the electrochemical gradient from the space between the mitochondrial membranes into its matrix. Some of the protons are able to leak through other parts of the inner membrane. This is called proton leak.

Proton leak is important in generating heat. In babies, in a special tissue known as brown fat, the inner mitochondrial membrane contains a transport protein called uncoupling protein (UCP), which allows protons to leak through the membrane. The energy involved is not used to make ATP – in other words, the movement of the protons has been uncoupled from ATP production. Instead, the energy is transferred to heat energy. Brown fat in babies can produce a lot of heat.

Some people's mitochondrial membranes are leakier than others, and it is likely that this difference can at least partly account for people's different metabolic rates.

During the First World War, women helped to make artillery shells. One of the chemicals used was 2,4-dinitrophenol. Some of the women became very thin after exposure to this chemical. For a short time in the 1930s, it was actually used as a diet pill. Now we know that dinitrophenol increases the leakiness of the inner mitochondrial membrane. It is banned from use as a diet pill because it increases the likelihood of developing cataracts and it can damage the nervous system. However, several pharmaceutical companies are still working on the development of drugs that could be used to help obese people lose weight, based on this same idea.

Anaerobic respiration

The processes described so far – glycolysis followed by the link reaction, the Krebs cycle and the electron transport chain – make up the metabolic reactions that we call **aerobic respiration**. They can all only take place when oxygen is present. This is because oxygen is needed as the final electron acceptor from the electron transport chain. If there is no oxygen, then the electron carriers cannot pass on their electrons, so they cannot accept any more from reduced NAD. So the reduced NAD cannot be reconverted to NAD, meaning that there is nothing available to accept hydrogens from the reactions in the link reaction or Krebs cycle. The link reaction, Krebs cycle and the electron transport chain all grind to a halt. It is like a traffic jam building up on a blocked road. The whole process of respiration backs up all the way from the formation of pyruvate.

However, glycolysis can still take place – so long as something can be done with the pyruvate. And, indeed, pyruvate does have an alternative, unblocked route that it can go down. In many organisms it can be changed into **lactate**.

pyruvate + reduced NAD ⟶ lactate + NAD

This reaction requires the addition of hydrogen, which is taken from reduced NAD. The pyruvate is acting as an alternative hydrogen acceptor.

These NAD molecules can now accept hydrogen as glycolysis takes place, just as they normally do. So at least some ATP can be made, because glycolysis can carry on as usual.

The oxidation of glucose by means of glycolysis and the lactate pathway is known as **anaerobic respiration** (Figure 6.12).

You can probably see that anaerobic respiration only generates a tiny amount of ATP compared with aerobic respiration. None of the ATP that could have been generated in the Krebs cycle or electron transport chain is made. Instead of the theoretical maximum of 32 molecules of ATP from each molecule of glucose, anaerobic respiration produces only 2. (Remember that the reduced NAD produced in glycolysis is not able to pass on its hydrogens to the electron transport chain – it gives them to pyruvate instead.)

Dealing with the lactate

The lactate pathway is most likely to occur in skeletal muscle cells. When they are exercising vigorously, they may need more oxygen than can be supplied to them by the blood. They carry on using whatever oxygen they can in aerobic respiration, but may also 'top up' their ATP production by using the lactate pathway. This means that lactate can build up in the muscle cells.

The lactate diffuses into the blood, where it dissolves in the plasma and is carried around the body. A high concentration of lactate can make a person feel disorientated and nauseous, as it affects the cells in the brain. If it builds up too much, it can stop the muscles from contracting. A 400 m race is notorious for producing high concentrations of lactate in the blood, and some athletes actually vomit after running this race.

When the lactate reaches the liver, the hepatocytes absorb it and use it. They first convert it back to pyruvate. Later, when the exercise has stopped and oxygen is plentiful again, they will oxidise the pyruvate using the link reaction and the Krebs cycle. They also convert some of it to glycogen, which they store as an energy reserve.

This removal of the lactate by the hepatocytes requires oxygen. This is why you go on breathing heavily after strenuous exercise. You are providing extra oxygen to your liver cells, to enable them to metabolise the lactate. The extra oxygen required is often known as the **oxygen debt**.

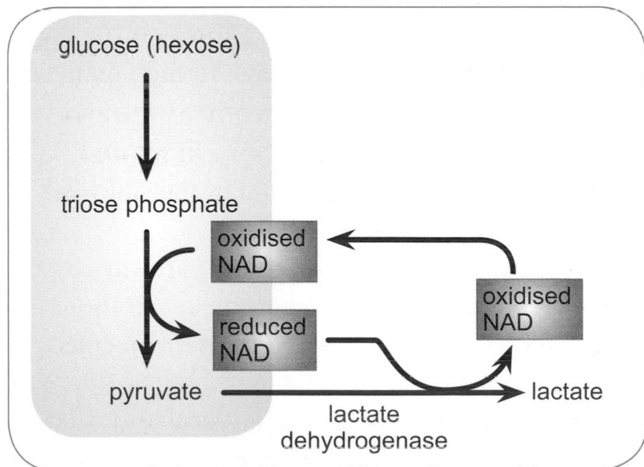

Figure 6.12 Anaerobic respiration; producing lactate from pyruvate generates NAD and allows glycolysis to continue.

Anaerobic respiration in yeast

All mammals use the lactate pathway in anaerobic respiration. Fungi and plants, however, have a different pathway, in which **ethanol** is produced (Figure 6.13).

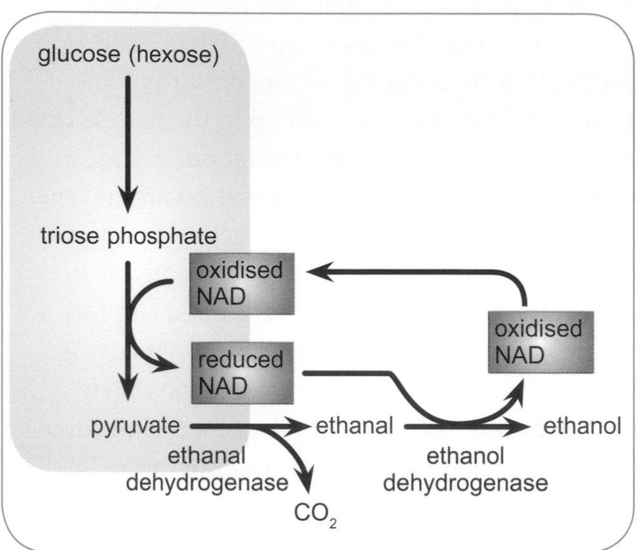

Figure 6.13 Anaerobic respiration in yeast.

SAQ

7 a Outline the differences between the metabolism of pyruvate in humans and in yeast, in anaerobic respiration.

b How are these two processes similar?

Answer

Respiratory substrates

The substance that is used to produce ATP in a cell by respiration is known as a **respiratory substrate**. So far, we have described respiration as if the only respiratory substrate was glucose. In fact, many cells in the body are able to use other substances as respiratory substrates, especially lipids and proteins. (Brain cells are unusual in that they can use only glucose.)

Figure 6.14 shows the metabolic pathways by which glucose is oxidised in aerobic respiration. You can also see how other substrates can enter into these reactions.

Lipids can be hydrolysed to glycerol and fatty acids, and then enter glycolysis and the link reaction. Amino acids, produced from the hydrolysis of proteins, are fed into the link reaction and the Krebs cycle.

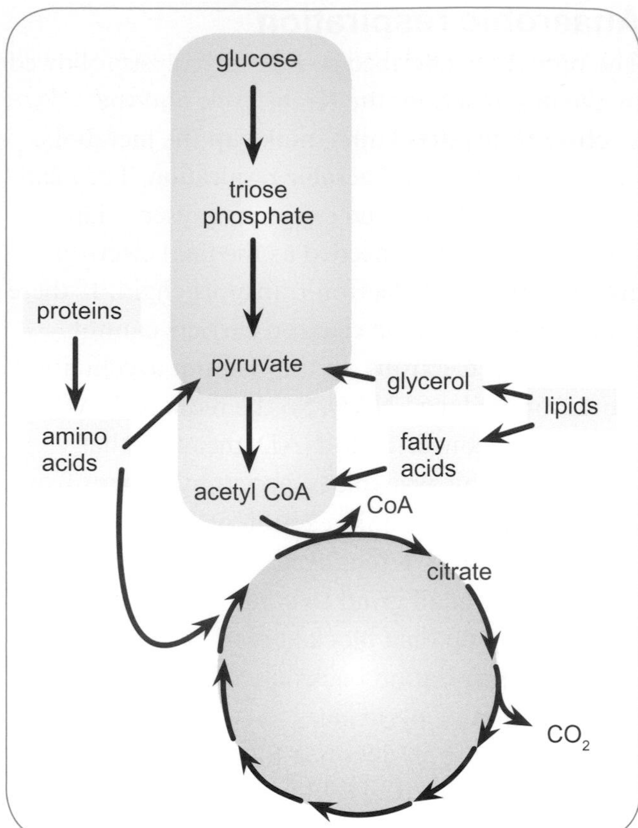

Figure 6.14 How fats, fatty acids and proteins are respired.

These different respiratory substrates have different energy values. Carbohydrates and proteins have very similar energy yields, releasing about $17\,kJ\,g^{-1}$. The values for fats are much higher, around $39\,kJ\,g^{-1}$. The reason for this greater energy content is mainly due to the higher proportion of H atoms compared with C and O atoms in fat molecules. Most of the energy of respiration is obtained from the electron within each H atom.

Different tissues in the body tend to use different substrates. Red blood cells and brain cells are almost entirely dependent on glucose. Heart muscle gets about 70% of its ATP by using fatty acids as the respiratory substrate. Other muscles readily use fatty acids, as well as carbohydrates.

SAQ

8 Which respiratory substrates shown in Figure 6.14 can be used only when there is a supply of oxygen? Explain your answer.

Answer

SAQ

9 Carbohydrates, lipids and proteins can all be used as substrates for the production of ATP. Suggest why migratory birds and the seeds of many plants tend to use lipids as an energy store, rather than carbohydrates.

Answer

Extension

Summary

Glossary

- Respiration is the release of energy from the oxidation of respiratory substrates, such as glucose. Energy is needed for many processes, such as active transport and some metabolic reactions.
- The energy is used to synthesise ATP, which is the energy currency of every cell. ATP is a nucleotide containing adenine, the sugar ribose and a phosphate group.
- The first stage of respiration is glycolysis, and this takes place in the cytoplasm of a cell. Glucose is phosphorylated to produce hexose bisphosphate, which is then split to form two triose phosphates. These are oxidised to form pyruvate. The oxidation of one glucose molecule to pyruvate uses two ATP molecules and generates four, so there is a net gain of two ATPs per glucose.
- The hydrogens that are removed during oxidation are taken up by the coenzyme NAD.
- If oxygen is available, the pyruvate is actively transported into the matrix of a mitochondrion where the link reaction takes place. This produces acetyl CoA, carbon dioxide and hydrogen. The carbon dioxide is lost from the cell and transported to the gas exchange surface, where it is excreted.
- Still in the matrix of the mitochondrion, the acetyl CoA combines with the four carbon compound oxaloacetate to form citrate, which is gradually converted to oxaloacetate again in the Krebs cycle. This generates some ATP directly. Hydrogens are picked up by NAD and FAD. Carbon dioxide is given off and excreted.
- The reduced NAD and reduced FAD pass on electrons to the electron transport chain in the inner membrane of the cristae in the mitochondrion. As they pass down the chain, their energy is used to pump hydrogen ions into the intermembranal space. The hydrogen ions then diffuse back down the electrochemical gradient through ATPases, and ATP is produced from ADP and Pi. This is called oxidative phosphorylation. The process is known as chemiosmosis.
- The existence of a pH gradient across the membrane, the fact that thylakoids can generate ATP in the dark so long as a pH gradient is produced across their membranes, and the way in which hydrogen ion transfer can be decoupled from ATP production all provide evidence for the chemiosmotic theory.
- A theoretical 32 molecules of ATP can be made from each molecule of glucose respired aerobically.
- When oxygen is unavailable, the electron transport chain and the Krebs cycle stop. Glycolysis continues as usual, but the pyruvate produced is converted into either lactate (in mammals) or ethanol (in plants and yeast). This reaction also converts reduced NAD to NAD, so that NAD continues to be available and glycolysis can continue to take place. This is anaerobic respiration, and it generates only a tiny fraction of the ATP that could be generated by aerobic respiration.
- The substance that is oxidised in respiration is called the respiratory substrate. About twice as much ATP can be made from the complete oxidation of one gram of lipid compared with one gram of either carbohydrate or protein.

Stretch and challenge question

1 Outline the methods by which ATP is produced in animals and plants.

Questions

1 The diagram is an outline of the glycolytic pathway.

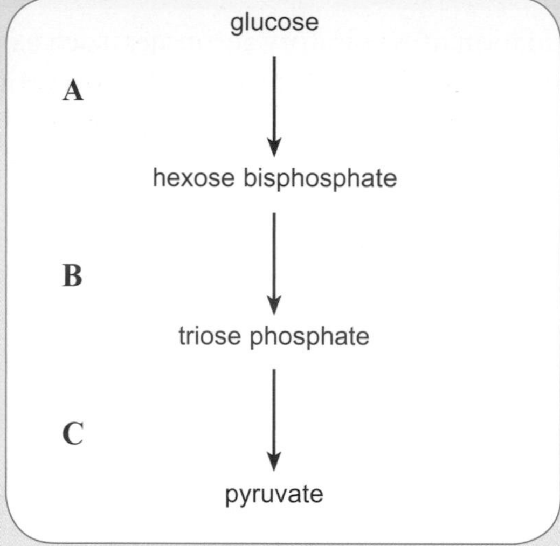

a With reference to the diagram, state the letter, **A**, **B** or **C**, in the glycolytic pathway where the following processes occur.
- phosphorylation using ATP
- dehydrogenation
- formation of ATP
- splitting of a hexose [4]

b State where glycolysis occurs in a cell. [1]

c State the net gain in ATP molecules when one molecule of glucose is broken down to pyruvate in glycolysis. [1]

d Describe what would happen to the pyruvate molecules formed under anaerobic conditions in mammalian muscle tissue. [3]

e Explain why, under aerobic conditions, lipids have a greater energy value per unit mass than carbohydrates or proteins. [2]

f Many chemicals will 'uncouple' oxidation from phosphorylation. In this situation, the energy released by oxidation of food materials is converted into heat instead of being used to form ATP. One such compound is dinitrophenol, which was used in munition factories for the manufacture of explosives during the First World War. People working in these factories were exposed to high levels of dinitrophenol.
Suggest and explain why people working in munitions factories during the First World War became very thin regardless of how much they ate. [3]

OCR Biology A (2804) January 2006 [Total 14]

Answer

Chapter 7

Cellular control

e-Learning

Objectives

Looking at where we are now, with the ability to use genetic engineering to alter the structures and functions of living organisms, it is amazing to realise that until the middle of the 20th century few believed that DNA was an important substance. The structure of DNA was worked out by Watson and Crick in 1953. Once this was known, understanding of the way in which DNA contains information, which is passed on from parents to offspring, began to develop at a tremendous rate. Today, new discoveries and insights continue to be made, and new technologies are developing so fast that we don't seem to have to time to decide whether we really want them or not.

You learned about the structure of DNA in your AS course. Figure 7.1 shows the structure of a very small part of a DNA molecule. You will probably remember that it is made of two strands of **nucleotides**. The deoxyribose–phosphate backbones form the 'uprights' and the nitrogenous bases form the 'rungs' in this ladder-like structure. The nitrogenous bases come in four varieties – **adenine** and **guanine**, which are purines, and **cytosine** and **thymine**, which are pyrimidines. They are generally known by their abbreviations, A, G, C and T.

Hydrogen bonds between the bases hold the two strands together. A always bonds with T, and C always bonds with G. This is called **complementary base pairing**, and it is because of this that DNA can be copied over and over again, and that it can serve as the **genetic code**.

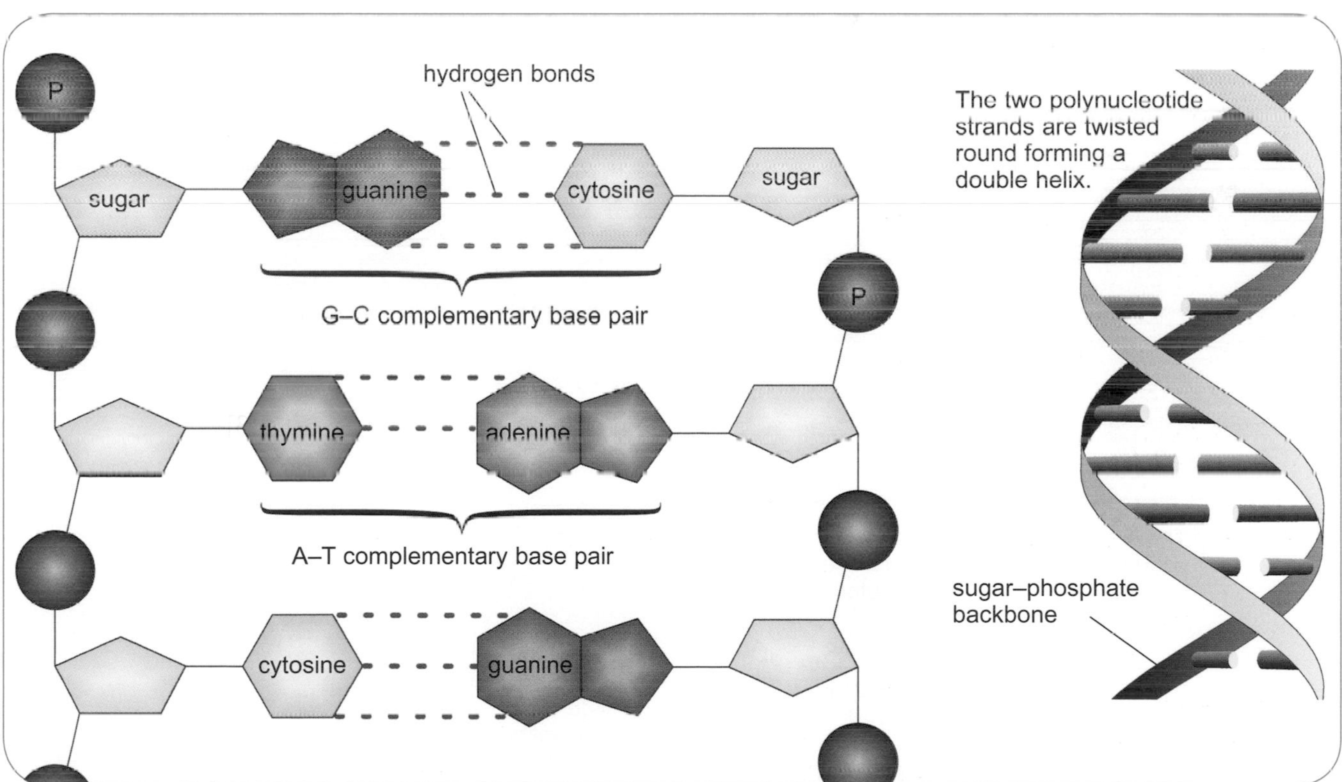

Figure 7.1 Part of a DNA molecule.

The genetic code

To understand how the genetic code works, you first need to think back to the structure of proteins. Proteins are made of polypeptides, which are long chains of amino acids. There are about 20 different amino acids, and the sequence in which they are strung together determines the structure – and therefore the function – of the protein molecule that is made.

DNA determines this sequence. The sequence of bases in a DNA molecule determines the sequences of amino acids in the proteins that the cell makes. A length of DNA that codes for one polypeptide is called a **gene**.

Some of the proteins for which DNA codes are structural ones, such as keratin or collagen. Others have physiological roles, such as haemoglobin or the hundreds of different enzymes that control our metabolic reactions. As you will see later in this chapter, even a small change in a DNA molecule that codes for a protein can have a very large effect on the appearance or body chemistry of an organism, and may even mean that it cannot survive at all. If, for example, the DNA coding for a particular enzyme is faulty, then the enzyme may not be able to catalyse its reaction and a whole bundle of other metabolic reactions that depend on that one could also be affected.

How the genetic code works

The four different bases in a DNA molecule can be put together in any order along one of the polynucleotide chains that make up the DNA. Normally, only one of these strands is used as the code for making proteins. We will refer to this strand as the **reference strand**.

The code is a three-letter code. A sequence of three bases, known as a base **triplet**, on the reference strand of part of a DNA molecule codes for one amino acid. This is shown in Figure 7.2.

The genetic code is almost universal – the same DNA triplets code for the same amino acids in almost every kind of organism. This indicates that it evolved very, very early on in the evolution of life on Earth. The triplets of bases on the DNA reference strand that code for each amino acid are shown in Table 7.1.

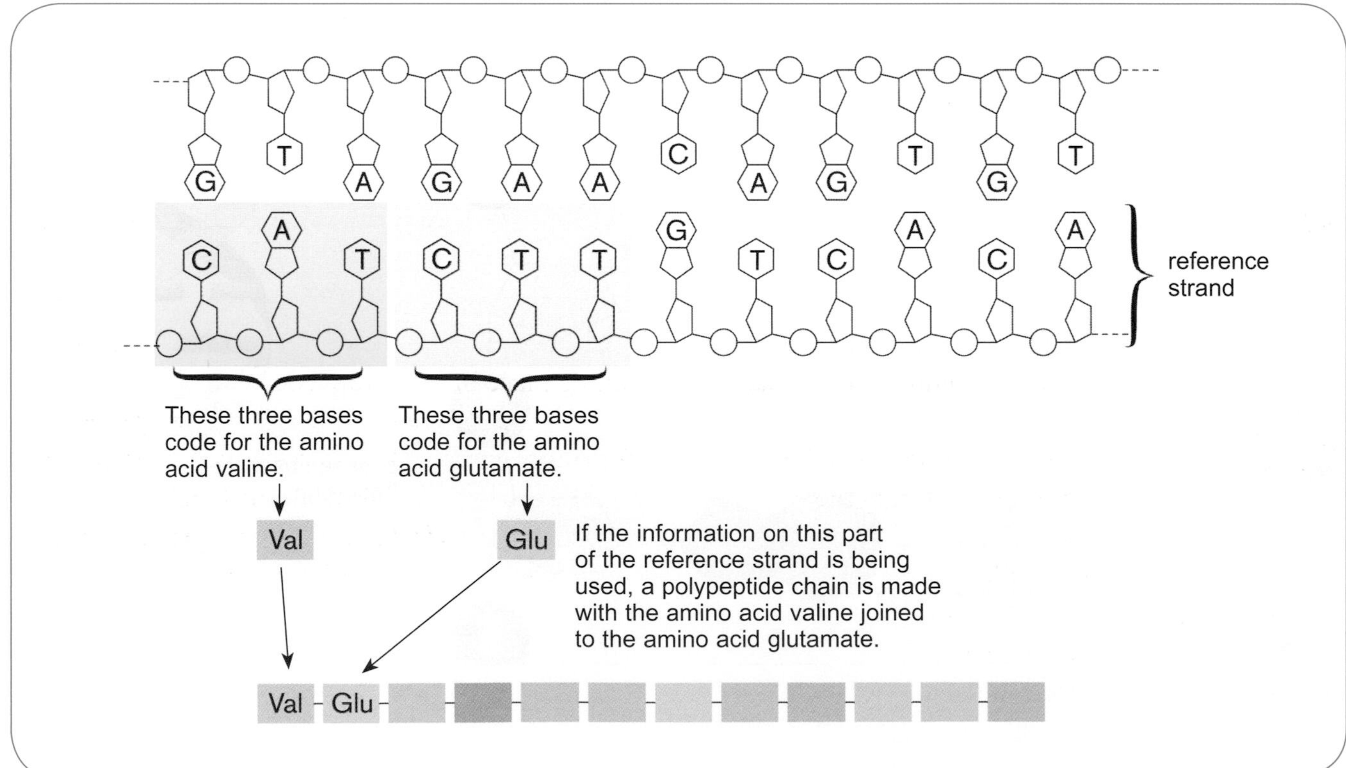

Figure 7.2 How DNA codes for amino acid sequences in proteins.

First base		Second base: A		G		T		C	
A		AAA	Phe	AGA	Ser	ATA	Tyr	ACA	Cys
		AAG	Phe	AGG	Ser	ATG	Tyr	ACG	Cys
		AAT	Leu	AGT	Ser	ATT	*Stop*	ACT	*Stop*
		AAC	Leu	AGC	Ser	ATC	*Stop*	ACC	Trp
G		GAA	Leu	GGA	Pro	GTA	His	GCA	Arg
		GAG	Leu	GGG	Pro	GTG	His	GCG	Arg
		GAT	Leu	GGT	Pro	GTT	Gln	GCT	Arg
		GAC	Leu	GGC	Pro	GTC	Gln	GCC	Arg
T		TAA	Ile	TGA	Thr	TTA	Asn	TCA	Ser
		TAG	Ile	TGG	Thr	TTG	Asn	TCG	Ser
		TAT	Ile	TGT	Thr	TTT	Lys	TCT	Arg
		TAC	Met	TGC	Thr	TTC	Lys	TCC	Arg
C		CAA	Val	CGA	Ala	CTA	Asp	CCA	Gly
		CAG	Val	CGG	Ala	CTG	Asp	CCG	Gly
		CAT	Val	CGT	Ala	CTT	Glu	CCT	Gly
		CAC	Val	CGC	Ala	CTC	Glu	CCC	Gly

Key

alanine	Ala	glutamine	Gln	leucine	Leu	serine	Ser
arginine	Arg	glutamic acid	Glu	lysine	Lys	threonine	Thr
asparagine	Asn	glycine	Gly	methionine	Met	tryptopyhan	Trp
aspartic acid	Asp	histidine	His	phenylalanine	Phe	tyrosine	Tyr
cysteine	Cys	isoleucine	Ile	proline	Pro	valine	Val

Table 7.1 A DNA dictionary, showing the base triplets on the DNA reference strand that code for each amino acid.

SAQ

1 a There are 20 different naturally occurring amino acids. There are four different bases. Remembering that the sequence of bases is always read in the same direction, work out how many different base triplets there can be.

Hint

b There are many more possible base triplets than there are amino acids. Using the information in Table 7.1, explain how these 'spare' triplets are used.

c Explain why a two-letter code, rather than a three-letter code, would not work.

Answer

Protein synthesis

The DNA is in the nucleus. It is good to keep the DNA safely shut away from the rest of the cell, because it makes it much less likely that the DNA might be affected by any of the metabolic reactions taking place in the cytoplasm.

But proteins are made in the cytoplasm, on the ribosomes. So there needs to be a messenger to take the instructions from the DNA to the ribosomes. This is done by a substance called **messenger RNA**, **mRNA** for short.

The process of using the DNA code to make a polypeptide or protein takes place in two stages.

- First, the instructions on part of a DNA molecule are transferred to a mRNA molecule. This is called **transcription**.
- Next, the mRNA takes the instructions to a ribosome, and they are used to build a polypeptide. This is called **translation**.

Transcription

Usually, only a small part of a DNA molecule is transcribed at one time – a section that contains the code for making one polypeptide, called a gene.

The process begins as this part of the DNA molecule 'unzips'. An enzyme called **DNA helicase** breaks the hydrogen bonds between the bases, and the helix unwinds (Figure 7.3).

Next, free RNA nucleotides slot into place against one of the exposed DNA strands. The nucleotides pair exactly. C and G always pair together, just as they did in the DNA molecule. However, there are no RNA nucleotides that contain the base T – they have a base called **uracil**, U, instead. So the base A on the DNA links up with the base U on an RNA nucleotide, and the base T on the DNA links up with the base A on the RNA.

As the RNA nucleotides slot into place and form hydrogen bonds with their complementary bases on the DNA strand, condensation reactions take place between the adjacent RNA nucleotides. These reactions are catalysed by **RNA polymerase**. This enzyme also checks that the bases have paired up correctly – it will not link the RNA nucleotides if they don't have the correct base pairing with the exposed DNA strand.

Working steadily along the DNA strand, a complementary RNA strand is built up. This is a messenger RNA molecule. When the end of the gene is reached, the complete mRNA molecule breaks away. The end is signalled by a particular triplet of bases on the DNA (Table 7.1) that, instead of coding for an amino acid, signifies 'stop here'.

The DNA molecule may stay unzipped so that more mRNA molecules can be made from the same gene, or it may zip back up again.

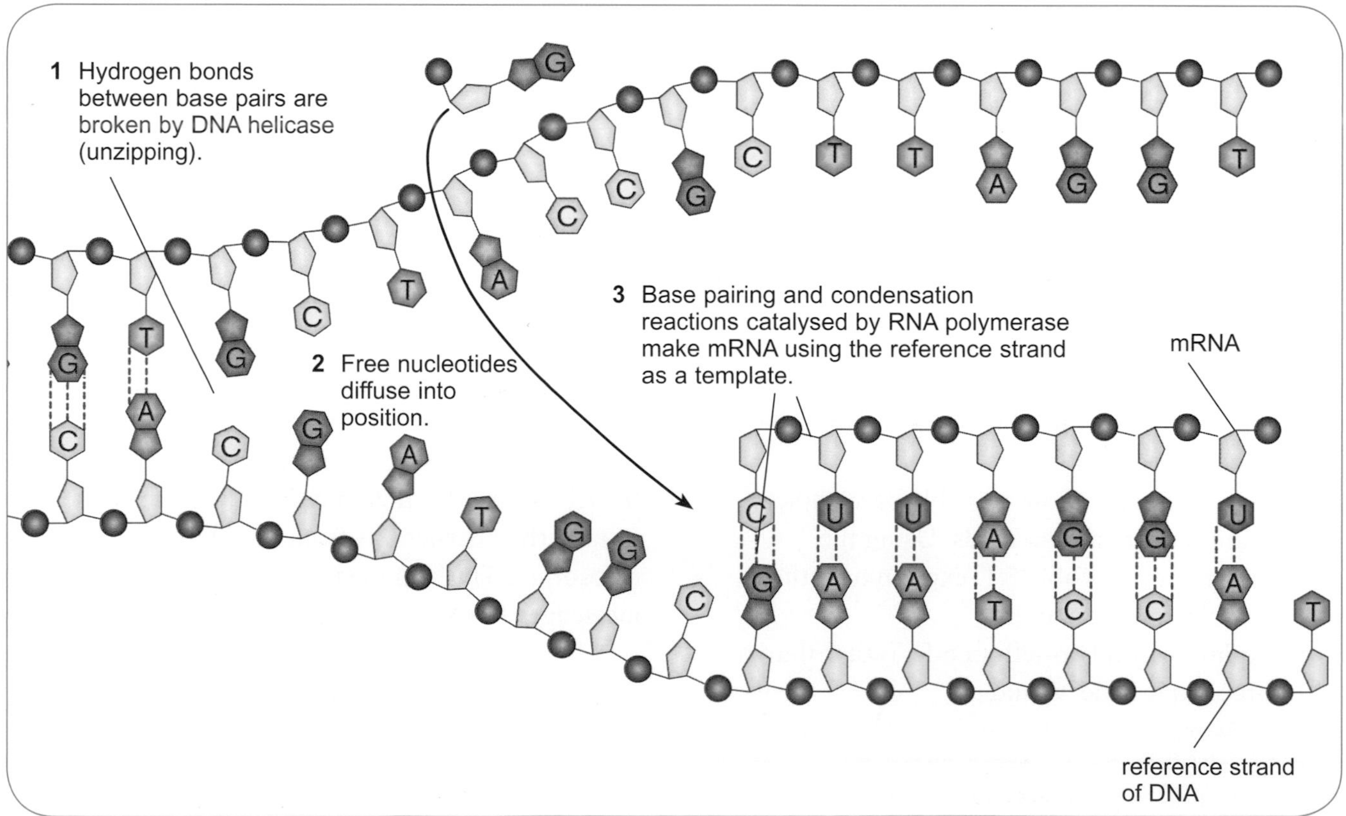

Figure 7.3 Transcription.

The mRNA molecule is now guided out of the nucleus through a pore in the nuclear envelope. It passes into the cytoplasm and arrives at a ribosome.

Translation

Translation is the process by which the code for making the protein – now carried by the mRNA molecule – is used to line up amino acids in a particular sequence and link them together to make a polypeptide.

Each group of three bases on the mRNA molecule is called a **codon**. Each codon stands for a particular amino acid (Figure 7.4). Some codons also act as 'stop' and 'start' codons. The sequence AUG, which denotes methionine, can indicate that this is where the amino acid chain should be begun. AUG is a 'start' codon.

SAQ

2 Using Table 7.1, work out which amino acid is coded for by each of these mRNA codons.

a AAA **b** ACG **c** GUG
d CGC **e** UAG

Answer

Transfer RNA

In translation, yet another type of nucleotide comes into play. This is a different kind of RNA, known as **transfer RNA**, **tRNA** for short.

Each tRNA molecule has a group of three exposed (unpaired) bases at one end (Figure 7.5). This is called an **anticodon**. An anticodon can undergo complementary base pairing with a codon on an mRNA molecule.

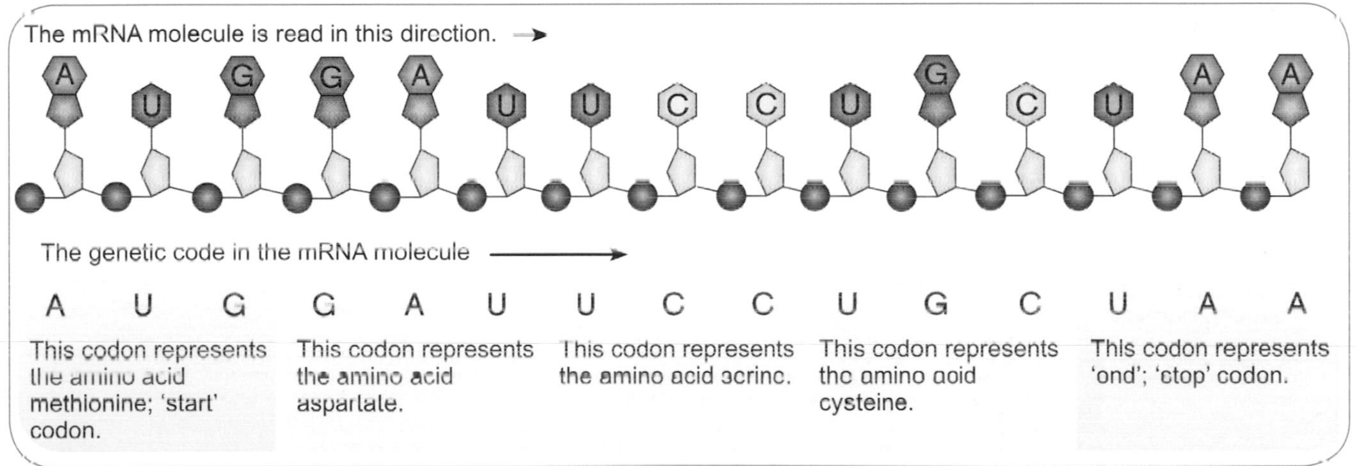

Figure 7.4 The genetic code in part of an mRNA molecule.

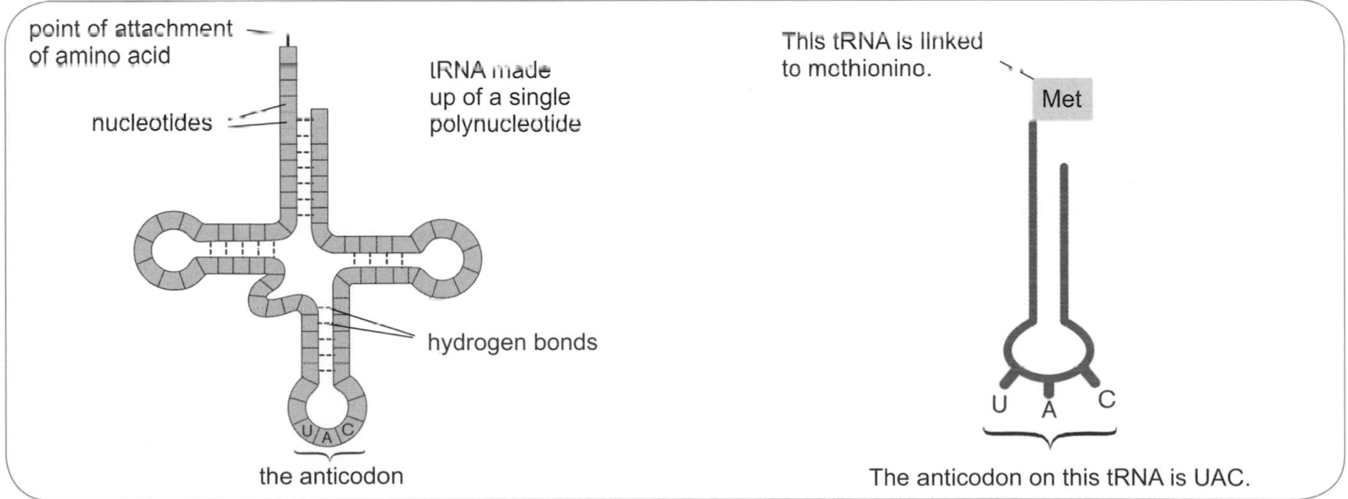

Figure 7.5 Transfer RNA.

At the other end of the tRNA molecule there is a site where an amino acid can bind. The crucial property of tRNA is that a tRNA molecule with a particular anticodon can only bind with a particular amino acid. This is what allows the sequence of bases on the mRNA molecule to determine the sequence of amino acids in the polypeptide that is made.

In the cytoplasm, specific enzymes load specific amino acids onto specific tRNA molecules. These enzymes are called **tRNA transferases**, and there is a different kind for each type of tRNA.

For example, a tRNA with the anticodon UAC will have the amino acid methionine loaded onto its amino acid binding site. You can imagine thousands of tRNA molecules in the cytoplasm, each loaded with its particular amino acid, waiting for the opportunity to offload it at the polypeptide-making production line on a ribosome.

Building the polypeptide

The mRNA molecule, carrying the code copied from part of a DNA molecule, is held in a cleft in the ribosome, so that just six of its bases are exposed. This is two codons.

A tRNA with an anticodon that is complementary to the first mRNA codon then binds with it (Figure 7.6). Complementary base pairing makes sure that only the 'correct' tRNA can bind. For example, if the mRNA codon is AUG, then a tRNA molecule with the anticodon UAC will bind with it. As we have seen, this tRNA will be carrying the amino acid methionine.

Another tRNA now binds with the next codon on the mRNA. Once again, the tRNA – and therefore the amino acid – is determined by the mRNA codon. If the mRNA codon is GAU, then the anticodon on the tRNA will be CUA and the amino acid will be aspartate.

Now the two amino acids are held in a particular position next to each other on the ribosome. A condensation reaction takes place and a peptide bond is formed between the two amino acids.

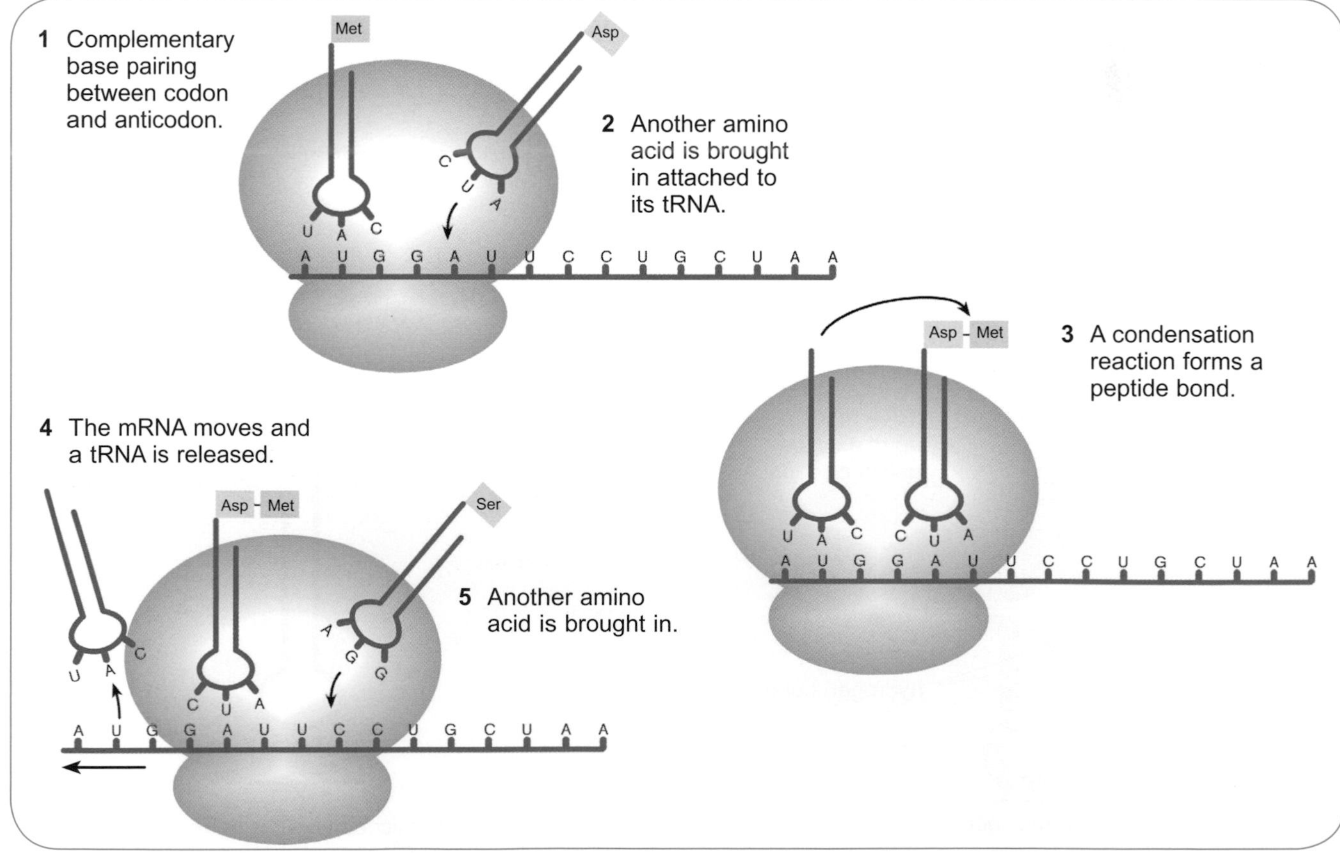

Figure 7.6 Translation on a ribosome.

The mRNA moves on through the cleft in the ribosome, bringing a third codon into place. A third tRNA binds with it, and a third amino acid is added to the chain. Meanwhile, the first tRNA (the one that brought methionine) has completed its role. It breaks away, leaving the methionine behind. This released tRNA is now available to be reloaded with another methionine molecule. In this way, the whole polypeptide chain is gradually built up. It is released when a 'stop' codon is reached on the mRNA.

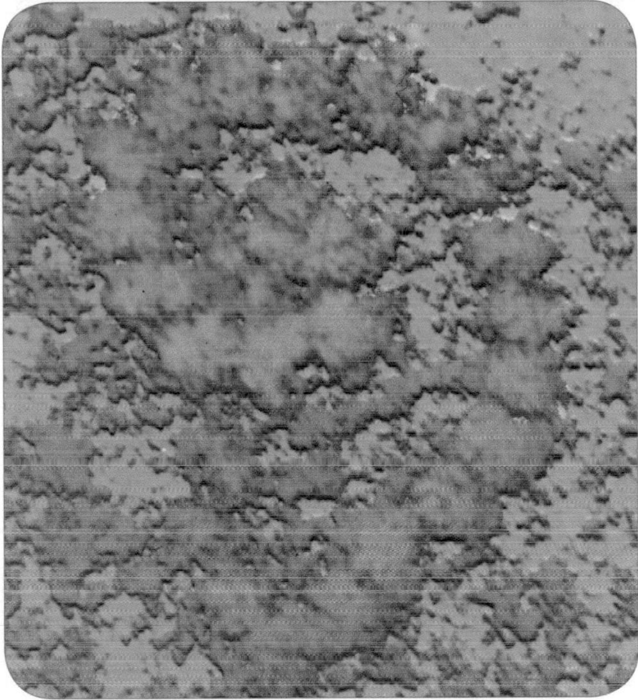

Figure 7.7 Each large blob in the spiral is a ribosome. They are all working on the same strand of mRNA, which is too thin to be seen. A group of ribosomes like this is sometimes called a polyribosome or polysome. This electronmicrograph is of a tiny part of the cytoplasm of a brain cell (× 15 000 000).

SAQ

3 A length of DNA has the base sequence ATA AGA TTG CCC.

a How many amino acids does this length of DNA code for?

b Using Table 7.1, write down the sequence of amino acids that is coded for by this length of DNA.

c What will be the base sequence on the mRNA which is made during the transcription of this length of DNA?

d Using your answers to **b** and **c**, work out the anticodons of the tRNA molecules which will carry these amino acids to this mRNA:

i tyrosine

ii asparagine.

Answer

4 These statements contain some very common errors made by A level candidates in examinations. For each statement, explain why it is wrong and then write a correct version of the statement.

a 'The sequence of bases in a DNA molecule determines which amino acids will be made during protein synthesis.'

b 'The amino acids in a DNA molecule determine what kind of proteins will be made in the cell.'

c 'The four bases in DNA are adenosine, cysteine, thiamine and guanine.'

d 'During transcription, a complementary mRNA molecule comes and lies against an unzipped part of a DNA molecule.'

Answer

5 Using the diagrams in Figure 7.6 as a guide, make annotated drawings of the next stage in the synthesis of the polypeptide shown in the figure. The codon UGC codes for cysteine.

Answer

Mutations

The processes of DNA replication, transcription of the code onto mRNA and the translation of this to an amino acid sequence are all very carefully quality-controlled by the cell. Nevertheless, things do sometimes go wrong.

Occasionally, the structure of a DNA molecule is damaged. There are many possible causes – it most often happens when the DNA is being copied. Despite the fact that DNA polymerase will not normally allow a 'wrong' base to be used, just occasionally a different one does creep in.

A random, unpredictable change in a DNA molecule like this is called a **mutation**.

Types of mutations

Figure 7.8 shows three different kinds of mutations that might take place.

Substitution of one base for another quite often has no effect. This is because the DNA code is **degenerate**, meaning that each amino acid is coded for by more than one triplet (Table 7.1). For example, GAA and GAG both code for the amino acid leucine.

Deletion however, is almost certain to make a big difference. Deletion involves the loss of one base pair from the DNA molecule. Because the bases are read as triplets, if one pair goes missing then the whole sequence is read differently. This is called a **frame shift** (Figure 7.9).

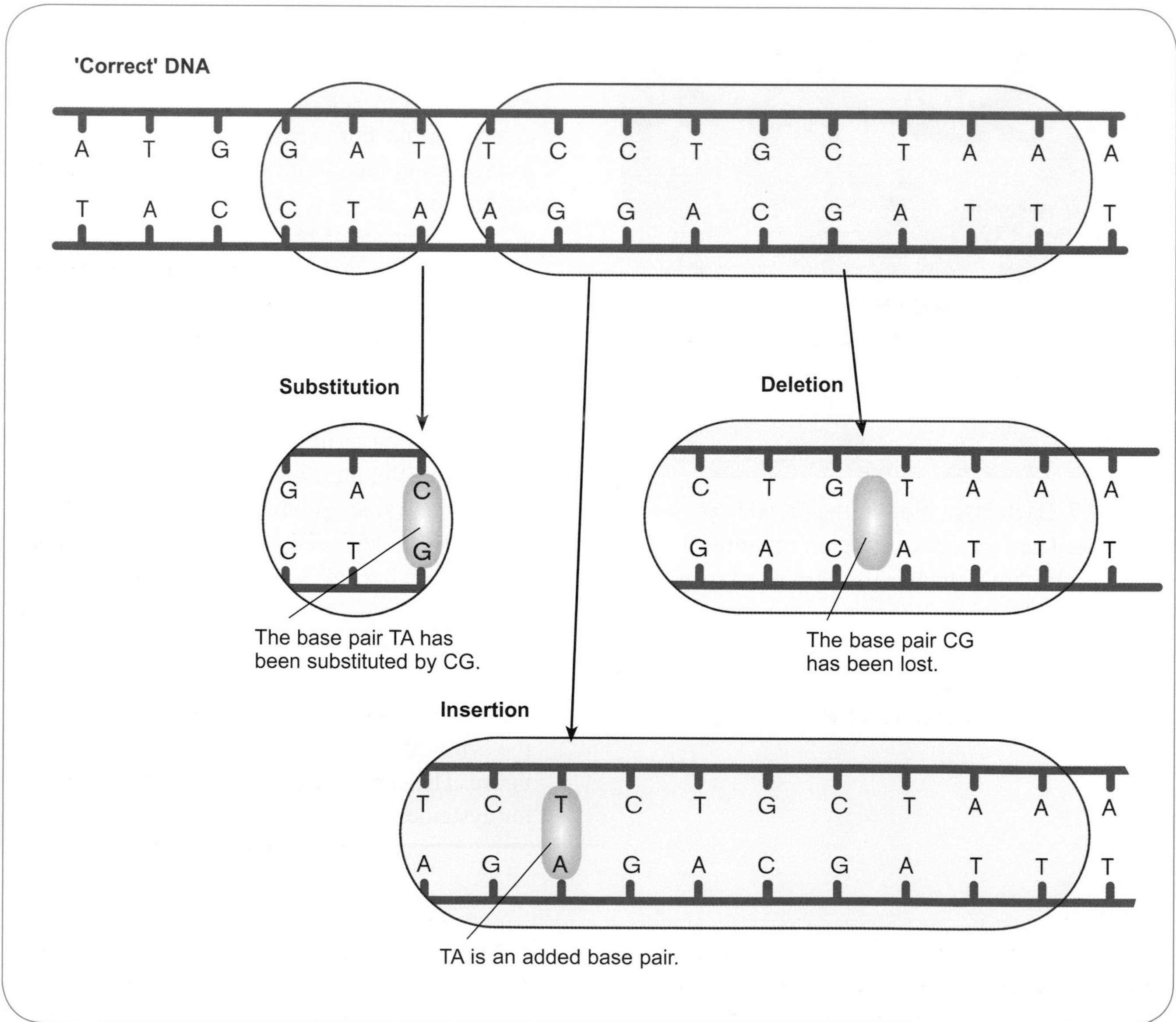

Figure 7.8 Mutations.

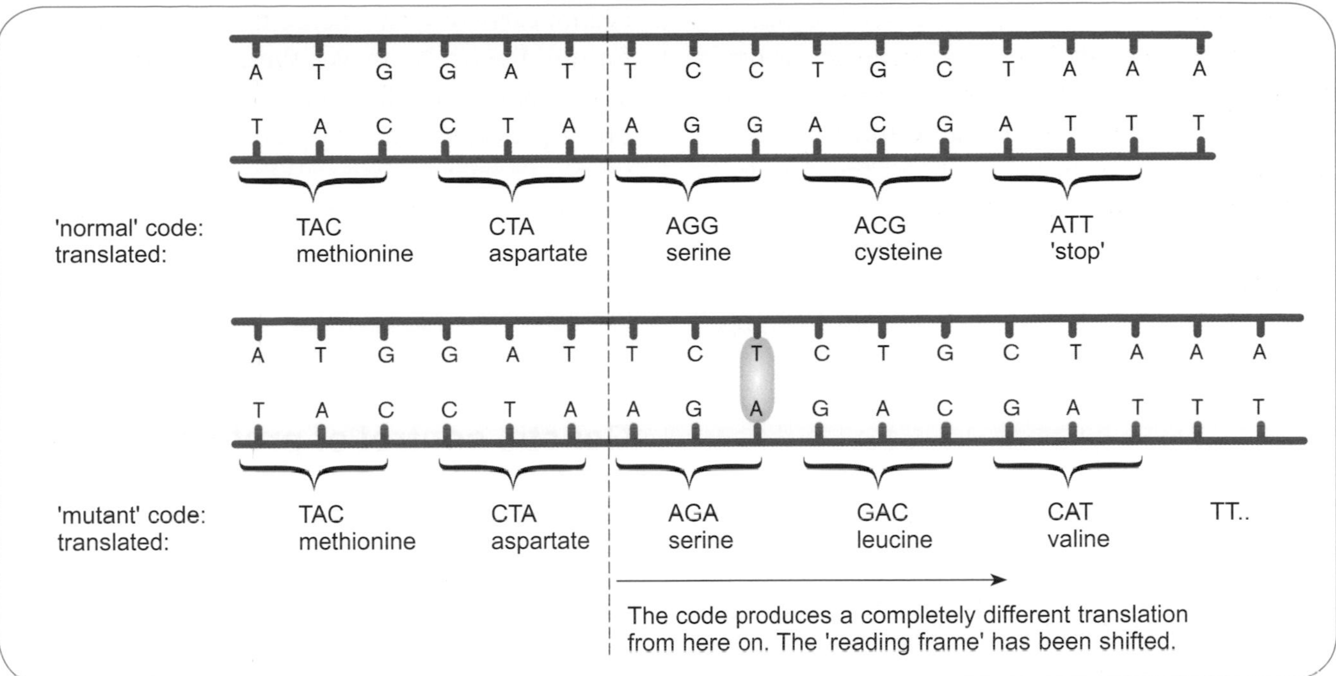

Figure 7.9 Deletion or insertion causes a frame shift in the DNA.

Insertion is the addition of a new pair of bases into the DNA. Like deletion, this always causes a frame shift and so is likely to have a big effect on the protein that is made.

Each of these kinds of mutation can produce a different amino acid sequence (primary structure) in the protein that the DNA is coding for. This may result in the secondary and tertiary structure of the protein being different. If so, the protein's function is likely to be disrupted. Usually, this is harmful, because the organism will have evolved over time, through the process of natural selection, to have proteins that behave in a particular way.

Occasionally, though, a mutation can be beneficial. You have seen, for example, how random mutations in bacteria can cause changes in their DNA that make them resistant to a particular antibiotic (*Biology 1*, page 224).

Sickle cell anaemia

An example of the way in which the substitution of just one base can cause huge and damaging changes in an organism's physiology is the genetic condition **sickle cell anaemia**. Sickle cell anaemia is an inherited disease caused by a single substitution in the gene that codes for one of the polypeptide chains in haemoglobin.

Haemoglobin is the red pigment, found inside erythrocytes, that transports oxygen around the body. It is a globular protein made up of four polypeptide chains. Two are α chains and two are β chains. A mutation in the gene coding for the β chains causes sickle cell anaemia.

Normally, part of this gene has a base sequence that codes for this amino acid sequence:

– valine – histidine – leucine – threonine
– proline – glutamate – glutamate – lysine –

The base sequence that codes for the first of the glutamates is usually CTT. But in the faulty gene the base sequence in this triplet has become CTA. And CTA does not code for glutamate. It codes for valine. So now the amino acid sequence will be:

– valine – histidine – leucine – threonine
– proline – valine – glutamate – lysine –

You might think that this would not make much difference. After all, there are 146 amino acids in each β chain, and only one has been changed. But it does, in fact, have a huge and sometimes fatal effect.

When the four polypeptide chains curl up and join to form a haemoglobin molecule, they form a very precise three-dimensional shape. One factor influencing this shape is that some amino acids have side chains that are hydrophilic, while others are hydrophobic. The polypeptides tend to curl up so that most of the hydrophobic amino acids are in the middle of the molecule, well away from the watery cytoplasm inside the erythrocyte. The hydrophilic side chains tend to be on the outside, where they interact with water molecules.

Glutamate has a side chain that is hydrophilic. In the 'correct' version of the haemoglobin molecule, it lies on the outside and helps to makes the haemoglobin soluble. Valine, however, has a side chain that is hydrophobic. So in the 'incorrect' version, the haemoglobin molecule has a hydrophobic side chain on its outer surface, where there should be a hydrophilic one.

The valine side chains cannot interact with water, but they *can* interact with each other. Most of the time, this does not happen. But if the oxygen level in the blood falls, then the valines form bonds between themselves that stick haemoglobin molecules together. Long fibres of stuck-together haemoglobin molecules are produced. As the fibres form inside the erythrocytes, they pull the cell out of its usual biconcave shape. Some cells become sickle shaped (Figure 7.10).

In this state, the erythrocytes are not only useless but also dangerous. The fibres of haemoglobin

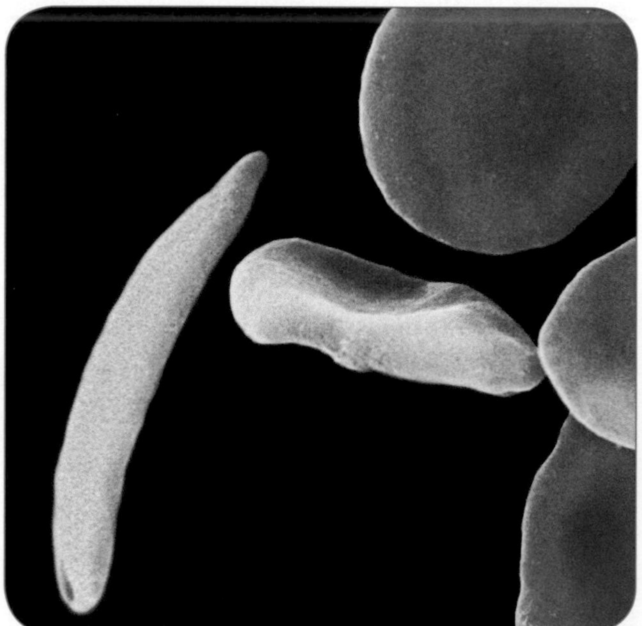

Figure 7.10 The cell at the left of this scanning electron micrograph is a sickled erythrocyte (× 5000).

cannot carry oxygen – hence the name 'anaemia' for this disease. Moreover, these misshapen cells cannot pass through capillaries. They cause blockages, which are very painful and can do serious damage to tissues. When this happens, a person is said to be having a 'sickle cell crisis'.

Extension

Genetic control of protein production

We have about 20 000 genes in each of our cells. Each cell has the same set of genes. But a particular cell does not make use of all of them. For example, only certain white blood cells use the genes that code for the production of antibodies – skin cells and heart cells don't make antibodies. Only certain cells in the skin produce the protein melanin – heart cells and nerve cells don't make it.

Each specialised cell in a multicellular organism uses only a particular set of genes. This is a very important concept, because it can explain how cells differentiate to become specialised for a particular function. It explains how a single cell, the zygote, can eventually produce a complete organism with so many different kinds of cells. In each cell type, a particular set of genes is switched on.

Even in a single-celled organism, not all its genes need to be switched on at the same time. For example, the bacterium *Escherichia coli* (*E. coli*) has genes that code for the synthesis of two enzymes that help with the digestion and absorption of the disaccharide lactose. One is called β **galactoside permease** (also known as **lactose permease)**, and it enables the cell to take up lactose. The other is called β **galactosidase** (also known as **lactase**), and this hydrolyses lactose to glucose and galactose.

If the bacterium is grown on a medium containing only glucose, it does not produce either of these enzymes. The genes that code for them are not expressed – they are switched off. However, if the bacterium is transferred to a medium containing only lactose, then the genes are switched on. Both lactose permease and β galactosidase are produced.

The genes that are involved in this regulatory process are part of a stretch of DNA called the ***lac* operon**. An operon is a length of DNA containing the base sequence that codes for the proteins, known as **structural genes**, and also other base sequences that determine whether or not the gene will be switched on. Figure 7.11 shows the structure of the *lac* operon in *E. coli*.

You can see that the longest length of DNA in the operon makes up the structural genes, which code for the production of lactose permease and β galactosidase. Close to this section (on its left in the diagram) is a short length of DNA called a **promoter**. This is the part of the DNA to which the enzyme RNA polymerase must bind in order to begin to catalyse the transcription of mRNA from the structural genes.

Next to the promoter is a region called the **operator**. If nothing is bound to the operator, then the promoter is available for RNA polymerase to bind to, and the structural genes can be expressed. However, in another part of the operon lies yet another stretch of DNA, a **regulator** gene. The regulator DNA codes for a protein called a **repressor protein**.

The repressor protein has two binding sites. One of these fits the operator DNA, and so binds with it. When this is happening, the promoter is blocked, RNA polymerase cannot bind to it, and the structural genes cannot be expressed. This is the normal situation in the bacterium.

The repressor protein can also bind with the sugar lactose. When this happens, the shape of the repressor protein changes, so that it no longer fits onto the operator DNA. So, if you grow *E. coli* on agar jelly containing lactose, the repressor protein leaves the operator, which frees the promoter site. Now RNA polymerase can bind and start transcribing the structural genes. Within a very short time, lactose permease and β galactosidase are synthesised, and the bacterium can begin to make use of the lactose on which it is growing.

SAQ

6 Suggest why it is an advantage to *E. coli* to produce lactose permease and β galactosidase only when lactose is present.

Answer

Extension

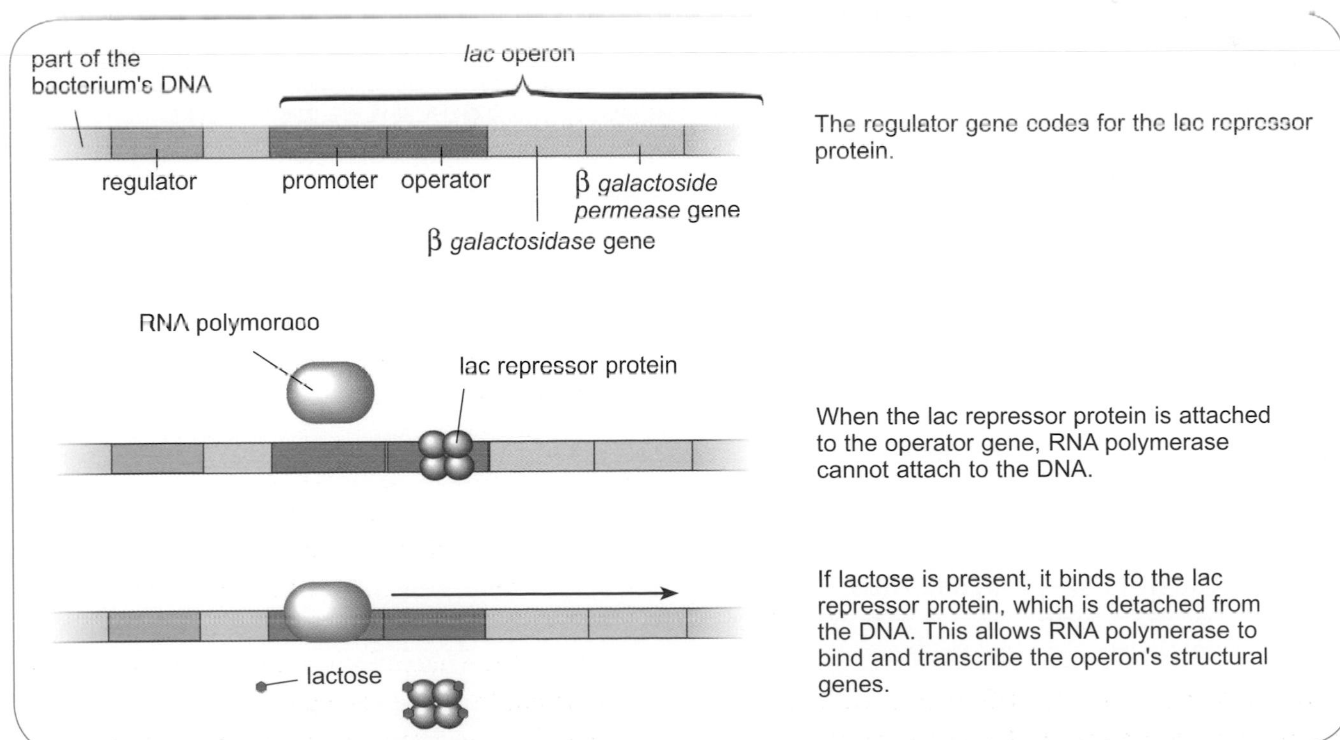
part of the bacterium's DNA
lac operon
regulator
promoter
operator
β *galactoside permease* gene
β *galactosidase* gene
The regulator gene codes for the lac repressor protein.
RNA polymerase
lac repressor protein
When the lac repressor protein is attached to the operator gene, RNA polymerase cannot attach to the DNA.
lactose
If lactose is present, it binds to the lac repressor protein, which is detached from the DNA. This allows RNA polymerase to bind and transcribe the operon's structural genes.

Figure 7.11 The *lac* operon in *E. coli*.

Controlling development

Your body contains hundreds of different kinds of specialised cells. Unless you are unlucky, they are all in the right place. You have skin cells where skin should be, muscle cells in your muscles, bone cells in your bones. And, probably, your organs are where they should be. You have a radius and ulna in your forearm, two eyes at the front of your head, a heart in your thorax between your lungs.

How do all these cells, tissues and organs manage to develop in the right place? This is a fascinating branch of biology, and one where there are still many puzzles to be solved. However, we do understand at least a small part of the process. It involves a set of genes called **homeobox genes**.

Homeobox genes were first discovered in 1983. They are genes that determine how an organism's body develops as it grows from a zygote into a complete organism. They determine the organism's **body plan**.

One intriguing thing about them is the tremendous similarity between homeobox genes in different organisms. All animals have homeobox genes that are recognisably similar – they are **homologous** with each other (Figure 7.12).

You may remember from your AS course that a scientist can take a homeobox gene that determines eye development from a mouse, and put it into a fruit fly's wing. The gene will make an eye develop in the fruit fly's wing.

This similarity in the homeobox genes in all animals is striking. We think that the last common ancestor of fruit flies and mice lived around half a billion years ago. Yet the base sequence on these genes has scarcely changed since then. We say that the genes are **highly conserved**. This implies that their activity is absolutely fundamental to the development of an animal body that actually works. It seems as though a mutation in a homeobox gene is so disastrous that the organism is usually not able to survive.

Homeobox genes have also been discovered in fungi and plants. Like animals, all plants share similar sets of homeobox genes. But the plant genes are not homologous to the animal ones. It looks as though each kingdom started pretty much from scratch in developing its own set of homeobox genes.

Extension

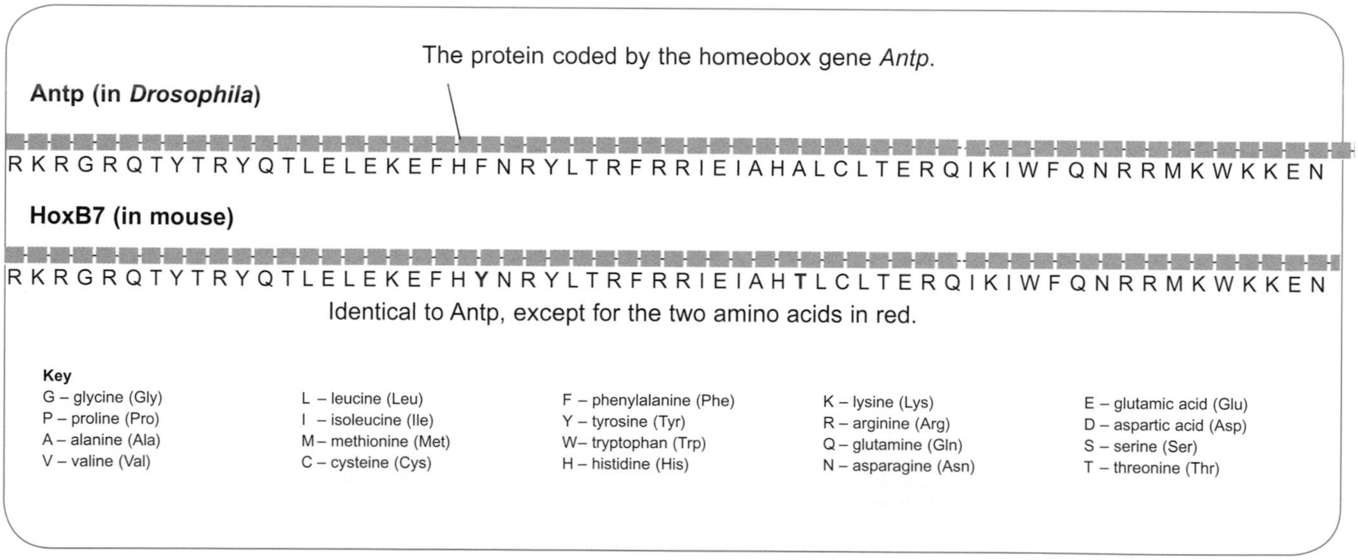

The protein coded by the homeobox gene *Antp*.

Antp (in *Drosophila*)

R K R G R Q T Y T R Y Q T L E L E K E F H F N R Y L T R F R R I E I A H A L C L T E R Q I K I W F Q N R R M K W K K E N

HoxB7 (in mouse)

R K R G R Q T Y T R Y Q T L E L E K E F H **Y** N R Y L T R F R R I E I A H **T** L C L T E R Q I K I W F Q N R R M K W K K E N

Identical to Antp, except for the two amino acids in red.

Key

G – glycine (Gly)	L – leucine (Leu)	F – phenylalanine (Phe)	K – lysine (Lys)	E – glutamic acid (Glu)
P – proline (Pro)	I – isoleucine (Ile)	Y – tyrosine (Tyr)	R – arginine (Arg)	D – aspartic acid (Asp)
A – alanine (Ala)	M – methionine (Met)	W – tryptophan (Trp)	Q – glutamine (Gln)	S – serine (Ser)
V – valine (Val)	C – cysteine (Cys)	H – histidine (His)	N – asparagine (Asn)	T – threonine (Thr)

Figure 7.12 These are the sequences of 60 amino acids in the proteins coded for by the homeobox genes *Antp* in a fruit fly (*Drosophila*) and *HoxB7* in a mouse.

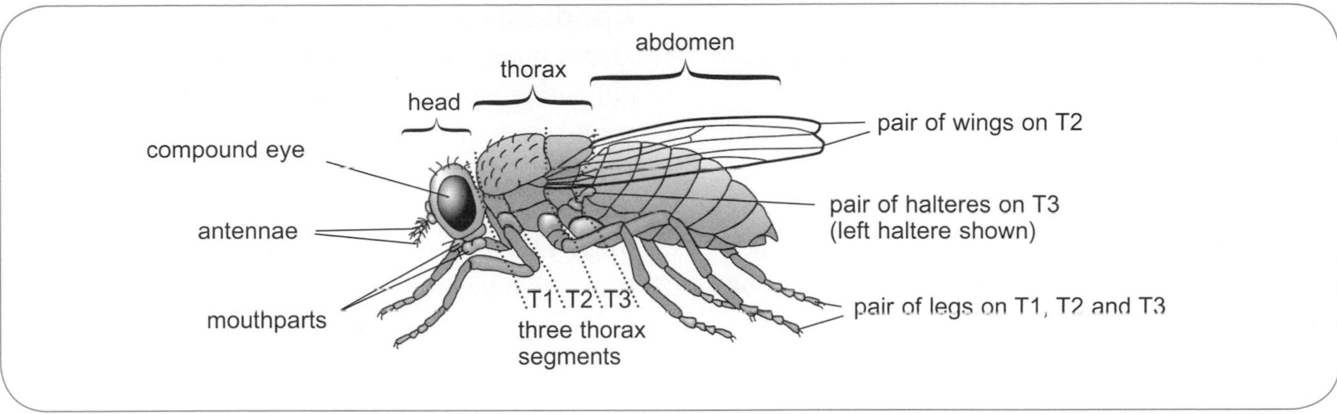

Figure 7.13 The general body plan of a fly.

The fruit fly body plan

One of the most useful ways of finding out how homeobox genes work is to study what happens when they go wrong.

The fruit fly *Drosophila melanogaster* has the body plan of a typical insect (Figure 7.13). Its body is divided into a head, thorax and abdomen. The thorax is made up of three segments, which we can call T1, T2 and T3. A pair of legs grows from each of these segments. A pair of wings grows from segment T2, and a pair of halteres (tiny gyroscopes that the fly uses to keep balance while it is flying) grows from segment T3.

The fruit fly has a homeobox gene called *Ubx*. This gene stops the formation of wings in T3. If the fly has a mutation in both copies of *Ubx*, then wings grow in T3 instead of halteres.

Figure 7.14 The fly on the left has the correct number of wings, plus halteres (which are too small to see in this photograph). The one on the right has grown a second pair of wings instead of halteres.

The fly ends up with two pairs of wings, and cannot fly (Figure 7.14). There is a similar story for the development of legs. A homeobox gene called *Antp* is usually turned on in the thorax, where it causes legs to develop. It is turned off in the head. However, in some types of mutant flies the *Antp* gene is switched on in the head. The fly grows legs from its head, instead of antennae (Figure 7.15).

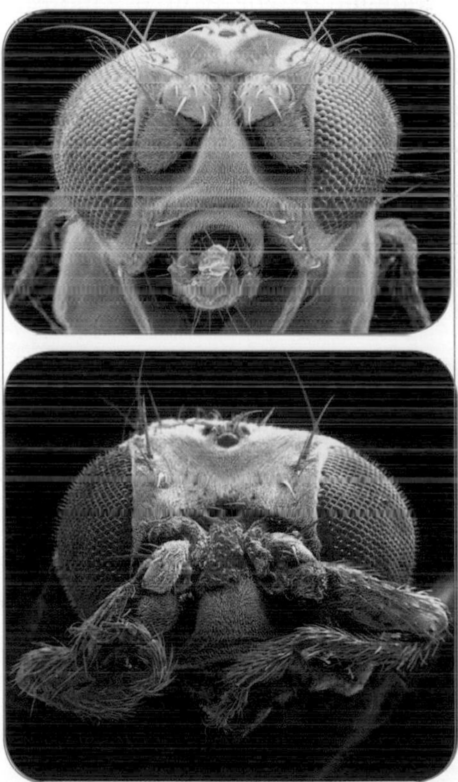

Figure 7.15 The fruit fly at the top has antennae (the small, yellow furry objects) between its eyes. The fly below has a mutation in its *Antp* gene, and has grown legs where its antennae should be (× 70).

There is a mouse homeobox gene that is very, very similar to the fruitfly *Antp* gene. If this mouse gene is put into the fruit fly head, the fly grows fruitfly legs instead of antennae, just as it would with the *Antp* gene switched on.

So, what are homeobox genes actually doing to bring about these effects? Homeobox genes code for the production of proteins called **transcription factors**. These proteins can bind to a particular region of DNA and cause it to be transcribed. In this way, a single homeobox gene can switch on a whole collection of other genes. The normal *Antp* gene, for example, switches on all the genes that are involved in the production of a leg. The normal *Ubx* gene switches off all the genes that are involved in the production of a wing.

We know that our homeobox genes work like this, too. Switching just one homeobox gene on or off results in the switching on or off of a complete set of other genes. For example, homeobox genes called *HoxA11* and *HoxD11* switch on the genes that cause a forelimb to develop. If a mouse has mutations in both of its copies of these two genes, it does not grow a radius or ulna in its forelimb. The effects of the drug thalidomide, taken by many pregnant women in the 1950s, appear to have been caused because it affected the behaviour of one or more homeobox genes at a particular stage of embryonic development when their activity was crucial (Figure 7.16).

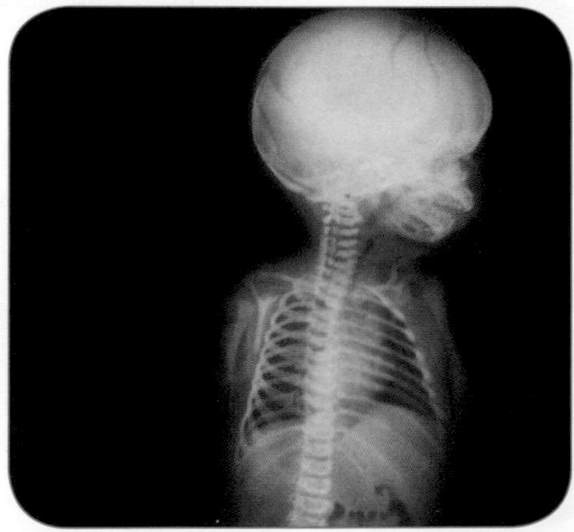

Figure 7.16 This is an X-ray of a child whose mother took thalidomide during pregnancy. The drug affected the activity of some of the fetus's homeobox genes, so that arms and legs did not develop properly.

Apoptosis in development

Development is not all about the production of differentiated cells in different parts of the body. At some stages of development, we actually need to get rid of cells.

You may have seen tadpoles changing into frogs. This is an example of **metamorphosis** – a major change in the structure of an organism as it develops from one stage of its life cycle to the next. The tadpoles of the common frog, *Rana temporaria*, live completely aquatic lives. They have streamlined bodies and a tail for swimming. As they grow, they develop legs, change their body shape and lose their tails (Figure 7.17).

The tail is lost because the cells in it die and are tidied up by phagocytic cells, which engulf and digest them. This cell death is not accidental. It is meant to happen – it is **programmed cell death**. The type of programmed cell death involved in development is called **apoptosis** (Figure 7.18). It is an essential part of the development of all animals.

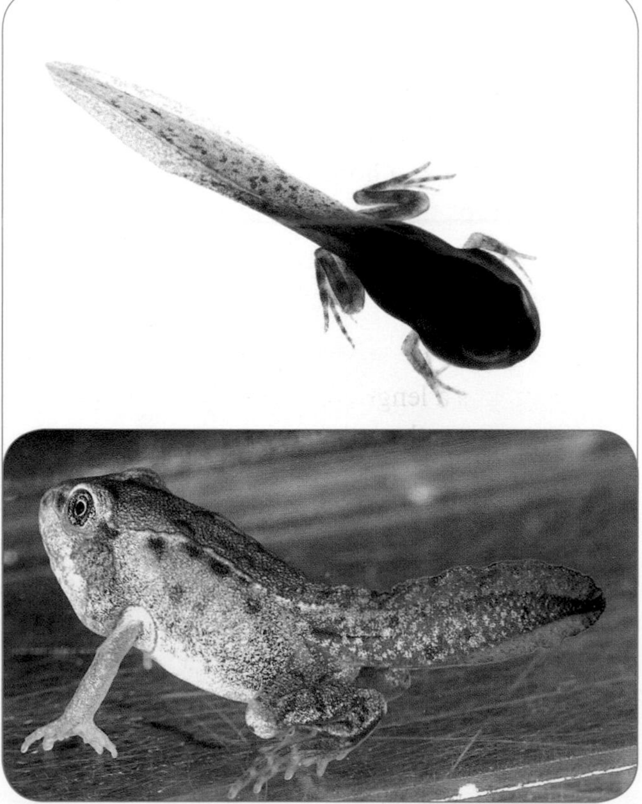

Figure 7.17 The tadpole, almost ready to metamorphose into a frog, still has a tail for swimming. The tail is reabsorbed as the young frog finally develops.

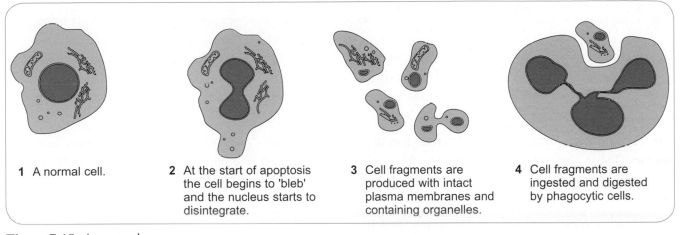

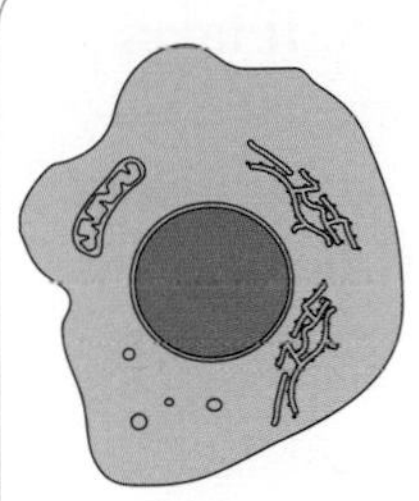

1 A normal cell.

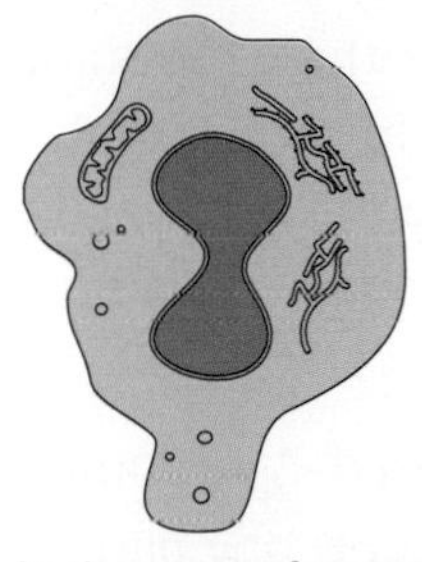

2 At the start of apoptosis the cell begins to 'bleb' and the nucleus starts to disintegrate.

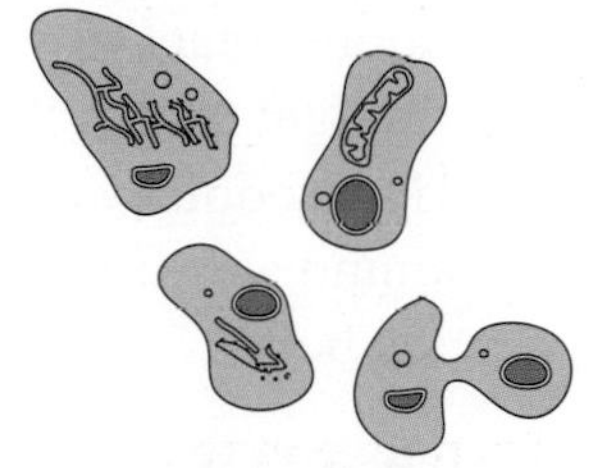

3 Cell fragments are produced with intact plasma membranes and containing organelles.

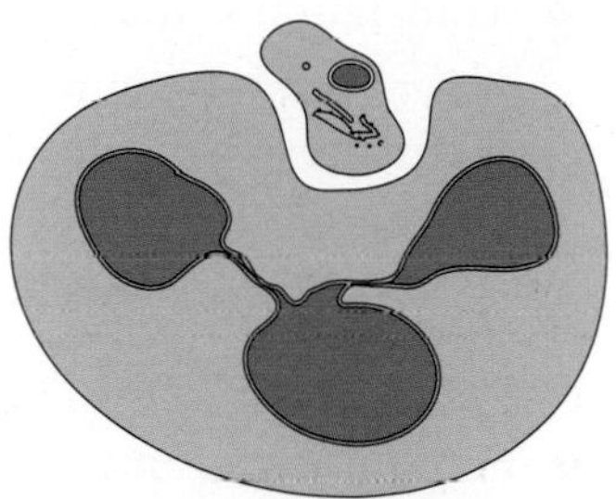

4 Cell fragments are ingested and digested by phagocytic cells.

Figure 7.18 Apoptosis.

For example, in humans, the fingers and toes develop as separate organs because of apoptosis of the cells between them, so that the tissue linking them together is lost. Sometimes this does not happen, and a baby is born with 'webs' between its fingers or toes (Figure 7.19). Usually this is easily remedied by a simple operation to separate the digits.

Extension

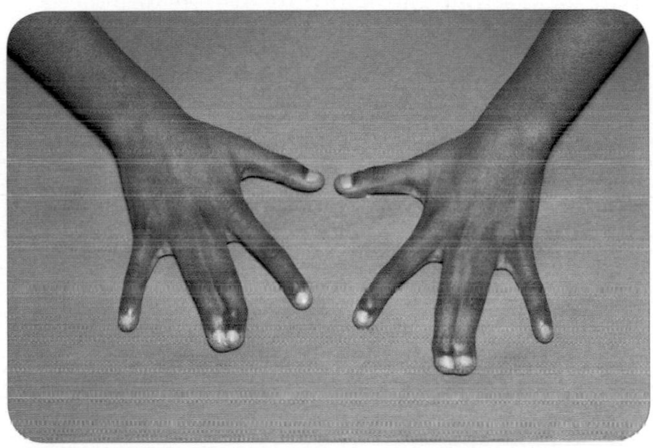

Figure 7.19 Webbed fingers can result when apoptosis does not occur as it should during the development of an embryo.

Summary

Glossary

- A gene is a length of DNA that codes for a polypeptide. The sequence of nucleotides in the DNA determines the sequence of amino acids in the protein.
- The genetic code is a three-letter code, in which a particular sequence of three bases in DNA stands for a particular amino acid.
- Protein synthesis takes place in two main stages, transcription and translation.
- Transcription is the production of a complementary mRNA molecule by building it against the reference strand of the DNA in a gene. The DNA strands are separated by DNA helicase, and free mRNA nucleotides line up against one of the exposed strands, with complementary bases pairing with each other. C and G pair. A on the DNA strand pairs with U on the mRNA. T on the DNA strand pairs with A on the mRNA. The mRNA nucleotides are then linked together by RNA polymerase.

continued

- Translation is the production of a polypeptide following the base sequence on the mRNA. It takes place on a ribosome, where two codons (that is, two sets of three bases) on the mRNA are exposed at one time. The amino acids are brought to the ribosome by tRNA molecules, each of which has an anticodon that binds with the mRNA codon by complementary base pairing. The anticodon on the tRNA determines which specific amino acid it brings. As successive amino acids are brought to the ribosome, they are linked by peptide bonds.
- A mutation is an unpredictable change in the genetic material. Mutations can involve changes in a single base pair in a DNA molecule. This may have no effect if one base is substituted for another but the triplet still codes for the same amino acid. However, if a base is added or lost, then a frame shift occurs and all the amino acids coded for beyond that point will be different.
- If the sequence of amino acids in a protein is different, then its tertiary structure is also likely to be different and the protein probably will not function normally. This is likely to be a harmful effect, but just occasionally it can be beneficial.
- Most genes are only expressed in certain cell types and under certain circumstances. In prokarotyes, gene expression is controlled by means of a number of other regions of DNA that lie close to the part that carries the code for the amino acid sequence of the protein. The whole structure is called an operon. In *E. coli*, for example, the *lac* operon ensures that the genes for lactose permease and β galactosidase are only expressed when lactose is present.
- All animals have similar genes that control the development of their general body plan, called homeobox genes. Plants and fungi also have them, but they are not homologous to those found in animals. Homeobox genes function by switching on or off whole sets of other genes that bring about processes resulting in the formation of a particular part of the body, such as a leg or an eye.
- A particular type of programmed cell death, called apoptosis, is important during development.

Stretch and challenge questions

1 Discuss the features of DNA that make it suitable as the genetic material. Hint

2 All cells (except those with no nuclei such as red blood cells) in the human body contain identical genetic material. Discuss how it is possible for cells in different parts of the body, and at different times, to have different structures and to behave differently from one another. Hint

Questions

1 **a** Proteins may be globular or fibrous.
Name <u>one</u> globular protein and <u>one</u> fibrous protein. [2]

b When enzymes are heated to high temperatures, they cease to function.
They are said to become denatured.
Describe the effect of high temperature on enzymes. [4]

continued

c During protein synthesis, amino acids are carried by transfer RNA (tRNA) molecules to ribosomes, where the tRNA binds to messenger RNA (mRNA).

The table shows the tRNA triplet code (anticodons) for some tRNA molecules and the amino acid each one carries.

tRNA triplet code (anticodon)	Amino acid carried
UCU	leucine
UCA	arginine
UUC	lysine
CCC	glycine
GGG	proline
AGC	serine
AUA	tyrosine
CAA	valine
CGC	alanine
AGG	serine

The diagram shows a stage in the synthesis of a polypeptide. The mRNA molecule is moving through the ribosome and the second and third tRNA molecules are lined up with the mRNA.

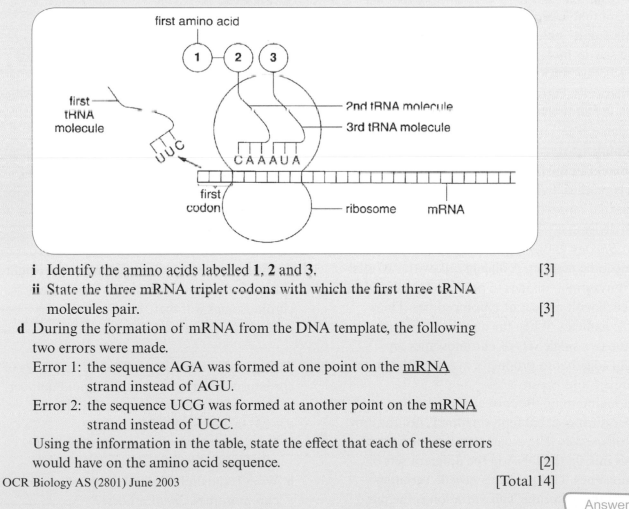

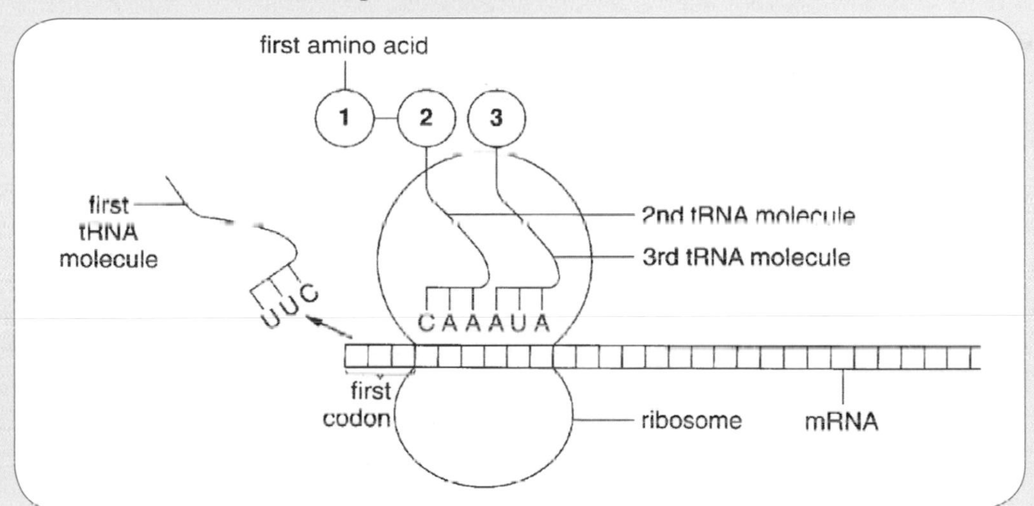

i Identify the amino acids labelled **1**, **2** and **3**. [3]

ii State the three mRNA triplet codons with which the first three tRNA molecules pair. [3]

d During the formation of mRNA from the DNA template, the following two errors were made.

Error 1: the sequence AGA was formed at one point on the mRNA strand instead of AGU.

Error 2: the sequence UCG was formed at another point on the mRNA strand instead of UCC.

Using the information in the table, state the effect that each of these errors would have on the amino acid sequence. [2]

OCR Biology AS (2801) June 2003 [Total 14]

Answer

Chapter 8

Meiosis and variation

e-Learning

Objectives

All species of living organisms are able to reproduce. This is how the species is perpetuated. Reproduction may be **asexual reproduction**, in which a single organism, or part of it, divides by mitosis to produce a new organism that is genetically identical to the parent. Animals, however, and also plants for much of the time, generally use **sexual reproduction**. This involves the production of specialised sex cells called **gametes**. The nuclei of two gametes (usually, but not necessarily, from two different parents) fuse together in a process called **fertilisation**. The new cell that is formed is called a **zygote**. The zygote then divides repeatedly by mitosis to form a new organism that is genetically different from its parents and its siblings.

You saw in *Biology 1* that, during mitosis, chromosomes are divided equally between the two daughter cells. Perfect copies of each chromosome are made before the division of the cell begins, so that each cell gets a complete set of chromosomes, containing an exact replica of all the DNA that was present in the parent cell. This is how most eukaryotic cells divide most of the time.

In sexual reproduction, however, another type of cell division is needed. This is **meiosis**. As we saw in *Biology 1*, this type of division halves the chromosome number. A **diploid** cell, with two sets of chromosomes, divides to produce four **haploid** cells, each with one set of chromosomes. These become gametes. When the nuclei of two gametes fuse, the two single sets of chromosomes are brought together to produce a zygote with two sets (Figure 8.1 and Figure 8.2).

But maintaining the correct chromosome number during sexual reproduction is not the only effect of meiosis. The events that take place during meiosis mix up the DNA in the different sets of chromosomes. This produces **genetic variation** amongst the offspring. This variation is the raw material on which natural selection acts, sometimes

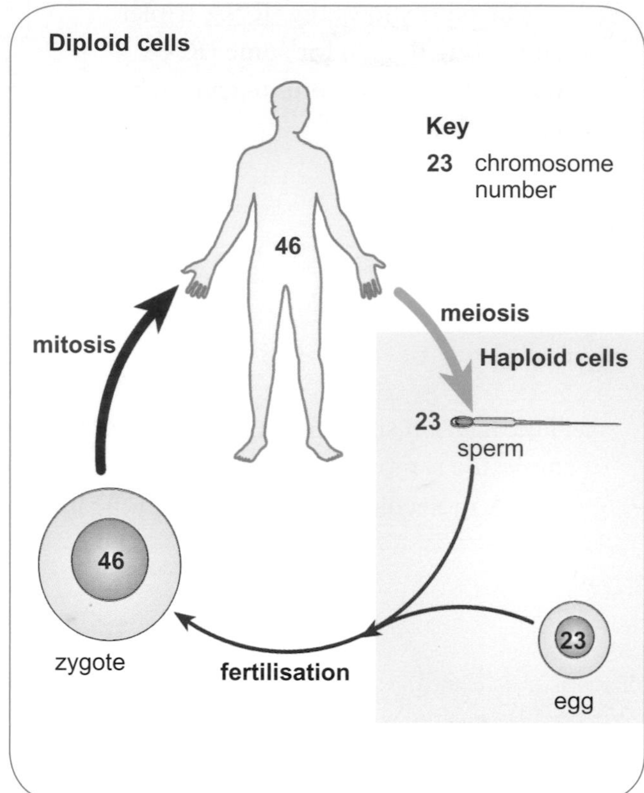

Figure 8.1 The human life cycle, typical of a sexually reproducing animal. Mitosis produces genetically identical diploid body cells, and meiosis produces genetically varying haploid gametes.

SAQ

1 The fruit fly *Drosophila melanogaster* has eight chromosomes in its body cells. How many chromosomes will there be in a *Drosophila* sperm cell?

Answer

2 The symbol n is used to indicate the number of chromosomes in one set – the haploid number of chromosomes. For example, in humans $n = 23$. In a horse, $n = 32$.

a How many chromosomes are there in a gamete of a horse?

b What is the diploid number of chromosomes, $2n$, of a horse?

Answer

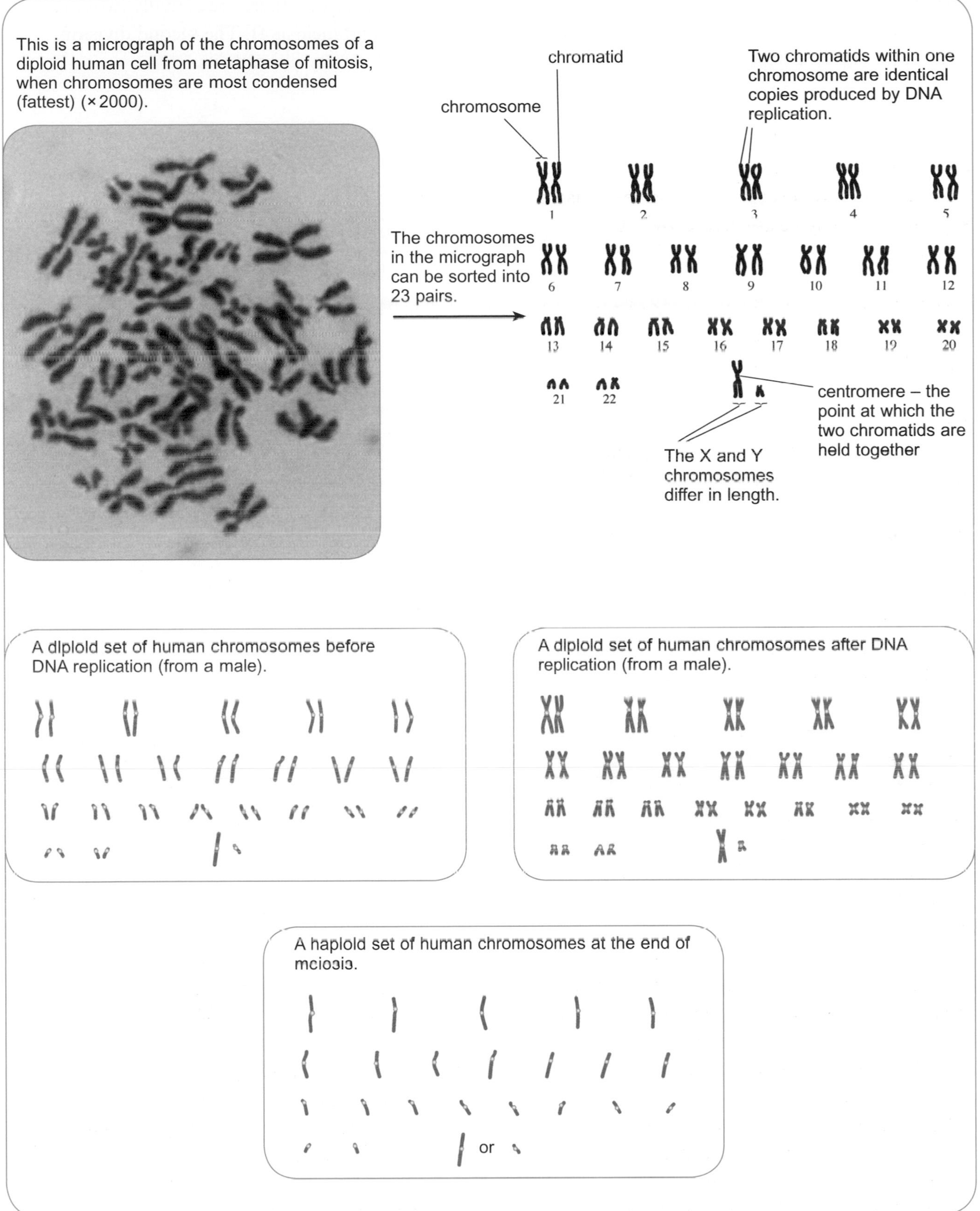
This is a micrograph of the chromosomes of a diploid human cell from metaphase of mitosis, when chromosomes are most condensed (fattest) (×2000).
chromatid
chromosome
Two chromatids within one chromosome are identical copies produced by DNA replication.
The chromosomes in the micrograph can be sorted into 23 pairs.
1
2
3
4
5
6
7
8
9
10
11
12
13
14
15
16
17
18
19
20
21
22
centromere – the point at which the two chromatids are held together
The X and Y chromosomes differ in length.
A diploid set of human chromosomes before DNA replication (from a male).
A diploid set of human chromosomes after DNA replication (from a male).
A haploid set of human chromosomes at the end of meiosis.
or

Figure 8.2 Chromosome structure.

Meiosis

The main events that take place during meiosis are shown in Figure 8.3. The diagrams show a cell with four chromosomes – that is, a haploid number of 2.

You will see that there are actually two divisions, meiosis I and meiosis II. The second division, meiosis II, is very like mitosis.

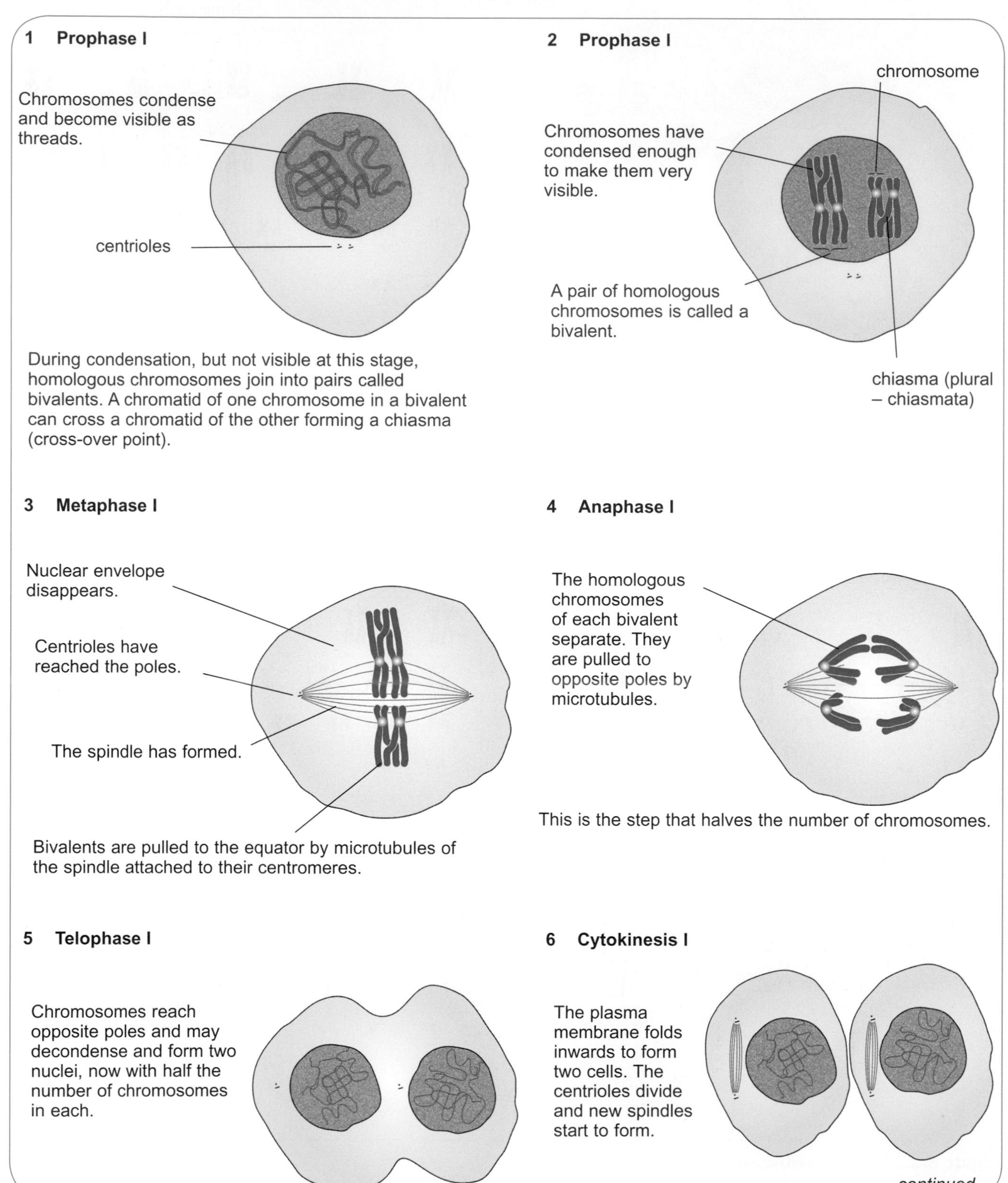

1 Prophase I
Chromosomes condense and become visible as threads.
centrioles
During condensation, but not visible at this stage, homologous chromosomes join into pairs called bivalents. A chromatid of one chromosome in a bivalent can cross a chromatid of the other forming a chiasma (cross-over point).
2 Prophase I
chromosome
Chromosomes have condensed enough to make them very visible.
A pair of homologous chromosomes is called a bivalent.
chiasma (plural – chiasmata)
3 Metaphase I
Nuclear envelope disappears.
Centrioles have reached the poles.
The spindle has formed.
Bivalents are pulled to the equator by microtubules of the spindle attached to their centromeres.
4 Anaphase I
The homologous chromosomes of each bivalent separate. They are pulled to opposite poles by microtubules.
This is the step that halves the number of chromosomes.
5 Telophase I
Chromosomes reach opposite poles and may decondense and form two nuclei, now with half the number of chromosomes in each.
6 Cytokinesis I
The plasma membrane folds inwards to form two cells. The centrioles divide and new spindles start to form.

continued

Figure 8.3 Meiosis.

7 Prophase II

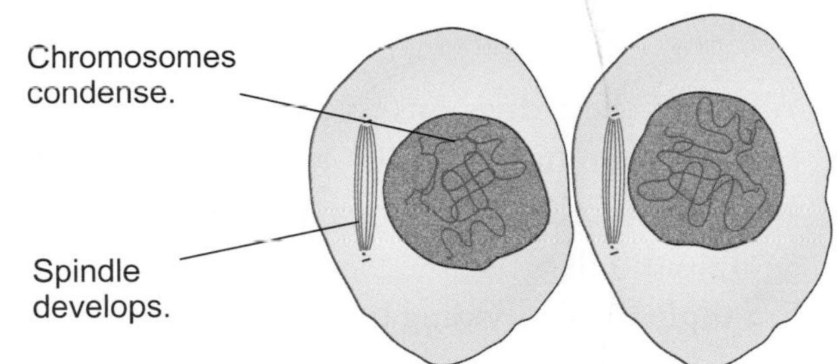

8 Metaphase II

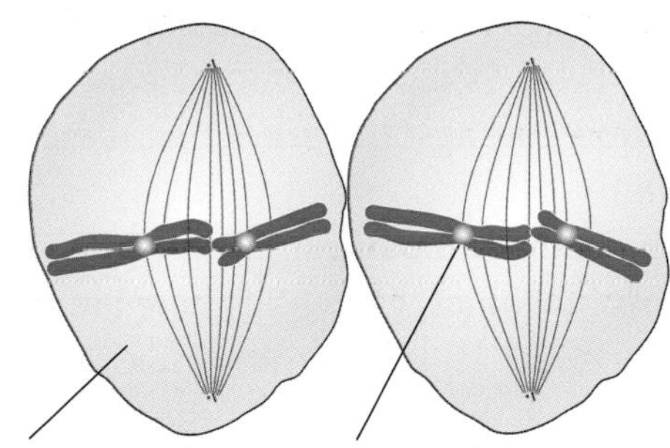

9 Anaphase II

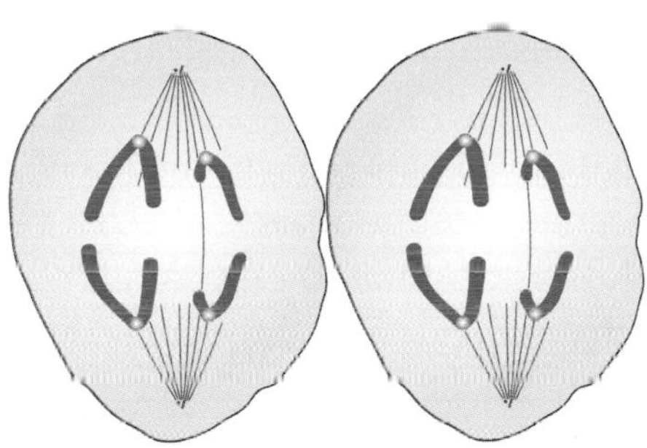

Centromeres divide so each chromatid is now a chromosome. These chromosomes move to opposite poles.

10 Telophase II

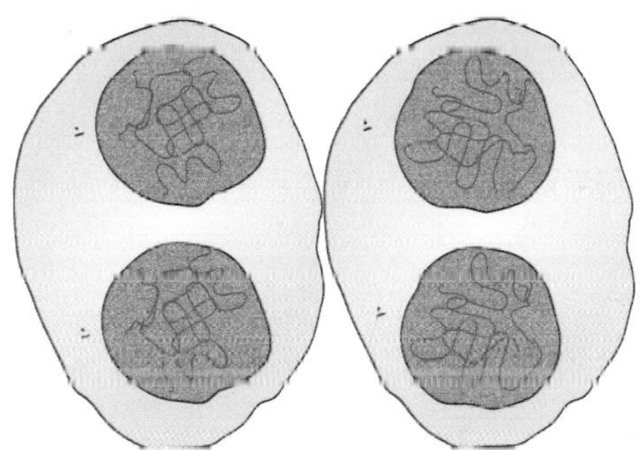

Chromosomes reach the poles, decondense and nuclei form.

11 Cytokinesis II

The original cell has now produced four cells. Each of the four has half the number of chromosomes of the parent cell. Each cell has one chromatid (now chromosome) from each homologous pair in the original cell.

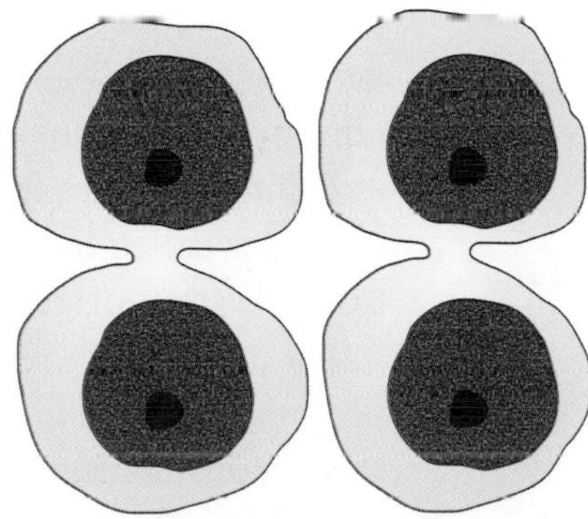

Figure 8.3 Meiosis continued.

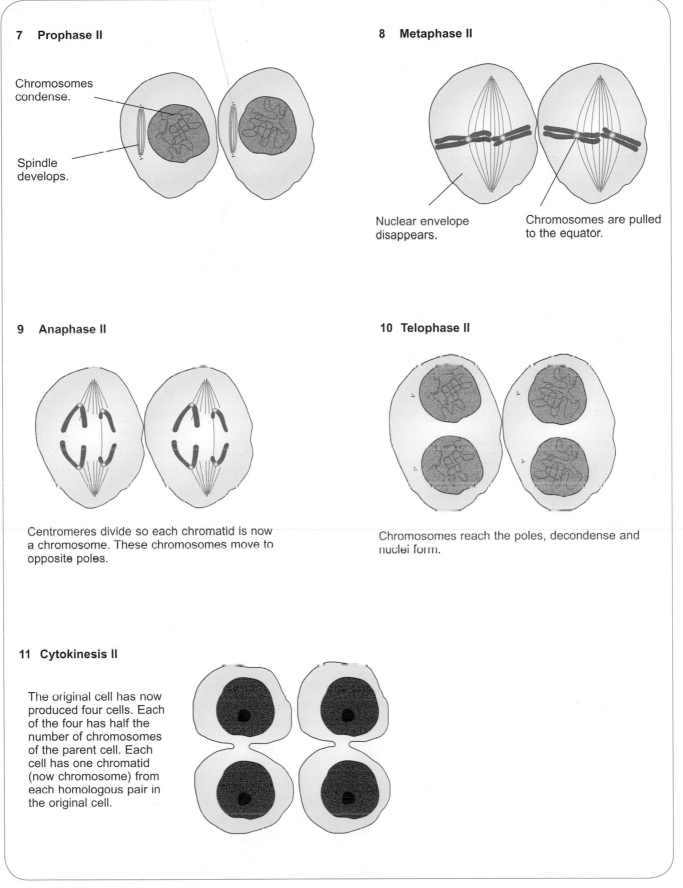

How meiosis causes variation

We have already seen one way in which the new cells formed by meiosis are different from their parent cell. The new cells are haploid whereas the parent cell was diploid. But meiosis also produces variation amongst the **genes** that these cells contain.

Consider a human cell, with two sets of 23 chromosomes, 46 in all. There are two chromosome 1s, two chromosome 2s and so on. One of each pair came from the father, and one from the mother. Both of the chromosomes of a homologous pair carry genes for the same feature at the same place, called a **locus**. For example, both chromosome 4s carry a gene that determines whether red hair will be produced.

Most genes exist in different versions, called **alleles**. The alleles have slight differences in the base sequences in their DNA. As a human cell has two copies of each chromosome, they have two copies of each gene. The cell could therefore contain two different alleles of that gene (Figure 8.4).

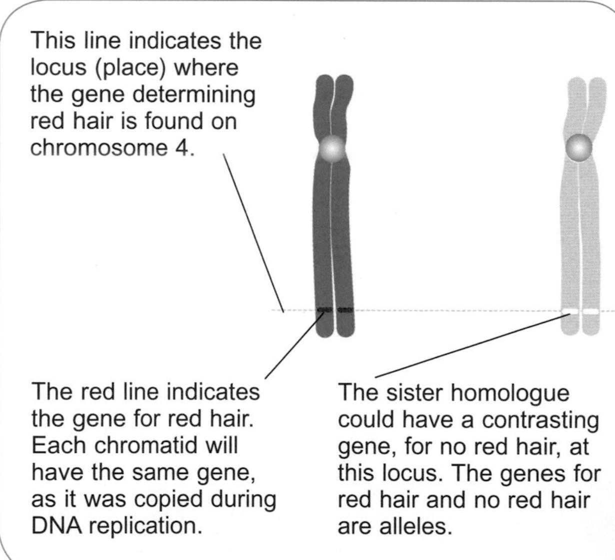

This line indicates the locus (place) where the gene determining red hair is found on chromosome 4.
The red line indicates the gene for red hair. Each chromatid will have the same gene, as it was copied during DNA replication.
The sister homologue could have a contrasting gene, for no red hair, at this locus. The genes for red hair and no red hair are alleles.

Figure 8.4 Different alleles for a gene can exist on homologous chromosomes.

SAQ

3 During which division, meiosis I or meiosis II, is the chromosome number halved?

Answer

4 Which of these divisions would be possible? Explain your answers.

a a diploid cell dividing by mitosis to form diploid cells

b a diploid cell dividing by meiosis to form haploid cells

c a haploid cell dividing by mitosis to form haploid cells

d a haploid cell dividing by meiosis to form haploid cells

Answer

5 Name the stage of meiosis at which each of these events occurs. Remember to state whether the stage is in meiosis I or meiosis II.

a Homologous chromosomes pair to form bivalents.

b Chiasmata form between chromatids of homologous chromosomes.

c Homologous chromosomes separate.

d Centromeres divide and chromatids separate.

e Haploid nuclei are first formed.

Answer

Independent assortment

During meiosis, as pairs of chromosomes line up on the equator, each pair behaves independently of every other pair. Figure 8.5 shows this for two pairs of chromosomes. One pair carries the gene for red hair, and the other pair carries the gene for colour blindness to blue. In Figure 8.5, chromosomes from the father are shown in blue, and chromosomes from the mother in grey.

This is called **independent assortment**. It mixes up alleles that originally came from an organism's father and its mother, so that the gametes it produces contain a mixture of alleles from both of the organism's parents. Each sperm or egg that you produce contains a mixture of alleles from your father and your mother.

And the number of combinations of different alleles in these gametes is vast. We can calculate the number of different combinations of *chromosomes* that can be present in the gametes using the formula 2^n, where n is the haploid number of chromosomes.

In the example shown in Figure 8.5, $n = 2$. The number of possible combinations is therefore $2 \times 2 = 4$. In this instance, these combinations of chromosomes mean that we have four possible combinations of the alleles that they carry for hair colour and colour vision. They are:

- red hair / blue colour blindness
- red hair / normal blue vision
- not red hair / blue colour blindness
- not red hair / normal blue vision

But in a human cell, the haploid number is 23. The number of different combinations of chromosomes is therefore 2^{23}. Try working this out (you have to multiply 2 by itself 23 times). No wonder we never look exactly like either of our parents, or our brothers or sisters. The only exception is identical twins, who each inherit exactly the same combination of genes.

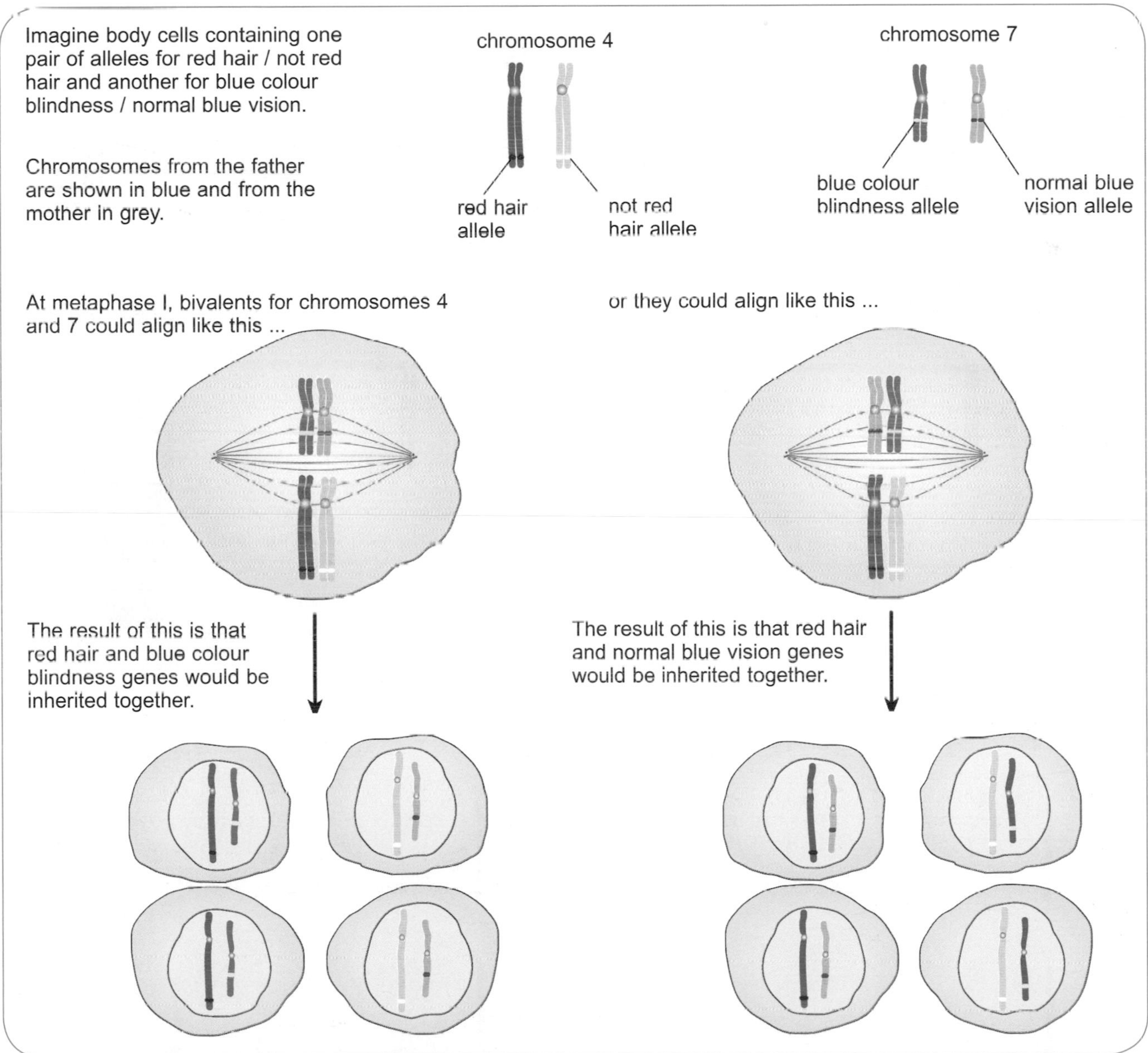

Figure 8.5 How independent assortment produces variation. As a result of the randomness of alignment of the bivalents during metaphase I, either of a pair of alleles of one gene may end up in the same cell as either of a pair of alleles of another gene on a different chromosome.

Crossing over

Crossing over happens during prophase I. It is a result of the chromatids within a bivalent (pair of homologous chromosomes) getting tangled up with one another. They form **chiasmata** (singular: chiasma). The chromatids break and rejoin at each chiasma, producing a different arrangement of alleles on each one (Figure 8.6).

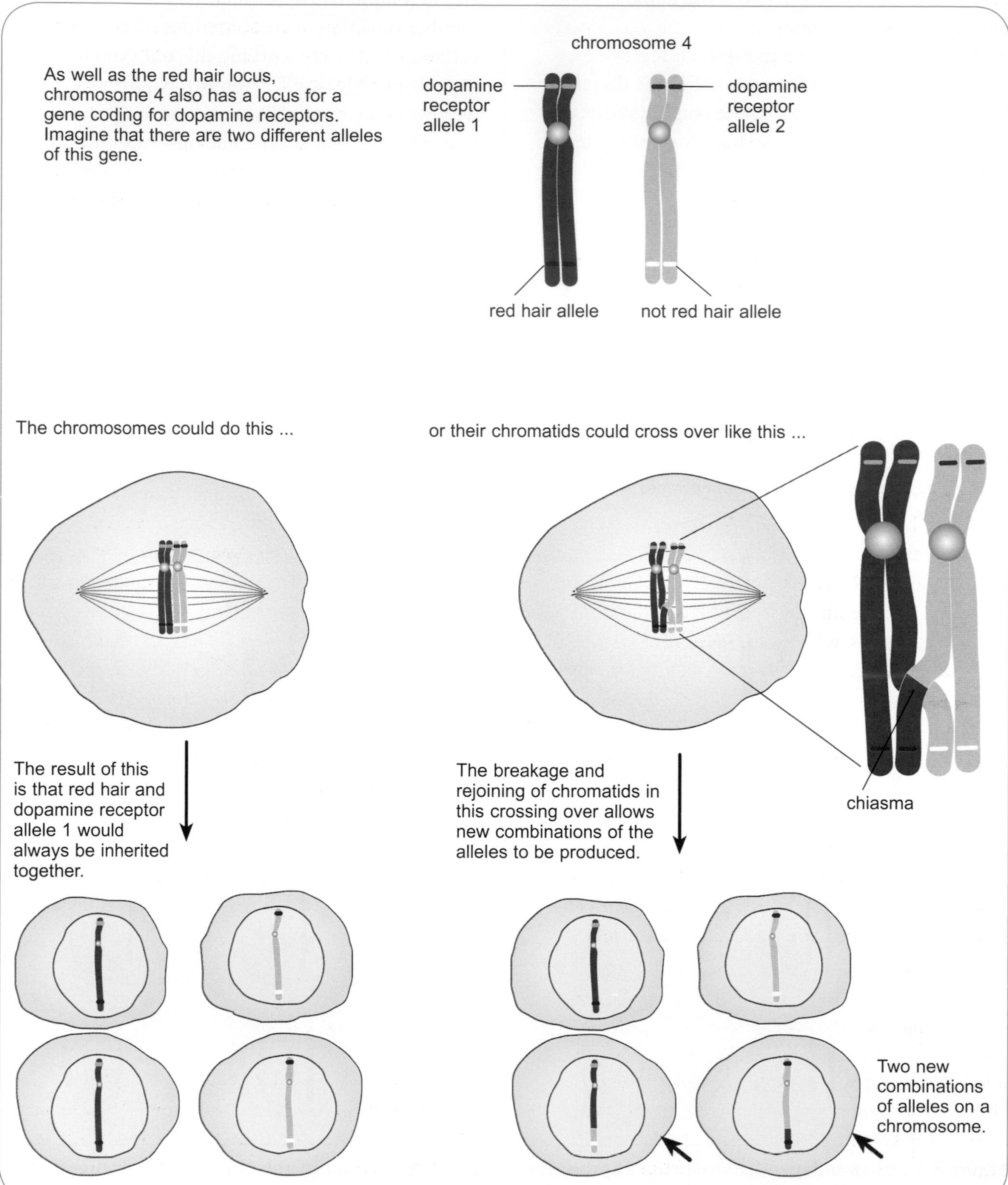

Figure 8.6 How crossing over produces variation.

Genetics and inheritance

The study of the inheritance of genes is called **genetics**. We will begin by looking at some characteristics that are affected by just one gene locus, and then consider some patterns of inheritance that may be seen when alleles found at two different gene loci interact with one another.

Single gene inheritance

You probably studied genetics at GCSE. If so, then this first section will be revision for you. However, it is very easy to get muddled in genetics so it is a good idea to work carefully through this again, as it will make sure you are on the right track and will eventually lead you to something new.

We will use the inheritance of **cystic fibrosis** as an example. This is a genetic disease in which abnormally thick mucus is produced in the lungs and other parts of the body. A person with cystic fibrosis is very prone to bacterial infections in the lungs because it is difficult for the mucus to be removed, allowing bacteria to breed in it.

Cystic fibrosis is caused by a faulty version of a gene that codes for the production of a protein called **CFTR**. The protein normally sits in the plasma membranes of cells in the lungs and other organs, where each protein molecule forms a channel that allows chloride ions to pass from inside the cell to the outside. The gene for CFTR is found on chromosome 7. It consists of about 250 000 bases. Mutations in this gene have produced several different alleles. The commonest of these is the result of the deletion of three bases. The CFTR protein made using this code is therefore missing one amino acid. The machinery in the cell recognises that this is not the right protein, and it does not place it in the plasma membrane.

This faulty allele is a **recessive allele**. The normal allele is a **dominant allele**. A recessive allele only has an effect on the phenotype when the dominant allele is not present. A dominant allele has an effect whether or not the recessive allele is present.

We can use symbols to represent these two alleles. Because they are alleles of the same gene, we should use the same letter to represent both of them. By convention, a capital letter is used to represent the dominant allele, and a small letter to represent the recessive allele. It is a good idea to choose letters where the capital and small letter look different, so that neither you nor an examiner is in any doubt about what you have written.

In this case, we will use the letter F for the allele coding for the normal CFTR protein, and the letter f for the allele coding for the faulty version.

Because we have two copies of each gene, there are three possible gene combinations – called **genotypes** – that may be present in any one person's cells. They affect the person's **phenotype** – their observable characteristics. The three possible genotypes are:

Genotype	Phenotype
FF	unaffected
Ff	unaffected
ff	cystic fibrosis

A genotype in which both alleles of a gene are the same is said to be **homozygous**. A genotype in which the alleles of a gene are different is **heterozygous**. FF and ff are homozygous, and Ff is heterozygous.

Inheritance of the *CFTR* gene

When gametes are made by meiosis, the daughter cells get only one copy of each pair of chromosomes. So they only contain one copy of each gene. A sperm or an egg can therefore contain only one allele of the *CFTR* gene.

Genotype of parent	Possible genotypes of their gametes
FF	all F
Ff	50% F and 50% f
ff	all f

At fertilisation, any gamete from the father can fertilise any gamete from the mother. We can show all of this by drawing a **genetic diagram**. This is a conventional way of showing the relative chances of a child of a certain genotype or phenotype being born to parents having a particular genotype or phenotype. The genetic diagram that follows shows the chances of a heterozygous man and a heterozygous woman having a child with cystic fibrosis.

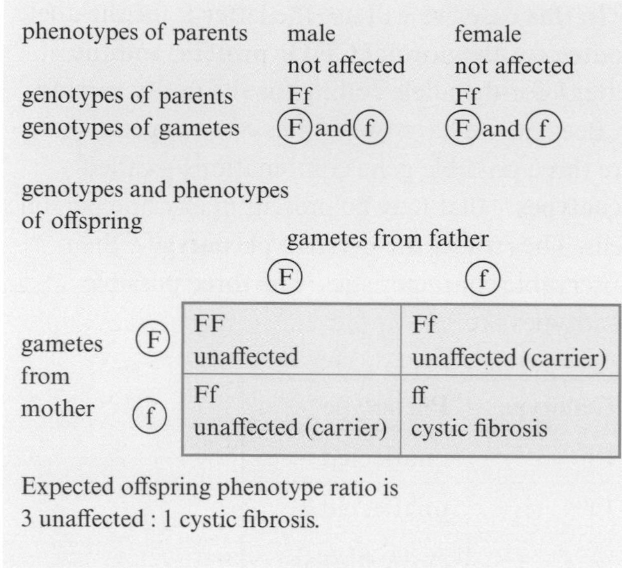

The genetic diagram shows that the phenotype ratio amongst the offspring is 3 unaffected : 1 affected. This means that every time the couple have a child, there is a 25% chance that the child will inherit the genotype FF and a 50% chance that it will inherit the genotype Ff. There is a 75% chance that the child will not have cystic fibrosis. The chance of the child inheriting the genotype ff and having cystic fibrosis is 25%.

Another way of expressing this is to say that the probability of the child *not* having cystic fibrosis is 0.75, while the probability of it having the disease is 0.25. This can also be stated as a probability of 1 in 4 that a child born to these parents will have this disease.

Yet another way of expressing this is to say that the expected ratio of children without cystic fibrosis to those with cystic fibrosis is 3 : 1.

SAQ

6 Explain what is wrong with each of these statements.

a 'A couple who are both carriers for cystic fibrosis will have four children, one with cystic fibrosis and three without.'

b 'If a couple's first child has cystic fibrosis, their second child will not have it.'

Answer

7 Copy and complete the genetic diagram to determine the chance of a heterozygous man and a woman with the genotype FF having a child with cystic fibrosis.

F is the normal allele; f is the cystic fibrosis allele

phenotypes of parents	male not affected	female not affected
genotypes of parents	Ff	FF
genotypes of gametes	(F) and (f)	all (F)

genotypes and phenotypes of offspring

	gametes from father ( )	( )
gametes from mother (F)		

Offspring phenotype ratio is ...

Chance of child with cystic fibrosis is ...

Answer

8 Explain why, in the genetic diagram you have drawn for SAQ 7, it is not necessary to show two gametes from the female parent.

Answer

The Hardy–Weinberg equations

In Britain, approximately one baby in 3300 is born with cystic fibrosis. What does this tell us about the frequency of the cystic fibrosis allele in the population? The Hardy–Weinberg equations allow this to be worked out.

In these equations, the letters p and q are always used to represent the frequency of the dominant allele and the recessive allele in the population respectively. So we can say:

p represents the frequency of allele F

q represents the frequency of allele f

The frequency of an allele can be anything between 0 and 1. If it is 0, then no-one has this allele. If it is 1, then it is the only allele of that gene in the population. If it is 0.5, then it makes up half of the alleles of that gene in the population. The other allele will make up the other half.

The first Hardy–Weinberg equation is:

$p + q = 1$

The second equation is a bit more complicated. It is:

$p^2 + 2pq + q^2 = 1$

where:

p^2 is the frequency of genotype FF

$2pq$ is the frequency of genotype Ff

q^2 is the frequency of genotype ff

Using these two equations, and our knowledge of the frequency of cystic fibrosis in the population, we can work out p and q (Worked example 1).

SAQ

9 Phenylketonuria, PKU, is a genetic disease caused by a recessive allele. About one in 15 000 people in a population are born with PKU. Use the Hardy–Weinberg equations to calculate the frequency of the PKU allele in the population. State the meaning of the symbols that you use, and show all your working.

Answer

Codominance

So far, we have looked at examples where one allele of a gene is recessive and another is dominant. The alleles controlling the ABO blood group phenotypes, and those responsible for sickle cell anaemia (Chapter 7), behave differently.

ABO blood group inheritance

Red blood cells contain a glycoprotein in their plasma membranes that determines the ABO blood group. There are two forms of this protein, known as antigens A and B. The gene that encodes this protein is on chromosome 9. It has three alleles, coding for antigen A, antigen B or no antigen at all.

The symbols for these alleles are written differently from those for CFTR.

Worked example 1

We know that 1 in 3300 babies are born with cystic fibrosis, and have the genotype ff. So:

$$q^2 = \frac{1}{3300}$$

$$= 0.0003$$

$$\text{so } q = \sqrt{0.0003}$$

$$= 0.017$$

We also know that

$$p + q = 1.$$

So:

$$p + 0.017 = 1$$

$$\text{so } p = 1 - 0.017$$

$$= 0.983$$

Now we can use this to work out how many people in the population are carriers for the cystic fibrosis allele, with the genotype Ff. We know that the frequency of this genotype is $2pq$ (see where we introduced the second equation). So:

$$\text{frequency of genotype Ff} = 2pq$$

$$= 2 \times 0.0983 \times 0.017$$

$$= 0.0334$$

This means that, out of every 100 people, 3.3 on average have the genotype Ff. In other words, about 1 in 30 people are carriers for the cystic fibrosis allele.

Each symbol includes the letter I to represent the gene locus. A superscript represents one particular allele.

I^A allele for antigen A
I^B allele for antigen B
I^o allele for no antigen

They are written like this because alleles I^A and I^B show **codominance**. They each have an effect when they are together. However, both I^A and I^B are dominant with respect to allele I^o, which is recessive. There are four possible phenotypes:

Genotype	Phenotype
$I^A I^A$	Group A
$I^A I^B$	Group AB
$I^A I^o$	Group A
$I^B I^B$	Group B
$I^B I^o$	Group B
$I^o I^o$	Group O

SAQ

10 Using the correct symbols, draw a complete and fully labelled genetic diagram to find the chance of a child with blood group O being born to a heterozygous man with blood group B and a heterozygous woman with blood group A.

Hint

Answer

Sex linkage

Genes whose loci are on the X or Y chromosomes (**sex chromosomes**) have different inheritance patterns from genes on all the other chromosomes (**autosomes**). Women have two X chromosomes, while men have one X and one Y.

The X chromosome is much larger than the Y chromosome. It has many genes that are not present on the Y. Most of these two chromosomes are therefore not homologous (Figure 8.7). These genes are said to be **sex-linked**, because their inheritance is affected by whether a person is male or female. If one of these genes has a recessive allele that causes a particular condition, then this condition is much more common in males than in females and, indeed, may not ever occur in females at all (Figure 8.8).

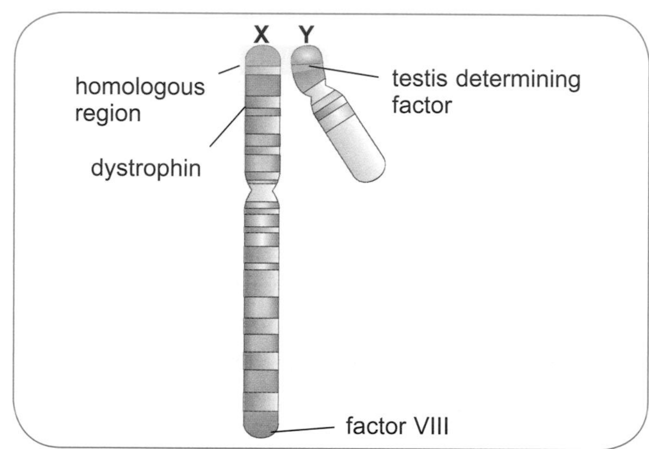

Figure 8.7 X and Y chromosomes showing the position of the gene for factor VIII.

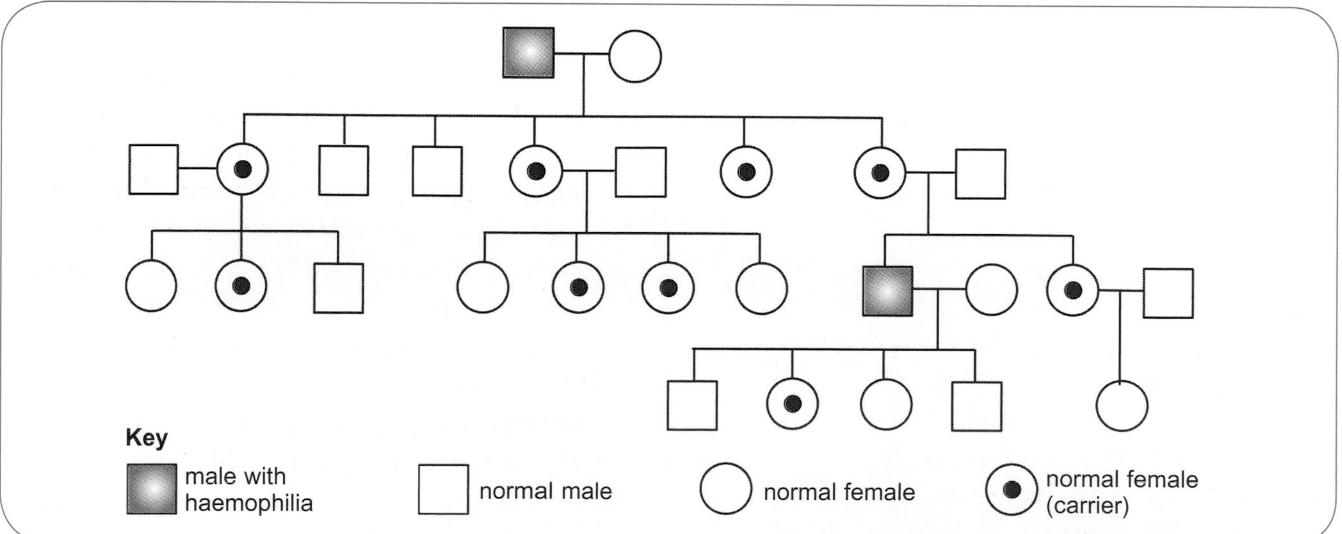

Figure 8.8 Pedigree for a sex-linked recessive disease, such as haemophilia.

One such gene determines the production of a factor that is needed to enable blood to clot, a protein called **factor VIII**. There is a recessive allele of this gene that codes for a faulty version of factor VIII. With this faulty version, blood does not clot properly, a condition called **haemophilia**. Bleeding occurs into joints and other parts of the body, which can be very painful and eventually disabling. Haemophilia can nowadays be treated by giving the person factor VIII throughout their life.

When writing symbols of genes carried on the X chromosome, they are written as superscripts. The symbol X^H can be used to stand for the normal allele, and X^h for the haemophilia allele.

In a woman, there are two X chromosomes, so a woman always has two factor VIII genes. Her possible genotypes and phenotypes are:

Genotype	Phenotype
X^HX^H	normal blood clotting
X^HX^h	normal blood clotting (but she is a carrier)
X^hX^h	lethal

A fetus with the genotype X^hX^h does not develop, so no babies are born with this genotype.

In a man, however, there is only one X chromosome present, so he can only have one allele of this gene. His possible genotypes and phenotypes are:

Genotype	Phenotype
X^HY	normal blood clotting
X^hY	haemophilia

The genetic diagram at top right shows how a woman who is a carrier for haemophilia, and a man who has normal blood clotting, can have a son with haemophilia.

SAQ

11 Explain why a man with haemophilia cannot pass it on to his son.

Answer

X^H is the normal allele; X^h is the haemophilia allele

	male	female
phenotypes of parents	normal clotting	normal clotting
genotypes of parents	X^HY	X^HX^h
genotypes of gametes	(X^H) and (Y)	(X^H) and (X^h)

genotypes and phenotypes of offspring

gametes from mother \ gametes from father	(X^H)	(Y)
(X^H)	X^HX^H normal female	X^HY normal male
(X^h)	X^HX^h normal (carrier) female	X^hY haemophiliac male

Expected offspring phenotype ratio is 3 normal : 1 haemophilia.

SAQ

12 The family tree shows the occurrence of a genetic condition known as brachydactyly (short fingers). Use the tree to deduce:

a whether the allele for this condition is dominant or recessive

b if this condition is sex-linked.

Explain your answers.

Answer

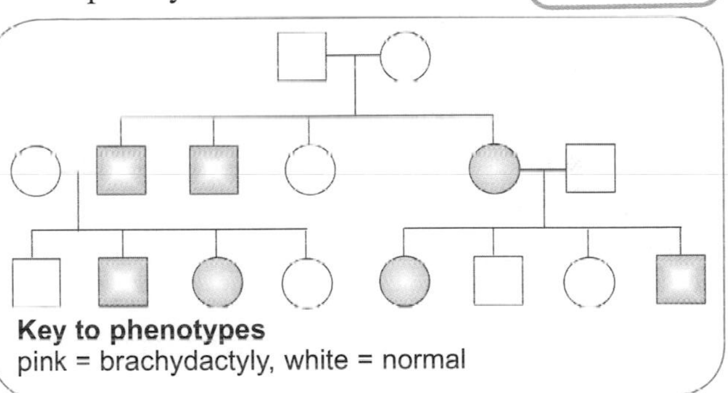

13 One of the genes for coat colour in cats is found on the X chromosome but not the Y. The allele C^O of this gene gives orange fur, while C^B gives black fur. The two alleles are codominant, and when both are present the cat has patches of orange and black, known as tortoiseshell.

a Explain why male cats cannot be tortoiseshell.

b Draw a genetic diagram to show the expected genotypes and phenotypes of the offspring from a cross between an orange male and a tortoiseshell female cat.

Answer

Dihybrid inheritance

Sometimes, we want to look at the inheritance of two genes at the same time. This is known as **dihybrid inheritance**.

We will begin by looking at the inheritance of two quite separate genes on different chromosomes, and then move on to **linkage**, in which the two genes are on the same chromosome.

Imagine that there is a gene on chromosome 4 that has two alleles, A and a. On chromosome 6 there is a different gene with two alleles B and b. Imagine that allele A, in the Rainbow family, codes for green ears and allele a for purple ears. Allele B codes for yellow hair and allele b codes for blue hair.

All the cells in the body have two complete sets of chromosomes. They will therefore have two chromosome 4s and two chromosome 6s, so they will have two copies of each gene. There are nine different genotypes that any one person could have, and four different phenotypes:

Genotype	Phenotype
AABB	green ears, yellow hair
AABb	green ears, yellow hair
AAbb	green ears, blue hair
AaBB	green ears, yellow hair
AaBb	green ears, yellow hair
Aabb	green ears, blue hair
aaBB	purple ears, yellow hair
aaBb	purple ears, yellow hair
aabb	purple ears, blue hair

When meiosis happens and gametes are made, only one copy of each gene goes into each gamete. So, if a man has the genotype AABB, all of his sperm will get one of the A alleles and one of the B alleles. If he has the genotype AaBB, half of his sperm will get allele A and the other half allele a, and they will all get allele B.

We saw on page 113 that independent assortment in meiosis I means that each pair of chromosomes behaves entirely independently. If these genes A/a and B/b are on different chromosomes, then either allele of one may find itself in a gamete with either allele of the other (Figure 8.9).

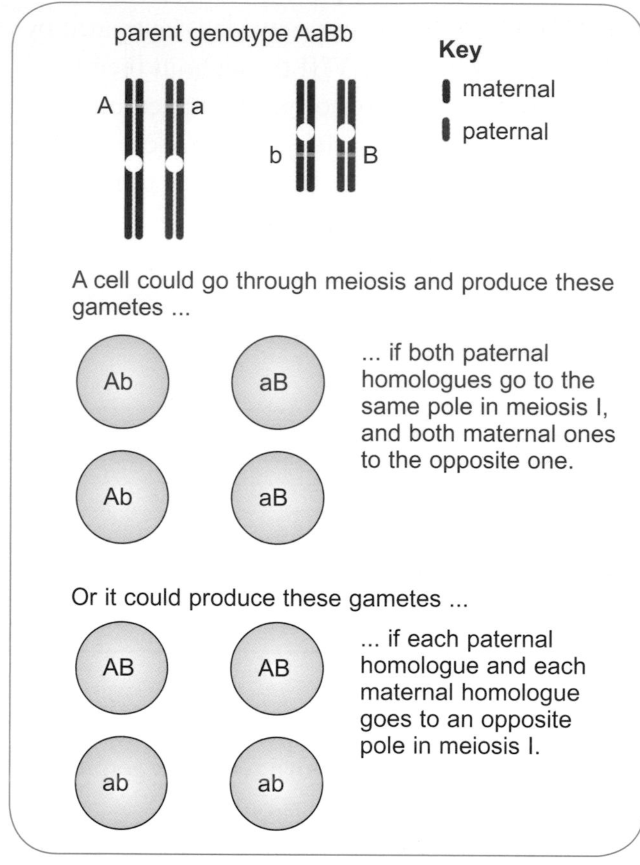

Figure 8.9 Independent assortment in dihybrid inheritance.

SAQ

14 Copy the two groups of four gametes in Figure 8.9 and draw the appropriate chromosomes inside each one. Answer

15 A woman has the genotype AAbb. What is the genotype of all the eggs that are made in her ovaries? Answer

16 A man has the genotype AABb. What are the possible genotypes that his sperm may have? Answer

We can work out the results of a dihybrid cross in just the same way as for a monohybrid cross, but showing the alleles of *both* genes. Notice that we always write the two alleles for one gene next to each other.

In the example shown below, both parents are heterozygous at both gene loci. The 9 : 3 : 3 : 1 ratio of phenotypes resulting from this cross is typical of a dihybrid cross between two parents who are both heterozygous at both gene loci.

A is the green ear allele; a the purple ear allele; B the yellow hair allele; b the blue hair allele

phenotypes of parents	green ears, yellow hair	green ears, yellow hair
genotypes of parents	Aa Bb	Aa Bb
genotypes of gametes	(AB) and (Ab) and (aB) and (ab)	(AB) and (Ab) and (aB) and (ab)

genotypes and phenotypes of offspring

gametes from mother	gametes from father: (AB)	(Ab)	(aB)	(ab)
(AB)	AABB green ears yellow hair	AABb green ears yellow hair	AaBB green ears yellow hair	AaBb green ears yellow hair
(Ab)	AABb green ears yellow hair	AAbb green ears blue hair	AaBb green ears yellow hair	Aabb green ears blue hair
(aB)	AaBB green ears yellow hair	AaBb green ears yellow hair	aaBB purple ears yellow hair	aaBb purple ears yellow hair
(ab)	AaBb green ears yellow hair	Aabb green ears blue hair	aaBb purple ears yellow hair	aabb purple ears blue hair

offspring phenotype ratio is:
9 green ears, yellow hair : 3 green ears, blue hair : 3 purple ears, yellow hair : 1 purple ears, blue hair

SAQ

17 A woman with cystic fibrosis has blood group A (genotype I^AI^o). Her partner does not have cystic fibrosis and is not a carrier for it. He has blood group O.

a Write down the genotypes of these two people.

b With the help of a full and correctly laid out genetic diagram, determine the possible genotypes and phenotypes of any children that they may have.

Answer

18 Tomato plants can have purple or green stems, and potato (smooth) or cut (jagged) leaves. Stem colour is controlled by gene A/a, where A is dominant and gives purple stem. Leaf shape is controlled by gene D/d, where D is dominant and gives cut leaves.
Use genetic diagrams to predict the ratios of phenotypes expected from each of the following crosses:

a a plant that is heterozygous at both loci with a plant that has green stems and potato leaves

b two plants that are heterozygous at both loci.

Answer

Autosomal linkage

Two genes that are both on the same chromosome tend to be inherited together. They do not show independent assortment. Genes on the same chromosomes are said to be **linked**. As this is different from sex linkage (in which you are usually just talking about one gene, which is present on the X chromosome) it is often referred to as **autosomal linkage**. (Remember that the autosomes are all the chromosomes except the sex chromosomes.)

An example in humans is the gene locus that determines ABO blood group and another that affects the development of fingernails and the kneecap (patella). These genes are both found on chromosome 9, and they are very close together (Figure 8.10).

These genes can cause a condition called **nail patella syndrome (NPS)**. The gene that affects the nails and patella codes for a protein that is involved in the development of limbs in the human embryo. Dominant alleles of these genes cause faults in the development of the nails and patella, in which the nails may not reach right to the end of the fingers, and the patella may not form correctly. There is also an increased risk of developing kidney disease.

During meiosis, when the homologous chromosomes separate, the blood group and nail patella alleles stay together, because they are on the same chromosome. Whatever the combination of alleles was in the parent cell, they nearly always stay in the same combination in the gametes that are formed.

So, when gametes are formed, the alleles do *not* assort independently. They stick together and stay in the same combinations as in the parent cell. The genetic diagram shows how blood group B and nail patella syndrome are inherited together.

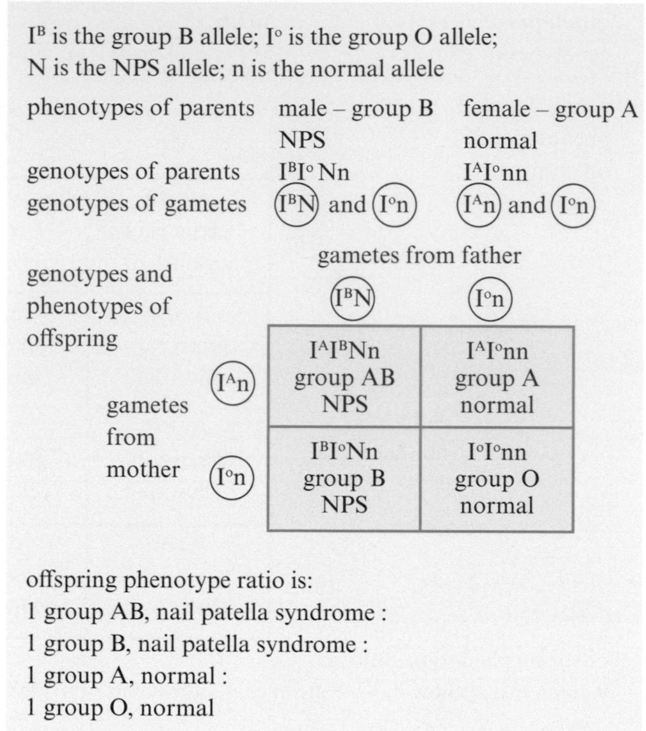

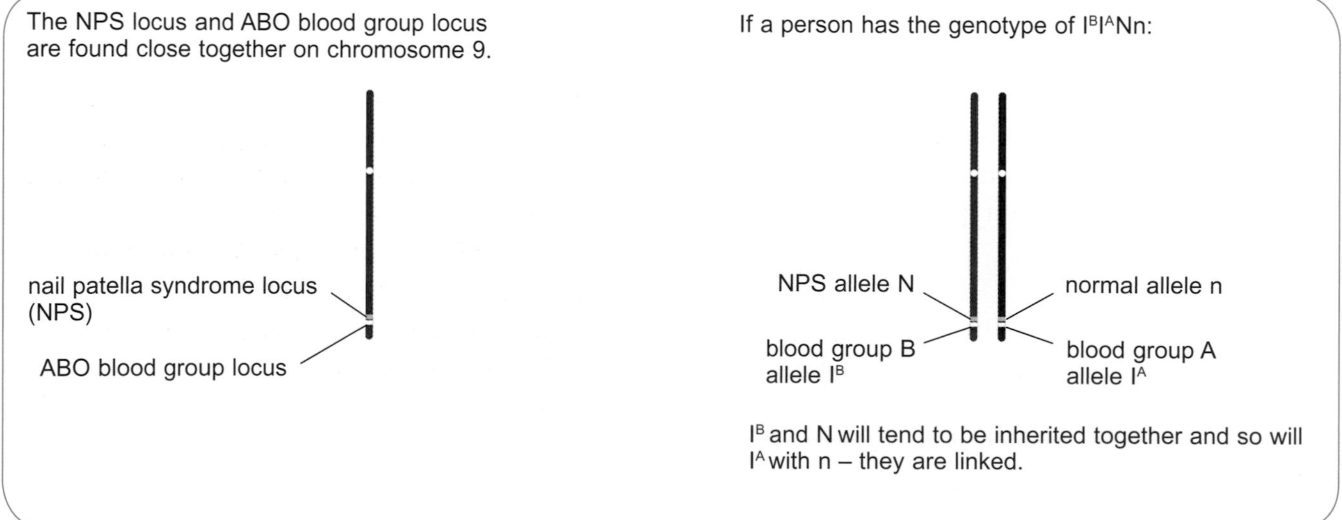

Figure 8.10 An example of autosomal linkage.

Crossing over

We have seen that the alleles of two different genes that are on the same chromosome are usually inherited together – they are linked. But this is not always the case.

If you look back at page 114, you will see that the chromatids of homologous chromosomes can cross over, break and rejoin during meiosis I. This swaps part of one chromatid with the equivalent part of a chromatid of the other chromosome in the pair (Figure 8.11). This mixes up the alleles so you can get different combinations in the gametes and therefore in the offspring.

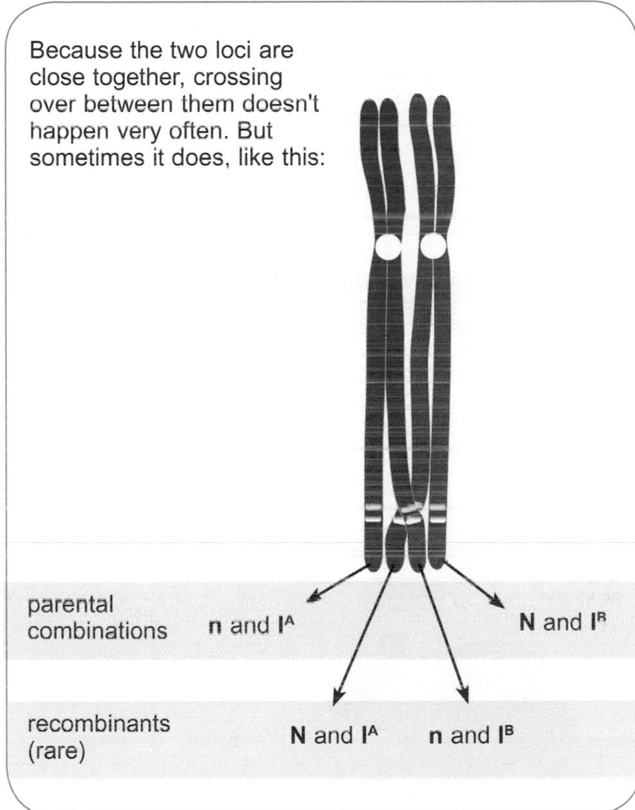

Figure 8.11 Crossing over.

For example, imagine a person who is blood group AB and has nail patella syndrome. The possible gametes they could produce are shown below.

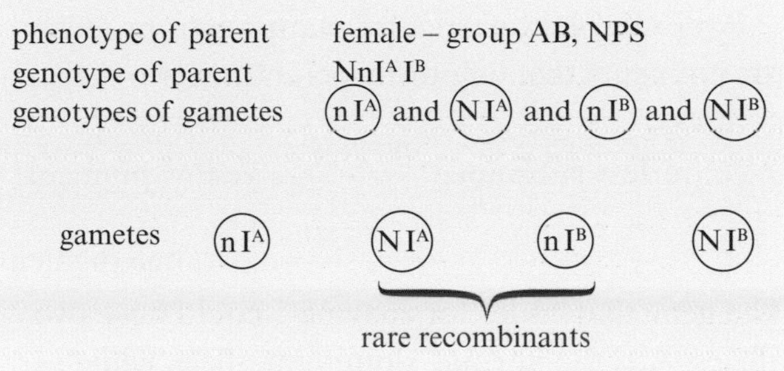

SAQ

19 The Rainbows only marry within the family. They have either yellow or blue hair, and either grey or orange toenails. The allele for yellow hair, Y, is dominant, as is the allele G, for grey toenails.

A man with the genotype YyGg has a partner who has the genotype yygg.

a Use a genetic diagram to find the possible genotypes and phenotypes of their offspring, if the two genes are on different chromosomes (i.e. they are not linked).

b Now construct another genetic diagram to find the possible genotypes and phenotypes of their offspring if the hair colour locus and the toenail colour locus are close together on the same chromosome.

Answer

20 In SAQ 19b, you worked out the possible genotypes and phenotypes of the offspring of a couple, assuming their genes for hair colour and toenail colour were always linked. Explain how crossing over could result in one of the children of this couple having a different combination of hair colour and toenail colour from either of their parents, even if the genes for these characteristics are linked.

Answer

Epistasis

Quite frequently, two different genes both affect the same characteristic. This is often because the two genes code for two enzymes that help to control the same metabolic pathway.

For example, a particular plant might produce the pigments that colour its petals in a two-step pathway:

$$\text{colourless substance} \xrightarrow{\textit{enzyme 1}} \text{yellow pigment} \xrightarrow{\textit{enzyme 2}} \text{orange pigment}$$

The gene that codes for enzyme 1 could have two alleles. A is the normal, dominant allele, while allele a does not produce a working enzyme. Similarly, B is the normal allele for enzyme 2, while b does not produce any enzyme 2.

Before the plant can produce any colour at all, it must have a working version of enzyme 1. So it must have at least one A allele. If it has the genotype aa, then it cannot produce any yellow pigment and its flowers will contain only the colourless substance and be white. It does not matter what alleles of the B/b gene it has, because there is no yellow pigment for them to work on in any case.

These are all the possible genotypes and phenotypes.

Genotype	Phenotype
AABB	orange
AABb	orange
AAbb	yellow
AaBB	orange
AaBb	orange
Aabb	yellow
aaBB	white
aaBb	white
aabb	white

You can see from this example that the genotype for one gene – the A/a gene – affects the expression of another quite separate gene – the B/b one. This situation is called **epistasis**.

Coat colour in animals is quite often determined by epistatic genes. Commonly, one gene determines whether there is any pigment produced at all, while another determines its pattern or precise colour. Obviously, the 'pattern' gene cannot have any effect unless there is some pigment there. In fact, the situation is often even more complicated than this, with many different genes all interacting to determine coat colour. You only have to look at all the different coat colours in cats and dogs to get an indication of this.

For example, the colours of 'wild type' and black mice are determined by a gene, A/a, which codes for the distribution of the pigment melanin in the hairs (Figure 8.12). The coat of a wild type mouse is made up of banded hairs, which produces a grey–brown colour called agouti. Allele A determines the presence of this banding. Allele a determines the uniform black colour of the hair of a black mouse.

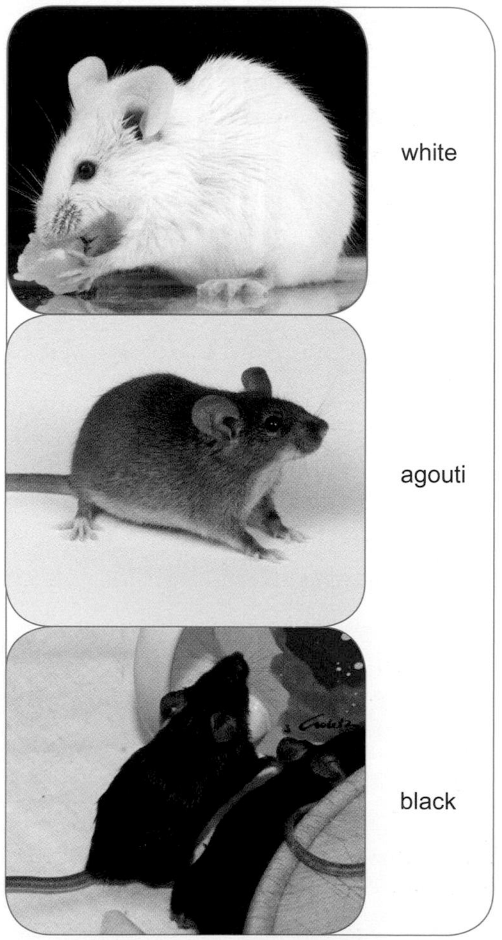

Figure 8.12 The coat colour of mice is controlled by epistatic genes.

A second gene, C/c, determines the production of melanin. The dominant allele C allows colour to develop, while a mouse with the genotype cc does not make melanin and so is albino.

SAQ

21 a List the three possible genotypes of each of the three mice in Figure 8.12.

b What would be the expected results of a cross between two agouti mice with genotypes AaCc? Hint

c Suggest how you could do a breeding experiment to determine if an agouti mouse was heterozygous for the C/c alleles. Answer

22 Feather colour in budgerigars is affected by many different genes.
One of these is the gene G/g, which determines whether the feathers are green or blue. Allele G is dominant and gives green feathers, while allele g gives blue feathers.
A second gene is C, which affects the intensity of the colouring. It has two codominant alleles, C^P which produces a pale colour and C^D which gives a dark colour.
The table shows the six colours produced by various combinations of the alleles of these two genes.

	Intensity of colour		
Colour	**pale**	**medium**	**dark**
green	light green	dark green	olive green
blue	sky blue	cobalt blue	mauve

a What is the genotype of:

i a dark green bird

ii a sky blue bird?

b Draw a genetic diagram to show the possible offspring produced from a cross between a dark green bird and a cobalt blue bird. Indicate the phenotype of each of the different genotypes produced in the cross. Answer

The chi-squared (χ^2) test

The results of the cross between two tomato plants which both have genotype AaDd (described in SAQ 18b), would be expected to show a 9 : 3 : 3 : 1 ratio of phenotypes in the offspring – 9 purple cut : 3 purple potato : 3 green cut : 1 green potato. It is very important to remember that this ratio is just a *probability*. We would be rather surprised if we got precisely this ratio amongst the offspring, just as you would not necessarily expect to get exactly five heads and five tails if you tossed a coin ten times.

But just how much difference might we be happy with, before we began to worry that the situation was not quite what we had thought? For example, let us imagine that the two plants produced a total of 144 offspring. If the parents really were both heterozygous, and if the purple stem and cut leaf alleles really are dominant, and if the alleles really do assort independently (that is, they are on different chromosomes and not linked) then we would expect the following numbers of each phenotype to be present in the offspring:

$$\text{purple, cut} = \frac{9}{16} \times 144 = 81$$

$$\text{purple, potato} = \frac{3}{16} \times 144 = 27$$

$$\text{green, cut} = \frac{3}{16} \times 144 = 27$$

$$\text{green, potato} = \frac{1}{16} \times 144 = 9$$

But imagine that, amongst these 144 offspring, the results we actually observed were as follows:

purple, cut 86
purple, potato 26
green, cut 24
green, potato 8

We might ask: are these results sufficiently close to the ones we expected that the differences between them have probably just arisen by chance? Or are they so different that something unexpected must be going on?

To answer these questions, we can use a statistical test called the **χ^2 (chi-squared) test**. This test allows us to compare our observed results with the expected results, and decide whether or not there is a significant difference between them.

The first stage in carrying out this test is to work out the expected results, as we have already done. These, and the observed results, are then recorded in a table like the one below. We then calculate the difference between observed and expected for each set of results, and square each difference. (Squaring it gets rid of any minus signs – it is irrelevant whether the differences are negative or positive.) Then we divide each squared difference by the expected value and add up all of these answers.

$$\chi^2 = \Sigma \frac{(O - E)^2}{E}$$

where Σ = the sum of

O = the observed value

E = the expected value

	Purple stems, cut leaves	Purple stems, potato leaves	Green stems, cut leaves	Green stems, potato leaves
Observed number, *O*	86	26	24	8
Expected number, *E*	81	27	27	9
$O - E$	+5	−1	−3	−1
$(O - E)^2$	25	1	9	1
$\frac{(O - E)^2}{E}$	0.31	0.04	0.33	0.11
$\Sigma \frac{(O - E)^2}{E} = 0.79$				
$\chi^2 = 0.79$				

So now we have our value for χ^2. Next we have to work out what it means.

To do this, we look in a table that relates χ^2 values to probabilities (Table 8.1). The table tells us *the probability that the differences between our expected and observed values are due to chance.*

For example, a probability of 0.05 means that we would expect these differences to occur in 5 out of every hundred experiments, or 1 in 20, just by chance. A probability of 0.01 means that we would expect them to occur in 1 out of every 100 experiments. For biological data, we usually take a probability of 0.05 as being the critical one. If our χ^2 value represents a probability of 0.05 or larger, then it is reasonable to assume that the differences between our observed and expected results may simply be due to chance – the differences between them are not **significant**. However, if our χ^2 value represents a probability smaller than this, then it is likely that the difference *is* significant, and we must reconsider our assumptions about what was going on in this cross.

Degrees of freedom	**Probability greater than**			
	0.1	**0.05**	**0.01**	**0.001**
1	2.71	3.84	6.64	10.83
2	4.60	5.99	9.21	13.82
3	6.25	7.82	11.34	16.27
4	7.78	9.49	13.28	18.46

Table 8.1 Table of χ^2 values.

There is one more aspect of our results to consider, before we can look up our value of χ^2 in the table. This is the number of **degrees of freedom** in our results. This takes into account the number of comparisons made. (Remember that to get our value of χ^2 we added up all our calculated values, so obviously the larger the number of observed and expected values we have, the larger χ^2 is likely to be. We need to compensate for this.) To work out the number of degrees of freedom, simply calculate: (number of classes of data – 1). Here we have four classes of data (the four possible phenotypes) so the number of degrees of freedom is 4 – 1 = 3.

Now, at last, we can look at the table to determine whether our results show a significant deviation from what we expected. The numbers in the body of the table are χ^2 values. We look at the third row in the table, because that is the one for 3 degrees of freedom, and find the χ^2 value that represents a probability of 0.05. You can see that this is 7.82. Our calculated value of χ^2 was 0.79. So our value is much, much smaller than the one we have read from the table. In fact, we cannot find anything like this number in the table – it would be way off the left-hand side, representing a probability of much more than 0.1 (1 in 10) that the difference in our results is just due to chance. So we can say that the difference between the observed and expected results could well be due to chance, and there is *no significant difference* between what we expected and what we actually got.

SAQ

23 The allele for grey fur in a species of mammal is dominant to white, and the allele for long tail is dominant to short.

a Using the symbols G and g for coat colour, and T and t for tail length, draw a genetic diagram to show the genotypes and phenotypes of the offspring you would expect from a cross between a pure-breeding (homozygous) grey animal with a long tail and a pure-breeding white animal with a short tail.

b If the first generation of offspring were bred together, what would be the expected phenotypes in the next generation, and in what ratios would you expect them to occur?

c In an actual cross between the animals in the first generation, the numbers of each phenotype obtained in the offspring were:

grey, long 54
grey, short 4
white, long 4
white, short 18

Use the χ^2 test to determine whether or not the difference between these observed results and the expected results is significant.

Answer

Variation

In *Biology 1*, Chapter 14, we saw that considerable variation can occur between organisms within a species. Some of this variation is caused by differences in their genes, and some by differences in their environments. The variation can be **discontinuous variation**, in which each organism falls into one of a few clear-cut categories (as for human blood groups, for example) or **continuous variation**, in which there are no definite categories but a continuous range of values between two extremes (as for human height).

Genes, environment and variation

In this chapter, we have seen how genes with different alleles can cause variation. In the examples we have used, this is discontinuous variation. For example, a person either has cystic fibrosis or they do not. Their blood group can be A, B, AB or O. A person has nail patella syndrome or they do not.

However, not all variation caused by genes is discontinuous. In some cases, where there are many genes at different loci, or many different alleles of a gene, there can be so many different possibilities that variation is effectively continuous. You can see that we came close to this situation with the budgerigar colours (page 125), where two genes each with two alleles help to determine colour. Although we can still place these colours into definite categories, you would only need another gene or two to be involved, or some more alleles of these same genes, for there to be so many different possible combinations of alleles that the variation in colour would be effectively continuous.

Genes can therefore produce continuous variation when:

- there are several different genes contributing towards a particular characteristic
- the genes affecting a characteristic have many different alleles.

When a characteristic is influenced by the combined effect of many genes, this is known as **polygenic** inheritance. Polygenic characteristics tend to show continuous variation and a normal distribution (*Biology 1*, page 220).

To illustrate this, we can consider the variation that can be produced with just two genes, each with two codominant alleles. This is not really polygenic inheritance, which requires at least three genes, but it will give you the idea of how things work, without getting too complicated.

Imagine that these genes help to determine a person's blood pressure. Let's say that allele A^M contributes 4 units to blood pressure, while allele A^N contributes 1. Allele B^R contributes 6 units, while allele B^S contributes 2. If the 'basic' blood pressure is 100 units, then the possible blood pressures are:

Genotype	Phenotype
$A^MA^MB^RB^R$	100 + 4 + 4 + 6 + 6 = 120 units
$A^MA^MB^RB^S$	100 + 4 + 4 + 6 + 2 = 116 units
$A^MA^MB^SB^S$	100 + 4 + 4 + 2 + 2 = 112 units
$A^MA^NB^RB^R$	100 + 4 + 1 + 6 + 6 = 117 units
$A^MA^NB^RB^S$	100 + 4 + 1 + 6 + 2 = 113 units
$A^MA^NB^SB^S$	100 + 4 + 1 + 2 + 2 = 109 units
$A^NA^NB^RB^R$	100 + 1 + 1 + 6 + 6 = 114 units
$A^NA^NB^RB^S$	100 + 1 + 1 + 6 + 2 = 110 units
$A^NA^NB^SB^S$	100 + 1 + 1 + 2 + 2 = 106 units

If this amount of variation can be produced with just two genes, each with just two alleles, it is not difficult to see that more genes with more alleles can produce an immense range. You might like to work out for yourself what variation you could expect to obtain with a truly polygenic example, where a third gene C has alleles C^T and C^U contributing 3 and 0 units respectively.

There are many human characteristics that are influenced by a large number of genes, each having a small effect. The tendency towards obesity is one example. The environment also often contributes towards these characteristics. Obesity, for example, is also affected by what we eat and how much exercise we do.

Variation and natural selection

In Chapter 14 in *Biology 1*, we saw how genetic variation is the basis on which natural selection acts. In a population, there will be a range of different alleles present for many of the genes. This set of alleles is called the **gene pool** of the population. Each individual can have any combination of the alleles in the gene pool, producing variation.

Where individuals within a species vary, it is likely that some forms will be more likely to survive than others. These are the ones that have the best chances of breeding and passing on their alleles to their offspring. Over time, the alleles that confer an advantage become more common in the population, while disadvantageous alleles become less common or even disappear completely.

Most of the time, in most populations, the individuals are already well adapted to their environment. The alleles present in the population are the ones that confer the most advantageous characteristics. If the environment remains fairly stable, then the same alleles will be selected for in every successive generation. Nothing changes. This is called **stabilising selection** (Figure 8.13).

However, if there is a change in the environment, this might result in a change in the selection pressures on the population. A variation that previously was not advantageous may begin to confer better survival value than another, resulting in **directional (evolutionary) selection** (Figure 8.13). Or perhaps a completely new, advantageous variation arises, by mutation. The change in the environment, or the appearance of a new allele, can bring about a change in the genetically determined characteristics of subsequent generations of the species, which we call **evolution**. We have seen this happen recently as bacteria have evolved to become resistant to antibiotics.

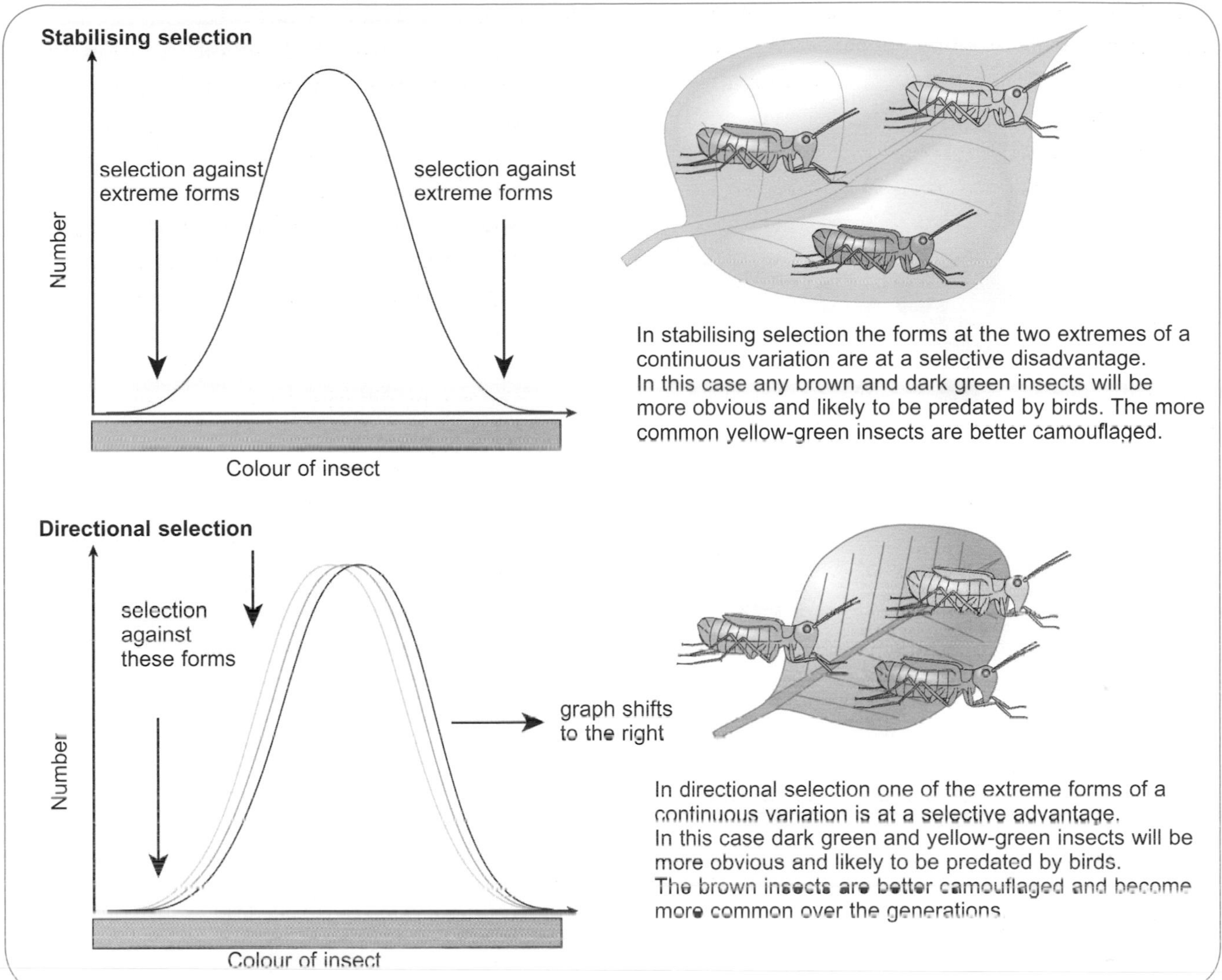

Figure 8.13 Stabilising and directional selection.

Genetic drift

Evolutionary change is not always the result of natural selection. Sometimes it appears to happen simply by chance.

This is most likely in a small population. If there are only a few individuals, and selection pressures are not very strong, then just by chance one or two individuals may have better breeding success than others. Over time, their alleles become more common in the population while other alleles, that just happened to be present only in individuals that were unlucky and did not have offspring, are lost. There is a change in the gene pool and characteristics within the population, and this change has occurred by chance, rather than as the result of natural selection. This is called **genetic drift**. Genetic drift can cause lasting changes in a gene pool, for no apparent reason other than chance.

Genetic drift is thought to happen relatively frequently in populations on islands, because they may be made up of quite a small number of individuals, and are geographically separated from other members of their species (Figure 8.14). It might help to explain, for example, why rabbits on offshore islands around Britain are more likely to have black or white coats than wild rabbits on the mainland. Many isolated islands have their own endemic species of plants and animals that are found nowhere else, and genetic drift has probably played a significant role in the evolution of many of them.

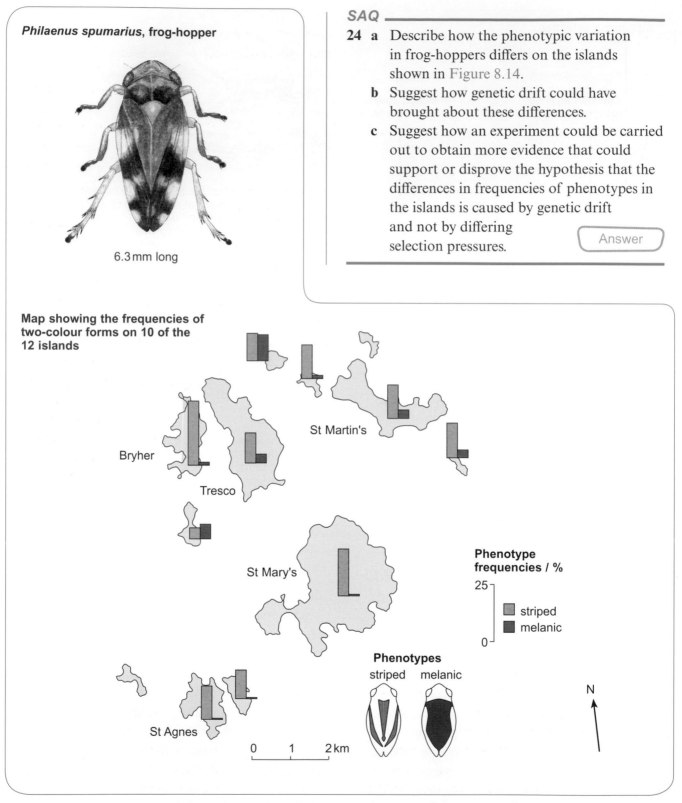

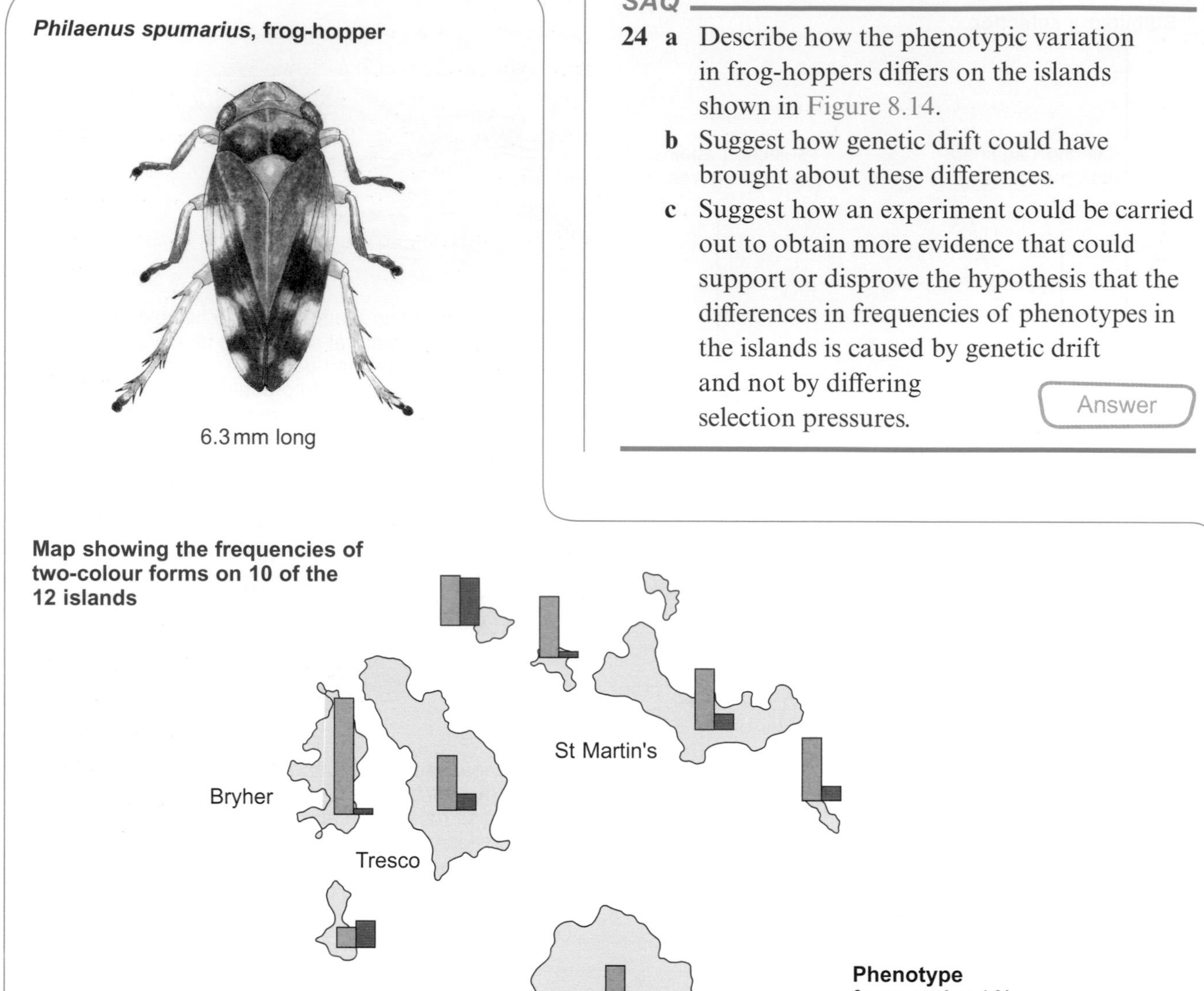

SAQ

24 a Describe how the phenotypic variation in frog-hoppers differs on the islands shown in Figure 8.14.

b Suggest how genetic drift could have brought about these differences.

c Suggest how an experiment could be carried out to obtain more evidence that could support or disprove the hypothesis that the differences in frequencies of phenotypes in the islands is caused by genetic drift and not by differing selection pressures.

Answer

Figure 8.14 The colours of the common frog-hopper are determined by seven different alleles of a single gene. The range of colours and their frequencies, on different islands in the Isles of Scilly, are very variable, almost certainly as a result of genetic drift rather than because there are different selection pressures on different islands.

Speciation

Speciation is the formation of a new species. In *Biology 1*, we saw that it is not easy to define exactly what we mean by a species, but one generally accepted definition is that it is a group of organisms, with similar morphology and physiology, which can interbreed with one another to produce fertile offspring. (This is discussed in more detail in *Biology 1* pages 227–228.) So, to produce a new species from an existing one, some of the individuals must:

- become morphologically or physiologically different from the members of the original species
- no longer be able to breed with the members of the original species to produce fertile offspring.

The splitting apart of this 'splinter group' from the rest of the species is known as **isolation**. Sometimes, the organisms are separated by a physical barrier, such as a mountain range or river, and this is called **geographical isolation**. However, it is not until the two groups are so different from each that they can no longer interbreed that they are said to show **reproductive isolation**, and have become different species. There is no gene flow between two different species – each is effectively genetically isolated from the other.

Examples of isolating mechanisms

In *Biology 1*, we saw that speciation is thought often to begin when a geographical barrier separates two populations of a species. The two groups then evolve along different lines, either because of different selection pressures in the two geographically separated areas, or because of genetic drift. If the barrier then breaks down and the two populations come together again, they may have changed so much that they can no longer interbreed, and can be said to be two different species.

What is it that prevents the two groups breeding, even when they are living in the same place? There are many different factors that can prevent interbreeding between two closely related species. One way of classifying them is to group them into **ecological**, **temporal** and **reproductive barriers**.

Ecological barriers

Two species may live in the same area at the same time, yet rarely meet. You have already met one example – the apple and hawthorn flies, *Rhagoletis pomonella*, which live on apple or hawthorn trees and do not interbreed because they do not meet (*Biology 1*, page 227). At the moment, these are still classified as the same species, but there is a strong case for the argument that they are already reproductively isolated from one another and so could be said to be different species.

Another example involves two different species of crayfish, *Orconectes virilis* and *Orconectes immunis*, which both live in freshwater habitats in North America (Figure 8.15). They look very similar to one another, but whilst *O. virilis* lives in streams and lake margins, *O. immunis* lives in ponds and swamps. They rarely meet and do not interbreed. It seems that *O. virilis* is less good at digging than *O. immunis*, and cannot easily burrow into the mud when a pond dries up, so it is less able to survive summer drying than *O. immunis*. *O. immunis* is able to live perfectly well in the lakes and streams where *O. virilis* lives, but *O. virilis* is more aggressive and drives *O. immunis* out of crevices where it tries to shelter.

Figure 8.15 **a** *Orconectes virilis*. **b** *Orconectes immunis*, sometimes called the nail polish crayfish.

Temporal barriers

Two species may live in the same place and even share the same habitat, but not interbreed because they are not active at the same time of day, or do not reproduce at the same time of year. For example, the spectacular flowering shrubs *Banksia attenuata* and *Banksia menziesii* both live in the same area of Western Australia (Figure 8.16) . *B. attenuata* flowers in summer, but *B. menziesii* flowers in winter, so they cannot interbreed.

Figure 8.16 **a** *Banksia attenuata*. **b** *Banksia menziesii*.

Reproductive barriers

Even if two species share the same habitat and are reproductively active at the same time, they still may not interbreed successfully. There are many ways in which this can be prevented. They include:

- different courtship behaviour, so that individuals of the two species are not stimulated to mate with each other (Figure 8.17) – they may make different movements, or sing different songs
- mechanical problems with mating – for example, one may be much smaller than the other or have different shapes or sizes of reproductive organs
- gamete incompatability, so that even if mating takes place successfully the sperm cannot fertilise an egg
- zygote inviability, so that even if a zygote is produced it dies
- hybrid sterility, so that even if a zygote develops successfully, the resulting hybrid cannot produce gametes and so cannot reproduce.

Figure 8.17 A mallard drake will only mate with a female who displays appropriate courtship behaviour. **a** A pair of mallards displaying to one another. **b** Although a pintail female looks very like a mallard female, her courtship behaviour will only interest a pintail male.

The species concept

The definition of a species that we gave on page 131 involves reproductive isolation between two groups. This is sometimes known as the **biological species concept**. The biological species concept is a useful one in trying to work out how new species can evolve. However, it has one major limitation – it can only be used for organisms that reproduce sexually. We cannot use it to determine whether groups of asexually reproducing organisms belong to the same or different species. Nor can we use it to classify extinct organisms that are only known as fossils, old bones or skins.

But we do still classify all organisms into a particular species. Each species is given a unique binomial, a name made up of its genus and its species – for example, *Homo sapiens*. Even organisms that do not reproduce sexually, or where we don't know enough about them to determine whether or not they can interbreed with other species, are classified in this way. Biologists use a variety of different methods to decide whether two groups of organisms belong to the same species or to different ones, often largely based on their morphology. The species taxon can be used even when we cannot apply the biological species concept to a group of organisms.

For example, birds that are clearly very closely related in an evolutionary sense, but live in different parts of the world and have different colouring, may be classified as different species even if nothing is known about whether they are able to breed together. This way of using the term 'species' is sometimes known as the **phylogenetic (evolutionary) species concept**. It is based on the fact that we can clearly see a difference between the two groups – we can tell them apart – and we are certain that they must have evolved from a common ancestor. We do not need to know how *far* they have evolved from one another. It is enough to know that they are clearly two distinct groups each with their own distinctive characteristics.

Using the phylogenetic species concept often means that many more groups are classified as separate species than if we restricted ourselves to using the strict biological species concept. Conservationists sometimes make use of this to make their case stronger. For example, using the biological species concept there are 101 bird species that are endemic to Mexico (that is, are found there and nowhere else). Using the phylogenetic species concept, there are 249.

So which is the better concept to use – the biological species concept, or the phylogenetic species concept? Most biologists would say that it depends on what you are using it for. The biological species concept gives a clear-cut definition, which can be applied rigorously and in the same way for different groups of organisms. But it is limited because it can only be used for sexually reproducing organisms and because we often don't have enough information to determine whether or not there is complete reproductive isolation. The phylogenetic species concept is not so rigorous, so that different people might make different decisions about whether particular groups of organisms are species or not. But it does at least allow us to make a decision, which we might not be able to do at all if we stuck rigidly to the biological species concept.

Artificial selection

People have been breeding animals and plants for their own purposes for thousands of years. On pages 152–155 in *Biology 1* we saw how **artificial selection** is used to produce varieties of bread wheat, *Triticum aestivum*, with desirable characteristics. The principles are very simple – the 'best' individuals are chosen to breed with each other, while the ones with less useful characteristics are not allowed to breed. The offspring are therefore likely to inherit some of the 'good' characteristics from their parents. If this continues generation after generation, then over time the desired characteristics become prevalent.

This, of course, only works if the desired characteristics are determined by genes, and not by environment. Despite the rapid increase in knowledge of DNA sequences and gene mapping in different species, in most cases we still do not know exactly which alleles of which genes contribute towards the characteristics we wish to breed for. For example, milk production in cows is probably affected by many different genes as well as by environment. We do not know what all of these genes are, let alone the alleles of them that lead to greatest milk production. The greatest advantage of using artificial selection to increase the performance of a breed of cattle is that we don't *need* to know this – we simply choose the cows with the highest milk production to breed, and there is a good chance that the alleles they possess will be passed on to their offspring.

Artificial selection is very like natural selection, in that individuals with 'advantageous' characteristics are more likely to breed and pass on their alleles to the next generation. The big difference is that in artificial selection we choose those characteristics. We often choose just one – for example, high milk yield – and ignore all others, such as resistance to disease or the ability to manage on a sparse diet – that might also be selected for in the wild. So, whereas natural selection tends to produce populations that are well-adapted to their environment in many different ways, artificial selection often produces populations that show one characteristic to an extreme – for example, very high milk yields – while other characteristics are retained that would be positively disadvantageous in a natural situation.

An example of this is shown by the results of a breeding experiment that was carried out with Holstein cattle in the USA (Figure 8.18). A large number of cows were used, and split into two groups. In the first group, only the cows that produced the highest milk yields were allowed to breed, and they were fertilised with sperm from bulls whose female relatives also produced high milk yields. This was called the 'selection line'. The second group was a control, in which all the cows were allowed to breed, and they were fertilised with sperm from bulls chosen more randomly. The selection was carried out in each generation for 25 years. All the cattle were kept in identical conditions and fed identical food. The results are shown in Figure 8.19 and Table 8.2.

The graph in Figure 8.19 shows the large increase in milk yield that was produced in the selection line. The results for the control line show that this increase must be due to the differences in the genes in the two groups, because environmental conditions were the same for both. It is interesting to see that the milk yield in the control line actually went down. Why could this be? Perhaps there is a selective *disadvantage* to having high milk yields, so that the cows with lower milk yields were more likely to have more offspring, all other factors being equal. Or perhaps this is just the result of random variation, or genetic drift.

The data in Table 8.2 support the hypothesis that very high milk yields would be disadvantageous in a natural situation.

Health costs for every kind of ailment were greater in the selection line than in the control line. Again, we don't know exactly why this is, but we can make informed guesses. Mastitis is inflammation of the udder, in which the milk is produced and carried. Larger quantities of milk in the udder could easily make it more likely to become inflamed. Heavier udders could also put

Figure 8.18 **a** Holstein cows grazing on pasture. **b** Holstein cows have been bred to produce large volumes of milk each day, which has to be carried in their enlarged udders between milking.

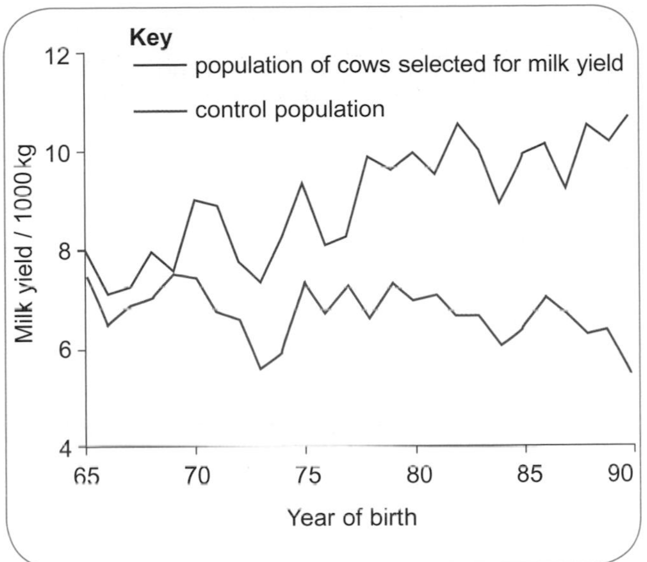

Figure 8.19 Graph showing the results of selection for milk yield in Holstein cattle between 1965 and 1990.

Health costs per year	Selection line / $	Control line / $
mastitis	43	16
ketosis and milk fever	22	12
reproductive	18	13
lameness	10	6
respiratory	4	1

Table 8.2 Health costs in the selection line and control line of Holstein cattle.

more strain on legs, so increasing the incidence of lameness. Perhaps, also, there are alleles that confer a greater likelihood of suffering these conditions and these were inadvertently selected for along with the selection for high milk yields.

Maximising breeding success

Various techniques in cattle breeding make it possible for chosen cows and bulls to produce more offspring than would be possible if they bred naturally.

Artificial insemination, generally known as AI, involves collecting semen from a chosen bull and then using it to inseminate cows. It is very widely used by farmers all over the world. The semen ejaculated on one occasion would, in natural conditions, fertilise just one cow. With AI, a large number of cows can be inseminated using sperm from a single ejaculation. The sperm can be frozen and kept for long periods before use. It can easily be transported over long distances. In this way, a high-quality bull can breed with a very large number of cows, over a long period of time and in many different parts of the world.

The bull may have been selected through **progeny testing**. His female offspring are scored according to the degree to which they show the desired characteristics – such as high milk yield. This, of course, will not be known until these offspring have grown to maturity, which can involve a wait of almost two years after fertilisation took place. This is another good reason for freezing and storing semen – farmers can wait until the characteristics of a bull's daughters are known, before choosing to use his semen in their own breeding programmes.

Embryo transplantion is much less commonly used than AI. Embyro transplants increase the number of offspring that can be produced by one cow. A cow with the desired characteristics can be treated with reproductive hormones to make her superovulate – that is, to produce a large number of eggs. She is then artificially inseminated with sperm from the chosen bull, and fertilisation takes place in her oviducts. The resulting embryos are then washed out of her uterus.

These embryos can then be transferred into the uteruses of a number of other, less valuable, cows. These cows will have been treated with reproductive hormones to ensure that their uteruses are ready to receive an embryo. The embryos develop normally and are born in the usual way.

To increase the number of embryos even more, it is possible to divide them before they are implanted into the surrogate mother. One embryo can give rise to two or more, which of course will be genetically identical with one another. Embryos can even be frozen and kept for quite long periods of time, for later use.

SAQ

25 The table shows the changes in milk yield and nutrient content in a herd of Jersey cattle in which artificial selection for high yields of high-quality milk was carried out. The figures in the table are the mean results per cow for one year.

a Display these results as line graphs.

b Calculate the mean change in milk yield per year over the 10-year period of the breeding experiment.

c Describe the trends in the nutrient content of the milk over the 10-year period.

d Discuss the welfare issues associated with selective breeding programmes such as this.

Answer

Year	Milk yield per cow / kg	Total protein content / kg	% protein content	Total fat content / kg	% fat content
1989	4104	157.5	3.83	221.6	5.40
1990	4104	157.6	3.84	221.8	5.40
1991	4123	158.4	3.84	223.6	5.42
1992	4151	159.3	3.84	224.7	5.41
1993	4182	160.2	3.83	225.9	5.40
1994	4245	162.2	3.82	228.1	5.37
1995	4281	163.0	3.81	229.0	5.35
1996	4311	164.3	3.81	230.7	5.35
1997	4370	166.2	3.80	233.8	5.35
1998	4412	167.4	3.79	235.1	5.33
1999	4470	169.3	3.79	237.6	5.32

Summary

Glossary

- Meiosis is a type of nuclear division that produces genetically different haploid cells from a diploid cell. There are two divisions. During the first, homologous chromosomes pair up and separate, often exchanging pieces of chromatids at chiasmata. During the second, each chromosome is separated into two chromatids.
- Meiosis produces genetic variation through crossing over and independent assortment of chromosomes during the first division. Fertilisation between gametes with different combinations of alleles also introduces variation.
- A gene for a particular characteristic is found at a specific locus on a chromosome. In a diploid cell, there are two copies of each gene. Different varieties of a gene are called alleles. An organism with two alleles that are the same is homozygous, and one with two different alleles is heterozygous. Dominant alleles have an effect on the phenotype whether or not a recessive allele is present, but recessive alleles only have an effect when the dominant allele is not present. Codominant alleles both have an effect in a heterozygous organism.
- The Hardy–Weinberg equations allow us to calculate the frequency of two alternative alleles in a population.
- There are numerous genes on the X chromosome that are not present on the Y chromosome. These are said to be sex-linked genes. In mammals, a male has only one copy, and so is more likely to show the recessive trait.
- Two genes that are on two different chromosomes assort independently. However, if they are on the same chromosome they tend to be inherited together and are said to be linked.
- Some characteristics are affected by two different genes. This is called epistasis.

continued

- If the results obtained in a cross do not exactly match the results that were predicted, we can check the significance of the difference between them using the χ^2 test. The value obtained tells us the likelihood that the difference is due purely to chance. In biology, we normally take a probability of 0.05 or larger as meaning we can accept the difference as due to chance, and that we can accept the hypothesis on which the expected results were calculated.
- Genes and the environment both affect phenotype, and are responsible for variation between organisms of the same species. Discontinuous variation occurs when the phenotype is caused by a small number of genes with a small number of alleles. Continuous variation can be caused by a large number of genes (polygenes) or genes with a large number of alleles, or may be caused by an interaction between genotype and environment.
- The gene pool of a population is all the alleles of all the genes present in it. Through interbreeding, all these alleles are available to be passed on to the next generation. If some alleles produce characteristics that confer a selective advantage, then organisms that possess them are more likely to survive and breed, so these alleles have a relatively high chance of being passed on to the next generation. This is called natural selection.
- Generally, when a population is already well adapted to its environment, natural selection keeps the relative proportions of alleles in the population fairly constant from generation to generation. This is called stabilising selection. However, if the environment changes so that selection pressures change, or if a new allele appears through mutation or immigration of an individual from another population, then natural selection may produce a change in allele frequency. This is called directional or evolutionary selection.
- In small populations, chance may determine which alleles are passed on and which are not. This is called genetic drift.
- Speciation is the formation of new species. It involves isolation of two or more populations, by geographical features, differences in their ecology, differences in the times of day or seasons at which they are reproductively active, or difficulties in interbreeding.
- The biological species concept defines a species as a group of organisms that are morphologically and physiologically similar, and that cannot breed with other groups to produce fertile offspring. This can only be determined for species that reproduce sexually. The phylogenetic species concept has a less rigorous definition, in which observable differences between two groups living in different parts of the world are sufficient for them to be classified as different species. Both concepts are useful in different situations.
- Artificial selection is carried out by humans to produce varieties of organisms that have features humans desire. It differs from natural selection in that it often selects for a single feature to be at its highest or lowest value. Other features are ignored or given little weight in the choice of which organisms are allowed to breed together.

Stretch and challenge question

1 Discuss the ways in which genetic variation can arise in sexual reproduction. Hint

Questions

1 a The following are different stages in meiosis. Each stage has been given a letter.

anaphase II	metaphase II	anaphase I	prophase I	telophase II	metaphase I
M	N	P	Q	R	S

i Using <u>only</u> the letters, arrange these stages in the correct sequence. [1]

ii State the letter of the stage when each of the following processes occur.

- pairing of chromosomes
- centromeres divide
- crossing over
- bivalents align on equator
- nuclear membrane reforms [5]

iii State <u>two</u> processes that occur in a cell during interphase to prepare for a meiotic division. [2]

b Haemophilia A is a sex-linked genetic disease which results in the blood failing to clot properly. It is caused by a recessive allele on the X chromosome. The diagram shows the occurrence of haemophilia in one family.

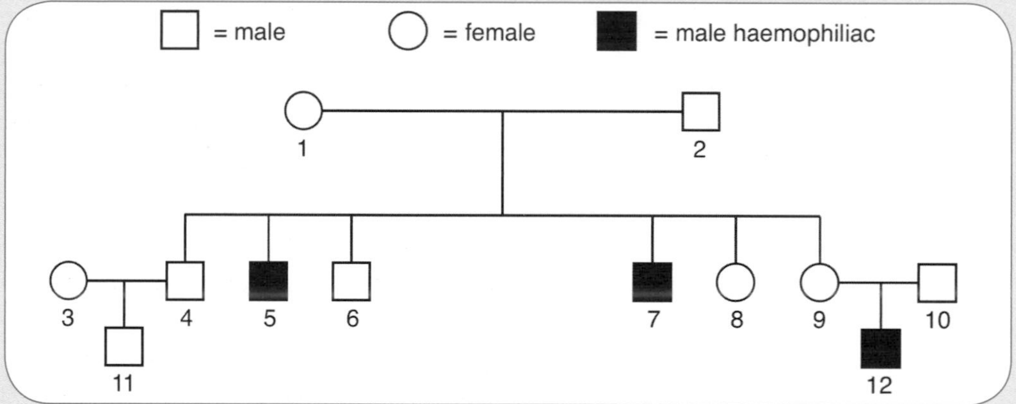

i Using the following symbols:
H = dominant allele h = recessive allele
state the genotypes of the following individuals. The first one has been completed for you.

individual	**genotype**
1	X^HX^h
2	....
5	....
6	....
9	....

[4]

ii State the probability of individual 8 being a carrier of haemophilia. [1]

iii Explain why only females can be carriers of haemophilia. [2]

OCR Biology A (2804) June 2006 [Total 15]

Answer

Chapter 9

Cloning in plants and animals

e-Learning

Objectives

Cloning is the production of genetically identical organisms. Many plants do this naturally, when they reproduce asexually. For example, strawberry plants put out runners, from which new plants grow (Figure 9.1). The cells that form the new plant have all been produced by mitosis, from cells that were originally part of the parent plant. The new plants therefore have exactly the same DNA as the parent plant. They are all genetically identical to the parent, and to each other.

Vegetative propagation

Asexual reproduction in plants is often known as **vegetative propagation**. Commercial plant growers often produce plants by vegetative propagation because it produces genetically identical plants. If the parent plant has a particular set of genetically determined features – size, colour, hardiness and so on – then the offspring will all have them too. Barring mutation, vegetative propagation does not introduce any genetic variation into the population. It is the only way in which most named varieties of a plant species, such as a named rose, can be propagated (Figure 9.2).

The lack of genetic variation that results from vegetative reproduction can also be advantageous to plants reproducing naturally. If a particular individual is well adapted to its environment and doing well, then any offspring produced vegetatively will inherit these same features and will also stand a good chance of surviving in that habitat. Vegetative propagation often produces many plants that remain close to the parent, so they may form a dense population. In contrast, sexual reproduction in plants produces genetically variable seeds, and these are often dispersed to considerable distances from the parent plant. This can be of value in allowing the plant to colonise new areas, perhaps with environmental conditions that differ from those in which the parent plant lives. If the seeds have different combinations of alleles, then there is a chance that a new variant will find itself in a place where its particular characteristics are well suited to the new environment.

English elm trees, *Ulmus procera*, have done very well in the UK using only vegetative propagation

Figure 9.1 Strawberry plants produce long stems called runners that grow sideways across the ground. New roots and shoots grow from the stems at several points along the runner. Eventually these become new, genetically identical strawberry plants.

Figure 9.2 To produce large numbers of identical roses of the same variety, growers use vegetative propagation.

(Figure 9.3). They were first introduced by the Romans, around 2000 years ago. They used wood from the tree for supporting grape vines from which they made wine. They may have chosen this strain of elms because it did not produce seeds, and therefore did not cause problems by producing young seedlings that had to be weeded out. The elm propagates itself only by **suckering**, the growth of new trees from the roots of the parent (Figure 9.4). Only mitosis is involved, and so the new suckers are genetically identical to the parent. DNA analysis has shown that all English elms are almost entirely identical to each other, and to a strain of elms that grows in Spain – where they were also used for vine-training by the Romans. It seems that all English elms are derived from a single clone, which the Romans transported from Italy first to Spain and then to the UK.

Figure 9.3 The English elm, *Ulmus procera*.

Roots from the parent tree spread out near the surface of the soil.
Stems (suckers) grow from these roots. In time, these can form new trees.

Figure 9.4 English elms do not produce seeds, and can only reproduce vegetatively by growing suckers.

English elms spread throughout England and became an important part of the landscape. However, you will have to search very hard now to find a mature one. In the late 1960s a new disease began to attack these trees. It was caused by a fungus called *Ophiostoma novo-ulmi,* which was accidentally introduced to the UK from the USA. It is transmitted by elm bark beetles, *Scolytus scolytus*. The beetles are native to Britain, and they reproduce by laying their eggs inside the bark of dying elm trees. The larvae that hatch from the eggs burrow through the bark, making extensive networks of tunnels (Figure 9.5).

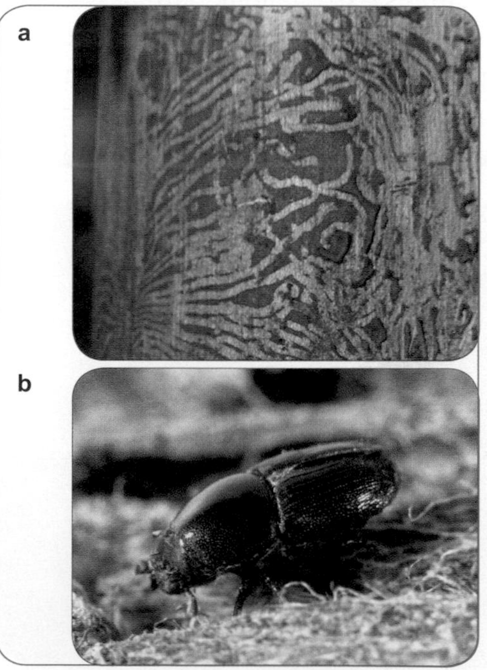

Figure 9.5 **a** The bare trunk of a dead elm tree, from which the bark has fallen. You can see the network of tunnels that were produced by the elm bark beetles that infected the tree with the Dutch elm disease fungus. **b** The elm bark beetle, *Scolytus scolytus*.

The fungus grows in the tunnels made by the elm bark beetles. It secretes enzymes that digest substances around it and then absorbs these nutrients into its mycelium. In time, it produces spores on the walls of the tunnels.

The beetle larvae eventually mature into adults, which fly to healthy elm trees to feed on their bark. They inadvertently carry spores of the fungus with them, and these infect the tree. The fungus grows in the outer layer of xylem vessels in the trunk of the tree, eventually blocking them so that water is no longer transported from the roots to the branches. The tree inevitably dies (Figure 9.6).

Before the American fungus was introduced, elms were often infected by a native fungus called *Ophiostoma ulmi*. This was able to grow in the trees without killing them – the two species had evolved so that both could survive together. But the introduced fungus is not the same, and there has been no time for the elm to evolve features that would allow them to co-exist. The fact that all English elms are genetically identical has meant that *all* of them are susceptible to the fungus. There is no variation on which natural selection can act.

Figure 9.6 Dead elms are a common sight in English hedgerows. Often, however, young trees grow up alongside the old ones, as suckers from their roots. These, too, soon die.

When an elm is killed by the fungus, the roots remain alive for some time and often produce new suckers. These grow well for some years, until they too are infected by the fungus and die. Instead of large, fully mature elm trees in our hedgerows, there are just small groups of trees that are only a few years old. With no genetic variation, apart from the possibility of a mutation occurring, there is little hope of a strain of English elms that is resistant to the fungus arising naturally.

Tissue culture

Traditional vegetative propagation of plants has often involved using the plant's own natural propagation methods. For example, new strawberry plants are propagated from runners; new potato plants are propagated from tubers. However, gardeners and commercial growers have also used techniques that bear little or no relation to the way the plant would naturally reproduce. For example, taking stem, leaf or root cuttings has been used for hundreds of years to propagate grape vines and other crop plants, and today cuttings are still used on a huge scale in some plant nurseries (Figure 9.7).

More recently, the technique of **tissue culture** has been developed to produce clones of a particularly desirable plant. This is vegetative propagation on a very large scale, and it is used by many producers of plants for sale to the agricultural or

Figure 9.7 African violets, *Saintpaulia*, can be quickly propagated by leaf cuttings. Whole leaves, or small pieces cut from them, are placed into compost, where they grow roots and then produce complete new plants.

horticultural industries. Very large quantities of genetically identical plants can be produced from just one – or at least very few – parents. Tissue culture enables large stocks of a particular variety to be built up quickly and relatively cheaply. It can be carried out at any time of year, in any country, as it takes place inside a laboratory. Plants are only moved outside or into the soil in glasshouses when they are well developed.

When a plant is wounded, cells close to the wound divide by mitosis to produce a **callus** – a fairly shapeless bundle of cells that seals the wound and prevents the entry of fungi or other potential pathogens. Tissue culture involves stimulating cells to behave in a similar way to callus cells. Plant growth substances are then used to stimulate the bundle of cells to differentiate to form the variety of different cell types which form themselves into root, stem and leaf tissues.

The process begins with the removal of a small group of cells from a plant. Not all plant cells are able to divide by mitosis, and those that do are called **meristematic cells**. Experience has enabled knowledge to be built up of the best source of cells to use in different plant species and varieties. The group of cells that is removed is called an **explant**. Care must be taken to ensure that the explant does not contain any cells infected by viruses.

There are various ways in which the explant can now be treated. A common procedure is to immerse it in a well-aerated solution containing a particular balance of **plant growth substances**, in particular **auxin** and **cytokinin**, which stimulate cell growth and division. The solution also contains nutrients needed by the cells (which will not be able to photosynthesise) – such as sucrose as an energy source, and inorganic ions such as potassium, magnesium and nitrate – and is sterile. It is very important to maintain sterile conditions throughout the procedure, as the tiny bundles of plant cells are highly vulnerable to attack by fungi or bacteria. The explants are usually dipped into a disinfectant solution immediately upon removal from the parent plant, and sterile techniques are used during their handling and their transfer into the sterile nutrient solution.

The explants can be kept in this solution for long periods of time, and these time periods can be extended almost indefinitely if a few cells are taken out every now and then and grown in a fresh culture solution. The undifferentiated cells in the explants divide repeatedly by mitosis, producing a callus (Figure 9.8). Every now and then some of the cells can be harvested for growing on into new plants. A complete callus could be used, or it could be subdivided to produce several smaller ones.

The calluses are now placed onto sterile agar jelly containing a particular mix of plant growth substances that stimulates them to grow roots and shoots (Figure 9.9 and Figure 9.10). The particular growth substances that are used, and their relative concentrations, have been found by trial and error. They vary from species to species and may be changed at different stages of the tiny new plant's growth – one mix might be used to stimulate production of roots, and then a different mix to stimulate production of shoots.

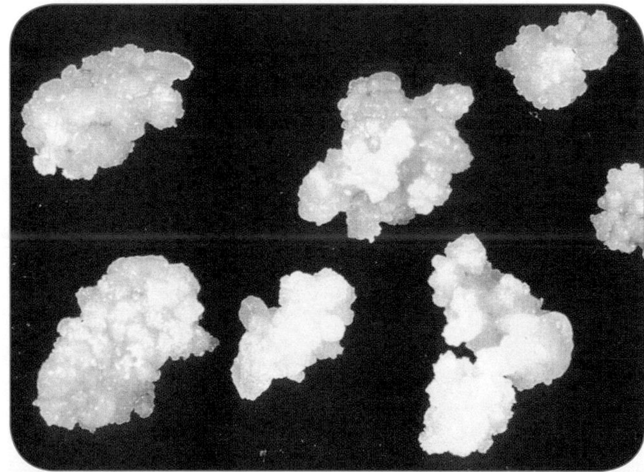

Figure 9.8 Calluses derived from onion cells.

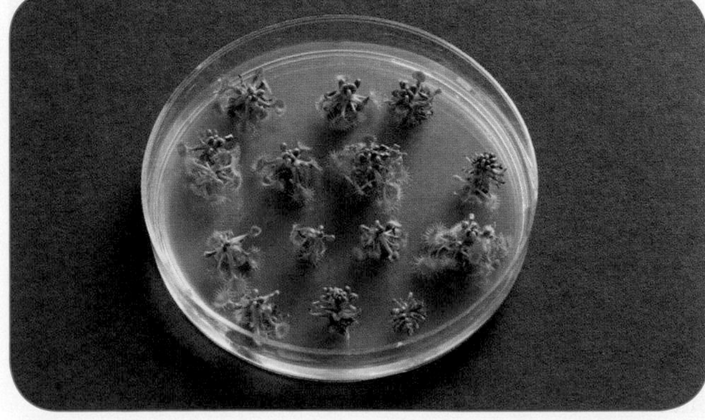

Figure 9.9 Sundew plants grown from explants.

Figure 9.10 Orchid plants are very difficult to propagate by any means other than tissue culture. Now they can be produced on a huge scale, as at this orchid nursery in Bangkok, Thailand. It is also easy to airfreight the small plants, still in their sterile environment inside a glass or plastic container, to other countries.

When the plant is large enough, it is transplanted into sterile soil. From now on, it should grow into a complete new plant. The biggest danger at this stage is infection by fungi, and it is important to maintain sterile conditions until the plant is large enough to be able to fend for itself.

Plant cloning in agriculture

The big advantage of cloning plants for commercial use in agriculture or horticulture is that all of the new plants are genetically identical. This is useful because the grower can choose a parent that has desirable features and produce almost endless quantities of identical plants. If they are grown in reasonably similar conditions, all of these offspring will have the same features – they will have flowers of the same colour, leaves of the same shape, be able to grow in particular types of soil and so on. This is also useful in agriculture, where a farmer can plant a known variety of potato, for example, and know that all of the potato plants that grow will produce potatoes like the ones that were planted. The features of that variety will be known by supermarkets and customers, so the farmer knows he will have almost guaranteed sales. The plants will all mature at the same time so can all be harvested and processed at the same time.

However, as we have seen with the English elm, genetic uniformity can have its downside too. If something changes in the environment – the arrival of a new pathogen, for example, or climate change – then if one plant is vulnerable all the others will be too. It is important that many different varieties of cultivated plant species are kept, each with its own particular combination of alleles, so that there is a large gene pool from which new varieties can be bred if required in the future.

In fact, almost all of the major crops grown in the UK are propagated by seed and not by cloning. This is true for all of the cereal crops – wheat, barley, oats and rye – as well as oilseed rape and linseed. These crops are all **annuals** – seed is sown in autumn or spring, and then the crop is harvested after around 6–10 months' growth. It would be much more labour-intensive to propagate these plants vegetatively, and then to plant the new plantlets out every year. Collecting and sowing seed is much faster and cheaper.

The only crops grown on a large scale in the UK for which vegetative propagation is the norm are potatoes. Potato plants form swollen stem tubers underground (Figure 9.11). The tubers are harvested, and some are saved to plant the following year. Each tuber that is planted produces one potato plant, on which many new tubers grow. Collecting and planting the tubers is no more difficult than collecting and sowing seed for cereal crops. However, there is one significant disadvantage, which is that the tubers may harbour viruses or fungi, which will then be able to infect the new plant that grows from them. Seeds, on the other hand, rarely carry pathogens from one generation to the next.

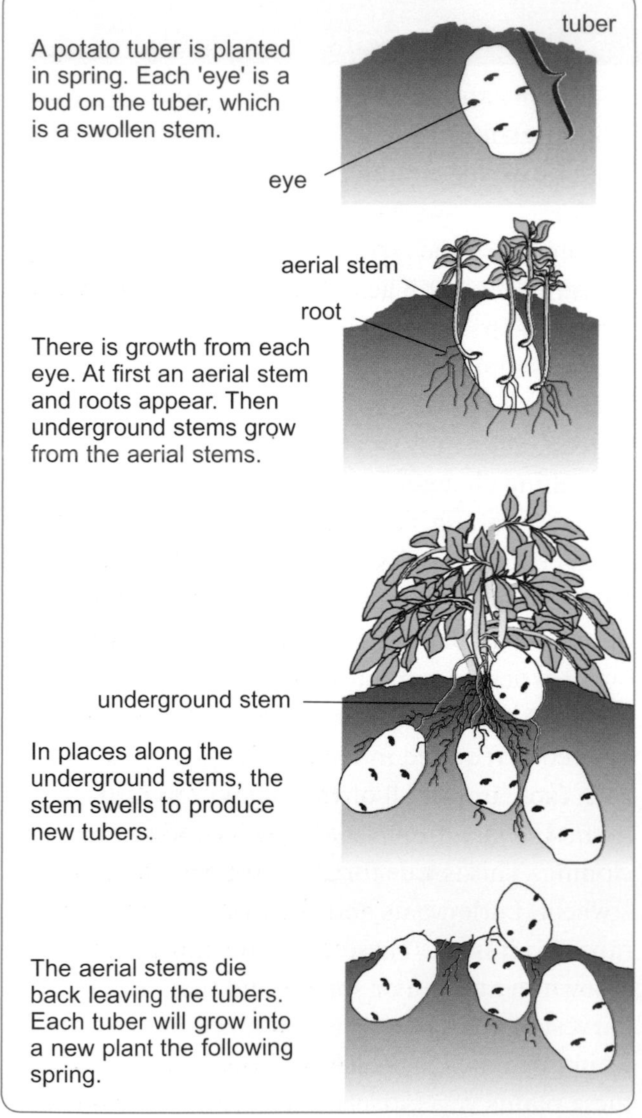

tuber
A potato tuber is planted in spring. Each 'eye' is a bud on the tuber, which is a swollen stem.
eye
aerial stem
root
There is growth from each eye. At first an aerial stem and roots appear. Then underground stems grow from the aerial stems.
underground stem
In places along the underground stems, the stem swells to produce new tubers.
The aerial stems die back leaving the tubers. Each tuber will grow into a new plant the following spring.

Figure 9.11 Potato plants grow vegetatively, from tubers.

Seed production always involves sexual reproduction, and so you would expect to get genetic variation. However, named varieties of crops have each been inbred so much that they have become genetically uniform. So, despite the fact that seed production involves the formation of gametes by meiosis, these gametes are all genetically identical and so there is no genetic variation in the offspring. This provides all the same advantages as cloning. For example, a farmer can sow seed of a particular wheat variety in a field, and know that the plants that grow will all reach about the same height and be ready to harvest at the same time. Sowing seed of cereal crops is much faster and easier than producing new plants by any form of vegetative propagation could be.

Vegetative propagation really comes into its own when you are growing crops that stay in the ground for years and years, or for which seed production is very difficult. For example, bananas have been bred to produce varieties that do not produce seeds at all. The only way of propagating them is vegetatively. In the UK, apart from potatoes, vegetative propagation is used for most named varieties of herbs or plants such as lavender, and for fruits such as apples, pears and cherries. These are perennial plants. Lavender is propagated from cuttings and fruit trees from grafts (Figure 9.12 and Figure 9.13). The high costs of vegetative propagation and planting out cuttings or grafted plants are offset by the long period for which the plants stay in the ground and the relatively high value of their products, such as lavender oil.

SAQ

1 Explain how the procedures involved in developing a new variety of a cereal crop such as wheat eventually produce genetic uniformity, even though propagation is by sexual reproduction. (You may want to refer back to *Biology 1 page 153*.) Answer

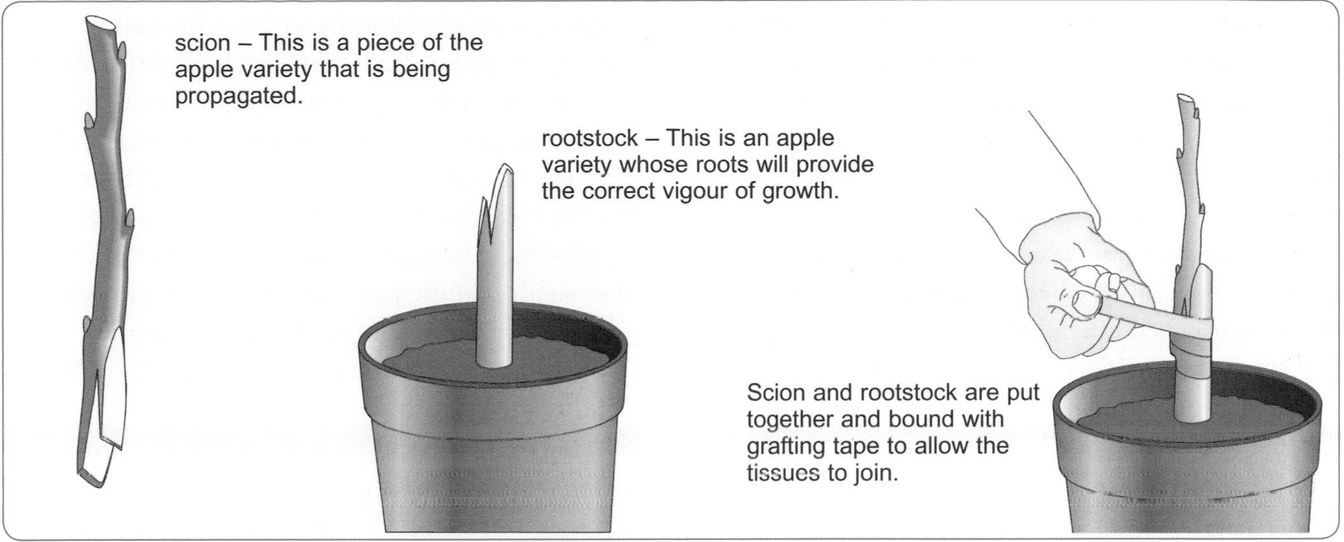

scion – This is a piece of the apple variety that is being propagated.
rootstock – This is an apple variety whose roots will provide the correct vigour of growth.
Scion and rootstock are put together and bound with grafting tape to allow the tissues to join.

Figure 9.12 Propagating a particular variety of an apple tree. The scion will grow, on the roots of the rootstock, to produce a new apple tree of the variety from which the scion was taken.

Figure 9.13 Lavender is propagated vegetatively from cuttings.

SAQ

2 Use bullet points to summarise:
 a the advantages
 b the disadvantages
 of plant cloning in agriculture.

Answer

Cloning animals

In the last 20 years or so, cloning has become an important ethical issue. This is because it has become possible for humans to produce clones of a wide range of species artificially. This is fine for plants and for most kinds of animals, but once it involves mammals and especially humans, then many people feel uncomfortable with the concept. Should we feel free to produce clones of 'intelligent' animals, such as cats, dogs or horses? Should we ever produce clones of humans?

Most people would say 'no' to cloning humans. But there are some areas in which cloning of human *cells* is desirable. Using cloning to produce a complete organism is called **reproductive cloning**. Using cloning to produce just some cells is called **non-reproductive cloning**. These two types of cloning raise very different moral and ethical issues.

Non-reproductive cloning

Non-reproductive cloning involves the production of genetically identical cells. The cells are not used to produce whole new organisms. Non-reproductive cloning of animal cells has been carried out routinely in many laboratories since the 1950s. The first human cell line was derived from cancer cells taken from Henrietta Lacks, who died from her cancer in 1951. The cells were taken without her permission, which today would be against the law. As they were cancer cells, they divided repeatedly in culture solution, producing large numbers of genetically identical cells. The cells, which became known as HeLa cells (Figure 9.14), have been used in medical research. Today there are thousands of cell lines grown in laboratories all over the world, from humans and also many other animal species. They can be used, for example, to test potential new drugs or to investigate the involvement of genes or external factors in the development of diseases such as cancer, diabetes or multiple sclerosis.

Non-reproductive cloning is also used in – the so far largely experimental – attempts at gene therapy (Chapter 11). For example, the genetic disease SCID, severe combined immunodeficiency disease, is caused by a faulty allele of a gene coding for an enzyme called adenosine deaminase or ADA. This enzyme is essential for the proper working of the immune system. Without it, the immune system is unable to fight off pathogens, and without treatment a child born with this condition will almost certainly die in infancy or childhood. Several methods of gene therapy have been trialled to treat this disease. They involve the removal of some of the patient's T cells and the insertion of the correct allele into them using a vector such as a retrovirus. The cells that have successfully taken up the allele are then cloned to produce large numbers of them, which can then be replaced into the patient's body. The technique is still in need of refinement, and several patients who appeared to have been successfully treated have gone on to develop leukaemia (a cancer involving white blood cells). However, as they would have died anyway the risk of cancer is generally seen as an acceptable, albeit very unfortunate, one in the treatment of this rare and inevitably fatal disease.

More recently, research has moved into the potential use of **stem cells** to treat diseases (*Biology 1*, page 40). Stem cells are undifferentiated cells that are able to divide and then form specialised cells. It is hoped that stem cells could be used to treat diseases in which a particular group of cells has ceased to function, such as diabetes (β cells in the islets of Langerhans) and Parkinson's disease (dopamine-producing cells in a particular part of the brain). The biggest hurdle in the development of such treatments is the difficulty in obtaining stem cells. Although there are some stem cells in adults, they are relatively few and most of them are only able to form a few different cell types. A more useful source of stem cells is very young embryos (Figure 9.15), where most or all of the cells have not yet differentiated and are still able to form almost any of the different cell types present in the human body. They are said to be **totipotent** (able to form every different kind of cell) or **pluripotent** (able to form most of the different kinds of cells).

Embryos at the blastocyst stage are potentially the best source of stem cells. These cells are known as **embryonic stem cells**. Theoretically, cells taken from a human blastocyst could be used to grow endless supplies of human stem cells that could be used to replace faulty cells in an adult. To avoid rejection, however, these stem cells would need to be genetically identical to the person's own cells.

Stem cells from human embryos were first isolated and grown in a laboratory in 1988. As their potential was realised, people began to

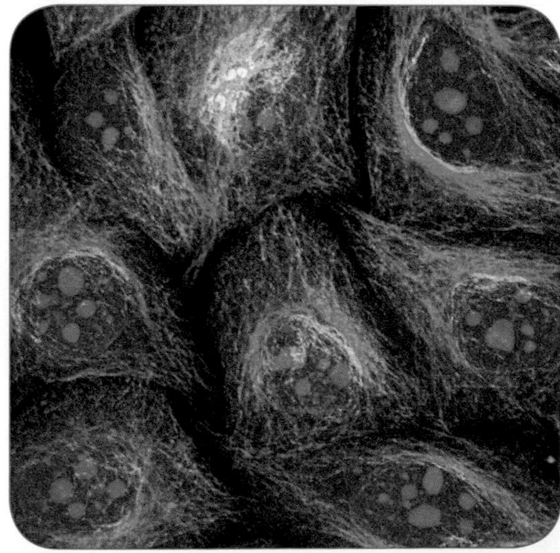

Figure 9.14 HeLa cells are immortal, and have been cultured continuously in laboratories since 1951. Magnification ×2100.

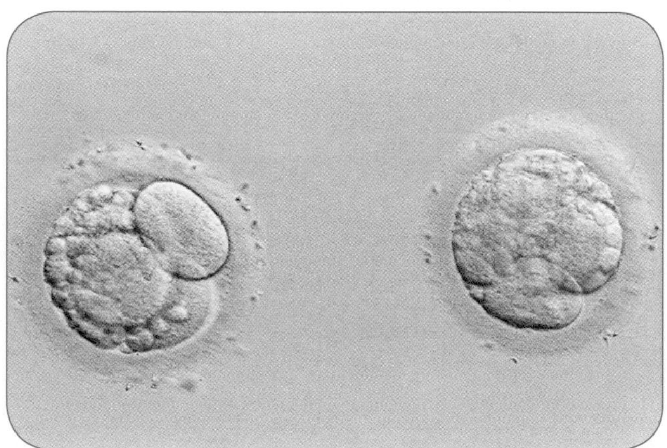

Figure 9.15 Human embryos four days after fertilisation. At this stage, all of the cells are pluripotent. Magnification ×410.

question the ethics of this research. The embryos from which the cells were taken were destroyed. They usually came from surplus embryos that were not placed into a woman's uterus during fertility treatment. Some people consider that it is unacceptable to use embryos for this purpose, even if there never was any chance of the embryo becoming a baby. Others feel that the potential benefits outweigh the ethical concerns.

Some researchers now take just a single cell from an eight-cell embryo. There is evidence that the remaining seven cells can grow into a normal fetus and eventually a normal person, but there are questions about this and it is not a perfect solution to the problem.

But there are other possibilities for finding sources of stem cells. When a cell differentiates, most of its genes are permanently switched off, so that only a particular set that is required for the running of that particular cell type remains active. What if it were possible to reverse this process? The genes required for every other type of cell are still there – they have just been switched off. If we could find ways to re-activate them, then we could re-programme a differentiated cell so that it regained its ability to develop into other types of cells. In 2007, several groups of researchers managed to turn back the clock for differentiated cells taken from mouse skin. By exposing them to different growth factors (chemicals produced by cells in the body at different stages of their development and differentiation) they managed to reset the cells to become stem cells again. If this process can be made to work reliably, and with human cells, then this will be a much better source of stem cells than using embryos. It is unlikely to raise serious ethical issues. Moreover, it means that stem cells can be produced from a person's own body, so that they will be genetically identical and not likely to be rejected by the immune system.

Reproductive cloning

Reproductive cloning of animals involves the production of a whole new animal. There are some animals – all of which are invertebrates, such as the cnidarian *Hydra* – that can do this naturally. However, for vertebrates it can only be done artificially.

We have seen how one type of cloning is used in the production of multiple embryos from a single embryo, in the technique of embryo transplantation in cattle (Chapter 8). The multiple embryos are all genetically identical to each other, but not to their parents. To produce a clone of mammals, a sophisticated technique is required.

Everyone has heard of Dolly the sheep, the first mammal to be produced by cloning (Figure 9.16). Despite the success of the researchers in producing her, the technique they used was far from perfect. They only managed to get 227 pairs of cells to fuse together, and of these only 29 developed into embryos. Only one of these 29 then went on to develop into a live lamb, which was Dolly. And even then there were problems. She was not particularly healthy, and died at a relatively young age.

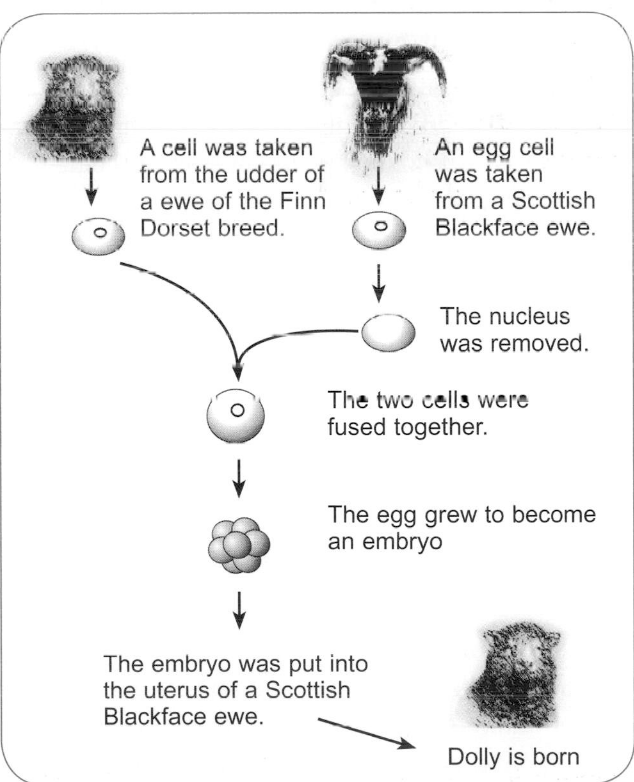

A cell was taken from the udder of a ewe of the Finn Dorset breed.
An egg cell was taken from a Scottish Blackface ewe.
The nucleus was removed.
The two cells were fused together.
The egg grew to become an embryo
The embryo was put into the uterus of a Scottish Blackface ewe.
Dolly is born

Figure 9.16 How the first cloned mammal was produced.

Even if the difficulties with making the technique work could be solved, there would still be major concerns about the health of mammals produced by this kind of cloning technique. Since Dolly, clones have been produced of many other mammals, including mice, horses and dogs. In all of these cases, there appears to be an increased likelihood of serious health problems developing at a relatively early age.

This brings into question the whole issue of cloning mammals. If the animals are not healthy, then should we do it at all? If we are producing these animals for our own pleasure – perhaps because someone wants to have a replica of a pet that is aging and expected to die soon, or to produce a racehorse that is genetically identical to one that wins races – then many would suggest that these are not good enough reasons to cause potential suffering. However, there may be other purposes, such as producing an animal from which cures for human diseases might be derived, for which there are stronger moral and ethical arguments.

SAQ

3 Use the internet to find the current regulations in the UK relating to cloning of cells from human embryos. What are your opinions on these regulations? Answer

4 Use the internet to investigate some of the current discussions and debates taking place about the use of reproductive cloning. Write a brief summary of your own views about whether reproductive cloning of any animals – or even humans – should be allowed to take place, and your justification for your opinions. Answer

Extension

Summary

Glossary

- Many plants reproduce naturally by vegetative propagation (asexual reproduction) producing genetically identical populations known as clones. The English elm, for example, reproduces by means of suckers.
- Humans use natural and artificial methods of vegetative propagation, such as tissue culture, to produce clones of plants for use in horticulture or agriculture. These are particularly useful for plants that are difficult to reproduce by seed (such as orchids) or where seeds would produce genetically variable plants (such as apples).
- Tissue culture involves the removal of a small group of cells, called an explant, and its subsequent growth in an aerated, sterile solution containing nutrients and plant growth factors. The resulting callus is then transferred to a medium such as sterile agar gel, containing plant growth factors that stimulate the growth of roots and shoots.
- The genetic uniformity of clones results in a crop with predictable characteristics, which is all ready for harvesting and processing at the same time. However, the lack of genetic variability means that the entire crop is vulnerable to the same diseases or unfavourable environmental conditions.
- Non-reproductive cloning involves the production of genetically identical cells. Reproductive cloning involves the production of genetically identical complete organisms.
- Non-reproductive cloning of human cells has been happening for almost 60 years – for example, using cells taken from human cancers. Recently, it has become possible to clone cells taken from human embryos. There has been considerable debate about the ethical issues associated with this practice, and various rules and regulations have been laid down about it in different countries at different times.

continued

- Reproductive cloning of mammals involves the fusion of a body cell with an enucleated egg, which then divides by mitosis as a normal zygote would. Reproductive cloning is technically difficult, and is not regularly carried out on a large scale. However, as techniques advance and become more reliable, there will need to be widespread discussions about what is, and is not, considered to be ethically acceptable.

Stretch and challenge question

1 Describe the ways in which genetic uniformity is maintained in named crop plants. What are the advantages to the farmer, seller and consumer of growing genetically uniform crops?

Hint

Questions

1 a Vast areas of tropical rainforests have lost their largest and best trees to the timber trade or to agriculture.

To help restore these forests, biologists are applying the traditional technique of using cuttings from trees in the rainforest to produce clones that might form the basis of new forests.

It is essential to grow trees with high productivity so that they are desirable to growers. One way to do this is to create clones of the most productive specimens. These can then be planted instead of using saplings grown from seed.

i Explain the meaning of the term *clone*. [2]

ii State two advantages of using clones instead of saplings grown from seed. [2]

iii Auxin stimulates the growing roots to develop root hairs. These are projections from specialised epidermal cells. Explain in detail why it is important for the cuttings to develop root hairs. [4]

b Micropropagation has been used to produce clones of some pine trees. New plants are grown by culturing tissues from trees with high productivity. The tissues from the trees are grown in artificial conditions in a culture medium.
List three constituents of the culture medium. [3]

c One disadvantage of micropropagation is that it can be more expensive than traditional methods.
Suggest three factors which may contribute to this extra cost. [3]

d Name one technique for producing clones of trees, other than taking cuttings, or micropropagation. [1]

OCR Biology A (2805/01) January 2006 [Total 15]

Answer

Chapter 10

Biotechnology

Objectives

e-Learning

Biotechnology can be defined as the industrial use of living organisms (or parts of living organisms) to produce food, drugs or other products. It is not new – microorganisms have long been used to make food and drink, such as bacteria to produce cheese or yeast to produce wine and beer – but until recently people did not realise that microorganisms were involved, let alone understand exactly what they were doing. Now, as our understanding of the biology of the organisms and metabolic reactions involved has increased, so have the breadth and scale of the production processes we can use them for.

Today, many biotechnological processes involve genetically modified microorganisms. Some of these are described in Chapter 11.

Using microorganisms

Many, but by no means all, biotechnological processes use microorganisms, including bacteria, archeans, fungi and – in a few cases – protoctists. Microorganisms have several features that make them particularly useful in large-scale industrial processes.

- They generally have rapid life cycles, so that large populations can be built up quickly.
- All prokaryotes (bacteria and archaea) reproduce asexually, as do many other types of microorganisms, so the populations are genetically identical and all the individuals carry out the same metabolic processes.
- They tend to have very specific and simple requirements for growth, so can be grown in fermenters under controlled conditions with the minimum of attention.
- They can often be grown using waste materials from industry that would otherwise have no use and could be costly to dispose of.
- No-one minds what is done to a microorganism, so their use does not usually raise ethical questions.
- Bacteria have only a single copy of each gene, so if a gene is altered through gene technology there will be no other copies of that gene to mask it.
- The ways in which the expression of genes is controlled are relatively simple in bacteria compared to eukaryotes, making them more straightforward for genetic modification (Chapter 11).
- Archaea and, to a lesser extent, bacteria have a very wide range of metabolic pathways, which may be developed for an equally wide range of human purposes.
- Many archaea, and also some bacteria, have evolved to live in very hot environments, and the enzymes and other substances that they produce are able to work at high temperatures.

Growth curves of microorganisms

Given appropriate environmental conditions, most microorganisms are capable of very rapid population growth. Figure 10.1 shows a typical growth curve for a population of the bacterium *Escherichia coli* in a closed culture.

E. coli is a bacterium that commonly lives in the human alimentary canal. It does no harm, and may even be beneficial to our health. It respires aerobically if oxygen is present, but can also respire anaerobically for long periods of time if oxygen is in short supply. *E. coli* can be grown in a liquid containing a variety of organic nutrients, such as glucose, amino acids and vitamins, called **nutrient broth**. The bacteria reproduce asexually, the cells splitting into two in a process called **binary fission**. The size of the population can be measured by counting the number of cells in a certain volume of broth.

The curve in Figure 10.1 shows the population size of *E. coli* in nutrient broth in a conical flask, over a period of two days. A small number of cells were introduced to the flask at time 0, and then samples taken at intervals after that. You can see that, at first, the number of bacterial cells was too small to detect in the samples, and that it is not until 8 hours after the beginning of the experiment that the population begins to grow significantly. This early stage, before population growth is detected, is known as the **lag phase**. During the lag phase, the bacteria are adjusting to the new conditions. For example, they have a wide variety of enzymes they can synthesise to allow the absorption and metabolism of nutrients, and it takes a while for appropriate genes to be switched on to make the enzymes required for the particular types of nutrients available. Even when the bacteria do begin to divide, it takes some time before their numbers increase sufficiently to be detected and reliably measured in the samples.

Once the lag phase is over, the numbers of bacteria increase rapidly. This stage is called the **log phase** or **exponential phase**. During the log phase, bacterial cells are growing and dividing at their maximum rate for the particular conditions they are in; they have plenty of nutrients and space, and the only limitation to their rate of reproduction is their own in-built capacity. The population growth in this phase is exponential – that is, it repeatedly doubles in a particular length of time. In the results shown in Figure 10.1, doubling is occurring about every 25 minutes.

Figure 10.1 shows that, after about 10 hours, the rate of growth of the population begins to slow down. This is usually because one or more of the nutrients are beginning to run out. By 12 hours, the population has stopped growing. The number of new cells being produced is matched by the number of cells dying. This is called the **stationary phase**. Eventually, nutrient levels become so low that more reproduction cannot take place. There may also be changes in the broth caused by the accumulation of waste products from the bacteria,

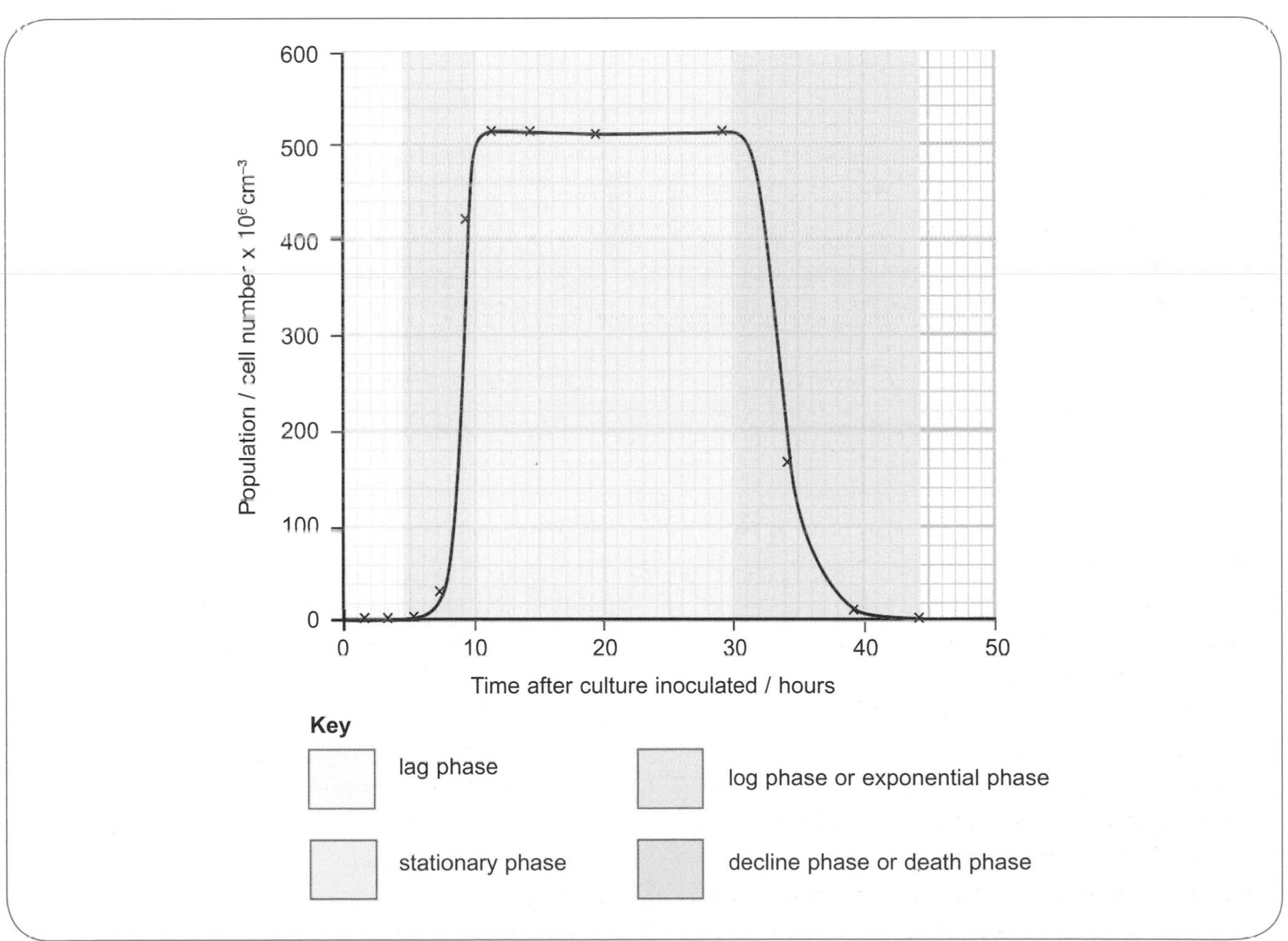

Figure 10.1 Growth curve of *E. coli* in a closed culture.

some of which may be toxic and prevent any more reproduction. Now death rate is greater than birth rate and the population begins to decline. This is called the **decline phase** or **death phase**.

The first three phases of this curve make up a **sigmoid growth curve**. This kind of growth pattern is typical of most microorganisms kept in a culture vessel in which supplies of nutrients are limited.

Large-scale production techniques

We use many different microorganisms to make products that can be used in medicine and as foods. This usually involves culturing the microorganisms in containers called **fermenters**.

The precise way in which this is done depends on the nature of the product that we want to make, and the kind of microorganism that is being used. We will look at three examples – the production of penicillin, the production of protease enzymes and the production of mycoprotein.

Manufacturing penicillin

The antibiotic penicillin is made by a microscopic fungus called *Penicillium*. Figure 10.2 shows a fermenter in which *Penicillium* can be grown and from which penicillin can be harvested.

Penicillium does not make penicillin all the time. Penicillin production only reaches high levels after the fungus has been growing in the medium for a while (Figure 10.3).

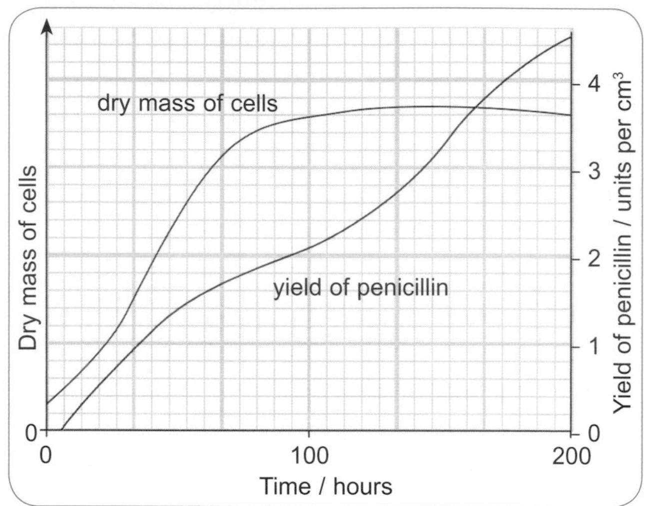

Figure 10.3 Yield of penicillin in a fermentation.

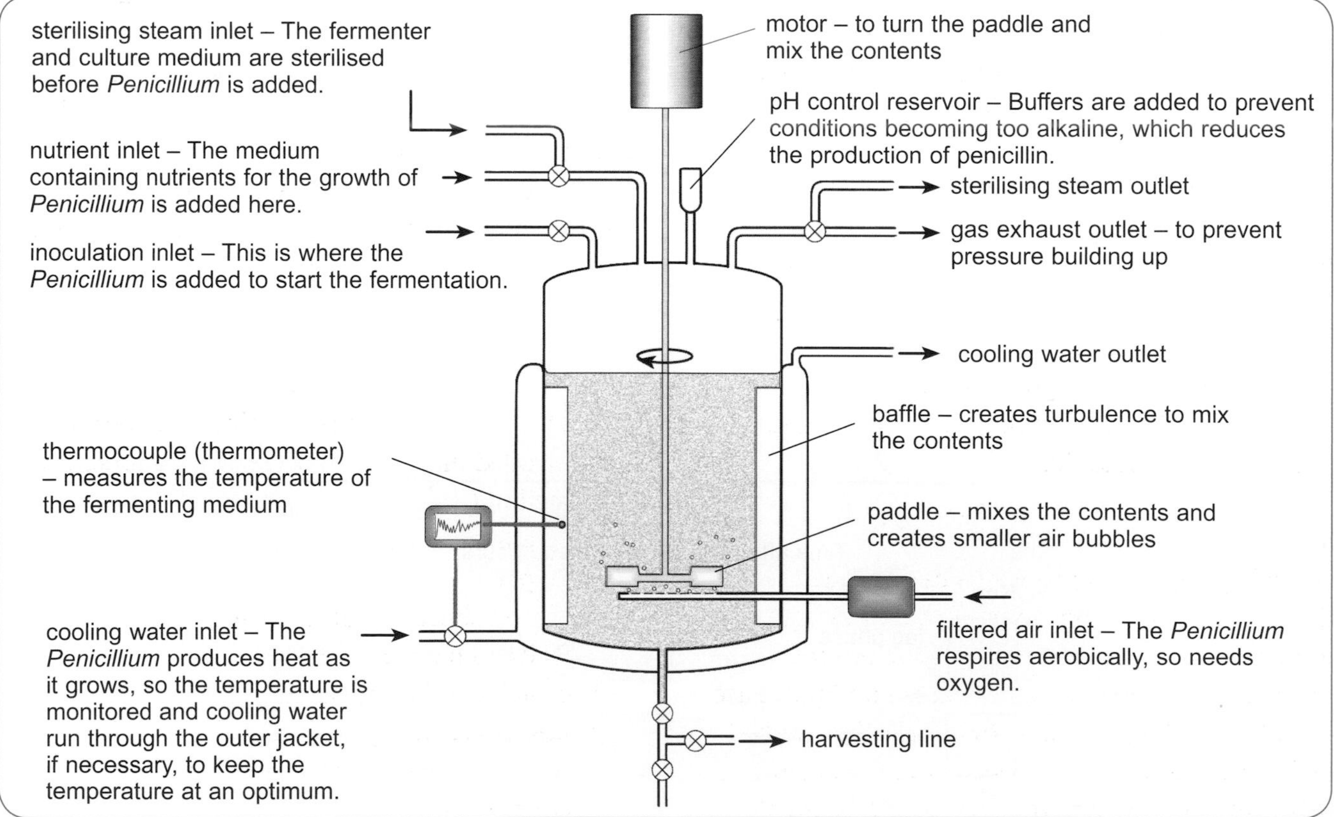

Figure 10.2 A batch fermenter used for the production of penicillin.

Penicillin is a **secondary metabolite**. A metabolite is a substance that is made by a cell in the course of its metabolism. The metabolite may remain inside the cell, or it may be secreted outside it. A **primary metabolite** is a substance that is produced by most of the cells in a culture most of the time, and is involved in 'normal' metabolic processes such as respiration or growth. A secondary metabolite can be defined as any metabolite that is not a primary one – in other words, it is only produced by some cells, or at a particular growth stage, and does not appear to have any direct involvement with fundamental metabolic processes.

Because penicillin is a secondary metabolite, it is only produced at certain stages of the fermentation. This means that we have to keep setting up new fermentations. The fungus is grown in the fermenter until the maximum amount of penicillin has been produced. Then the fermentation is stopped and the antibiotic harvested. The fermenter is cleaned out and then a new culture of *Penicillium* is put in and the whole process started again.

This is called **batch culture**. In 'standard' batch culture, the fermentation is set up and then left to proceed. Nothing is added or taken out while the fermentation takes place, except that waste gases are allowed to escape.

In practice, penicillin is produced by a variant of this technique called **fed batch culture**. During the fermentation process, a carbohydrate source (often corn steep liquor, a by-product of processing maize) is added about every 30 minutes. This can keep the fermentation going for a longer time, and therefore produces more penicillin than standard batch culture would do.

Manufacturing enzymes

All living organisms produce a huge range of different enzymes, and some of these can have important uses in industry, medicine or food technology. For example, proteases and lipases are added to washing powders to help in the removal of stains; digestive enzymes are added to some cattle feeds to increase the quantity of nutrients that the cattle can absorb; enzymes are used in the modern leather industry to prepare skins.

Enzyme production occurs in two stages. First, the microorganism that will produce the enzyme is grown. Then the enzyme is extracted, purified and concentrated (Figure 10.4).

Many different kinds of bacteria and fungi can be used to produce enzymes. Often, a thermophilic (heat-loving) organism such as *Bacillus stearothermophilus* is used. These bacteria live in hot springs and they have evolved enzymes that are not denatured until temperatures as high as 70 °C or more are exceeded. These heat-resistant enzymes are very useful in industrial processes in which higher temperatures are encountered.

To produce the enzymes, the bacteria are provided with a carbon source and a nitrogen source. The carbon source is often a waste product from an agricultural process or industrial process, such as left-over parts of maize plants after the grain has been harvested, remains of sugar cane (called bagasse) after sugar has been extracted from it or meal made from soya beans or potatoes. This helps to keep costs down. The nitrogen source can be protein, urea or ammonium salts, or the remains of other cells that have been used in other fermentations.

Usually, batch culture is used, as for the production of penicillin. The bacteria or fungi are almost always aerobic, so the contents of the fermenter are well aerated. Some organisms secrete the enzymes into the medium around them but in some cases the enzymes remain inside the cells.

SAQ

1 Each of the following conditions is carefully controlled in a fermenter used to manufacture penicillin (Figure 10.2):

- temperature
- pH
- concentration of nutrients
- oxygen concentration.

For each condition, explain:

a how it is controlled

b why it is important that it is controlled.

Answer

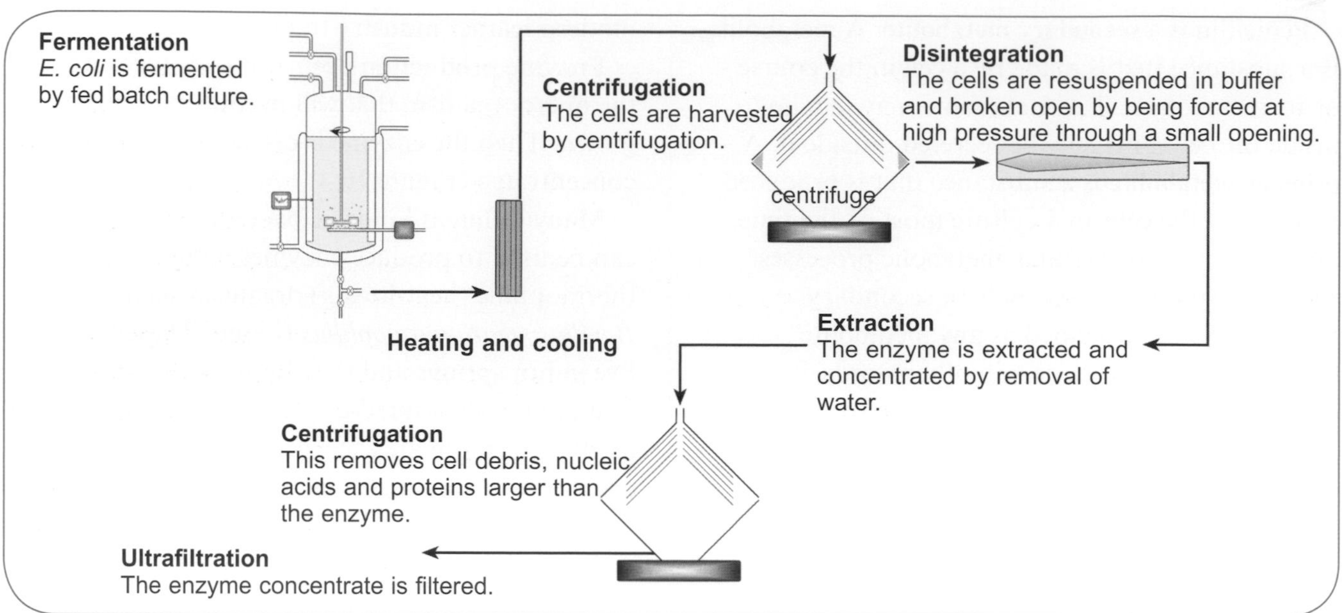

Fermentation
E. coli is fermented by fed batch culture.
Centrifugation
The cells are harvested by centrifugation.
centrifuge
Disintegration
The cells are resuspended in buffer and broken open by being forced at high pressure through a small opening.
Heating and cooling
Extraction
The enzyme is extracted and concentrated by removal of water.
Centrifugation
This removes cell debris, nucleic acids and proteins larger than the enzyme.
Ultrafiltration
The enzyme concentrate is filtered.

Figure 10.4 The extraction of β galactosidase (lactase) from *E. coli*. This enzyme is used to digest lactose in milk, to produce lactose-free milk suitable for people with lactose intolerance.

After the fermentation has finished, the culture is heated to kill the cells. If the enzyme is still inside the cells, the cells can be broken open to allow the enzyme to escape from them and dissolve in the culture medium. This can then be concentrated and filtered, leaving the cell fragments behind and collecting the enzyme in solution.

SAQ

2 Explain how each of the centrifugation steps in Figure 10.4 helps in the extraction of the enzyme.

Answer

Finally, the enzymes can be purified (if required – this is not always necessary) and packaged in a form that can be easily transported and used. Enzymes to be used in washing powders are formed into tiny capsules covered with a non-reactive substance. This is to prevent them coming into contact with the skin of the person using the washing powder, because they can cause irritation or allergies in some people.

Manufacturing mycoprotein

Mycoprotein means 'fungus protein'. The main mycoprotein product in Europe is called Quorn™.

Figure 10.5 shows a fermenter used to make mycoprotein. The fungus that is cultured is called *Fusarium*. It is made up of long, thin threads called **hyphae**.

The culture medium contains glucose, which is usually obtained from starch that has been hydrolysed by enzymes. This provides the growing fungus with a respiratory substrate for the release of energy, and also carbon that can be used to make new carbohydrate, protein and fat molecules for growth. Ammonium phosphate is added as

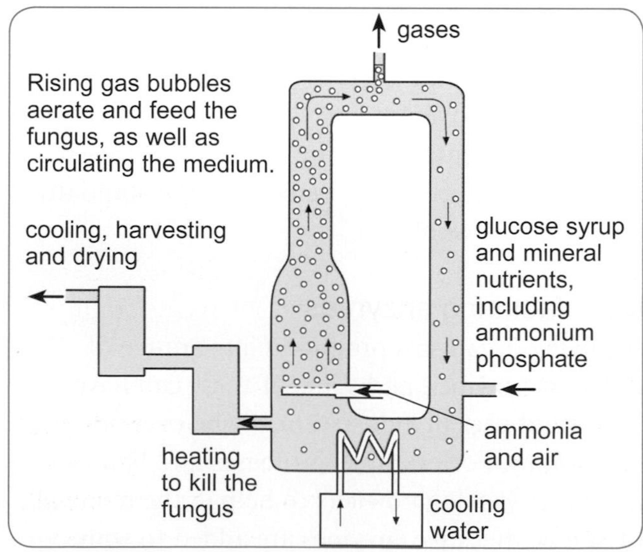

Figure 10.5 Fermenter used to make mycoprotein.

a nitrogen source, so that the fungus can make proteins and nucleic acids. Small amounts of trace elements such as zinc and copper are also provided. Ammonia gas may also be bubbled through the mixture.

The temperature, pH and oxygen content of the fermenter are kept constant, providing optimum growing conditions. No stirrer is used, because it would entangle and break the fungal hyphae.

Unlike the batch culture method used to produce penicillin and most enzymes, the production of mycoprotein uses **continuous culture**. This involves a steady input of nutrients into the fermenter and a steady harvest of the fungus from it. The liquid culture containing the fungus is run off from the base of the fermenter and then centrifuged to separate the hyphae from the liquid.

The hyphae contain high concentrations of RNA, which would give them an unpleasant taste. Enzymes are used to break this down. Filtration and steam treatment complete the process, after which the mycoprotein can be used in the production of many different foods. It is an excellent meat substitute, high in protein but low in fat.

SAQ

3 Suggest why trace elements such as zinc and copper are needed by the fungus in Figure 10.5. Answer

4 Suggest why ammonia gas is bubbled through the mixture. Answer

Advantages of batch and continuous culture

We have seen that, whereas penicillin and enzymes are produced using batch culture, mycoprotein production uses continuous culture. Each of these methods has its own advantages and disadvantages, and the choice of which one to use depends on the conditions that the microorganism requires in order to synthesise the desired product.

Batch culture

- It is relatively easy to set up the culture – you just provide the right nutrients at the right concentrations, and then allow fermentation to continue with minimum attention.
- Once the fermenter has been cleaned and sterilised, it can be used for a completely different process if required.
- If something goes wrong – for example, if the culture becomes contaminated with a different microorganism – then only that particular batch needs to be thrown away.
- In continuous culture, the cells can sometimes clump together and block inlet or outlet pipes, but this is less likely in batch culture.

Continuous culture

- Because the process is continuous, there is no 'down time' while the vessels are cleaned out and set up again.
- Relatively small vessels can be used, because the continual input and output means that less space is needed to grow enough microorganisms to give a good yield.

The importance of asepsis

Whatever technique is used to culture microorganisms, and on whatever scale, it is very important to use aseptic techniques. **Asepsis** means 'without microorganisms'. This means that no microorganisms other than the ones you want to grow are introduced into the culture. This is important because other microorganisms might metabolise the substrate in a different way, producing unwanted products in the fermenter. This is especially important when the product is to be used in medical techniques or as food, when unwanted substances produced in the culture could be hazardous to health.

If the microorganisms used are themselves potentially dangerous – for example, in a laboratory working on producing vaccines from live pathogens – then it is equally important that they do not come into direct contact with workers, or escape outside the laboratory. Special high-level containment facilities are used whenever hazardous microorganisms are being handled.

Some of the methods used to maintain asepsis for industrial-scale biotechnological processes are similar to those you will have used in the laboratory, while others are unlikely to be used in a normal school or college laboratory (Figure 10.6). These methods include:

- ensuring that all fermenters and attachments are sterile before the microorganisms or substrates are added. This generally entails cleaning with pressurised steam shortly before use. The high-temperature steam kills any microorganisms present. In some circumstances, chemical sterilisation may be used instead of, or as well as, steaming
- sterilising all liquids, solids and gases that enter the reaction vessel
- maintaining a small pressure difference between the air in the room where the fermentation is taking place and the air outside, so that there is a steady airflow *out of* the room; this reduces the chances of stray microorganisms entering on air currents from outside

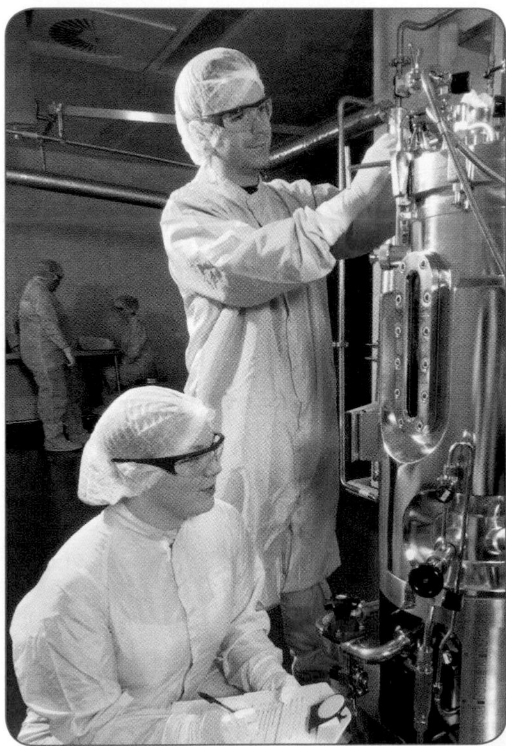

Figure 10.6 Inspectors checking a fermentation unit. The protective clothing is not only to ensure their own safety, but also to minimise the chances of them introducing unwanted microorganisms to the fermentation unit.

- for some processes, ensuring that the culture of microorganisms that is added to the vessels is a pure culture of just the one or two microorganisms that are required, uncontaminated with any others
- ensuring that workers do not introduce unwanted microorganisms from their skin, clothes or hair; they will normally wear clean lab coats over their clothing, and may also be required to wear latex gloves, and caps covering their hair.

Immobilising enzymes

Enzymes are expensive. No company that uses them in the manufacture of a product wants to have to keep buying them over and over again if they can recycle them in some way. One of the best ways of doing this is to use **immobilised enzymes**, which can be re-used many times.

Figure 10.7 shows one way in which enzymes can be immobilised. An enzyme solution is mixed with a solution of sodium alginate. Little droplets of this mixture are then added to a solution of calcium chloride. The sodium alginate and calcium chloride react to form jelly, which turns the droplet into a little bead. The jelly bead contains the enzyme. The enzyme is held in the bead, and is therefore immobilised.

These beads can be packed gently into a column. A liquid containing the enzyme's substrate can be allowed to trickle steadily over them. As the substrate runs over the surface of the beads, the enzymes in the beads catalyse a reaction that converts the substrate into product. The product continues to trickle down the column, emerging from the bottom, where it can be collected and purified.

For example, the enzyme lactase can be immobilised in this way. Milk is then allowed to run through the column of lactase-containing beads (Figure 10.7). The lactase hydrolyses the lactose in the milk to glucose and galactose. The milk is therefore lactose-free, and can be used to make lactose-free or lactose-reduced dairy products for people who cannot digest lactose.

You can see that this process has obvious advantages compared with just mixing up the enzyme with its substrate. If you mixed lactase with milk, you would have a very difficult task to get the lactase back again. Not only would you lose the lactase but you would also have milk contaminated with the enzyme. Using immobilised enzymes means that you can keep and re-use the enzymes, and that the product is enzyme-free.

Another advantage of this process is that the immobilised enzymes are more tolerant of temperature changes and pH changes than enzymes in solution. This may be partly because their molecules are held firmly in shape by the alginate in which they are embedded, and so do not denature as easily. It may also be because the parts of the molecules that are embedded are not fully exposed to the temperature or pH changes.

This kind of immobilisation is called gel entrapment. Figure 10.8 shows several methods of immobilising enzymes.

SAQ

5 Summarise the advantages of using immobilised enzymes rather than enzyme solutions.

Answer

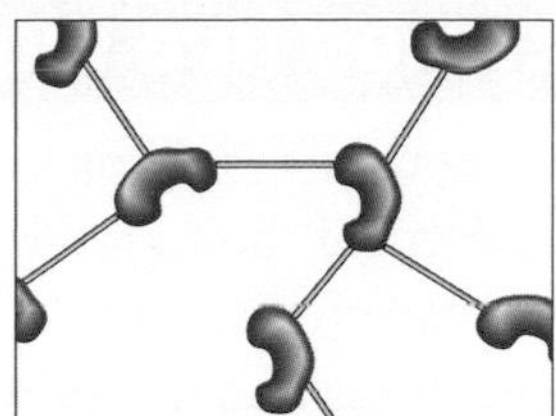

Cross-linked. Enzyme is immobilised by cross-linking amino groups of the enzyme using glutaraldehyde.

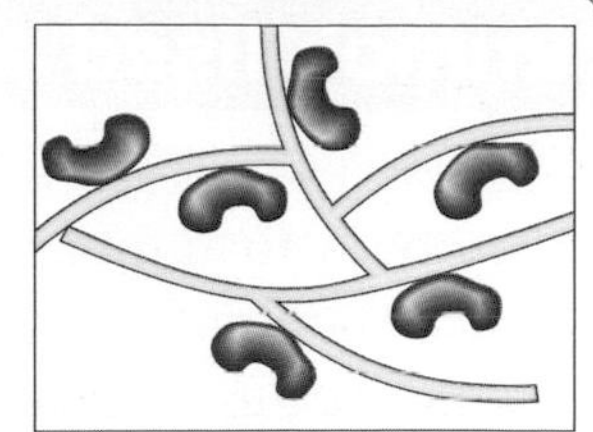

Carrier-bound. Enzyme is attached to a carrier, such as activated carbon, clay, minerals, glass beads or gold.

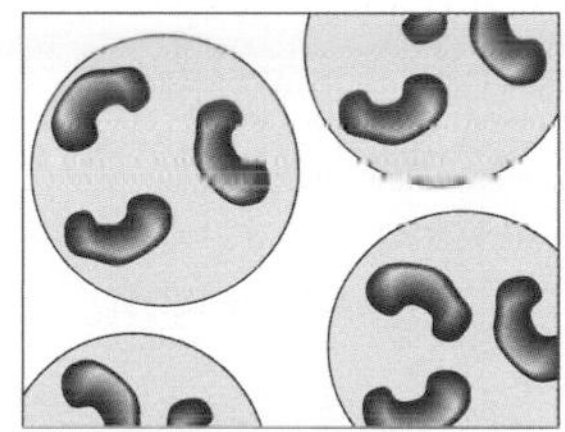

Microcapsule. Enzyme is trapped inside a semipermeable membrane, such as chitosan-alginate.

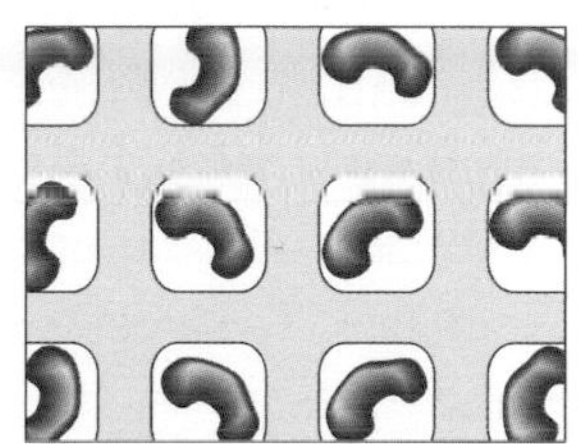

Inclusion. Enzyme is trapped within a gel, such as protein-alginate gels.

Figure 10.8 Methods of immobilising enzymes.

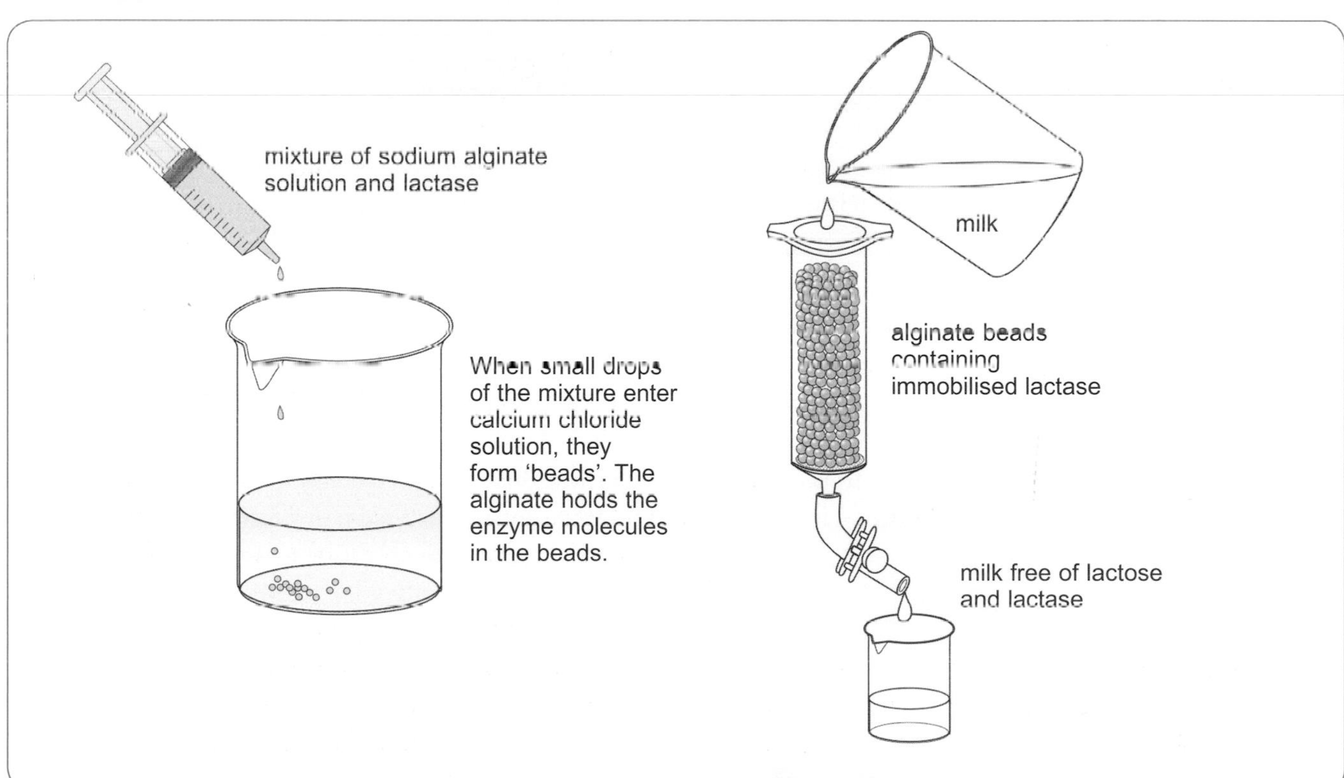
mixture of sodium alginate solution and lactase
When small drops of the mixture enter calcium chloride solution, they form 'beads'. The alginate holds the enzyme molecules in the beads.
milk
alginate beads containing immobilised lactase
milk free of lactose and lactase

Figure 10.7 Immobilising lactase in alginate.

Immobilised enzymes in a biosensor

A person with Type 1 diabetes cannot rely on their body to automatically control their blood glucose concentration. They have to do this themselves, using insulin injections and a careful diet to keep things under control.

Some people live fairly predictable lives, where their levels of activity are about the same each day, and they eat reasonably similar amounts and types of food at particular times of day. If they can do this, then they may get away with not needing to measure their blood glucose levels. They learn by experience just how much insulin they need to inject each day, and when is the best time to do it.

However, this is not true for everyone. If you eat less carbohydrate on a particular day, then you may need to inject less insulin. The same is true if you have a particularly active day, when you use up glucose in respiration more rapidly than usual.

To check blood glucose levels, and therefore to determine whether you need to eat more carbohydrate or inject more insulin, a tiny drop of blood is taken – for example, by jabbing a small needle into a fingertip. Up until around the 1970s, most people would then have used a dipstick to check the concentration of glucose in the blood sample. Glucose dipsticks have a little pad at one end that is impregnated with an immobilised enzyme called glucose oxidase. This enzyme oxidises any glucose in the blood, changing it to a substance called gluconolactone, and also producing hydrogen peroxide.

The little pad on the dipstick also contains a colourless chemical. When hydrogen peroxide is produced, it changes this chemical to another substance that has a brownish colour. The more glucose present, the darker the colour produced. A dipstick of this kind can be used to test for the presence of glucose in blood or in urine.

negative (no detectable glucose)

mg cm^{-3}	0	1.0	2.5	5.0	10.0	20.0 or more

But most people with diabetes now use a more sensitive method of testing for glucose, using a **biosensor**. Like the dipsticks, this relies on the use of immobilised glucose oxidase, which converts the glucose to gluconolactone. This reaction produces a tiny electric current, which is picked up by an electrode on the test strip. The more glucose that is present, the greater the current. This current is read by a meter, which provides a reading for blood glucose concentration within seconds. The user of the biosensor in the photograph has diabetes and the meter shows a high reading so she will need an injection of insulin.

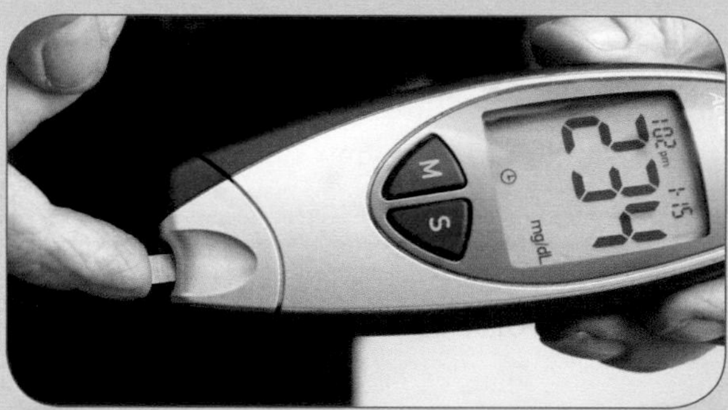

An automatic insulin pump can make life even easier for a person who needs to inject insulin. This involves a biosensor that remains permanently on the body – for example, with a sensor fixed just underneath the skin on the arm. The sensor is attached to a container of insulin. If the current produced by the biosensor goes above a certain level, then insulin is automatically injected. This is a much better method than just measuring blood glucose intermittently, because it can keep glucose concentrations much more steady. It also avoids having to repeatedly stick needles into yourself.

Perhaps one day it will be possible to use completely non-invasive techniques to measure blood glucose levels, avoiding the need for blood or tissue fluid to come into direct contact with a sensor.

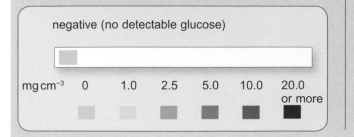

SAQ

6 Papain is a protein-hydrolysing enzyme found in pawpaw fruit and pineapples. It is often used in the preparation of processed food products. The graph shows the effect of temperature on the activity of papain in free solution and when immobilised on the surface of a gel.

a Describe the effect of temperature on the activity of the enzyme when in free solution.

b Explain the reasons for these effects.

c Compare the effect of temperature on the free and immobilised enzyme.

d Suggest reasons for the differences you have described.

e Suggest how these differences could make the use of immobilised papain preferable to free papain in the production of processed foods.

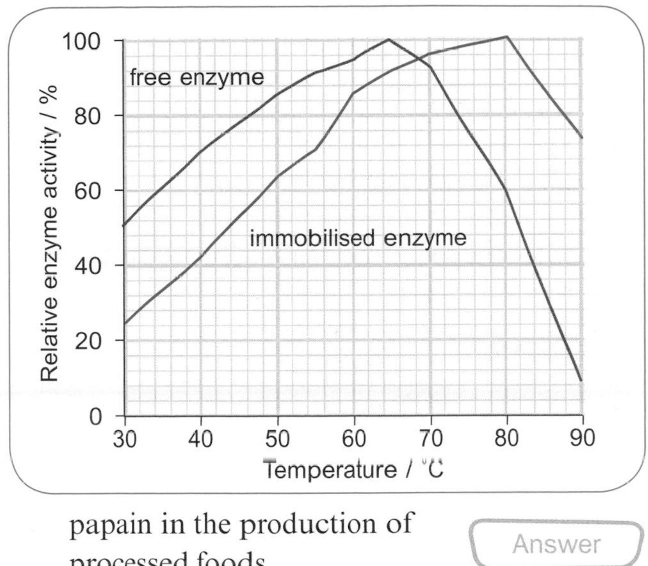

Answer

Summary

Glossary

- Biotechnology is the industrial use of living organisms, or parts of organisms, to produce food, drugs and other products.
- Microorganisms are widely used in biotechnology because of their short life cycles, ease of handling and culture, ability to use materials that might otherwise be wasted, unusual metabolic pathways and the perceived reduction in the number of ethical issues associated with their use.
- The growth of a population of microorganisms in closed culture generally follows a sigmoid curve. During the lag phase, the small initial population synthesises enzymes appropriate to the conditions in which they have been placed, and begins to multiply. Population growth then follows a log (exponential) phase, in which the rate of growth of the population is limited only by the reproductive capabilities of the organisms. As nutrients run out, or as toxic waste products build up, growth rate slows down and eventually stops.
- Many biotechnological processes involve growing microorganisms in large vessels called fermenters. The conditions inside the fermenter, especially temperature, pH, concentration of nutrients and oxygen supply, are carefully controlled to maximise the yield of the desired product.
- In batch culture, the microorganism and culture solution are placed inside the fermentation vessel and then the fermentation is allowed to proceed without the addition of any new microorganisms or nutrients, or the removal of any product. This is especially useful when the required product is a secondary metabolite that is only produced (or produced at a greater rate) at certain stages of population growth. It is used for the production of penicillin (in a modified form of batch culture where nutrients are added at intervals) and many enzymes.
- In continuous culture, a steady addition of nutrients is made to the culture throughout the fermentation, and the product is steadily collected. This is used for the production of mycoprotein.

continued

- It is important to maintain asepsis in setting up and carrying out biotechnological processes with microorganisms, because unwanted microorganisms could metabolise the nutrient sources in a different way and produce unwanted products.
- Enzymes used in biotechnology are often immobilised by fixing them within or on the surface of a solid material. This enables the enzymes to remain functional over a wider range of temperature and pH, and it avoids the problem of having to remove enzyme from the product. It also allows the re-use of the same enzymes over and over again.

Questions

1 a A number of organic chemicals are produced commercially using microorganisms. Citric acid is produced by certain fungi and is a secondary metabolite.

i Name one other secondary metabolite produced commercially from a fungus. [1]

ii State what is meant by the term *secondary metabolite*. [1]

iii State which method of fermentation would be used to produce a secondary metabolite and explain your answer. [3]

The diagram shows a 'pilot plant' assembled by a student in a school laboratory.

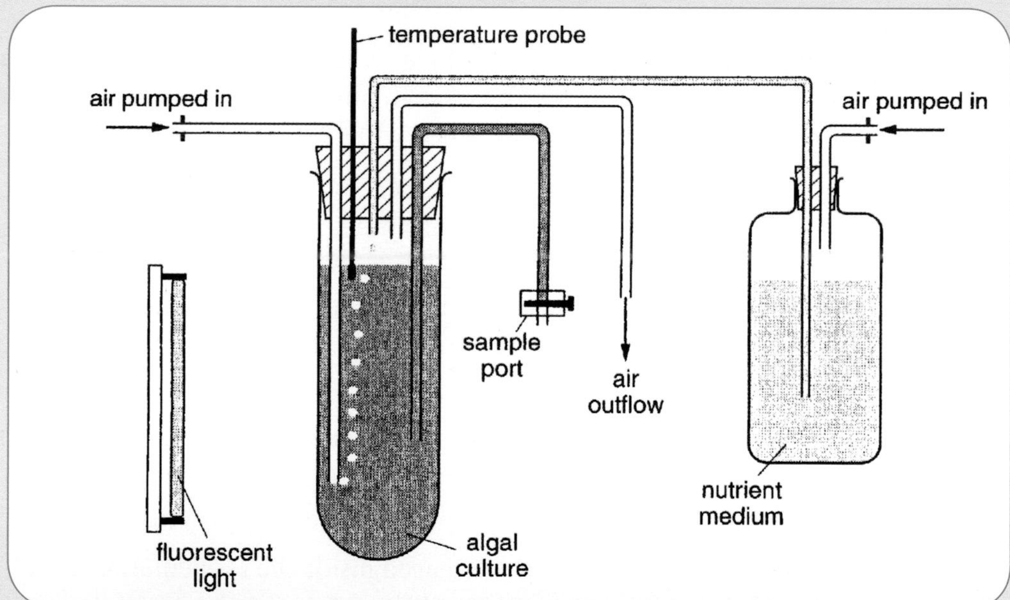

b The student has undertaken a project to culture an alga called *Chlorella* to feed brine shrimps for use as fish food. If it works, the student hopes to produce a continuous culture of algae.
Explain how the apparatus shown in the diagram allows a continuous culture of *Chlorella*. [6]

c Suggest the major problems of developing this project to enable the large-scale production of *Chlorella*. [4]

OCR Biology A (2805/04) January 2005 [Total 15]

Answer

Chapter 11

Genomes and gene technologies

e-Learning

Objectives

We first learned that DNA is the genetic material in the 1950s. Since then, our ability to understand how it works, and then how to manipulate it for our own purposes, has increased at a phenomenal rate. The use of DNA – genes – to produce something that we want is called **gene technology**. It is developing very rapidly. We are becoming more and more able to alter genes within organisms. It is very important to think about what we should do and what we should not do. The fact that we *can* do something does not mean that we *should*.

Sequencing a genome

The term **'genome'** can mean all the genes possessed by an individual organism, or by a population of organisms. It can also be used to mean the whole sequence of bases in all of the DNA in an organism.

There are many different methods of **sequencing** DNA. Figure 11.1 shows one of these methods. In this example, the purpose of the sequencing was to look for similarities and differences in the base sequences in a particular stretch of DNA in different plant species, to try to work out the relationships between them.

The human genome

In 1988, an enormous international project set out to discover the sequence of bases in each of the 23 different types of chromosomes found in human cells. In the year 2000, the project achieved its objective of producing a working draft sequence. As the programme continues, ever more detailed 'maps' are being drawn showing the DNA sequences and known genes in each human chromosome.

There are some strange facts about the human genome. For example, 99.9% of the base sequence in our DNA seems to be identical in all humans. The differences between us must be caused by the variable 0.1% and by our different environments. This 0.1% is *very* variable, and the variations in it are used in DNA profiling ('fingerprinting'), which can pin down a particular base sequence as having a very high probability of belonging to a particular person.

It is thought that only about 2% of the human genome actually codes for the manufacture of proteins – perhaps around 20 000 different proteins. As a gene can be thought of as the code for one protein, this means that there are around 20 000 genes in the human genome. There is uncertainty about this because researchers are still trying to sort out which bits of the code belong to each gene, and the number may be lower. It was not expected that the number of genes in a human would be as low as 20 000, as even mice have around 21 000 genes.

All the rest of the DNA was at first classified as 'junk', but it is now thought that a lot of it does have very important functions. Some of it, for example, may be involved in regulating the expression of other genes.

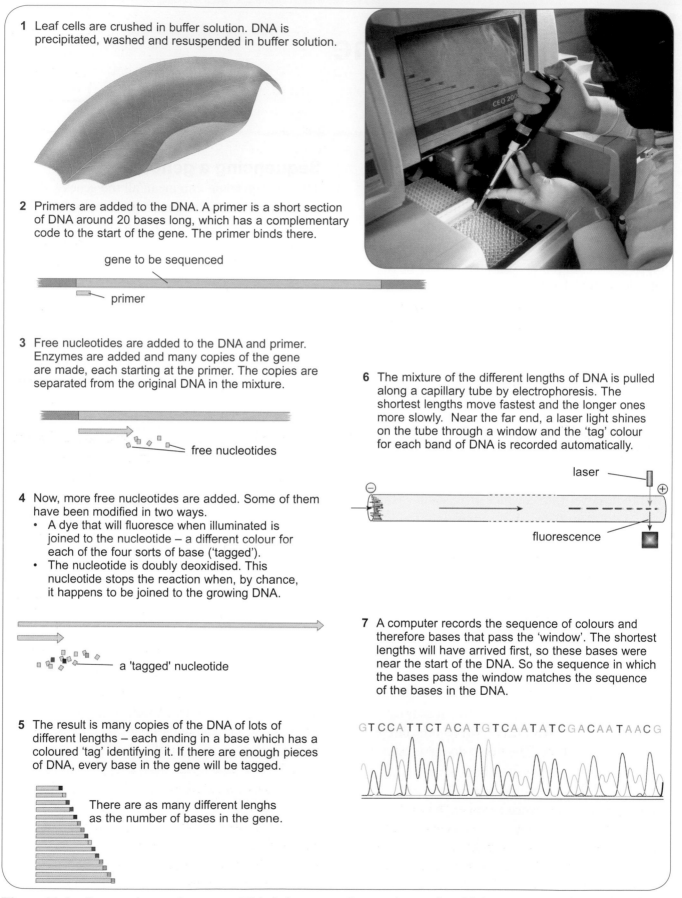

1 Leaf cells are crushed in buffer solution. DNA is precipitated, washed and resuspended in buffer solution.

2 Primers are added to the DNA. A primer is a short section of DNA around 20 bases long, which has a complementary code to the start of the gene. The primer binds there.

gene to be sequenced

primer

3 Free nucleotides are added to the DNA and primer. Enzymes are added and many copies of the gene are made, each starting at the primer. The copies are separated from the original DNA in the mixture.

free nucleotides

4 Now, more free nucleotides are added. Some of them have been modified in two ways.

- A dye that will fluoresce when illuminated is joined to the nucleotide – a different colour for each of the four sorts of base ('tagged').
- The nucleotide is doubly deoxidised. This nucleotide stops the reaction when, by chance, it happens to be joined to the growing DNA.

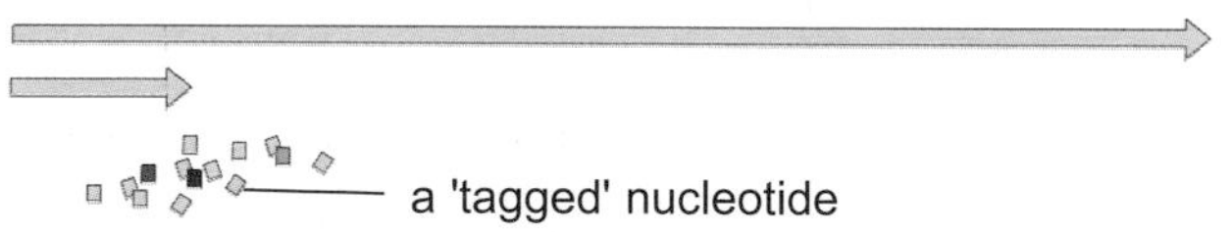

5 The result is many copies of the DNA of lots of different lengths – each ending in a base which has a coloured 'tag' identifying it. If there are enough pieces of DNA, every base in the gene will be tagged.

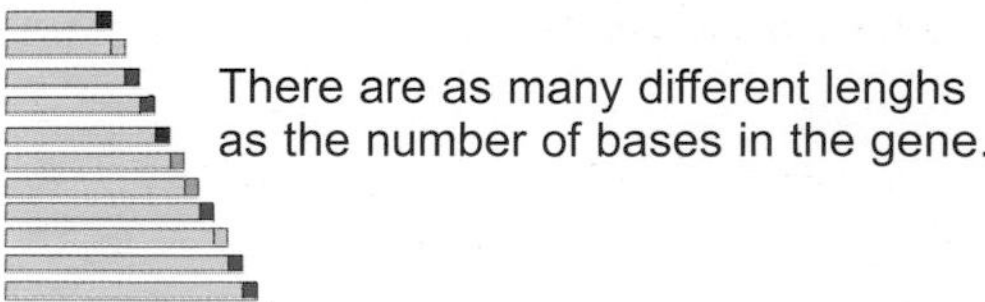

There are as many different lenghs as the number of bases in the gene.

6 The mixture of the different lengths of DNA is pulled along a capillary tube by electrophoresis. The shortest lengths move fastest and the longer ones more slowly. Near the far end, a laser light shines on the tube through a window and the 'tag' colour for each band of DNA is recorded automatically.

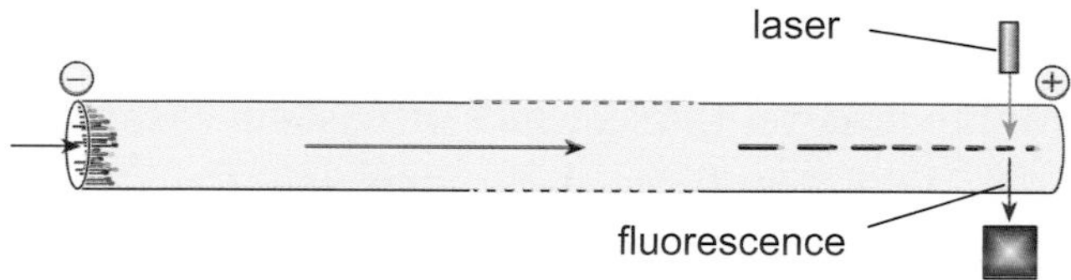

7 A computer records the sequence of colours and therefore bases that pass the 'window'. The shortest lengths will have arrived first, so these bases were near the start of the DNA. So the sequence in which the bases pass the window matches the sequence of the bases in the DNA.

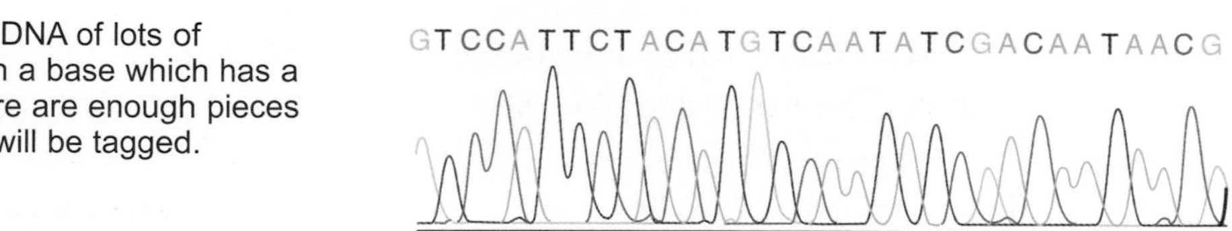

Figure 11.1 Sequencing a plant gene. This is just one of several ways in which a gene can be sequenced.

- If the whole genome is to be sequenced, multiple copies of it (that is, multiple copies of all the DNA in an organism's nuclei) are made, using a technique called PCR (described on pages 171–172). All of this DNA is then squeezed through a tiny hole under high pressure. This breaks it up, randomly, into lengths ranging from about 2000 bp (base pairs) to 10 000 bp long. These lengths may be then be cut up into smaller lengths, as this makes it easier to sequence them.
- The next step involves making multiple labelled copies of each of these small lengths of DNA. To do this, they are mixed with an enzyme called DNA polymerase, a primer, some 'normal' DNA nucleotides and some nucleotides that have been 'labelled' by attaching a fluorescent dye to them. Four colours of dye are used, a different one for each of the bases A, C, T and G. These labelled nucleotides are also modified so that when they are incorporated into a growing nucleotide chain, the chain cannot be increased any more – it has to stop.
- The DNA polymerase uses the nucleotides in the mixture to make multiple copies of each of the lengths of DNA. However, most of these copies will not be *full* copies, because if a labelled nucleotide is added in at any point, then the chain stops growing. The result is many different chains, all different lengths. Each chain ends with a labelled nucleotide.
- This mixture of lengths of DNA is then separated using electrophoresis (explained on page 170). A voltage is applied across a capillary tube, which draws the DNA towards the positively charged end. The shorter the length of the DNA fragment, the faster it travels.
- A computer records the colours as they pass the end of the tube. The first colour to pass represents the base at the end of the shortest fragment. The last colour to pass represents the base at the end of the longest fragment. If there are enough fragments, then every base in the complete chain will be represented. The computer then works out the sequence of bases in that particular length of DNA.
- This is done for every piece of the DNA that was originally produced from the whole genome. A computer programme then uses the results to work out the overall sequence of nucleotides in the whole genome.

These processes are now largely automated. You put your DNA sample into the sequencing machine, and get a print-out like the one at the bottom of Figure 11.1. Nevertheless, the preparation of the DNA and the analysis of the results is still a time-consuming process requiring considerable human skill. By 2007, researchers had sequenced the genomes of many different organisms, including humans, mice, fruit flies, a nematode worm *Caenorhabditis elegans* and a small weed called *Arabidopsis.*

Using gene sequencing

When the idea of sequencing the entire human genome was dreamt up, some people thought that if we only knew the whole sequence of bases in our DNA, we would be able to work out how a human being is made, and why there are differences between us. In practice, things are (as usual in biology) not quite so simple. We may well know the entire sequence of bases in our DNA, but finding out exactly what they do is another matter altogether. We do not even know for certain all of the lengths which are genes coding for proteins. Of the remainder, we believe that some lengths are involved in switching other genes on or off, some lengths code for mRNA that is not used for making proteins, and the functions of yet others are still to be determined. It certainly is not all just 'junk' as some people originally thought.

However, if we have gene sequences from different organisms, then we can use them to *compare* the genome of one organism with that of another. This can give us insights into the evolutionary relationships between them. We have already seen, for example, how the DNA sequences in homeobox genes in humans are very similar to those in fruit flies, implying that we share a common ancestor. DNA sequencing is now widely used when determining how closely related two species are. The example shown in

Figure 11.1 was used – together with comparisons of their morphology (structure) – to work out the relationships between several different species of rushes, to decide how they should be classified.

Extension

Genetic engineering

Genetic engineering means using technology to change the genetic material of an organism. It may involve taking genes from an organism of one species and placing them in another, where they are expressed. The DNA that has been altered by this process, and which now contains lengths from two different species, is called **recombinant DNA**.

The organism to which the new gene has been added is said to be a recombinant organism, or a genetically **transformed organism**, or a **transgenic organism**. The term **genetically modified organism** (GMO) is also used. This is not restricted to organisms into which genes from other species have been placed. GMOs can also be organisms that have had their own genes altered using gene technology.

Mitochondrial Eve

As well as the DNA in the chromosomes in the nucleus, we also have a much smaller quantity of DNA in our mitochondria. It is known as mitochondrial DNA, mtDNA.

All of our mtDNA comes from our mothers. All the mtDNA in a zygote comes only from the egg, not the sperm. So your mtDNA is exactly the same as your mother's, her mother's and her mother's before her, back and back over hundreds of generations. Your brothers and sisters have identical mtDNA to yours. So do your mother's brothers and sisters, and their children, because they have all inherited their mtDNA from your mother's mother.

The only way in which mtDNA can change is by mutation. In the 1990s, researchers used this idea to work out how long ago our first common female ancestor may have lived. They looked at differences between the base sequences in the mtDNA of 147 people from different parts of the world. Then they used the so-called 'mitochondrial clock' to work how long it would have taken for these differences to build up. They arrived at a value of between 140 000 and 290 000 years ago. They suggested that, at this date, a woman lived who could have been a common ancestor to all of us. She has been named 'mitochondrial Eve'.

The 'mitochondrial clock' is an estimate of how often mutations happen in mtDNA. At first it was assumed that all of the nucleotides in the mtDNA were equally likely to mutate. More recent studies have found that different sites in the mtDNA actually have different mutation rates. Some sites, called 'fast sites', have an average of 274 mutation events per million generations. (A generation is defined as 30 years.) But most sites mutate much more slowly than this, at between 23 and 1 mutation events per million generations. This has required recalculations of the time at which 'mitochondrial Eve' lived. Some estimates put her at only 10 000 years ago, but most suggest a much earlier date of at least 140 000 years ago.

These studies don't suggest that 'mitochondrial Eve' was once the only woman on Earth. They simply show that it is possible that all the mtDNA found in modern humans could have been derived from one set of mtDNA that was in existence at a particular time in the past, and that has since been passed down through the female line. The calculations make a great many assumptions, and most archaeologists and researchers into human evolution take the conclusions with a large pinch of salt. All the same, this is a useful tool that can add to our understanding of how human evolution may have taken place, and the timescales involved.

Gene technology is an expensive process, and it still runs a very poor second to conventional selective breeding in terms of numbers of new varieties of crop plants and farm animals that are being produced. There has been considerable opposition to it from many people in the UK and other countries, which has greatly slowed down the widespread introduction of genetically modified organisms into food production and some other industries, too. Nevertheless, there are several instances where a product made using genetic engineering is literally a life-saver, such as the human insulin secreted by genetically modified bacteria.

We will look first at the general principles involved in genetic engineering, and then at some of the techniques in more detail.

An overview of gene transfer

1 The gene that is required is identified. It is either cut out of the chromosomes, or it is made by 'reverse transcription' of mRNA.
2 Multiple copies of the gene are made using a technique called PCR, which stands for polymerase chain reaction.
3 The gene is inserted into a vector – an organism or structure that is able to deliver the gene into the required cells.
4 The vector inserts the gene into the cells.
5 The cells that have been successfully transformed are identified and cloned.

Now let's look at how this has been done in order to produce bacteria that secrete human growth hormone, HGH.

Extracting the gene

A length of DNA that is known to contain the HGH gene is treated with **restriction enzymes**. These enzymes are made by bacteria. They are used by the bacterium to attack and destroy DNA that has been inserted into them by viruses. (Viruses called bacteriophages, or phages, can infect bacteria.) There are many different kinds of restriction enzymes, and each kind cuts DNA at a particular base sequence. For example, a restriction enzyme called *Bam*H1 always cuts DNA where there is a GGATCC sequence on one DNA strand and, of course, the complementary sequence CCTAGG on the other (Figure 11.2). If you know the base sequences near the ends of the gene you require, then you can use a particular restriction enzyme to cut at these points.

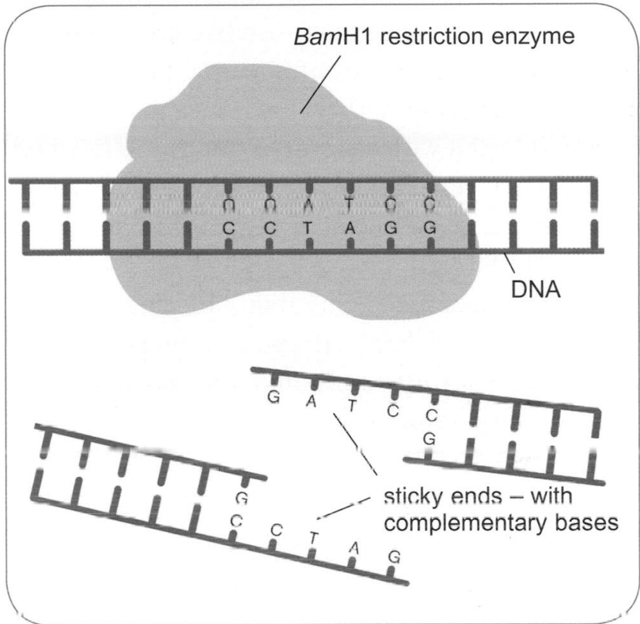

Figure 11.2 Cutting DNA with a restriction enzyme.

You can see that the restriction enzyme does not cut straight across the DNA molecule, but cuts the two strands of the DNA at different points. This leaves short lengths of unpaired bases on both pieces. These are called **sticky ends** (because they can easily form hydrogen bonds with, and therefore 'stick' to, similar ends on other pieces of DNA) and, as you will see, they have an important function in the next step in the process.

You are still likely to get a mixture of different lengths of DNA, so you will still have the problem of identifying the bits that you need. The way in which the technique of electrophoresis and the use of DNA probes can help with this is described on pages 170–171. Multiple copies of the required length of DNA can then be made using a technique called the **polymerase chain reaction, PCR**. This is described on pages 171–172.

Inserting the gene into a vector

In order to get the gene into the recipient cell, a go-between called a **vector** often has to be used.

One commonly used vector, used if the gene is to be inserted into bacteria, is a **plasmid**. A plasmid is a small, circular piece of DNA that occurs naturally in bacteria (Figure 11.3). Plasmids often contain genes that confer resistance to antibiotics. They can be exchanged between bacteria – even between different species of bacteria. (This is a concern for humans, because it means that a person infected with a strain of antibiotic-resistant bacteria may also become a breeding ground for a different species of bacterium that is also resistant to that antibiotic.)

We can make use of this ability of plasmids to get inside bacterial cells. If you can put your piece of human DNA into a plasmid, the plasmid can deliver it into a bacterium.

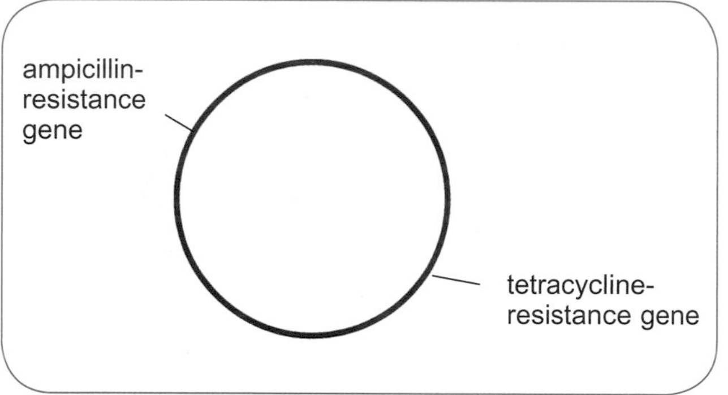

Figure 11.3 Plasmid pBR322.

To get the plasmids, the bacteria containing them can be treated with enzymes to dissolve their cell walls. The 'naked' bacteria are then centrifuged, so that the relatively large bacterial chromosomes are separated from the much smaller plasmids and the cell debris.

The circular DNA molecule making up the plasmid is then cut open using the same restriction enzyme as was used for cutting out the HGH gene from the original DNA. This leaves sticky ends that are complementary to those on the required gene.

The plasmids and HGH genes are then mixed up together. Some of the plasmid sticky ends will pair up with some of the HGH gene sticky ends. The enzyme DNA **ligase** is then used to link together the deoxyribose–phosphate backbones of the DNA molecule, producing a closed circle of double-stranded DNA containing the HGH gene (Figure 11.4).

Not all the plasmids will take up the HGH gene like this. Some of them just join up with themselves again.

Plasmids are not the only kind of vector that can be used. Viruses can also be used as vectors as

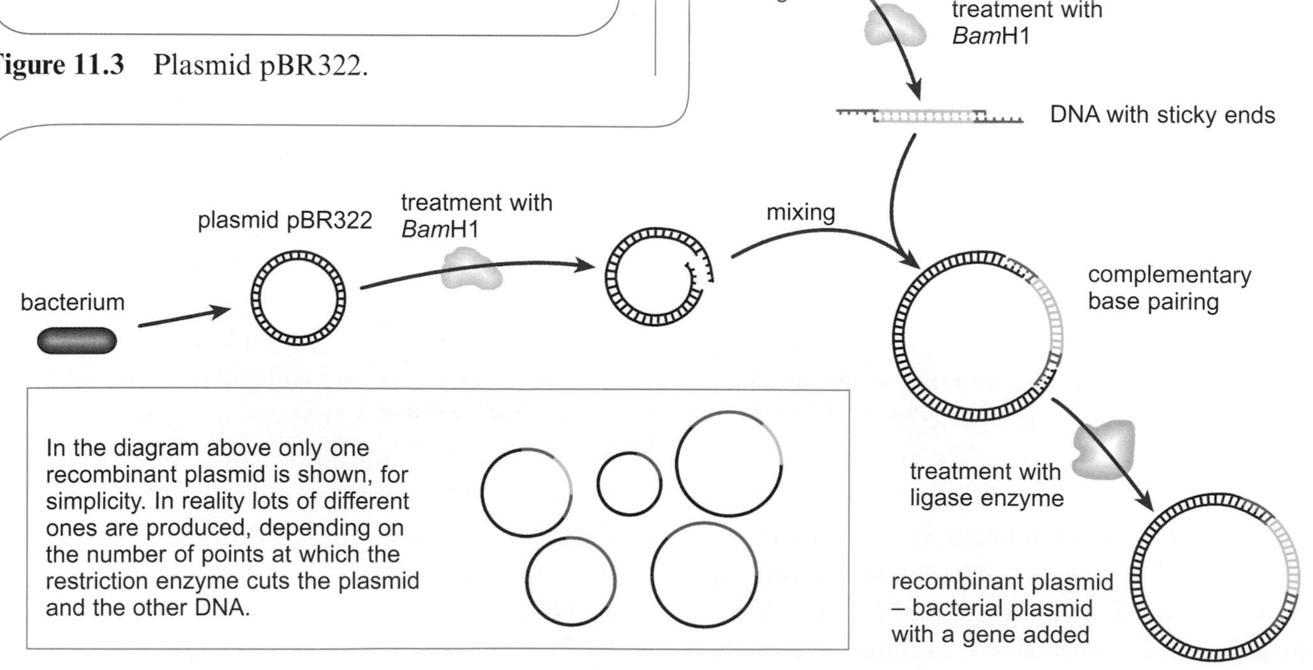

Figure 11.4 Inserting the HGH gene into a plasmid.

they, too, have the ability to insert their DNA into other cells. Yet another type of vector is **liposomes**. These are tiny balls of lipids containing the DNA. They have been used in some attempts at gene therapy in humans. Gene therapy is described on pages 176–177.

Getting the plasmids into bacteria

Now the plasmids are mixed with a culture of the bacterium that is to be transformed. Calcium ions are added to the mixture, because they affect the cell walls and plasma membranes of the bacteria, making it easier for them to take up the plasmids. A small proportion of the bacteria, perhaps 1%, take up plasmids containing the HGH gene. The rest either do not take up plasmids at all, or take up ones that did not contain the HGH gene.

To sort out the bacteria that have been transformed (i.e. contain the HGH gene) from those which have not, the fact that the plasmid contains antibiotic-resistance genes is used. For example, the plasmid pBR322 contains two resistance genes, one for tetracycline and one for ampicillin. It just so happens that, if the restriction enzyme *Bam*H1 is used to cut the DNA of the plasmid, it cuts right through the middle of the tetracycline-resistance gene. So, when the HGH gene is inserted, it inactivates the tetracycline-resistance gene (Figure 11.5).

The bacteria are then grown on agar jelly to which ampicillin has been added. Any that survive must have taken up the plasmid. However, we don't know which have taken up the transformed plasmids (containing the HGH gene) and which have just taken up the unaltered plasmids.

To sort these out, a sample of each colony of bacteria is now placed on another agar plate, this time containing tetracycline (Figure 11.6). This is called **replica plating**. Only the ones that have a working resistance gene to tetracycline will survive – and these must be the ones that have *not* taken up the transformed plasmids. So now we can go back to the first plate, and select just the colonies of bacteria that were *not* able to grow on the tetracycline plate. These are the ones that contain the required gene.

These genetically modified bacteria are now cultured on a large scale, in fermenters (Chapter 10). They secrete HGH, which is extracted, purified and sold.

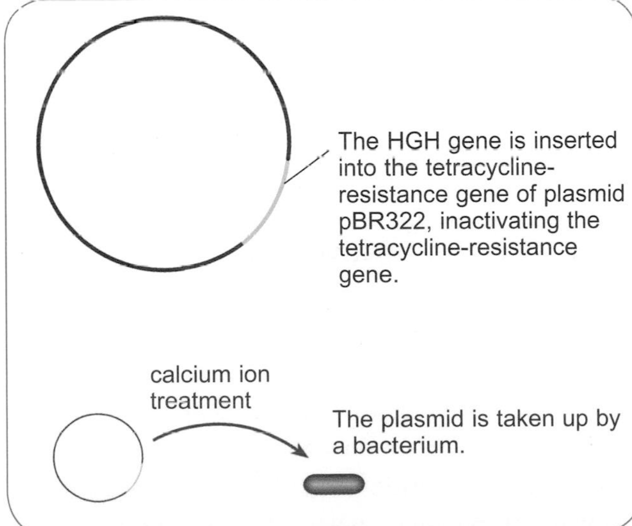

Figure 11.5 Inserting the gene into a bacterium.

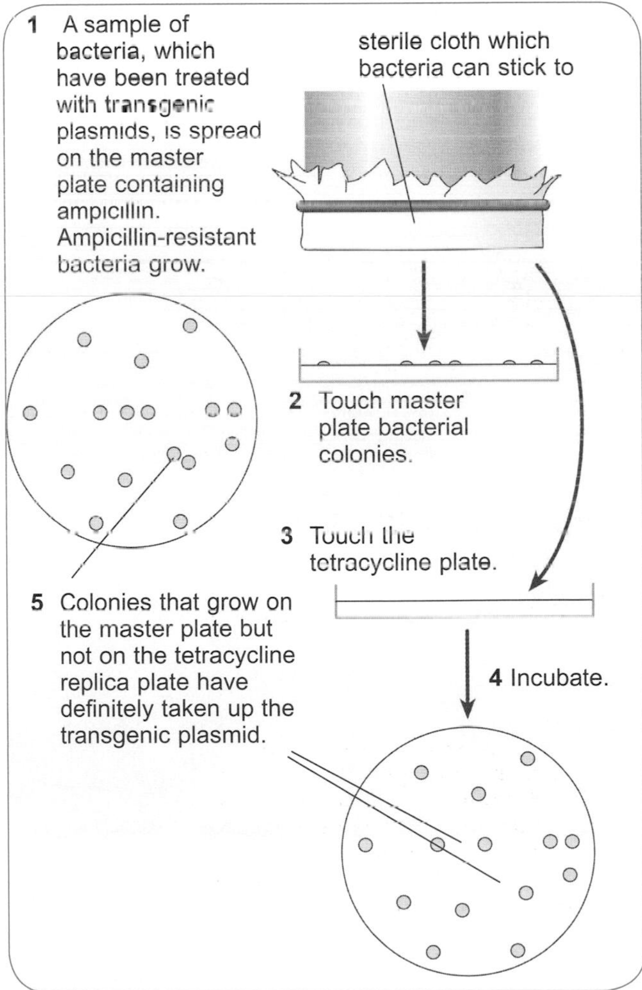

1 A sample of bacteria, which have been treated with transgenic plasmids, is spread on the master plate containing ampicillin. Ampicillin-resistant bacteria grow.
sterile cloth which bacteria can stick to
2 Touch master plate bacterial colonies.
3 Touch the tetracycline plate.
4 Incubate.
5 Colonies that grow on the master plate but not on the tetracycline replica plate have definitely taken up the transgenic plasmid.

Figure 11.6 Replica plating.

Other genetic markers

In the technique described on page 167, antibiotic resistance genes were used to identify the bacteria that had been successfully transformed. However, there has been some concern about this, because it could increase the risk of other, potentially pathogenic, bacteria taking up these genes and becoming resistant to antibiotics. So other markers now tend to be used.

One of the most widely used types of marker is a gene that causes fluorescence. The gene was first found in jellyfish, and it codes for the production of an enzyme that produces a protein that fluoresces bright green in ultraviolet light. The gene for the enzyme is inserted into the plasmids. So all that needs to be done to identify the bacteria that have taken up the plasmids is to shine ultraviolet light on them. The ones that have been transformed will glow (Figure 11.7).

Producing human insulin from bacteria

One of the very first successes of genetic engineering was the production of clones of the bacterium *Escherichia coli* that contained the human insulin gene. Biotechnology companies began to work on this idea in the 1970s. They tried several different approaches, finally succeeding in the early 1980s. The complete process is shown in Figure 11.8.

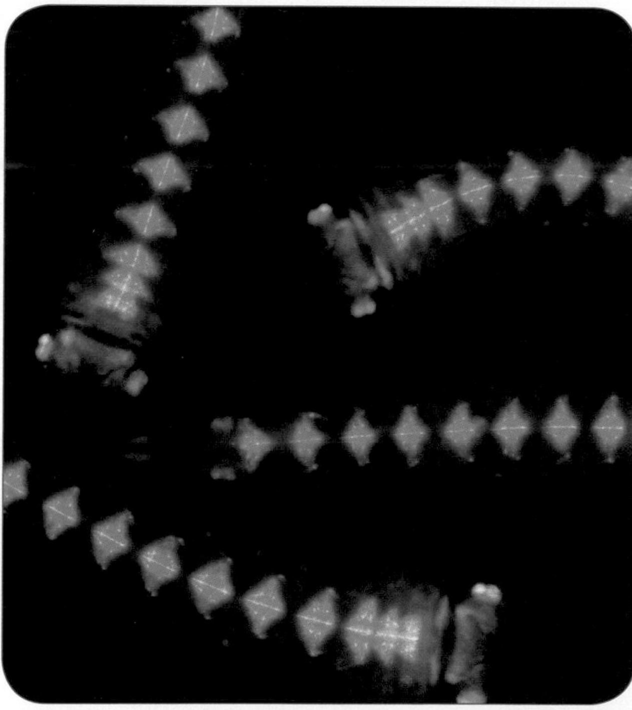

Figure 11.7 These mosquito larvae have been genetically modified for research into their role in transmitting malaria. Genes for a green fluorescent protein were inserted into the eggs from which they developed, so the transformed larvae glow green.

The first task was to isolate the gene coding for human insulin from all the rest of the DNA in a human cell. We have seen how this can be done using restriction enzymes, which can cut out lengths of DNA. However, insulin is only a small protein, and the insulin gene is a very tiny portion of the huge quantity of DNA in the nucleus of each cell, and at that time techniques for identifying particular lengths of DNA were still quite difficult to use. Another approach was taken, which made it much easier to isolate the insulin gene.

The approach made use of the fact that this gene is only expressed by beta cells in the islets of Langerhans in the pancreas, and these cells really specialise in doing just that. This means that a very high proportion of the mRNA in these cells has been transcribed from the insulin gene.

So mRNA was extracted from these cells. The mRNA was then incubated with an enzyme called **reverse transcriptase**. This comes from a group of viruses called **retroviruses** – HIV is an example of one. As the name suggests, this enzyme does something that does not normally happen in human cells – it makes DNA using RNA as a template. In this instance, complementary single-stranded DNA molecules were made, using the mRNA as a template. These single-stranded molecules were then converted to double-stranded DNA molecules, which carried the code for insulin – they were insulin genes.

We have seen that we need to have sticky ends on each end of the gene, so that it can be successfully inserted into a vector. In the first successful production of bacteria genetically engineered to produce insulin, the sticky ends on the insulin gene were made not by using restriction enzymes, but by adding lengths of single-stranded DNA made up of guanine nucleotides. Then similar lengths, but made up of cytosine nucleotides, were added to the cut ends of the plasmids used as vectors.

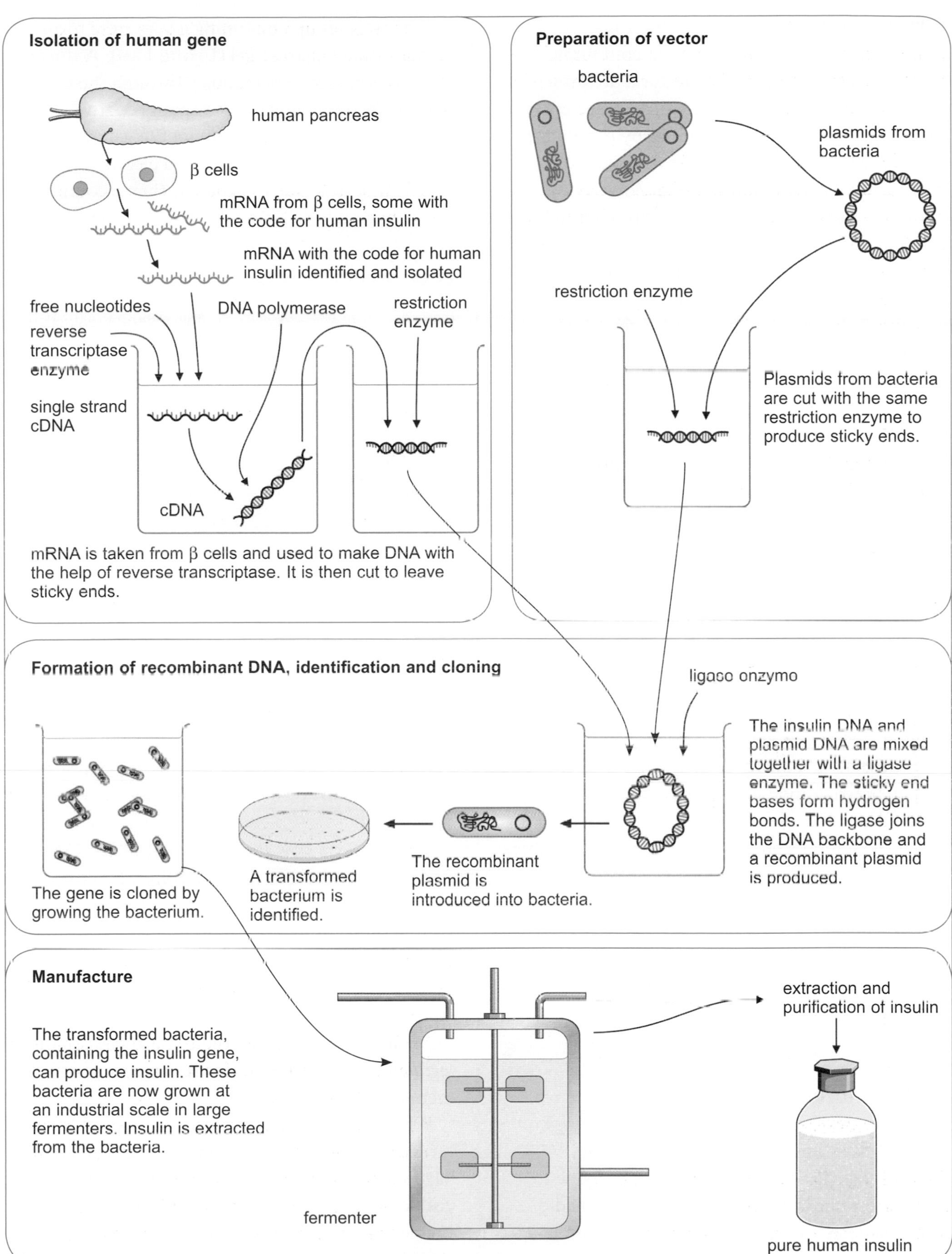

Isolation of human gene
human pancreas
β cells
mRNA from β cells, some with the code for human insulin
mRNA with the code for human insulin identified and isolated
free nucleotides
DNA polymerase
restriction enzyme
reverse transcriptase enzyme
single strand cDNA
cDNA
mRNA is taken from β cells and used to make DNA with the help of reverse transcriptase. It is then cut to leave sticky ends.
Preparation of vector
bacteria
plasmids from bacteria
restriction enzyme
Plasmids from bacteria are cut with the same restriction enzyme to produce sticky ends.
Formation of recombinant DNA, identification and cloning
ligase enzyme
The insulin DNA and plasmid DNA are mixed together with a ligase enzyme. The sticky end bases form hydrogen bonds. The ligase joins the DNA backbone and a recombinant plasmid is produced.
The recombinant plasmid is introduced into bacteria.
A transformed bacterium is identified.
The gene is cloned by growing the bacterium.
Manufacture
The transformed bacteria, containing the insulin gene, can produce insulin. These bacteria are now grown at an industrial scale in large fermenters. Insulin is extracted from the bacteria.
fermenter
extraction and purification of insulin
pure human insulin

Figure 11.8 Producing insulin from genetically modified bacteria.

Today, several different biotechnology companies have produced bacteria containing the human insulin gene. The bacteria are grown in fermenters, and the insulin that they secrete is collected, purified and sold for use by people with diabetes. This is a much cheaper and more efficient way of obtaining insulin than the old way – which involved collecting up pancreases from animals that had been slaughtered (usually pigs or cattle) and extracting insulin from them. It also has the advantage that the insulin is absolutely identical to human insulin, because it is made using the base sequence on the human insulin gene.

SAQ

1 Outline the use of each of these enzymes in gene technology:

a restriction enzymes

b DNA ligase

c reverse transcriptase.

Answer

Promoters

Bacteria contain many different genes, which make many different proteins. But not all these genes are switched on at once. We saw in Chapter 7 that genes are switched on by **promoters**. If we want the gene that we have inserted into a bacterium to be expressed, then we also have to insert an appropriate promoter for it.

When bacteria were first transformed to produce human insulin, the insulin gene was inserted next to the β galactosidase (lactase) gene, so that they shared a promoter. The promoter switches on the gene when the bacterium needs to metabolise lactose. If the bacteria are grown in a medium containing lactose, they synthesise both β galactosidase and human insulin.

Electrophoresis

One of the techniques used in gene technology – for example, in sequencing a genome, in genetic fingerprinting or in identifying a gene to be transferred to another organism – is called **electrophoresis**. This separates different fragments of DNA according to their sizes.

A tank is set up containing a very pure form of agar called **agarose gel** (Figure 11.9). A direct current is passed continuously through the gel. The DNA fragments carry a small negative electric charge. They are pulled through the gel towards the anode (the positively charged electrode). The smaller the fragments, the faster they move.

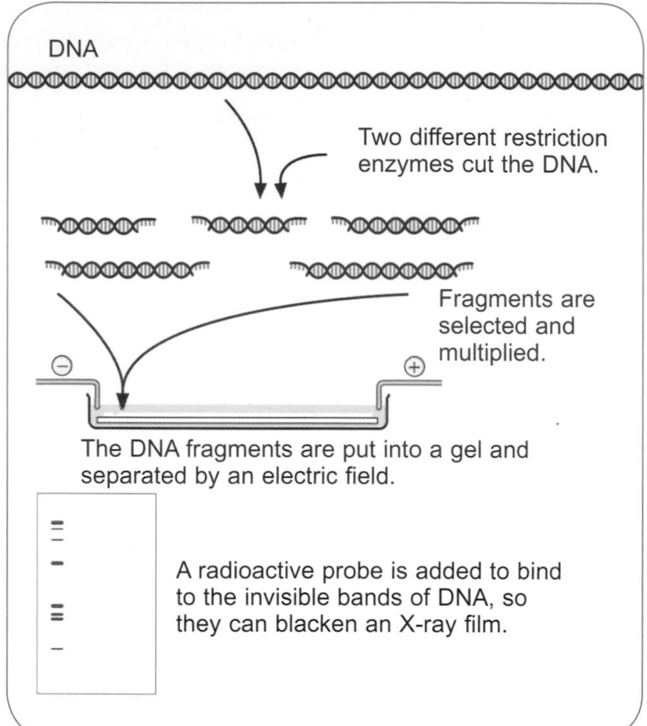

DNA
Two different restriction enzymes cut the DNA.
Fragments are selected and multiplied.
The DNA fragments are put into a gel and separated by an electric field.
A radioactive probe is added to bind to the invisible bands of DNA, so they can blacken an X-ray film.

Figure 11.9 Using electrophoresis to separate DNA fragments of different lengths.

We have seen how the movement of the DNA fragments can be tracked by noting when they pass a particular point – using nucleotides labelled with fluorescent markers (Figure 11.1). This uses the *time* at which the fragments pass a particular point to sort out the longer from the shorter ones. Another method allows the fragments to move for a particular length of time, and then uses the *distance* they have moved in this time to sort them out.

When the current in the tank in Figure 11.9 is turned off, the gel contains DNA fragments that have ended up in different places. These are not visible straight away. One way of making them visible is to transfer them, very carefully, onto absorbent paper, which is placed on top of the gel.

Now the paper is heated just enough to make the two strands in each DNA molecule separate from one another. Short sequences of single-stranded DNA, called **probes**, are added. These may be 'labelled' using fluorescence, or using radioactive isotopes. The probes pair up with the DNA fragments on the paper. The positions of the DNA fragments can now be detected, either by shining ultraviolet light onto them or by placing the paper against an X-ray film. The radiation emitted by the probes makes the film go dark. So we end up with a pattern of dark stripes on the film, matching the positions of the DNA fragments in the agarose gel (Figure 11.10).

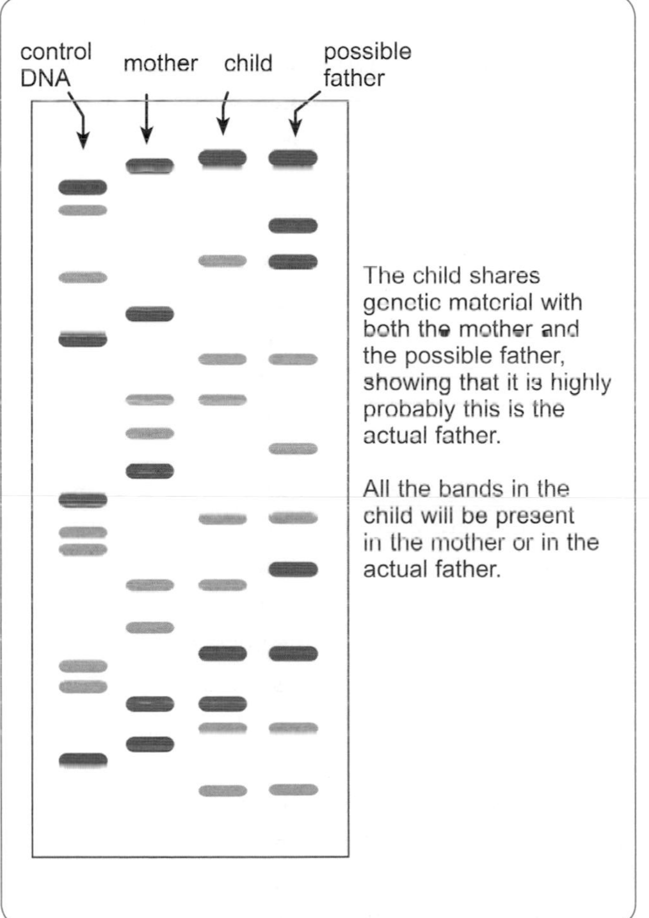

Figure 11.10 These patterns were made following electrophoresis and labelling of DNA samples taken from four individuals. The same sections of the genome were tested for each person. This process is called DNA profiling.

DNA probes

Probes are used in all kinds of gene technology. They help to pick out the required piece of DNA from amongst a whole collection of different DNA fragments in a mixture.

A probe is a length of single-stranded DNA, often a few hundred base pairs long, that has a base sequence complementary to the one you want to extract. It does not have to be *perfectly* complementary, so it does not matter if you don't know the precise base sequence of the required DNA.

The probe is 'labelled' in some way. It might, for example, be made with nucleotides containing an isotope of phosphorus, ^{32}P, which emits beta radiation that can be detected using X-ray film.

When the probe is mixed with the DNA fragments, it forms hydrogen bonds with any stretches of DNA that are mostly complementary to its own base sequence. If we can see where the probes are, then we also know where these DNA fragments are.

The polymerase chain reaction

The polymerase chain reaction, generally known as **PCR**, is used in almost every application of gene technology. It is a method for rapidly producing a very large number of copies of a particular length of DNA.

Figure 11.11 shows the various steps in PCR. First, the DNA is denatured, usually by heating it. This separates the DNA molecule into its two strands, leaving bases exposed.

The enzyme **DNA polymerase** is then used to build new strands of DNA against these exposed ones.

However, DNA polymerase will not just begin doing this with no 'guidance' – it needs to know where to start. A **primer** is used to begin the process. This is a short length of DNA, often about 20 base pairs long, that has a base sequence complementary to the start of the part of the DNA strand that you want to copy. The primer attaches to the start of the DNA strand, and then the polymerase will continue to add nucleotides all along the rest of the DNA strand.

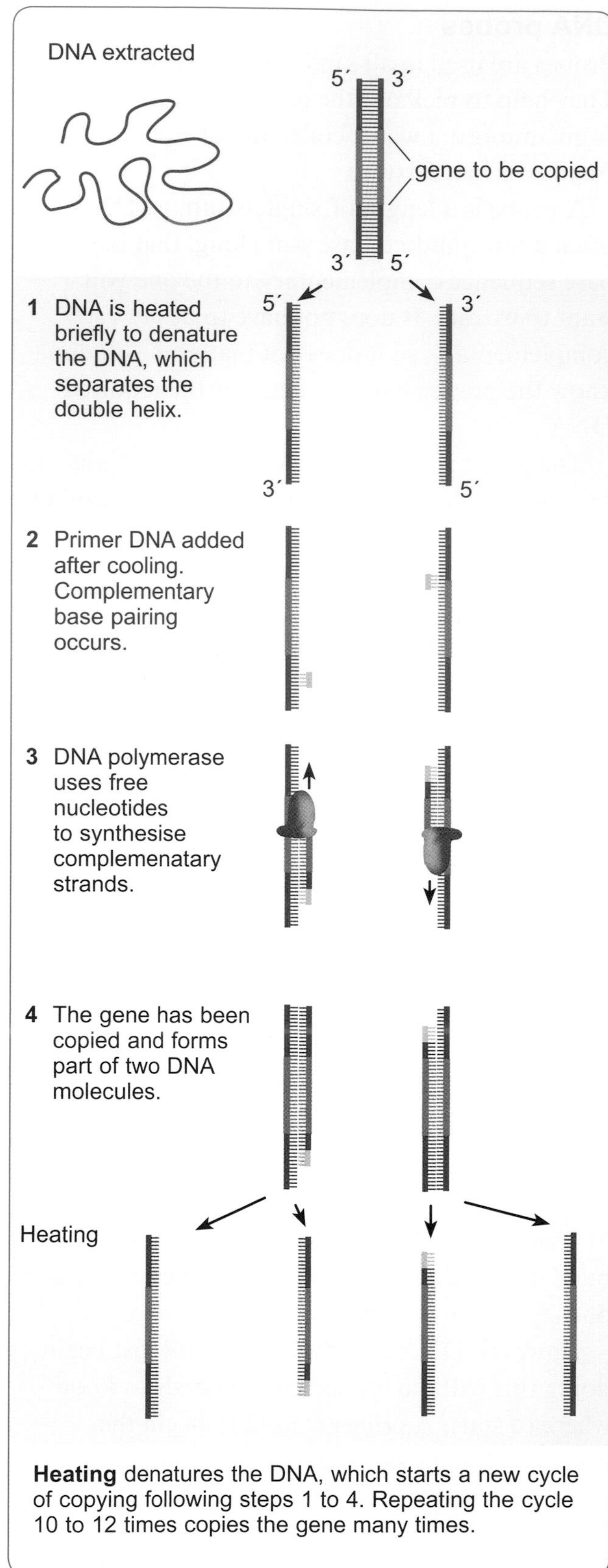

DNA extracted
5′
3′
gene to be copied
3′
5′
1 DNA is heated briefly to denature the DNA, which separates the double helix.
5′
3′
3′
5′
2 Primer DNA added after cooling. Complementary base pairing occurs.
3 DNA polymerase uses free nucleotides to synthesise complemenatary strands.
4 The gene has been copied and forms part of two DNA molecules.
Heating
Heating denatures the DNA, which starts a new cycle of copying following steps 1 to 4. Repeating the cycle 10 to 12 times copies the gene many times.

Figure 11.11 The polymerase chain reaction.

Once the DNA has been copied, the mixture is heated again, which once more separates the two strands in each DNA molecule, leaving them available for copying again. Once more, the primers fix themselves to the start of each strand of unpaired nucleotides, and DNA polymerase makes complementary copies of them.

The three stages in each round of copying need different temperatures:

- Denaturing the double-stranded DNA molecules to make single-stranded ones requires a high temperature, around 95 °C.
- Attaching the primers to the ends of the single-stranded DNA molecules (known as **annealing**) requires a temperature of about 65 °C.
- Building up complete new DNA strands using DNA polymerase requires a temperature of around 72 °C. (The polymerases used for this process come from microorganisms that have evolved to live in hot environments.)

Most laboratories that work with DNA will have a machine that automatically changes the temperature of the mixture. You simply place your DNA sample into a tube together with the primers, free nucleotides, a buffer solution and the DNA polymerase, switch on the machine and let it run. The tubes are very small (they each hold about 1 mm^3) and have very thin walls, so as the temperature in the machine changes, the temperature inside the tubes also changes very quickly.

You can see how this could theoretically go on forever, making more and more copies of what might originally have been just a tiny number of DNA molecules. A single DNA molecule can be used to produce literally billions of copies of itself in just a few hours. PCR has made it possible to get enough DNA from a tiny sample – for example, a microscopic portion of a drop of blood left at a crime scene – to carry out sequencing.

SAQ

2 Explain the difference between a primer and a probe. Answer

Another example of genetic engineering – making Golden Rice™

A lack of vitamin A, **retinol**, in the diet causes health problems to hundreds of thousands of people, in developing countries in South East Asia, for example. Vitamin A is required for the formation of the visual pigment rhodopsin, responsible for the reception of light energy by rod cells in the retina of the eye. Vitamin A deficiency therefore causes night blindness. It also reduces resistance to bacterial and viral infections, and so increases the risk of a person dying from infectious diseases such as measles, or diarrhoea caused by microorganisms.

Most of us get plenty of vitamin A in our diets. It is present in most meat products, especially liver. We can also make retinol from a precursor called **β carotene**, an orange pigment found in plant foods such as carrots. However, people who eat diets based on rice may get insufficient amounts of either β carotene or retinol.

In an attempt to address this problem, by providing an affordable way of improving dietary intake of β carotene to people who eat a rice-based diet, a new variety of rice, called **Golden Rice™**, has been developed through genetic engineering (Figure 11.12).

The idea was to insert genes into rice plants that would increase the amount of β carotene made by the plants, and that would be expressed in their seeds. The first type of Golden Rice™ that was produced, in 1999–2000, used a gene from daffodils that coded for the production of an enzyme called phytoene synthase, and another from the bacterium *Erwinia uredovora* that coded for the enzyme carotene desaturase. This worked, but the quantities of β carotene that were produced were not high enough to make a significant increase in the vitamin A levels in children who ate the rice. The rice only contained about 1.6 μg of β carotene per gram. As a child requires about 300 μg of vitamin A per day, and as you need 12 μg of β carotene to make 1 μg of vitamin A, they would have to eat a lot of rice to get this amount. The low level of β carotene in the Golden Rice™ helped to fuel the criticisms which were already being made of the project – that this was not the

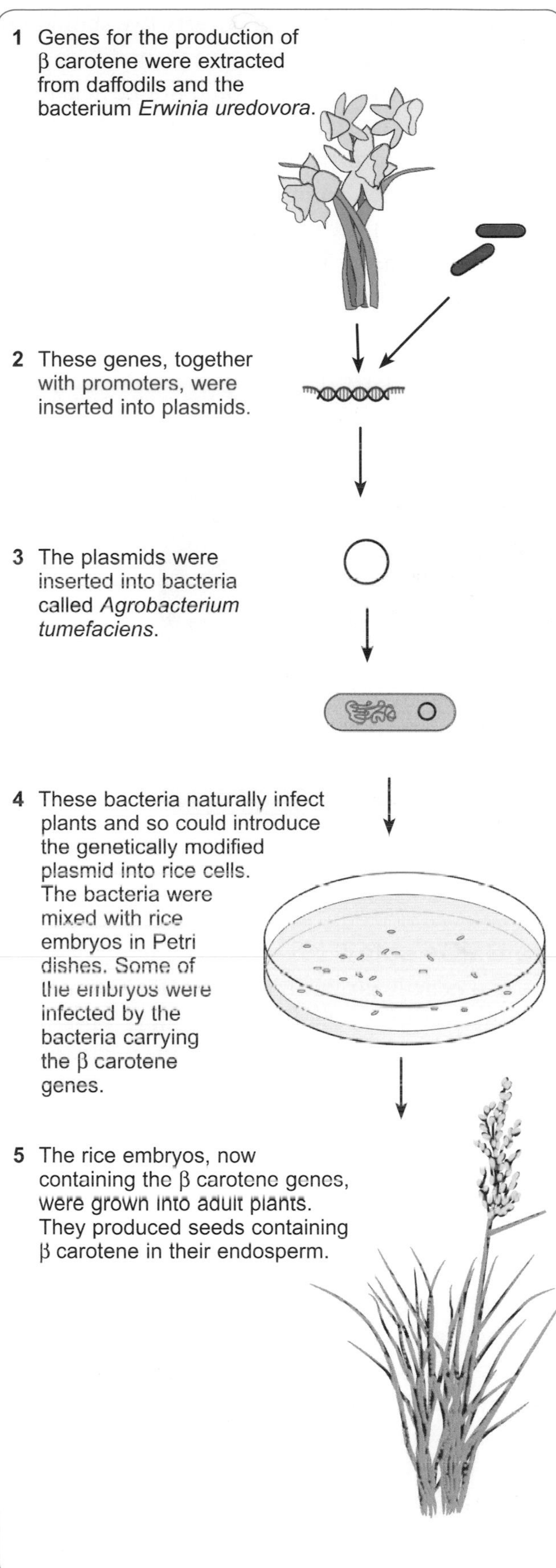

1 Genes for the production of β carotene were extracted from daffodils and the bacterium *Erwinia uredovora*.
2 These genes, together with promoters, were inserted into plasmids.
3 The plasmids were inserted into bacteria called *Agrobacterium tumefaciens*.
4 These bacteria naturally infect plants and so could introduce the genetically modified plasmid into rice cells. The bacteria were mixed with rice embryos in Petri dishes. Some of the embryos were infected by the bacteria carrying the β carotene genes.
5 The rice embryos, now containing the β carotene genes, were grown into adult plants. They produced seeds containing β carotene in their endosperm.

Figure 11.12 How Golden Rice™ was developed.

way to help people suffering poverty (we should lift them out of poverty, not just give them different food to eat) or that the rice would not be able to help those who need it.

The researchers experimented with other sources of these two genes, and in 2004 produced a better version of golden rice using genes taken from maize plants and rice itself. This produces up to 31 μg of β carotene per gram of rice (Figure 11.13). In many countries, children eat between 100 g and 200 g of rice per day, so they could get more than half (in some cases all) of their vitamin A requirement by eating Golden Rice™.

Figure 11.13 Three types of rice – 'ordinary' rice and the first and second versions of Golden Rice™.

Are GMOs safe?

The first genetically modified crops for commercial use were planted in the 1990s, and more varieties have been developed steadily since then. Their introduction immediately sparked controversy in several countries, including the UK. Many people are vehemently opposed to them, sometimes because they think they pose risks to health and sometimes because they think they may damage the environment. Some think they are potentially hugely beneficial to humans, and to the environment. In between are the great majority of people, who do not have sufficient scientific background to think through these issues for themselves, and who do not know which of the many competing claims they see or hear in the media to believe.

So, *are* genetically modified crop plants 'safe'? There are really two issues here. First, could genetically modified crops cause harm to other organisms in the environment? Secondly, is it safe to eat food made from genetically modified plants?

At the moment, most genetically modified crop plants have had genes inserted into them to make them resistant to insect or other pests, or to herbicides. Resistance to insect pests, for example, is conferred by a gene introduced from a bacterium called *Bacillus thuringiensis*, which causes the plant to produce a substance called Bt toxin that is toxic to insects. When these plants are grown, there is no need to spray insecticides onto the crop, so in theory this should mean that other insects are not unnecessarily destroyed. It also reduces the risks that pesticides that could harm human health will be present on the food that we eat. Resistance to herbicides means that the farmer can spray herbicide to kill weeds without harming the crop amongst which the weeds are growing. This should reduce costs and lead to cheaper food.

There is absolutely no evidence that such GM plants are unsafe to eat, or less nutritious. However, the quantity and quality of research on the environmental impact of these crops is not very great. One worry is that these crops might 'invade' a habitat and reduce the numbers or variety of other, native, plants growing there. Or their genes might somehow spread into other plants, perhaps by wind or pollinating insects. This could change the plants and the ecosystems in which they live in unpredictable ways.

In 2003, the results were published of a large-scale UK study of the effects on biodiversity of growing genetically modified crops. They showed that the effects were fairly small. One GM crop even appeared to increase biodiversity on the farm where it was grown.

In general, the risk of the GM plants, or their genes, spreading into the wider environment appears to be small. After all, the features that have been introduced into the crops would be very unlikely to give them an advantage in a natural situation. There is no reason to expect that they could compete successfully with native plants. Moreover, gene transfer is not likely unless close relatives of the crop plants are growing nearby. For most of our crops – all of the cereals, potatoes, cotton – it is not usual for the crops to be grown in the vicinity of any close, wild relatives.

However, things will be changing in the next few years. Some of the GM crops expected to be introduced in the future *will* have features that could enhance their ability to survive in the wild. For example, varieties of maize are being developed that have the ability to grow in very dry situations, and varieties of rice that are able to grow in salty water. Any genetically modified rice – including Golden Rice™ – could pose a threat, as there are often wild relatives of rice growing right next door to the paddy fields where rice is cultivated, meaning that there is a risk of genes being transferred into the wild plants. It will be important to carry out large-scale field trials on these new GM crops, if safety is to be ensured and public fears allayed.

On the whole, people have more positive views towards GM crops when they can see a benefit to the consumer. The first GM crops almost all had no obvious benefit to the consumer at all – they benefited only the grower or retailer. This undoubtedly contributed to the public opposition to their introduction. Crops like Golden Rice™, however, may be more acceptable, if benefits to health can be clearly demonstrated.

It is important to remember that a genetically modified plant is really not that different from one that has been produced by traditional selective breeding. Both of them contain genes that are different from those found in natural populations of the wild plants from which the crop plant has been developed. We could, for example, develop drought-resistant varieties of maize by selective breeding over many generations, and end up with plants that are very similar to those produced by genetic engineering. We need to be just as careful in our use of plants bred traditionally as we are with those produced by gene technology.

Animals for xenotransplantation

If a human organ such as a heart, kidney or liver becomes so damaged that it can no longer carry out its function, the best option for the person may be a transplant. This involves taking an organ from another person (the donor) and placing it in the recipient's body.

Human organs for transplantation are in very short supply, and many people die each year while they are waiting for a suitable organ to become available. One proposal for a partial solution to the shortage is to use organs from other animals (**xenotransplantation**). In particular, pigs have been suggested, because the size and structure of their organs is quite close to those of humans.

We have already seen that transplanted organs need to have a very close tissue-typing match between donor and recipient before the recipient's body can accept them. If not, then the immune system mounts a concerted attack against the 'invading' cells and destroys them. The vigour of this immune response against an organ taken from a completely different species would be massive.

When such an attack is made on pig tissues by the human immune system, the human antibodies attach to the surface of the pig cells by means of the sugars that are part of glycoproteins in the pig plasma membranes. One of these sugars is made by an enzyme called GGTA1 (1,3-galactosyltransferase). If the sugar isn't there, then the antibodies don't attach to the cells and the attack is greatly weakened.

Researchers have identified the gene that codes for the GGTA1 enzyme in pigs, and have genetically engineered pigs that do not contain this gene. The hope is that organs taken from these pigs could be transplanted into humans.

There are many potential difficulties, both technical and ethical, that need to be thought carefully about if this procedure is to be adopted.

- Is it right to genetically modify pigs in this way, just for our own benefit? If the genetically modified pigs are in any way less healthy than normal pigs, can we justify the suffering caused?
- Is it acceptable to place an organ from another animal into a human body? In particular, should pigs – regarded as 'unclean' animals by several major religions – be used for this purpose?
- Will just knocking out one gene be enough to reduce the size of the immune response sufficiently? Will the recipients need to take huge doses of immunosuppressant drugs for the rest of their lives?

- Might the pig cells in the transplant contain pig viruses that could be transmitted to humans, and then perhaps mutate to produce a virus that causes disease in humans?
- Will the pig organs last long enough to be of genuine use in the recipient? After all, pigs have much shorter lifespans than humans.

The possible use of animals for xenotransplantation is in the early stages of research and discussion, and by the time you read this there may well have been major developments in the science and the arguments for or against it. If you are interested, you will be able to find plenty of up-to-date information about the whole issue on the internet.

Gene therapy

Gene therapy is the treatment of a disease by manipulating the genes in a person's cells. We have already looked at this briefly in Chapter 9, where the treatment of SCID by gene therapy was described.

Attempts have also been made to treat **cystic fibrosis** by gene therapy. It is worth looking at the story in some detail, as it shows how a thorough knowledge of the biology underlying a disease, and of genetic engineering techniques, can open up new possibilities for treating previously untreatable diseases. It also shows how unexpected problems can greatly lengthen the time taken to put a new idea into practice.

Cystic fibrosis is a genetic disease in which abnormally thick mucus is produced in the lungs and other parts of the body. A person with cystic fibrosis is very prone to bacterial infections in the lungs because it is difficult for the mucus to be removed, and bacteria can breed in it. The thick mucus adversely affects many other parts of the body. The pancreatic duct may become blocked, and people with this disease often take pancreatic enzymes by mouth to help with digestion. Around 90% of men with cystic fibrosis are sterile because thick secretions block ducts in the reproductive system.

In Chapter 8, we saw that cystic fibrosis is caused by a recessive allele of the gene that codes for a transporter protein called **CFTR**. This protein sits in the plasma membranes of cells – for example, in the alveoli – and allows chloride ions to pass out of the cells. The recessive alleles (there are several different faulty ones) code for an incomplete or faulty version of this protein, which does not act properly as a chloride ion transporter.

In a healthy person, the cells lining the airways and in the lungs pump out chloride ions through the channel in the membrane formed by CFTR. This results in a relatively high concentration of chloride ions outside the cells. This reduces the water potential below that of the cytoplasm of the cells. So water moves out of the cells by osmosis, down the water potential gradient. It mixes with the mucus there, making it thin enough for easy removal by the sweeping movements of cilia (Figure 11.14).

However, in someone with cystic fibrosis, this does not happen. Much less water moves out of the cells, so the mucus on their surfaces stays thick and sticky. The cilia, or even coughing, can't remove it all.

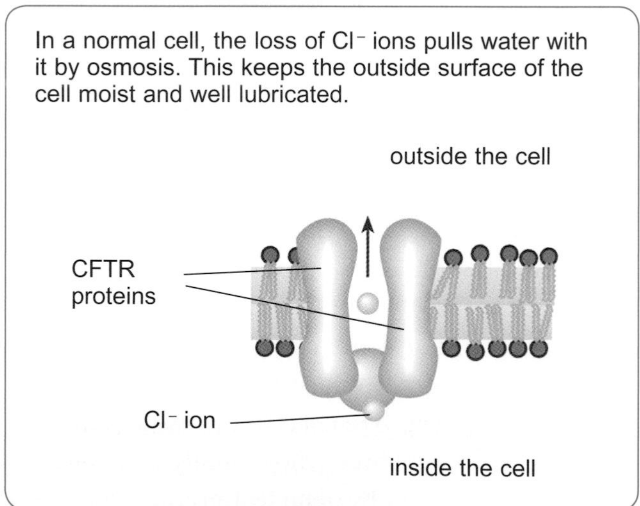
In a normal cell, the loss of Cl^- ions pulls water with it by osmosis. This keeps the outside surface of the cell moist and well lubricated.
outside the cell
CFTR proteins
Cl^- ion
inside the cell

Figure 11.14 The CFTR protein forms channels for chloride ions in the plasma membrane.

The *CFTR* gene

The gene that encodes the CFTR protein is found on chromosome 9. The commonest defective allele is the result of the deletion of three bases. The CFTR protein made using this allele is therefore missing one amino acid. The machinery in the cell recognises that this is not the right protein, and does not place it in the plasma membrane.

Because the faulty *CFTR* alleles are recessive, someone with one faulty allele and one normal allele is able to make enough CFTR to remain healthy. This makes it a good potential candidate for gene therapy. We don't need to remove the genes that are already there – we just need to get a correct, dominant allele into the cell, and it should – in theory – be able to make enough of the CFTR protein to allow the cell to work properly.

In practice, all attempts to do this so far have run into major difficulties. Trials in the UK began in 1993. The normal allele was inserted into liposomes, which were then sprayed as an aerosol into the noses of nine volunteers. The hope was that the liposomes would be able to move through the lipid layers in the plasma membranes of the cells lining the respiratory passages, carrying the gene with them. The trial succeeded in introducing the gene into a few cells lining the noses of the volunteers, but the effect only lasted for a week because these cells have only a very short lifespan and are continually replaced.

Researchers in the USA tried a different vector. In a trial involving several people with cystic fibrosis, they introduced the gene into normally harmless adenoviruses and then used these to carry the gene into the passages of the gas exchange system. The gene did enter some of the cells, but some of the volunteers experienced unpleasant side-effects as a result of infection by the virus. As a result, the trials were stopped.

Work has not been completely abandoned, however, and research continues into other possible ways of introducing working copies of the correct *CFTR* allele into human cells.

Somatic and germ line gene therapy

The two examples of gene therapy that we have looked at – for SCID and for cystic fibrosis – involve **somatic gene therapy**. This means that the cells that are being genetically modified are body cells. They are not involved in reproduction. If the genes in them are modified, the effect stops there, in that person. The modified genes will not be passed on to any offspring that person has (Figure 11.15).

Germ line gene therapy would involve changing the genes in cells that would go on to form gametes, and therefore possibly zygotes. If this was done, then *all* of the cells in the new organism would carry the genetic modification. At the moment, this kind of gene therapy for humans is banned in most countries, including the UK and the USA. However, some people think this type of therapy could bring huge benefits. You may like to think about what these could be, and consider your opinion on whether or not germ line therapy should be allowed to take place.

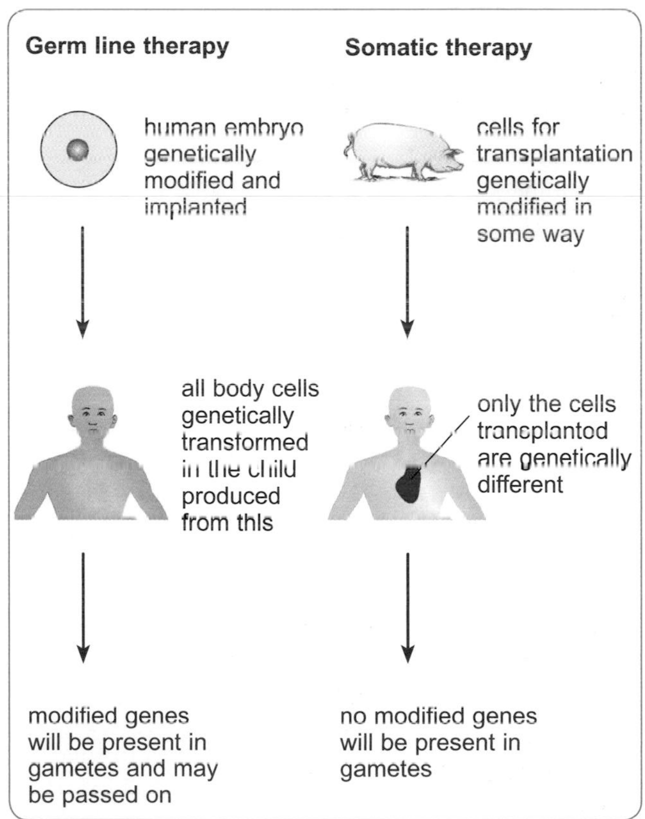

Figure 11.15 Germ line and somatic gene therapy compared.

Summary

Glossary

- An organism's genome can be sequenced by cutting up the DNA into many short pieces. These pieces are then copied using some normal and some labelled nucleotides, using different labels for each of the four bases. The labelled nucleotides stop the chain from being made any longer, so many chains of different lengths are produced, each ending with a labelled nucleotide. The lengths are then separated using electrophoresis. The labelled nucleotides at the ends of the shortest ones indicate which bases are present near the start of the DNA fragment, while those at the ends of the longest ones show which bases are present at the other end of the DNA fragment.
- DNA sequences can be used to compare the DNA of different organisms within the same species, or of different species. The more similar the DNA, the more closely related the organisms are considered to be.
- Genetic engineering involves the production of recombinant DNA, which contains genes inserted from a source other than the organism itself. The genes need to be inserted in such a way that they will be expressed in the genetically transformed organism, which may mean that a promoter is also added to the DNA.
- Restriction enzymes make staggered cuts in DNA at points where particular bases sequences are present. The short lengths of unpaired bases that they leave are known as sticky ends. If another piece of DNA is cut with the same kind of restriction enzyme, then the two lots of sticky ends will be complementary to one another and able to join by hydrogen bonding between the bases.
- Electrophoresis can be used to separate DNA fragments of different lengths. The DNA is placed in agarose gel and a voltage applied across it. The fragments are pulled to the positive end, shortest fragments first.
- A probe is a short length of DNA, labelled in some way to make it 'visible' (for example, containing ^{32}P), which is complementary to the single-stranded DNA you wish to detect. The probe attaches to single-stranded DNA, so the position of the probe indicates the position of that particular DNA.
- The polymerase chain reaction, PCR, is a method of making very large numbers of copies of DNA. The DNA is first separated out into its single strands. A primer then attaches to one end of the strand, and polymerase enzymes make a copy of each of the DNA strands. These copies are then separated into single strands and the process is repeated many times.
- Plasmids may be used as vectors to carry DNA into bacterial cells. The plasmids are cut open with restriction enzymes, and then the required DNA is added to them. DNA ligase links the new DNA with the rest of the DNA in the plasmid. The plasmids can be taken up by bacterial cells, which are therefore transformed by the addition of the new DNA. If the DNA has come from another organism, the bacteria are now said to be transgenic.
- Viruses and liposomes can also be used as vectors.
- Many plasmids contain genes that confer resistance to antibiotics, and can be passed from one bacterium to another. These resistance genes can be used as markers to check which bacteria have successfully taken up plasmids containing the required gene. Genes that code for green fluorescent protein are being increasingly used as markers.

continued

- Human insulin is now produced by transgenic *E. coli* bacteria, which have been genetically engineered to contain and express the human insulin gene.
- Golden Rice™ has been genetically engineered to contain genes that produce large amounts of β carotene in the grains. It is hoped that growing and eating this rice will help some of the many people in developing countries who suffer from vitamin A deficiency.
- Research is being carried out on producing genetically engineered pigs and other animals whose transplanted organs will not produce a massive immune response in humans, and could therefore be used as a source of organs for transplants.
- Gene therapy involves the addition of genes to human cells that could cure, or reduce the symptoms of, diseases such as cystic fibrosis or SCID. There are difficulties to be surmounted in getting enough genes into enough cells for the therapy to be worthwhile, and also in avoiding some of the side-effects that may be caused, such as an increased risk in developing cancer. Somatic cell gene therapy involves the genetic modification of body cells, whereas germ cell gene therapy (which is not currently allowed in the UK) involves genetic modifications that would be present in gametes or a zygote, and would therefore be passed on to subsequent generations.
- Genetic manipulation of animals, plants and microorganisms raises important ethical issues, such as the balance between potential suffering to other organisms and benefits to humans. The use of genetically modified crop plants also raises issues relating to human health, and to damage that might be caused to the environment or to other species.

Stretch and challenge question

1 Describe some of the uses that have been made of microorganisms in gene technology, and discuss the moral, ethical and safety issues that could be associated with these uses.

Hint

Questions

1 Using genetically engineered bacteria, a synthetic insulin molecule has been produced which has over 20% of the activity of naturally produced insulin. The gene for the synthetic molecule has been used in an experimental gene therapy for insulin-dependent diabetes.

DNA coding for the synthetic molecule was combined, as shown in the diagram, with a promoter region taken from a gene for an enzyme found <u>only</u> in liver cells. The promoter is sensitive to blood glucose concentration and switches on its associated gene as blood glucose concentration rises above the normal concentration.

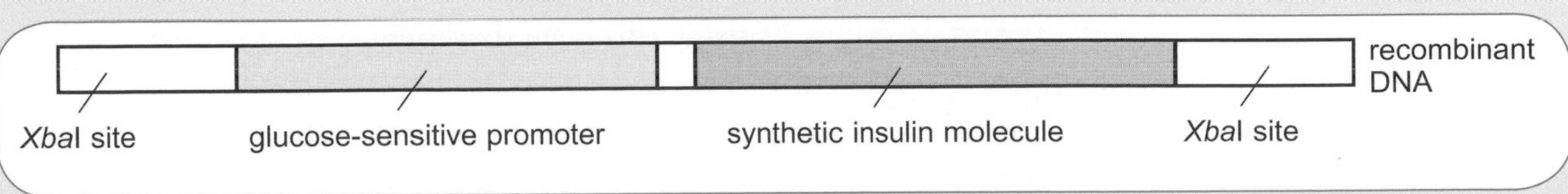

continued

The recombinant DNA shown in the diagram was cut with the restriction enzyme, *Xba*I, at the two sites shown and inserted into a virus. Cloned virus particles were injected into diabetic rats which expressed the gene only in liver cells.

a **i** State what is meant by *recombinant* DNA. [1]

ii Describe the roles of a restriction enzyme, such as *Xba*I, in genetic engineering. [4]

iii Explain the advantage of being able to produce the synthetic insulin molecule in response to a rise in blood glucose concentration. [2]

b Four weeks after receiving this gene therapy, the experimental diabetic rats were given a glucose meal. The concentrations of blood glucose and synthetic insulin in their blood were measured at intervals for eight hours.

A control group of non-diabetic rats, which had not received gene therapy, were also given a glucose meal and the concentrations of blood glucose and insulin measured at the same time intervals. The results are shown below.

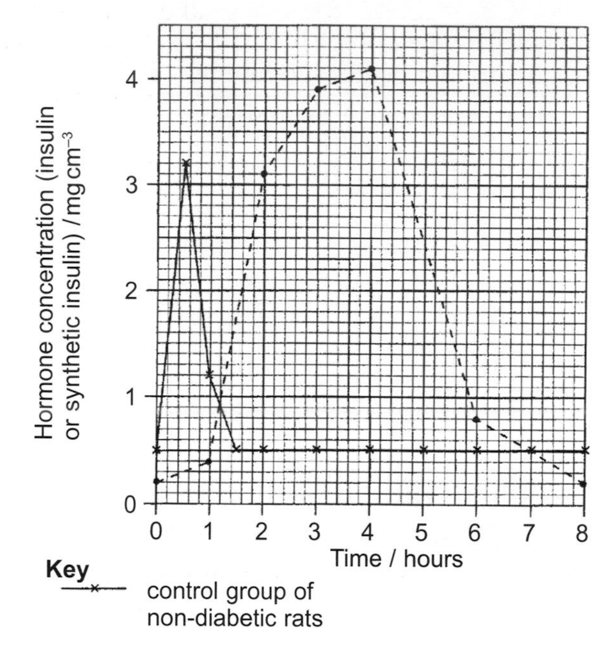

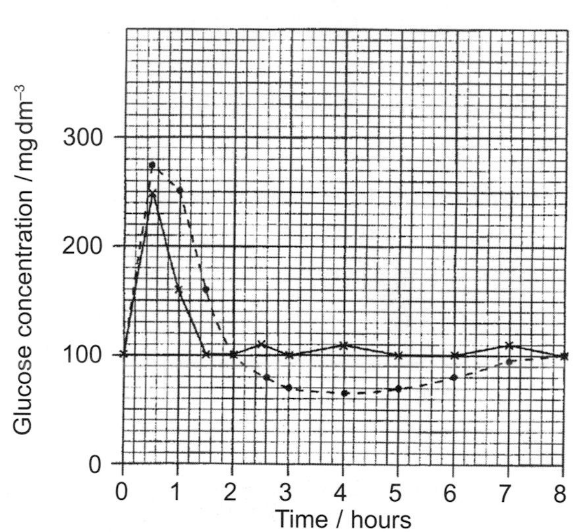

With reference to the graphs,

i compare the concentrations of glucose and hormone in the blood of experimental and control rats [4]

ii discuss the potential benefits and problems of using this gene therapy for the treatment of diabetes. [4]

OCR Biology A (2805/02) June 2003 [Total 15]

Answer

Ecosystems

e-Learning

Objectives

In *Biology 1*, we defined an ecosystem as a relatively self-contained system including all the living organisms and the environment, interacting with each other. The word 'interacting' is very important. An ecosystem is a system, not just a place. You cannot really 'visit' an ecosystem in the way that you can visit a habitat. An ecosystem is dynamic – changes are happening in it all the time, as interactions take place. Energy constantly flows through it, from one organism to another and between organisms and the non-living environment. Materials, too, pass between the environment and the organisms, and between the different organisms in the ecosystem.

Biotic and abiotic factors

The components of an ecosystem that affect the organisms within it can be divided into **biotic factors** and **abiotic factors**.

Biotic factors are ones that involve other living organisms (Figure 12.1). They include:

- the **feeding** of herbivores on plants
- **predation**, in which one organism (the predator) kills and eats another (the prey)
- **parasitism**, in which one organism (the parasite) lives in close association with an organism of a different species (the host) and does it harm
- **mutualism**, in which two organisms of different species live in close association, both benefiting from the relationship
- **competition**, in which two organisms both require something that is in short supply.

Zebras are affected by intraspecific competition (between themselves) and interspecific competition (with other species) for food and water.

Grazing by herbivores such as zebras is a biotic factor affecting grass. Similarly, zebras are affected by the quality and availability of grass.

Zebras are affected by predation by lions, and lions by the availability of their prey.

Zebras are affected by parasites such as ticks. A mutualistic relationship with oxpeckers, which feed on the ticks, benefits both zebra and oxpecker.

Figure 12.1 Examples of biotic factors affecting organisms in an ecosystem.

Abiotic factors are ones that involve non-living components of the environment (Figure 12.2). They include:

- **temperature**, which affects the rate of metabolic reactions in both endothermic and ectothermic organisms
- **light intensity**, which affects the rate of photosynthesis in plants and also the behaviour of animals
- **oxygen concentration**, which affects any organism that respires aerobically
- **carbon dioxide concentration**, which affects photosynthesising plants
- **water supply**, which affects all organisms
- **pH** of water or soil, which affects all organisms living in them
- **availability of inorganic ions** such as nitrate or potassium, which affects the growth of plants
- **factors relating to the soil**, known as **edaphic** factors, such as aeration, size of soil particles, drainage and mineral content
- **atmospheric humidity**, which affects the rate of water loss by evaporation from an organism's body
- **wind speed**, which affects transpiration rate of plants and can also greatly increase cooling effects if the environmental temperature is low.

Some plants, such as ferns, are able to live beneath trees where the light intensity is too low for other plant species.

All organisms are affected by the temperature of their environment.

Relatively few species of plants are able to survive where water is in short supply.

Growing in a low cushion shape helps plants in the high Andes to survive the strong, cold, drying winds.

Figure 12.2 Examples of abiotic factors affecting organisms in an ecosystem.

As you can imagine, the ways in which all of these different kinds of factors interact within even the simplest of ecosystems is extraordinarily complex. Studies of ecosystems usually confine themselves to some small part of these interactions – for example, the way in which energy flows through the system, or the way in which interactions between a predator and its prey affect the population sizes of the two species. In this chapter, we will concentrate on two main issues – the flow of energy through an ecosystem, and the cycling of nitrogen within it. In Chapter 13, we will look at some examples of biotic factors affecting populations in an ecosystem, and how human intervention can affect ecosystems in both negative and positive ways.

SAQ

1 Classify each of these factors as biotic or abiotic.

a The speed of water flow in a river.

b The density of seaweed growing in a rock pool.

c The oxygen availability on a high altitude mountainside.

Answer

Energy flow through an ecosystem

Within most living cells, the immediate source of energy is ATP. Most metabolic reactions within cells require input of energy from ATP. We have seen how this molecule is used to fuel active transport and the synthesis of proteins. In Chapter 15, you will see how it is used to make muscles contract.

The initial entry of energy into most ecosystems takes place during photosynthesis (Figure 12.3). Some of the energy in the sunlight hitting a plant's leaves is used to make carbohydrates, proteins and fats whose molecules contain a proportion of this energy. Plants are **producers**. The carbohydrates and other organic substances that they synthesise serve as supplies of chemical energy to all of the other organisms in the ecosystem. These other organisms, which include all the animals and fungi, and many of the microorganisms, consume the organic substances made by plants. They are **consumers**.

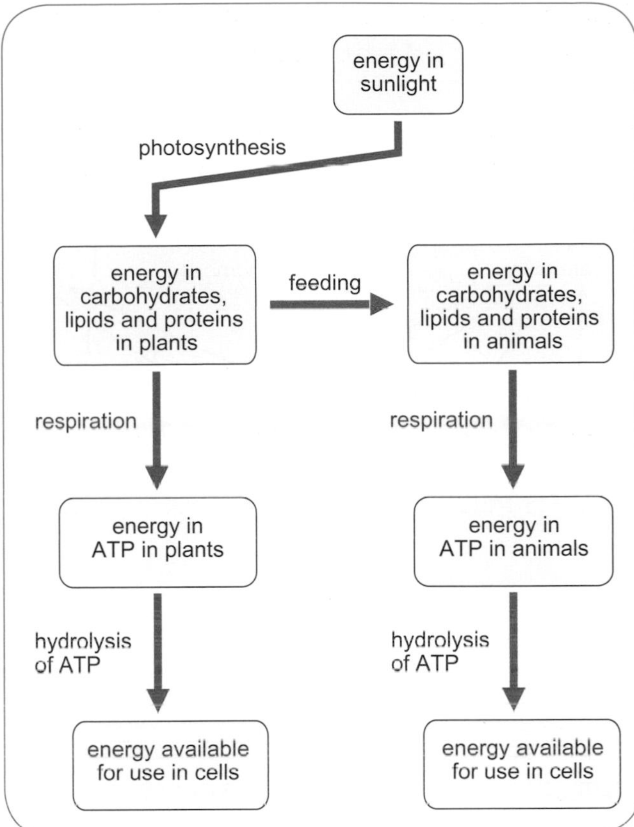

Figure 12.3 Energy flow through organisms and ecosystems.

Food chains and food webs

The way in which energy flows from producer to consumers can be shown by drawing a **food chain**. Arrows in the food chain indicate the direction in which the energy flows. A simple food chain in a wood could be:

oak tree ⟶ winter moth caterpillar ⟶ great tit ⟶ sparrowhawk

The oak tree is the producer, and the three animals are consumers. The caterpillar is a **primary consumer**, the great tit a **secondary consumer** and the sparrowhawk is a **tertiary consumer**. These different positions in a food chain are called **trophic levels**. ('Trophic' means 'feeding'.)

Within this woodland ecosystem, there will be a large number of other food chains. The interrelationships between many food chains can be drawn as a **food web**. Figure 12.4 shows a partial food web for such an ecosystem. You can pick out many different food chains within this web.

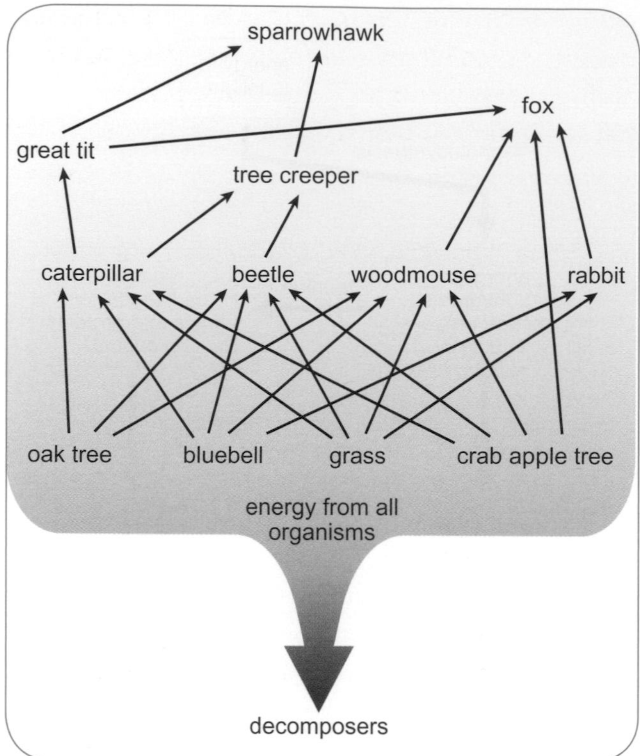

Figure 12.4 A food web in oak woodland.

You may notice that a particular animal does not always occupy the same position in a food chain. While herbivores such as caterpillars and rabbits tend *always* to be herbivores, and therefore always primary consumers, carnivores often feed at several different levels in a food chain. The fox, for example, is a primary consumer when it eats a fallen crab apple, a secondary consumer when it eats a rabbit, and a tertiary consumer when it eats a great tit. Animals that regularly feed as both primary and higher level consumers, such as humans, are known as omnivores.

The food web also shows the importance of a group of organisms called **decomposers**. Most decomposers live in the soil or in the leaf litter that covers the soil in woodland. Their role in the ecosystem is to feed on **detritus** (organic matter in dead organisms and waste material, such as dead leaves, urine and faeces). You can see that energy from every organism in the ecosystem flows into the decomposers. Decomposers include many bacteria, fungi and also some larger animals such as earthworms. Sometimes, the term 'decomposer' is reserved for bacteria and fungi, which feed saprotrophically (that is, by secreting enzymes onto the substances around them and then absorbing the digested products), while the larger animals are called **detritivores**, meaning 'detritus feeders'. Decomposers are a largely unseen but vitally important group within every ecosystem. You will find out more about their roles in the nitrogen cycle on pages 193–196.

Energy losses along food chains

Whenever energy is transferred from one form, or one system, to another, some is always lost as heat. As energy passes along a food chain, large losses from the food chain occur at each transfer, both within and between the organisms. Figure 12.5 shows these losses for a simple food chain.

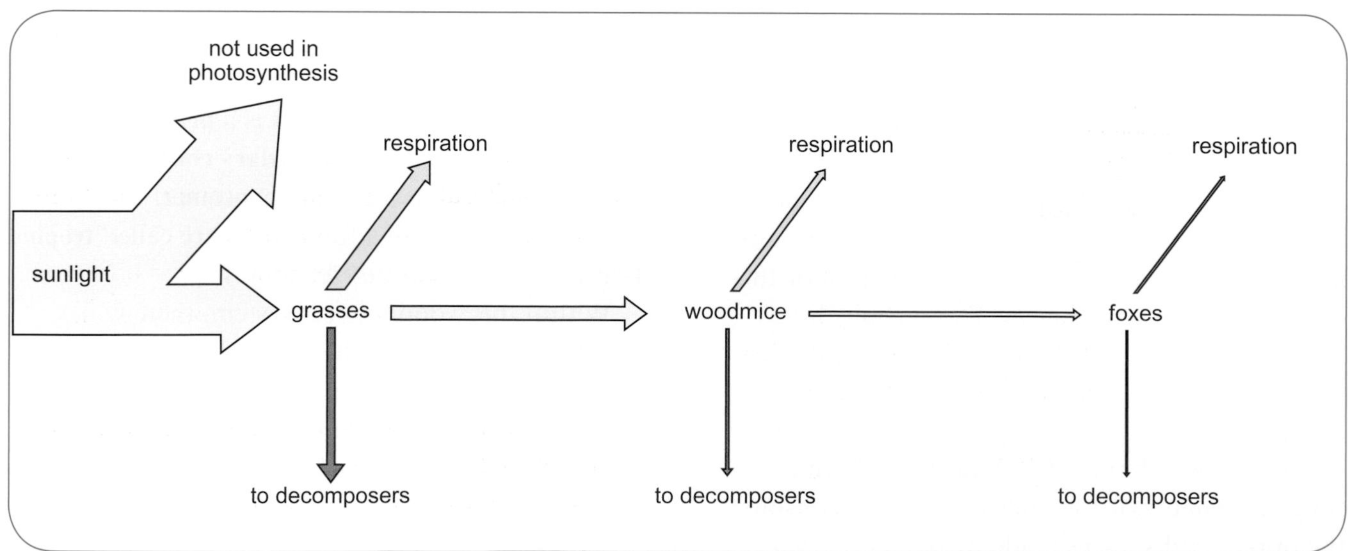

Figure 12.5 Energy losses in a food chain.

Of all the sunlight falling onto the ecosystem, only a very small percentage is converted by the green plants into chemical energy (Figure 12.6). In most ecosystems, the plants convert less than 3% of this sunlight to chemical energy. The reasons for this inefficiency include:

- some sunlight missing leaves entirely, and falling onto the ground or other non-photosynthesising surfaces
- some sunlight being reflected from the surfaces of leaves
- some sunlight passing through leaves, without encountering chlorophyll molecules
- only certain wavelengths of light being absorbed by chlorophyll
- energy losses as energy absorbed by chlorophyll is transferred to carbohydrates during the reactions of photosynthesis.

The chemical potential energy, now in the plant's tissues, is contained in various organic molecules,

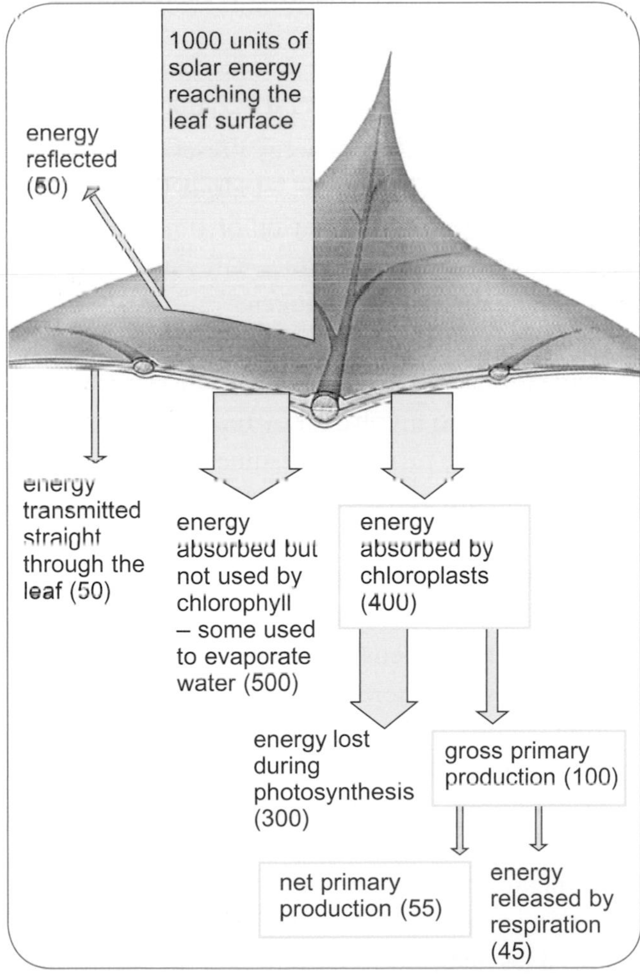

Figure 12.6 Photosynthetic efficiency.

especially carbohydrates, lipids and proteins. It is from these molecules that the primary consumers in the ecosystem obtain all of their energy. However, in most plants, almost half of the chemical potential energy that they store is used by the plants themselves. They break down the organic molecules by respiration, releasing some of the energy from them and using it to make ATP. During this process, and also when the energy in the ATP is used for activities in the plant cells, much energy is lost to the environment as heat.

What is left is then available for other organisms, which feed on the plants. Once again, losses occur between the plants and the primary consumers. The reasons for these losses include:

- not all parts of all the plants being eaten – for example, woody tissues or roots may be left
- not all the plant material that is eaten being fully digested, so that not all of the molecules are absorbed by the consumer (the rest is lost as faeces, and therefore becomes available to decomposers)
- energy being lost as heat within the consumer's digestive system as the food molecules are hydrolysed.

As a result of the loss of energy during respiration in plants, and the three reasons above, the overall **efficiency** of transfer of energy from producers to primary consumers is rarely greater than 10%.

Similar losses occur at each trophic level. So, as energy is passed along a food chain, less and less is available at each successive trophic level. Food chains rarely have more than four or five links in them, because there simply would not be enough energy left to support animals so far removed from the original energy input to the producers. If you *can* pick out a five-organism food chain from a food web, you will probably find that the 'top' carnivore also feeds at a lower level in a different food chain – or that it is extremely scarce.

SAQ

2 Energy losses from mammals and birds tend to be significantly greater than from other organisms. Suggest why this is.

Answer

Productivity

The *rate* at which plants convert light energy into chemical potential energy is called **productivity**, or **primary productivity**. It is usually measured in kilojoules of energy transferred per square metre per year (kJ m^{-2} $year^{-1}$).

Ecologists often differentiate between **gross primary productivity (GPP)** and **net primary productivity (NPP)**. GPP is the total quantity of energy transferred by plants from sunlight into plant tissues. NPP is the energy that is left as chemical energy after the plants have supplied their own needs by respiration.

SAQ

3 Table 12.1 shows some information about energy transfers in three ecosystems.

	Mature rain forest in Puerto Rico	Alfalfa field in the USA	Young pine forest in England
GPP/ kJ m^{-2} $year^{-1}$	188 000	102 000	51 000
Respiration by plants/ kJ m^{-2} $year^{-1}$	134 000		20 000
NPP/ kJ m^{-2} $year^{-1}$	54 000	64 000	

Table 12.1

a Calculate the figures for respiration by plants in the alfalfa field, and the NPP of the young pine forest.

b How much energy is available to be passed on to the primary consumers in the rain forest?

c Suggest why the GPP of the rain forest is so much greater than that of the pine forest. (You should be able to think of several possible reasons.)

d Suggest why the NPP of the alfalfa field is greater than that of the rain forest. (Again, you may be able to think of several reasons.)

Answer

4 Table 12.2 shows some typical values for NPP in a range of different ecosystems.

Type of ecosystem	NPP/kJ m^{-2} $year^{-1}$
desert	280
subsistence farming	3 000
temperate grassland	15 000
temperate forest	26 000
intensive agriculture	30 000
tropical rainforest	40 000

Table 12.2

a Explain why the NPP in desert is so low.

b Suggest why the NPP of temperate forest is greater than that of temperate grassland.

Answer

Measuring energy transfers between trophic levels

Values for energy transfers in ecosystems are not at all easy to measure. It is not even very easy to measure the quantity of energy present in a trophic level at one moment in time, let alone the quantity that is transferred over a period of time.

Although precise techniques will vary, in general the following steps will be taken.

- The food chain is worked out. A decision is made about which organisms to investigate. Is the study to involve all of the producers and all of the primary consumers, or just one producer and one consumer that feeds on it? Obviously the latter is much easier to do, and the results obtained are much easier to interpret – but it will only give a very partial picture of what really happens in a complete ecosystem. We will assume here, for simplicity, that we are just looking at one producer that is eaten by only one consumer, and that this consumer feeds entirely on that producer and nothing else. Often, these measurements are made in an artificial laboratory situation, because in the outside world there are too many uncontrolled variables involved to be sure that the results are at all reliable.

- The population size of each species is measured. If this is being undertaken outside the laboratory, it will probably involve sampling (*Biology 1* page 200) and then a calculation to estimate the size of the whole population.
- The mean dry mass of a single organism is calculated. This involves killing a sample of organisms, then drying to constant mass by heating to drive off water.
- The energy content per gram of dry mass is calculated for each kind of organism. This is done by burning a sample of dry material of known mass in a calorimeter, and measuring the heat that is produced.
- The total energy content in the population is then calculated:

  energy content = number of organisms × mean dry mass of one organism × energy content of 1 g of dry mass

Manipulating energy flow

With so much energy being lost as it passes along a food chain, there is a lot to be gained if we try to minimise these losses when producing our own food. Intensive agriculture does just that.

Intensive agriculture involves growing a lot of plants, or a lot of animals, in a relatively small area. Inputs – what the farmer spends on growing the crops – are high. This includes the application of fertilisers, water, herbicides and pesticides. Outputs – what the farmer gets back when he sells the crop – are also high, because yields and quality are likely to be better than if inputs were lower. Table 12.2 shows how intensive agriculture can greatly raise productivity, compared with subsistence farming, where people grow crops and keep animals for their own uses and inputs are minimal.

We grow many of our crops as **monocultures** (Figure 12.7). This means that we grow just a single variety of plant in one area. All of the light falling on that area is available for those plants to grow. The crop is often sprayed with herbicides to kill weeds, which might compete with the crop plants for light, water or minerals. It may also be sprayed with pesticides to kill insects and fungi that might feed on the plants, diverting energy flow into themselves rather than towards us, the intended consumers.

We have seen that plants only use a small fraction of the light energy that falls onto the area where they are growing, generally something in the region of 2–5%. This can be calculated as **photosynthetic efficiency**, where:

$$\text{photosynthetic efficiency} = \frac{\text{amount of light energy falling onto a crop}}{\text{amount of light energy converted to carbohydrate}}$$

Agricultural systems can increase photosynthetic efficiency. Crop plants can be planted close together, so that less sunlight falls onto the bare ground between them and more is absorbed by their leaves. They can be given more water than might be naturally available in the soil, so that water does not become a limiting factor for photosynthesis. They can be given extra mineral ions as fertilisers – particularly ions containing nitrogen, potassium and phosphorus – so that, once again, these are not limiting factors for

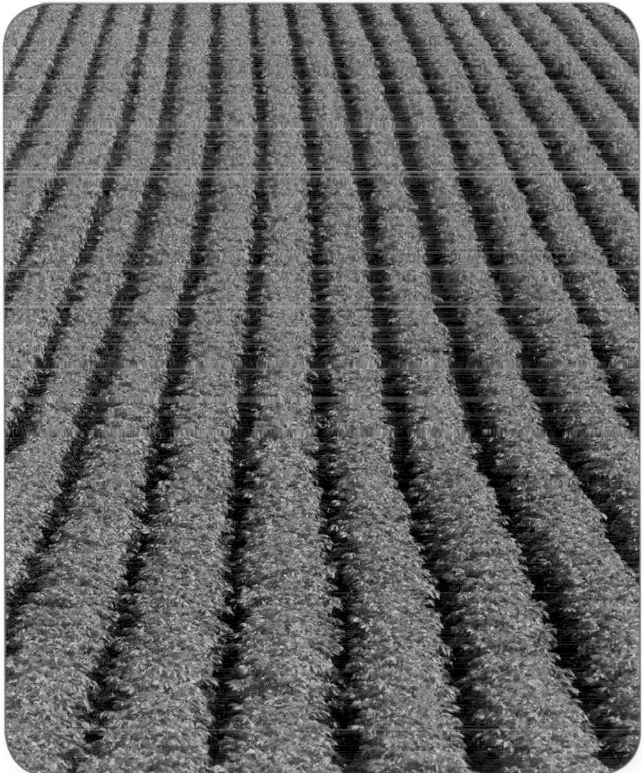

Figure 12.7 A potato crop growing in Norfolk. This is an example of a monoculture – a single variety of one species covering a large area of land.

their growth and usage of light energy. For example, a natural beech woodland may have a photosynthetic efficiency of only around 3%, but a sugar beet crop (one of the most efficient temperate crops) can have an efficiency of more than 8%.

Similar principles are employed when farming animals – farmers use various techniques to increase the energy flow into the animals rather than into other organisms or into the environment as waste heat. Almost all of the animals that are reared for food – cattle, sheep, pigs, goats – are primary consumers. They feed at the first available level in the food chain, minimising energy losses in transfer between trophic levels. An exception is fish such as salmon, which feed at the second or even third trophic level.

Many animals are reared extensively, where they are allowed to graze outdoors on naturally growing grass or other plants. However, these plants will generally have fertiliser applied, to increase their growth and therefore the energy available to the animals. The animals will probably be treated with medicines to kill parasites such as intestinal worms, which would divert energy into themselves, and away from the meat or milk that the farmer expects to harvest from the animals. Animals may also be reared intensively, kept indoors in controlled conditions, and perhaps deliberately limited in their movements; the more they move around, the more they respire, and the more energy is lost to the environment rather than being used to build animal tissues.

Succession

Glaciers are rivers of ice. As they slowly flow over the ground, they scrape away the soil and even the upper layers of rock over which they pass.

Many glaciers have been in retreat over the past 200 years, and the rate and extent of these retreats are increasing as carbon dioxide levels in the atmosphere rise and cause global warming. When a glacier retreats, ground that was previously covered with ice and completely devoid of plant life becomes exposed. It is littered with debris that the glacier had carried along with it, made up of a scatter of rocks of various sizes. This is called **moraine** (Figure 12.8a).

As the glacier begins to retreat, completely bare moraine is exposed.

Over time, the pioneer plants alter the soil so that shrubs can grow.

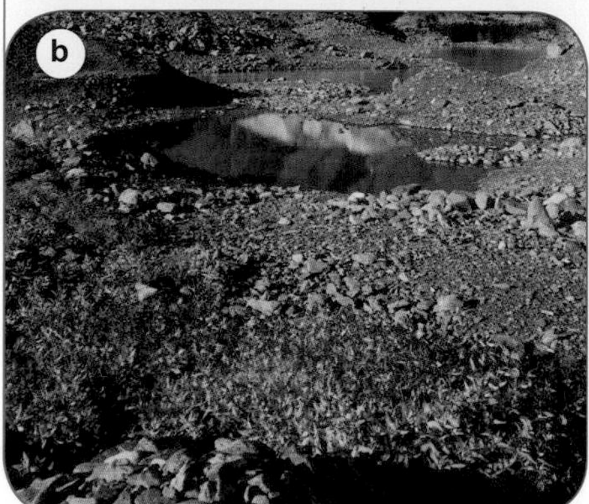

Dwarf fireweed is one of the first plants to colonise the moraine.

Eventually, poorly drained soils become covered with sphagnum bog, and drier areas with conifer forest.

Figure 12.8 Succession on soil exposed by a retreating glacier.

For the last 90 years, ecologists have been studying how living organisms gradually colonise the newly uncovered moraines in Glacier Bay, in Alaska. In fact, it is possible to look even further back in time than this. Because the glaciers are retreating steadily, you can find areas of moraine that were first uncovered at different times, up to 200 years ago.

The first living organisms to colonise the newly exposed moraine are mosses, willow-herbs (called fireweed in America), mountain avens, and dwarf willows (Figure 12.8b). They are called **pioneer plants**. They grow sparsely in the almost non-existent soil. The rocky ground is very low in nitrate ions, but mountain avens has a mutualistic relationship with nitrogen-fixing bacteria (pages 193–194), which take nitrogen gas from the air and convert it into ammonium ions that the plant can use to build amino acids and then proteins. This helps the mountain avens to outcompete many other pioneer plants, and it can sometimes form huge carpets over the moraine.

The presence of the pioneer plants alters the soil. As they shed leaves and remains of flowers, these provide nutrients for decomposers, which therefore increase in numbers. Proper soil begins to form, containing humus (partly decayed plant remains), which helps to hold water and contains mineral ions. The humus also helps to hold together the rock particles that make up the soil, stabilising it. Some of the ammonium ions produced by the nitrogen-fixing bacteria in the mountain avens roots seep into the soil, providing an available nitrogen source for other plants that can now begin to colonise the moraine. About 50 years after the moraine was first exposed, it is covered with shrubs, now able to survive on the thin but more fertile soil (Figure 12.8c).

Many of these shrubs are alders. These, like mountain avens, have nitrogen-fixing bacteria in their root nodules. The quantity of nitrogen-containing ions in the soil continues to increase. The alders also alter the pH of the soil. The rocks carried by the glaciers in Glacier Bay contain carbonates, and they produce a pH of 8 in the soil. Alder leaves, however, decay to produce a slightly acidic humus, releasing acids into the soil. Once alder thickets are established, the soil pH rapidly falls to about 5 (Figure 12.9). The pioneer plants are not suited to this kind of soil. Nor can they compete with the much taller alders for light, and they disappear.

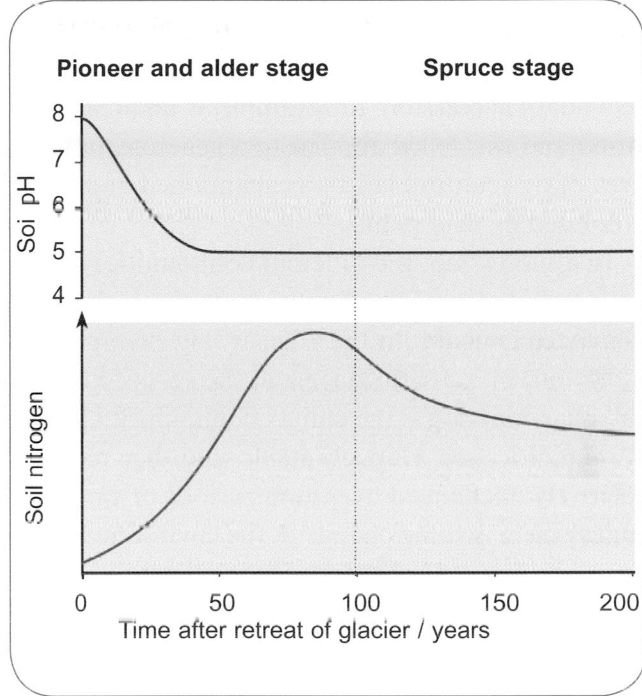

Figure 12.9 Change in soil pH and nitrogen content in Glacier Bay moraines.

Tall conifer trees, such as hemlock and sitka spruce, now begin to grow amongst the alders. They eventually crowd the alders out. By around 170 years after the moraine was first exposed, the ground is covered with spruce forest. Spruce trees are not nitrogen-fixers, and they depend on the nitrate left in the soil by the alders.

What happens next depends largely on the drainage of the soil. In areas of good drainage, the spruce forest remains (Figure 12.8d). In areas of poor drainage, *Sphagnum* mosses invade. These mosses hold water, making the ground even more waterlogged. This lowers the pH, and also lowers oxygen availability. The trees die, and the area ends up as a sphagnum bog.

The predictability of succession

The gradual change in the plant communities on the exposed moraines in Glacier Bay is an example of **succession**. Succession is a directional change in a community (all the different species living in an area) over time. If the original area had no soil and no living organisms present, the change is known as **primary succession**. If the area was simply disturbed, and there was soil present, then the change is a **secondary succession**. You could get secondary succession, for example, if an area of woodland was felled and left to regenerate, or if an area of agricultural land was abandoned and then colonised by wild plants.

In a succession, the different communities are called **seral stages**. The final community is the **climax community**. In the Glacier Bay example, the alder thicket is a seral stage and the spruce forest or sphagnum bog is the climax community. Climax communities are relatively stable, and they remain relatively unchanged over long periods of time unless there is some change in the environment, such as a forest fire or a change in climate.

Succession often follows a predictable course. One community alters the environment in such a way that it becomes possible for a different community to take over. This is what happens on the Glacier Bay moraines. First, the pioneer species come in. These are plants that have good dispersal mechanisms, so they are likely to arrive early. For example, mountain avens and willow herbs produce large quantities of fluffy fruits, which can disperse the seeds over long distances on the wind. Pioneer species must be adapted to grow and reproduce in poor soils and exposed conditions. However, they are unlikely to be adapted to compete with taller, stronger-growing species on good soils.

The presence of the pioneer plants changes the soil and other aspects of the environment. We have seen that mountain avens adds nitrogen-containing ions to the soil. The plants provide shelter, and their waste materials produce humus. This allows alder to colonise, which again changes the soil and allows spruce and hemlock to colonise. A similar pattern is seen on almost every exposed moraine in Glacier Bay.

In the early stages of succession, abiotic factors tend to be much more important than biotic ones in determining what can survive. The availability of nutrients in the soil, wind exposure, water availability and temperature are likely to be far more influential than competition or grazing. Later, as more and more species colonise the area, biotic factors – especially competition – become more important.

SAQ

5 Look at the photographs in Figure 12.8. Suggest and explain what happens to each of the following during the process of succession.
  a The number of different species in the community.
  b The quantity of biomass per unit area.

Answer

Studying succession

One way of studying a succession such as that on the Glacier Bay moraines would be to keep sampling the communities that live there over a 200-year period. Luckily, it is actually a bit easier than that. Because the glaciers retreat gradually, at any one time we can look at pieces of ground at almost every stage in the succession. Some were just uncovered yesterday as a glacier retreated, some have been uncovered for 10 years, some for 15 years and so on.

This is true of many examples of succession. You may, for example, be able to study succession on sand dunes near the sea (Figure 12.10). The exposed gravel or sand nearest to the sea represents the very early stages of succession, while the ground further away from the sea represents later stages. We can use the distribution of the communities in *space* on the ground to show us what they look like at different *times* during a succession.

In *Biology 1* Chapter 12, we saw how quadrats, point quadrats and transects can be used to sample plant and animal communities. Transects are an excellent way of studying succession. We can run a measuring tape along the area in which we can see different seral stages (for example, from the edge of the sea across the beach and deep into the sand dunes) and record what is growing at different points along the line. If we record what is growing right next to or touching the tape, we have a **line transect**. If we place quadrats at certain points along the tape and record what is growing inside them, we have a **belt transect**. Transects can be either **continuous transects** – a record along the whole length of the tape – or **interrupted transects** – a record at intervals along the tape (Figure 12.11).

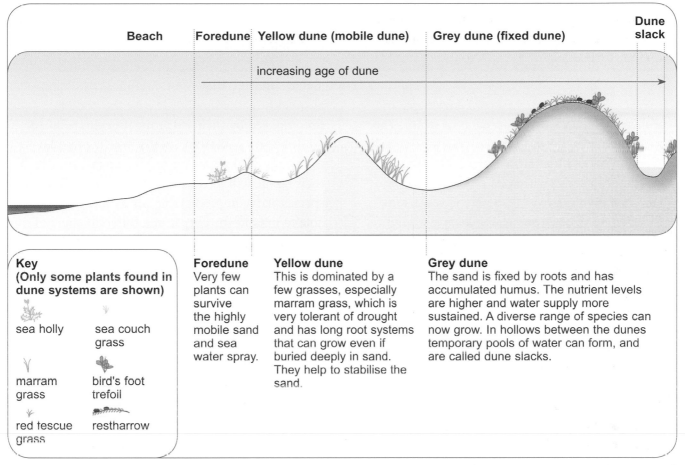

Beach | **Foredune** | **Yellow dune (mobile dune)** | **Grey dune (fixed dune)** | **Dune slack**

increasing age of dune →

Key
(Only some plants found in dune systems are shown)

sea holly
sea couch grass
marram grass
bird's foot trefoil
red fescue grass
restharrow

Foredune
Very few plants can survive the highly mobile sand and sea water spray.

Yellow dune
This is dominated by a few grasses, especially marram grass, which is very tolerant of drought and has long root systems that can grow even if buried deeply in sand. They help to stabilise the sand.

Grey dune
The sand is fixed by roots and has accumulated humus. The nutrient levels are higher and water supply more sustained. A diverse range of species can now grow. In hollows between the dunes temporary pools of water can form, and are called dune slacks.

Figure 12.10 Succession on sand dunes.

Figure 12.11 Using a transect to study succession.

Succession as a forensic tool

When an organism dies, its body becomes available for various kinds of organisms to feed on it. Each kind of organism changes the body in some way, which in turn makes it suitable for colonisation by another kind. The body is a small ecosystem, progressively invaded by wave after wave of other organisms that live and feed on it.

When a person dies, their own enzymes start to digest their cells within minutes of death. Then bacteria quickly begin to feed on the dead tissues, releasing odours that attract bluebottle flies. The flies can arrive within an hour after death. They can even arrive when a person is still alive, attracted by smells from a suppurating wound.

The flies are there not to feed themselves, but to lay their eggs. The eggs hatch into maggots (fly larvae), which feed on the corpse by secreting enzymes onto it and then sucking up the liquefied nutrients.

The life cycle of these flies has been extensively studied. The maggots grow and shed their skins several times, and then become pupae, which eventually hatch into flies. Forensic entomologists know exactly how long each of these stages takes in different conditions. For example, the warmer the conditions, the faster the maggots grow. If the person has been taking heroin, this also speeds up the maggots' development. Data tables built up from this knowledge can be used to work out how long a body has been dead.

Shortly after the bluebottles, the fleshflies arrive – indeed, they are sometimes there almost as quickly as the bluebottles. As the body is decomposed by their maggots, it begins to attract adult beetles and tabby moths, which again lay their eggs on the now putrefying corpse on which their larvae will feed. As time goes on, different species arrive in predictable waves, each one able to inhabit the corpse at a different stage of decomposition. It is the predictability of this succession that makes it possible to estimate the time since death.

What's more, the presence of these species depends not only on the length of time the body has been dead, but also on where it has been. For example, the fly *Calliphora vomitoria* is found in rural situations, never indoors. So if remains of its larvae are found on the corpse, the corpse must have been outdoors at some stage, no matter where it was eventually found.

Cycling matter in ecosystems

Earlier in this chapter, we saw how energy flows through ecosystems. It enters as light energy, and is converted to chemical potential energy by plants. It is then passed from one organism to another as they eat each other. All along the food chain, a great deal of energy is lost to the environment as heat. This heat energy is lost from the ecosystem. 'New' sunlight coming in to the system brings in fresh supplies of energy.

Organisms also pass matter between themselves – atoms of various elements that they use to build their bodies. Carbon, oxygen and hydrogen are needed to make carbohydrates and fats and also proteins, which in addition require nitrogen. Other elements, such as potassium, calcium, magnesium and iodine are needed in smaller quantities to make particular molecules, to act as enzyme cofactors or to produce potential differences across membranes.

These substances, unlike energy, tend to be cycled *within* the ecosystem rather than passing through it. When an organism dies or sheds a part of itself, excretes or egests, the molecules from its body are used as nutrients by decomposers. The decomposers break down the organic molecules and liberate atoms and ions that can be used by other organisms. Decomposers have a vital part to play in returning 'used' materials to the ecosystem so that they become available to other organisms.

We will look at just one example of how an element is cycled within an ecosystem – the nitrogen cycle.

The nitrogen cycle

Nitrogen is an essential element for all living organisms, because of its presence in proteins and nucleic acids. There is a large quantity of nitrogen in the air, which is around 78% nitrogen gas. However, most organisms cannot use this nitrogen. This is because nitrogen gas exists as molecular nitrogen, in which two nitrogen atoms are linked with a triple covalent bond. In this form, nitrogen is very unreactive. With each breath you take in around 350 cm^3 of nitrogen gas, but this is completely useless to you. It simply passes in and out of your body unchanged. Similarly, N_2 passes freely in and out of a plant's stomata, with the plant unable to make any use of it.

Before nitrogen can be used by living organisms it must be converted from N_2 into some more reactive form, such as ammonia (NH_3) or nitrate (NO_3^-). This conversion is called **nitrogen fixation** (Figure 12.12).

Nitrogen fixation by living organisms

Only prokaryotes and archeans are capable of fixing nitrogen. One of the best-known nitrogen-fixing bacteria is *Rhizobium* (Figure 12.13). This bacterium lives freely in the soil, and also in the roots of many species of plants, especially leguminous plants (belonging to the pea family) such as peas, beans and clover. When living freely in the soil, *Rhizobium* can only fix nitrogen to a very limited extent. Most nitrogen fixation by *Rhizobium* occurs when it is living in plant roots. The plant and the bacterium coexist in a rather remarkable way, each benefiting from the presence of the other.

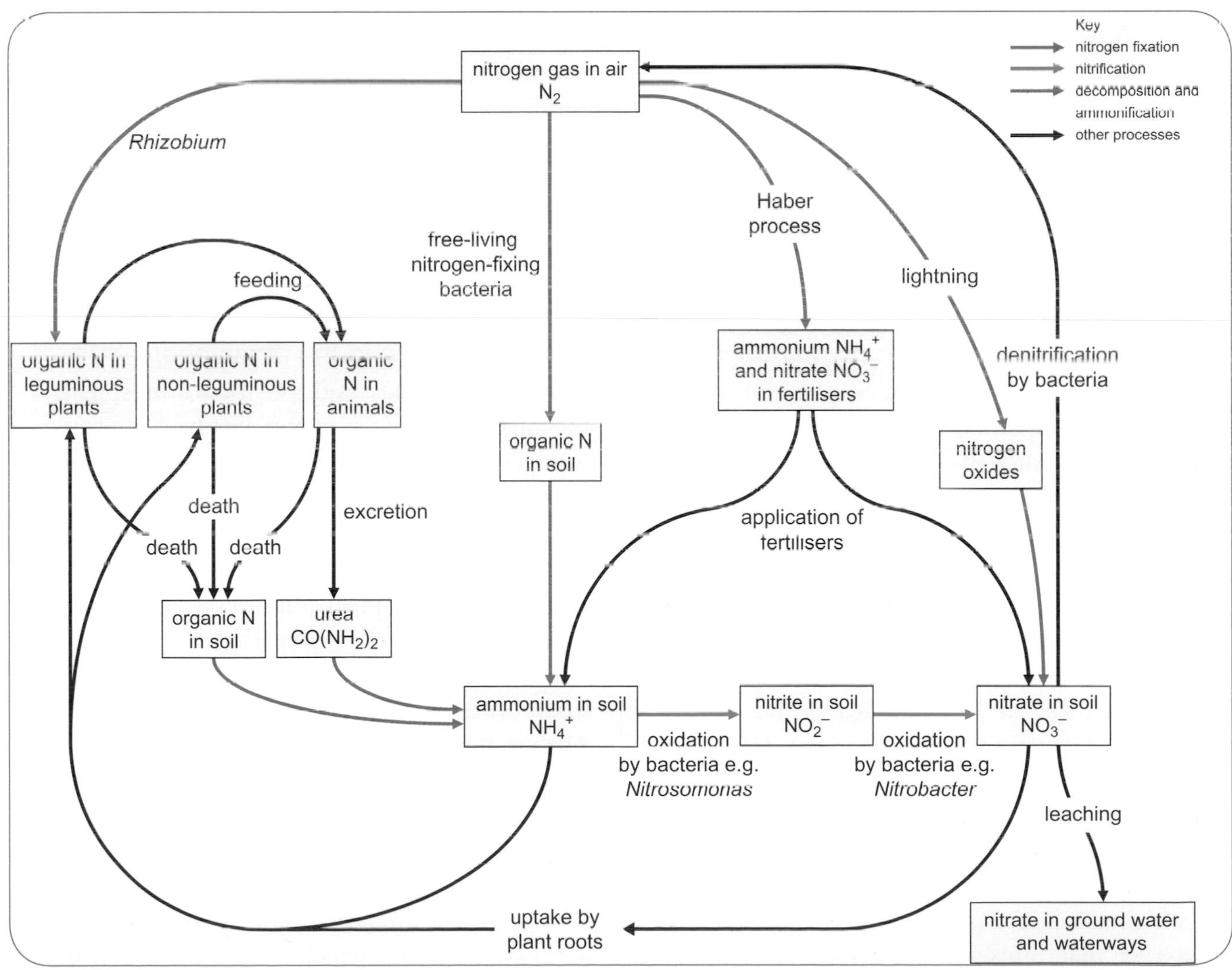

Figure 12.12 The nitrogen cycle.

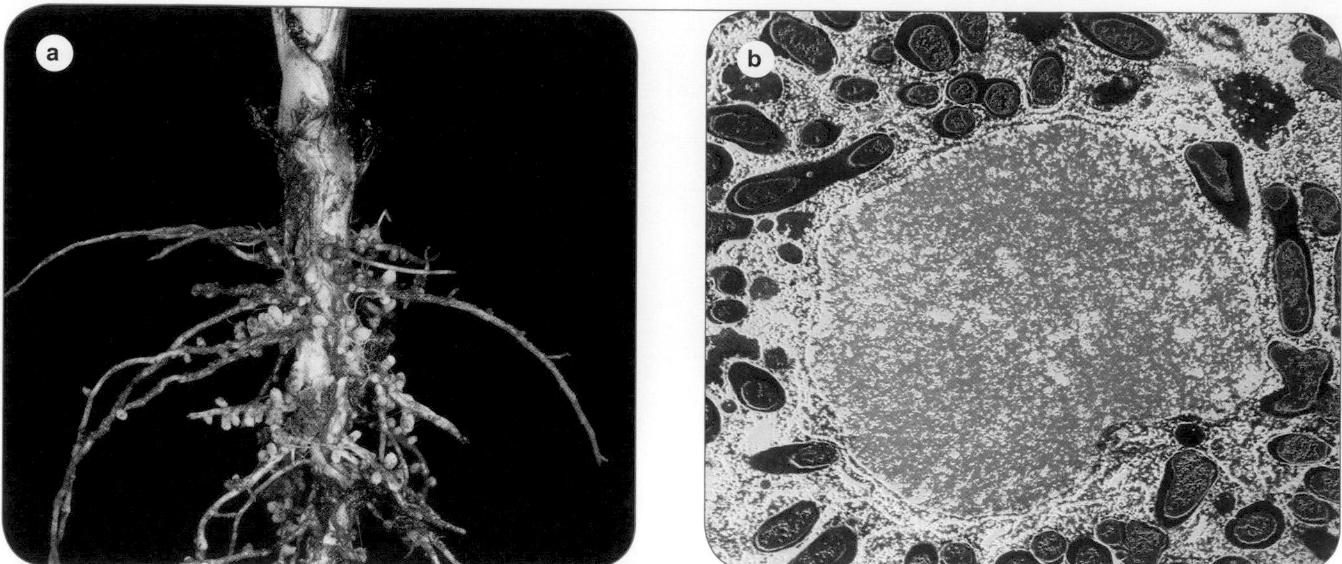

Figure 12.13 **a** Root nodules on the roots of a broad bean plant. **b** Electron micrograph showing *Rhizobium* bacteria inside the cytoplasm of a root nodule cell. The large green area is the cell nucleus. The bacteria are red. Magnification ×4480.

Rhizobium is found in most soils. When a leguminous plant germinates, its roots produce proteins called lectins, which bind to polysaccharides on the cell surface of the bacteria. The bacteria invade the roots, spreading along the root hairs. They stimulate some of the cells in the root to divide and develop into small lumps called nodules, inside which the bacteria form colonies.

The bacteria fix nitrogen with the help of an enzyme called **nitrogenase**. This enzyme catalyses the conversion of nitrogen gas, N_2, to ammonium ions, NH_4^+. To do this, it needs:

- a supply of hydrogen
- a supply of ATP
- anaerobic conditions – that is, the absence of oxygen.

The hydrogen comes from reduced NADP, which is produced by the plant. The ATP comes from the metabolism of sucrose, produced by photosynthesis in the plant's leaves and transported down into the root nodules. Here the sucrose is processed and used in respiration to generate ATP. Anaerobic conditions are maintained through the production, by the plant, of a protein called leghaemoglobin. This molecule has a high affinity for oxygen, and effectively 'mops up' oxygen that diffuses into the nodules.

The relationship between the plant and the bacteria is therefore a very close one. The plant supplies living space, and the conditions required by the bacteria to fix nitrogen. The bacteria supply the plant with fixed nitrogen. This is an example of **mutualism**, in which two organisms of different species live very closely together, each meeting some of the other's needs.

Nitrogen fixation in the atmosphere

When lightning passes through the atmosphere, the huge quantities of energy involved can cause nitrogen molecules to react with oxygen, forming nitrogen oxides (Figure 12.12). These dissolve in rain, and are carried to the ground. In countries where there are frequent thunderstorms – for example, many tropical countries – this is a very significant source of fixed nitrogen.

Fixation by the Haber process

The production of fertilisers containing fixed nitrogen is a major industry. In the Haber process, nitrogen and hydrogen gases are reacted together to produce ammonia This requires considerable energy inputs, so the resulting fertilisers are not cheap. The ammonia is often converted to ammonium nitrate, which is the most widely used inorganic fertiliser in the world.

Use of fixed nitrogen by plants

In legumes, the fixed nitrogen produced by *Rhizobium* in their root nodules is used to make amino acids. These are transported out of the nodules into the xylem, distributed to all parts of the plant and used within cells to synthesise proteins (Figure 12.14).

Other plants rely on supplies of fixed nitrogen in the soil. Their root hairs take up nitrate ions by active transport. In many plants, the nitrate is converted in the roots, first to nitrite (NO_2^-), then to ammonia and then to amino acids which are transported to other parts of the plant through the xylem. In other plant species, the nitrate ions are transported, in xylem, to the leaves before undergoing these processes. Again, most of the nitrogen ends up as part of protein molecules in the plant, especially in seeds and storage tissues.

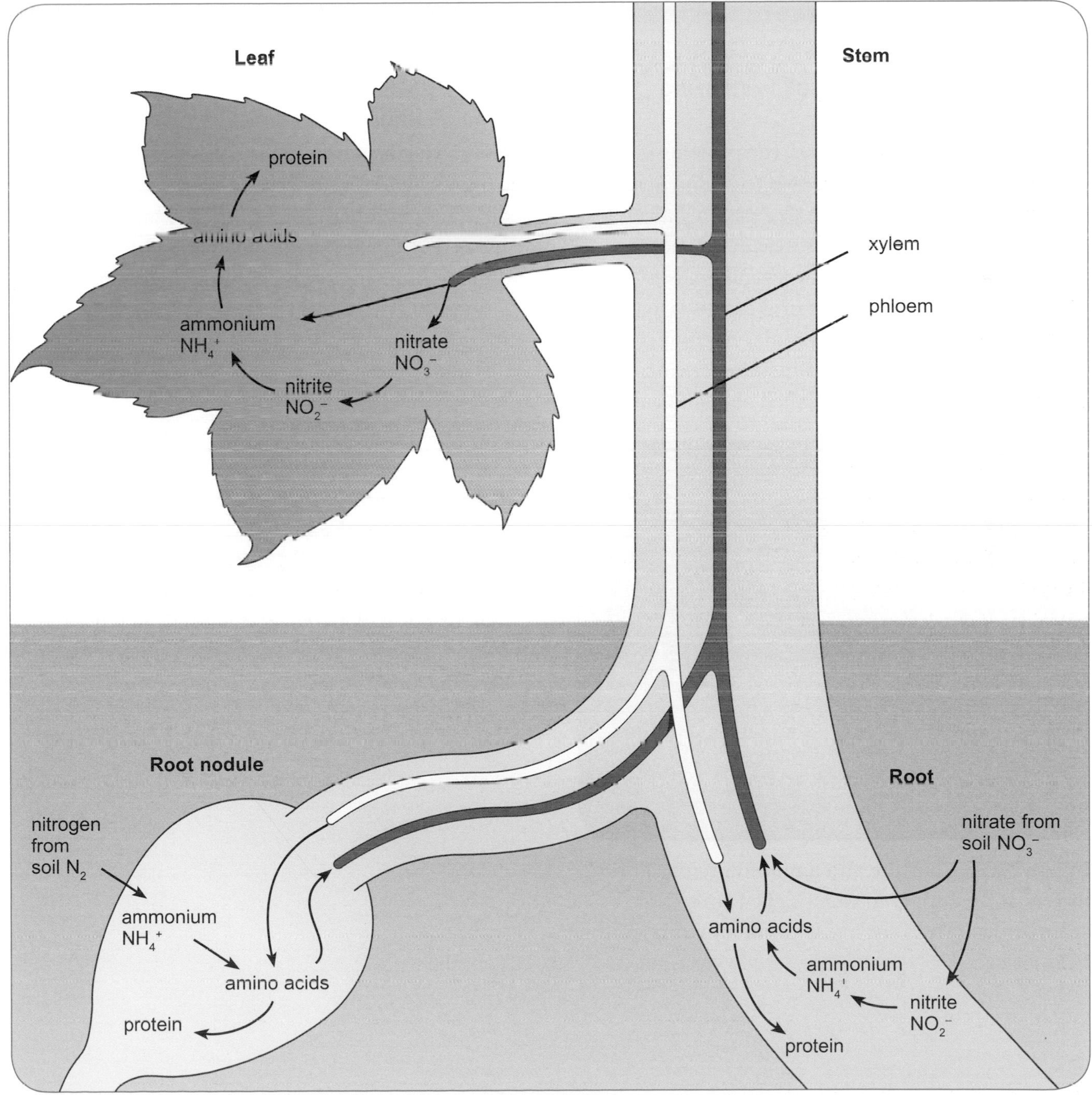

Figure 12.14 A summary of nitrogen metabolism and transport in plants.

Assimilation of nitrogen by animals

Animals, including humans, can only use nitrogen when it is part of an organic molecule. Most of our nitrogen supply comes from proteins in the diet, with a small amount from nucleic acids. During digestion, proteins are broken down to amino acids, before being absorbed into the blood and distributed to all cells in the body. Here they are built up again into proteins. Excess amino acids are deaminated in the liver, where the nitrogen becomes part of urea molecules. These are excreted in urine.

Return of nitrate to the soil from living organisms

When an animal or plant dies, the proteins in its cells are gradually broken down to amino acids. This is done by decomposers, especially bacteria and fungi, which produce protease enzymes. The decomposers use some of the amino acids for their own growth, while some are broken down and the nitrogen released as ammonia. Ammonia is also produced from the urea in animal urine. The production of ammonia is called **ammonification**.

Figure 12.15 Nitrate and ammonium ions are in very short supply in waterlogged soils, but carnivorous plants survive by obtaining nitrogen from insects.

Ammonia in the soil is rapidly converted to nitrite ions (NO_2^-) and nitrate ions (NO_3^-) by a group of bacteria called **nitrifying bacteria**. They include *Nitrosomonas* and *Nitrobacter*. These bacteria derive their energy from **nitrification**. In contrast to nitrogen fixation, this only occurs freely provided the soil is well aerated. Boggy soils are therefore often short of nitrates. Some plants have become adapted to growing in such soils by supplementing their nitrogen intake using animal protein. These carnivorous plants trap insects, whose proteins are digested and absorbed by the plant (Figure 12.15).

Denitrification

Denitrifying bacteria provide themselves with energy by reversing nitrogen fixation and converting nitrate to nitrogen gas, which is returned to the air (**denitrification**). They are common in places such as sewage treatment plants, compost heaps and wet soils. This brings the nitrogen cycle full circle.

Extension

Stretch and challenge question

1 Describe the roles of microorganisms in the nitrogen cycle. To what extent do their activities affect the distribution of plants and animals in a habitat?

Hint

Summary

Glossary

- An ecosystem is a self-contained system including living organisms and environment interacting with one another. Ecosystems are dynamic.
- Biotic factors are factors affecting an organism that involve other organisms. They include predator–prey relationships, parasitism, mutualism and competition.
- Abiotic factors are factors affecting an organism that involve non-living components of its environment. They include light, temperature, oxygen, carbon dioxide, water supply and the inorganic components of the soil.
- Energy enters nearly all ecosystems in the form of light energy, and is transferred between living organisms in the form of organic nutrients. It is lost from ecosystems as heat energy.
- Plants are producers, capturing energy from sunlight and transferring it into organic compounds during photosynthesis. Animals and fungi are consumers, taking in their energy as organic compounds in the food that they eat. The level at which an organism feeds is known as a trophic level.
- A great deal of energy – often around 90% of it – is lost during transfer from one trophic level to the next. The percentage of energy transferred is known as the efficiency of transfer.
- Gross primary productivity is the rate at which plants transfer light energy into chemical potential energy during photosynthesis. Net primary productivity is the quantity of energy remaining after the plant has used some for its own metabolic processes.
- The energy transferred between trophic levels can be measured by estimating the population sizes of the organisms involved. A value for the energy content of each organism is calculated, by drying to constant mass and then heating in a calorimeter. The energy content times the number of organisms gives a value for the energy content of each population.
- In agriculture, energy flow is manipulated so that the maximum quantity is channelled along food chains involved in the production of edible crops or animal products. Parasites, predators and other plants – which in a natural ecosystem would use some of the energy – are excluded, so that more energy flows into the parts of the food chain leading to humans. Factors that could reduce the proportion of the light energy used by plants, such as only partial coverage of the ground or shortage of mineral ions, are typically dealt with by close planting and the application of fertilisers.
- Succession is a gradual, directional change in the communities living in an area. Each community affects the environment in such a way that it becomes possible for different species to live in it. Each step in the succession is called a seral stage, and the final, stable community at the end of the succession is called a climax community.
- Nitrogen is an essential element in all living organisms, and is found in proteins and nucleic acids. Nitrogen gas is too unreactive for most organisms to use, but nitrogen-fixing bacteria such as *Rhizobium* are able to convert it to ammonium ions. Plants use these ions to make amino acids, which are then passed along the food chain to consumers. Decomposers break down nitrogen-containing compounds in plants and animals, often releasing ammonia or ammonium ions in the process. Nitrifying bacteria, such as *Nitrosomonas* and *Nitrobacter*, convert ammonium to nitrite and then to nitrate ions, which can be taken up by plants. Denitrifying bacteria convert nitrate ions to nitrogen gas.

Questions

1 a Nitrifying and denitrifying bacteria are involved in the nitrogen cycle.
Explain the role in the nitrogen cycle of:
i nitrifying bacteria
ii denitrifying bacteria. [4]

b Read the following passage carefully, then answer the questions below.

Rhizobium is a bacterium that is closely associated with the roots of certain plants known as legumes. These plants produce chemicals to attract the bacteria and extra root hairs are produced. The bacteria attach to the surface of the root hairs. Chemical links are formed between a complex polysaccharide on the bacterial surface and lectin, a protein, formed by the plants. The bacteria penetrate the cell walls of the root hairs and enter the cells. The presence of the bacteria stimulates the cells of the root to divide, forming swellings known as nodules.

The bacteria produce an enzyme, nitrogenase, that is the catalyst for the conversion of nitrogen gas to ammonia. The bacteria use carbon compounds manufactured by the plant to respire, making energy available for this conversion. The ammonia is then used to form amino acids. Nitrogenase only functions in low oxygen concentrations. The root cells produce a pigment, leghaemoglobin, that is very similar to haemoglobin. Leghaemoglobin absorbs oxygen, leaving low concentrations in the nodules.

i *Rhizobium* is a prokaryotic organism.
State <u>one</u> characteristic that is typical of prokaryotes, but not of eukaryotes. [1]

ii Lectin (line 5) and polysaccharides are compounds that are formed from small molecules joined together by chemical bonds.
Explain how the small molecules are joined together to form these compounds. [3]

iii Leghaemoglobin contains the same metal element as haemoglobin.
Name this metal element. [1]

iv State the names of <u>two</u> proteins, <u>other than lectin</u>, mentioned in the passage. [2]

v Name the process that occurs in *Rhizobium* to convert nitrogen gas into ammonia. [1]

vi It has been suggested that oxygen is an inhibitor of nitrogenase.
Explain <u>one</u> way in which oxygen could act as an inhibitor. [2]

c Genetic engineers have tried to introduce genes for nitrogenase into wheat, which is <u>not</u> a legume.
Suggest the possible advantages of developing this wheat. [2]

OCR Biology A (2801) January 2004 [Total 16]

Answer

Chapter 13

Populations and sustainability

e-Learning

Objectives

We can define a **population** as a group of organisms of the same species, which live in the same place at the same time and can interbreed with one another. In this chapter, we will look at some of the factors that can influence the size of a population, and also at some of the ways in which human activities can threaten or help to sustain populations of plants and animals.

Population growth curves

In Chapter 10, we saw how the pattern of growth of a population of bacteria in a closed system follows a pattern known as a **sigmoid growth curve** (Figure 10.1). This general pattern is found in many other populations of different organisms living in different environments. The population tends to increase until it reaches the maximum number that can live in that habitat. Various factors come into play in determining what this number is.

Anything that stops a population from increasing in size is said to be a **limiting factor**. In the case of the bacteria in the nutrient broth, the limiting factor is the amount of nutrients in the broth. Once these begin to be in short supply, the population can no longer increase at its maximum rate and eventually stops growing completely.

In a wild population, many different factors may limit population growth at different times and in different ways. Imagine, for example, a population of song thrushes in the gardens of a small town (Figure 13.1). The thrushes feed on snails, slugs and other small invertebrates, so if there is a limited supply of these, this may prevent the population from growing beyond a certain level. They need nesting sites, and if these are in limited supply this, too, may act as a limiting factor for their population size. They are predated by cats and birds such as kestrels and sparrowhawks; if the number of predators is high, this may keep the thrush numbers down. Parasites could also affect them. Between them, these factors place an upper limit on the size of the population that can be sustained. This upper limit is known as the **carrying capacity** of that particular area.

You could imagine what might happen if some thrushes were introduced into a suitable area where there had previously been none. Like the bacteria in the flask, their population would probably go through a lag phase and then a log phase, until the limiting factors described above (or perhaps others that we have not thought of) begin to slow down and eventually limit their population growth.

However, unlike the bacteria in the flask, it is unlikely that the thrush population will enter a decline or death phase, because in the wild it is probable that the supply of food and nest sites will never entirely run out – they will just remain in short supply. The thrush population will probably stay in the stationary phase. Having said that, the population size is unlikely to remain absolutely constant; it will fluctuate up and down a little, perhaps in response to particularly cold or wet winters, or summers when snails are in especially good supply.

Although we have made what seem like sensible suggestions about what factors might be important in limiting a population such as the thrushes,

Figure 13.1 Snails are an important part of the diet of the song thrush, *Turdus philomelus*.

you can imagine how very difficult it would be to obtain experimental evidence to test these ideas. If we thought, for example, that food supply might be limiting the thrush population, we could try supplying lots of extra snails and then see if this has an effect on population size. But it would be virtually impossible to control all the other variables, such as size of predator or parasite populations, and we certainly cannot control the weather. So it would be extremely difficult to interpret the results we observed with any great confidence. We are therefore only very rarely sure that one particular factor really does have a significant influence on population size. In most populations that have been studied, the evidence points to many different factors interacting with each other to limit the size of the population.

Predator–prey relationships

In some cases, there is evidence that the size of a predator population is influenced by the size of the population of its prey, and also vice versa – that is, the size of the prey population is influenced by the size of the population of its predator.

Again, laboratory experiments are much easier to interpret than data obtained from wild populations, because we can control the conditions more carefully. A classic experiment carried out in 1958 investigated the relationship between a predatory mite *Typhlodromus occidentalis* and a mite on which it preys, *Eotetranychus sexmaculatus*. (Mites are small arthropods.) The prey species was fed on oranges. Figure 13.2 shows the results of one such experiment, where the predatory mite and its prey were introduced into a complex environment containing a large number of oranges, with partial barriers of Vaseline between the oranges, but also some small upright sticks that allowed the mites to disperse gradually from one orange to the next. You can see that the populations of both mites oscillate.

SAQ

1 a At what trophic level does each of the mite species feed?

b From what you know about energy transfer between trophic levels, explain why the size of the population of the predatory mite is always lower than that of its prey.

Hint

Answer

Closer examination of the graph reveals some other patterns. The population of the prey species rises first, followed by that of the predator. This makes sense, because we would expect the population of the predatory mite to be able to grow only when it has plenty of food – so the rise in the predator population *follows* that of the prey. As the predator population rises, this begins to limit the prey population, so that begins to fall. This reduction in food supply limits the predator population, so that then begins to fall. As the predator population decreases, the prey population can begin to increase again, and so on.

There are relatively few cases where populations of predator and prey behave like this in 'wild' situations. It only seems to work where the predator specialises in feeding on one type of prey. Clearly, if the predator eats many different types of prey, then it can just switch to a different one if the population of one particular type begins to fall. For example, dog whelks (predatory snails

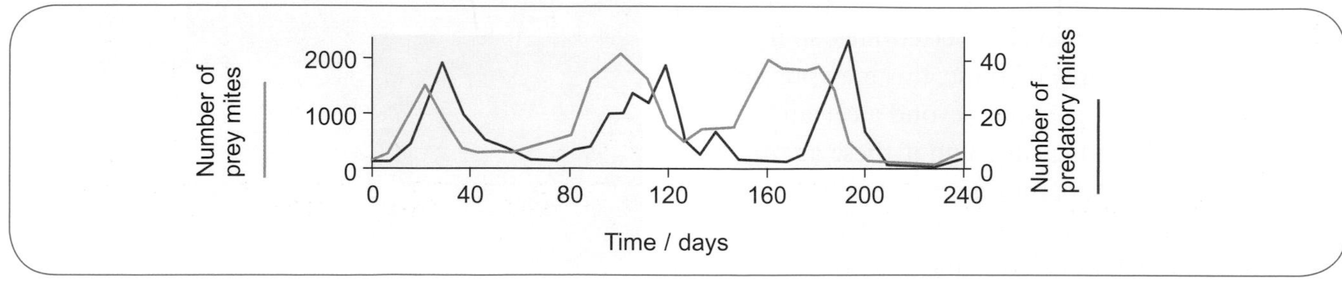

Figure 13.2 Changes in population size of a predatory mite (*Typhlodromus occidentalis*) and its prey (*Eotetranychus sexmaculatus*).

that live on rocky sea shores) prefer to feed on mussels when these are available, but if the mussel population is not very large then they will feed on barnacles instead.

This type of close relationship between predator and prey populations also only happens when predation is the main limiting factor for the prey population (not disease, or food supply, or anything else) and where food supply is the main limiting factor for the predator population. Predator–prey interactions may, for example, be the main factors affecting populations of lynxes (predators) and snowshoe hares (prey) in northern Canada (Figure 13.3).

SAQ

2 a Describe the changes in population size of the lynx between 1850 and 1935, shown in Figure 13.3.

b What evidence is there from these data that the lynx and hare populations influence one another? Could there be another explanation for these population changes?

Answer

Competition

Organisms are said to **compete** whenever a resource that they need is in short supply. For example, the thrushes that we discussed earlier may compete for food if there is not enough for all of them, or for nesting sites. This is an example of **intraspecific competition**. 'Intra' means 'within', so intraspecific competition occurs between members of the same species. It can be an extremely important factor in limiting population sizes. We have seen (*Biology 1*, Chapter 14) that intraspecific competition is also involved in the process of natural selection, in which organisms with variations that make them better competitors are more likely to survive, passing on their genes (and therefore their characteristics) to their offspring.

Competition can also occur between organisms of *different* species. This is known as **interspecific competition**. Interspecific competition will only occur when the niches of the two species overlap. The **niche** of an organism is its role or position in the ecosystem of which it is part; it involves not only its particular habitat but also what the organism does and all the different ways in which it affects, and is affected by, the biotic and abiotic

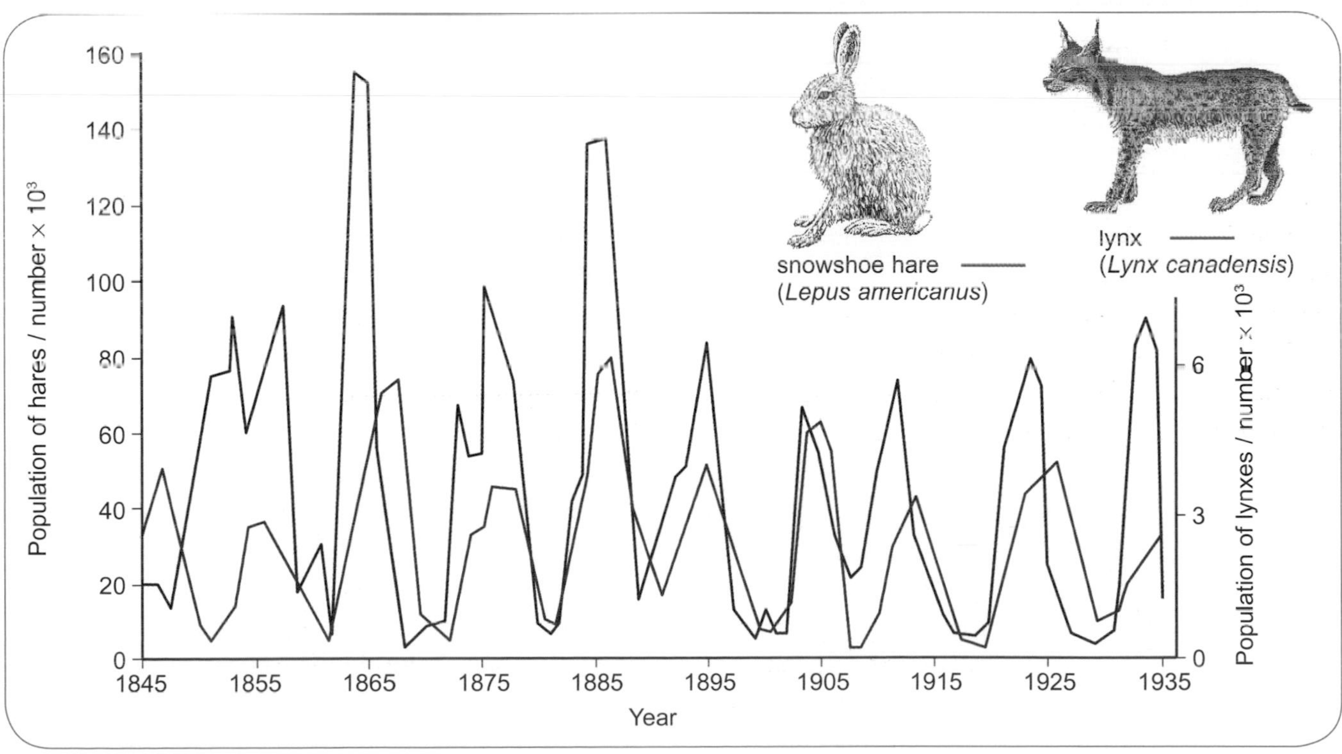

Figure 13.3 The relationship between the numbers of lynx (predator) and snowshoe hares (prey) between 1845 and 1935, as shown by the number of animals trapped for the Hudson's Bay Company.

factors of its environment. The more the niches overlap, the more likely competition is to occur. Once again, we have learned most about this from relatively simple situations set up as laboratory experiments, rather than from trying to unravel the complex situations that occur in the wild.

One such experiment, first carried out in 1948, involved two species of small beetles that live and breed in flour. The adults and larvae live entirely on dry flour, which makes them very useful as experimental organisms. They are sometimes found in houses, where you might see them as tiny, slow-moving dark dots in bags of flour that have been kept for rather too long.

The two species of flour beetles in this particular experiment were *Tribolium confusum* and *Tribolium castaneum*. If small numbers of both species were placed in some wholemeal flour to which a little yeast had been added, then the population of *T. castaneum* almost always rose and then oscillated, while that of *T. confusum* gradually fell until it died out altogether (Figure 13.4). Similar results have been found in many other cases when two species with very similar requirements are living and breeding in the same restricted habitat. One very often out-competes the other, so that they cannot

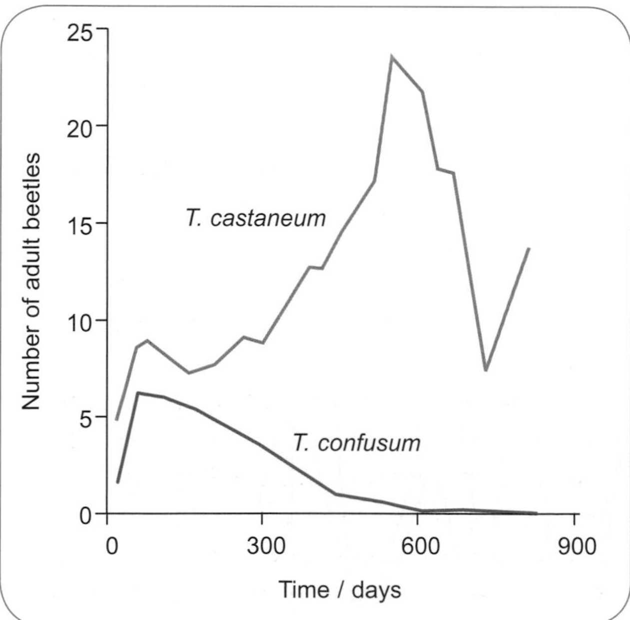

Figure 13.4 Changes in population size of two species of flour beetle, *Tribolium confusum* and *Tribolium castaneum*, competing for food and space in a container of wholemeal flour.

coexist. However, in the *Tribolium* experiments, it was found that a very small change in the conditions in which they lived could alter *which* species survived. For example, if the temperature was above 29 °C then it was *T. castaneum* that survived while at temperatures below 29 °C *T. confusum* survived. If a protozoan that parasitised both species was introduced, then *T. castaneum* was almost always the species to die out.

SAQ

3 Suggest reasons for the changes in population size for *Tribolium confusum*, shown in Figure 13.4.

Hint

Answer

In other similar experiments, however, it has been found that two species with very similar niches can survive indefinitely together. For example, two different species of beetles, *Oryzaephilus* sp. and *Rhizopertha* sp., that live and feed in stored wheat grain, can coexist in laboratory conditions for long periods of time. Although the adults of both species feed on the outside of the wheat grains and therefore compete directly with one another, the larvae of *Rhizopertha* feed from inside the grains while *Oryzaephilus* larvae feed from the outside. This small difference in their niches seems to be enough to enable the two species to live alongside one another.

Interacting factors

In natural situations, it is rare that competition or predation alone have a major effect on the size of a population. Generally, several different factors interact to affect population size and distribution. One example that has been well studied is the distribution of two species of barnacles, *Chthamalus stellatus* and *Balanus balanoides*.

You can often find these barnacles on rocky shores around Britain. Adult barnacles live fixed firmly to rocks, lying on their backs inside their strong outer shells and waving their legs in the water around them to catch food when the tide comes in. Their larvae are planktonic – that is, they are very small and float in the sea, from which some of them will be washed onto rocks where they settle down to spend the rest of their lives. These larvae are produced in huge numbers.

Figure 13.5 shows the distribution of these two species of barnacles on a rocky shore in Scotland. The tide comes in twice a day, covering the rocks, before retreating again. So each part of the shore is under water for part of each day, and exposed to the air for the rest of the time. The higher up the shore a barnacle lives, the less time it is covered by water. Another problem for barnacles living high up a shore is that temperatures fluctuate much more here than when they are close to, or covered by, water. It seems that neither *Chthamalus* nor *Balanus* is able to live any higher up the shore than they do, because they cannot cope with the temperature fluctuations or long periods of exposure to drying air they would experience there. *Chthamalus*, however, is better than *Balanus* at coping with this, so it is found higher up.

At the bottom end of their range on the shore, *Balanus* is unable to live any further down because here it becomes more likely to be eaten by the predatory dog whelk, *Nucellus*, which is only active when covered by water. Moreover, algae (seaweeds) grow on these rocks that spend much of their time covered by water, and *Balanus* is not good at competing with these algae for space on the rocks.

In the middle of the range, there is only a very small area where both *Chthamalus* and *Balanus* are found together. If all the *Balanus* are removed from the region below the bottom of *Chthamalus*'s range, or if rocks with *Chthamalus* on them are placed lower down the shore, then it is found that *Chthamalus* is perfectly capable of surviving there. What normally stops it is competition with *Balanus* – in this part of the shore, *Balanus* grows faster than *Chthamalus* and so wins the competition for limited space on the rocks.

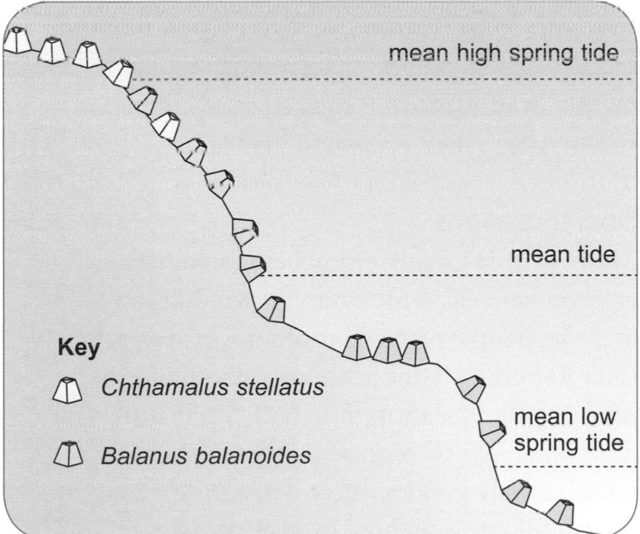

Figure 13.5 The distribution of two species of barnacles, *Chthamalus stellatus* and *Balanus balanoides*, on a rocky shore.

SAQ

4 Summarise the main factors limiting the distribution of:

a *Chthamalus* at the top of its range on the shore

b *Chthamalus* at the bottom of its range on the shore

c *Balanus* at the top of its range on the shore

d *Balanus* at the bottom of its range on the shore.

Answer

Conservation

No-one can fail to be aware of the real and potential damage we are doing to the environment on Earth, as our population increases and we place ever-increasing demands on environmental resources. Yet there is hope that we can slow, stop or – in some cases – even reverse the harm we cause. There are signs that our population growth is slowing, and as we learn more and more about how our behaviour affects the environment, we should be able to bring into play more effective measures to conserve it.

Conservation involves the active management of habitats in order to maintain, or even increase, the biodiversity within them. Biodiversity, as we saw in *Biology 1* Chapter 12, can be defined as the range of habitats, communities and species that are present in an area, and the genetic variation that exists within each species.

Conservation is far more than just 'preservation', which means keeping things as they are. Ecosystems are not static entities; they involve dynamic interactions between organisms and their environment. They change over time. Just 'preserving' a wood, or a pond, with no active management, may not be the best thing to do. In the UK today there is scarcely a single wood or pond that has not already been influenced by human activities. None of them are entirely 'natural'. If we put a fence around the pond and ignore it, it will gradually become filled with sediment and cease to be a pond at all. If we wish to maintain the biodiversity in the pond then we need to play an active role in periodically removing sediment from it, stopping succession from taking its natural course. Similarly, the variety of woodlands in the UK now has been heavily affected by human activities in the past. There is probably no genuine 'wild wood' in the UK today. Woodland management has produced and then maintained the complex communities that we see in our woodlands and forests. If we stop managing the woodland, then it will cease to exist in the form with which we are familiar.

This is not to say that there is never a time and place for just leaving things alone. In some parts of the world, there may still be ecosystems which have never been significantly influenced by humans, and which for the moment seem to be relatively safe from human interference. The best way of conserving these may indeed be to keep well away from them.

Whether this can be done is another matter altogether. Once discovered, these undisturbed habitats – perhaps a tract of tropical rainforest in inaccessible mountains in New Guinea, or a plateau in South America that is almost impossible to get to – seem to become irresistible magnets for researchers and film crews who want to tell the world all about them. These may not cause much damage themselves, but they can sometimes encourage the opening up of the area to tourism, which can have damaging effects on a vulnerable environment.

Most of us feel uncomfortable watching a wildlife film showing a wild animal being 'tagged' with a heavy radio-transmitting collar, so that we can find out more about its way of life. The researchers argue that this information will make it easier for us to find ways of conserving this species. But there must always be a lingering doubt that an even better way of conserving it is to leave it alone. In most cases, though, the researchers are right. We simply have to accept that people will infiltrate even the wildest places on Earth, and that it is rarely going to be possible for us just to leave somewhere completely alone and unaffected by humans.

Reasons for conservation

In *Biology 1* Chapter 15, we saw that there are a variety of different reasons for conservation. We can summarise these as follows. These are not mutually exclusive categories, and you will see that they merge into each other.

Economic reasons

Conservation can ensure that we can carry on using resources that we obtain from our environment for long into the future. For example, good conservation practice in the harvesting of timber from woodland (described below) enables us to continue to use this resource indefinitely. We have already seen (*Biology 1*, page 235) that the hugely diverse flora of tropical rainforests is the source of many of our medicinal drugs, and has the potential to provide many more. Conservation of fish stocks in the sea should allow us to keep harvesting fish in the future. If we do not do this, then the resource will eventually run out. Conservation can also help to maintain biodiversity in places that provide income for local people from tourism – such as the Galapagos Islands, described on pages 209–212.

Social reasons

Many people greatly enjoy being in a natural environment. Research has shown that, on average, people report a more positive effect on their happiness after a walk in woodland than after a walk in a shopping mall. Surprisingly, at least one piece of research suggests that there is a measurably greater effect if the biodiversity in the woodland is greater, even if people are not biologists and are not consciously aware of the number of different species that are present.

Economic reasons for conservation are often

also social ones. For example, failing to conserve fish stocks by careful management of the number of fish that we take from the sea, or by reducing pollution or protecting fish breeding sites, means that many people lose their jobs connected to the fishing industry. Conserving wildlife in the Galapagos Islands can continue to draw in tourists, providing employment and income for local people.

Ethical reasons

For many people, there is no need to justify conservation for any reason other than the fact that it is our responsibility to look after the planet on which we live. We share our planet with a huge number of other species, large and small, loveable (like koalas) and not so loveable (such as liverworts and slugs). We have no right to make these species extinct, just because we want to use their habitat in a way that will not allow them to coexist with us.

Sustainable production and conservation

'Conservation' does not always mean that we cannot make use of a particular environment. There are circumstances in which it may be possible, and sometimes even beneficial, to use a natural resource without harming an ecosystem. One such example is the careful management of woodland to provide us with timber.

In Britain, woodland and forests have long been used as a source of many different resources, including wood used for making ships, buildings and furniture. Although we now import a lot of our timber, there are still many woodlands that are managed to provide a sustainable supply of wood. With care, we can ensure that these woodlands continue to survive indefinitely.

Coppicing is a method of woodland management that has been in use in Britain for thousands of years (Figure 13.6 and Figure 13.7). It enables wood to be taken year on year, without destroying the woodland or the biodiversity within it. It may even increase biodiversity.

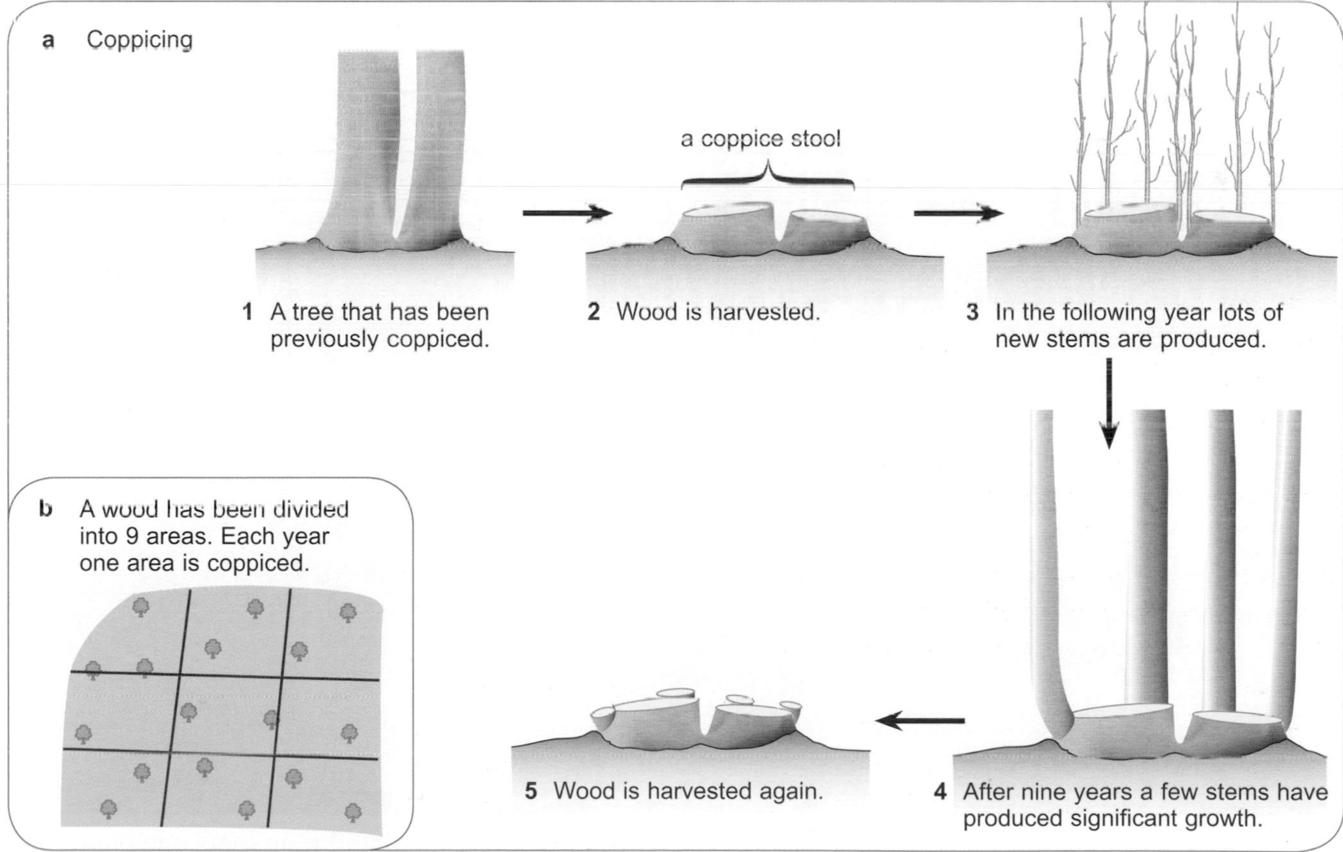

a Coppicing
a coppice stool
1 A tree that has been previously coppiced.
2 Wood is harvested.
3 In the following year lots of new stems are produced.
4 After nine years a few stems have produced significant growth.
5 Wood is harvested again.
b A wood has been divided into 9 areas. Each year one area is coppiced.

Figure 13.6 Coppicing: **a** the coppice cycle – this cycle would be repeated for 100 years or more; **b** how a wood could be coppiced on a nine-year cycle.

This traditional woodland management system exploits the fact that most deciduous trees don't die when they are cut down. They regrow from the base. The tree – for example, sweet chestnut, ash, lime or hazel – is cut down close to the ground and then left for several years to regrow. The new growth consists of several stems, so the wood that can be harvested from these is normally quite small in diameter, which limits its use. It cannot be used to make large planks, for example, although it is ideal for making items such as garden furniture or fencing, or for use as firewood or for making charcoal.

Within a wood, it is normal to coppice just part of it in any one year. Each year, a different area is coppiced, until all of it has been done and the first area is coppiced again. This is called **rotational coppicing**. The length of the coppice cycle can be varied according to the species involved, and the use that is required of the timber. Often, a system called **coppice with standards** is used, where some trees in each area are not coppiced but are left to grow into full-sized trees called standards. For example, a wood might contain a mix of hazel that is regularly coppiced, and oak that is left to grow as standards. The oak trees can be harvested when they are big enough to provide large timber. They may then be left to regrow from the cut stumps, or new ones can be planted.

Rotational coppicing is an excellent way of maintaining and even increasing biodiversity in woodlands. Left to itself, a deciduous wood in Britain is likely to become populated with large trees, whose canopies prevent much light reaching the woodland floor. This limits the number of species that are able to grow there. Coppicing opens up parts of the woodland, increasing light levels on the woodland floor and so providing

Figure 13.7 Sweet chestnut coppice. Each ring of trunks is one coppice stool and represents one plant that has been coppiced several times. Sweet chestnut is split to produce fence posts that are resistant to rot and so do not need treating with chemicals.

conditions in which species such as bluebells and other herbaceous plants can thrive. The fact that different parts of the wood are at different stages of the coppice cycle at any one time helps to maximise species diversity.

While coppicing is a very good way of providing a sustainable supply of timber from a woodland, it is very labour-intensive and is nowadays usually done on a relatively small scale, in circumstances where conservation is more important than profit-making. It is more difficult to carry out large-scale forestry in a sustainable way.

'Sustainable forestry' can have different meanings. It may simply mean providing a sustainable timber harvest – in other words, timber is removed from a forest in such a way that similar amounts can be removed year after year for long periods of time. It may also mean that the forest *ecosystem* is maintained, with all the different habitats and species able to live in the forest even though timber is being extracted from it.

Maintaining a sustainable forest ecosystem while timber extraction is carried out on a large scale is extremely difficult. However, it is possible to take steps to minimise damage to the ecosystem and still make good profits. For example, rather than **clear felling**, which is the removal of all the trees in an area at once, **selective cutting** can be used. This involves felling only some of the largest, most commercially valuable trees, while leaving the others alone. This does help to leave most habitats largely intact, but it is obviously impossible to do without considerable disturbance, especially if large machinery is used to fell and drag out the harvested trees. Selective cutting is very useful on steep slopes, where clear felling would leave the soil extremely vulnerable to erosion. Selective cutting helps to maintain nutrients in the forest soil, which is beneficial to the plants growing in the forest, and also reduces pollution of nearby waterways.

Another practice that increases sustainability is using a long **rotation time** – that is, leaving each part of the forest for many years before re-harvesting it. For example, traditional forestry would have left trees to grow for up to 100 years or more, while in some modern forestry industries, such as those which provide wood for making paper, the trees grow for only 10 years before harvesting. Short rotations do not allow much time for species diversity to build up, and the frequent disturbance by machinery can cause great damage to the soil. Unfortunately, short rotations are usually more profitable than long ones.

Good forestry practice can increase efficiency. This means that the most use possible is made of each tree that is planted and that there is minimum wastage. Efficiency can be improved in many ways, including:

- matching the tree species to be grown to the climate, topography and soil type – for example, willow or poplar will grow well on low-lying wetland, whereas oak requires drier conditions
- planting trees at the best distance apart – if they are planted too close, they will tend to grow very tall and thin, and competition between them may result in all of the trees producing poor-quality timber; if they are planted too far apart, then a bigger area of land will be used than is necessary to obtain the same amount of timber
- controlling pests and pathogens, so that the trees grow well and provide a good-quality harvest of timber
- using every part of each tree that is felled – branches that are too small for use as timber can be chipped and used as a source of fuel or mulch.

By increasing efficiency in these ways, the very best use is made of the land, thus reducing the total area of land required. It also means that fewer trees need to be felled, as one well-grown tree may provide as much good-quality timber as two or more poorly grown ones.

Active management – conservation at Wildmoor Heath

Across the UK, various organisations work hard to conserve particular habitats and environments. As we saw in *Biology 1* (page 241), every part of the country has drawn up Biodiversity Action Plans, setting out priorities for conservation of species and habitats. At a local level, a variety of organisations take on responsibility for determining precise targets for conservation in their area, and for drawing up detailed plans for how this will be done.

For example, the UK Biodiversity Steering Group has identified 17 habitat types that should be considered for conservation. One of these is heathland and bogs. There has been a huge loss of this type of habitat across the whole of Europe, and the situation is particularly bad in the UK, where we have lost about 80% of our lowland heath since the 1800s.

The Berkshire Conservation Forum is just one of many organisations across the UK whose remit is to interpret the UK Biodiversity Steering Group's ideas and aims, and translate them into action at a local level. Berkshire has some important heathland and bog areas, including some within an area called Wildmoor Heath, near Bracknell (Figure 13.8).

This heathland has already been designated a Site of Special Scientific Interest, which gives it some protection from developers and others who might damage it. Wildmoor Heath is jointly managed by Bracknell Forest Borough Council and the Berks, Bucks and Oxon Wildlife Trust. Together, they have responsibility for the care of this 99-hectare reserve, of which 60 hectares is mostly made up of heath and bog. The reserve contains many species that have been identified as 'key species' to be considered when management plans for conservation areas are drawn up. These include Dartford warblers, nightjars, woodlarks, bog bush crickets and raft spiders (Figure 13.9).

Before conservation can begin, it is important to know exactly what you are dealing with. Detailed

Figure 13.9 Nightjars nest on the ground in heathland, and are threatened by habitat loss and disturbance by humans and dogs. These chicks are 11 days old.

Figure 13.8 **a** Volunteers at Wildmoor Heath help to clear trees and shrubs from the heathland. **b** Heather provides a habitat for a particular community of organisms that would not survive if the heathland was allowed to become woodland.

surveys have been carried out, so that we know what lives where at Wildmoor Heath, and what each species needs from its habitat. Threats have been identified; they include disturbance to animals caused by humans (for example, dogs running loose and disturbing ground-nesting birds such as nightjars), pollution leading to nutrient enrichment (which allows a few vigorous plant species to out-compete some of the rarer ones) and a drop in ground water levels, which would mean a loss of plants that are adapted to living in wet soil. The aims of the conservation programme have been decided in some detail – firstly what it is hoped the conservation will achieve, and then detailed plans for how these aims will be realised.

The overall aims are to maintain and even increase the biodiversity at Wildmoor Heath, and to restore some of the former heathland that has been lost. For example, in some of the wetter areas, the vegetation is dominated by a grass called *Molinia*. These areas are being managed to increase biodiversity there, allowing other plants to grow as well as *Molinia*, which should in turn bring in more species of insects and other animals. This is being done by maintaining a high water table and also by allowing cattle to graze the area at certain times of year. In other areas, trees have colonised areas that were once heathland. These areas are being reclaimed by removing the trees and allowing the heath flora to re-colonise.

Local people are strongly involved in the management of the Wildmoor Heath Reserve. This is a very important feature of conservation – if people who live near and use the conservation area are involved in its management, the conservation is much more likely to be successful. Bracknell Conservation Volunteers regularly turn out to clear trees from areas where heath is to be restored, and to maintain paths – which should keep dogs away from sensitive areas where they are more likely to disturb birds and other animals. The volunteer group is made up of all kinds of different people, with an age range from 17 to 70.

Their work will never be done. There will not be a day when everyone can just sit back and leave Wildmoor Heath to itself. Ecosystems, as we have seen, are dynamic and ever-changing, and if the Heath is simply abandoned then it is likely that the restored heathland will gradually revert to woodland again – the natural climax community – with the loss of the rare species that the heathland supported. Conservation is an on-going process, its demands changing as the ecosystem itself changes. Constant monitoring of the habitat and its biodiversity, and the threats to it, will be needed in order to keep management plans up to date and able to fulfil their aims.

Conservation on the Galapagos Islands

The Galapagos Islands are a small group of isolated islands lying on the equator to the west of Ecuador, which owns them (Figure 13.10). There are about 24 islands (some are very small, so it depends on what you count as an 'island') – all of

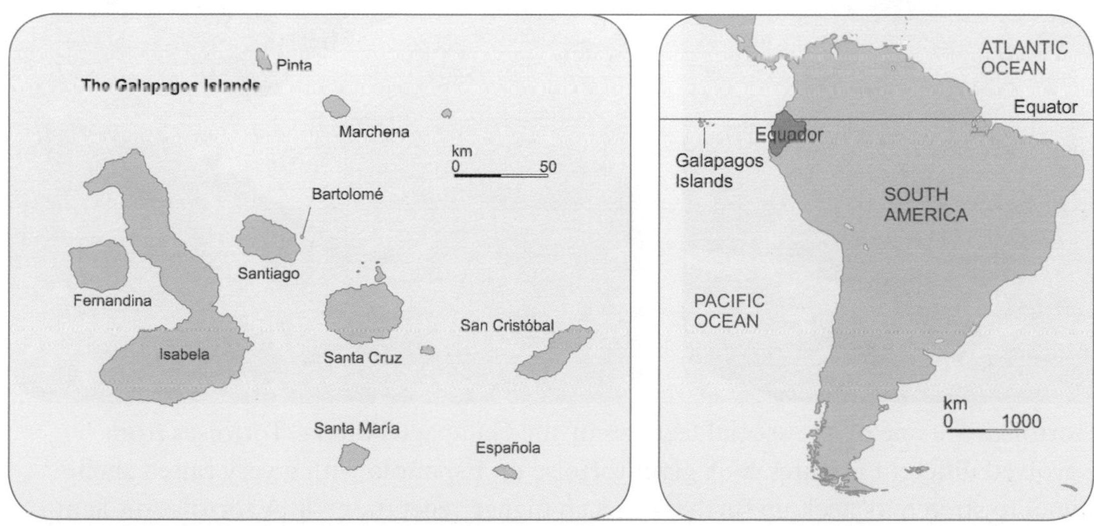

Figure 13.10 The Galapagos Islands.

them are the tips of volcanoes that erupted under the sea millions of years ago. They are famous for the many species of plants and animals that live only there – **endemic species** – and because they were visited by Charles Darwin on the *Beagle* in 1835. What Darwin saw there was important in developing his ideas on evolution.

The plants and animals of Galapagos have been living in isolation from the mainland for hundreds or even thousands of years. Many of the small islands have species that are different from similar species on other islands (Figure 13.11). They provide excellent examples of speciation, and some of these species – for example, the many species of finches – have been the subject of important research on how speciation can occur both with and without geographical isolation.

However, the unique ecosystems and communities of the Galapagos Islands are under threat. Although they are very remote and isolated, people do live there, and increasing numbers of tourists visit each year.

Threats to species on the Galapagos

The activities of humans on and around the Galapagos Islands are posing serious threats to their biodiversity.

- Population growth is occurring at an ever-increasing rate. More and more people are leaving mainland Ecuador because they cannot find work, hoping to find work in the tourist industry on Galapagos. In 1990, just under 10 000 people lived on the Galapagos Islands. By 2008, there were more than 20 000, and the human population is estimated to reach 40 000 by 2014. This large human population puts immense pressure on the fragile ecosystems on the islands. For example, the huge quantities of rubbish the people generate are disposed of in open dumps, or burned, releasing potentially harmful gases.
- Over-fishing is one of the results of this huge population growth. Many of the new immigrants do not manage to find work, and they have increasingly taken up fishing in order to try to make a living. In particular, they have targeted sea cucumbers, for which there is a thriving Asian market. So many were taken that the sea cucumber population has come under threat. Measures such as quotas have been brought in to curb the fishing activities, but these have not been accepted by the fishermen and there have been violent confrontations. This is not an issue that will be solved easily.

Figure 13.11 Giant tortoises are one of the special features of the Galapagos fauna. Tortoises from different islands have evolved different features. **a** A giant tortoise on Española with a very raised shell front, enabling the animal to stretch its neck up further to reach higher vegetation. **b** A tortoise on Santa Cruz with a low shell front suitable for the low and lush vegetation on the island.

- Tourism is a growing industry in the Galapagos. It is a very expensive but also very desirable tourist destination, especially for people who are interested in the animals and plants that live there. Unfortunately, their very interest is increasing the threats to these species. The National Park Service places strict regulations on where tourist boats can land and where tourists can be taken, and this has certainly reduced many of the potential problems that their presence can cause (Figure 13.12).

Figure 13.12 Bartolomé Island is regularly visited by tourists. Steps and walkways have been built to reduce the damage to the natural vegetation.

- Exotic species are probably the greatest immediate threat to biodiversity on the Galapagos. Ever since people first visited the islands, they have brought with them – not always intentionally – species from elsewhere (Figure 13.13). On many of the islands, rats, feral cats, feral dogs and feral goats are causing serious problems. For example, feral dogs eat tortoise eggs. Goats eat almost any kind of vegetation, and cause erosion. On several islands, the effects of goats pose a severe threat to the tortoise populations, because there is less food, water and shelter for the tortoises.

Figure 13.13 On Santa Cruz island, giant tortoises compete with cattle and other livestock for food.

Conservation projects

The Galapagos Islands are an internationally important area; their large number of endemic species makes them a prime conservation target. Organisations from all over the world help Ecuador to develop and fund conservation projects. One of the most ambitious of these was named Project Isabela, and was targeted on the islands of Santiago and northern Isabela in a bid to save the tortoises and other species there before they became extinct.

The major problem on Isabela was the huge feral goat population (Figure 13.14). Goats first got onto the island in the early 1970s, and by the mid 1990s there were thousands of them. Attempts to get rid of goats had already been made on other islands, with no real success. You only need to leave three or four goats, and their population will simply expand again.

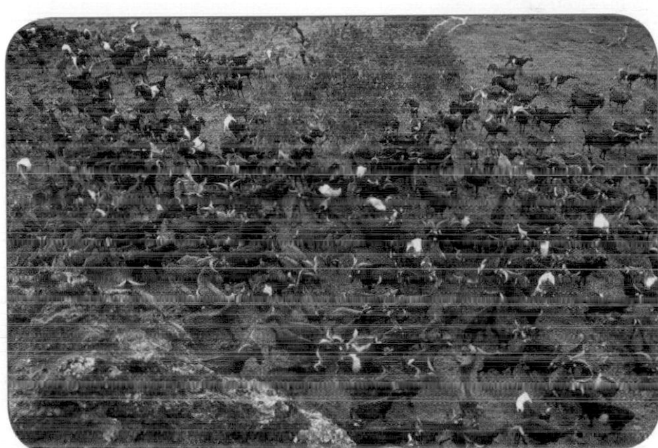

Figure 13.14 On Isabela, a large and growing population of feral goats was destroying vegetation and threatening endemic species.

So ecologists all over the world were consulted, and a plan was made to destroy the entire goat population on Santiago and Isabela, using specially trained hunters with high-performance weapons and information gleaned from aerial surveys and global positioning satellites. So-called 'Judas goats' were released; they had radio collars on, so that the hunters would know exactly where they were, which would almost certainly be with other goats. It was also important that the goats were dispatched as humanely as possible. The techniques were first tried out on a smaller island,

and fine-tuned before the big project began on Santiago and Isabela.

By 2006, all the goats had been destroyed. This was an amazing success story; these are the largest islands anywhere in the world from which introduced mammals have been eradicated. There are already noticeable increases in the growth of tree ferns and other vegetation (Figure 13.15), and there are signs of several insect species returning that had been thought to be extinct. The tortoise population is expected to thrive now that the vegetation is back to something like it should be. It is hoped that Isabela will make a full recovery, returning to the level of biodiversity that it had before it was discovered by humans.

Figure 13.15 These two photos show protected and unprotected areas on Isabela before and after removal of the feral goats.

There are other tortoise conservation success stories. On another island, Española, there were only 14 giant tortoises left by the late 1990s. These were all captured and kept for captive breeding (Figure 13.16). Now more than 100 of their offspring have been returned to Española and the population is increasing. This can only work, however, if the habitat on Española is conserved, making sure that the tortoises can continue to live and breed successfully.

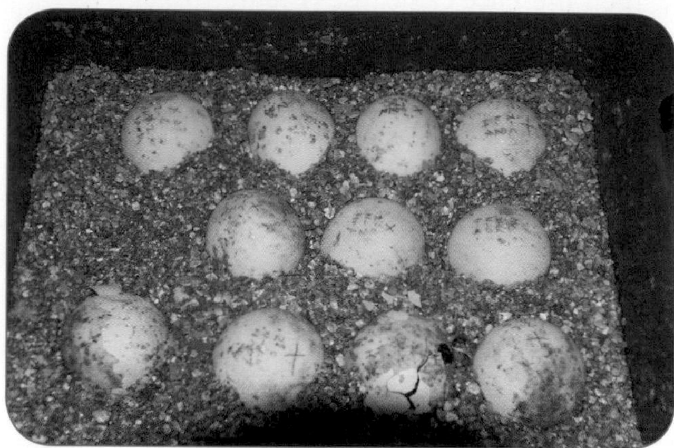

Figure 13.16 Captive breeding projects are carried out at the Charles Darwin Research Station on Santa Cruz island. These are eggs of the giant tortoise *Geochelone nigra*.

But there is still much work to be done, both on Isabela and other islands in the archipelago. For example, there is currently a concern about the indigenous mangrove finch, *Camarhynchus heliobates*. This finch has never been common, but by 2007 it appeared that there were only 50 pairs left. Their habitat is mostly mangrove swamps, and these are under threat from human activity and – like the tortoises – from introduced exotic species. Plans are being drawn up to try to conserve this species before it is too late.

Summary

Glossary

- The maximum sustainable population size in a particular area is known as its carrying capacity. Population sizes are determined by limiting factors such as food supply or nesting sites.
- When one species of predator feeds almost exclusively on one species of prey, the populations of the two may oscillate just out of synchrony with one another.
- Competition occurs whenever two or more organisms require a resource that is in short supply. Intraspecific competition (within a species) is often very important in limiting population size. Interspecific competition (between species) often influences distribution as well as population sizes.
- Conservation involves the maintenance and perhaps increase of biodiversity in a habitat. It is more than simply preservation, and often needs to be an active and dynamic process, involving management and reclamation of habitats that have lost some of their biodiversity.
- There are many different reasons for conservation, including economic, social and ethical ones. Frequently, these reasons overlap and reinforce one another.
- Conservation does not mean that we cannot continue to use resources from the conserved habitat, but we do need to do this with care. Coppicing is a good example of how careful management of a resource can help to maintain biodiversity in deciduous woodland.
- The Galapagos Islands provide an example of how increasing human populations and introductions of exotic species can have devastating effects on many different species and threaten them with extinction.

Stretch and challenge questions

1 With reference to specific examples, discuss the importance of intraspecific competition in: Hint

a natural selection and evolution

b the control of population size.

2 With reference to the conservation activities described in this chapter and the project that is returning the scimitar-horned oryx to the wild (*Biology 1*, pages 238–239), discuss the extent to which conservation must be an active and dynamic process. Hint

Questions

1 a Define the term *interspecific competition*. [1]

The shag, *Phalacrocorax aristotelis*, and the cormorant, *Phalacrocorax carbo*, feed in the same waters and nest on the same cliffs. The table shows the prey eaten by these two birds.

continued

Prey		% of prey taken by	
		Shag	**Cormorant**
surface swimming	sand eels	33	0
	herring	49	1
bottom feeding	flat fish	1	26
	shrimps, prawns	2	33

b State why the results for each species of bird do not add up to 100%. [1]

c With reference to the diagram and the table, describe how the behaviour of shags and cormorants avoids direct competition. [4]

d Suggest a resource for which these two species show interspecific competition. [1]

OCR Biology A (2804) January 2005 [Total 7]

Answer

2 Lemmings are small mammals that live near the Arctic circle. Their populations show regular patterns of increase and decrease. In 2003, scientists published results based on a long-term project in East Greenland. They made the following observations.

- Population peaks occurred in regular four year cycles.
- Four main predators feed on the lemmings: Arctic owls, Arctic foxes, long-tailed skuas and stoats.
- Stoats feed only on lemmings; the other predators feed on a range of prey species.
- Stoats reproduce more slowly than lemmings.

a The graph shows the changes in the population of lemmings in the East Greenland project area from 1990 to 2002.

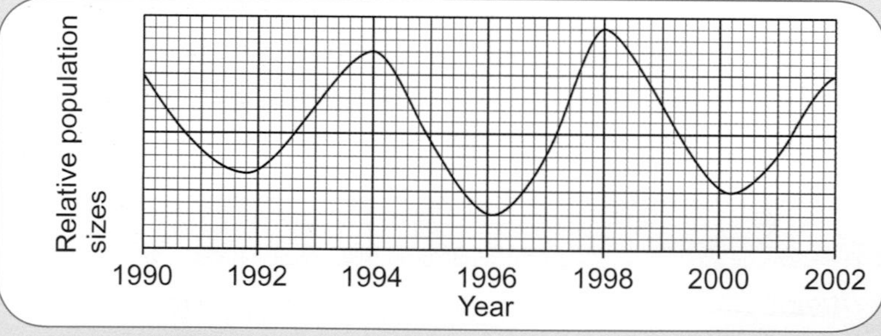

i Copy the graph and sketch on the copy the likely changes in population size of stoats. [2]

ii Suggest three environmental conditions, other than climatic, that are required for a population explosion of lemmings. [3]

b With reference to the species studied in the East Greenland project, distinguish between interspecific and intraspecific competition. [3]

c The carrying capacities for lemmings and for the various predators in this area are all different.

Explain the term *carrying capacity*. [2]

OCR Biology A (2804) June 2006 [Total 10]

Answer

Chapter 14

Plant responses

e-Learning

Objectives

It's not entirely easy being a plant. While most animals are able to move around to avoid danger or unpleasant environmental conditions, plants have to stay put and take whatever their environment throws at them. Abiotic stress factors, such as high temperatures or drought, simply have to be survived – they cannot be avoided. However, this does not mean that plants cannot respond to these threats or environmental changes. Plants have evolved a very wide range of responses to a large variety of stimuli, which help them to survive.

Nastic movements and tropisms

Some plant responses can be quite rapid. These are usually brought about by changes in the turgidity of cells. As a cell takes up water, it swells, and this can cause movement. For example, in Chapter 2 we saw how action potentials in Venus fly traps are produced in response to contact of insects with the trigger hairs in their leaves. The action potentials cause certain cells at the 'hinge' of the leaf to take up water and swell, which causes the leaf to close. Similar types of movement occur when a flower closes its petals at night (Figure 14.1). These leaf and petal movements are examples of **nastic movements**.

SAQ

1 Think back to your work on xerophytes (*Biology 1*, page 96 in Chapter 6). Can you think of a nastic response made by marram grass? Describe the response and its adaptive value to the plant.

Answer

Other responses are much slower. They sometimes involve the switching on of certain genes – even if this is done quite quickly, it takes a while for the gene to be transcribed and translated and for its products to appear in the cell. For example, when insects chew on the leaves of some species of plants, particular transcription factors are activated in the plant's cells. These switch on the transcription of genes that code for the production of proteinase inhibitors. If the insects keep on eating the leaves, they will also eat the inhibitors, which will stop their protein-digesting enzymes from working and either kill them or encourage them to move elsewhere and eat something else.

Many of a plant's responses to changes in their environment are carried out through growth. These growth responses are called **tropisms**. A fundamental feature of a tropism is that the

Figure 14.1 An example of a nastic movement. Osteospermums open their flowers during daylight to display their bright petals and allow insects access to the pollen on their anthers. As the light fades, the petals fold over to cover the pollen and keep it dry over night.

direction of the growth is always related to the direction of the stimulus. For example, a shoot may grow towards light, a response known as **positive phototropism** (Figure 14.2). Shoots generally grow away from the direction of gravity, and this is **negative geotropism**. We can therefore define a tropism as a directional growth response to a stimulus.

Figure 14.2 The seedlings in the pot on the left of the photo have been grown in uniform light. Those on the right have been grown in unidirectional light, and have responded by growing towards the light source.

Unlike tropisms, nastic responses are not directional – the direction of the movement is not determined by the direction of the stimulus. A Venus fly trap does not change the way its leaf folds up if a fly happens to be on one particular part of it rather than another.

Another difference is that, whereas tropisms always involve growth, nastic responses involve temporary changes in cell volume, caused by the uptake or removal of water. Tropisms, unlike nastic movements, don't go into reverse when conditions change because growth is, by definition, a permanent change. If a shoot has grown towards the light then, if the light is moved so that it comes from the opposite side, the shoot will now grow towards that side – but the first 'bend' in its stem will stay there.

Plant hormones

Although action potentials do occur in plants, it seems that the majority of communication between plant cells is carried out by means of chemicals. There are a number of these that are classified as **plant hormones**; you may also come across the terms 'plant growth substance' and 'plant growth regulator'. Unlike animal hormones, plant hormones are not made in glands, most of them being produced by groups of cells in certain parts of the plant. Nor do they always travel very far from their point of production before they have their effects. But in other respects they frequently act in similar ways to animal hormones. Like them, they bind with receptors either in the plasma membrane of a cell or within its cytoplasm, and set off a series of reactions in the cell, which results in some kind of response.

Numerous different plant hormones have been discovered, and just recently there has been a rapid increase in our understanding of how they work. All the same, there are still only a few simple or completely understood stories to be told. This is at least partly because plant hormones are often present in very tiny quantities, which makes it difficult to know exactly where they are in a plant. You may be able to detect a hormone in a leaf, but in which cells is it present? And in exactly which part of the cell? Another complication is that two or more hormones often act together, having very different effects than when either of them is present alone. And, just to complicate things even further, they often have different effects in different species of plants, in different parts of the same plant, or at different stages of its life cycle.

In this chapter, we will look at just a few examples of some plant responses involving hormones. Between them, they illustrate several important features of the ways in which plants respond to environmental stimuli, and coordinate the growth and other activities of their different parts.

Phototropism

Phototropism is a growth response towards or away from light. Most plant shoots grow towards light, whereas many roots grow away from it. Phototropism has been known about for hundreds of years, and some of the classic experiments on it were carried out in the 1880s by Charles Darwin, and by the Danish physiologist Boysen-Jensen in the early years of the 20th century. Some of these early experiments are shown in Figure 14.3.

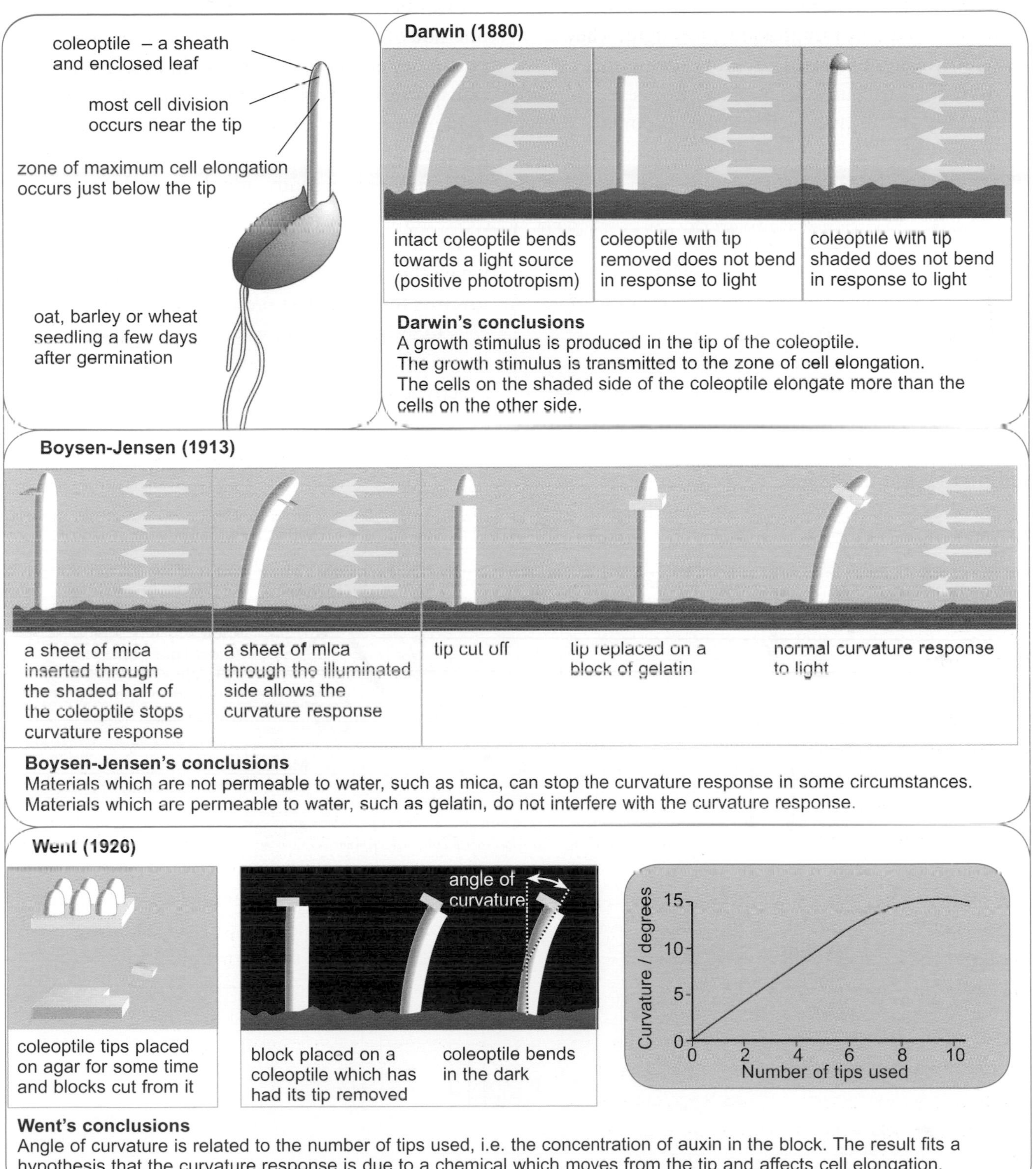

Figure 14.3 Some early experiments on phototropism using oat, barley or wheat coleoptiles.

It is only recently, however, that we have really begun to understand just how this response happens – and we are still far from a full understanding. As you might expect, cell signalling (*Biology 1*, pages 26–27) is involved.

A major step forward was the discovery of proteins that act as receptors for blue light. They are named **phototropins**. They sit in the plasma membrane of certain cells in plant shoots. When they are hit by blue light, they become phosphorylated. If the blue light is coming from one side, then the phototropin on the side receiving the light becomes phosphorylated, while that on the shady side does not.

We don't yet understand exactly what happens next. Somehow, the phosphorylation of phototropin brings about a sideways movement of the plant hormone **auxin**, so that more auxin ends up on the shady side of the shoot than on the light side (Figure 14.4). This involves a transporter protein in the plasma membranes of some of the cells in the shoot, which actively moves auxin out of the cell. It seems that phosphorylation of phototropin changes the location and/or the activity of this transporter. The transporters are found mostly in the plasma membranes at the sides (not top or bottom) of some of the cells in the growing shoot, and it may be that the phototropin activation causes the transporters to collect up on one side of the cells rather than another. Another possibility is that the phototropin causes the transporters to work harder on one side of a cell than on the other. Either of these could produce a gradient of auxin concentration across the shoot, with more on the shady side than on the bright side.

The final step in the chain of events is the way in which this auxin gradient causes the shoot to bend towards the light. The presence of auxin stimulates cells to grow longer, so where there is more auxin there is more growth. Once again, we don't know exactly how this happens, but it seems that as well as some immediate effects of auxin on the cell, it also affects gene expression.

Extension

blue wavelengths of light
The phototropin receptors in plasma membranes detect light equally on each side.
active transport of auxin
Phototropin receptors detect light from one side, causing auxin to be transported from cell to cell to the shaded side.
More auxin is transported down the shaded side, causing the cells to elongate more on this side.

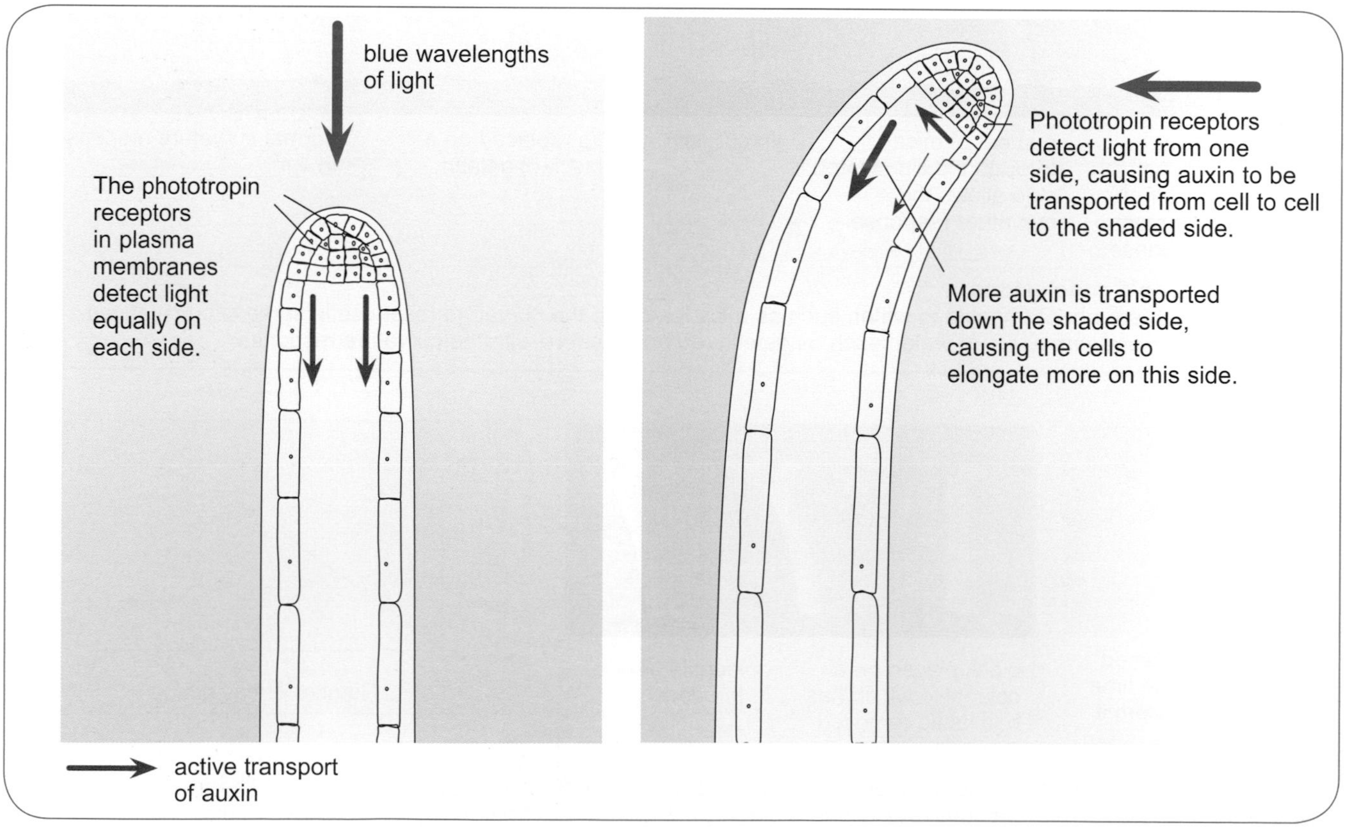

Figure 14.4 Phototropin, auxin and phototropism.

The cells in the shoot have receptors in their plasma membranes to which auxin binds. This affects the transport of ions through the plasma membrane. One of the results of this is a build-up of hydrogen ions in the cell walls. This produces a lower pH, which activates enzymes that break cross-linkages between molecules in the walls, making it easier for them to be stretched. As the cell takes up water by osmosis, it is able to swell and become longer. This is a permanent effect (the cell doesn't shrink again afterwards).

SAQ

2 In what ways is auxin similar to an animal hormone, such as insulin? How is it different?

Answer

Extension

Apical dominance

Plant shoots grow lengthways by the division and elongation of cells. A region near the tip of the shoot, called the **apical meristem**, contains small, undifferentiated cells that are constantly dividing. Some of the new cells then grow longer, so that the length of the shoot steadily increases.

Most plant shoots have buds on either side of them, called **lateral buds**. These buds contain groups of cells that are also meristems, but they often don't become active as long as the apical meristem is in position and functioning. So the presence and growth of the apex of the shoot inhibits sideways growth from the lateral buds. This is called **apical dominance** (Figure 14.5).

Apical dominance is easy to demonstrate, and many gardeners make frequent use of it. If you want a plant to stop growing upwards and branch out sideways, you simply need to cut off the tip of the main shoot. This removes the apical dominance and the lateral buds are able to grow.

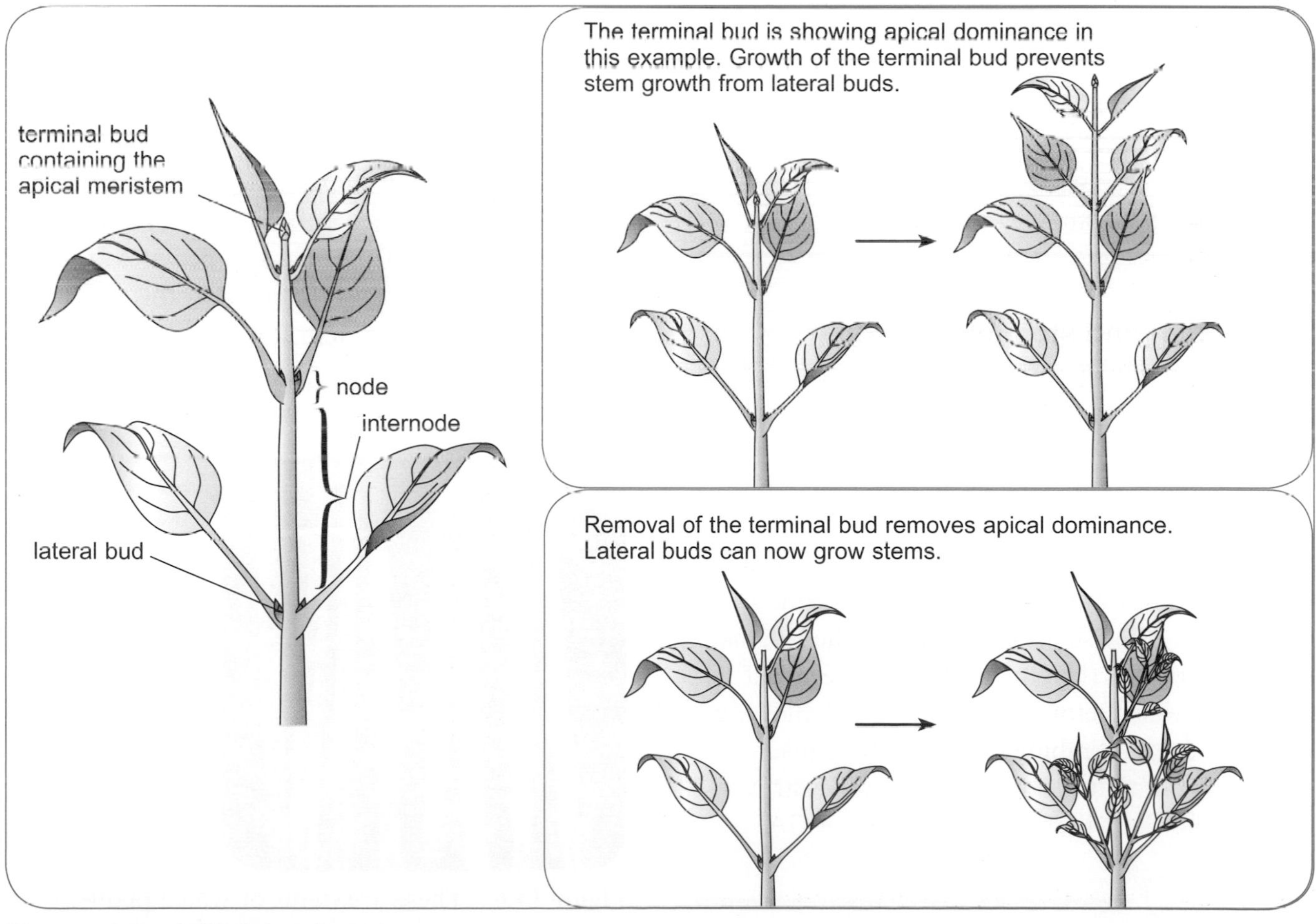

Figure 14.5 Apical dominance.

The exact way in which the inhibition of the lateral buds is caused has not yet been worked out. However, we do know that it involves auxin. Auxin is constantly made by cells at the tip of the shoot. It is then transported downwards, from cell to cell. The auxin accumulates in the nodes beside the lateral buds. Somehow, its presence here inhibits their activity.

Two simple experiments provide evidence for this mechanism.

- If we cut the tip off two shoots, and apply **indole-3-acetic acid, IAA** (synthetic auxin) to one of them, this one will continue to show apical dominance and the side shoots will not grow. The other one will branch out sideways.
- If a growing shoot is tipped upside down, apical dominance is prevented and the lateral buds start to grow out sideways. This can be explained by the fact that auxin is not transported *upwards* against gravity, but only downwards. So in the upside-down shoot the auxin produced in the apical meristem does not reach the lateral buds and therefore cannot affect them.

SAQ

3 Suggest how apical dominance could be an advantage to a plant. Answer

Gibberellin and stem elongation

Auxin is just one of many different plant hormones. In the 1930s, a substance was found that caused rapid growth of the stems of some kinds of plants. It was named **gibberellin, GA** for short.

If a low concentration of gibberellin is applied to the stems of dwarf beans, the beans begin to grow rapidly. The stems get longer, as the lengths of the internodes (lengths of stem between leaf stalks) increase. Before long, the bean plants have grown as tall as climbing (non-dwarf) beans.

It turns out that the dwarf beans are dwarf because they lack the gene for producing GA.

Extension

You may have come across Gregor Mendel's early experiments with genetics in peas. We now know that Mendel's short and tall pea plants actually differed in this way, too. The short pea plants lacked the dominant allele that encodes GA production. Recently, dwarf varieties of rice and wheat have been bred that lack one of more of the enzymes needed for GA production (Figure 14.6). Their shorter height means that they can put more energy into producing grain rather than stalk, allowing farmers to get higher grain yields from the same area of land.

SAQ

4 What would you expect to happen if you applied GA to the stem of a genetically tall pea plant? Explain your prediction. Answer

Gibberellin works by affecting gene expression. Gibberellin moves through the plasma membrane and into a cell, where it binds to a receptor protein. This in turn binds to other receptor proteins, eventually resulting in the breakdown of a DELLA protein. DELLA proteins usually bind to transcription factors, needed to allow a particular gene to be transcribed. Once the DELLA protein is broken down, the transcription factor is released and transcription of the gene can begin. At the moment, we don't know exactly how this makes the cells grow and the stem elongate.

Extension

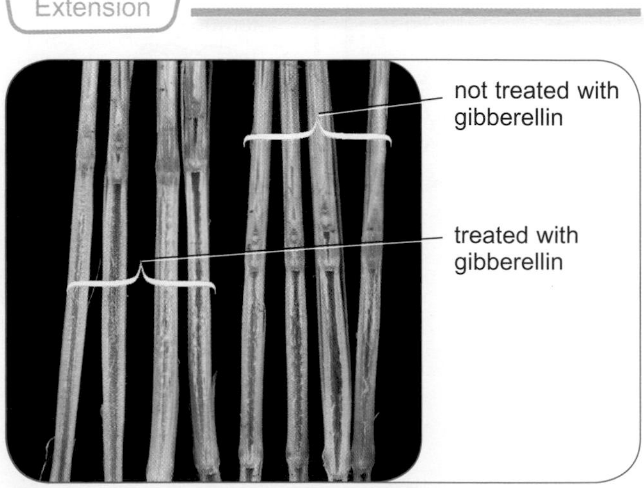

Figure 14.6 These are stems of wheat plants, from the same dwarf variety of wheat, cut open.

Leaf abscission

Many trees and other plants in temperate countries drop their leaves in autumn. This is called **leaf abscission**. It helps the plants to survive the winter by reducing water loss through their leaf surfaces, avoiding frost damage and avoiding fungal infections through damp, cold leaf surfaces. In the cold temperatures and low light levels of winter, leaves cannot photosynthesise to any great extent, so they may become more of a potential hazard and a drain on resources rather than a help to the tree.

Abscission is affected by at least three different plant hormones – auxin, ethene and abscisic acid.

We have already seen that auxin is produced by the young cells near the growing points of a stem. Auxin is also made by young leaves and fruits. Auxin inhibits abscission. As long as a leaf is making plenty of auxin, it will not fall off the tree.

Ethene is a very unusual hormone, because it is a gas. It moves through a plant by diffusion through the air spaces between cells. It tends to be produced by maturing or aging plant tissues, such as maturing fruits or aging leaves.

Abscisic acid, **ABA** for short, is sometimes known as the plant 'stress hormone'. It is produced when the plant is under stress, such as suffering a lack of water or very low temperatures. ABA is involved in many processes other than leaf abscission, including the control of stomatal closure when the plant is short of water.

So what makes deciduous trees drop their leaves in autumn? Young leaves produce auxin. As autumn approaches and the leaves age, the rate of auxin production declines. This drop in auxin concentration makes the leaf more sensitive to ethene. More ethene is then produced, and this in turn inhibits auxin production.

There has therefore been a change in the balance of auxin and ethene – less auxin and more ethene are present in the leaf. As a result, an **abscission layer** begins to grow at the base of the leaf stalk (petiole). This is made of thin-walled cells, which are then weakened by enzymes that hydrolyse the polysaccharides in their walls. Eventually this layer of cells is so weak that the petiole breaks and the leaf falls off (Figure 14.7). Before this happens, the tree grows a layer of protective tissue where the

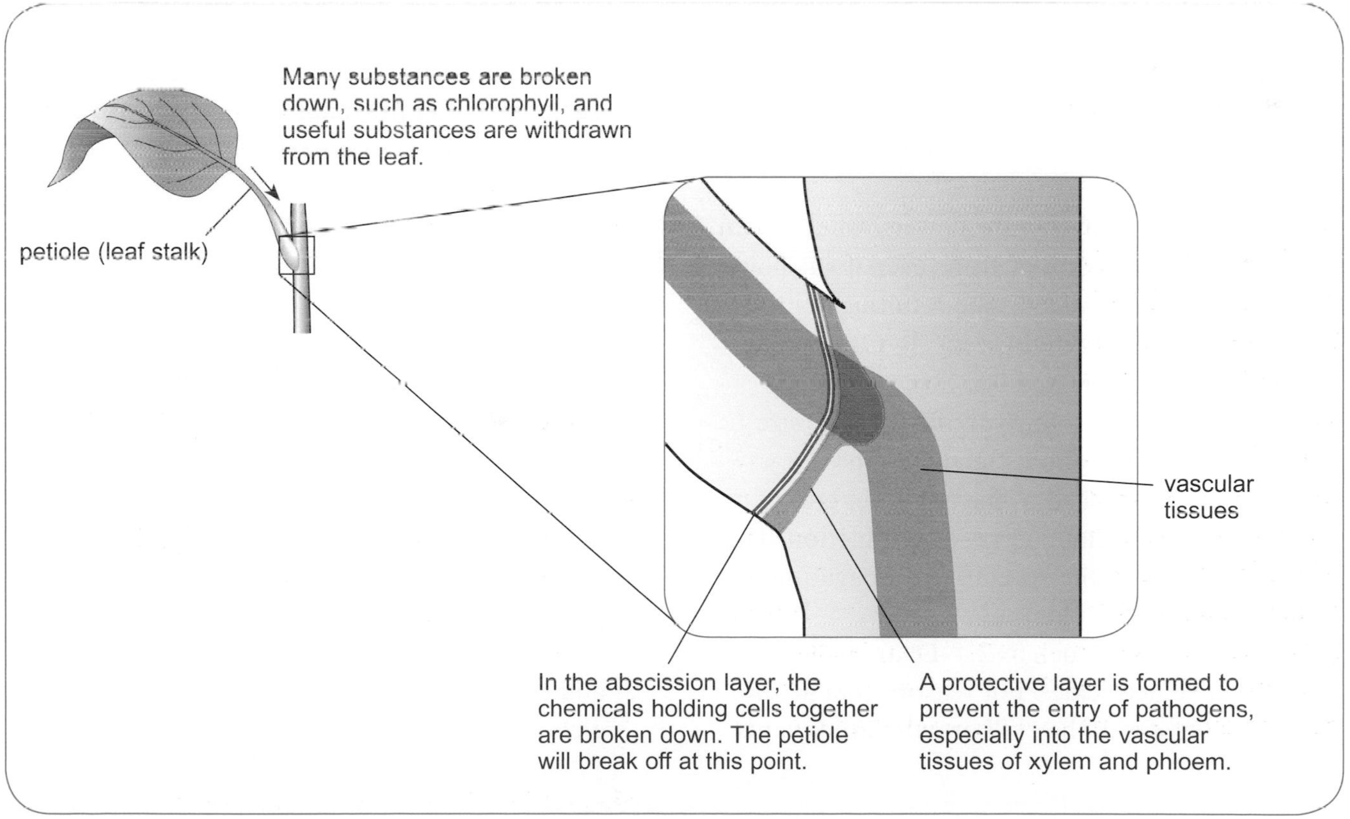

Many substances are broken down, such as chlorophyll, and useful substances are withdrawn from the leaf.
petiole (leaf stalk)
vascular tissues
In the abscission layer, the chemicals holding cells together are broken down. The petiole will break off at this point.
A protective layer is formed to prevent the entry of pathogens, especially into the vascular tissues of xylem and phloem.

Figure 14.7 Leaf abscission.

leaf will break off, leaving a scar which prevents the entry of pathogens. The cells in this layer have **suberin** in their cell walls. (Suberin is a waxy, waterproof substance, also found in the cell walls of cork cells in tree bark.)

Although abscisic acid obtained its name through its involvement in leaf abscission, it now appears that its role here is perhaps not quite as important as those of auxin and ethene. Abscisic acid does cause leaf abscission in some plants, but in others it actually reduces it. It may have its effects through influencing the production or action of ethene on plant tissues.

Commercial uses of plant hormones

We have been using synthetic versions of plant hormones for various purposes for decades, even before we knew anything about how they bring about their effects in plants. Indeed, for many of them we still don't know how they work – we just know that they do, and make use of that. The list below includes most of the more wide-ranging and economically important uses, but you will be able to find many more if you search the internet.

Auxins

- Auxins are sprayed onto developing fruits to prevent abscission; the fruits stay on the plant longer and so can be harvested when they are fully ripe.
- Auxin can be sprayed onto flowers, where it can initiate the formation of fruits even if the flower has not been pollinated. The resulting fruits therefore do not contain seeds. In California, grapes are often treated like this, producing seedless grapes of a fairly uniform, large size which all ripen at about the same time.
- Auxin can be applied to the cut lower end of a shoot, where it stimulates root production. This is widely used in the vegetative propagation of many varieties of plants.
- Synthetic auxins, such as 2,4–D, are widely used as selective herbicides. For reasons that are not fully understood, they kill broad-leaved plants such as dandelions and daisies, but not grass and cereal crops. It is thought that they work because the 2,4–D can get *into* cells through the auxin transporters in the plasma membranes, but not *out* of them through the different set of transporters that allow the natural auxins to pass out by facilitated diffusion. 2,4–D therefore builds up inside the cells, and this may be what kills the plant.

Ethene

- Ethene promotes ripening. Fruits such as bananas can be harvested before they are ripe, allowing them to be transported long distances without deteriorating. When they are close to their sale point, they can be exposed to ethene, which causes them to ripen.

Gibberellin

- GA is sprayed onto fruit crops to promote their growth. For example, it is used to produce seedless grapes by causing the fruits to grow even if they are not fertilised (an effect similar to that of auxin). The GA also increases the movement of sucrose into the growing fruits, which in turn brings in more water by osmosis. As a result, the grapes are larger and sweeter.
- GA is sprayed onto some types of citrus trees to allow the fruit to stay longer on the tree. This allows the grower to let the fruit grow to its maximum size before picking.
- GA is widely used to increase the yield of sucrose from sugar cane. Sugar cane produces sucrose in its stems. In cool temperatures, the stems do not grow as long, so less sucrose is stored. The application of GA makes the stems grow longer, so there is more sucrose present.
- GA stimulates germination in seeds. This is used in the beer-making industry, where GA may be sprayed onto barley grains to make them germinate. The germinating grains produce enzymes that break down starch to maltose, and the action of yeast on the maltose produces alcohol.

Agent Orange

Between 1965 and 1975, the United States of America supported South Vietnam in a war against communist-led North Vietnam. The war ended in defeat for the USA and its allies.

Much of the war was fought over thickly forested areas. The USA adopted a policy of spraying defoliants (chemicals that cause plants to lose their leaves) over trees and crops. The idea was to deprive their enemy of food, and also to destroy the jungle that provided cover for the Vietcong fighters.

The defoliant they used most frequently was called Agent Orange (this was the colour of the label on the drums in which it was stored). Agent Orange was a mixture of two synthetic auxins, 2,4–D and 2,4,5–T. They were very effective, generally causing complete leaf loss from the plants onto which they were sprayed within around two weeks. Huge quantities were sprayed over huge areas. Spraying stopped in 1971.

Although 2,4–D and 2,4,5–T appear to be harmless to humans, unfortunately the manufacture of 2,4,5–T often also produces small amounts of another substance – dioxin. This is formed when the temperature of the reaction mixture is allowed to rise above 160 °C. Small quantities of dioxin are formed whenever biological material is burned – you will breathe it in at barbecues, for example – but the amounts contained in the huge volumes of Agent Orange added up to rather more than 'small quantities'.

And dioxin is most certainly *not* harmless. Even in quite small concentrations, experiments show it to be a carcinogen, mutagen and teratogen (causing defects in developing embryos). Dioxin is a very persistent chemical (it does not easily break down) and accumulates up the food chain.

In the areas of Vietnam where Agent Orange was sprayed, the incidence of cancer and genetic or birth defects in children is much higher than elsewhere. Studies have shown concentrations

of dioxin well above recommended maximum levels in some of the food eaten by people who live there. And these problems don't appear to be confined to the Vietnamese; it also seems that American soldiers who were involved in the spraying have a greater chance of health problems developing in themselves (for example, diabetes) or in their children.

Still, 37 years after the spraying stopped, there are vast tracts of land where the vegetation has never recovered and where the land cannot be farmed.

Was the spraying of Agent Orange a war crime? Many people think so. However, the USA states firmly that, at that time, the spraying of defoliants was not illegal. At one point, they agreed to fund a multimillion-dollar research programme in Vietnam to investigate the claims that dioxin contaminants in Agent Orange had caused long-lasting health problems, but the project was cancelled in 2005. The USA does not accept liability for the prolonged health problems and environmental damage that are still present in Vietnam.

Summary

Glossary

- Plants cannot move away from herbivores or a stressful environment, but they are able to respond to their environment in ways that increase their chances of survival.
- Movements such as stomatal closure, the closure of flowers at night or the rolling of a marram leaf are fairly fast-acting, reversible movements caused by changes in turgidity of cells. They are called nastic movements.
- Tropic responses, or tropisms, are directional growth responses to a stimulus. Positive phototropism is growth towards light, and is shown by plant shoots.
- Plant responses are often coordinated by hormones. Unlike animal hormones, these are not made in glands, nor are they always transported far from their site of production.
- Phototropin molecules in the plasma membranes of some of the cells in a shoot respond to blue light. Their activation affects the distribution of auxin, which collects on the shady side of the shoot. The auxin causes an increase in the ability of the cell walls to expand, and also switches on certain genes, which between them cause the cells where there is more auxin to grow faster than those where there is less. As a result, the shady side of a shoot grows more than the light side and the shoot bends towards the light.
- Apical dominance is the repression of growth of lateral buds so long as the apical bud is present. Removing the apical bud allows the lateral buds to grow, so the plant branches sideways. If the apical bud is removed and a synthetic hormone such as IAA applied to the cut, the lateral buds do not grow. In an intact shoot, auxin produced in the apical meristem is transported down the shoot through the cells, and accumulates at the nodes, where its presence inhibits growth of the nearby buds.
- Gibberellin encourages stem elongation. In plants that do not produce normal quantities of gibberellin, application of gibberellin to the stem makes it grow longer. Gibberellin has its effects by switching on certain genes, which cause cell lengthening.
- In a temperate climate, deciduous trees shed their leaves in autumn. This happens as a result of a decrease in auxin production and an increase in ethene production. This causes an abscission layer to build up at the base of the petiole of each leaf, which eventually becomes so weak that the leaf falls off. Abscisic acid also plays a role in leaf abscission in some plants.
- Plant hormones have many commercial uses. For example, auxin is used to control fruit production and fruit drop, to encourage rooting of stem cuttings and as a selective weedkiller. Ethene is used to ripen fruits before sale. Gibberellin helps to increase fruit size and sweetness in grapes, and increases the growth of sugar cane stems and so increases yield. It is also used in the brewing industry to stimulate germination of barley grains to produce malt.

Stretch and challenge questions

1 With reference to specific examples, compare nastic movements and tropisms.

Hint

2 Describe the effects of auxin on plant tissues. How are these effects made use of by humans?

Hint

Questions

1 Rice, *Oryza sativa*, is a grass that is grown as a cereal crop in many parts of the world. In most rice-growing regimes, the rice fields are flooded with water while the rice is actively growing.

a An investigation was carried out into the effect of flooding on the growth of the submerged stems of rice plants.

Young rice plants were grown in a container in which the level of water was increased in 10 cm steps, over a period of seven days. The mean length of the submerged internodes (lengths of stem between two leaves) and the concentration of ethene in the rice stems was measured each day. As a control, rice plants were grown in identical conditions but the water level was kept constant throughout the seven days. The results are shown in Graphs A, B and C.

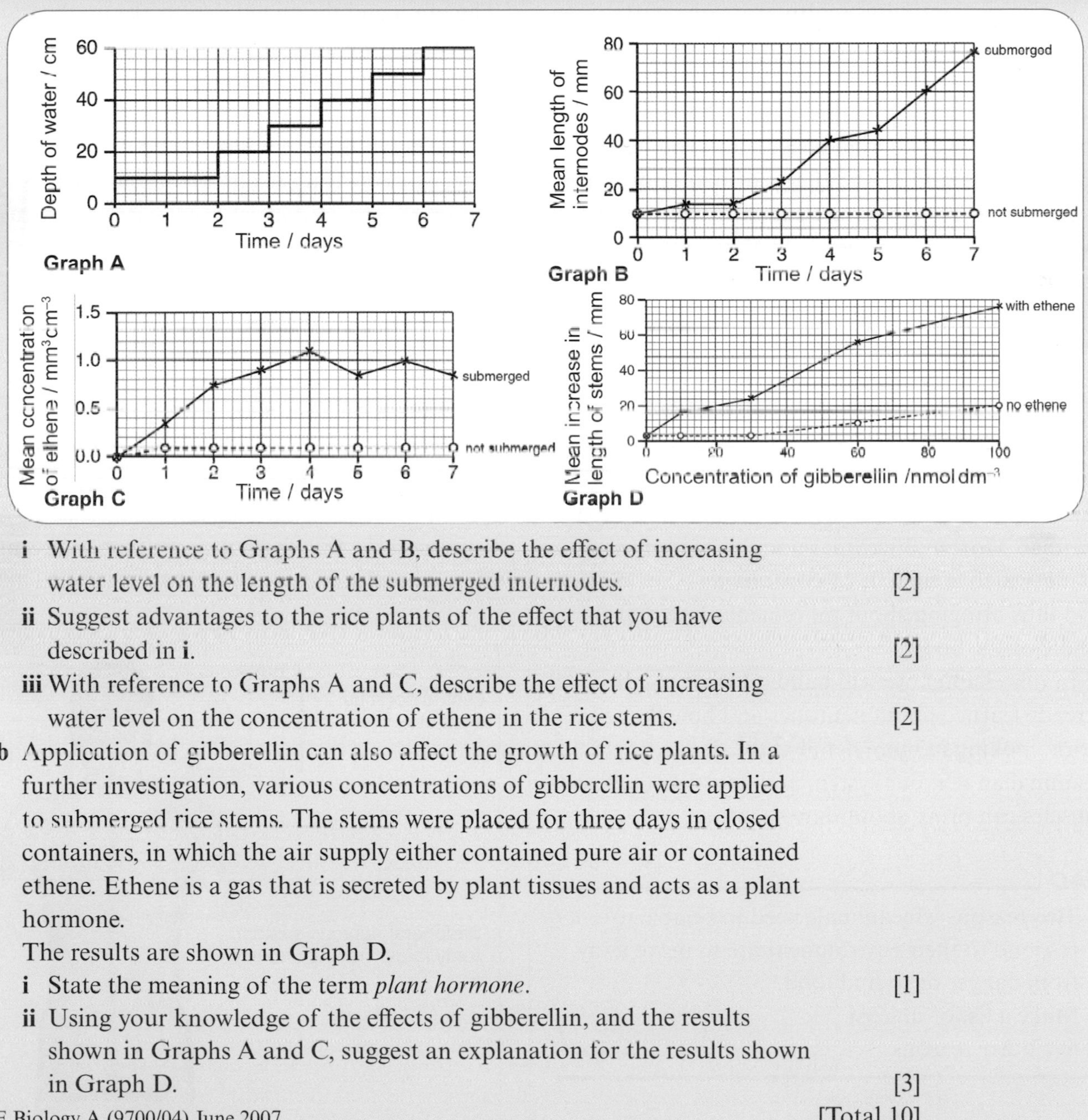

i With reference to Graphs A and B, describe the effect of increasing water level on the length of the submerged internodes. [2]

ii Suggest advantages to the rice plants of the effect that you have described in **i**. [2]

iii With reference to Graphs A and C, describe the effect of increasing water level on the concentration of ethene in the rice stems. [2]

b Application of gibberellin can also affect the growth of rice plants. In a further investigation, various concentrations of gibberellin were applied to submerged rice stems. The stems were placed for three days in closed containers, in which the air supply either contained pure air or contained ethene. Ethene is a gas that is secreted by plant tissues and acts as a plant hormone.

The results are shown in Graph D.

i State the meaning of the term *plant hormone*. [1]

ii Using your knowledge of the effects of gibberellin, and the results shown in Graphs A and C, suggest an explanation for the results shown in Graph D. [3]

CIE Biology A (9700/04) June 2007

[Total 10]

Answer

Chapter 15

Animal responses

e-Learning

Objectives

In Chapter 1, we saw how important it is that different parts of a multicellular organism can communicate with one another, ensuring that different parts of the body can act in a coordinated way. In Chapter 2, we looked at how neurones pass electrical impulses swiftly from one part of the body to another, allowing fast responses to changes in the environment, and complex behaviour controlled by the brain. Chapter 3 considered the endocrine system, and you have probably just studied the effects of plant hormones – which have many features similar to hormones in animals – and how they help plants respond to their environment.

All organisms need to be able to respond to changes in their environment. Plants can do so by making nastic movements or tropic responses, or by switching on genes to step up the production of a particular protein. Animals, however, have a wider variety of possible responses, because they can often move their whole body from one place to another. Most multicellular animals have muscle tissue, which is capable of contracting (shortening) and thus bringing about movement of part or the whole of the body.

In this chapter, we will build on what you have already learned about neurones and how they work, looking in more detail at the design of the mammalian nervous system and how neurones and muscles can bring about movement.

SAQ

1 Two reasons why animals need to be able to respond to their environment are to move away from danger or to find food.
Make a list of at least five other reasons.

Answer

The organisation of the human nervous system

The human nervous system is very similar to that of all mammals, except that certain parts of our brains are more highly developed than most. The brain and the spinal cord make up the **central nervous system**, while all the rest of the nervous system is the **peripheral nervous system** (Figure 15.1).

The nervous system is made up of two major types of cells. You are already familiar with **neurones** – specialised cells that carry electrical impulses, in the form of action potentials, throughout the body. They can be classified as sensory, motor and intermediate neurones (Chapter 2). The other type of cells are called **glial cells**, and they appear to have a variety of functions, such as helping nutrients from the blood pass to neurones (especially in the brain and spinal cord) and maintaining the correct balance of ions in the tissue fluid that surrounds them. The Schwann cells that form the myelination around the axons of some of our neurones are glial cells.

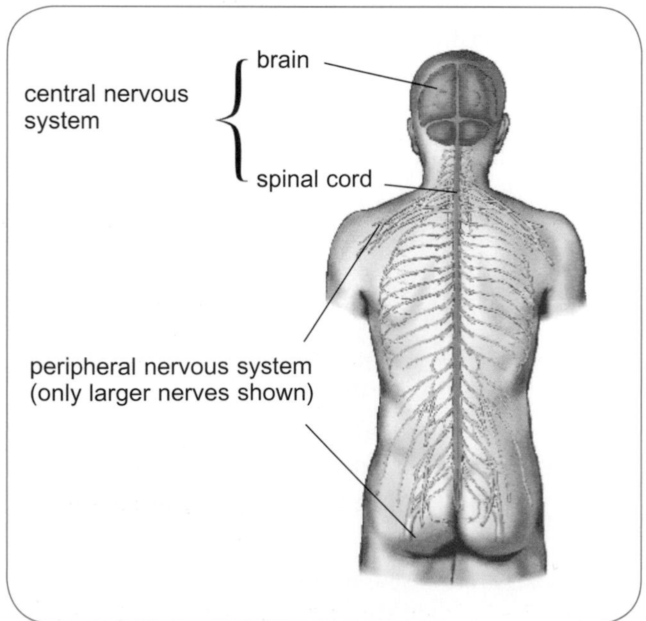

Figure 15.1 The human nervous system.

The central nervous system

Within the central nervous system, most neurones are intermediate neurones (Figure 15.2). They have many short dendrites forming synapses with many other cells. One neurone may have as many as 200 000 synapses. The function of these neurones is to receive and integrate information arriving via their synapses, and then to pass on action potentials to other neurones. Some of the synapses are excitatory – when an impulse arrives at them, this depolarises the postsynaptic membrane. Others are inhibitory – the arrival of an action potential prevents the postsynaptic membrane from depolarising. Within the neurone, the balance between the excitation and inhibition that is happening at all the synapses will determine whether or not the neurone passes an action potential along its axon to other neurones. As there are around 2×10^{14} neurones in a human brain, you can probably imagine that the possible number of different patterns of excitation and inhibition of different neurones is, to all intents and purposes, infinite.

The **spinal cord** extends from the base of the brain, lying inside the neural arches of the vertebrae. In the centre of the cord is a canal containing **cerebro-spinal fluid**. A butterfly-shaped region in the centre of the cord contains unmyelinated neurones, and therefore appears grey (Figure 15.3). Around this are axons and dendrons

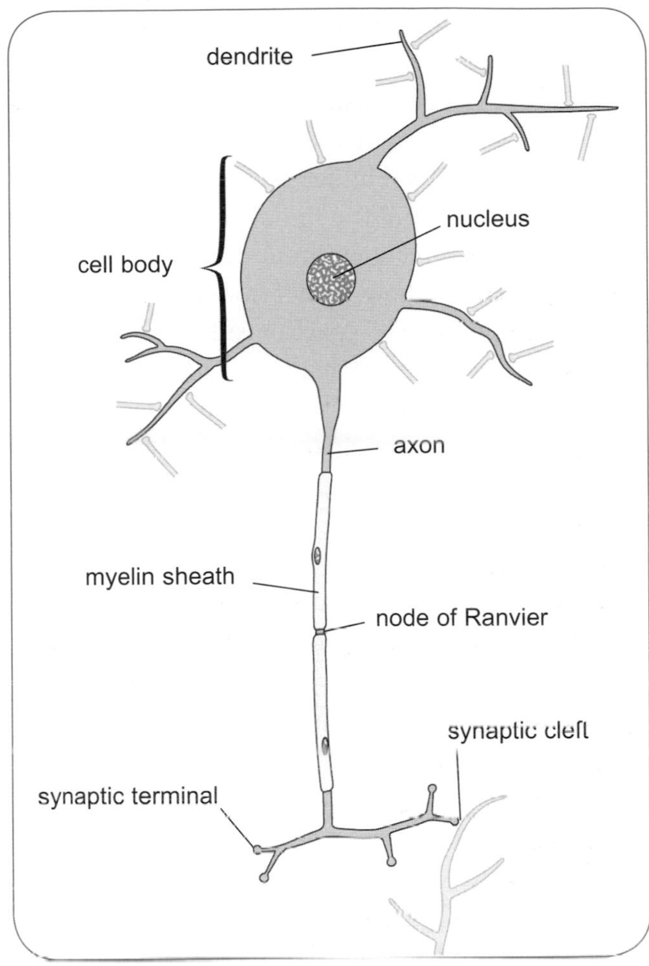

Figure 15.2 A neurone in the central nervous system.

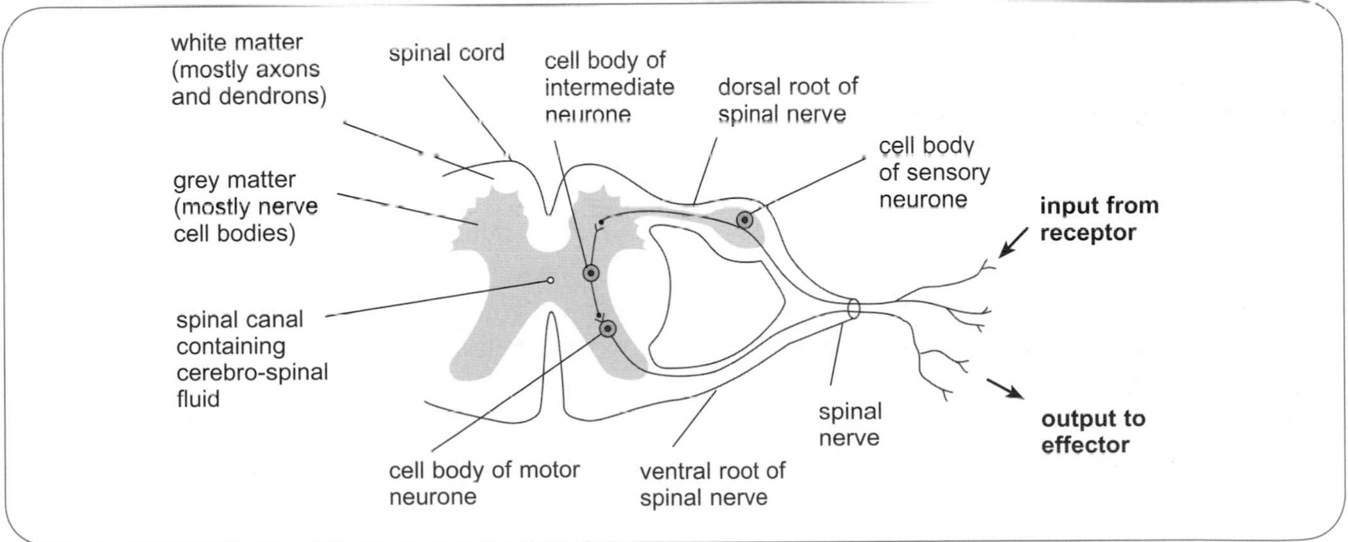

Figure 15.3 Diagrammatic section of the spinal cord and spinal nerve, showing the arrangements of neurones forming a reflex arc.

that are mainly myelinated, and so this area appears white.

The **brain** can be considered to be a highly specialised extension of the spinal cord. Its structure is described in detail on pages 233–236.

Both the brain and the spinal cord are surrounded by three membranes called **meninges**. These membranes help to secrete cerebro-spinal fluid, which fills all the spaces inside the brain and spinal cord and also the space beneath the bones of the skull. The fluid helps to absorb mechanical shocks to the brain (such as when you hit your head on something) and also to provide nutrients and oxygen to the brain cells.

The peripheral nervous system

The **peripheral nervous system** is made up of sensory neurones that carry action potentials from receptors towards the central nervous system, and motor neurones that carry action potentials from the central nervous system to effectors.

The cell bodies of sensory neurones are situated just outside the spinal cord, in the **dorsal root ganglia**. They have long cytoplasmic processes that pick up information at receptors (for example, sense organs in the skin) and transmit action potentials from the receptor towards their cell bodies. From here, action potentials pass along their axons into the central nervous system. The cell bodies of many motor neurones are in the spinal cord and their long axons pass out of the spinal cord and towards effectors such as muscles and glands.

In Chapter 2, we saw that the cytoplasmic processes (axons and dendrons) of neurones generally lie in bundles, forming **nerves** (Figure 2.6). Axons and dendrons leave and enter the spinal cord in **spinal nerves**, which occur between each pair of vertebrae. Each spinal nerve has a **dorsal root**, which carries impulses from receptors towards the spinal cord, and a **ventral root**, which carries impulses outwards to effectors. Nerves that arise from the brain are known as **cranial nerves**.

The peripheral nervous system is made up of two systems with rather different functions. These are the **somatic nervous system** and the **autonomic nervous system**.

The somatic nervous system includes all the sensory neurones and also the motor neurones that take information to the skeletal muscles. So the neurones in a typical reflex arc (Figure 2.5 and Figure 15.3) are all part of the somatic nervous system. The autonomic nervous system includes all the motor neurones that supply the internal organs.

The autonomic nervous system

The autonomic nervous system carries action potentials to all of the internal organs – sometimes called the **viscera**. It controls the activity of all the smooth muscle (page 244) in the body – for example, in the walls of arterioles and in the wall of the alimentary canal. It also controls the rate of beating of the cardiac muscle in the heart and the activities of exocrine glands such as the salivary glands. 'Autonomic' means 'self-minding' and this refers to the fact that most of the activities that are controlled by the autonomic nervous system are not usually under our voluntary control.

As well as having a different *function* from the somatic nervous system, the autonomic nervous system also has a different *structural organisation* (Figure 15.4). As we have already seen, the motor neurones of the somatic nervous system have their cell bodies in the central nervous system, and long axons that lead from the cell bodies all the way to an effector. The cell bodies of the motor neurones of the autonomic nervous system, however, have their cell bodies outside the central nervous system, in **autonomic ganglia**. Another type of neurone, called a **preganglionic neurone**, carries action potentials from the central nervous system to this ganglion.

The autonomic nervous system is itself divided into two components – the **sympathetic** and **parasympathetic nervous systems** (Figure 15.5).

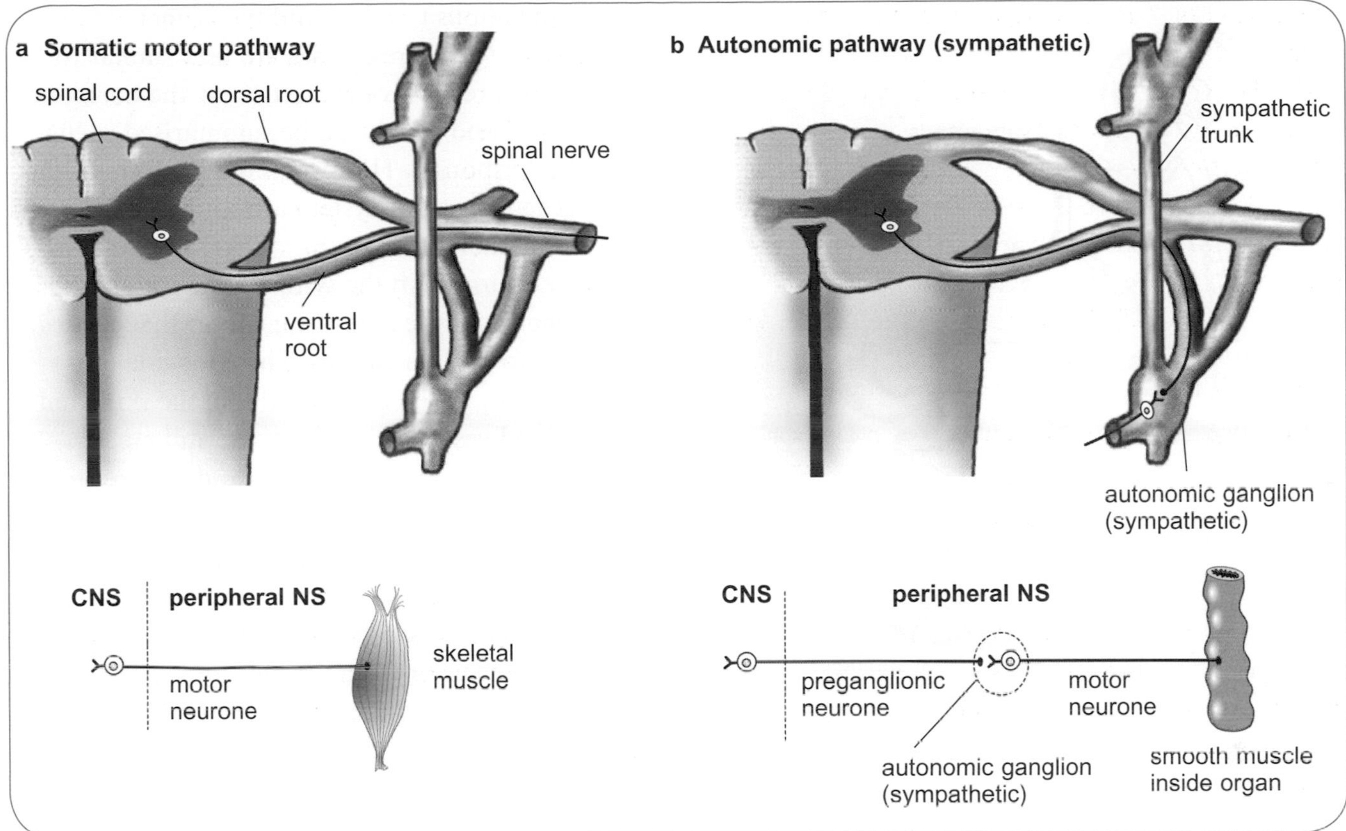

Figure 15.4 The layout of motor pathways (that is, the pathways along which impulses travel from the CNS to an effector) in **a** the somatic nervous system and **b** the autonomic nervous system. In each case, the actual arrangement of the spinal cord and nerves is shown at the top, with a diagrammatic simplification below.

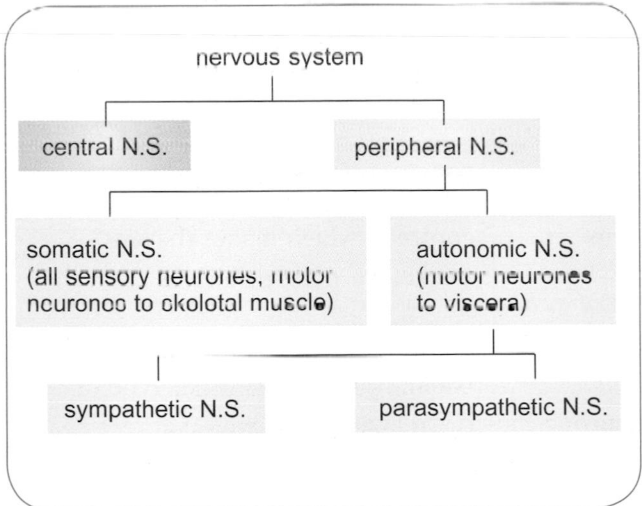

Figure 15.5 The components of the human nervous system.

The sympathetic nervous system

Figure 15.6 shows the structure of the sympathetic nervous system. We have already seen that the cell bodies of its motor neurones lie in ganglia outside the spinal cord. The axons of the preganglionic neurones pass out of the spinal cord through the ventral root, and synapse with the motor neurone cell bodies in these ganglia. There are also neurones that directly connect each ganglion with the next.

From these ganglia, axons pass to all the organs within the body. Here they form synapses with the muscles (cardiac muscle in the heart, smooth muscle elsewhere). The transmitter substance that carries the impulses across most of the synapses is **noradrenaline**, which is very similar to adrenaline. You will probably not be surprised, therefore, that the effect of nerve impulses arriving at organs via the sympathetic system is generally to *stimulate* them. For example, they cause the heart to beat

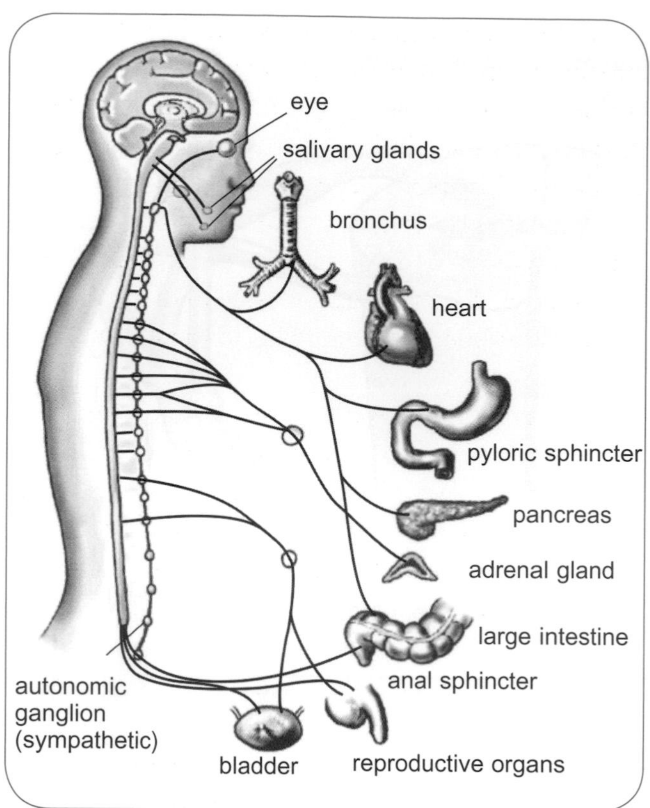

Figure 15.6 The structure of the sympathetic nervous system.

faster, the pupils to dilate and the bronchi to dilate. All of these responses are very similar to those which result from secretion of the hormone adrenaline, and which can be summarised as 'fight or flight' responses. However, not all effects of the sympathetic nervous system are stimulatory, as you can see in Table 15.1.

Some neurones in the sympathetic system use **acetylcholine** as the neurotransmitter that carries impulses to effector organs. These include the sweat glands, the erector muscles in the skin, and some blood vessels. The effects are still mostly stimulatory, causing the sweat glands to produce more sweat and the erector muscles to contract and make the hairs stand on end.

The 'fight or flight' response is initiated when we are under stress, or when we see something that frightens us or makes us feel angry. These stimuli cause the sympathetic nervous system to be activated. As well as the direct activation of various target organs, the sympathetic nerves supplying the adrenal glands cause these glands to secrete the hormones adrenaline and noradrenaline into the blood. Between them, the sympathetic nervous system and these hormones bring about a

Organ		**Effect of sympathetic stimulation**	**Effect of parasympathetic stimulation**
heart		increases rate and force of contraction	reduces rate and force of contraction
eye	pupil	dilates (gets wider)	constricts (gets narrower)
	ciliary muscles	relax, which makes the lens thinner for distant vision	contract, which makes the lens thicker for near vision
digestive system	glands	little or no effect	stimulates secretion
	sphincter muscles	contraction	relaxation
	liver	release of glucose to blood	small increase in glycogen production
skin	sweat glands	increases sweating	little effect, except to increase sweating on palms of hands
	erector muscles	contract, making hairs stand on end	no effect
	arterioles	vasoconstriction	no effect

Table 15.1 Effects of the sympathetic and parasympathetic nervous systems.

wide range of responses. They include:

- speeding of the heart rate and breathing rate
- contraction of the radial muscles in the irises, widening the pupils
- relaxation of the sphincter muscle of the urethra, causing urination
- defecation
- constriction of arterioles supplying the alimentary canal, and dilation of arterioles supplying the skeletal muscles
- cessation of secretion of saliva from the salivary glands.

While these responses may be very useful in a genuine 'fight or flight' situation, they are not so useful in some of the situations that we find stressful in modern life. They are really geared up to help us to get away from or to deal quickly with the threat. If we find ourselves in a prolonged stressful situation – such as family problems, a stressful job, or a series of examinations – then the 'fight or flight' response can be counterproductive. There is considerable evidence that prolonged, unavoidable and uncontrollable stress can have widespread negative effects on health.

SAQ

2 Explain how each of the effects of the 'fight or flight' response prepare the body for fast action in a dangerous situation.

Answer

The parasympathetic nervous system

Figure 15.7 shows the structure of the **parasympathetic nervous system**. Unlike the sympathetic system, the nerve pathways involved in the parasympathetic system all begin in the brain, the top of the spinal cord or the very base of the spinal cord.

As in the sympathetic system, two different neurones carry the impulse on its way from the central nervous system to the effector organ. However, whereas the synapses between these neurones in the sympathetic system are inside ganglia close to the spinal cord, this is not the case in the parasympathetic system. Instead, the neurone that carries the impulse out of the brain or spinal cord just keeps on going, until it is right inside the wall of the organ that it will stimulate. It is here, actually in the organ, that this neurone synapses with an effector neurone.

Many of the axons of the neurones of the parasympathetic nervous system are in the **vagus nerve**, which leaves the brain and carries information to all of the organs in the thorax and abdomen.

The neurotransmitter released into the organs from the parasympathetic axons is **acetylcholine**. This often has an inhibitory effect on the activities of the organ. Once again, however, the situation is not entirely cut-and-dried, and you will see from Table 15.1 that impulses arriving through the parasympathetic system have an inhibitory effect on some organs, and a stimulatory effect on others.

It may help to remember that the sympathetic nervous system tends to prepare the body for 'fight or flight', while the parasympathetic nervous system tends to help it to 'rest and digest'.

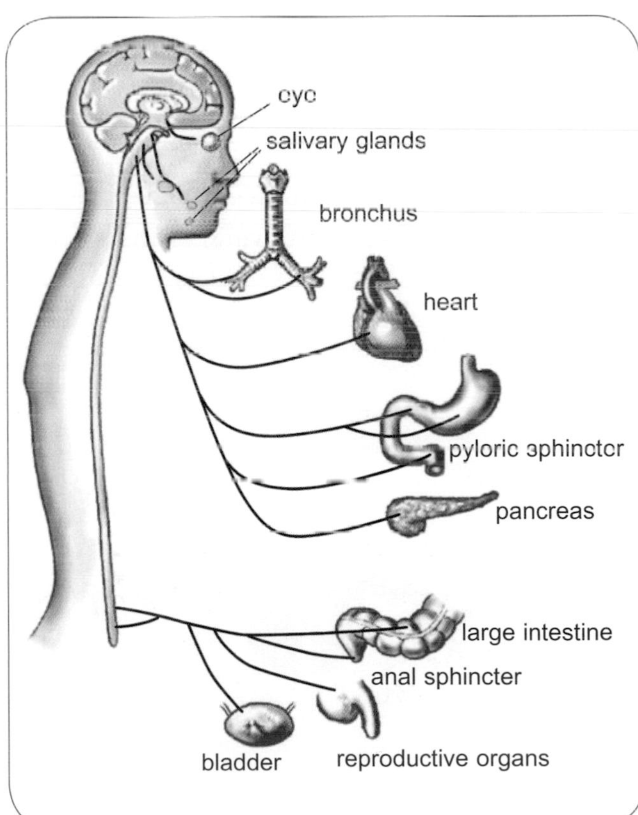

Figure 15.7 The structure of the parasympathetic nervous system.

Some examples of effects of the autonomic nervous system

The digestive system

The walls of the alimentary canal contain nerve endings from both the sympathetic and parasympathetic nervous systems. In general, stimulation from the parasympathetic system tends to stimulate digestive activity, by causing sphincter muscles to open and causing the smooth muscle involved in peristalsis to contract. It also causes the salivary glands and gastric glands to increase their secretion of saliva and gastric juice.

SAQ

3 Suggest one stimulus that might result in action potentials being carried to the salivary glands via the parasympathetic nervous system.

Answer

The sympathetic nervous system is not normally very significant in the working of the alimentary canal. Strong stimulation from it can, however, reduce peristalsis and cause sphincters to close, so that food passes through the digestive system much more slowly. It can also have an indirect effect on the secretory glands, because it can bring about vasoconstriction (narrowing) of the blood vessels that supply them, thus reducing their rate of secretion.

The action of the heart

You will remember that cardiac muscle is myogenic – it contracts and relaxes automatically with no need for stimulation by the nervous system (*Biology 1*, page 70). The patch of muscle known as the **sino-atrial node (SAN)**, in the wall of the right atrium, has a faster natural rate of contraction than all the other muscle in the heart, so the SAN sets the pace and rhythm for the rest of the heart muscle.

The SAN receives impulses from both the sympathetic and parasympathetic nervous systems. Impulses from the latter reach it via the vagus nerve. Impulses arriving from the sympathetic system increase the rate of contraction of the SAN, and therefore the whole heart. This also increases the force of contraction of the heart muscle, so the overall effect is for the heart to beat faster and to push more blood into the arteries with each beat. Impulses from the parasympathetic system have exactly the opposite effect.

SAQ

4 Suggest how parasympathetic stimulation of the SAN might affect blood pressure.

Answer

The pupil in the eye

The pupil is the dark space in the centre of the eye (Figure 15.8). The iris contains circular and radial

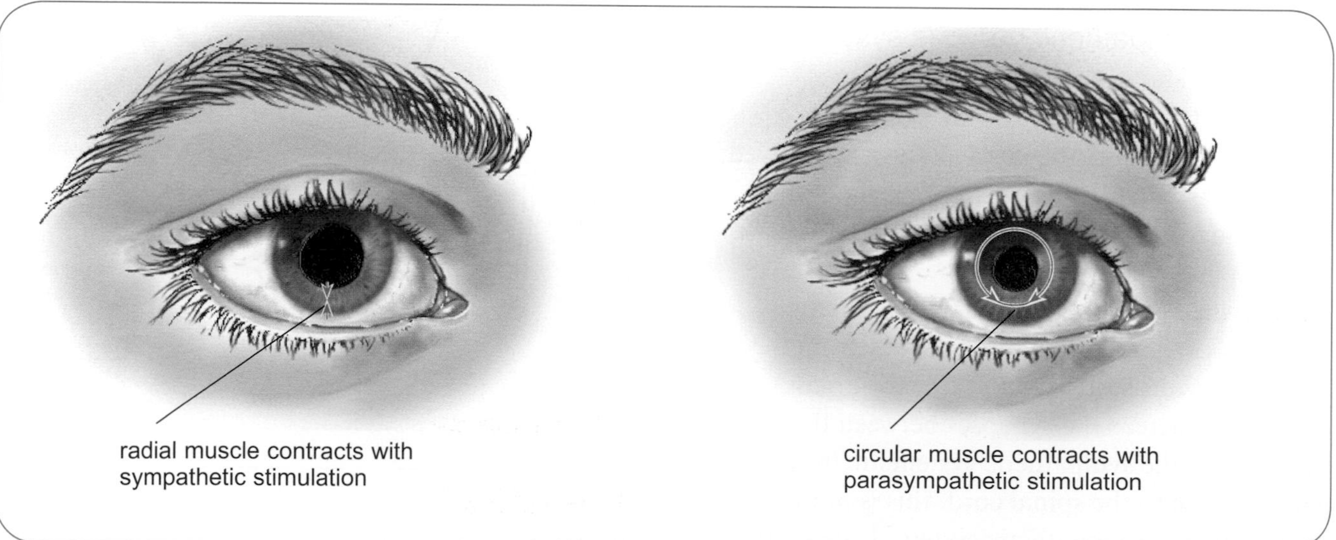

Figure 15.8 The effects of sympathetic and parasympathetic stimulation on the iris.

muscles, and their activity can widen or narrow the diameter of the pupil. It tends to widen in dim light, to allow more light onto the retina, and to narrow in bright light, to prevent too much light damaging the cells within the retina.

Stimulation from the sympathetic system causes the radial muscle fibres in the iris to contract, which widens the pupil. This can happen if a person is excited or nervous, as well as when light is dim. Stimulation from the parasympathetic system causes the circular muscles to contract, narrowing the pupil. This can be a reflex action resulting from stimulation of the retina with bright light.

The brain

The human brain is currently, as it always has been, an object of tremendous interest. Events occurring in the brain underlie virtually all of our behaviour. We would love to know how these events affect what we do. How do we perceive, think, learn and remember? What exactly is 'consciousness'? How does the brain control behaviour such as walking and talking, and emotions such as anger, fear, love, happiness and despair?

Considerable progress has been made in recent years in our knowledge of the anatomy and physiology of the brain, and we are beginning to understand a little about how these may affect behaviour. However, we are still a very long way from being able to explain precisely how even such simple behaviour as walking is controlled, let alone more complex behaviour such as the creation of works of art.

The structure of the brain

Figure 15.9 shows the structure of the human brain. The relationship between the different parts of the brain, however, is best illustrated in a simplified way, as shown in Figure 15.10. This shows the brain 'stretched out' into a line, rather than folded as it really is.

The brain is a cream-coloured organ, surrounded and protected by the bones of the cranium and also by the three membranes known as **meninges**. As we have seen, these membranes help to secrete **cerebro-spinal fluid**, which provides protection and cushioning of the brain. The fluid also fills the spaces inside the brain, known as **ventricles**.

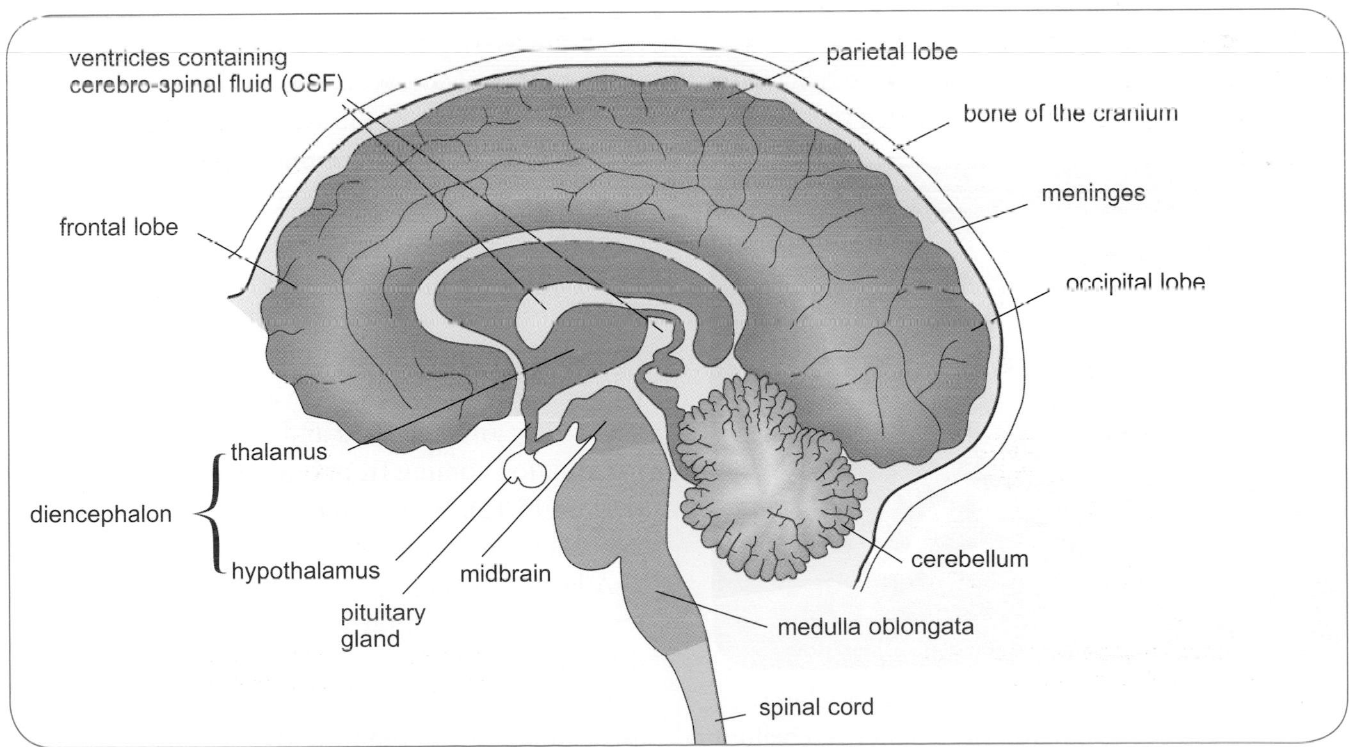

Figure 15.9 The structure of the human brain.

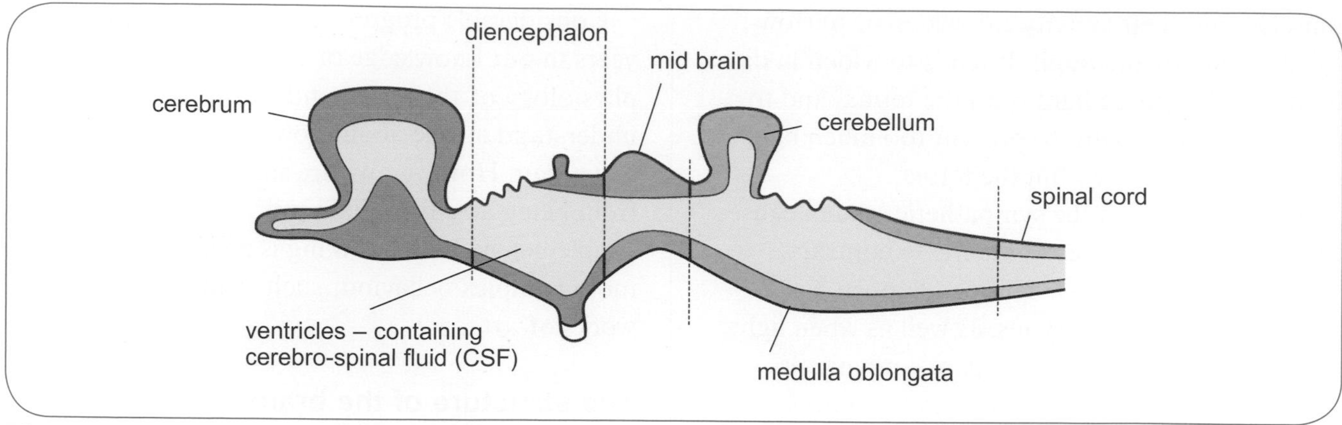

Figure 15.10 The arrangement of the main parts of the brain, shown as though it has been 'unfolded'.

Most organs in the body are supplied with blood in capillaries with leaky walls – the leakiness helps the rapid transfer of substances between the blood and the tissues. In the brain, however, the capillaries are much less leaky and many substances are not able to pass through their walls. This barrier to easy exchange with the blood is known as the **blood–brain barrier**, and it helps to isolate the brain from potentially damaging substances in the blood.

The cerebrum

The **cerebrum** is the highly folded area at the front of the brain. It is so large in humans that it covers most of the rest of the brain (Figure 15.11). It is made up of two **cerebral hemispheres**, connected to each other by a 'bridge' of tissue called the **corpus callosum**. The area just beneath the wrinkled surface of the cerebral hemispheres is called the **cerebral cortex**, and it is largely this part of the brain that is responsible for the characteristics that we consider make us human – such as speech, emotions, logical thought and decision-making.

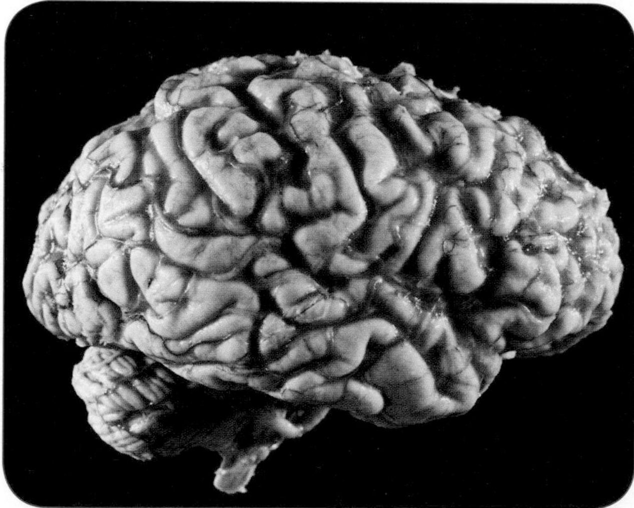

Figure 15.11 The human brain. The very large, greatly folded cerebrum and the smaller cerebellum can be clearly seen.

In the past, the only way people could work out the functions of different parts of the brain was to study changes in the behaviour of people whose brains had been damaged, and link those changes to the particular area of damage. Now it is possible to watch live images of the brain using MRI or PET scanning, and this has given us much more information about how we use the various parts of the brain as we perform different activities.

The cerebral cortex receives information from sense organs, such as the eyes and ears. The left hemisphere receives nerve impulses from the right side of the body and the right hemisphere from the left side.

The parts of the cerebral cortex that first receive this information are known as **primary sensory areas**. Nerve impulses from these areas and other parts of the brain are sent to **association areas**, where they are processed and integrated with other information coming from other parts of the brain (Figure 15.12). In the **motor areas**, nerve impulses are generated and sent to effectors.

A large association area in the parietal, temporal and occipital lobes is involved in determining what our sense organs tell us about the position of different parts of the body. Another association area in the frontal lobe is involved in planning actions and movements. The third main

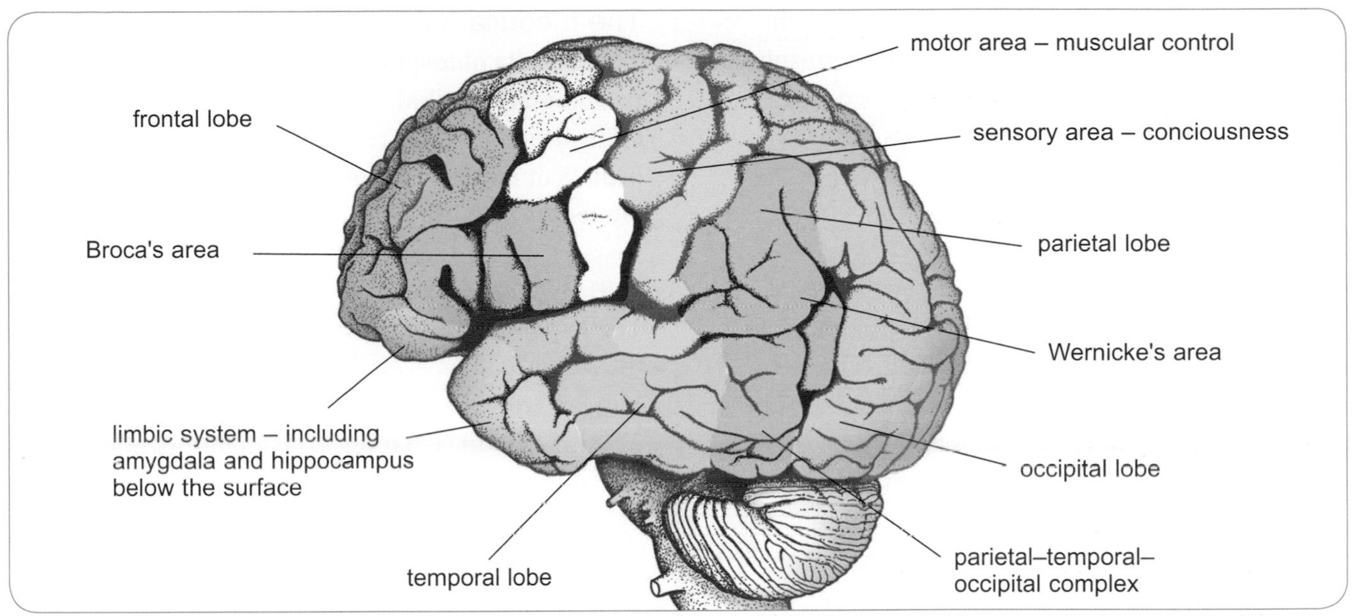

Figure 15.12 Primary sensory areas (green), association areas (blue) and motor areas (white) of the cerebrum.

association area, known as the **limbic system**, is concerned with emotions and memory. The limbic system contains the **hippocampus**, which plays an important role in memory, and the **amygdala**, which coordinates the actions of the autonomic and endocrine systems, and is involved in determining our emotions. (These strange names come from the early anatomists, who named the parts of the brain according to the shapes they could see in them. 'Hippocampus' means 'seahorse', and 'amygdala' means 'almonds'.)

There are some differences between the left and right hemispheres. The association areas of the left hemisphere are responsible for our understanding and use of language. One small area, known as **Broca's area**, has long been known to be involved in the production of language in speaking and writing. **Wernicke's area** is responsible for the understanding of language. PET scans of active brains show that different parts of the brain are active depending on whether we are thinking of words, speaking words or listening to them (Figure 15.13). This is a good example of how the different parts of the cerebral cortex interact to carry out even the simplest of thoughts or actions.

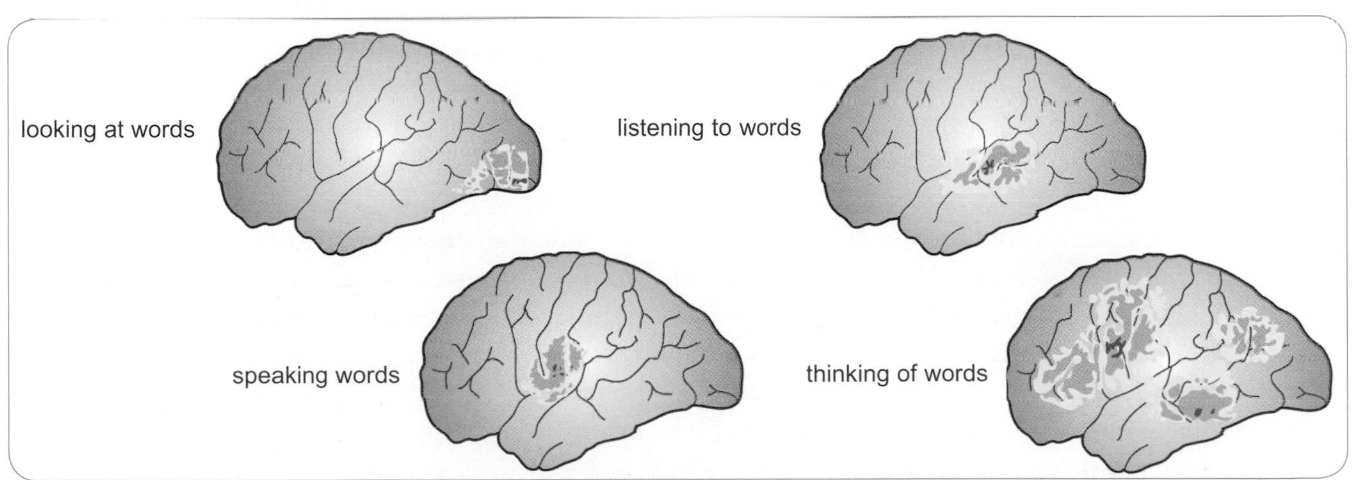

Figure 15.13 PET scanning allows us to show how much work is being done in different areas of the brain while different tasks are done. Yellow – some activity; orange – high activity; purple – most activity.

While the left hemisphere tends to deal with language, the parietal lobe of the right hemisphere is more concerned with non-verbal processes, such as being able to visualise objects in three dimensions and to recognise faces.

The cerebellum

The **cerebellum**, like the cerebrum, has a folded surface – but is much smaller. It is here that movement and posture are controlled. The cerebellum receives impulses from the ears, eyes and stretch receptors in muscles and also from other parts of the brain. The information is integrated and used to coordinate the timing and pattern of skeletal muscle contraction and relaxation. Thus this area is responsible for balance, coordination, eye movement and fine manipulation.

The medulla oblongata

The **medulla oblongata** forms a link between the brain and the spinal cord. It coordinates and controls involuntary movements such as breathing, heartbeat and movements of the wall of the alimentary canal.

The hypothalamus

The **hypothalamus** is a small region that regulates the autonomic nervous system (page 228) and also controls the secretion of hormones from the pituitary gland (Chapter 4). It therefore effectively controls many of our homeostatic processes, such as temperature regulation and the water content of body fluids.

Memory

Most of us take memory for granted until we know someone whose memory is severely impaired; then we begin to understand how essential it is to us. A person with Alzheimer's disease loses the ability to form new memories and may not be able to remember what day it is or even what they ate for breakfast 15 minutes ago. Without our memories, we cease to be the person we have previously been.

One area of the brain that is essential in forming new memories is a part of the limbic system called the hippocampus. This is used when we make new memories. Scientists are not sure how it does this, but it is certain that synapses are involved. Synapses may be 'strengthened' in some way, or perhaps completely new synapses are made.

These new memories are often short-term memories, and most of us don't keep all of them for very long. But some are converted into long-term memories, and this involves other parts of the brain. Memories of events and facts are stored in the temporal and frontal lobes of the cerebral cortex. Facts or events are most likely to be converted into long-term memories if we 'play them back' in our heads. We may make an effort to replay them consciously, or it may happen while we are asleep. The involvement of the hippocampus in making new memories, but not storing old memories or facts or events, helps to explain why people with damage to the hippocampus may not remember what happened five minutes ago but often still have vivid memories of the distant past.

We also store emotional memories – the kind of memory where a smell or a sound or an event can trigger emotions of love, fear or anger. These memories involve another part of the limbic system, called the amygdala. And spatial memories, the mental maps that help us to find our way from one room to another or from home to work, seem to be stored in the hippocampus itself. Yet another kind of memory, called procedural memories, such as how to ride a bike, do not involve the hippocampus at all and are formed and stored in the cerebellum.

Muscular movement

Movements of various parts of the body are caused by specialised tissues called **muscles**. Muscles have the property of being able to use energy to **contract** (get shorter).

You have already seen how the specialised **cardiac muscle** in the heart contracts and relaxes automatically, with no need for action potentials arriving from neurones. The other two types of muscle in our bodies, **smooth muscle** (page 244) and **skeletal (voluntary) muscle**, only contract when action potentials reach them from motor neurones. And even cardiac muscle is affected by neurones, because they help determine the rate of activity of the muscle in the SAN and therefore control the rate of heartbeat.

It is obviously very important that the activities of the different muscles in our bodies are coordinated. When a muscle contracts, it exerts a force in a particular direction pulling on particular body parts. The nervous system ensures that the behaviour of each muscle is coordinated with all the other muscles, so that together they can bring about the desired movement without causing damage to any parts of the skeletal or muscular system.

Bones, muscles and joints

You will probably remember, from GCSE, the basic structure of the bones and muscles in the arm (Figure 15.14). Bones are solid and strong, and cannot bend. The place where two bones meet is called a **joint**. The elbow joint in the arm is an example of a **synovial joint**, adapted to allow smooth movement between the two bones. The elbow joint is a **hinge joint**, allowing movement in one plane. You can't make your elbow joint bend sideways.

There are several muscles in the arm that help to produce movement. The two main muscles that act across the elbow joint are the **triceps** and **biceps** muscles, so-called because of the number of **tendons** that attach them to the humerus and scapula. These are **antagonistic muscles**. When the biceps contracts, it pulls the radius and ulna closer to the scapula, bending – that is, **flexing** – the arm. When the triceps contracts, it pulls them away from each other, straightening – **extending** – the arm. The two muscles generally work in a coordinated way: when the biceps contracts the triceps relaxes, and vice versa. However, in some movements both of the muscles contract to some degree. For example, the triceps may contract to act as a steadying force ensuring that the contraction caused by the biceps produces a controlled and steady movement.

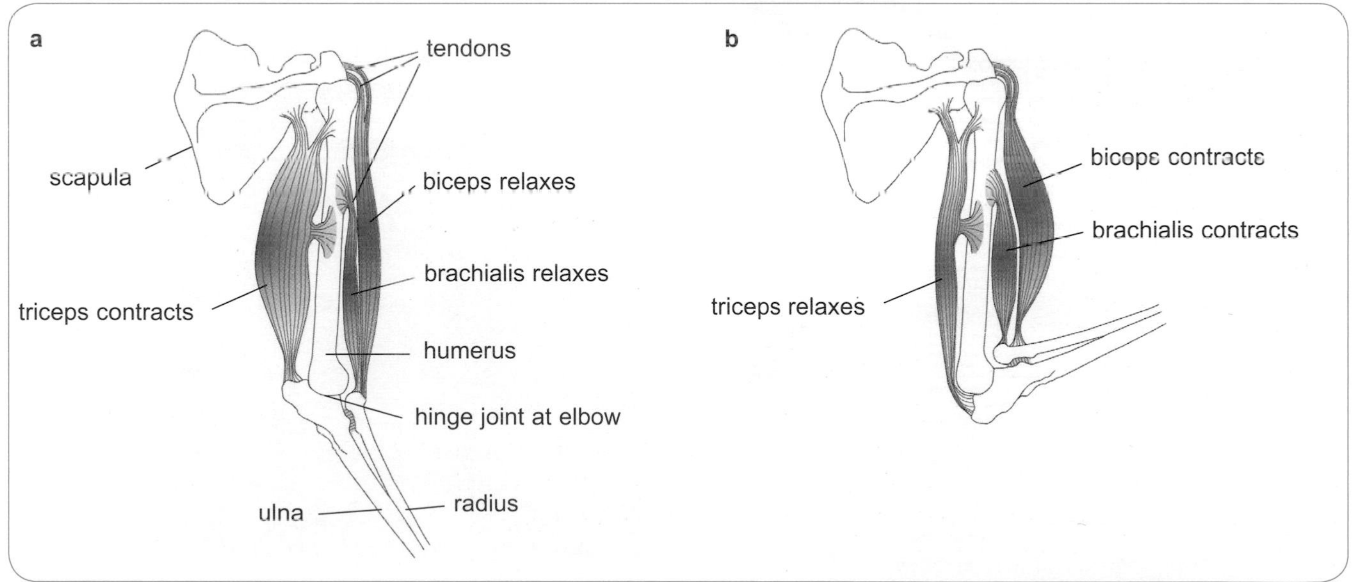

Figure 15.14 Movement of the elbow joint: **a** contraction of the triceps muscle lowers the arm (extension); **b** contractions of the biceps and brachialis muscles raises the lower arm (flexion).

The structure of skeletal muscle

The type of muscle that helps to move the bones in our body is sometimes called **skeletal muscle**. Other names are **voluntary muscle** (because we can decide when to make it contract) and **striated muscle** (because it looks stripy under the microscope).

A muscle such as a biceps is made up of thousands of **muscle fibres** (Figure 15.15). Each muscle fibre is a very specialised 'cell'. Some biologists prefer not to call it a cell, because it contains many nuclei. A name for this kind of structure is a **syncitium**.

Each muscle fibre is surrounded by a plasma membrane, often known as the **sarcolemma**. ('Sarco' means 'to do with muscle'. Another term meaning muscle is 'myo', and you will see that many of the structures in muscle have one of these two words in their names.) The plasma membrane has many deep infoldings into the interior of the fibre, called **T-tubules** (Figure 15.16). These run close to the endoplasmic reticulum, which again is often given a special name, the **sarcoplasmic**

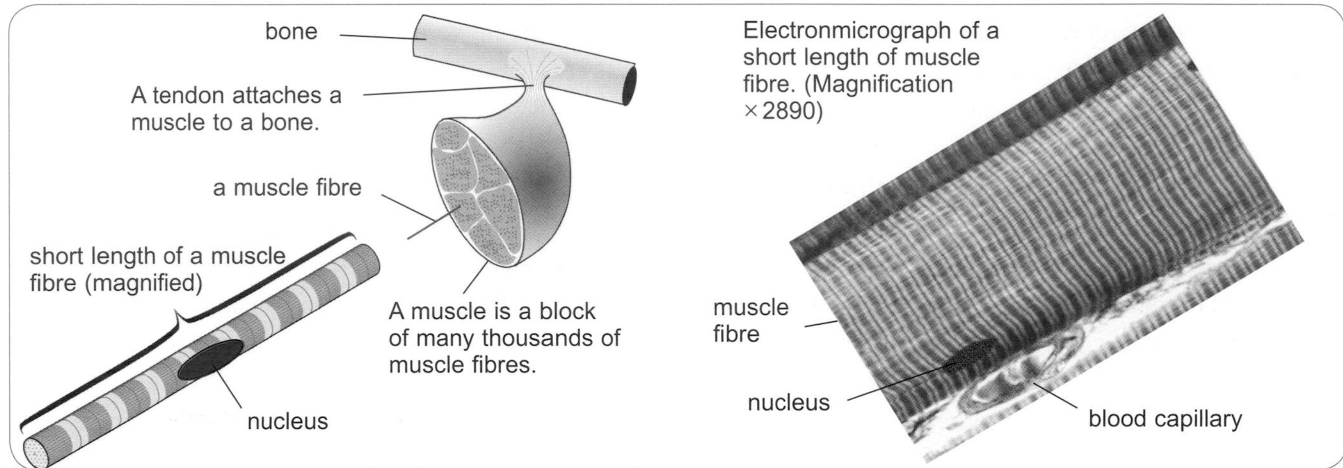

Figure 15.15 The structure of a muscle.

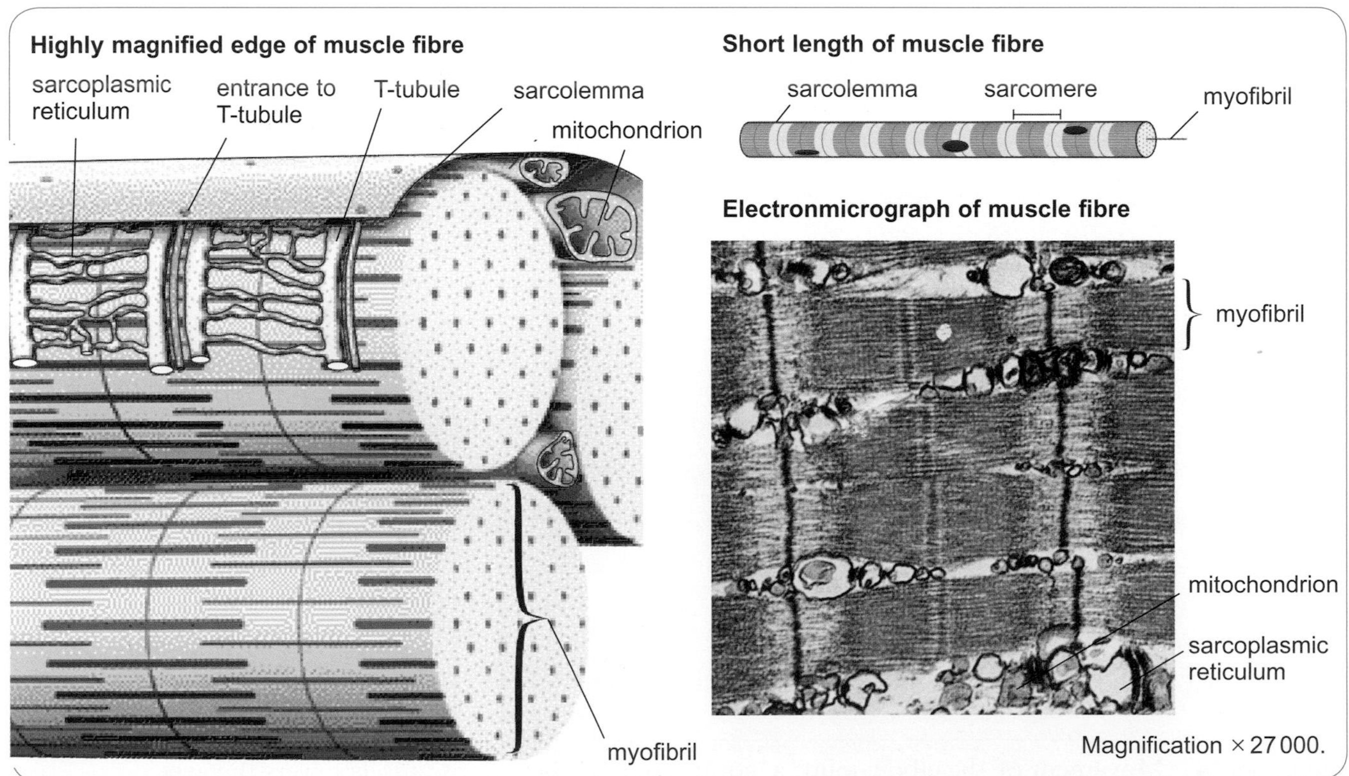

Figure 15.16 Ultrastructure of part of a muscle fibre.

reticulum. The cytoplasm (**sarcoplasm**) contains a large quantity of mitochondria, often packed in as tightly as they possibly could be. These carry out aerobic respiration, generating the ATP that is required for muscle contraction.

The most striking thing about a muscle fibre is its stripes. These are produced by a very regular arrangement of many small fibrils, called **myofibrils**, in its cytoplasm. Each myofibril is striped in exactly the same way, and is lined up precisely against the next one, so producing the pattern shown in the whole fibre.

This is as much as we can see using a light microscope, but with an electron microscope it is possible to see that each myofibril is itself made up of yet smaller components, called **filaments** (Figure 15.16). Parallel groups of thick filaments lie between groups of thin ones.

Both thick and thin filaments are made up of protein. The thick filaments are made of **myosin**, whilst the thin ones are made of **actin**. Now we can understand what causes the stripes. The darker parts of the stripes, the **A bands**, are where the myosin filaments are. The lighter parts, the **I bands**, are where the actin filaments are (Figure 15.17). The very darkest parts of the A band are produced by the overlap of myosin and actin filaments, while the lighter area within the A band, known as the **H band**, represents the parts where only myosin is present. A line known as the **Z line** provides an attachment for the actin filaments, while the **M line** does the same for the myosin filaments. The part of a myofibril between two Z lines is called a **sarcomere**.

SAQ

5 All cells, not only muscle cells, contain actin, in the form of microfilaments.
What is their role?

Hint

Answer

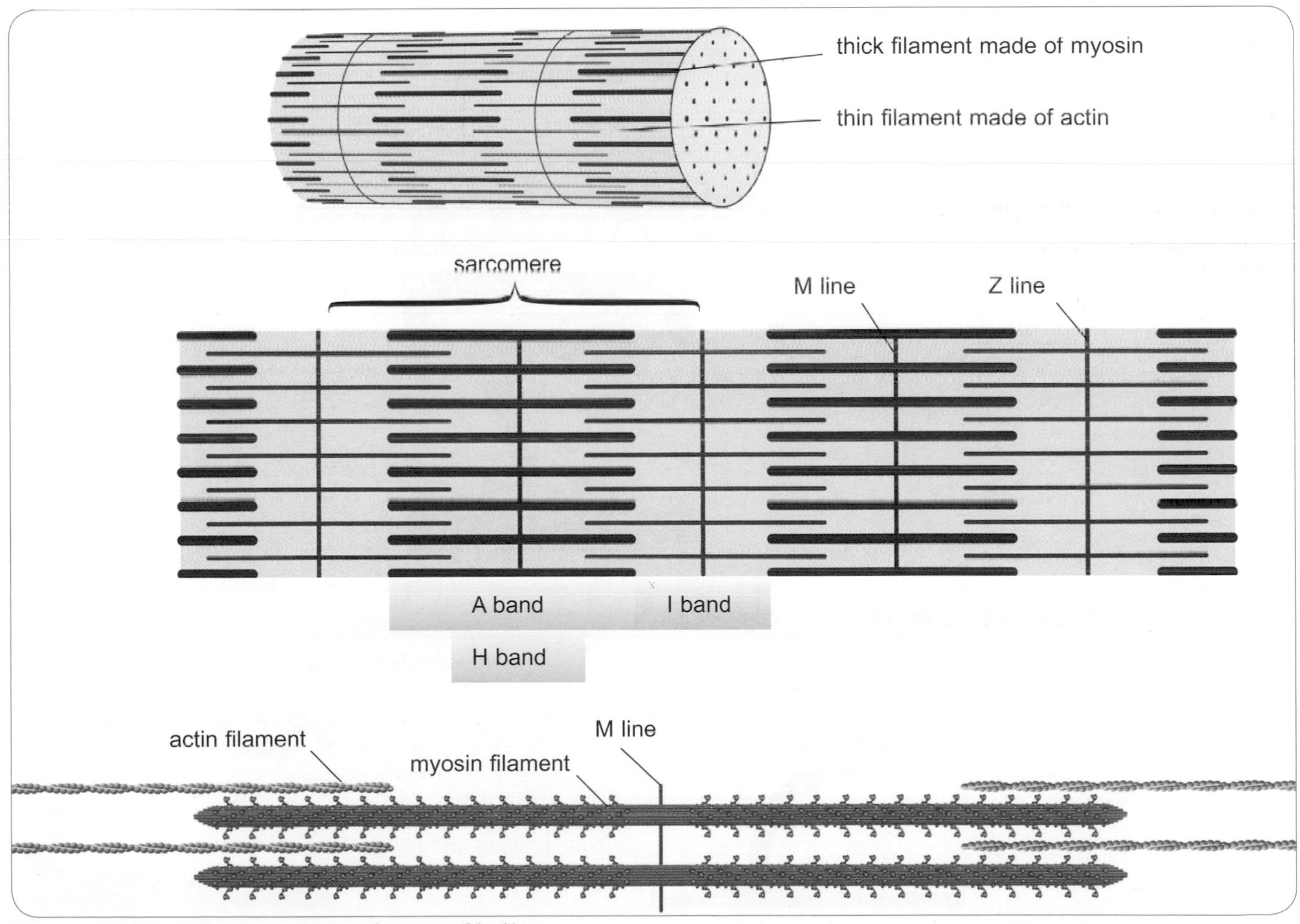

Figure 15.17 The structure of a myofibril.

Structure of thick and thin filaments

Myosin is a fibrous protein. Each myosin molecule has a tail (attached to the M line) and a head. Several myosin molecules all lie in a bundle together, heads all pointing away from the M line, forming a myosin filament.

Actin is a globular protein, but many actin molecules link together in a long chain. Two of these chains twist together to form an actin filament.

Also twisted around the actin chains is a fibrous protein called **tropomyosin**. And a fourth protein, **troponin**, is attached to the actin chain at regular intervals (Figure 15.18).

How muscles contract

Muscles cause movement by contracting. The sarcomeres in each myofibril get shorter as the Z lines are pulled closer together. Figure 15.18 shows how this happens. It is known as the **sliding filament model** of muscle contraction.

Energy for this comes from ATP attached to the myosin heads, which act as **ATPases**.

When a muscle contracts, the troponin and tropomyosin molecules change shape (Figure 15.18). They move to a different position on the actin filaments, and this exposes parts of the actin molecules that act as binding sites for myosin. The myosin heads bind with these sites, forming cross-bridges between the two types of filament.

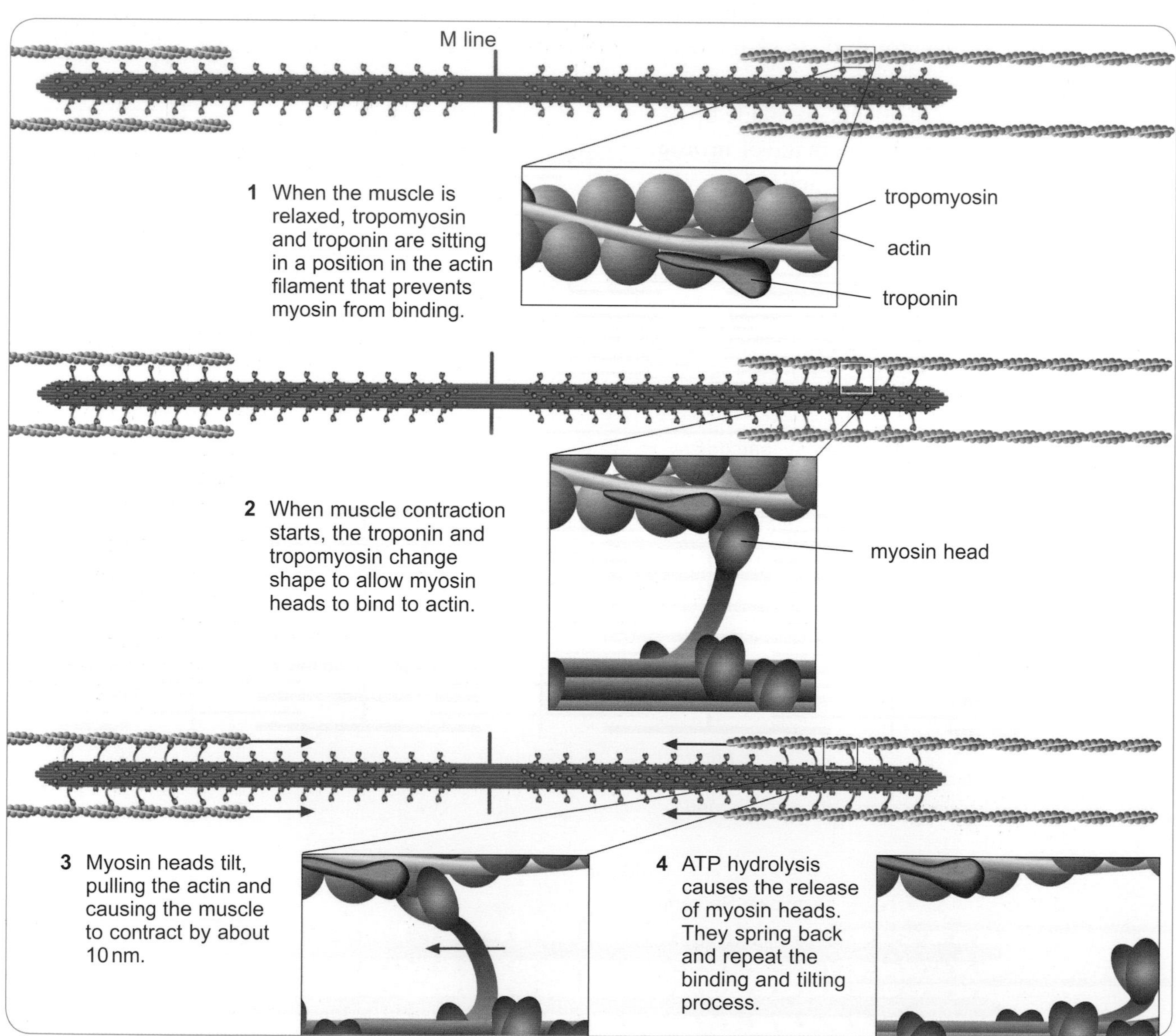

M line
1 When the muscle is relaxed, tropomyosin and troponin are sitting in a position in the actin filament that prevents myosin from binding.
tropomyosin
actin
troponin
2 When muscle contraction starts, the troponin and tropomyosin change shape to allow myosin heads to bind to actin.
myosin head
3 Myosin heads tilt, pulling the actin and causing the muscle to contract by about 10 nm.
4 ATP hydrolysis causes the release of myosin heads. They spring back and repeat the binding and tilting process.

Figure 15.18 The sliding filament model of muscle contraction.

Next, the myosin heads tilt, pulling the actin filaments along towards the centre of the sarcomere. The heads then hydrolyse ATP molecules, which provides enough energy to force the heads to let go of the actin. They tip back to their previous positions and bind again to the exposed sites on the actin. But, of course, the actin has moved along by now, so the heads are now binding to a different part of the actin filaments. They tilt again, pulling the actin filaments even further along, then hydrolyse more ATP molecules so that they can let go again. This goes on and on, so long as the troponin and tropomyosin molecules aren't blocking the binding sites, and so long as the muscle has a supply of ATP.

Extension

Stimulating muscle to contract

Now you have seen what happens when a muscle contracts, but what makes it do this? Skeletal muscle contracts when it receives an impulse from a neurone. Neurones and muscles meet at specialised synapses called **neuromuscular junctions**. An action potential sweeps along the axon of a motor neurone and arrives at the presynaptic membrane (Figure 15.19). A neurotransmitter, generally acetylcholine, diffuses across the synaptic cleft and slots into receptors on the postsynaptic membrane – which is the sarcolemma (the plasma membrane of the muscle fibre). This depolarises the membrane and generates an action potential, which sweeps along the sarcolemma.

The action potential plunges down into the centre of the muscle fibre, along the membranes of the T-tubules. Here it is picked up by the membranes of the sarcoplasmic reticulum. Here, in the cisternae of the reticulum, calcium ions have been collecting up, pumped in by active transport. The arrival of the impulses causes this

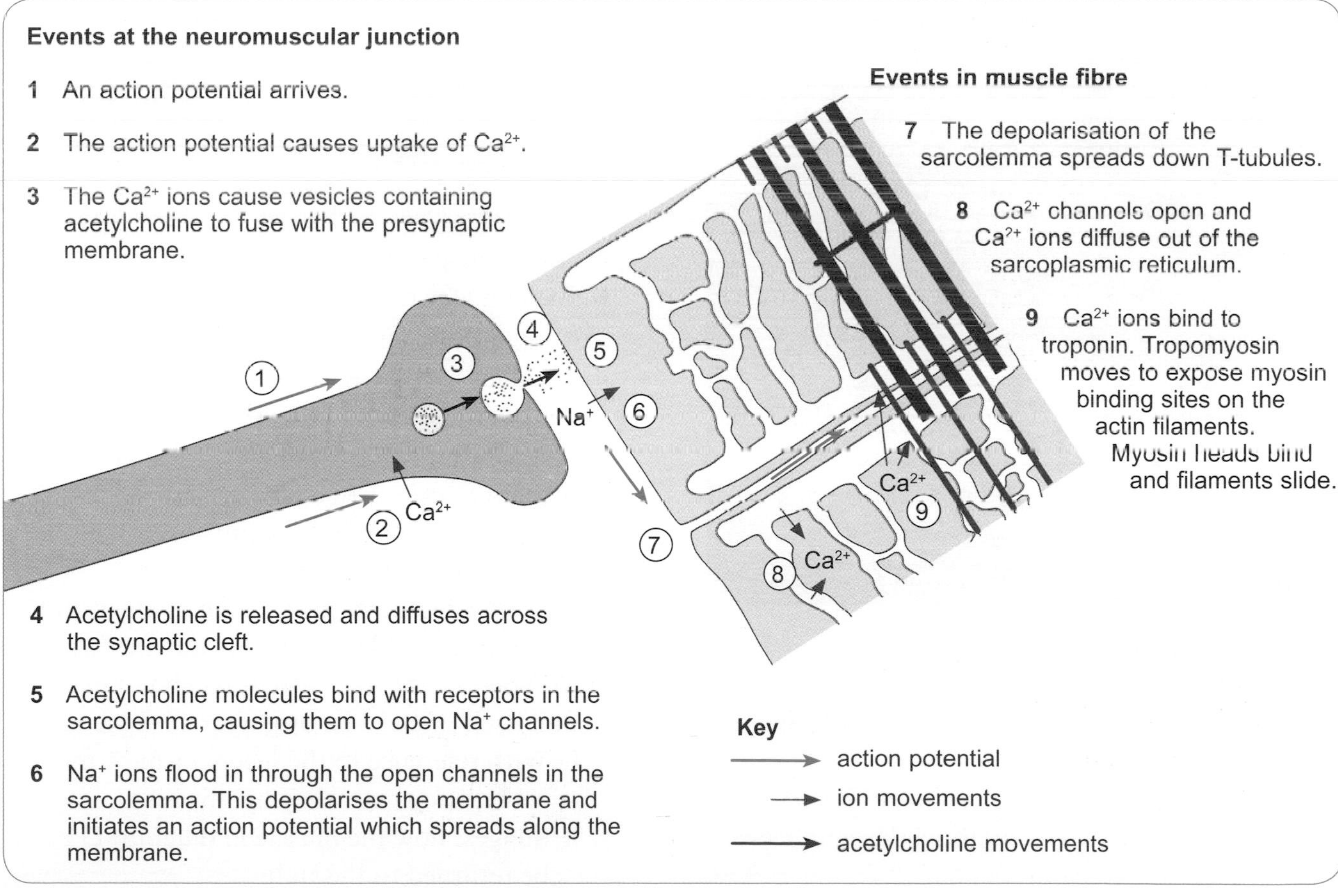

Events at the neuromuscular junction
1 An action potential arrives.
2 The action potential causes uptake of Ca^{2+}.
3 The Ca^{2+} ions cause vesicles containing acetylcholine to fuse with the presynaptic membrane.
Events in muscle fibre
7 The depolarisation of the sarcolemma spreads down T-tubules.
8 Ca^{2+} channels open and Ca^{2+} ions diffuse out of the sarcoplasmic reticulum.
9 Ca^{2+} ions bind to troponin. Tropomyosin moves to expose myosin binding sites on the actin filaments. Myosin heads bind and filaments slide.
1
2
3
4
5
6
7
8
9
Na^+
Ca^{2+}
Ca^{2+}
Ca^{2+}
4 Acetylcholine is released and diffuses across the synaptic cleft.
5 Acetylcholine molecules bind with receptors in the sarcolemma, causing them to open Na^+ channels.
6 Na^+ ions flood in through the open channels in the sarcolemma. This depolarises the membrane and initiates an action potential which spreads along the membrane.
Key
action potential
ion movements
acetylcholine movements

Figure 15.19 How a nerve impulse causes muscle contraction.

active transport to stop, and calcium ion channels in the membranes open. The calcium ions flood out, down their concentration gradient, into the sarcoplasm. The calcium ions rapidly bind with the troponin molecules that are attached to the actin filaments. This changes the shape of the troponin molecules, which causes the troponin and tropomyosin to move away and expose the binding sites for the myosin heads. These attach, and the process of muscle contraction begins.

SAQ

6 Compare and contrast the action of synapses between neurones and synapses between neurones and muscles at neuromuscular junctions.

Hint

Answer

7 The electron micrograph shows some sarcomeres in part of a muscle that has contracted.

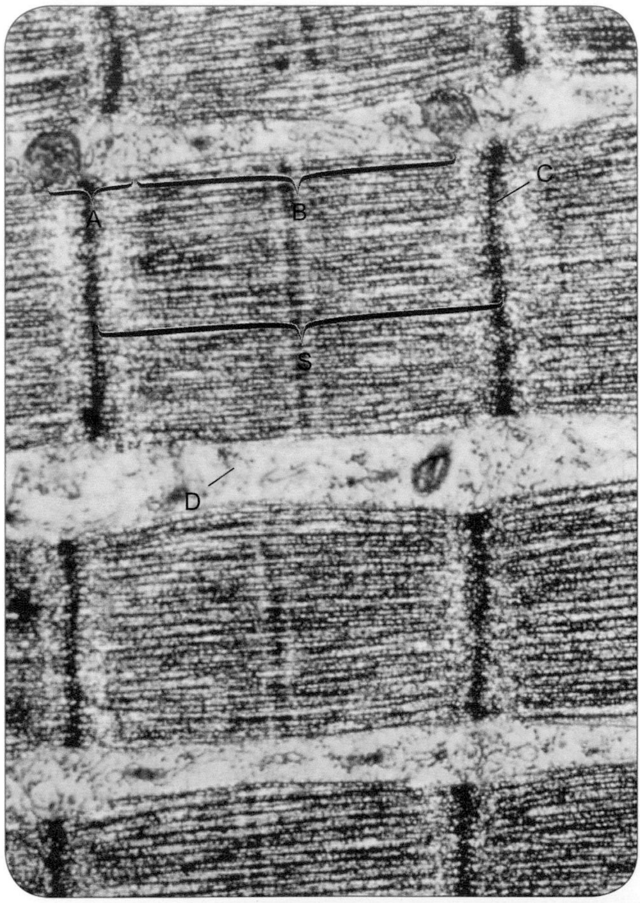

a Name the parts labelled A to D.

b Describe how you can tell that this electron micrograph is from contracted muscle and not relaxed muscle.

c The electron micrograph is magnified 33 500 times. Calculate the length of the sarcomere labelled S. Give your answer in μm.

Answer

8 The diagrams show a sarcomere in different states of contraction.

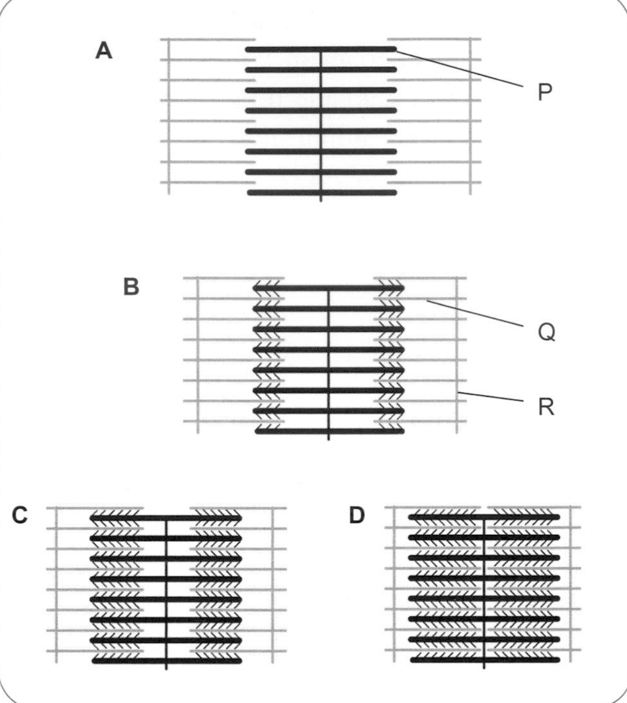

a Name the parts labelled P to R.

b Explain why there are no actin–myosin cross-bridges visible in diagram A.

c Muscle fibres are able to contract with more force in some states of contraction than others. Suggest which of the diagrams shows the state that can develop the greatest force, and explain the reasons for your answer.

Hint

d Explain why the muscle shown in diagram D would not be able to contract any further.

e Muscle can contract with force, but it cannot pull itself back to its original relaxed length.

i With reference to the mechanism of muscle contraction, explain why this is so.

ii Suggest how the muscle in diagram D could be returned to the state shown in diagram A.

Answer

Rigor mortis

Rigor mortis means 'rigidity of death'. After death, muscles become rigid. The time it takes for rigor mortis to develop and then fade away can be used to help determine the time of death.

In resting muscle, most myosin heads are not attached to actin filaments. Transporter proteins pump calcium ions into the cisternae of the sarcoplasmic reticulum, so troponin and tropomyosin cover the attachment sites.

When an animal or person dies, respiration in the muscles stops and ATP production ceases. Calcium ions are no longer pumped into the cisternae of the sarcoplasmic reticulum, so they build up in the sarcoplasm. This causes troponin and tropomyosin to move away from their blocking positions on the actin filaments, so myosin heads bind with the actin. Because there is no ATP left, they stay attached and the muscle is held rigidly.

Rigor mortis lasts for around one to three days. By the end of this time, enzymes leaking out of lysosomes will have partially destroyed the cells, and the actin–myosin bridges will have broken apart.

Extension

Providing ATP for muscle contraction

A contracting muscle gets through a lot of ATP. Muscles do keep a very small store of ATP in the muscle fibres, but this is used up very rapidly once the muscle starts working. More ATP is produced by respiration – both aerobic respiration inside the mitochondria and, when that cannot supply ATP fast enough, also by anaerobic respiration in the cytoplasm (Figure 15.20). Muscles also have another source of ATP, produced from a substance called **creatine phosphate**. They keep stores of this substance in their cytoplasm. It is their immediate source of energy once they have used up their small store of ATP. A phosphate group can quickly and easily be removed from each creatine phosphate molecule and combined with ADP to produce more ATP:

creatine phosphate + ADP ⟶ creatine + ATP

Later, when the demand for energy has slowed down or stopped, ATP molecules produced by respiration can be used to 'recharge' the creatine:

creatine + ATP ⟶ creatine phosphate + ADP

In the meantime, however, if energy is still being demanded by the muscles and there is no ATP spare to regenerate the creatine phosphate, the creatine is converted to creatinine and excreted in urine.

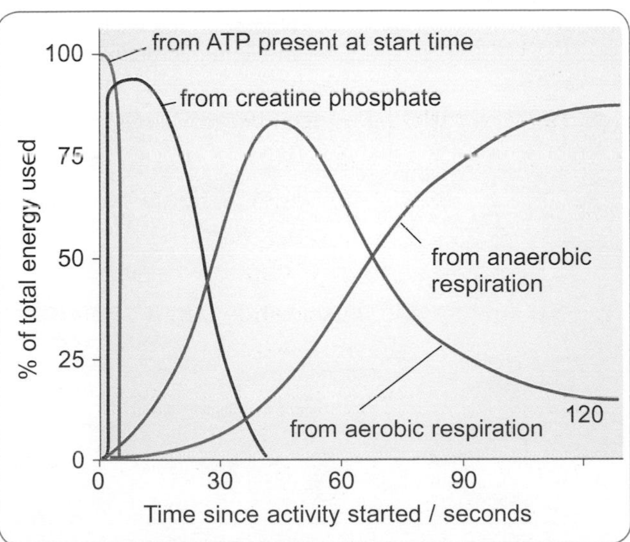

Figure 15.20 Energy sources used in muscle at high power output.

Other types of muscle

Skeletal (also known as voluntary muscle) is not the only type in the body. As we have seen, we also have cardiac and smooth muscle.

Figure 15.21 shows the structure of **cardiac muscle**. It is found only in the heart. Like skeletal muscle, it is striated, each cell containing fibrils made up of sarcomeres. The mechanism of contraction is very similar to that described for skeletal muscle.

However, cardiac muscle differs from skeletal muscle in several ways. The cells, or fibres, are smaller, each one being about 80 μm long and 15 μm in diameter. Each cell has just the one nucleus. These cells branch and form connections with adjacent cells. Thick structures that are continuous with the plasma membranes (sarcolemmas), called **intercalated discs**, separate the end of each fibre from its neighbour. These discs include specialised joining points between the cells called **gap junctions**. Tiny channels through these gap junctions connect the cells directly and allow the wave of depolarisation to sweep rapidly along through the wall of the heart (*Biology 1*, pages 70–72).

Cardiac muscle has more mitochondria than skeletal muscle. Most skeletal muscles do not have to contract for long periods of time and, in any case, they can if necessary respire anaerobically. Cardiac muscle must have a continuous supply of oxygen and can only perform its repetitive, regular contractions if it respires aerobically. It uses fatty acids rather than glucose as a respiratory substrate.

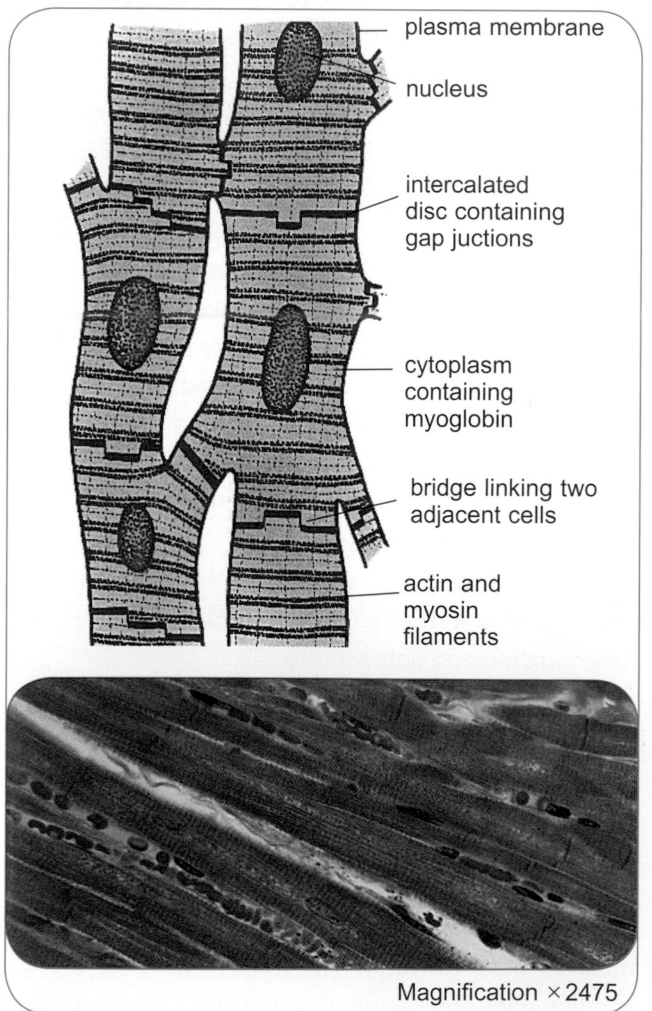

Figure 15.21 The structure of cardiac muscle.

Smooth muscle is rather different in structure from both skeletal and cardiac muscle (Figure 15.22). It does not look stripy under the microscope, and so is sometimes called **non-striated muscle**. It is made up of individual cells each with their own nucleus. The cells are quite long and thin (about 400 µm long and 5 µm wide) and lie parallel to each other. Smooth muscle is found in many places in the body, including the walls of the alimentary canal, blood vessels and uterus. It is not under voluntary control.

Smooth muscle cells contract more slowly and steadily than other types of muscle. As in other muscles, the contraction is caused by the sliding of actin and myosin filaments, but these are not arranged to form myofibrils or sarcomeres. Contraction is initiated by action potentials arriving along neurones of the autonomic nervous system and may also be brought about by hormones such as adrenaline and oxytocin.

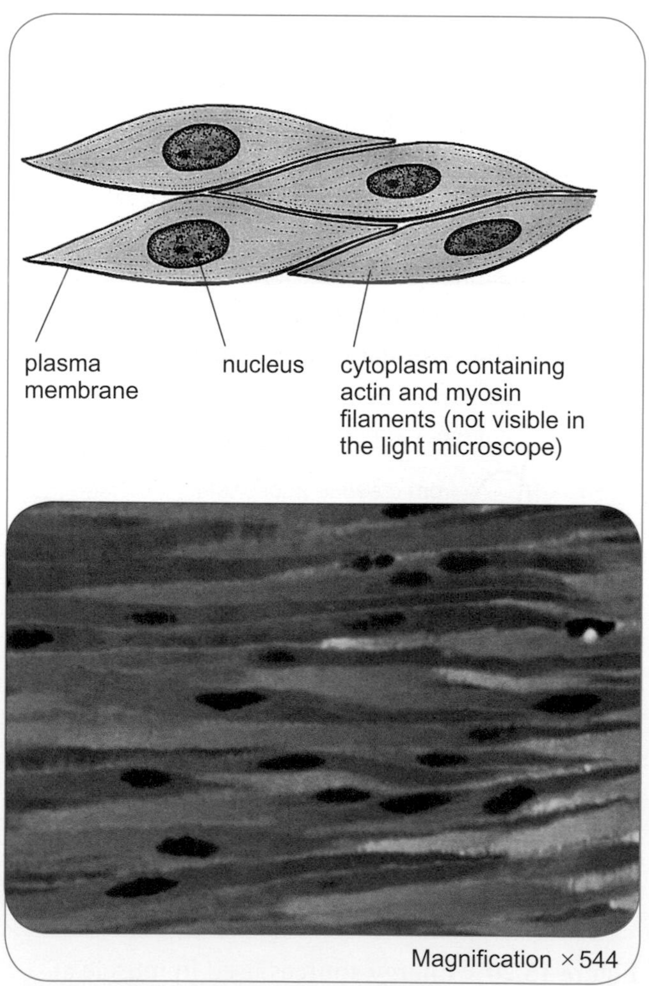

Figure 15.22 The structure of smooth muscle.

Creatine supplements

If you walk around any health food store, you are likely to see big tubs of creatine supplements for sale, generally in the form of creatine monohydrate. People sometimes take it because they think it may improve their general health, or to give them more energy or enable them to perform better in their sport.

A muscle's own store of ATP and creatine phosphate is only enough to provide energy for around 10 seconds. This is just about long enough for a world-class sprinter to complete a 100 m sprint. If the quantity of creatine phosphate in the muscles can be increased, this can improve the performance of sprinters and others who take part in events requiring short bursts of high-intensity performance. It has not been shown to have any beneficial effects in events lasting for more than one minute.

It is possible to increase the quantity of creatine phosphate in muscles by taking creatine monohydrate supplements. Creatine monohydrate is absorbed from the blood by muscle fibres, where it is converted to creatine phosphate. One investigation showed that taking 20 g of creatine monohydrate daily for six days increases creatine phosphate stores in muscles by up to 20%. However, this amount taken over longer periods of time may damage the muscles' ability to take up and metabolise creatine, and studies have shown that, if the effect is to be maintained, then much lower doses of about 2 g each day are preferable.

Taking creatine supplements is perfectly legal in all sports. There is no evidence that it is dangerous, as the kidneys easily eliminate any excess in the form of creatinine.

Summary

Glossary

- Animals respond to their environment in a wide variety of ways, such as fleeing from dangerous situations or moving towards potential rewards such as food or a mate. The responses of animals to environmental stimuli are brought about and coordinated by activities of the nervous system and the endocrine system.
- The human nervous system is made up of the central nervous system (brain and spinal cord) and the peripheral nervous system (nerves). The peripheral nervous system is made up of the somatic and autonomic nervous systems.
- The brain and spinal cord are mostly made up of intermediate neurones and glial cells. The brain and spinal cord contain spaces filled with cerebro-spinal fluid, secreted by protective membranes known as meninges. They are protected within the bones of the skull and vertebral column.
- Nerves leave the brain (cranial nerves) and spinal cord (spinal nerves). A spinal nerve splits to form a dorsal root, which contains axons of sensory neurones carrying action potentials towards the spinal cord, and a ventral root containing axons of motor neurones carrying action potentials away from the spinal cord towards an effector.
- The somatic nervous system includes all the sensory and motor neurones that supply the skeletal muscles, and which are generally under our voluntary control. The autonomic nervous system includes all the motor neurones supplying the viscera.

continued

- The autonomic nervous system is made up of the sympathetic and parasympathetic nervous systems. The sympathetic nervous system tends to bring about stimulation of various organs, such as increasing the heart rate. Widespread activity of the sympathetic nervous system results in a 'fight or flight' response, in which adrenaline released from the adrenal glands adds to the effects of the nervous system. The parasympathetic nervous system tends to have an inhibitory effect on various internal organs, bringing about a set of responses that allow the body to 'rest and digest'.
- The largest part of the brain is the cerebrum, divided into two cerebral hemispheres with deeply folded surfaces. This is responsible for language, conscious thought, memory, emotions and decision-making. The cerebellum controls movement and posture. The medulla oblongata regulates activities of the internal organs, such as the rate of heart beat and breathing. The hypothalamus is involved in homeostasis and in the regulation of the autonomic nervous system.
- Skeletal muscles are attached to bones by tendons. Contraction of a muscle pulls on the tendon and therefore on the bone, bringing two bones closer together as movement occurs at the joint between them. Skeletal muscles generally work in pairs, in which the contraction of one brings the bones closer together (flexion) and contraction of the other pulls them further apart (extension).
- Skeletal muscle is made up of many multinucleate cells called muscle fibres, which in turn contain many myofibrils. These contain regularly arranged filaments of myosin and actin. The arrangement of the myosin and actin filaments produces the striations seen in the muscle. Regions containing myosin filaments look darker than actin filaments, and the darkest areas of all contain both types. Myosin filaments are attached to Z lines, and a length of a myofibril between two Z lines is known as a sarcomere.
- The arrival of an action potential at a neuromuscular junction causes the release of acetylcholine which diffuses across the synaptic cleft and slots into receptors on the sarcolemma. This causes depolarisation, and an action potential sweeps along the sarcolemma, whose T-tubules carry it deep into the myofibril.
- The arrival of the action potential causes the cisternae of the sarcoplasmic reticulum to become permeable to calcium ions, so these diffuse out. Calcium ions bind with troponin molecules, causing troponin and tropomyosin to move from their normal position on the actin filaments. This exposes binding sites for myosin, and the myosin heads bind with the actin, forming cross-bridges.
- The myosin heads then tilt, pushing the actin filaments along. ATPases in the myosin heads then hydrolyse ATP, providing energy that causes the myosin heads to detach. The heads flip back to their normal position and bind with actin again. The process is repeated over and over, pulling the actin filaments between the myosin filaments and causing the sarcomere to shorten.
- Muscles contain a very small store of ATP, which is ready for immediate use. Once this is used up, the next supply comes from creatine phosphate, which can rapidly donate phosphate to ADP molecules. When this in turn has been used up, the muscle uses ATP newly generated from aerobic respiration in the many mitochondria packed into each muscle fibre. If the demand for ATP is even greater than can be generated in this way, then anaerobic respiration may also be used.
- Cardiac muscle is also striated, but is formed from branched cells which link with each other through intercalated discs containing gap junctions through which action potentials can rapidly pass.
- Smooth muscle is made up of individual, elongated cells, which are not striated, although they do contain actin and myosin fibres. It is adapted for slow, prolonged contraction.

Stretch and challenge questions

1 Compare and contrast the structure and activity of the somatic and autonomic nervous systems. Hint

2 With reference to synapses, muscle contraction and the control of hormone secretion, discuss the roles of calcium ions in the control of cell activity. Hint

Questions

1 The human brain is an organ, protected by the skull. The largest part of the human brain is the cerebrum. The surface of the cerebrum is covered by a highly folded region of tissue, called the cerebral cortex. The cerebrum contains regions of mostly myelinated axons, called white matter, and regions of mostly cell bodies and dendrites, called grey matter.

a Explain why the cerebral cortex is a tissue, whereas the brain is an organ. [3]

b Explain the advantage of the cerebral cortex being highly folded. [2]

c Cerebrospinal fluid (CSF) surrounds the brain and fills the central cavities, known as ventricles.
Suggest two functions of CSF. [2]

d Which of the following list of functions are performed by the cerebrum? You may choose more than one.

- control of the autonomic nervous system
- coordination of posture
- planning a task
- control of heart rate [1]

e Hydrocephalus is a disease in which children produce a large volume of CSF, which accumulates, putting pressure on the brain and causing damage to neurones. The table shows how hydrocephalus affects the total amount of white and grey matter within the cerebrum.

Region of cerebrum	Mean total amount of white and grey matter as a percentage of cerebrum volume	
	Unaffected children	Children with hydrocephalus
front	88.8	90.7
middle	90.4	85.3
rear	90.7	84.0

Children with hydrocephalus show the following features:

- poor understanding of written and spoken words
- loss of fine motor skills
- poor memory of objects
- normal hearing
- normal speech production.

Explain, using information from the table and your knowledge of the localisation of functions in the brain, the features seen in children with hydrocephalus. [4]

OCR Biology A (2805/05) June 2005 [Total 12]

Answer

Chapter 16

Animal behaviour

Objectives

e-Learning

The study of animal behaviour is concerned with everything that an animal does – sleeping, being aggressive, standing still, making sounds and so on. Although people have been interested in animal behaviour for thousands of years, its beginnings as an area of scientific investigation can probably be said to have occurred in the early years of the 20th century.

These early studies grew partly out of Darwin's ideas on evolution by natural selection – some people began to look for the ways in which particular patterns of behaviour might adapt living organisms to their environment. This type of study became known as **ethology**. Ethologists tended to study the natural behaviour of animals in their natural environment. They were interested in the evolutionary basis of behaviour, and they started by focusing on simple, inherited behaviour patterns.

At the same time, other investigators were taking a very different approach. They carried out their experiments in laboratories, under controlled conditions. They were especially interested in how animals learned new patterns of behaviour. This type of study became known as **psychology** and it often focused on differences between the behaviour patterns of different species, when it was known as comparative psychology. Some psychologists concentrated on studying behavioural events involving stimuli and responses, and how rewards and punishments could affect these responses. These studies were known as **behaviouralism**.

Throughout the first half of the 20th century, these two different approaches to studying animal behaviour – those of ethologists and of psychologists and behaviouralists – gave rise to the so-called 'nature–nurture debate'. Is an animal's behaviour largely controlled by its 'nature' (that is, its genes) or by its 'nurture' (that is, the experiences it has during its lifetime)? Humans, of course, are animals and the nature–nurture debate in relation to human behaviour raged quite fiercely for a while. Are aspects of our behaviour largely determined by our genes – and therefore not 'our fault'? Or are they largely determined by our environment? To what extent does choice – 'free will' – allow us to override any innate tendencies to particular behaviour patterns?

Today, there is no sharp divide between these two approaches to studying and interpreting animal behaviour. We understand that both 'nature' and 'nurture' probably contribute to most behavioural patterns. Other ways of studying animal behaviour have also emerged. These include the physiological approach, in which the roles of receptors, neurones, effectors and neurotransmitters that contribute to behaviour are investigated. More recently, as more and more is learned about the human genome, we have been able to look at how particular alleles of genes appear to be linked with particular types of human behaviour.

The study of animal (including human) behaviour is now a very diverse and extensive branch of science. This chapter will give you just a very small taste of this diversity.

Innate behaviour

As we watch the behaviour of animals, we often find ourselves amazed at how they seem to 'know' what to do. For example, a dragonfly nymph crawls out of the pond in which it has spent the first few years of its life, and drags itself up a plant stem until it is well above the water surface. It attaches its feet very firmly, and hangs on as its skin splits. As its body emerges from the old skin, it at first hangs downwards, until a moment arrives when it suddenly twists upwards and grabs onto the stem with its newly emerged legs. It stays in this position for quite a long time, as its new wings gradually expand and dry. After some time – sometimes several hours – it quickly cleans its large eyes with its front pair of legs then takes off on its very first flight (Figure 16.1).

All dragonfly nymphs of a particular species follow exactly the same pattern of behaviour. How do they 'know' what to do? Until the moment that the nymph crawls up onto the plant stem, it has spent all of its life under water. Until the moment that it first takes off, it has never used wings. Yet these actions are carried out with near perfection, the very first time that they are used.

This behaviour is an example of **innate** behaviour. 'Innate' means 'inborn'. Innate behaviour can be defined as a pattern of inherited, pre-set behaviour that does not require learning or practice. We must assume that the dragonfly nymph does not 'know' what to do in the sense that it does not think about it, nor make decisions. The pattern of behaviour that it shows is simply a result of the 'wiring' of its nervous system, and it is inherited in just the same way as, for example, the growth of its wings, the colour of its body or the structure of its excretory system.

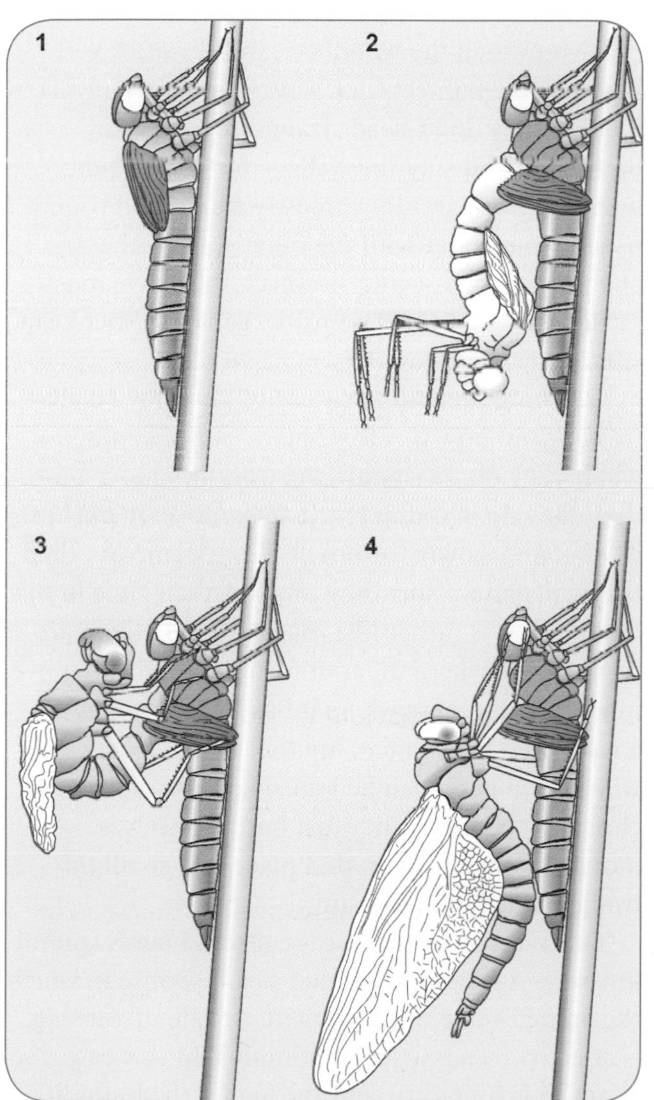

Figure 16.1 A dragonfly nymph follows an innate, complex pattern of behaviour as it changes into an adult.

Genes and behaviour

Truly innate behaviour must be 'hard-wired' into an organism's nervous system. If it is genuinely innate, then it is largely determined by genes.

It is possible to pick out seemingly innate behaviour in most animal species. Some of the simplest types of genetically determined innate behaviour are seen in invertebrates. Three examples are escape reflexes, kineses and taxes.

The escape reflex

In Chapter 2, we saw that a reflex action is a fast, automatic response to a stimulus. An excellent and easily observed example is the **escape reflex** of an earthworm (Figure 16.2).

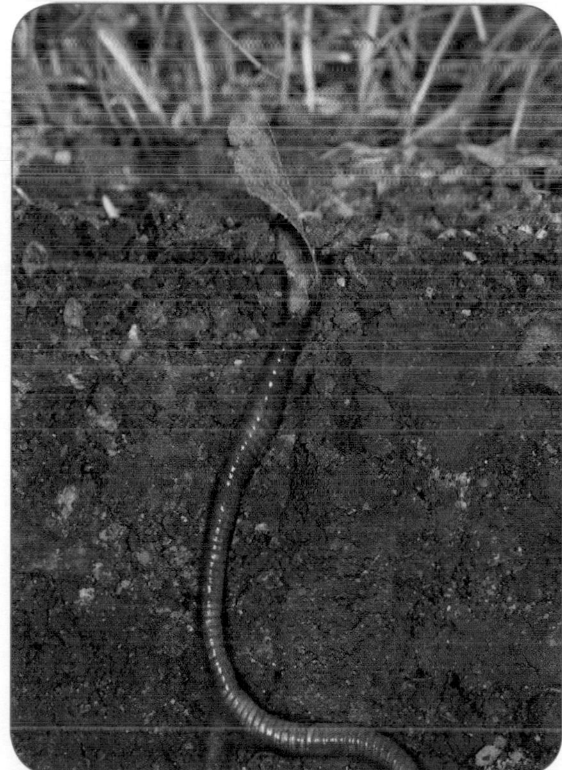

Figure 16.2 A light touch on the front end of an earthworm produces a very fast escape response in which it withdraws into the safety of its burrow.

Earthworms spend most of their time underground, but several species, including *Lumbricus terrestris*, come up to the surface to feed at night or when it is damp. They pull dead leaves down into their burrows, where they can eat them in safety. They have many predators. Birds such as thrushes and blackbirds, and mammals such as hedgehogs and badgers, readily eat earthworms. You have probably seen a thrush or blackbird on a lawn, head cocked, listening and watching for a movement that might mean there is an earthworm close to the entrance of its burrow.

Earthworms do not have eyes that produce images, but they do have numerous other sense organs, including light-sensitive cells and a concentration of highly touch-sensitive receptors in their heads. Neurones run from these receptors to the simple brain at the front of the body, and then along the ventral nerve cord down the whole body length. This nerve cord contains three especially wide axons, which are adapted to allow action potentials to pass along them very swiftly. (Having very wide axons is an alternative method of speeding up a nerve impulse in neurones that are not myelinated.)

If the worm receives a touch on its anterior end, nerve impulses race along these neurones. As they reach the muscles in the body wall, they cause the longitudinal muscles to contract. The worm's body immediately shortens. Its chaetae – tiny stiff bristles on its underside – stick into the wall of its burrow so that this part is anchored as the body contracts. The result is a very rapid withdrawal of the worm into its burrow, away from the danger.

Kineses

You may have carried out some simple experiments into the behaviour of woodlice (Figure 16.3 and Figure 16.4). If you put woodlice into a choice chamber, in which one side is damp and the other is dry, you will probably find that they all eventually end up on the damp side. This has adaptive value because most species of woodlice are not good at conserving water. They need to spend most of their time in areas where humidity is high so as to avoid desiccation.

Figure 16.3 Given the choice, woodlice tend to congregate in damp, dark areas, such as the cracks in this piece of bark.

If you watch the woodlice carefully after you have put them into the choice chamber, you will see that they don't head straight towards the damp side and stay there. They bumble around, wandering apparently aimlessly round and round, usually in contact with the outer wall of the chamber. After a while, however, they have mostly settled down on the damp side, generally in a heap with the other woodlice.

Watching even more carefully, you may be able to work out how it is that the woodlice end up where they do. In dry air, the woodlice move more than they do in damp air. If they move quickly in dry air, and slowly (or not at all) in damp air, then they will end up spending most of their time in the damp air. It is rather like road traffic. If there are some places where the traffic on the road can move quickly, and others where it has been brought to a halt, then the chances are that most of the cars will end up in the traffic jam. Their drivers haven't chosen to be there; they just find themselves moving more slowly in that place and so all the traffic builds up in the jam.

This kind of behaviour is called a **kinesis** (plural kineses). A kinesis is defined as a response in which the animal's rate of movement, or rate of turning, is affected by a particular stimulus. In this case, the stimulus is humidity, and the higher the humidity the slower the rate of movement.

SAQ

1 Woodlice tend to move into dark areas rather than light ones.

a Suggest how a kinesis could cause this effect.

b Suggest the adaptive value of this kinesis.

Hint

Answer

Taxes

In a kinesis, the direction of movement of the animals is not affected by the direction of the stimulus. The woodlice do not move *towards* the damper areas – they just move *less* when they get there.

A **taxis** (plural taxes), however, does involve movement whose direction is related to the direction of the stimulus. A good example is the movement of maggots (fly larvae) away from a light source.

Maggots have simple photoreceptors at their anterior ends (Figure 16.4). If light shines onto them, they move their heads from side to side, 'sampling' the light intensity. They then move towards the direction in which the receptors detect the lowest intensity light. They keep on sampling, and keep on moving, until their movement takes them directly away from the light source.

Learning

At the beginning of the 20th century, many ethologists considered that much of the behaviour they observed, especially in animals other than mammals, was entirely innate. Such behaviour patterns are often stereotyped – that is, they are performed in the same way by all the members of a particular species. The animal has inherited genes that somehow programme its nervous system to carry out this behaviour pattern.

The evolution of this kind of behaviour can be thought of in just the same way as the evolution of any other characteristic. Animals that have alleles that produce behaviour patterns that give them a selective advantage are more likely to survive and breed than animals whose alleles produce less well-adapted behaviour patterns. So, over time and generations, the alleles that produce the behaviour with the greatest survival value become more and more common in a population.

a Kinesis

A response involving changed level of activity

Woodlice tend to spend more time in humid areas, if they have previously been in an area that is too dry.

The woodlouse moves more slowly in more humid conditions and randomly turns more frequently in more humid conditions. The combined effects of this mean the woodlouse will spend most time in the humid area. This response is a hygrokinesis.

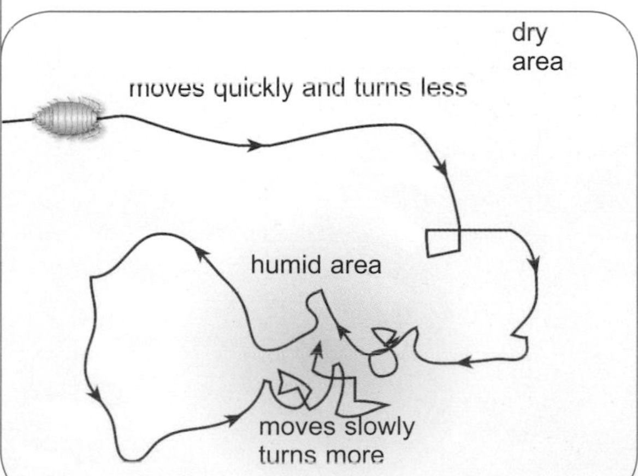

b Taxis

A directional locomotory response

Fly maggots move directly away from a light source. This response is a phototaxis. As it is away from the light, it is a negative phototaxis.

Maggots have two light receptors at the anterior end. As the maggots move they wave their heads from side to side. If the light reaching the two receptors is not equal in strength, the maggot turns. If the light is equal in strength at the two receptors, the maggot keeps moving straight on.

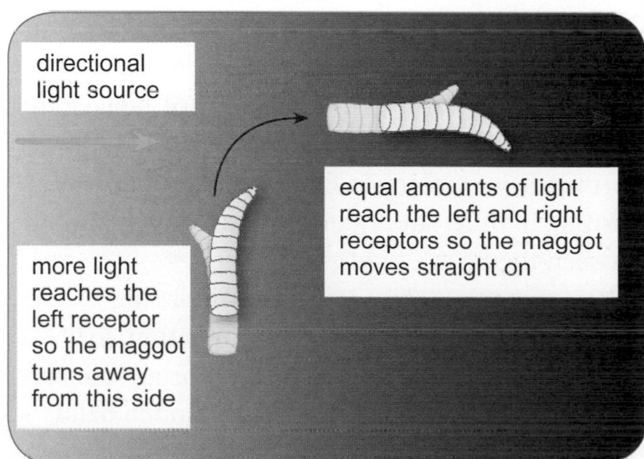

Figure 16.4 Kinesis and taxis.

Today, however, it is recognised that it is not easy to be absolutely sure that a particular pattern of behaviour is *totally* innate. Much of the behaviour of animals is the result of an interaction between genes and the environment. An animal's genes produce the basic structure and physiology of its nervous system and muscles, but the precise development of these may be affected by its environment. The behaviour of the animal is a result of interaction between genetically programmed features and the environment in which it has developed. There is not really a sharp dividing line between innate behaviour and learned behaviour.

What exactly is 'learned behaviour'? There is no single, totally accepted definition, but a useful working description would be that it is behaviour that has been modified by experience. Every animal that has so far been studied (and even some much simpler organisms than animals) has shown some ability to learn.

SAQ

2 Suggest advantages and disadvantages to an animal of having behaviour patterns that are innate, rather than learned. Answer

3 Genes are not the only way in which behaviour patterns can be passed on from generation to generation. How else can this occur? Answer

Different kinds of learning

Biologists have an intrinsic need to classify the things that they study, and the study of behaviour is no different. It makes it easier to understand learning if we can try to find particular kinds of learning in different organisms, and draw parallels between them.

You may think of learning as memorising – learning your biology for an examination, for example. Memory is certainly an important part of learning. Learning and memory go hand in hand. An animal cannot change its behaviour as a result of experience if it does not remember the experience.

Whether or not that memory is conscious is another matter altogether. There is more to learning than memorising. The memory of an animal with a relatively simple nervous system is likely to be of a very different kind from the memory that we can summon up into our consciousness. And even organisms that have no brains – even ones with no nerve cells – can learn (page 260). So conscious learning, involving conscious memory, is certainly not the only kind of learning there is. Even in humans, there is a great deal of evidence that a lot of what we learn is happening outside our consciousness. There is a lot of activity going on in our brains that we never become 'aware of'.

Human brains and behaviour are so complex that we are not the best starting point to try to understand how animals learn. It is often very revealing to look at learning in simpler organisms, where there is less happening and the relationships between stimulus and response are easier to interpret.

Habituation

One species of the marine ragworm, *Nereis*, lives in burrows from which it stretches out its head to capture prey (Figure 16.5). If a shadow passes over it, the worm quickly withdraws back into its tube. This is an innate response – an escape reflex.

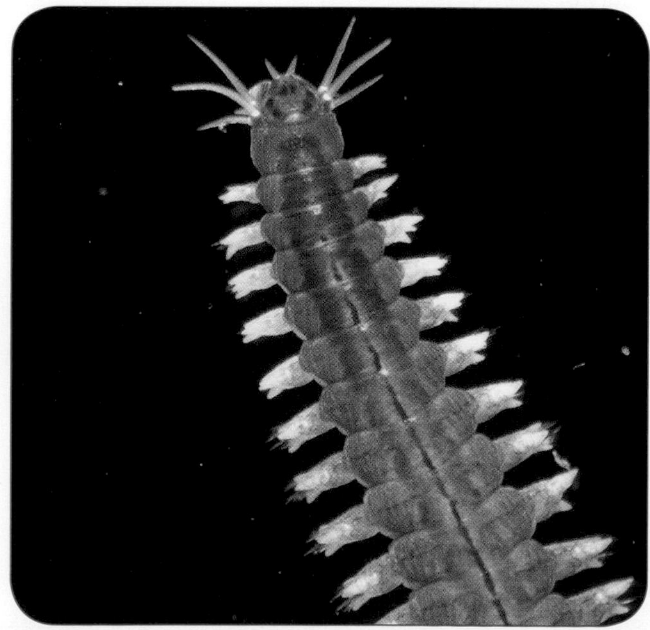

Figure 16.5 The marine ragworm, *Nereis*.

If a similar shadow passes over the worm again and again, and nothing else happens, then the worm eventually stops responding to it (Figure 16.6). It has learned not to respond to this stimulus. Certainly there must be some form of 'memory' in the worm's nervous system, but you should not imagine that it is consciously thinking 'Shadows haven't hurt me before, so I do not need to respond to them'.

SAQ

4 What is the adaptive value to the ragworm of this example of learning?

Answer

Figure 16.6 shows an example of experiments on habituation in ragworms. A group of 20 worms were treated as described above. A shadow was passed over them every minute. The first time, 60% of the worms responded by withdrawing into their tubes. By the eighth shadow, all of them had stopped responding.

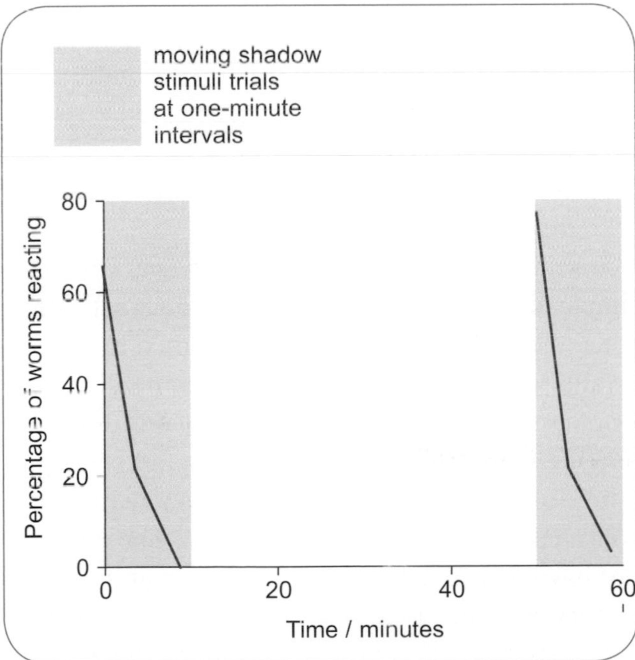

Figure 16.6 Changes in the response of *Nereis* to a moving shadow. During the ten minutes at the start of the experiment, and again during the last ten minutes, a shadow was passed over the worms at one-minute intervals.

The worms were then left for 40 minutes, and the trials repeated. They had apparently completely 'forgotten' the first group of trials, and behaved exactly as they had first time round.

The type of learning shown by *Nereis* is known as **habituation**, and it is the simplest form of learning. The relatively short period of time for which habituation lasts is fairly typical. Another feature of it is that it is very specific – it only applies for that particular stimulus. If, after the ten trials with the moving shadow, the worms were given a different stimulus such as a mechanical shock, they behaved just as though they had never been given any previous stimulus at all (Figure 16.7).

SAQ

5 Suggest possible explanations for only 60% of the worms showing the escape response during the first exposure to shadow during the experiment.

Hint

Answer

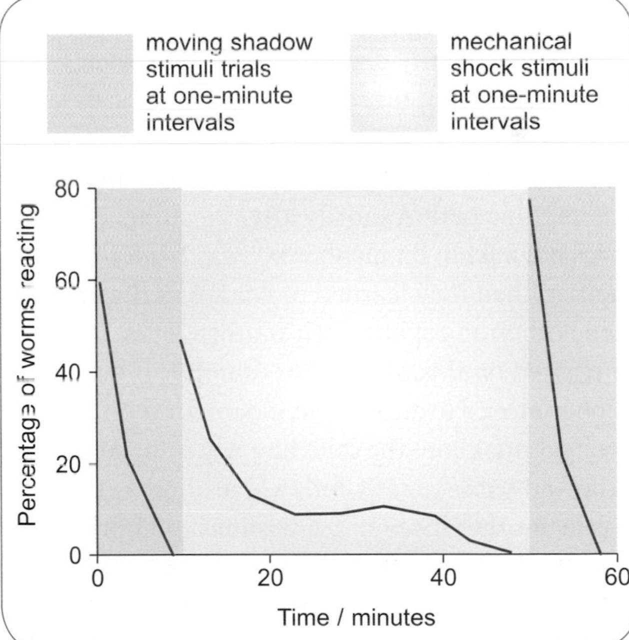

Figure 16.7 Responses of *Nereis* to mechanical shock stimuli after being habituated to a moving shadow.

Imprinting

One of the earliest scientists to study behaviour carefully was Konrad Lorenz. He worked in Austria during the early part of the 20th century, and won the Nobel Prize for Medicine in 1973 for his work on animal behaviour.

Lorenz is perhaps most famous for his work on **imprinting**. Although he was not the first person to recognise this type of behaviour, he brought a rigorous scientific method to its study that enabled us to describe and understand it more.

Imprinting, like most forms of animal behaviour, is impossible to define exactly (because one type of behaviour always grades imperceptibly into another). However, a useful working definition is that it is a modification of behaviour that happens during a relatively short 'window' of time early in an animal's life.

Lorenz used birds for many of his experiments. Hens, ducks and geese all have young (chicks, ducklings and goslings) that are able to run around quite quickly after hatching. In the wild, they quickly learn to keep close to their mother as she moves around to look for food. They stay together as a 'family' for many weeks, until the young have become sufficiently developed to live on their own.

It is clearly important that the young birds learn who their mother is, so they know to stick close to her. Lorenz found that this happened during a critical time period shortly after hatching. If the birds hatched in an incubator, away from their mother, then they learned to behave as though some other object was their mother. They became imprinted on this object. For example, if a wooden cube is moved around in an incubator with a newly hatched duckling, the duckling will imprint on the cube and subsequently follow it around as though it is its mother. Lorenz got goslings to imprint on himself (Figure 16.8).

Imprinting lasts well into adult life. This has proved to be a problem in the captive breeding of animals. It seems that many young animals need to imprint on a member of their own species if they are to recognise a member of this species as a potential mate. Animals that have imprinted on humans may fail to show appropriate sexual behaviour with other members of their own species, and be unable to breed. Captive breeding programmes therefore often involve keeping humans as far as possible from the young animals, or perhaps 'disguising' their keepers and handlers so that they are not recognised as humans.

Figure 16.8 This famous photo shows Konrad Lorenz with a family of goslings. The goslings had imprinted on him and behaved as though he was their mother.

Classical conditioning

A few decades before Lorenz began his experiments into behaviour, Ivan Pavlov had carried out important work on learning in dogs, in his native Russia. He was not initially interested in their behaviour, but was trying to find out about their digestive processes.

Like many experiments, Pavlov's began with a simple observation, in this case that dogs salivate when they are given food. Pavlov wanted to be able to measure the degree of salivation in response to different stimuli, and this was done by making a small hole in a dog's cheek and placing a tube in it so that saliva flowed out and could be collected and measured (Figure 16.9). The dog, not having been fed for some time so that it was hungry, was then placed in a harness and presented with a stimulus. Everything around the dog was controlled – sound, light, temperature and so on. A standard quantity of meat powder was then puffed into the dog's mouth through a tube, and the degree of salivation measured.

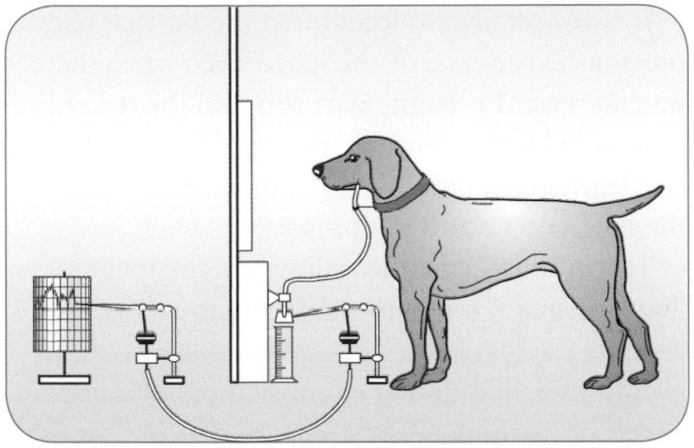

Figure 16.9 One of Pavlov's experiments into classical conditioning. A tube in the dog's cheek collects saliva, and the volume that is collected is recorded on the kymograph drum. Pavlov used this apparatus to investigate the response of the dog's salivary glands to different types and strengths of stimuli.

On succeeding days, before the food was puffed into the dog's mouth, Pavlov provided another stimulus first. He tried different stimuli – perhaps the most famous one is the sound of a bell. He found that at first the dog just pricked up its ears when it heard the bell, but did not salivate. However, after several sessions in which the ringing bell preceded the giving of food, the dog began to salivate when it heard the bell – that is, before the food arrived. The more times this was done, the more saliva the dog produced at the sound of the bell alone, and the more quickly the saliva was produced.

The dog had learned to associate the sound of the bell with the arrival of food. This kind of learning is called **classical conditioning**.

To begin with, the dog had a reflex action – the production of saliva in response to the taste or smell of food. As far as we know, this is an innate reaction – the dog was just born with it and did not have to learn it. The stimulus of the taste or smell of food is known as the 'unconditioned' stimulus. The new stimulus that the dog learned to associate with food – the sound of the bell – is known as the 'conditioned' stimulus. The whole reflex – that is, the response to the new stimulus – is called a **conditioned reflex**.

Operant conditioning

Even though Pavlov's experiments were very well controlled, he found that his dogs were learning rather more than he had intended. For example, hungry dogs quickly realised that they were going to be fed when the experimenter came to take them to the laboratory and would run ahead, tail wagging, ready to be placed in their harness. This involves a more complex process than is measured with the salivation reflex, because here the dog is making a decision about where and how to move. Such an activity, where an animal learns to carry out a behaviour that makes something good happen to it (or something bad not happen to it), is known as **operant conditioning**.

Experiments on operant conditioning sometimes involve a so-called 'Skinner box' (Figure 16.10), after B. F. Skinner who carried out some important experiments on operant conditioning. This is a cage in which an animal can be placed, containing a bar that the animal can press, or a key that it can peck. A reward of some kind – often food – is provided when the animal carries out this action.

At first, the animal simply moves around in its box looking for a way out. Eventually, often just by chance, it presses the bar and a reward appears. After this has happened once, twice or a few times, the animal begins purposefully to press the bar. It has learned to associate this behaviour with the reward.

Figure 16.10 A rat in a Skinner box. The photo was taken in the 1930s, when experiments into operant conditioning were first carried out.

Similar results are seen if, instead of being presented with a reward, the animal avoids something unpleasant by pressing the bar. For example, a rat in a Skinner box will quickly learn to press a bar to switch off a very bright light just above its head, or to avoid a mild electric shock.

The adaptive value of conditioning

Both classical conditioning and operant conditioning can be described as **associative learning**. In each case, the animal learns to associate a stimulus or an action that previously had meant nothing to it with some rewarding result. It changes its behaviour in such a way that the rewarding result – often known as a **reinforcer** – is achieved more often.

It is not too difficult to see that associative learning has an adaptive value. An animal that can learn in this way may have a better chance of survival than one that does not. For example, imagine a young insect-eating bird that tries to eat a wasp. This is likely to be an unpleasant experience, and the bird quickly learns to associate yellow and black stripes with something that is best not tasted. In the future, it will probably avoid not only real wasps, but also yellow and black caterpillars, yellow and black beetles and anything else that has yellow and black stripes or bands.

Latent learning

Some kinds of learning, however, have no obvious association with the acquiring of a reward or the avoidance of something unpleasant. For example, if you put a rat into a maze, it will just run around randomly. It apparently has no reason to learn anything – there is no reward or unpleasant stimulus in one particular part of the maze. As far as the rat is concerned, there is no advantage in going in any one direction more than another.

But learning has been going on. We can take this rat, and another rat that has never been in the maze, and put them each into mazes that are identical with the first one. This time, there is a reward in one particular position in the maze. Each time the rat finds the reward, the rat is taken out. Each time it is replaced in the maze, it finds the reward a little faster than on the first occasion.

It is almost always found that the rat that had previous experience of the maze, even when there was no reward present, learns to find the reward more quickly than the inexperienced rat. The rat had learned the pattern of the maze even when there was no reward in doing so.

This is called **latent learning**. 'Latent' means 'hidden', and it refers to the fact that we can't actually *see* that learning is taking place at all. It is only later, in different circumstances, that the effects of learning become apparent.

Insight learning

In 1927, Wolfgang Kohler wrote a book called *The Mentality of Apes*. This book described his work on the behaviour of chimpanzees. Some of the results of his experiments indicated that relatively 'intelligent' animals, such as primates, can learn in a more complex way than the types of associative learning we have so far looked at.

One of Kohler's chimps was called Sultan. When a banana was placed on the ground outside his cage, Sultan quickly learned to use a long stick to reach the banana and work it into his cage, where he would eat it. When he had learned to do this, Kohler gave him not one but two sticks that could be made to fit together end-to-end. Again a banana was placed outside his cage, but this time too far away to be reached with one stick.

Sultan tried to reach the banana with one stick, and failed. He then tried putting one stick down outside the cage, and pushing it forward with the second stick until it touched the banana. But of course he could not rake the banana back. After an hour or so, he eventually gave up and moved off to a different part of the cage to play, taking his two sticks with him.

While playing, Sultan suddenly discovered that the end of one stick could be pushed into the end of the other. Straight away, he rushed back to the side of the cage and used his extended stick to rake in the banana.

Other chimps showed similar abilities – for example, discovering that they could stack up boxes and stand on them to take a banana hanging above their reach.

This type of learning seems to be something altogether more complex than the simple associative learning described by Pavlov or seen in a Skinner box. It has been termed **insight learning**, because it seems as though inspiration suddenly struck the chimps, often while they were doing something not directly connected with obtaining the food. Some form of reasoning seemed to be going on in the animals' brains. They worked out how a particular pattern of behaviour might solve a problem.

Many investigators see insight learning in chimps as evidence that the chimps are *thinking* about the problem, in a similar way to the ways that we go about problem-solving. Perhaps the chimps think through the possible things that they might do to reach the high banana, and work out in their heads that *this* action might produce *that* result. From watching other forms of behaviour in chimps, many biologists would agree that this is probably true. We do not find it difficult to imagine that the processes going on inside a chimpanzee's brain might be similar to what we know happens inside our own brain. You do not necessarily need language to think out the solution to a problem.

However, it is not easy to be sure that insight learning really does provide evidence of rational thinking. A real difficulty with an experiment into insight behaviour is that it cannot, by its very nature, be repeated. The description of Sultan's use of two sticks to reach the banana is really no more than an anecdote – a story describing something interesting happening, that does not have the rigour and repeatability that we would ideally like to see from a scientific investigation. The chimp's behaviour could just have happened by chance.

Other experiments suggest that insight learning can occur in several species of birds, including pigeons. For example, some pigeons were trained to push a box towards a green spot on the floor of their cage, but not to push the box if there was no green spot. This was done by rewarding them for the action when there was a green spot, but not when there wasn't a green spot. They were also trained to stand on a box placed underneath a banana hanging above them, so that they could reach it and peck at it.

When each pigeon was put into a cage with a box but no green spot, and a banana hanging above it, the pigeon first of all tried to reach the banana by standing on the floor underneath the banana. Then, quite suddenly, as though it had just 'seen' the solution, the pigeon pushed the box underneath the banana and stood on the box.

This behaviour is not all that different from that of Sultan. So, do pigeons show insight learning? Do birds think rationally? Only pigeons that had been taught both to push a box and to stand on one to reach a banana were able to come up with the solution of pushing the box underneath the banana. Pigeons that had been taught just one of these actions never did find a solution to the problem. So the pigeons' prior learning was certainly very important in bringing about this new response. But whether or not any conscious, rational thought was going on in their brains is a question that is very difficult to answer.

Primate behaviour

We are primates, a group that we share with lemurs, monkeys, chimpanzees, gorillas, orang-utans and gibbons. As a group, primates show some of the most complex behaviour shown by any animals.

Many, but by no means all, primates are social animals. They live in close groups, interacting with one another in many different ways. We can see many parallels between the social behaviour of some species of primates and our own. In particular, chimpanzees have wide-ranging social behaviour that can provide a mirror in which we can see some aspects of our behaviour from a different angle. Much of what we know about the social behaviour of chimps was first discovered by Jane Goodall, who studied chimps in the wild at Gombe in Tanzania over many years. You may like to find out about this amazing scientist and her work – the Jane Goodall Institute at www.janegoodall.org is a good starting point.

Many different kinds of animals, not just primates, live in groups. Perhaps the most well known are ants, wasps and bees, most of which live in complex societies in which each individual has a particular role to play. By sharing out different tasks between workers, queen and drones, ants are hugely successful and are some of the commonest animals in a very wide range of habitats. The relationships between the different members of the groups are called **social relationships**, involving interactions between individuals within the society.

The benefits of social behaviour

There are very many benefits to be had from living in a group. Different tasks can be shared out between different individuals (Figure 16.11). Between them, the group may be much more successful at finding food, avoiding predators or defending their territory than one animal on its own could be.

Chimpanzees have complex and highly developed brains, so it is not surprising that their social behaviour is also very complex. There are two species, *Pan troglodytes* (the common chimp) and *Pan paniscus* (bonobos). We'll look at some aspects of social behaviour in *P. troglodytes* and consider how this behaviour gives them a survival advantage.

Chimpanzees spend most of their time in the company of other chimpanzees. Within an area, there may be several hundred individuals that make up the community. Different groups form and break up within this community, forming temporary groups whose membership may change quite frequently. The groups may be all male or all female or – most frequently – a mix of both sexes.

Figure 16.11 Meerkats take turns to be on sentry duty, while others in the group look after the young in a crèche or look for food.

If you watch a group of chimps, it is immediately obvious that they pay a great deal of attention to each other. This is typical social behaviour – they don't just happen to be in the same place at the same time but are in constant communication. The behaviour of each individual is greatly affected by the behaviour of others in the group. Chimps have very mobile, expressive faces and their facial expressions are important in communication. A large 'grin' with closed lips indicates that a chimp has seen or heard something unexpected and frightening, and other chimps will react by showing fear responses themselves. Body postures – body language – are also important in communication, as are vocalisations such as hoots and grunts. Each chimp has a particular place and rank in the society, so that some are more dominant and others more subordinate. These rankings are maintained in several ways – for example, by grooming relationships – and this helps to keep the group together and stable (Figure 16.12). Each young chimp grows up knowing its place in the society.

Figure 16.12 Grooming helps to maintain social rankings in chimpanzee society.

What are the advantages to chimps of this kind of social behaviour? Chimps are largely herbivorous, eating fruits and other plant material, but they do occasionally hunt for meat – red colobus monkeys are a favourite prey. Living in a group means that searching for food becomes more efficient. If one member of the group finds a good food source, then all the others become aware of it and can share. The group can also cooperate to defend a particularly good food source against other groups.

Another clear benefit of group living is protection from predators. There is a high chance that at least one chimp in a group will become aware of a predator before it strikes, and can warn the others. The group also has a better chance of fighting off an attack from a predator than a chimp on its own.

Living in a socially cohesive group increases an individual chimp's likelihood of mating and having young. This is especially important for males, whose reproductive success appears to be limited by their access to females. The reproductive success of females is limited by their access to food. For both sexes, group living makes it more likely that they will breed, passing on their genes to the next generation.

Chimp societies do not only pass on their genes to the next generation, but also their behaviour. Particular behaviour patterns learned by individuals in a group will be picked up and copied by the young. Chimps are highly intelligent, and have a great capacity for learning. For example, in one area the chimps use long, thin branches from which they have stripped off the leaves to extract termites from their nests – they push a stick into the nest and then gently pull out the stick, to which termites are likely to be clinging (Figure 16.13). We don't know when this behaviour first began, but we can imagine it might have been a case of insight learning, perhaps in just one chimp. Others copied the behaviour, and now it is passed on to each generation. This is called cultural learning. It can really only happen in animals that live in social groups.

Figure 16.13 These chimpanzees are fishing for termites using simple tools that they have made.

Genes and human behaviour

Like chimpanzees, we are social animals. Much of our behaviour is influenced by others, with whom we are in constant communication. A great deal of our behaviour is due to cultural learning. We have long childhoods, during which we gradually learn how to behave in ways that fit us into the society in which we live. We all need to feel that we belong somewhere. Our behaviour as adults has been shown to be significantly influenced by our childhood experiences.

But human behaviour is hugely complex, and no-one would suggest that everything we do is a result of the influence of what happened to us as we grew up. We like to feel that we are able to make choices in our behaviour and are in control of it – we make conscious decisions about what to do and how to do it. The ways in which these decisions are made is of enormous interest, and the subject of a great deal of research.

With such complex brains and such a complex society with such extensive communications, it would be reasonable to think that our genes have only a minor effect on how we behave. But, perhaps surprisingly, an increasing number of studies suggest that this is not so and that particular alleles of particular genes can have significant effects on our behaviour. One such gene is one of several that codes for dopamine receptors.

Dopamine is a neurotransmitter found in the brain. It is involved in the autonomic nervous system. Given as a drug, it increases the activity of the sympathetic neurones, causing effects such as an increase in heart rate.

Like acetylcholine, dopamine is released from the presynaptic membrane at a synapse and diffuses across the synaptic cleft to slot into receptors in the postsynaptic membrane. So far, five different types of dopamine receptors have been discovered. They are all G-protein coupled receptors (*Biology 1*, page 27). One of them, called the **DRD4 receptor**, has shown some interesting possible links with behaviour.

The DRD4 receptor is coded for by a gene that is known to have at least 18 different alleles. Various studies have shown that people with particular alleles of this gene have a greater risk of developing attention deficit hyperactivity disorder (ADHD). This is a condition seen mostly in young children, characterised by an inability to concentrate for any length of time and a tendency to act on impulse. Other studies have also linked these alleles with intelligence, with novelty-seeking behaviour, with obesity and the likelihood of drug addiction.

However, the results of these studies are not clear-cut. They are carried out by looking for particular alleles of particular genes in people showing a particular characteristic, and then looking for correlations between the presence of an allele and the presence of a characteristic. Quite often, a particular study shows no association, and it is only when you put together the results from a very large number of different studies that a statistically significant correlation can be picked up. It certainly is not the case that having a particular allele of the DRD4 gene makes you become a drug addict or obese. It is much more likely that this allele, together with many other alleles of many other genes, increases the risk of developing these traits. The next step will be to try to find out *how* the DRD4 alleles might be having these effects. What are they actually doing in the brain, and how is this affecting behaviour? The answers are likely to be very complex.

Even slime moulds can learn

How easy do you find it to learn? Humans have the greatest capacity of all organisms to learn, and we have the most highly developed brains of all animals. It is estimated that we have around 100 billion neurones in our brain. The number of possible connection pathways between these neurones is practically infinite. We believe that learning involves the formation of new synapses between neurones, or the strengthening of particular pathways between them.

So just how many neurones do you need in order to be able to learn? The answer is 'none'. Recent experiments have shown that even a slime mould, which has not a single neurone, can learn.

At the beginning of this book, in Chapter 1, you may have read about the life history of a slime mould. Japanese researchers have found that they can 'teach' a slime mould to remember and anticipate a stimulus.

The slime mould that they used moves around very slowly, at about one centimetre per hour. It moves more slowly in dry air than in moist air. In the laboratory, they passed dry air over the slime mould for a very short time, and then repeated this each hour for the next two hours. The slime mould duly slowed down each time the dry air passed over it. And it did the same after one more hour when the next experience of dry air would have been due – even though the researchers did not do anything to it at this point. Some slime moulds did this on the next hour and then the next one – three more times, even after the dry air stimulus was no longer being applied.

If the stimulus stopped being applied for some time, then the slime mould stopped slowing down and just went back to moving normally. But then, if the dry air stimulus was applied again, it clearly 'remembered' what had happened before; just a single dry air stimulus now elicited the hourly slowing down pattern again.

How can such a simple organism learn? What is going on in its apparently simple cells? We

continued

don't know. However, it is fairly certain that it is something to with the slime mould's biological clock. We all have systems in our cells that 'oscillate' in a regular pattern with time. This is the basis of our body clock, which results in changes in hormonal concentrations and other features at different times of day and night. Slime moulds have a simple body clock, too.

The researchers think that the regular exposure to dry air somehow modifies the slime mould's body clock, so that a new rhythm is imposed on it. We have no idea, though, how it is that this is 'remembered'. Finding out how a simple organism such a slime mould learns could give us useful starting points for looking at our own, greatly more complex, methods of learning.

Summary

Glossary

- Innate behaviour is inbuilt, genetically determined and 'hard-wired' into an organism's nervous system. It provides a basic pattern of behaviour that helps an organism to survive in its environment from a very early age, before any learning has taken place.
- Reflexes are automatic, stereotyped responses to a particular stimulus. Many reflexes, such as the escape reflex of an earthworm, are very rapid and help an organism to react to danger.
- A kinesis is a response by an organism to differences in the environmental factors around it, such that it moves faster or turns less often where the factor is less conducive to survival. This results in the organism spending more time where the factor is favourable.
- A taxis is a response by an organism resulting in it moving towards, or away from, an environmental stimulus such as light.
- The modification of behaviour as a result of experience is known as learning.
- Habituation is a simple form of learning in which an organism fails to continue to respond to a stimulus if this is repeated several times without anything harmful or beneficial happening to the organism.
- Imprinting is a form of learning in which, during a particular 'window' of time early in its development, an organism comes to treat a particular object or organism as something to which it should remain close, as though it were its mother. Imprinting usually has an effect that lasts throughout the organism's life.
- Conditioning is a form of learning in which an organism learns to associate a particular stimulus with a beneficial or harmful event, and changes its behaviour accordingly. In classical conditioning, a reflex action is elicited by a new stimulus that is associated with the original one – for example, the salivation reflex can be elicited by a ringing bell which comes to be associated with food. In operant conditioning, the organism learns to modify its behaviour in order to achieve a reward or avoid something unpleasant – for example, a pigeon learning to peck a lever in order to obtain food.
- Latent learning occurs when an organism learns within an environment where there is no apparent reward; the learning only becomes apparent in a subsequent situation where a reward can be obtained through the organism's behaviour.
- Insight learning is the apparently spontaneous bringing together of previously learned behaviours to produce a new response that brings reward.

continued

- Primates live in social groups in which there is a great deal of communication between the members. Advantages include greater likelihood of finding a mate and being able to breed; better vigilance and therefore a greater chance of spotting predators; greater fighting power and therefore ability to deal with predators or defend territory against other groups; greater likelihood of finding good food sources; and the ability to pass on advantageous learned behaviour culturally, from one generation to the next.
- There is some evidence that particular alleles of particular genes may have effects on human behaviour. For example, certain alleles of the DHD4 gene appear to be correlated with a slightly greater likelihood of developing ADHD, novelty-seeking behaviour, drug addiction and obesity.

Stretch and challenge questions

1 Compare and contrast tropisms, kineses and taxes. Hint

2 Classical conditioning and operant conditioning are both examples of associative learning. Explain what is meant by this term, and discuss the potential benefits of classical and operant conditioning to the survival of an animal in its natural environment. Hint

Questions

1 The diagram shows an apparatus called a double-choice learning box with sound-proofed walls and doors.

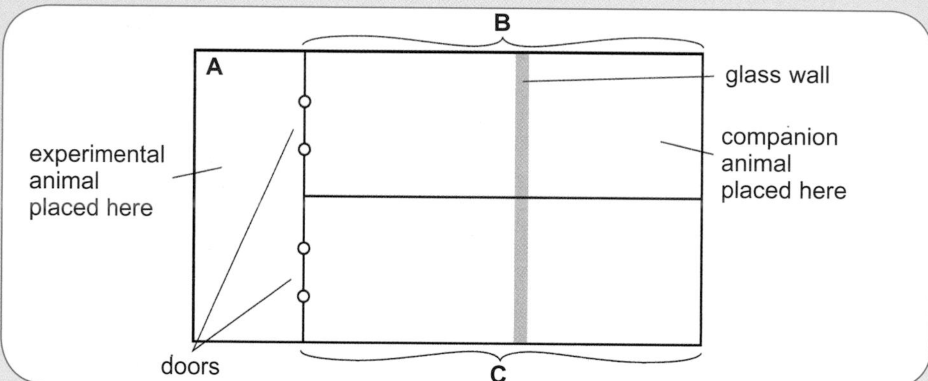

- Two young mice were kept in separate, identical home cages and were accustomed to being handled.
- One mouse was used as the experimental subject and the other acted as a companion.
- The companion mouse was placed in chamber B behind a glass wall.
- Chamber C was left empty.
- The experimental mouse was placed in chamber A and the stop clock was started.
- The time taken for the experimental mouse to enter chamber B or C was noted.
- The experimental mouse was allowed to explore chamber B or C for 10 seconds and was then removed.
- The experiment was repeated a further 14 times with the same two mice.

continued

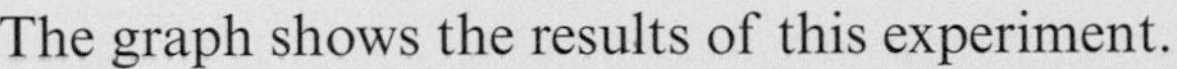

The graph shows the results of this experiment.

chamber B

Time taken to enter chamber / s

chamber C

250 200 150 100 50 0 50 100 150 200 250

1 2 3 4 5 6 7 8 9 10 11 12 13

Trial number

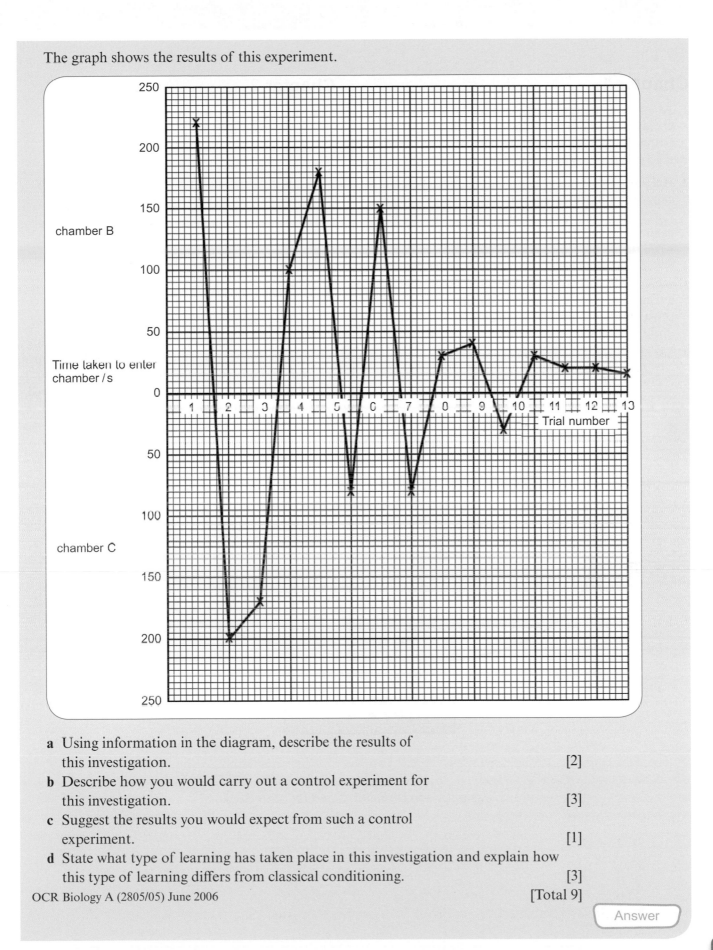

a Using information in the diagram, describe the results of this investigation. [2]

b Describe how you would carry out a control experiment for this investigation. [3]

c Suggest the results you would expect from such a control experiment. [1]

d State what type of learning has taken place in this investigation and explain how this type of learning differs from classical conditioning. [3]

OCR Biology A (2805/05) June 2006 [Total 9]

Answer

Answers to SAQs

Chapter 1

1 At low temperatures, particles have less kinetic energy. They move more slowly, so collisions are less frequent and less energetic. This reduces the rate of reactions between particles.

2 Animals that maintain a constant body temperature can remain active during both day and night, even if the external temperature falls at night. Animals that cannot regulate their temperature can only be active when their body temperature is sufficiently high, which is likely to be only at certain times of day. The same is true for activity at different times of year; in a temperate climate, animals that cannot maintain a constant body temperature are unlikely to be active during the winter.

3 See the figure at the bottom of this page.

Chapter 2

1
- Motor neurones have a single long axon, while sensory neurones have a long axon and a long dendron.
- Motor neurones have many short dendrites – short cytoplasmic processes from the cell body – but sensory neurones do not have these.

2 There are many different possible answers to each section of this question.

3 a The line should be drawn at about −70 mV.

b The inside of the axon has a charge of −70 mV compared with the outside.

c By active transport using ATP to power the sodium–potassium pumps in the membrane of the axon. Both sodium and potassium ions are positively charged. Three sodium ions are pumped out for every two potassium ions pumped in, so this builds up a positive charge outside compared with inside the axon.

continued

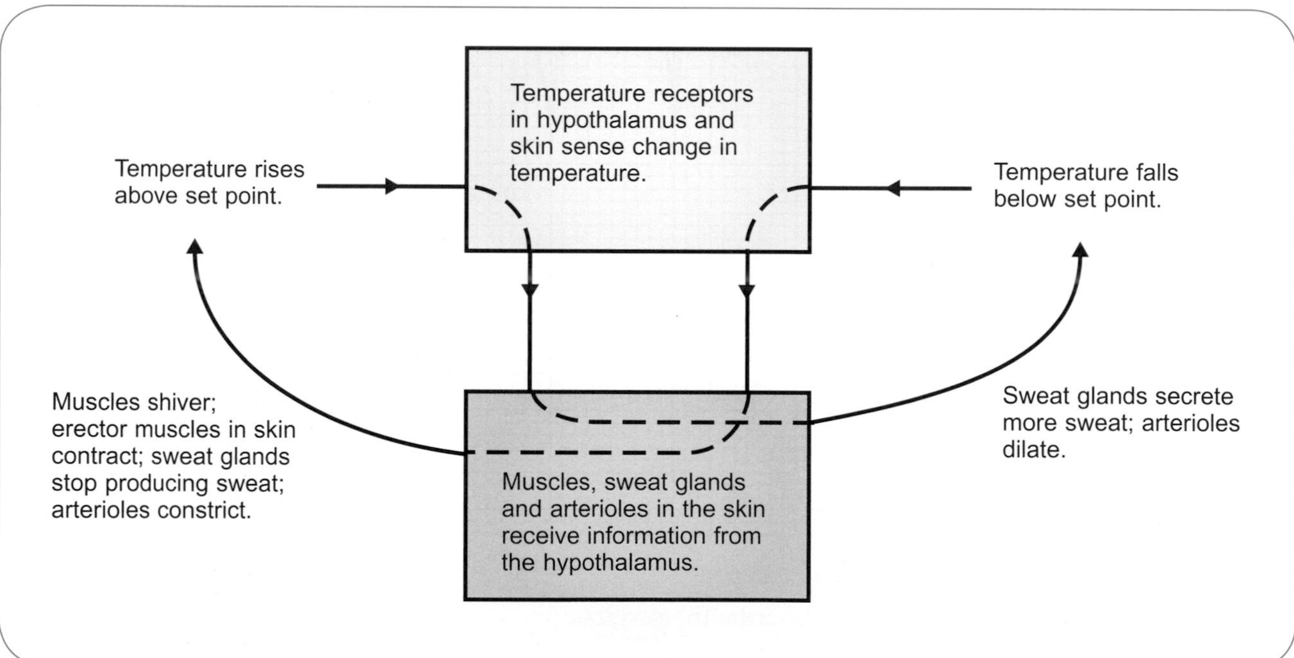

d i It is called depolarisation because the axon was polarised so that it had a negative charge inside and a positive charge outside. Now this is altered and there is a negative charge outside and a positive charge inside.

ii Sodium channels in the membrane open and allow sodium ions to flow in down their electrochemical gradient. As they enter the axon, their positive charge causes the negative charge inside the axon to be brought to zero and then continue to become more positive until it reaches about 40 mV.

e Between 1 ms and 2 ms the axon is repolarised. The sodium channels close again, and potassium channels open. Potassium ions flood out of the axon and therefore make the outside more positive than the inside. The potential overshoots the resting potential, temporarily becoming even more negative inside than it was before. Then the sodium–potassium pump kicks in again and the resting potential is restored (see Figure 2.9 on page 16).

f About 4 ms.

Chapter 3

1 Steroids are soluble in lipids, so they can diffuse through the phospholipid bilayer. Protein hormones are not lipid-soluble.

2 The adrenal glands can keep on secreting new adrenaline over a long period of time.

3 Glucose stimulates beta cells to produce insulin; insulin stimulates muscle cells and adipose tissue to put more glucose transporters in their plasma membranes; insulin stimulates liver cells to produce glycogen from glucose; glucagon stimulates liver cells to break down glycogen; glucagon stimulates gluconeogenesis in liver cells.

4 Both processes involve opening or closure of ion channels in the plasma membrane, in response to a signal. In both, there is a potential difference across the membrane, negative inside when at rest. In both, the arrival of a signal molecule (a neurotransmitter or glucose) causes this potential difference to become less, and this causes other ion channels to open.

However, in a neurone the signal can also be the arrival of an action potential. In the synaptic knob of a presynaptic neurone, calcium channels are opened when an action potential arrives there, and calcium channels also open in a beta cell. However, in a neurone along which an action potential is travelling, and at a postsynaptic membrane, the ion channels that open are sodium channels, while in a beta cell they are calcium channels.

In both processes, the opening of calcium channels causes vesicles containing a chemical (neurotransmitter in the presynaptic neurone, insulin in a beta cell) to move to the plasma membrane and to fuse with it, emptying their contents.

5 a i The glucose in the drink travels swiftly through the alimentary canal and is absorbed through the walls of the small intestine. It takes about 10 minutes for the glucose to be detected in a blood sample. The rise is spread out over 20 minutes because it takes time for all of the glucose to be absorbed.

ii As the blood glucose level begins to rise, this is detected by beta cells in the pancreas, and they respond by secreting insulin.

iii The blood glucose level falls in part because insulin increases the rate at which glucose is taken from the blood by cells in the liver, muscles and adipose tissue. Another reason for the fall is that cells use the glucose in respiration.

iv There is a time lag between the fall of glucose concentration in the blood, its detection by the beta cells and their response (secreting less insulin).

b i In the second graph, blood glucose levels continue rising until 60 minutes, in contrast to the first graph where they stop increasing at 20 minutes. In the person with diabetes, the blood glucose level reaches a maximum value of $195\,\text{mg}\,100\,\text{cm}^{-3}$, almost twice as great as the value of $110\,\text{mg}\,100\,\text{cm}^{-3}$ seen in the person without diabetes. It also fell more slowly, and had reached $110\,\text{mg}\,100\,\text{cm}^{-3}$ by the end of the experiment, in contrast with the person without diabetes for whom it fell to $65\,\text{mg}\,100\,\text{cm}^{-3}$ by this time.

ii The pattern of blood insulin concentration in the person without diabetes follows a similar pattern to that for blood glucose. It rises higher in the person with diabetes, and then plateaus at its highest value (200 arbitrary units) at 90 minutes, 30 minutes later than in the person without diabetes. By the end of the experiment at 240 minutes, the blood insulin concentration in the person with diabetes has only fallen to 90 arbitrary units, whilst in the person without diabetes it is only just above its starting value by this time.

iii In the person with diabetes, it appears that the pancreas is secreting insulin normally – that is, more insulin is secreted as the blood glucose concentration increases. However, this rise in insulin appears to be having very little effect on the blood glucose concentration. In the person without diabetes, the graph shows that as insulin concentration rises the glucose concentration soon falls. Because the insulin secreted by the person with diabetes does not reduce blood glucose concentration, insulin continues to be secreted at high levels, until something else brings the blood glucose concentration down.

6 There will only be glucose in urine when it has risen above a particular level in the blood, so testing urine for glucose won't tell you anything about blood glucose levels below this value. Glucose in urine has moved into the urine from the blood over a period of time, whereas if you test blood directly for glucose you know what the blood value is at a particular moment in time.

7 a Bread contains starch, which is made up of thousands of alpha glucose units linked together. When the bread is eaten, amylase in the saliva begins to hydrolyse the starch to maltose. When the food reaches the small intestine, amylase from pancreatic juice continues the conversion of starch to maltose, and then the maltose itself is hydrolysed to glucose by maltase. Only then can the glucose be absorbed. This explains the fact that a peak in blood glucose concentration does not occur until 30 minutes after the bread has been ingested.

The fall from 30 minutes up to 120 minutes will have been brought about by increased secretion of insulin by the beta cells in the islets of Langerhans in the pancreas. This takes a short while to happen, which is why the blood glucose does not begin to fall until 30 minutes after ingestion.

b All three foods produced a maximum level of blood glucose after 30 minutes. This maximum increase was much lower in the lentils and soya, at 13 and 5 mg 100 cm^{-3} respectively, compared with a value of 52 mg 100 cm^{-3} when bread was eaten. The blood glucose level then fell very rapidly for bread, but much less so for lentils and soya, and these continued to provide a relatively steady blood glucose level throughout the rest of the 120 minutes. At the end of this time, the blood glucose increases for bread and soya were identical at −2 mg 100 cm^{-3}, while that for lentils was still relatively high at 11 mg 100 cm^{-3}.

c It appears that the carbohydrate in the lentils and soya is less easy to digest, so it takes longer for glucose to be produced and for it to be absorbed into the blood. This would explain the fact that the blood glucose level did not rise as quickly, and, for lentils, stayed at a relatively high value throughout the rest of the experiment; we can guess that it might have continued at this level for some time afterwards.

Another possibility is that some of the carbohydrate in the lentils and soya could be cellulose, which we are not able to digest at all.

Another possibility is that some of the carbohydrate in the lentils and soya was made up of monosaccharides other than glucose – fructose, for example.

8 High carbon dioxide levels or low oxygen levels indicate that body tissues are respiring rapidly. They therefore require fast deliveries of oxygen (and perhaps also respiratory substrates such as glucose). This can be achieved by a raised heart rate, pushing blood around the circulatory system more rapidly and therefore delivering more oxygen per unit time to the tissues, and removing more carbon dioxide.

Chapter 4

1 The blood in the hepatic artery will contain more carbon dioxide and may also contain more dissolved nutrients, such as glucose or amino acids.

2 a The ammonia will quickly dissolve in the large volumes of water around them, and be so diluted that it will not harm the fish.

b Turning ammonia into urea requires energy in the form of ATP, so by excreting ammonia rather than urea energy is saved.

3 A large percentage of the water in the fluid is reabsorbed in the proximal convoluted tubule, so the volume of water in which the urea is dissolved decreases. This decrease in the volume of water is greater than the decrease in the quantity of urea, so this increases the concentration of urea in the fluid.

4 a The *y*-axis is shown as 'number of times greater'. This is done because the actual concentrations of each substance are very different from each other, so each would need a separate scale. It is also a logarithmic scale, so that it can accommodate a very wide range of values. It has no 0, because a value of ×1 means 'no greater'. Values above 1 represent an increase in concentration, and values below 1 represent a decrease.

b Amino acids and glucose are virtually all reabsorbed into the blood from the proximal convoluted tubule.

A small amount of urea is reabsorbed in the proximal convoluted tubule, but its concentration increases because there is now less water present. As more water is reabsorbed throughout the loop of Henlé, the concentration of urea continues to increase.

Although both sodium ions and potassium ions are reabsorbed in the proximal convoluted tubule, their concentration does not change because water is also reabsorbed here. The concentrations of both increase as they go down the descending limb of the loop of Henlé, because water is lost from here by osmosis into the tissue fluid around it. As the fluid passes up the ascending limb, sodium ions are actively pumped out, so their concentration inside the tubule decreases. More water is lost in the distal convoluted tubule and collecting duct, so the concentrations of both ions increase. (Potassium ions are actively transported into the distal convoluted tubule, which explains why their concentration rises more than that of sodium ions.)

5 Flow rate is highest at the beginning of the proximal convoluted tubule, where fluid is entering via filtration into the renal capsule. As the fluid flows along the proximal convoluted tubule, a large percentage of it is reabsorbed, thus decreasing its volume. There is thus less fluid to flow, so less passes a given point in unit time; in other words, its flow rate decreases.

This reabsorption happens all along the nephron, which is why the flow rate continues to drop. The rate of flow decreases rapidly in the collecting duct, as a high proportion of the water may be reabsorbed here.

6 a There appears to be a positive correlation between the percentage of long loops of Henlé and the dryness of a mammal's environment. For example, desert mice have 100% long loops, while beavers (which spend a lot of time in fresh water) have none.

b There appears to be a positive correlation between the percentage of long loops of Henlé and the maximum concentration of urine that can be produced. However, jerboas don't quite fit this pattern: they have only 33% long loops but still produce urine of a higher concentration than desert mice, which have 100% long loops.

c Long loops of Henlé can produce very high concentrations (low water potentials) in the kidney medulla. The lower the water potential here, the more water can be drawn out of the collecting duct rather than being lost in urine. Animals that live in conditions where water is in short supply therefore benefit by having long loops of Henlé because more of their water can be kept in the body and less lost in urine.

7 If this region changes colour, it shows that the dipstick is working – that is, that urine has moved up the stick and that the antibodies on the stick are present and active.

8 a Na^+, K^+, Mg^{2+}, urea.

b Ca^{2+}, HCO_3^-, glucose.

c Water.

d If there was no glucose in the dialysis fluid, all the glucose would be lost from the patient's blood. Her cells would have no respiratory substrate and would not be able to respire and make ATP.

e Most of it will have come from the carbon dioxide produced by respiring cells; carbon dioxide dissociates and reacts with water to form hydrogencarbonate ions.

f Blood proteins such as fibrinogen and immunoglobulins (antibodies), which have molecules too big to pass through the dialysis membrane.

Chapter 5

1 a Chlorophyll absorbs red and blue light, but only a very small amount of green light. We therefore see the green light that is reflected from it.

b Carotenoids absorb blue and green light, but do not absorb yellow or red. They therefore appear yellow, orange or red.

2 See the table at the top of page 268.

3 They can all be used in the light-dependent stage. The ADP and inorganic phosphate can be used to make more ATP, in photophosphorylation. The NADP can be reduced.

4 The light-dependent reactions are fuelled by energy from light. Their rate depends almost entirely on the amount of light available, not temperature.

5 a The first part, as it rises.

b This shows that the plant cannot make use of these higher levels of carbon dioxide. Some other factor – possibly light intensity – is holding it back and acting as the limiting factor.

2

	Cyclic photophosphorylation	Non-cyclic photophosphorylation
Is PSI involved?	yes	yes
Is PSII involved?	no	yes
Where does PSI obtain replacement electrons from?	from the electron that it emitted itself	from the electron emitted from PSII
Where does PSII obtain replacement electrons from?	n/a	from the photolysis of water
Is ATP made?	yes	yes
Is reduced NADP made?	no	yes

6 a As there is no light, ATP and NADP are not being made. GP cannot therefore be converted to TP. Therefore RuBP cannot be regenerated. The Calvin cycle stops.
b RuBP levels follow a similar pattern to TP levels.

7 A fall in temperature will reduce the rate of the reactions of the Calvin cycle. However, it should not affect any one step more than another, so the relative levels of the compounds in the cycle should not change much.

Chapter 6

1 a For active transport of sucrose from a source into the phloem sieve tube (sucrose loading.)
b For active transport of sodium ions and potassium ions across the membrane to create the resting potential (sodium–potassium pump).
c For active transport of sodium ions out of the furthest membranes of the cells in the wall of the proximal tubule, so that sodium ions will diffuse into the membrane next to the lumen of the tube and take glucose molecules with them (co-transport).

2 a, b Both have a five-carbon sugar molecule, but in DNA it is deoxyribose and in ATP it is ribose. Both have a phosphate group, but in ATP there are three whereas in a DNA nucleotide there is only one. Both have a base, but in ATP it is always adenine, whereas in a DNA nucleotide it could also be cytosine, guanine or thymine.

3 a Sodium ions and potassium ions are moved up their concentration gradients, by active transport.
b These are anabolic reactions. Energy is needed to form the bonds between the monomers in these polymers.
c There are many different possibilities, for example: moving organelles around inside cells; active transport of substances other than sodium and potassium; synthesis of molecules other than protein, RNA or DNA; contraction (of muscle cells); movement of cilia.

4 a ATP is used to phosphorylate glucose, providing it with energy required for it to undergo the next step of the reaction.
b 2
c 4
d 2

5 a Across the inner membrane (on the cristae).
b The intermembranal space contains more hydrogen ions, so it has a lower pH.
c Across the thylakoid membranes.
d In the space between the thylakoid membranes.

6 a The experiment is looking to see if the thylakoids can make ATP even when there is no electron transport going on. If they were in the light, then the light-dependent reaction of photosynthesis could take place, and so would electron transport.
b The hydrogen ions diffuse across the membrane until their concentrations are equal on both sides. This actually takes a little time, because the membrane is not very permeable to these ions.
c Greater.
d There was a greater concentration of H^+ ions inside the thylakoids than outside in the buffer.
e The hydrogen ions inside the thylakoids diffused through the ATPases in their membranes, into the buffer, down their concentration gradient. This transferred energy to the production of ATP.

7 a In the production of lactate, there is only one step, catalysed by lactate dehydrogenase. In the production of ethanol, there are two steps, catalysed by ethanal dehydrogenase and ethanol dehydrogenase. In the ethanol pathway, carbon dioxide is produced, but this does not happen in the lactate pathway.
  b In both, hydrogen is taken from reduced NAD and reacts with pyruvate. This regenerates NAD so that it can continue to be used in glycolysis.

8 Amino acids and fatty acids can only be used when oxygen is available, because they enter the link reaction and the Krebs cycle. These reactions can only take place when oxygen is available to take up electrons at the end of the electron transport chain.

9 Lipids contain twice as much energy per gram as carbohydrates and proteins. They are therefore the best energy store for anything that needs to be light, such as a flying bird or a seed that is dispersed by wind.

Chapter 7

1 a 64
  b In some cases, more than one triplet codes for the same amino acid. There are also triplets indicating 'start' and 'stop'.
  c A two-letter code could only code for 16 different amino acids.

2 a AAA would be formed from a TTT triplet on DNA, which codes for lysine.
  b ACG would be TGC on DNA, which codes for threonine.
  c GUG would be CAC on DNA, which codes for valine.
  d CGC would be GCG on DNA, which codes for arginine.
  e UAG would be ATC on DNA, which codes for 'stop'.

3 a 4
  b Tyrosine, serine, asparagine, glycine.
  c UAU UCU AAC GGG
  d i AUA
    ii UUG

4 a Amino acids are not 'made' during protein synthesis. They are already there, in the cytoplasm. During protein synthesis they are simply linked together. A better statement would be: 'The sequence of bases in a DNA molecule determines the sequence in which amino acids are linked together during protein synthesis.'
  b DNA does not contain amino acids. DNA is a polynucleotide, made of many nucleotides linked together. Amino acids are found in proteins. A better statement would be: 'The sequence of bases in a DNA molecule determines what kind of proteins are formed in a cell.'
  c The names of the bases are spelt incorrectly. The student has confused their names with those of other substances. For example 'thiamine' is a vitamin, not a base. The correct names of the bases are adenine, cytosine, thymine and guanine.
  d During transcription, an mRNA molecule is built up. It is not already made, so it cannot 'come and lie' next to the DNA strand. A better statement would be: 'During transcription, a complementary mRNA molecule is built up against part of a DNA molecule.'

5 The diagram should show the RNA moved to the left, so that the codon UCC is now on the left inside the ribosome, and the next codon (UGC) is on the right. The tRNA molecule with the anticodon AGG is sitting directly above the UCC codon, and its amino acid (serine) has now joined the chain. Another tRNA molecule, with the anticodon ACG and carrying the amino acid cysteine is about to bond with the UGC codon on the mRNA.

6 It takes energy and materials to make these enzymes, both of which would be wasted if they were made when not needed.

Chapter 8

1 Four.

2 a 32
  b 64

3 Meiosis I.

4 a Possible. Any cell with chromosomes in its nucleus can divide by mitosis, as chromosomes do not pair up.
  b Possible. Chromosomes can pair up.
  c Possible, as for **a**.
  d Not possible. Each chromosome needs to be able to pair up with its homologous partner in order to undergo meiosis, and in a haploid cell there is only one copy of each chromosome.

5 a Prophase I.
  b Prophase I.
  c Anaphase I.
  d Anaphase II.
  e Telophase I.

6 a We have no idea how many children they will have – they may have none or a large number. Nor can we tell how many will have cystic fibrosis and how many will not. The genetic diagram tells us only the probability of any one child having cystic fibrosis. All we can say is that, each time they have a child, there is a one in four chance that it will have cystic fibrosis.

b If their first child has cystic fibrosis, this does not affect the chances of the next one having it as well. For that second child, the chances are still one in four that it will have cystic fibrosis.

7 The gametes from the father are F and f. The genotypes of the offspring are FF and Ff, in equal proportions (you could write this as 1:1). Therefore the chance of a child with cystic fibrosis is zero.

8 All of the gametes from the female parent are the same. If we show the same one twice over, we just end up doing unnecessary work in doubling up everything in the diagram.

9 The symbol q represents the frequency of the recessive allele for PKU in the population.

$q^2 = 1 \div 15000$
$= 0.000067$
$q = 0.0082$

10 You should find that one in four children born to this couple would be expected to have blood group O. This can be expressed as a probability of 0.25 or 25%.

11 A son is conceived when a sperm carrying a Y chromosome fuses with an egg (all eggs contain an X chromosome). Therefore none of the genes on a man's X chromosome, including the haemophilia gene, can be passed on to his son.

12 a The condition appears to be dominant, as it seems to appear in the sons and daughters of everyone who has it. A mutation may have occurred in the ovaries or testes of one of the two original parents; they did not show the condition themselves as the mutant allele was not present in their body cells, but it was passed on to some of their children in their gametes. It would be possible for this pedigree to arise if the allele was recessive, but this is unlikely.

b Equal numbers of males and females have brachydactyly, so it does not appear to be sex-linked. However, as it is a dominant allele, it could possibly produce most of this pattern even if it was on the X chromosome. (Try this out on one or two parts of the pedigree.) The piece of evidence against this possibility is that a man in the middle row has a son who has the condition, even though the man's wife did not have it. As we have seen, it is not possible for a man to pass on an allele on his X chromosome to his son.

13 a Male cats cannot be tortoiseshell because a tortoiseshell cat must have two alleles of this gene. As the gene is on the X chromosome, and male cats have one X chromosome and one Y chromosome, they can only have one allele of the gene.

b C^O is the allele for orange fur; C^B is the allele for black fur

	male	female
phenotypes of parents	male orange fur	female tortoishell fur
genotypes of parents	$X^{C^O}Y$	$X^{C^O}X^{C^B}$
genotypes of gametes	(X^{C^O}) and (Y)	(X^{C^O}) and (X^{C^B})

genotypes and phenotypes of offspring

gametes from mother \ gametes from father	(X^{C^O})	(Y)
(X^{C^O})	$X^{C^O}X^{C^O}$ female orange fur	$X^{C^O}Y$ male orange fur
(X^{C^B})	$X^{C^O}X^{C^B}$ female tortoishell fur	$X^{C^B}Y$ male black fur

The kittens would therefore be expected to be in the ratio of 1 orange female : 1 tortoiseshell female : 1 orange male : 1 black male.

14 Each cell should be shown with two chromosomes (each chromosome will be a single thread, not with two chromatids), one long with one of the A/a alleles and one short with one of the B/b alleles.

15 All Ab.

16 AB and Ab.

17 a She is ffI^AI^o. He is FF I^oI^o.

b The woman's gametes will have genotypes fI^A and fI^o in equal proportions.
The man's gametes will all be FI^o.
The possible genotypes of the children are therefore FfI^AI^o and FfI^oI^o, with an equal chance of each combination arising.
The phenotypes corresponding to these two genotypes are 'no cystic fibrosis with blood group A', and 'no cystic fibrosis with blood group O'.

18 a The expected offspring would be 1 purple cut : 1 purple potato : 1 green cut : 1 green potato.

b The expected offspring would be 9 purple cut : 3 purple potato : 3 green cut : 1 green potato.

19 a The possible genotypes of the father's gametes are YG, Yg, yG and yg. All the mother's gametes are yg.

The possible genotypes and phenotypes of their children are YyGg (yellow, grey), Yygg (yellow, orange), yyGg (blue, grey) and yygg (blue, orange), in equal proportions.

b As the mother is yygg, we should assume that the y and g allele are on the same chromosome.

If we assume that the same linkage pattern is present in the father, then the father's gametes have only two possible genotypes, YG and yg.

The possible genotypes and phenotypes of their children are now YyGg (yellow, grey) and yygg (blue orange) in equal proportions.

20 If crossing over took place during meiosis to form the man's sperm, then a few of his sperm cells could end up with a different combination of alleles – that is, Yg and yG. Therefore there would be a small possibility that children with genotypes Yygg (yellow, orange) and yyGg (blue, grey) could be born.

21 a Albino could be AAcc, Aacc or aacc.
Black could be aaCc or aaCC.
Agouti could be AACc, AaCc, AACC or AaCC.

b The Punnett square of offspring genotypes and phenotypes will look like this:
You would therefore expect a ratio of

genotypes and phenotypes of offspring	gametes from father: AC	Ac	aC	ac
gametes from mother: AC	AACC agouti	AACc agouti	AaCC agouti	AaCc agouti
Ac	AACc agouti	AAcc albino	AaCc agouti	Aacc albino
aC	AaCC agouti	AaCc agouti	aaCC black	aaCc black
ac	AaCc agouti	Aacc albino	aaCc black	aacc albino

9 agouti : 3 black : 4 albino.

c The mouse could have any genotype with both an A allele and a C allele. We are not interested in the A allele. To find out if the mouse is CC or Cc, cross it with an albino mouse. We know that an albino mouse must have the genotype cc. If we get any albino mice in the offspring, then both parents must have contributed a c allele, so our unknown mouse must have been Cc. If we do not get any albino offspring, then the unknown mouse is probably CC – but we cannot be sure, as it is possible that just by chance none of its c gametes was involved in fertilisation.

22 a i GGC^DC^P or GgC^DC^P

ii ggC^DC^P

b The genotypes of the parents are GgC^DC^P or GGC^DC^P (dark green) and ggC^DC^P (cobalt blue).

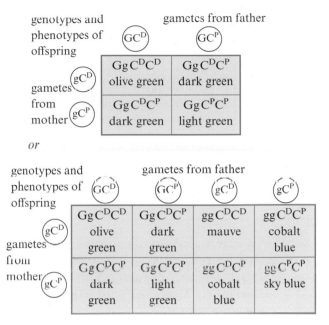

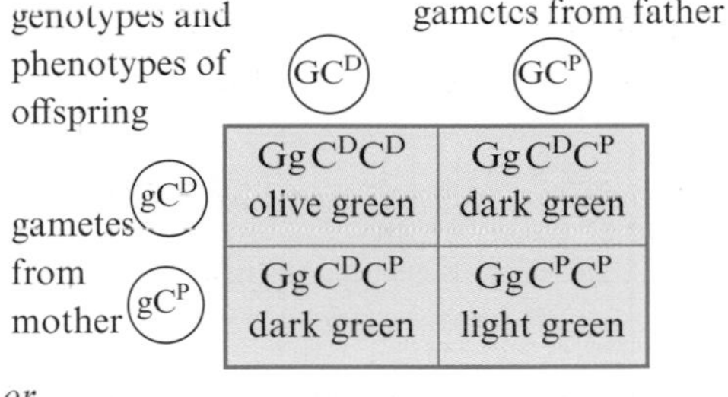

genotypes and phenotypes of offspring	gametes from father: GC^D	GC^P
gametes from mother: gC^D	GgC^DC^D olive green	GgC^DC^P dark green
gC^P	GgC^DC^P dark green	GgC^PC^P light green

or

genotypes and phenotypes of offspring	gametes from father: GC^D	GC^P	gC^D	gC^P
gametes from mother: gC^D	GgC^DC^D olive green	GgC^DC^P dark green	ggC^DC^D mauve	ggC^DC^P cobalt blue
gC^P	GgC^DC^P dark green	GgC^PC^P light green	ggC^DC^P cobalt blue	ggC^PC^P sky blue

23 a The offspring would all have genotype GgTt, and phenotype grey fur and long tail.

b Grey long, grey short, white long, white short in a ratio of 9 : 3 : 3 : 1.

c The total number of offspring is 80, so we would expect $\frac{9}{16}$ of these to be grey long and so on.

Expected numbers:

$\frac{9}{16 \times 80}$ = 45 grey long

$\frac{3}{16 \times 80}$ = 15 grey short

$\frac{3}{16 \times 80}$ = 15 white long

$\frac{1}{16 \times 80}$ = 5 white short

This gives a huge value for χ^2.

Now look at Table 8.1 on page 126. We have four classes of data, so there are 3 degrees of freedom. Looking along this line, we can see that our value for χ^2 is much greater than any of the numbers there, and certainly well above the value of 7.82, which is the one indicating a probability of 0.05 that the difference between the observed and expected results is due to chance.

Look at the table at the top of page 272.

	Grey long	Grey short	White long	White short
Observed number, *O*	54	4	4	18
Expected number, *E*	45	15	15	5
O* – *E	+9	– 11	– 11	+13
$(O-E)^2$	81	121	121	169
$\frac{(O-E)^2}{E}$	1.8	8.1	8.1	33.8
$\Sigma \frac{(O-E)^2}{E} = 51.8$				
$\chi^2 = 51.8$				

Our value is way off the right-hand end of the table, so we can be certain that there is a significant difference between our observed and expected results. Something must be going on that we had not predicted.

(In fact, these results suggest that these two genes are linked.)

24 a On St Agnes and St Mary's, all the frog-hoppers are striped. On all the other islands, there are some frog-hoppers with the striped phenotype, and some melanic. The proportions of these two forms vary. On all of the islands except one, there are more striped frog-hoppers than melanic ones.

b The populations of frog-hoppers on each island are small. If, just by chance, one individual on an island has more offspring than others (which might have been eaten by a predator or did not find a good place to breed) then its alleles will become more common in the population. On different islands, the proportion of luck that fell on individuals with different alleles varied.

It could also happen that, on each island, just two or three individuals invading from the mainland started off the population. The population would therefore contain their alleles, but not others. This is sometimes called the 'founder effect'.

c This is not at all easy to do. One approach could be to investigate the environmental factors that are thought to influence the reproductive success of frog-hoppers to look for any differences between the islands. Another could be to carry out laboratory-based experiments in which small populations of frog-hoppers kept in identical conditions are allowed to breed, and in which random removal of a few individuals each generation was carried out, to see if differences emerged between different populations. Or you might move frog-hoppers from one island to another, and use the mark, release, recapture technique (*Biology 1*, pages 203–204) to find out whether they are able to survive and breed as well on that island as on the one from which they were removed. You may be able to think of other approaches.

25 a A suitable line graph should be drawn.

b The increase in milk yield over the 10 years is 4470 – 4104 = 366 kg per cow. This works out at a mean value of 36.6 kg per cow per year.

c The total mass of protein in the milk has increased from 157.5 kg to 169.3 kg, an increase of 11.8 kg per cow per year. However, this represents a small decrease in the percentage of protein in the milk, from 3.83% down to 3.79%. Similarly, the total mass of fat in the milk increased from 221.6 kg to 237.6 kg, an increase of 16 kg per cow per year, but the percentage of fat in the milk fell from 5.40 to 5.32.

d Producing such large quantities of milk puts considerable demands on the body of a cow, and can lead to health problems such as mastitis and lameness. To keep these cattle healthy, considerable attention needs to be given to their health so they do not suffer discomfort as a result of their high productivity. They will need milking at more regular intervals, so that the udder does not remain painfully full of milk. They will need larger quantities of high-quality food, to provide them with the materials and energy to synthesise such large quantities of milk. Overall, these cattle will need more care and better living conditions in order to remain healthy, than would be needed for cows producing more normal quantities of milk.

Chapter 9

1 In each generation, only a small number of plants, each showing a particular set of desirable features, are bred to produce the next generation. Self-pollination is used, which limits the number of different alleles in the offspring. Each generation, any plant showing an unwanted feature – which will have been caused by an allele not present in the other plants, or by the coming together of two recessive alleles that are masked by dominant ones in the other plants – is discarded. Over many generations, only the plants with a particular set of alleles are left.

2 a *Advantages:*

- The grower can produce large quantities of plants with the same features (as long as they are grown in similar conditions).
- Cultivation and harvesting are easier, as all the plants are likely to be at a similar stage of development at the same time, and will all grow to similar dimensions.
- It is much easier to market a crop with predictable, uniform features than a variable one.
- Tissue culture can be used to produce very large numbers of genetically identical plants which can be left inside their sterile containers for transport to the places where they will be grown, including overseas, while they are still very small.
- Tissue culture can be carried out at any time of year in controlled conditions.
- Tissue culture can avoid the transmission of plant diseases, so long as the material taken from the parent plant is free of pathogens.
- Some plants are difficult or impossible to produce from seeds – for example, bananas and orchids.

b *Disadvantages:*

- If one plant is susceptible to a particular pathogen, then so will all the others be.
- There is no genetic variation on which either natural or artificial selection can act to produce new varieties suitable for growing in different conditions.
- The vegetative propagation of plants using tissue culture, grafting or most other methods is very labour intensive and expensive, and so is not suitable for most crop plants.
- Tissue culture requires the use of sterile facilities and highly trained staff, adding to the costs.

3 Answers will depend on the current state of the development of techniques and debate about therapeutic cloning. You will probably find that these vary in different countries, and you could compare, say, the way the issues are viewed in the UK and the USA.

4 Answers will depend on the current state of the development of techniques and debate about the cloning of mammals. There is no correct answer, but you should try to justify your opinions using biological information about the methods used and the results obtained, as well as moral or ethical arguments.

Chapter 10

1 *Temperature:*

a A thermocouple measures the temperature of the contents of the fermenter, which controls the rate at which cold water flows into the jacket around the fermenter.

b Many metabolic reactions are exothermic, causing the temperature inside the fermenter to increase. This could denature enzymes and therefore slow the process down.

pH:

a Buffers can be added to the mixture.

b The products of the metabolic reactions taking place inside the fermenter could alter the pH, which could reduce the activity of enzymes.

Concentration of nutrients:

a Nutrients can be added at intervals through tubes leading into the fermenter.

b The concentration of nutrients will affect the rate at which the product is formed. A high concentration may slow the formation of secondary metabolites such as penicillin, while in other applications a high concentration may increase productivity.

Oxygen concentration:

a Air, containing oxygen, can be bubbled into the fermentation vessel.

b Many microorganisms used in biotechnological processes are aerobic, and so need a constant supply of oxygen for respiration. In some cases, different products may be made if conditions become anaerobic.

2 The first centrifugation process separates the cells from the medium in which they were growing. The second centrifugation process removes the remains of the cells that were broken up to extract the enzyme. In the first centrifugation, it is the solid material that is required and the liquid discarded. In the second one, it is the liquid that is required and the solids discarded.

3 Zinc and copper are probably needed as cofactors for enzymes that catalyse some of the fungus's metabolic reactions.

4 Ammonia, NH_3, could be used as an additional source of nitrogen (as well as ammonium phosphate) for the fungus, which requires nitrogen to make amino acids and nucleotides.

5 The enzyme can be re-used. It does not contaminate the product. The enzyme is more stable in a wider range of temperature and pH than a free enzyme.

6 a As temperature increases from 30 °C to 64 °C, the relative enzyme activity increases from 50% to 100%. If temperature increases above 64 °C, enzyme activity decreases. For the free enzyme, 64 °C is therefore the optimum temperature. The rate of change of activity per °C is greater for temperatures above the optimum than for temperatures below the optimum. We do not have data beyond 90 °C, but if the graph was extrapolated we could predict that enzyme activity might stop completely at about 94 °C.

b As temperature rises, the kinetic energy of the enzyme molecules and substrate molecules increases. They therefore collide more frequently, and with greater energy. This increases the chance of a reaction occurring, so rate increases as temperature increases.

Above the optimum, an increase in temperature causes hydrogen bonds within the enzyme molecule to break. The enzyme begins to lose its shape. As the shape of the active site begins to be lost, it becomes less able to catalyse the reaction of the substrate. It may eventually become completely unable to bind with the substrate. The effect is gradual because the shape of an individual enzyme molecule is only changed a little at relatively low temperatures, and may still be able to bind with some substrate and catalyse some reactions. As temperature continues to increase, the shape change becomes more and more severe.

c The shape of the curve for the immobilised enzyme is very similar to that for the free enzyme. However, the optimum is 16 °C higher for the immobilised enzyme, at 80 °C.

At temperatures between 30 °C and 68 °C, the activity of the free enzyme is greater than that of the immobilised enzyme.

d The higher optimum for the immobilised enzyme is due to the fact that the immobilised enzyme molecules are prevented from losing their shape as easily as the free enzyme, because they are held firmly to the gel. This also explains the greater activity of the immobilised enzyme at temperatures above 68 °C.

The lower activity of the immobilised enzyme at temperatures up to 68 °C could be because the immobilised enzyme is not free to move around, so an increase in temperature does not increase the kinetic energy of the enzyme molecules as much as if they were in free solution. Frequency of collisions is therefore less for the immobilised enzyme than the free enzyme. Perhaps, too, some of the enzyme molecules are held in such a position that their active sites are not accessible to the substrate.

e Food processing could involve some relatively high-temperature cooking procedures. If papain is able to work at higher temperatures, its use may avoid having to cool the food down at a particular stage. This could make the procedure faster and perhaps cheaper.

Chapter 11

1 a Restriction enzymes are used to cut DNA into shorter lengths. There are many different kinds, and each cuts DNA at a particular sequence of bases. They therefore cut each strand at a different point, leaving sticky ends. If the same kind of restriction enzyme is used to cut another piece of DNA, then the sticky ends will be complementary and will form hydrogen bonds with the first piece.

b DNA ligase is used to link together different lengths of DNA. It catalyses the formation of bonds between the phosphate and deoxyribose groups in the backbone of the DNA molecule.

c Reverse transcriptase is used to synthesise DNA molecules using mRNA as a template.

2 A primer is a short length of DNA that attaches to one end of a single strand of DNA and allows DNA polymerase to begin to make a complementary copy of the single strand.

A probe is also a short length of DNA that attaches to a single strand of DNA. The probe, however, is labelled in some way, often with a form of phosphorus that emits beta radiation. The position of the probe indicates the position of that DNA – for example, on the surface of agarose gel after electrophoresis has been carried out.

Chapter 12

1 a Abiotic.

b Biotic.

c Abiotic.

2 Mammals and birds are endothermic. They use a great deal of glucose (and other substrates) to generate heat to keep their core body temperature above that of the environment.

3 a $38\,000\,kJ\,m^{-2}\,year^{-1}$ and $31\,000\,kJ\,m^{-2}\,year^{-1}$

b $54\,000\,kJ\,m^{-2}\,year^{-1}$

c For example, higher light intensity, higher temperatures and higher rainfall allow photosynthesis to take place at a greater rate; there are few seasonal variations in these factors, so photosynthesis can continue all the year round. Coniferous trees in the pine forest must be adapted to withstand cold and water shortage in winter, so they have narrow needles, limiting maximum rates of light absorption even when environmental conditions are ideal for photosynthesis. Tropical rain forest has a greater density of plants.

d Alfalfa plants are young and growing, so much of the carbon they fix in photosynthesis is incorporated into new cells rather than being respired. In the rain forest, the trees are mostly mature and amounts of growth will be small. Alfalfa is a nitrogen-fixer and this, together with the probable application of fertiliser to the crop, could allow greater rates of growth than in the rain forest.

4 a The lack of water in a desert limits the density of plants that can grow there, and also their rate of photosynthesis.

b There is a much greater total leaf surface area in a forest than in grassland, so more light is intercepted and more of it is transferred to chemical potential energy during photosynthesis.

5 a The first species to colonise an area of bare ground – the pioneer plants – are specialists. Relatively few species have adapted to be able to grow in these conditions, so at the beginning of the succession only two or three species are usually present. These organisms gradually change the environment so that it becomes more suitable for a range of other species to survive there, so the number of different species increases. This continues throughout the process. Each new plant species that comes into the community provides habitats for a new range of animal species. The final, climax community generally has the largest species diversity of all the stages.

b To begin with, the biomass is very low, as it takes time for organisms to colonise the new ground, and even when they do, there are very few of them. There are likely to be shortages of substances such as mineral ions or water which limits the population sizes of the pioneer species. As the community becomes more complex, more and more humus is added to the soil and more and more organisms are able to survive in the habitat, so biomass steadily increases.

Chapter 13

1 a *Typhlodromus* is a secondary consumer and *Eotetranychus* is a primary consumer.

b Energy is lost as it is transferred between trophic levels. There is therefore less energy to support secondary consumers than primary consumers, so the total biomass of secondary consumers is less than that of primary consumers. In this case, as the biomass of an individual of each species is roughly the same, this means that the *number* of secondary consumers will be smaller than the number of primary consumers.

2 a The lynx population, as measured by the number of lynxes trapped, oscillated on a cycle of roughly 7–8 years. It never rose above about 6000 animals trapped, but in some years almost none were trapped.

b The lynx and hare populations both oscillate on a similar timescale, with the lynx peaks often just a year or two after the hare peaks. This could happen because a high lynx population means that more hares are killed for food by these predators, and that a low hare population reduces the amount of food available for lynxes. However, there could be another factor that influences both of them, for which we do not have records. For example, a high lynx population might mean that more of them are infested by parasites, reducing their breeding success and bringing numbers down. Trapping effort might have varied in different years.

3 The *T. confusum* population rises rapidly at first, as food is in plentiful supply and there is little competition. However, as the population of *T. castaneum* also increases, interspecific competition for food or some other resource increases. *T. confusum* is outcompeted by *T. castaneum*. Individuals are less likely to survive and reproduce, and so the population falls and eventually, at around 600 days, dies out.

4 a, c At the top of the shore, both *Chthamalus* and *Balanus* cannot live higher because here they would be covered by water for only a very short time each day, and they cannot tolerate desiccation or wide temperature fluctuations. (You could also refer to why temperature fluctuations pose a threat, with reference to enzyme activity – see *Biology 1*, Chapter 9.) *Chthamalus* tolerates these better than Balanus and so can live a little higher up the shore.

continued

b At the bottom of its range, *Chthamalus* has to compete with *Balanus* for space on rocks, and in this area *Balanus* is the better competitor. So interspecific competition limits the lower range of *Chthamalus*.

c See answer for part **a**.

d At the bottom of its range, where it is covered by water for long periods of time, *Balanus* is more exposed to predation by dog whelks, and also to competition with algae for space on the rocks. So interspecific competition and predation limit the lower range of *Balanus*.

Chapter 14

1 Marram grass leaves roll up when water is in short supply. This is brought about by loss of turgor of the hinge cells. The leaf rolls so that its stomata are inside the cylinder, reducing water loss. This helps marram to survive in the sharply draining sand where it usually grows.

2 *Similarities:* Auxin and insulin are produced in one part of the organism and transported to another, where they have their effect. They affect cells by binding with receptors and bringing about changes in membrane permeability and some of the metabolic reactions within the cell.
Differences: Auxin is not a protein (or steroid), whereas insulin is a protein (and other animal hormones are often steroids). Auxin is not made in a gland. It is not transported through a bloodstream, but moves from one cell into another.

3 Apical dominance results in upward growth, ensuring that the part of the plant above ground obtains light. If all the buds on the plant grew at once, it would become so bushy that many of its leaves would be shaded. This would be wasteful, as the overall rate of photosynthesis per unit leaf area would be greatly reduced.

4 Adding more GA is unlikely to have any effect. The genetically tall pea plant will already have plenty of GA to which it will already be responding.

Chapter 15

1 You can probably think of many possibilities. They could include: responding to changes in temperature or daylength to begin breeding activity, seeking a mate, performing courtship behaviour with a potential mate, responding to behaviour of offspring (for example, feeding them), or moving into a warmer area to avoid low temperatures.

2 An increased heart rate and breathing rate increases the rate of supply of oxygen to the skeletal muscles. This allows more aerobic respiration, and therefore faster generation of ATP for muscle contraction. This would mean the animal could run away more quickly or fight more fiercely.

Widening of the pupils allows more light into the eyes, which could provide better image formation and clearer vision of whatever is perceived as being a danger. This could allow better decision-making about whether to stay and fight or to flee.

Urination and defaecation could possibly help by decreasing the weight the organism has to carry when running or fighting. In some organisms, it could deter potential predators.

Reduction of blood supply to the alimentary canal means that more blood can be transported to muscles, which need energy more than the digestive system does at that time. The reduction of saliva secretion is probably just part of this effect; as much energy as possible needs to be put into muscles and brain, and other functions that don't have an immediate useful effect in the 'fight or flight' situation can be put on hold.

3 The smell or taste of food.

4 Parasympathetic stimulation reduces the rate and force of heartbeat, and therefore tends to reduce blood pressure.

5 Microfilaments help to hold the cell in shape.

6 At neuromuscular junctions and at synapses between nerves, the arrival of an action potential causes calcium ion channels to open in the plasma membrane of the presynaptic neurone, so that calcium ions flood into the cytoplasm. This causes vesicles of transmitter substance to move to the presynaptic membrane and dock with their receptors. This in turn causes depolarisation of the postsynaptic membrane.

The neurotransmitter at a neuromuscular junction is usually acetylcholine. This is also found at many neurone–neurone synapses, but there are also many other neurotransmitters that may be found here, such as GABA and dopamine.

At a neuromuscular junction, the postsynaptic membrane is the plasma membrane (sarcolemma) of a muscle fibre, whereas at a neurone–neurone synapse it is the plasma membrane of a neurone.

At a neuromuscular junction, the action potential in the muscle fibre is carried deep into the cell along the T-tubules, eventually affecting the endoplasmic reticulum. This does not happen in the postsynaptic neurone of a neurone–neurone synapse.

7 a A = I band, B = A band, C = Z line, D = myosin.

b The H band is very narrow.

c a value between 1.58 and 1.63 μm.

8 a P = myosin or thick filament, Q = actin or thin filament, R = Z line.

b The muscle is relaxed. The troponin and tropomyosin molecules are covering the sites on the actin to which the myosin heads can bind.

c Diagram C, because there is the greatest overlap of the myosin and actin filaments, which means the maximum number of cross-bridges and therefore the greatest force applied by the movement of the myosin heads. In the state shown in D, it cannot contract any more.

d The sarcomere cannot shorten any more, without crumpling the actin and myosin filaments.

e i The myosin heads can only tilt in one direction. They are arranged so that when they do this they pull on the actin in such a way that the sarcomere is shortened. They can't pull the actin the other way. When the muscle relaxes, the relative positions of the actin and myosin fibres will stay exactly as they are unless something else pulls them back again.

ii In the human body, most skeletal muscles are arranged in antagonistic pairs. For example, when the biceps has contracted (shortened), it can be pulled back into its longer state by contraction of the triceps muscle. You can also make this happen just using the weight of your lower arm, or by placing a heavy weight on the hand.

Chapter 16

1 a The woodlice could move faster or turn less often when they are in a light area than in a dark one.

b Remaining in a dark area could help to avoid detection by predators. Dark areas, such as beneath a stone or a piece of tree bark, are also more likely to be humid and therefore present a reduced risk of desiccation.

2 Innate behaviour means that an animal can show appropriate behaviour – which could result in finding food or avoiding danger – at an early stage of its life, before it has had time to learn.

3 Young animals may learn to copy the behaviour of older ones. This is called cultural learning.

4 The worm stops wasting energy in responding to a stimulus unnecessarily. It can also spend more time feeding.

5 The worms may have been genetically different, and have different innate responses to the shadow. They may have had different previous experiences, so that some had already learned not to respond to shadows.

Glossary

A band: the part of a myofibril in which myosin filaments are present
abiotic factor: a non-living component of the environment that affects the distribution and abundance of a species
abscisic acid (ABA): a plant hormone produced in conditions of stress, which brings about responses such as stomatal closure
abscission layer: a layer of weak, thin-walled cells that grows across the base of a petiole and eventually allows the leaf to fall from the plant
absorption spectrum: a graph showing the wavelengths of light absorbed by a pigment
accessory pigment: a pigment other than the main light-absorbing pigment (chlorophyll) – for example, carotenoids; it helps to absorb more wavelengths of light than would be absorbed by chlorophyll alone, and may also have a protective effect
acetyl CoA: coenzyme A with an acetate group attached
acetylcholine (ACh): a transmitter substance
acetylcholinesterase: an enzyme that breaks down (hydrolyses) acetylcholine to acetate and choline
actin: the protein that makes up the thin filaments in a muscle fibre
action potential: a fleeting reversal of the resting potential, generally to about +40 mV inside, which sweeps along an axon
active transport: the movement of molecules or ions through transport proteins across a cell membrane, against their concentration gradient or electrochemical gradient, involving the use of energy from ATP
adenine: one of the four nitrogenous bases found in DNA and RNA
adenosine triphosphate (ATP): an energy-containing substance that acts as the energy currency of a cell, supplying an instantly available energy source that the cell can use
adenylyl cyclase: an enzyme that produces cAMP in the cytoplasm, in response to the binding of a signal molecule with the plasma membrane
adrenal glands: endocrine glands situated just above the kidneys, which secrete adrenaline
adrenaline: a catecholamine hormone, secreted by the adrenal glands in times of stress, fear or excitement, and which prepares the body for fight or flight
aerobic respiration: the sequence of reactions – including glycolysis, the link reaction, the Krebs cycle and the electron transport chain – that result in the complete oxidation of glucose in a cell
afferent arteriole: the blood vessel that delivers blood to a glomerulus
agarose gel: a type of agar jelly used in electrophoresis
alcohol dehydrogenase: an enzyme found in liver cells that converts ethanol to ethanal
aldehyde dehydrogenase: an enzyme found in liver cells that converts ethanal to ethanoate
allele: one of two or more alternative forms of a gene
alpha cells: cells in the islets of Langerhans that secrete glucagon
ammonification: the production of ammonia from nitrogen-containing compounds such as proteins, amino acids or urea
amygdala: a part of the limbic system that is important in determining our emotions; it also helps to coordinate the activities of the autonomic and endocrine systems
anabolic steroids: steroid hormones that stimulate anabolic reactions, such as those that result in a gain in muscle
anaerobic respiration: the partial oxidation of glucose to produce a small amount of energy; it involves glycolysis followed by either the lactate pathway or the ethanol pathway
annealing: a term used to describe the attachment of a primer to a DNA molecule in PCR
annual: a plant that completes its life cycle in one year
antagonistic muscles: a pair of muscles at a joint, in which the contraction of one causes the extension of the other
anticodon: a sequence of three bases on a tRNA molecule that determines the specific amino acid it can pick up, and the mRNA codon with which it can bind
anti-diuretic hormone (ADH): a hormone that is secreted by the posterior pituitary gland, which increases the permeability of the collecting duct walls and so allows the production of small volumes of concentrated urine
apical dominance: the inhibition of the growth of lateral buds by the presence of an active apical meristem
apical meristem: the region near the tip of a plant shoot where cells are constantly dividing
apoptosis: controlled process by which cells die, which is important in the development of an embryo to an adult; also called programmed cell death
aquaporins: protein-lined pores in plasma membranes that allow water to diffuse through
arteriole: a small artery
artificial insemination: the use of semen collected from a male animal to fertilise a female
artificial selection: the choice by humans of individual animals or plants from which to breed over successive generations in order to improve the characteristics of the population to suit the requirements of humans
ascending limb: the part of the loop of Henlé which carries fluid upwards from the medulla to the cortex

asepsis: the absence of microorganisms; used in biotechnology to mean the absence of all microorganisms apart from the one you wish to culture
asexual reproduction: reproduction in which genetically identical individuals are produced by mitosis; no gametes or fertilisation are involved
association area: a part of the cerebrum that integrates information from the primary sensory areas and other parts of the brain
associative learning: learning as the result of the association of a new stimulus with a reward or unpleasant effect
ATP: adenosine triphosphate; a substance that acts as the energy currency of a cell, supplying an instantly available energy source that the cell can use
ATPase: an enzyme that can catalyse the conversion of ADP and P_i into ATP or the reverse reaction; sometimes known as ATP synthase
autonomic ganglion: a swelling just outside the spinal cord containing cell bodies of motor neurones of the autonomic nervous system; plural, ganglia
autonomic nervous system: the part of the peripheral nervous system made up of the motor neurones supplying the viscera (internal organs)
autosome: any chromosome other than a sex chromosome
autotroph: an organism that makes its own organic nutrients using an inorganic carbon source
auxin: a hormone produced by young plant tissues – for example, in young leaves or at the apical meristem; it affects different tissues in different ways – for example, encouraging growth in stems, inhibiting growth of lateral buds; it has direct effects on cell membrane permeability and also affects gene transcription
axon: a long cytoplasmic process that transmits action potentials away from the cell body of a neurone
β carotene: an orange pigment found in carrots and in Golden Rice™, which can be used by the human body to produce retinol
β galactosidase: an enzyme produced by *Escherichia coli*, which catalyses the hydrolysis of lactose to glucose and galactose; also known as lactase
β galactoside permease: an enzyme produced by *Escherichia coli* which allows lactose to enter the cell; also known as lactose permease
batch culture: culturing microorganisms in a closed fermenter to which nothing is added during the fermentation; at the end of the process the product is harvested, the fermenter cleaned out and a new fermentation is set up
behaviouralism: the study of stimuli and responses, and their modification by rewards and punishments
belt transect: taking samples from quadrats placed along a line running across the area to be surveyed
beta cells: cells in the islets of Langerhans that secrete insulin
biceps: the muscle that causes flexion of the arm when it contracts
bile: a substance that is made in the liver and stored in the gall bladder, before passing along the bile duct into the duodenum; it contains bile salts which help to emulsify lipids in the alimentary canal
bile canaliculi: channels between cells in the liver, that carry bile
bile duct: a tube that carries bile from the gall bladder to the duodenum
binary fission: the principal method by which bacteria reproduce, splitting into two; it is not the same as mitosis because bacteria do not have linear chromosomes
biological species concept: the idea of a species as being a group of organisms with similar morphology and physiology, which are unable to breed successfully with other species
biosensor: a device that uses immobilised enzymes to detect and measure the concentration of a substance – for example, glucose
biotechnology: the industrial use of living organisms (or parts of living organisms) to produce food, drugs or other products
biotic factor: a living component of the environment that affects the distribution and abundance of a species
bladder (urinary): the organ in which urine is stored before being released from the body through the urethra
blood–brain barrier: the barrier to movement of substances from the blood and into the brain, produced by the relatively impermeable walls of the capillaries that supply the brain
body plan: the overall design of an organism's body
Bowman's capsule: also known as a renal capsule; the cup-shaped part at the beginning of a nephron, into which ultrafiltration takes place
brain: the part of the central nervous system found in the head
Broca's area: a part of the left cerebral hemisphere involved in speaking and writing
callus: a group of undifferentiated plant cells
Calvin cycle: the cyclic series of reactions that makes up the light-independent stage of photosynthesis; it takes place in the stroma of chloroplasts and produces triose phosphate using carbon dioxide, ATP and reduced NADP
cardiac muscle: the type of muscle found in the heart; it is striated, made of cells each with a single nucleus, connected with other cells by intercalated discs
carotenoids: accessory pigments found in chloroplasts, generally red, orange or yellow in colour
carrying capacity: the maximum population size that can be sustained within an area

cell signalling: communication between one cell and another
central nervous system: the brain and spinal cord
cerebellum: the part of the brain responsible for the coordination of movements, and posture
cerebral cortex: the outer layer of the cerebrum
cerebral hemispheres: the two halves of the cerebrum
cerebro-spinal fluid: the fluid between the meninges, within the ventricles of the brain and in the central canal of the spinal cord
cerebrum: the large, folded part of the brain which, in humans, covers most of the rest of the brain; it is where neuronal activity associated with language, emotions, personality and decision-making takes place
CFTR: a protein that acts as a transporter for chloride ions from inside a cell to the outside
chemiosmosis: the way in which the diffusion of protons down a proton gradient produced across the inner membrane of a mitochondrion, or across a thylakoid membrane in a chloroplast, provides energy for the synthesis of ATP
chiasma: a point at which a chromatid of one of a pair of homologous chromosomes breaks and rejoins to the chromatid of the other one of the pair, swapping genes between them; plural, chiasmata
chi-squared (χ^2 test): a statistical test that can be used to determine whether differences between observed and expected results are statistically significant or could simply be due to chance
chlorophyll: a green, light-absorbing pigment essential for the light-dependent stage of photosynthesis in most plants; it comes in two main forms, which absorb a slightly different range of light wavelengths, called chlorophyll *a* and chlorophyll *b*
cholinergic synapse: a synapse at which the transmitter substance is acetylcholine
cirrhosis: the formation of fibrous tissue in the liver, often as a result of the excessive consumption of alcohol; it can cause liver failure and death
citrate: a six-carbon compound that is involved in the Krebs cycle
classical conditioning: a type of learning in which an animal learns to respond to a stimulus which is different from the one that normally elicits a response
clear felling: cutting down all the trees in a wood at the same time
climax community: the final stage at the end of the process of succession
cloning: producing genetically identical copies of an organism
codominance: a situation in which both alleles have an effect on the phenotype in a heterozygous organism
codon: a sequence of three bases in mRNA that codes for one amino acid
coenzyme: a non-protein substance that is required for an enzyme to catalyse a reaction
coenzyme A (CoA): a coenzyme required for the removal of carbon dioxide by decarboxylase enzymes
collecting duct: the final part of a nephron, which joins the ureter
competition: the requirement by two different organisms of a resource that is in short supply
complementary base pairing: the pattern of pairing between the nitrogenous bases in a polynucleotide; in DNA, A pairs with T and C with G
conditioned reflex: a reflex action in which the original, innate reflex has been modified so that a different stimulus brings about the response
conservation: the management of the environment to maintain and, where possible, increase biodiversity; it is an active, dynamic process and not simply 'preservation'
consumer: an organism that obtains its energy from organic compounds such as carbohydrates, fats and proteins
continuous culture: culturing microorganisms in a closed fermenter to which nutrients and other requirements are added steadily throughout the fermentation, and products are steadily harvested
continuous transect: a line along which the organisms at every point on the line are recorded
continuous variation: variation in which a feature of an individual does not fit into a definite category, but can have any value between two extremes; it is likely to be caused partly by the environment and/or by polygenes or multiple alleles
contraction: the shortening of a muscle involving the use of energy
coppice with standards: regularly cutting most of the trees and shrubs close to the ground in an area of woodland, but allowing some trees to grow to their full height
coppicing: the management of woodland by cutting down the trees or shrubs in part of the wood to almost ground level and then allowing them to regrow; different parts of the wood are coppiced each year, so that at any one time the wood is made up of many different areas in different stages of regrowth
core temperature: the temperature deep inside the body
corpus callosum: a band of tissue containing neurones that connects the two sides of the cerebrum
cortex: the outer part of a kidney, in which renal capsules are found
co-transport: a form of active transport in which the active movement of one ion provides a gradient which can provide energy for the movement of another ion or molecule up its concentration gradient

counter-current system: an arrangement in which fluid flows in two vessels close to one another, in opposite directions; it maximises the concentration difference that can be built up between the two ends of the system, by maintaining a concentration gradient between the two vessels at all points along the pathway

cranial nerve: a nerve arising from the brain

creatine phosphate: a substance found in muscle tissue, which is able to donate phosphate to ADP to produce ATP

cristae: folds in the inner membrane of a mitochondrion, on which the electron transport chain is found

crossing over: the exchange of alleles between chromatids of homologous chromosomes as a result of chiasma formation during prophase of meiosis I

cyclic AMP (cAMP): a second messenger produced as a result of adrenaline binding with a receptor in the plasma membrane; it is also produced as a result of many other interactions between signal molecules and their receptors

cystic fibrosis: a genetic disease caused by the recessive allele of a gene that codes for a membrane protein responsible for the passage of chloride ions out of cells

cytokinin: a plant growth substance (hormone) that stimulates cell division

cytosine: one of the four nitrogenous bases found in DNA and RNA

deamination: the removal of the amino group from an amino acid; it takes place in the liver and results in the formation of ammonia

death phase: the stage in the growth of a population of organisms in closed culture in which death rate exceeds birth rate; also called decline phase

decarboxylation: the removal of carbon dioxide from a substance

decline phase: the stage in the growth of a population of organisms in closed culture in which death rate exceeds birth rate; also called death phase

decomposer: an organism that breaks down organic remains of other organisms, returning matter from them to the soil and air

degenerate: a term used to describe the genetic code, in which more than one triplet of bases codes for the same amino acid

dehydrogenase: an enzyme that can remove hydrogens from a substance

deletion: the loss of one base pair from a DNA molecule

dendrites: short cytoplasmic processes that transmit action potentials from other neurones to a motor neurone

dendron: a long cytoplasmic process that transmits action potentials towards the cell body of a neurone

denitrification: the production of nitrogen gas from nitrite or nitrate ions

denitrifying bacteria: bacteria that convert nitrite or nitrate ions to nitrogen gas

depolarisation: the loss or reversal of the resting potential

descending limb: the part of the loop of Henlé which carries fluid downwards from the cortex to the medulla

detritivore: an organism that feeds on detritus

detritus: remains of plants and animals, such as dead leaves, used as a nutrient source by decomposers and detritivores

diabetes mellitus: a condition in which blood glucose levels are not fully controlled; in Type 1 diabetes, insulin is not secreted, while in Type 2 diabetes insulin is secreted but has little effect on the target tissues

dialysis: the use of a partially permeable membrane to allow certain substances to diffuse from one fluid to another, down their concentration gradients

dihybrid inheritance: the study of the inheritance of two different genes

diploid: containing two sets of chromosomes

directional selection: natural selection in which a change in environment or a change in the alleles present in the gene pool selects for a different feature than in the past, so that this feature becomes more common in successive generations; also called evolutionary selection

discontinuous variation: variation in which a feature of an individual fits into one of a few definite categories; it is likely to be caused by a small number of genes with a small number of alleles

distal convoluted tubule: the second coiled part of a nephron

DNA helicase: an enzyme that unwinds and separates the two strands of a DNA molecule

DNA polymerase: an enzyme that makes complementary copies of DNA

dominant allele: an allele having an effect on the phenotype even when a recessive allele is also present

dopamine: a neurotransmitter substance found in the brain

dorsal root: the branch of a spinal nerve that enters the spinal cord nearest to the upper surface of the organism (the back, in humans); it contains the axons and dendrons of sensory neurones

dorsal root ganglion: a swelling on the dorsal root of the spinal nerve in which cell bodies of sensory neurones are found; plural, ganglia

DRD4 receptor: one of several types of G-protein coupled receptors for dopamine, found in the membranes of postsynaptic neurones

duct: a tube leading from one part of the body to another

ecological barrier: the prevention of interbreeding between two populations because of ecological differences between them, for example they live in different parts of a habitat

ectotherm: an organism that does not fully control body temperature by physiological means; its body temperature changes with the environmental temperature

edaphic: relating to soil

effector: an organ that carries out an action in response to a stimulus, such as a muscle that contracts or a gland that secretes a substance

efferent arteriole: the blood vessel that carries blood away from a glomerulus

efficiency: the total energy put into a system divided by the useful energy obtained; it is often multiplied by 100 and stated as a percentage

electrochemical gradient: a situation in which the concentration and charge on one side of a membrane differs from that on the other

electron carrier: one of the components of the electron transport chain, that picks up electrons from one substance and passes them on to another

electron transport chain: a series of molecules that successively gain and release electrons provided by a reduced coenzyme such as NADP; as the electron is passed along it loses energy, and the energy is used to synthesise ATP

electrophoresis: the separation of fragments of DNA according to their lengths, by applying a voltage across them; the DNA fragments are pulled towards the positive end, smallest first

embryo transplantation: the collection of embryos from one animal and their transfer for subsequent development into a surrogate mother

embryonic stem cells: stem cells taken from an early embryo

endemic species: a species that is found naturally in only one country or area

endocrine gland: an organ that secretes hormones directly into the blood

endocrine system: the body organs that secrete hormones

endotherm: an organism that generates heat inside the body to maintain a constant body temperature no matter what the temperature of the environment

envelope: a pair of membranes surrounding an organelle; mitochondria, chloroplasts and nuclei have envelopes

epinephrine: American term for adrenaline

epistasis: the interaction of two or more different genes to produce a particular phenotype

erector muscle: a muscle that raises a hair when it contracts

escape reflex: a fast, automated response to a stimulus resulting in a sudden movement that helps the animal to escape a predator

ethene: a gaseous plant hormone that enhances fruit ripening and leaf abscission

ethology: the study of the behaviour of an animal in its environment

evolution: a directional change in the characteristics of a population over time

evolutionary selection: natural selection in which a change in environment or a change in the alleles present in the gene pool selects for a different feature than in the past, so that this feature becomes more common in successive generations; also known as directional selection

excretion: the removal of toxic waste products of metabolism

exocrine gland: a gland that secretes something into a duct

explant: a small group of cells taken from a parent plant to be used in tissue culture

exponential phase: the stage in the growth of a culture of microorganisms in which their numbers double at regular intervals; this occurs while nutrients, oxygen and space are not limiting factors; also known as log phase

extending: straightening; extending the arm involves straightening it at the elbow joint

factor VIII: a protein required for blood clotting, encoded by a gene found on the X chromosome and therefore sex-linked

FAD: flavine adenine dinucleotide; a coenzyme that is required to allow dehydrogenases to remove hydrogens; the FAD accepts them and becomes reduced

fatty liver: a condition in which fat deposits are formed in the liver, often as a result of the excessive consumption of alcohol

fed batch culture: a modified form of batch culture in which nutrients are added at intervals during the fermentation process

fermenter: an enclosed vessel in which microorganisms are cultured; industrial fermenters are frequently very large and made of stainless steel

fertilisation: the fusion of the nuclei of two gametes to form a zygote

filament: a long protein molecule in a myofibril; thin filaments are made of actin and thick filaments of myosin

first messenger: a molecule that binds to a receptor in the plasma membrane and causes changes to happen in the cell; adrenaline is an example of a first messenger

flexing: bending; flexing the arm involves bending it at the elbow joint

food chain: a diagram showing a sequence of organisms in which chemical energy passes from one organism to the next

food web: many interconnecting food chains
frame shift: the result of adding or removing one base pair from a DNA molecule, so that the way in which every subsequent triplet is read is altered
G-protein: a protein inside the plasma membrane of a cell, which is affected by the binding of a signal molecule with a receptor in the plasma membrane
gametes: haploid cells specialised for reproduction; the nuclei of two gametes fuse together at fertilisation to form a diploid zygote
gap junction: a channel connecting the cytoplasm of one animal cell directly with another – for example, in cardiac muscle cells
gene: a sequence of DNA nucleotides that codes for a polypeptide
gene pool: all the alleles of all the genes present in a population of interbreeding organisms
gene technology: the manipulation of an organism's DNA to produce an organism or a product that can be made use of in some way
gene therapy: changing the DNA in some of a person's cells – for example, to attempt to cure a disease caused by faulty genes
genetic code: the three-letter code by which information is contained in a DNA molecule; a group of three bases specifies a particular amino acid to be added to a growing polypeptide chain
genetic diagram: a conventional way of showing the genotypes of parents, their gametes and the genotypes and phenotypes of the offspring they would be expected to produce
genetic drift: a change in the characteristics of a population, or the proportions of different alleles in the population, as a result of chance; it is most likely to happen in small, isolated populations
genetic engineering: using technology to change the genetic material of an organism
genetically modified organism: an organism whose DNA has been modified using gene technology – for example, by the removal of some of its genes or by the addition of DNA from another organism
genetics: the study of inheritance
genome: the complete DNA of an organism, or of a species
genotype: the alleles of a particular gene or genes possessed by an organism
geographical isolation: the separation of two populations by a geographical barrier
geotropism: a tropic response to gravity
germ line gene therapy: gene therapy that involves changing the DNA in cells whose DNA could be passed on to the next generation
gibberellin (GA): a plant hormone that affects stem elongation and seed germination; it acts by causing certain genes to be transcribed
glial cell: a cell within the nervous system that is not a neurone – for example, a Schwann cell
glomerular filtrate: the fluid that is filtered from the blood and passes into a renal capsule
glomerulus: a network of blood capillaries in the cup of a renal capsule
glucagon: a hormone secreted in response to low blood glucose levels, which brings about an increase in the rate of production of glucose from glycogen and other substances in the liver
glucokinase: an enzyme that adds a phosphate group to a glucose molecule
gluconeogenesis: the production of glucose from non-carbohydrate substances, such as amino acids or lipids
glutamate: a transmitter substance found in the brain
glycerate 3-phosphate (GP): a three-carbon substance formed following the reaction between RuBP and carbon dioxide, in the Calvin cycle
glycogen: a storage polysaccharide found in liver cells and muscle cells, made of many alpha glucose units linked by glycosidic bonds
glycogen phosphorylase: an enzyme found in liver cells that breaks down glycogen to glucose
glycogen phosphorylase kinase: an enzyme found in liver cells that activates glycogen phosphorylase
glycolysis: the first set of reactions in respiration; it takes place in the cytoplasm and results in the conversion of glucose to pyruvate, with the net gain of two ATPs per glucose molecule
GM insulin: insulin produced by genetically modified bacteria
Golden Rice™: a variety of rice that has been genetically engineered to produce large amounts of β carotene
grana: stacks of thylakoids; singular, granum
gross primary productivity (GPP): the total quantity of energy transferred by plants from sunlight into plant tissues
guanine: one of the four nitrogenous bases found in DNA and RNA
H band: the darkest part of the A band, where myosin and actin filaments overlap
habituation: a type of learning in which an animal learns not to respond to a repeated stimulus
haemodialysis: the treatment of kidney failure by passing the patient's blood through dialysis tubing surrounded by dialysis fluid
haemophilia: a sex-linked genetic disease caused by a recessive allele of the gene that encodes factor VIII
haploid: containing one set of chromosomes
Hardy–Weinberg equations: a pair of equations that allow the frequency of an allele in a population to be calculated
hepatic artery: the blood vessel that delivers oxygenated blood to the liver
hepatic portal vein: the blood vessel that carries blood from the alimentary canal to the liver

hepatic vein: the blood vessel that carries deoxygenated blood from the liver towards the heart
hepatocytes: liver cells
heterotroph: an organism that requires organic nutrients to supply it with a source of carbon
hexose bisphosphate: a six-carbon sugar with two phosphate groups attached
hinge joint: a joint that allows movement in one plane, e.g. the elbow joint
hippocampus: a part of the limbic system especially important in the formation of short-term memories
histology: the study of tissues
homeobox gene: a gene whose activity switches a whole set of other genes on or off, affecting an organism's body plan; all animals have very similar homeobox genes, as do all plants
homeostasis: the maintenance of a stable internal environment
homologous: having similar base sequences (in genes)
hormone: a chemical secreted by an endocrine gland, which brings about a response in an organ elsewhere in the body
human chorionic gonadotrophin (HCG): a hormone that is secreted during pregnancy, and whose presence in urine indicates that a woman is pregnant
hyperglycaemia: having a blood glucose level that is too high
hyphae: the long, thin threads that make up the body of a fungus
hypoglycaemia: having a blood glucose level that is too low
hypothalamus: a small part of the brain in the very centre of the head, which contains receptors involved in temperature regulation and osmoregulation; it is closely associated with the pituitary gland and controls the secretion of hormones from that gland
I band: the part of a myofibril in which only actin filaments are present
immobilised enzymes: enzymes that have been trapped into or onto a solid, for example in gel beads
imprinting: a form of learning in which, during a particular 'window' of time early in its development, an organism comes to treat a particular object or organism as something to which it should remain near, as though it were its mother.
independent assortment: the result of the random orientation of each pair of homologous chromosomes on the equator of the spindle in metaphase of meiosis I, ensuring that either one of a pair of homologous chromosomes can be found with either one of another pair
indole-3-acetic acid (IAA): a type of auxin
innate: inborn; innate behaviour is genetically determined and 'hard-wired' into an organism's nervous system
insertion: the addition of one base pair to a DNA molecule
insight learning: a type of learning in which an animal appears to integrate memories arising from two or more pieces of behaviour, in order to produce a new response that achieves a reward
insulin: a hormone secreted in response to high blood glucose levels, which brings about an increase in the uptake of glucose from the blood and its conversion to glycogen
intercalated disc: a structure found where two cardiac muscle cell membranes join
intermediate neurone: a neurone in the central nervous system that transmits nerve impulses between a sensory neurone and a motor neurone
interrupted transect: taking samples at intervals along the length of a line
interspecific competition: competition between members of different species
intraspecific competition: competition between members of the same species
islets of Langerhans: groups of cells in the pancreas that secrete insulin and glucagon
joint: a place where two bones meet
ketoacidosis: a dangerous condition caused by the presence of ketone bodies in the blood
kidney transplant: the replacement of a kidney with a kidney taken from another person
kinesis: a response to a difference in an environmental factor in one place compared with another, in which the organism moves more quickly and/or turns less often where the conditions are less favourable; plural, kineses
Krebs cycle: the cycle of reactions that takes place in the matrix of a mitochondrion, in which pyruvate is oxidised to oxaloacetate; ATP, reduced NAD and reduced FAD are produced, and carbon dioxide is given off
Kupffer cells: phagocytic cells found in the liver; they are macrophages and destroy bacteria
***lac* operon**: the length of DNA in *Escherichia coli* which controls the production of lactose permease and β galactosidase
lactase: an enzyme produced by *Escherichia coli*, which hydrolyses lactose to glucose and galactose; also known as β galactosidase
lactate: a three-carbon compound produced by the addition of hydrogen to pyruvate during anaerobic respiration
lactose permease: an enzyme produced by *Escherichia coli*, which allows lactose to enter the cell; also known as β galactosidase permease
lag phase: the initial stages in the growth of a culture of microorganisms, in which they synthesise suitable enzymes for the conditions in which they have been placed and begin to reproduce
lamellae: sheets; in a chloroplast, the lamellae are membranes within it

latent learning: learning that occurs in the absence of an obvious reward, and which is only manifested later in different circumstances

lateral bud: a bud on the side of a stem, generally in the angle between a petiole (leaf stalk) and the stem

leaf abscission: the loss of leaves from a plant following the growth of an abscission layer at the base of the petiole

ligase (DNA ligase): an enzyme that links nucleotides together by catalysing the formation of covalent bonds between the deoxyribose and phosphate groups

light-dependent stage: the stage of photosynthesis in which light energy is absorbed by chlorophyll and used to split water and make ATP and reduced NADP

light-independent stage: the stage of photosynthesis in which carbon dioxide reacts with RuBP, and carbohydrates are produced; it requires ATP and reduced NADP from the light-dependent stage

limbic system: an association area in the cerebrum, which is concerned with emotion and memory

limiting factor: a factor that is preventing a reaction or other process from going any faster; if the supply of the factor is increased, then the reaction rate will increase; with respect to populations, any factor that prevents the growth of the population above a certain value

line transect: taking samples along a line running across the area to be surveyed

link reaction: a reaction taking place in the matrix of a mitochondrion, in which pyruvate reacts with CoA to form acetyl CoA and carbon dioxide

linkage: the presence of two genes on the same chromosome, so that they tend to be inherited together and do not assort independently

liposome: tiny ball of lipid, which contains other substances such as DNA or protein

liver: a large organ situated just beneath the diaphragm; its cells carry out a very wide range of metabolic reactions, including deamination and the interconversion of glucose and glycogen

lobule: a unit of structure in the liver

locus: the position on a chromosome at which a particular gene is found

log phase: the stage in the growth of a culture of microorganisms in which their numbers double at regular intervals; this occurs while nutrients, oxygen and space are not limiting factors; also known as exponential phase

loop of Henlé: the section of a nephron that dips down into the medulla and then back up into the cortex of the kidney

M line: a structure within a sarcomere in which the ends of the myosin molecules are attached

matrix: the 'background material' inside a mitochondrion, where the link reaction and the Krebs cycle take place

medulla (of kidney): the inner part of a kidney, in which loops of Henlé and collecting ducts are found

medulla oblongata: the part of the brain from where breathing, heart rate and peristalsis are controlled

meiosis: reduction division; a type of nuclear division in which the nucleus divides twice to form four genetically different daughter cells from one parent cell, each containing half the number of chromosomes of the parent cell

meninges: three membranes that surround the brain and the spinal cord; they secrete cerebro-spinal fluid and provide protection

meristematic cell: a plant cell that is able to divide by mitosis

messenger RNA (mRNA): RNA that is made in the nucleus, complementary to the DNA of a gene, before travelling to a ribosome and taking part in protein synthesis

metabolic pathway: a series of chemical reactions taking place in an organism, in which each step is usually catalysed by an enzyme

metabolic reactions: the chemical reactions that take place in living organisms

metamorphosis: a major change in an organism's body plan as it moves from one stage in its life cycle to another – for example, a tadpole to a frog, or a caterpillar to a butterfly

monoclonal antibodies: antibodies (immunoglobulins) all of one type

monoculture: an area covered by a single variety of a single plant species

moraine: the jumble of rocks left behind by a retreating glacier

motor area: a part of the cerebrum which generates nerve impulses that are sent to effectors

motor neurone: a neurone that transmits action potentials from the central nervous system to an effector

multicellular: made up of many cells

muscle: an organ containing contractile tissue

muscle cells: cells making up muscle tissue; they contain the proteins actin and myosin that are able to use energy from ATP to slide along each other and shorten the cell

muscle fibre: one of the multinucleate cells making up muscle tissue

mutation: an unpredictable change in the structure of DNA, or in the structure and number of chromosomes

mutualism: a close relationship between two organisms in which both benefit

mycoprotein: a type of food made from the hyphae of fungi

myelin sheath: an insulating layer around an axon or dendron

myofibril: one of many similar bundles of filaments inside the cytoplasm of a muscle fibre

myosin: the protein that makes up the thick filaments in a muscle fibre

NAD: nicotinamide adenine dinucleotide; a coenzyme that is required to allow dehydrogenases to remove hydrogens; the NAD accepts them and becomes reduced

NADP: nicotinamide adenine dinucleotide phosphate; a coenzyme that picks up hydrogen ions when they are removed from a compound, and passes them to another substance

nail patella syndrome: an inherited condition caused by recessive alleles of two linked genes that affect the development of fingernails and the patella

nastic movement: a relatively rapid response of a plant to a stimulus – for example, petals closing as it gets dark; generally brought about by changes in turgor of specialised cells

negative feedback: a mechanism by which a change in a parameter is detected and which brings about a response that moves the parameter back towards the norm

negative tropism: a tropic response in which growth is away from the direction of the stimulus

nephron: a kidney tubule

nerve: a group of axons and dendrons, surrounded by a protective covering

net primary productivity (NPP): the energy left as chemical energy after plants have supplied their own needs by respiration

neuromuscular junction: a synapse between a motor neurone and a muscle fibre

neurone: a nerve cell, specialised for the rapid transmission of electrical impulses called action potentials

niche: the role of an organism in an ecosystem; the effects that it has on other components of the ecosystem, and the effects that they have on it

nicotine: a substance found in cigarette smoke, whose molecules have a similar shape to part of the acetylcholine molecule, and that can slot into acetylcholine receptors on postsynaptic membranes

nitrification: the production of nitrate and nitrite ions by the oxidation of ammonium ions

nitrifying bacteria: bacteria that oxidise ammonium ions to nitrite or nitrate; they include *Nitrobacter* and *Nitrosomonas*

nitrogen fixation: the conversion of nitrogen from unreactive nitrogen gas to a more reactive form such as ammonium or nitrate ions

nitrogenase: an enzyme that catalyses the conversion of nitrogen gas to ammonium ions

node of Ranvier: a gap in the myelin sheath

non-reproductive cloning: the production of a group of genetically identical cells, rather than a whole organism, by cloning

non-striated muscle: muscle that does not appear stripy under the microscope; smooth muscle

noradrenaline: a transmitter substance

nucleotide: a molecule consisting of a five-carbon sugar, a phosphate group and a nitrogenous base

nutrient broth: a liquid containing the full range of nutrients required by a population of microorganisms, in which they can be cultured

operant conditioning: a type of learning in which an animal learns to carry out a particular action in order to obtain a reward or avoid an unpleasant effect

operator: in a prokaryotic cell, part of an operon to which another molecule can bind, covering the promoter and preventing transcription

ornithine cycle: a metabolic pathway that takes place in liver cells, in which urea is produced from excess amino acids

osmoreceptors: cells that detect changes in the concentration of a fluid

osmoregulation: the regulation of the water content of body fluids

oxaloacetate: a four-carbon compound that is involved in the Krebs cycle

oxidative phosphorylation: the production of ATP via the electron transport chain in a mitochondrion

oxygen debt: the extra oxygen required by the body after exercise has taken place partly fuelled by anaerobic respiration; the extra oxygen is needed to convert the lactic acid that has been formed to pyruvate

pancreatic juice: a digestive secretion produced by the pancreas; it contains several digestive enzymes that act in the duodenum

parasympathetic nerve: a nerve that is part of the parasympathetic system; stimulation of the SAN by the parasympathetic nerve decreases heart rate

parasympathetic nervous system: the part of the autonomic nervous system that tends to prepare the body to rest and digest; its neurones generally secrete acetylcholine; many of the neurones of the parasympathetic nervous system are in the vagus nerve

pelvis (of kidney): the innermost part of a kidney, where the nephrons merge into the ureter

perineurium: protective connective tissue surrounding neurones

peripheral nervous system: all of the nervous system apart from the brain and spinal cord, made up of nerves (containing axons and dendrons of neurones)

peripheral receptors: cells in the skin that detect a stimulus

peritoneal dialysis: the treatment of kidney failure by infusing dialysis fluid into the patient's abdominal cavity, and then removing the fluid after it has exchanged solutes with the body fluids

phenotype: the characteristics of an organism

phosphorylation: the addition of a phosphate group to a molecule

photolysis: the splitting of water molecules using energy from light

photophosphorylation: the production of ATP using energy from light; it takes place on the thylakoid membranes in a chloroplast

photorespiration: an undesirable reaction between RuBP and oxygen, which takes place at high temperatures and high light intensities in some plants

photosynthesis: the manufacture of carbohydrates from inorganic substances (carbon dioxide and water) using energy from light; the light is transformed to chemical energy

photosynthetic efficiency: the amount of light falling onto a plant divided by the amount of energy the plant transfers into carbohydrate during photosynthesis

photosynthetic pigment: a molecule that absorbs some colours of light but not others, and transfers the light energy to chemical energy

photosystem: a cluster of pigment and protein molecules that harvest light energy and channel it to chlorophyll molecules

phototropin: a protein present in the plasma membranes of some plant cells, which is receptive to blue light

phototropism: a tropic response to light

phylogenetic species concept: the idea of a species as being a group of organisms that is geographically separated and morphologically or behaviourally distinct from other species, even if they may still be able to interbreed with individuals of another species; also called evolutionary species concept

phytoplankton: microscopic photosynthetic protoctists that float in the upper layers of the sea or fresh water

pioneer plant: a plant that is adapted to grow on newly exposed ground, and therefore often found in the very early stages of primary succession

plant growth substance: a chemical produced in one part of a plant that affects the growth or development of another part of the plant – examples include cytokinin, gibberellin and auxin; plant growth substances are also known as plant growth regulators and plant hormones

plant hormone: a substance produced in plant cells that coordinates growth and other activities of different parts of the plant; unlike animal hormones, plant hormones are not made in glands and often do not travel far from their point of synthesis

plasmid: a small, circular piece of DNA found in bacteria; plasmids often contain genes for antibiotic resistance, and can be transferred between bacteria

pluripotent: a stem cell is said to be pluripotent if it is able to divide to form many different types of specialised cell

podocytes: cells that make up the inner wall of a renal capsule

polymerase chain reaction (PCR): a method of making a large number of copies of a DNA molecule in a relatively short time; it involves the denaturation of DNA (i.e. the separation of its two strands), the attachment of a primer and then the construction of a complementary DNA strand against each exposed strand; this sequence is carried out repeatedly

population: a group of organisms of the same species, living in the same place at the same time and able to breed with each other

positive feedback: a mechanism by which a change in a parameter is detected and which brings about an action that takes the parameter even further away from the norm

positive tropism: a tropic response in which growth is towards the direction of the stimulus

preganglionic neurone: a neurone of the autonomic nervous system that carries impulses from the central nervous system to the autonomic ganglia

primary consumer: the first consumer in a food chain; a herbivore

primary metabolite: a substance produced by an organism as part of its basic metabolism – for example, by respiration

primary productivity: the energy transferred from sunlight to chemical potential energy by plants, usually measured in $kJ\,m^{-2}year^{-1}$

primary sensory area: a part of the cerebrum that receives information from various sense organs

primary succession: succession that occurs on a piece of ground that began with no soil

primer: a short length of DNA with a base sequence complementary to the start of a length of DNA that is to be copied

probe: a short length of DNA that is labelled – for example, by being radioactive; it binds to complementary lengths of DNA and so indicates their position

producer: an organism that transfers energy from light or an inorganic compound to organic compounds; plants are producers, using light energy to produce carbohydrates and other organic substances

productivity: the energy transferred from sunlight to chemical potential energy by plants, usually measured in $kJ\,m^{-2}year^{-1}$

progeny testing: the determination of the characteristics of the offspring of an animal that is to be used in selective breeding but which, for some reason, is not able to show those characteristics itself, for example the milk yield of the daughters of a bull

programmed cell death: controlled process by which cells die, which is important in the development of an embryo to an adult; also called apoptosis

promoter: a length of DNA that is needed for a gene to be transcribed; in a prokaryotic cell, part of an operon to which RNA polymerase binds in order to initiate transcription of the gene
protein kinase: an enzyme involved in some cell signalling pathways
proximal convoluted tubule: the first, highly coiled, part of a nephron
PSI: photosystem I, involved in both cyclic and non-cyclic photophosphorylation
PSII: photosystem II, involved in non-cyclic photophosphorylation but not cyclic photophosphorylation
psychology: the study of mental processes and their effects on behaviour
pyruvate: a three-carbon molecule that is the end-product of glycolysis
reaction centre: the part of a photosystem to which light energy is funnelled; it contains two chlorophyll *a* molecules that emit electrons
receptor: a cell that detects a stimulus
recessive allele: an allele having an effect on the phenotype only when a dominant allele is not present
recombinant DNA: DNA that has had DNA from a different source (often from a different species) inserted into it
reduced NAD: NAD that has picked up hydrogens
reduced NADP: NADP that has picked up hydrogen ions
reduction: the loss of oxygen, the gain of hydrogen or the gain of electrons
reference strand: the strand of a DNA molecule against which mRNA is built up during transcription
reflex action: a fast, stereotyped response to a stimulus, not involving conscious thought
reflex arc: the path travelled by an action potential from a receptor to an effector to bring about a reflex action
refractory period: the time immediately following an action potential when an axon cannot transmit another action potential, because of the time needed to restore the resting potential
regulator gene: part of an operon that codes for a repressor protein
reinforcer: a reward or unpleasant effect that an animal learns to associate with a particular behaviour pattern
relay neurone: a neurone in the central nervous system that transmits nerve impulses between a sensory neurone and a motor neurone
renal artery: the blood vessel that carries oxygenated blood to a kidney
renal capsule: also known as a Bowman's capsule; the cup-shaped part at the beginning of a nephron, into which ultrafiltration takes place
renal vein: the blood vessel that carries deoxygenated blood from a kidney towards the heart
replica plating: a technique used to determine which of several colonies of bacteria have successfully taken up a plasmid containing the desired gene, by testing for antibiotic resistance
repolarisation: the recovery of the resting potential following depolarisation
repressor protein: a protein that can bind to the operator in an operon, blocking the promoter and preventing transcription
reproductive barrier: the prevention of interbreeding between two populations because of problems in courtship, mating, fertilisation or development or because of hybrid sterility
reproductive cloning: the production of a complete new organism (usually applied only to animals) by cloning
reproductive isolation: the inability of two populations to interbreed successfully
respiration: the release of chemical energy from glucose or other substrates by oxidation; most of the energy is used to make ATP; respiration takes place in all living cells
respiratory substrate: a substance that can be oxidised in respiration to release energy for the synthesis of ATP
resting potential: the potential difference, usually about −70 mV inside, across the plasma membrane of a neurone while it is not transmitting an action potential
restriction enzymes: enzymes produced by bacteria to destroy viral DNA entering the cell; they are widely used in gene technology to cut DNA into smaller lengths
retinol: vitamin A; a substance required for the formation of the visual pigment rhodopsin
retrovirus: a virus whose genetic material consists of RNA, and which makes DNA using the RNA as a template when it has entered a host cell
reverse transcriptase: an enzyme that uses RNA to make a single-stranded molecule of complementary DNA
ribosomes: tiny organelles, sometimes free in the cytoplasm and sometimes attached to rough endoplasmic reticulum, where protein synthesis takes place
RNA polymerase: an enzyme that links together RNA nucleotides during transcription
rotation time: the time for which a woodland is left after harvesting, before being harvested again
rotational coppicing: coppicing different parts of a woodland each year, on a regular cycle
rubisco: ribulose bisphosphate carboxylase; an enzyme that catalyses the reaction of RuBP with carbon dioxide
RuBP: ribulose bisphosphate; a substance found in leaves that combines with carbon dioxide during the Calvin cycle

saltatory conduction: conduction of an action potential along a myelinated neurone by 'jumping' from one node of Ranvier to the next

sarcolemma: the plasma membrane of a muscle cell

sarcomere: the part of a myofibril between two Z lines

sarcoplasm: the cytoplasm of a muscle fibre

sarcoplasmic reticulum: the endoplasmic reticulum of a muscle fibre; calcium ions are stored in its cisternae

Schwann cell: a cell that wraps itself around an axon producing a multiple layer of membranes, called myelin

second messenger: a molecule that is affected by the binding of a first messenger to a receptor; cAMP is an example of a second messenger

secondary consumer: a carnivore that feeds on herbivores

secondary metabolite: a substance produced by an organism only at certain stages of its growth or development; it is not required for its normal day-to-day metabolism

secondary succession: succession that occurs following the clearance of land that already has soil

secretion: the production and release of a useful substance from a cell

selective cutting: cutting down only chosen trees in a woodland, leaving the rest to continue to grow

selective reabsorption: the absorption of wanted substances from the glomerular filtrate into the blood

sensory neurone: a neurone that transmits action potentials from a receptor to the central nervous system

sequencing (gene): working out the order of nucleotides in a length of DNA

seral stage: one of the communities that exists during a succession

sex chromosomes: the chromosomes that determine gender; in mammals, males are XY and females are XX

sex-linked: a characteristic caused by a gene that is found on the non-homologous portion of the X chromosome

sexual reproduction: reproduction in which two gametes (usually but not necessarily from two different parents) fuse to form a zygote; the offspring are genetically different from each other and their parent or parents

shivering: the rapid contraction and relaxation of muscles, generating heat

sickle cell anaemia: a genetic disease caused by a faulty allele of the gene that codes for the β chains in haemoglobin

sigmoid growth curve: the pattern of growth shown by many organisms when first introduced into a new environment – for example, a population of microorganisms in a closed culture

significant: in statistics, a significant difference between numbers indicates that there is a biological or other factor causing the difference; the difference is not purely due to chance

sino-atrial node (SAN): the pace-maker of the heart

sinusoids: channels between cells in the liver, that carry blood

skeletal muscle: striated muscle attached to the skeleton, generally under the control of the will; also known as voluntary muscle

sliding filament model: an explanation of how muscle contracts, based on the relative movement of actin and myosin filaments

smooth muscle: the type of muscle found in the walls of arterioles and the alimentary canal; it is not striated, and is made of cells with a single nucleus

social relationships: interactions between organisms living in a group

somatic gene therapy: gene therapy in which body cells are transformed, but with no effects on cells that will become gametes

somatic nervous system: the part of the peripheral nervous system containing all the sensory neurones, plus the motor neurones supplying skeletal muscles

spinal cord: the part of the central nervous system that runs from the base of the brain and through the vertebral column

spinal nerve: a nerve arising from the spinal cord

spinal reflex arc: reflex arc in which the nerve impulses are carried into and out of the spinal cord (without involving the brain)

stabilising selection: natural selection that tends to maintain the status quo

starch grain: a structure containing large numbers of starch molecules, inside a chloroplast; it is an energy store

stationary phase: the stage in the growth of population of organisms in closed culture in which birth rate equals death rate, so the population size remains constant; it occurs when an environmental factor, such as nutrient supply or concentration of toxins, becomes limiting

stem cell: an animal cell that has not differentiated, and is able to divide to form specialised types of cells

stem cell therapy: using stem cells to treat or cure a disease

steroid: a substance derived from cholesterol; many hormones, including testosterone, are steroids

sticky ends: short stretches of unpaired nucleotides at the end of a DNA molecule

striated muscle: muscle that looks stripy under the microscope; skeletal muscle and cardiac muscle are striated

stroma: the 'background material' in a chloroplast, in which the light-independent stage of photosynthesis takes place

structural gene: the part of an operon that codes for the amino acid sequence in a protein

suberin: a waxy, waterproof substance found in tree bark, abscission layers and in some of the cells surrounding xylem vessels in roots

substitution: the replacement of one base pair from a DNA molecule with another

substrate-level phosphorylation: the production of ATP directly from a reaction in the Krebs cycle, not involving the electron transport chain

succession: a directional change in a community over time

sucker: an outgrowth from the roots of a plant that is capable of growing into a complete new plant; suckering is a natural method of vegetative propagation, as occurs for example in the English elm

sweat gland: a gland in the dermis of the skin that extracts fluid from blood plasma and secretes this into a duct that carries the fluid onto the surface of the skin

sympathetic nerve: a nerve that is part of the sympathetic system; stimulation of the SAN by the sympathetic nerve increases heart rate

sympathetic nervous system: the part of the autonomic nervous system that tends to prepare the body for fight or flight; its neurones secrete noradrenaline or acetylcholine

synapse: an area where a nerve impulse can be passed from one neurone to another, or from a neurone to an effector

synaptic cleft: the tiny gap between two neurones, or between a neurone and an effector, at a synapse

syncitium: a cell containing many nuclei – for example, a muscle fibre

synovial joint: a joint that allows movement between two bones; it is lined by a synovial membrane which produces synovial fluid for lubrication

T-tubules: parts of the plasma membrane of a muscle cell that plunge deep inside it

target tissue: a group of cells that contain receptors for a particular hormone and are therefore affected by it

taxis: a movement towards or away from a stimulus; plural, taxes

telomerase: an enzyme that can synthesise new telomeres, normally only found in stem cells and cancer cells

telomere: a length of DNA, made up of repeating sequences of nucleotides, which protects the end of a chromosome; telomeres shorten each time a cell divides by mitosis

temporal barrier: the prevention of interbreeding between two populations because of differences in the times at which they are reproductively active

tendon: a strong, inelastic cord made of collagen, which connects a muscle to a bone

tertiary consumer: a carnivore that feeds on a secondary consumer

thylakoids: membrane-enclosed spaces inside a chloroplast, where the light-dependent stage of photosynthesis takes place

thymine: one of the four nitrogenous bases found in DNA (but not RNA)

tissue culture: the growth of many genetically identical plants from a small group of cells; the cells are grown in sterile nutrient medium before transfer to agar gel where they are stimulated to grow roots and shoots; the technique is also known as micropropagation

totipotent: a stem cell is said to be totipotent if it is able to divide to form any of the different types of specialised cell in the body

transcription: producing an mRNA molecule with a complementary base sequence to one strand of a length of DNA

transcription factor: a substance that can bind with a particular region of DNA and either initiate or prevent transcription

transfer RNA (tRNA): a type of RNA found in the cytoplasm, made of a single strand looped back on itself; each tRNA molecule has a particular anticodon that pairs with an codon on mRNA, and also determines the type of amino acid with which the tRNA will bind

transformed organism: an organism that has had foreign DNA inserted into it

transgenic organism: an organism that has had foreign DNA inserted into it

translation: the synthesis of proteins on a ribosome; the sequence of amino acids is determined by the sequence of bases in the mRNA

transmitter substance: a chemical that is released by a presynaptic neurone and diffuses across the synaptic cleft to slot into receptors on the postsynaptic neurone

triceps: the muscle that causes extension of the arm when it contracts

triose phosphate (TP): a three-carbon phosphorylated sugar, the first carbohydrate to be produced in photosynthesis

triplet: a group of three bases in a DNA molecule, coding for one amino acid

tRNA transferase: an enzyme that loads a specific amino acid onto a specific tRNA molecule

trophic level: the stage of a food chain at which an organism feeds

tropism: a response to a stimulus, brought about by growth, in which the direction of growth is related to the direction of the stimulus

tropomyosin: a fibrous protein closely associated with actin filaments in a myofibril

troponin: a protein closely associated with actin filaments in a myofibril

ultrafiltration: filtration on a molecular scale, as happens in the renal capsules of the kidney nephrons

uracil: one of the four nitrogenous bases found in RNA (but not DNA)
urea: the main nitrogenous excretory product of mammals, made in the ornithine cycle following the deamination of amino acids
ureter: one of the tubes that carries urine from the kidneys to the bladder
urethra: the tube that carries urine from the bladder to the outside of the body
urine: liquid produced by the kidneys, containing urea and other waste products dissolved in water
vagus nerve: a nerve running from the brain to many internal organs; it is part of the parasympathetic nervous system and slows heart rate when it carries impulses to the SAN
vasoconstriction: the contraction of the smooth muscle in the walls of arterioles supplying blood to capillaries near the surface of the skin, narrowing the lumen and reducing blood flow
vasodilation: the relaxation of the smooth muscle in the walls of arterioles supplying blood to capillaries near the surface of the skin, widening the lumen and increasing blood flow
vector: in gene technology, anything that is used to transfer DNA into the organisms to be genetically transformed; plasmids, viruses and liposomes can be used as vectors
vegetative propagation: asexual reproduction of plants, either natural or artificial, producing a clone
ventral root: the branch of a spinal nerve that enters the spinal cord nearest to the lower surface (the front, in humans) of the organism; it contains the axons of motor neurones
ventricles: fluid-filled spaces within the brain
viscera: the internal organs, such as stomach, kidneys and so on
voltage-gated channel: an ion channel in a plasma membrane that responds to a change in voltage (potential difference) across the membrane by opening or closing
voluntary muscle: striated muscle attached to the skeleton, generally under the control of the will; also known as skeletal muscle
Wernicke's area: a part of the left cerebral hemisphere involved in the understanding of language
xenotransplant: a transplant from one species to another
xenotransplantation: the use of organs from a different species for transplant into humans
Z line: a structure found at each end of a sarcomere, in which the ends of the actin molecules are fixed
Z-scheme: a diagram illustrating the changes in energy levels of electrons during the light-dependent reactions of photosynthesis
zygote: a diploid cell formed by the fusion of the nuclei of two haploid gametes

Index

Extension topics, which are to be found only on the accompanying CD-ROM, are shown in **bold**.